Critical Connections

Critical Connections

Promoting Economic Growth and Resilience in Europe and Central Asia

David Michael Gould

WORLD BANK GROUP

Contents

Boxes

Figures

Maps

Tables

About the Authors

David M. Gould (World Bank) is currently Lead Economist in the World Bank's Europe and Central Asia Region and the lead author of the ECA *Critical Connections* flagship. He is the author of several books and peer-reviewed journal articles on international trade and finance, migration, and economic policy. Currently, he is leading Europe and Central Asia regional studies on the development impact of disruptive technologies. During his 15 years at the World Bank, he has led teams to deliver country development strategies and analytical and lending operations in Europe, Latin America, and South Asia. Prior to joining the World Bank, he served as the Director of Global Economic Analysis at the Institute of International Finance and as Senior Economist and Policy Advisor at the US Federal Reserve. He has held visiting research positions at the Central Banks of Mexico and Chile. He holds a PhD in International Economics (with honors) from the University of California at Los Angeles and is a Chartered Financial Analyst charter holder.

Megersa Abate (World Bank) is a Transport Economist in the World Bank's Transport and Digital Development Global Practice. He has extensive expertise and interest in various topics, including freight demand modeling, air transport regulation, and transport connectivity. His research has been published in leading transportation economics journals. Before joining the Bank in 2016, he worked as a researcher at VTI, the Swedish National Road and Transport Research Institute, and at the VU University of Amsterdam. Earlier in his career, he worked at the Ethiopian Civil Aviation Authority as an air transport expert. He received his PhD in Transport Economics from the Technical University of Denmark in 2013; during his PhD studies, he was also a visiting student in the Institute of Transport Studies at the University of Leeds.

Erhan Artuc (World Bank) is a Senior Economist in the World Bank's Development Research Group. Prior to joining the World Bank in 2011, he was a faculty member at Koç University in Istanbul, Turkey. His most recent research focuses on international trade and migration policies and their effects on labor markets and development. His work has been published in leading academic and policy journals such as the *Journal of International Economics, Economic Journal,* and *American Economic Review.* He received his undergraduate degree from Bilkent University and a PhD in Economics from the University of Virginia.

Omar Bamieh (University of Vienna) is an Assistant Professor of Economics at the University of Vienna. His research focuses on labor market institutions and the interaction between legal frameworks and labor markets. He holds an MS in Economics and Social Sciences from Bocconi University in Milan and a PhD in Economics from the European University Institute in Florence, where he also worked as a Research Fellow in Global Economics at the Robert Schuman Centre for Advanced Studies.

Cecilia Briceno-Garmendia (World Bank) is a Lead Economist in the World Bank's Transport and ICT Global Practice, where she leads the economic research agenda in logistics and transport in the Latin America region and globally advises teams and governments in strategic issues pertaining to prioritization and planning of infrastructure investments, including aspects related to spending efficiency, green trucking and trucking sector performance, multimodal development corridors, and adaptation of transport networks to climate change. Previously, she led the economic team in the Office of the Director for Sustainable Development of the Latin America region, where she provided leadership for the analytical agenda on infrastructure, urban, and disaster risk management and climate change adaptation issues. She has worked extensively on issues pertaining to connectivity, logistics, and port performance and co-led the pathbreaking Africa Infrastructure Country Diagnostic. She has worked on projects and research in more than 70 countries. Before joining the World Bank, she worked in software engineering and the design of information and organizational systems for both private and public sector enterprises in República Bolivariana de Venezuela. She has an MBA from the Instituto de Estudios Superiores en Administración in Caracas, República Bolivariana de Venezuela, and a doctorate in Economics from Georgetown University.

Matteo Fiorini (European University Institute) is a Research Fellow in Global Economics at the Robert Schuman Centre for Advanced Studies of the European University Institute in Florence, Italy. His research focuses on international trade, trade policy, migration, and development. Prior to joining the Schuman Centre, he worked as a researcher at the Institute's Migration Policy Centre, the World Trade Organization, and Bocconi University. He holds an MS in Economics and Social Sciences from Bocconi University in Milan and a PhD in Economics from the European University Institute in Florence.

Bernard Hoekman (European University Institute) is a Professor at the Robert Schuman Centre for Advanced Studies of the European University Institute. He is also a Research Fellow at the Centre for Economic Policy Research, a member of the World Economic Forum Council on Trade and Investment, and a Senior Fellow at the Centre for International Governance Innovation. His research focuses on trade and development, economic integration, and the multilateral trading system.

Dror Y. Kenett (World Bank) is a multidisciplinary financial economist and an expert on financial networks, financial stability, and systemic risk. He is a consultant to the World Bank, Adjunct Professor at Johns Hopkins University, a research associate at the London School of Economics Systemic Risk Centre, and a visiting researcher at Boston University and at the Israel Securities Authority. He has also held a researcher position in the US Department of the Treasury's Office of Financial Research. He applies his scientific background to financial stability questions, focusing on network-based models, market structure, financial contagion and spillovers, and correlation-based models. He has extensive policy experience and has contributed to the Office of Financial Research *Financial Stability Report* and participated in the development of the Office's monitoring tools. He has published more than 40 papers in financial, physics, and engineering journals, including the *Journal of Banking and Finance, Journal of Risk and Financial Management, Quantitative Finance, Nature Physics,* and *Scientific Reports.* He has a PhD in Physics from Tel Aviv University in Israel.

Mathilde Lebrand (World Bank) is an Economist in the World Bank's Transport Global Practice. Currently she is working on the Belt and Road Initiative, economic corridor development, and connectivity. Previously she worked for the Europe and Central Asia Chief Economist office and contributed to several upcoming regional studies. Her research focuses on economic geography, international trade and global value chains, networks, and political economy. She has taught at the University of Montreal and has worked at the World Trade Organization in Geneva. She is a Research Fellow at the Center for Economic Studies ifo Institute (CESifo). She holds a PhD in economics from the European University Institute.

Paloma López-Garcia (European Central Bank) has been a Senior Economist in the Directorate-General—Economics at the European Central Bank since 2015. Before that she was Coordinator of the Competitiveness Research Network (CompNet) in the Directorate-General—Research, and she has also worked at the Instituto de Empresa Business School and in the Research and Economics Department of the Central Bank of Spain. She has published articles in the *European Economic Review, Small Business Economics,* and *Economics of Innovation and New Technology,* among other peer-reviewed journals. Her research topics are microanalysis of productivity and employment growth, innovation, and trade and competitiveness. She earned her PhD at the London School of Economics in 2003.

Çağlar Özden (World Bank) is a Lead Economist in the World Bank's Research Department. His research explores the nexus of globalization of product and labor markets, government policies, and economic development. His current research projects explore the determinants and patterns of global labor mobility; impacts of migrants on destination labor market outcomes; linkages between migration, trade, and foreign direct investment flows; medical brain drain; and linkages between aging and global economic integration. He has edited three books and published numerous papers in leading academic journals such as the *American Economic Review* and the *Economic Journal.* He is a Fellow of the Institute of Labor Economics (IZA) and of the Centre for Research and Analysis of Migration (CreAM) and serves on the advisory board of the Economic Research Forum. He received his undergraduate degrees in Economics and Industrial Engineering from Cornell University and his PhD in Economics from Stanford University.

Georgi Panterov (World Bank) is a Research Analyst in the World Bank's Office of the Chief Economist for Europe and Central Asia. His research interests are focused on machine learning, econometrics, blockchain, and cryptocurrencies. During his time at the World Bank, he has contributed to the *Golden Aging* flagship report, the *Critical Connections* flagship report, and the Europe and Central Asia economic update reports. Before joining the World Bank, he worked at Google, the US Department of Agriculture, and American University. He is currently a PhD candidate in Economics at American University in Washington, DC.

Nadia Rocha (World Bank) is a Senior Economist in the World Bank's Macroeconomics, Trade and Investment Global Practice. Prior to joining the Bank in 2016, she worked for five years in the World Trade Organization's Economic Research and Statistics Division. She was seconded to the Colombian Ministry of Trade to serve as a Senior Advisor on Trade during 2015. Her current work focuses on regionalism, trade costs, global value chains, and trade and gender. She holds a BA in economics from Bocconi University in Milan, an MA in Economics from Pompeu Fabra University of Barcelona, and a PhD in International Economics from the Graduate Institute, Geneva.

Daria Taglioni (World Bank) is the Principal Economist for the Europe and Central Asia and East Asia and Pacific Regions in the Economics and Private Sector Development Vice Presidency of the World Bank Group's International Finance Corporation. Prior to joining the World Bank Group, Daria worked at the European Central Bank and at the Organisation for Economic Co-operation and Development. Her research focuses on trade and competitiveness. She has published articles in the *American Economic Review* and *Journal of International Economics*, among other peer-reviewed journals. She holds a PhD in International Economics from the Graduate Institute of Geneva.

Shawn Tan (World Bank) is an Economist in the World Bank's Finance, Competitiveness and Innovation Global Practice and is currently working on private sector development and trade issues in the countries of Eastern Europe and the Western Balkans. He has worked on reports such as the *World Development Report 2016: Digital Dividends, Reaping Digital Dividends: Leveraging the Internet for Development in Europe and Central Asia,* and the high-growth entreneurship report and has written papers on international trade, firm productivity, and high-growth firms. Before joining the World Bank, he worked at the Singapore Economic Development Board, where he was a negotiator for Singapore's free trade agreements and bilateral investment treaties and worked on trade facilitation issues for multinational companies in Singapore. His research interests are broadly in international trade, economic geography, and firm productivity and performance. He holds a PhD in Economics from the University of Melbourne.

Gonzalo Varela (World Bank) is a Senior Economist in the Global Trade and Regional Integration Unit of the World Bank's Macroeconomics, Trade and Investment Global Practice. Prior to joining the World Bank, he was a Lecturer at the University of Sussex and at Uruguay's Ministry of Industry, Energy, and Mining.

His work agenda focuses on global integration and economic performance and on the analysis of trade policy and competitiveness. He holds a BSc in Economics from the Universidad de la República in Uruguay and both an MA in International Economics and a PhD in Economics from the University of Sussex.

Hernan Winkler (World Bank) is a Senior Economist in the World Bank's Jobs Group. He specializes in applied microeconomics, with a particular focus on issues related to labor markets, technological change, and the sources and consequences of poverty and inequality. His research has been published in peer-reviewed economics journals, including the *Review of Economics and Statistics* and the *Journal of Development Economics*. He was a lead author of the World Bank regional report *Reaping Digital Dividends: Leveraging the Internet for Development in Europe and Central Asia*. He has been part of the core teams of several regional reports, including *Diversified Development, Golden Aging*, and *Risk and Returns*. He was previously a researcher at the Center for Distributive, Labor and Social Studies (CEDLAS) at the National University of La Plata in Argentina, where he conducted research on poverty and distributional issues affecting countries in Latin America and the Caribbean. He holds a master's degree in Economics from the National University of La Plata and a PhD in Economics from the University of California at Los Angeles.

Thea Yde-Jensen (World Bank) is a Researcher in the World Bank Group's Poverty and Equity Global Practice, where she conducts research on issues related to livelihoods, labor market outcomes, and displacement. Her expertise and research interests particularly focus on examining the interlinkages of labor markets and inequality and poverty. Previously she worked as a Researcher in the Bank's Office of the Chief Economist for Europe and Central Asia, focusing on issues related to employment and firms' access to finance and international networks. Prior to joining the World Bank, she worked in the International Monetary Fund's Statistics Department and in the Department of Economics at Copenhagen Business School. She has a BS and an MS in Economics from the University of Copenhagen.

Foreword

In mid-2014 when *Critical Connections* was first contemplated, the Europe and Central Asia (ECA) region was still emerging from the global financial crisis, growth was uncertain and tepid, and policy makers were largely focused on mitigating further financial and macroeconomic risks from ongoing weakness in the banking sector and large fiscal deficits. Appropriately, the policy discourse was largely targeted to shoring up near-term challenges, rather than to assembling the building blocks that would provide the foundation for restoring the promise of long-term resilient growth.

Critical Connections was born out of the desire to help policy makers focus their attention on their long-term goals of regional and global integration to capture the benefits of connectivity, from which ECA countries had advanced so far during the early years of market expansion in the 1990s and early 2000s.

What started simply as an exploration into policies to capture the gains of specialization and knowledge transfers has taken on much greater meaning in recent times. The trend toward regional and global integration is under serious threat as many voters, particularly in high-income countries, see nationalism and protection as a remedy to greater economic uncertainty. But as former UK Prime Minister Gordon Brown noted in a 2015 speech, "the problems that give rise to nationalism can't be solved by nationalism and in an interdependent world the problems that give rise to isolationism and protectionism cannot be solved by isolationism and protectionism."

While *Critical Connections* does not provide answers to assuage all the concerns about our changing global economy, it does provide an invaluable insight into understanding—at the firm and country level—the interdependence of our world and how it has historically operated, and currently operates, to advance economic growth and shared prosperity.

A key insight of this report is that ECA's international connectivity through trade, foreign direct investment, migration, telecommunications, transportation, and other avenues facilitates the transfers of knowledge and technology that are critical to long-term growth and shared prosperity. These connections complement one another because of the tacit (learning by doing), rather than explicit (contained in books or blueprints), nature of knowledge transfers. Migration, for example, enhances knowledge spillovers through trade and foreign investment by migrants transferring information on foreign markets and supporting connections to them. Similarly, the internet and efficient transport links are both necessary for successful e-commerce.

Moreover, the depth of ECA's connections and the geographic composition of the connections both matter. Knowledge transfers are greater from countries that themselves have strong links to third countries. These transfers also emerge from linkages between firms in global value chains as well as foreign ownership and management practices that generate local spillovers.

While these connections are important for prosperity, however, one should not be naive about their impact. Despite its overall benefits, increased connectivity exposes ECA countries to shocks, particularly those emanating from countries at the center of international economic transactions, which may have contributed to economic insecurity. However, by providing alternative sources of external demand and financing, a broad range of connections can reduce those risks and help countries cope with both domestic and external shocks.

The European side of the ECA region is an ideal laboratory for observing the role of multidimensional connectivity in action. Regional supply chains are strong, and links between countries across the various forms of connectivity allow observations on how connectivity opens doors for the knowledge transfers that support resilient growth. Nonetheless, in many European countries, progress on deepening connectivity has stalled since the global financial crisis, and productivity growth attributed to connectivity has suffered.

In Central Asia, despite recent moves toward building greater interconnectedness, the region remains among the least connected globally. Because of both its geographical position and its limited infrastructure, many Central Asian countries are only weakly connected to other ECA countries and the global economy. The vast distances between Central Asia, Europe, and East Asia will remain an obstacle to connectivity. However, infrastructure investments and policies to improve integration through freer trade, infrastructure, and investment policies are likely to provide large growth benefits in Central Asia.

Many ECA countries can be proud of what they have achieved in building greater connectivity and advancing development during the past 25 years. But because the economic benefits of connectivity through knowledge and technology transfers are not obvious, while the challenge of economic uncertainty is, building the case for deepening connections requires solid and clear evidence. By recognizing the challenges as well as making explicit the potential opportunities of greater connectivity through various channels, *Critical Connections* can assist ECA's policy makers in building the foundations for deepening important connections in the coming decades.

Cyril Muller
Vice President
Europe and Central Asia Region
World Bank Group

Acknowledgments

This report was written by a team led by David Michael Gould, Lead Economist in the World Bank's Office of the Chief Economist for Europe and Central Asia. The core team members were Erhan Artuc, Cecilia Briceno-Garmendia, Bernard Hoekman (European University Institute), Mathilde Lebrand, Çağlar Özden, Georgi Panterov, Nadia Rocha, William Shaw, Daria Taglioni, Shawn Tan, Ekaterina Ushakova, Gonzalo Varela, Hernan Winkler, and Thea Yde-Jensen. The work was carried out under the overall supervision and guidance of Hans Timmer, Chief Economist for the Europe and Central Asia Region.

The Macroeconomics, Trade, and Investment team benefited from the guidance of Jose Guilherme Reis and comments and discussions with Jean Francois Arvis, Cordula Rastogi, and Daniel Saslavsky. The Transport team appreciates the general guidance of Juan Gaviria and comments and discussions with Baher El-Hifnawi, Carolina Monsalve, and the Global Practice Transport team at large. Many thanks go to Rashmi Shankar for her extremely helpful contributions during the early stages of the report and Moritz Meyer for his generous time and discussions on applied network analysis. Peer reviewers Luis-Felipe Lopez-Calva, Caroline Freund, Bill Maloney, Aaditya Mattoo, and Russell Hillberry provided very helpful advice and comments on the report.

This report would not have been timely or relevant without the insights and inputs of European Central Bank staff members, who provided data, analysis, and technical support for the work on "Knowledge Transfers from International Openness in Trade and Investment: The European Case," and staff members of the International Civil Aviation Organization, particularly Dr. Ananthanarayan Sainarayan and colleagues, who generously provided data on origin-to-destination airline connectivity. Private and public sector organizations and experts in Romania and Moldova also provided significant inputs and insights; in Romania: Startnet, Softelligence, Fondul Proprietatea, the Foreign Investors Council, Oracle România, the Ministry of Transport, the Ministry of External Commerce, the Ministry of Communications and Information Society, UPC Romania, Dr. Adrian Curaj (UNESCO), AmCham, H. Essers, Robin Martens (International Project Management), Kuijken Logistics Group, and Autonom Rent-A-Car; in Moldova: Ionel, Andragrup SRL, the European Business Association, GIZ (German Cooperation for International Development), the Ministry of Transport and Roads Infrastructure, APIUS, Moldova Investment and Export Promotion Organization, the Ministry of Finance, Star Legal Consulting, AmCham, Danube Logistics, and the Bureau for Relations with the Diaspora.

Many people participated in the writing of the report. The main authors and contributors were

- **Overview:** David Michael Gould
- **Chapter 1:** David Michael Gould, Dror Kenett, and Georgi Panterov (with contributions from Angel Bogoev [American University], Michael Danziger [Center for Complex Network Research and Department of Physics, Northeastern University], Dobrina Gogova, Xin Yuan [Boston University], and Tlek Zeinullayev [Harvard University])
- **Chapter 2:** Paloma López-Garcia (European Central Bank) and Daria Taglioni (with contributions from Francesco Chiacchio [European Central Bank], Alvaro Espitia, Katerina Gradeva [European Central Bank], Laura Gomez-Mera, Asier Mariscal [Carlos III University of Madrid], Nadia Rocha, and Gonzalo Varela)
- **Chapter 3:** Shawn Tan, Hernan Winkler, and Thea Yde-Jensen
- **Chapter 4:** Erhan Artuc and Çağlar Özden (with contributions from Gnanaraj Chellaraj, Julio Elias, David Michael Gould, Bingjie Hu, Zovanga Kone, Tu Chi Nguyen, and Michael Packard)
- **Chapter 5:** Cecilia Briceno-Garmendia, Mathilde Lebrand, and Megersa Abate (with contributions from Rodrigo Archondo, Gözde Isik, and Tetyana Kuchma)
- **Chapter 6:** Mathilde Lebrand
- **Chapter 7:** Omar Bamieh (University of Vienna), Matteo Fiorini (European University Institute), and Bernard Hoekman (European University Institute)
- **Spotlights 1 and 2**: Gonzalo Varela and Nadia Rocha
- **Spotlight 3:** Hernan Winkler
- **Content and Technical Editing:** William Shaw
- **Overview Editing:** Richard Alm

Ekaterina Ushakova oversaw the production and support of the report. Many thanks go to all the commentators and reviewers in the initial stages of the report, particularly Europe and Central Asia Country Directors and Managers and Cyril Muller, Vice President of the World Bank's Europe and Central Asia Region.

Abbreviations

AMI	average management index
BIT	bilateral investment treaty
BRI	Belt and Road Initiative
BvD	Bureau van Dijk
CIS	Commonwealth of Independent States
CMEA	Council for Mutual Economic Assistance
DCFTA	Deep and Comprehensive Free Trade Agreements
EBRD	European Bank for Reconstruction and Development
ECA	Europe and Central Asia
EEA	European Economic Association
EEC	European Economic Community
EU	European Union twenty-eight member countries
EU13	Bulgaria, Croatia, Cyprus, Czech Republic, Estonia, Hungary, Latvia, Lithuania, Malta, Poland, Romania, Slovakia, and Slovenia
EU15	Austria, Belgium, Denmark, Finland, France, Germany, Greece, Ireland, Italy, Luxembourg, Netherlands, Portugal, Spain, Sweden, and the United Kingdom
EU15+	EU15 plus Norway and Switzerland
FDI	foreign direct investment
FDIRRI	FDI Regulatory Restrictiveness Indicators
GATS	General Agreement on Trade in Services
GDP	gross domestic product
GVC	global value chain
HIC	high-income country
ICT	information and communication technologies
LMIC	lower-middle-income country
MBI	Mobility Barriers Index
MDC	multidimensional connectivity
MFN	most favored nation
MIPEX	Migrant Integration Policy Index
MNE	multinational enterprise
NACE	European Classification of Economic Activities
NAFTA	North American Free Trade Agreement
NTM	nontariff measures
NUTS-3	nomenclature of territorial units for statistics (Nomenclature des Unités territoriales statistiques), level 3

OECD	Organisation for Economic Co-operation and Development
OLS	ordinary least squares
PMR	product market regulation
PPML	Poisson pseudo–maximum likelihood
PTA	preferential trade agreement
RTA	revealed technology advantage
SPS	sanitary and phytosanitary
TBT	Technical Barriers to Trade
TFP	total factor productivity
TiVA	Trade in Value Added
TRIMS	Trade Related Investment Measures
UMIC	upper-middle-income country
WDI	World Development Indicators
WEF	World Economic Forum
WITS	World Integrated Trade Solution
WMS	World Management Survey
WTO	World Trade Organization

Countries and Economies

International Organization for Standardization three-letter country codes; italics designate countries in the Europe and Central Asia region

AFG	Afghanistan
ALB	*Albania*
ARE	United Arab Emirates
ARG	Argentina
ARM	*Armenia*
ATG	Antigua and Barbuda
AUS	Australia
AUT	*Austria*
AZE	*Azerbaijan*
BEL	*Belgium*
BEN	Benin
BFA	Burkina Faso
BGD	Bangladesh
BGR	*Bulgaria*
BHS	Bahamas, The
BIH	*Bosnia and Herzegovina*
BLR	*Belarus*
BLZ	Belize
BRA	Brazil
BRB	Barbados
BWA	Botswana
CAN	Canada
CHE	Switzerland
CHL	Chile

CHN	China
COL	Colombia
CMR	Cameroon
CRI	Costa Rica
CYP	*Cyprus*
CZE	*Czech Republic*
DEU	*Germany*
DNK	*Denmark*
DOM	Dominican Republic
DZA	Algeria
ECU	Ecuador
EGY	Egypt, Arab Rep.
ESP	*Spain*
EST	*Estonia*
ETH	Ethiopia
FIN	*Finland*
FRA	*France*
GAB	Gabon
GBR	*United Kingdom*
GEO	*Georgia*
GHA	Ghana
GRC	*Greece*
GUY	Guyana
HKG	Hong Kong SAR, China
HRV	*Croatia*
HUN	*Hungary*
IDN	Indonesia
IND	India
IRL	*Ireland*
ISL	Iceland
ISR	Israel
ITA	*Italy*
JAM	Jamaica
JOR	Jordan
JPN	Japan
KAZ	*Kazakhstan*
KEN	Kenya
KGZ	Kyrgyz Republic
KWT	Kuwait
LBN	Lebanon
LTU	*Lithuania*
LUX	*Luxembourg*
LVA	*Latvia*
MDA	*Moldova*
MEX	Mexico
MKD	*Macedonia, FYR*
MLT	*Malta*

MNE	*Montenegro*
MOZ	Mozambique
MUS	Mauritius
MYS	Malaysia
NAM	Namibia
NGA	Nigeria
NIC	Nicaragua
NLD	*Netherlands*
NOR	Norway
NZL	New Zealand
OMN	Oman
PAK	Pakistan
POL	*Poland*
PRT	*Portugal*
PRY	Paraguay
ROU	*Romania*
RUS	*Russian Federation*
SAU	Saudi Arabia
SGP	Singapore
SRB	*Serbia*
SWE	*Sweden*
SVK	*Slovak Republic*
SVN	*Slovenia*
SWZ	Swaziland
THA	Thailand
TJK	*Tajikistan*
TKM	*Turkmenistan*
TTO	Trinidad and Tobago
TUR	*Turkey*
TZA	Tanzania
UKR	*Ukraine*
UZB	*Uzbekistan*
XKX	*Kosovo* (not listed as an ISO standard country; the unofficial two- and three-digit codes are used by the European Commission and others until an ISO code is assigned)
YUG	*Serbia and Montenegro (former Yugoslavia)*
ZAF	South Africa
ZMB	Zambia

Regional Classifications Used in This Report

Europe and Central Asia

Northern Europe	Southern Europe	Central Europe	Western Europe	Western Balkans
Denmark	Greece	Bulgaria	Austria	Albania
Estonia	Italy	Croatia	Belgium	Bosnia and Herzegovina
Finland	Portugal	Czech Republic	France	Kosovo
Latvia	Spain	Hungary	Germany	Macedonia, FYR
Lithuania	Cyprus	Poland	Ireland	Montenegro
Sweden	Malta	Romania	Luxembourg	Serbia
		Slovak Republic	Netherlands	
		Slovenia	United Kingdom	

South Caucasus	Central Asia	Russian Federation	Turkey	Other Eastern Europe
Armenia	Kazakhstan			Belarus
Azerbaijan	Kyrgyz Republic			Moldova
Georgia	Tajikistan			Ukraine
	Turkmenistan			
	Uzbekistan			

Overview

The countries of the Europe and Central Asia (ECA) region, along with much of the rest of the world, find themselves engaged in a revival of one of the fundamental questions of economic policy: how much to open to the rest of the world. At the turn of the century, the issue seemed largely settled, and most nations viewed greater openness as a key component of the path to prosperity. In these heady days, the European Union (EU) deepened with a drive toward greater integration and expanded by incorporating nations transitioning to market-based economies. More recent events—most notably, the global financial crisis and the tough times that followed—sowed the seeds of doubts about the benefits of globalization, leading to a rise of protectionist and nationalist economic sentiments, exemplified by Britain's referendum to withdraw from the EU. In 2018, how much to open to the rest of the world now dominates the political economy of the ECA region, not just within the advanced EU economies, but also among the emerging economies of the region. Deciding where to draw the line between openness and protectionism has become a pivotal and divisive issue, often tinged with emotion. With this publication, the World Bank offers new research on the process of economic integration, showing its potential benefits without ignoring the downsides.

Main Findings of *Critical Connections*

- The ECA region's international connectivity through trade, foreign direct investment (FDI), migration, telecommunications, transportation, and other avenues

1

facilitates the transfers of knowledge and technology that are critical to long-run growth and shared prosperity. These connections complement each other. For example, migration encourages trade and foreign investment by providing knowledge spillovers between host and home country markets and supporting connections to them. Similarly, the internet and efficient transport links are both necessary for successful e-commerce. Therefore, a balanced approach to increasing all dimensions of connectivity is desirable.

- The depth of overall connections and the geographic composition of the connections both matter. Knowledge transfers are greater from countries that themselves have strong links to third countries. These transfers also emerge from firm linkages in global value chains as well as foreign ownership and management that generate local spillovers.

- Deep integration of countries into the EU along many dimensions has generated important benefits to growth through knowledge transfers. Central Asia, the South Caucasus, and the Western Balkans have benefited from regional connections as well, but the gains have been less pronounced. Much of the difference is due to the lack of direct and indirect connectivity to the wider global economy in the eastern part of ECA.

- Despite its overall benefits, increased connectivity has encountered opposition—most notably, Britain's June 2016 vote to exit the EU. National challenges often contribute to the backlash, but increased connectivity can expose ECA countries to external shocks, particularly those emanating from countries at the center of international economic transactions. By providing alternative sources of external demand and financing, however, a broad range of connections can reduce those risks and help countries cope with both domestic and external shocks.

Introduction

The ECA region has a rich history of regional integration and connectivity to the broader world economy, which has stimulated the growth of knowledge and technological innovation. Indeed, through migration, trade, investments, and other interactions, ECA countries have depended on, and benefited from, connectivity with other countries for centuries. The Silk Road, formally established during China's Han Dynasty in the second century BCE, facilitated more than the exchange of commercial goods. It was also a conduit for art, religion, philosophy, technology, language, science, and architecture (Starr 2015). Similarly, the Age of Discovery (1453–1660 CE) led to the deepening of a global community that was associated with profound advances in commerce and culture. As new navigation technology made sailing long distances possible, Europeans took to the seas to forge direct trading relationships with China, Indonesia, and Japan. Historians contend that it was the spice trade that fueled the development of faster boats, encouraged the discovery of new lands, and fostered new diplomatic relationships between East and West (Parthesius 2010; Bernstein 2013).

In recent times, the most prominent feature of ECA connectivity has been regional integration through the gradual expansion of what is now the EU. The 1951 European Coal and Steel Community, a sectoral integration initiative among six European states, led to a much more ambitious agreement to form a European

Economic Community in 1957. Over the next half century, the Community grew incrementally in geographic reach, issue coverage, and depth of policy cooperation. Within the EU, economic connections have progressively deepened from the initial lowering of trade barriers through the Single Market's convergence of regulation and finally the adoption of the euro as a common currency by 19 member states. Today, the 28-country EU incorporates the free movement of goods, services, capital, and people, with associated supranational common institutions—all the hard-won results of a multigenerational push toward greater connectivity.

A major feature of European integration in the past 20 years has been the process of EU accession—most notably by 10 Baltic and Central European countries (the Czech Republic, Estonia, Hungary, Latvia, Lithuania, Poland, the Slovak Republic, and Slovenia in 2004, followed by Bulgaria and Romania in 2007). Until the dissolution of the Soviet Union in 1991, the 10 nations that joined the EU had in one form or another been part of the ECA region's second major regional bloc: the Council for Mutual Economic Assistance. The perceived advantages of connectivity led to a looser form of economic integration and cooperation between Russia and the former Soviet republics—the Commonwealth of Independent States (CIS). In the past decade, Russia has sought to deepen the CIS into a common market and economic union and pursued a process of deepening economic integration with a subset of its neighbors through the creation of a Eurasian Economic Union. However, while progress has been made, the strength of global connectivity in the CIS remains much lower than in the EU.

The ECA region's growing participation in global and regional supply chains has greatly increased the importance and variety of international economic connections across the region. These forces have expanded ECA countries' regional connections more rapidly than their connections outside the region. Nevertheless, as shown in the example of trade connectivity (figure O.1), many ECA countries have achieved substantial increases in global connectivity through their links to other ECA countries, such as Germany (DEU in the figure), France (FRA), or the United Kingdom (GBR), that have strong global connections.

The ECA region's persistent efforts to integrate reflect at the very least an intuitive appreciation of the potential benefits from greater connectivity. More formally, economists have recognized the superiority of openness over autarky. In studying linkages between nations, they have focused on how knowledge transfers through international connectivity boost long-term growth, rather than one-time jumps in output due to gains from specialization (Romer 1990). Much of the knowledge gain from connectivity comes from "tacit" knowledge—the kind that comes through learning by doing and face-to-face interactions. Unlike "explicit" knowledge, it cannot be transferred in texts and blueprints.

When looking at connectivity and knowledge transfers, analysts typically consider one channel at a time—such as trade, FDI, migration, telecommunications, or transport links. While many cross-country studies find, for example, that the level of trade or FDI relative to gross domestic product (GDP) is positively associated with growth, they generally do not consider how many forms of connectivity work together. For example, it is hard to imagine trade taking place on the historic Silk Road without migration and transportation networks, or the recent development of e-commerce without high-speed internet and an efficient means of transferring goods from one country to another.

FIGURE O.1 **Exports of manufactured goods**

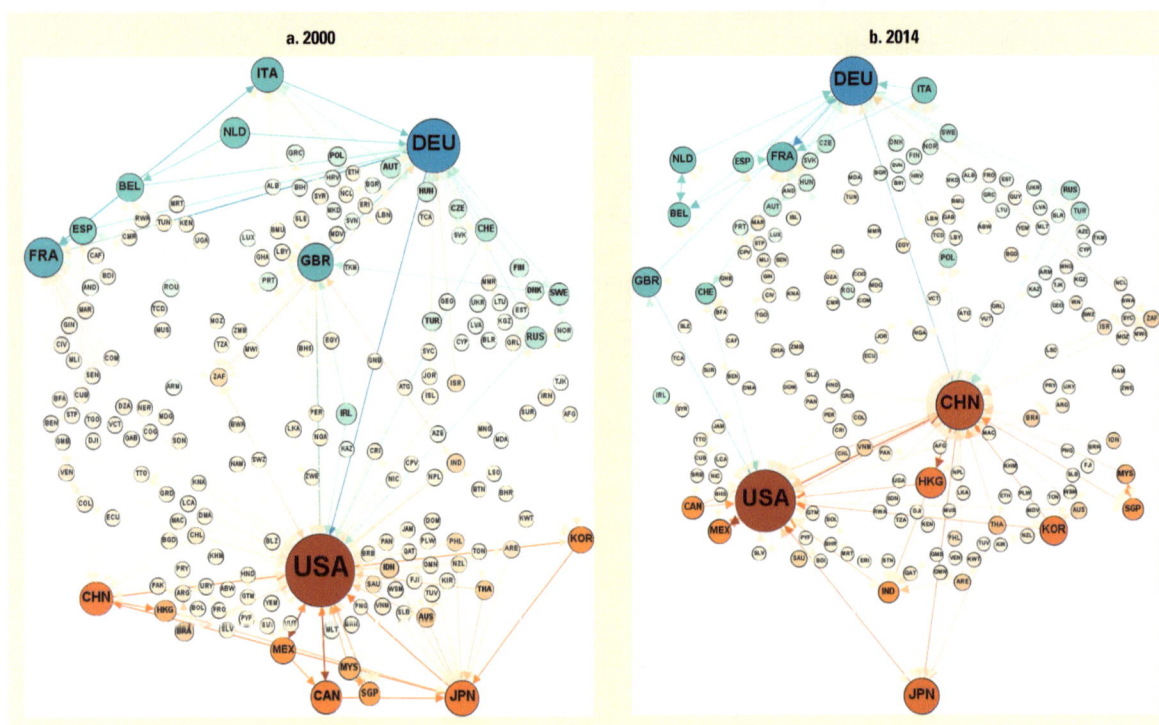

Source: Calculations based on data from the United Nations Conference on Trade and Development.
Note: The size of each country node reflects the total volume of trade. Each node has two outgoing links, which point to the country's two top export partners. Countries in the Europe and Central Asia region are shown in shades of blue. The methodology for plotting the countries attempts to show clearly the connections between countries in the global network of countries. The largest country nodes are pulled to the outer boundaries of the figure, but the pull is counterbalanced by the number and strength of connections with partner countries. Consequently, country nodes will tend to be grouped together if they share common connections.

The importance of each connectivity channel for growth is likely to be affected by the strength of other channels—particularly when technology transfers depend on both tacit and explicit knowledge. For example, FDI by higher-income ECA economies in those with lower incomes can be an important source of knowledge transfers through exposure to sophisticated production techniques and management styles that are learned "on the job." Migrants often learn important skills working abroad, and workers and managers from the investing country typically accompany the FDI. Thus, FDI and migration can work together to accelerate technology transfers within ECA. In Moldova, for example, connections developed through migration to Northern, Western, and Southern Europe in the 1990s subsequently generated Italian investment in the garment industry as well as German investment in factories for the assembly of electronic car components. Because of these initial connections and foreign investments, Moldova is now developing a service and manufacturing industry for the local market, creating its own brands, and exporting to other ECA countries.

In addition to being mutually reinforcing, connectivity channels vary in depth and geographic composition. Being well connected to highly connected countries can provide benefits beyond being well connected to comparatively isolated countries. The advanced economies in Europe have provided a gateway for knowledge transfers from outside of ECA. Poland, for example, leveraged its growing ties to Germany to develop connections with that country's trading partners and expand trade to broader markets within Europe and beyond. In the ECA region and other parts of the world, greater connectivity has delivered overall economic benefits for growth and development. Regional and global connectivity have been a tremendous "convergence machine," raising living standards in lower-income countries to those of wealthier middle- to high-income countries (see World Bank 2012).

The gains, however, are not evenly distributed or universally recognized. The 2007 global economic crisis and various commodity price shocks underscored the importance of understanding the potential risks of increased connectivity transmitting shocks from one country to another.[1] Voters, both in Europe and elsewhere, are now questioning whether the benefits of greater connectivity are worth the costs. In addition to the United Kingdom's 2016 vote to exit the EU (Brexit), recent elections in several European countries reflect an underlying skepticism regarding the benefits of deepening cooperation, with voters increasingly favoring parties seeking greater national autonomy instead of greater regional integration. Some analysts have attributed the lack of enthusiasm to concerns over the large migration flows and recent influx of refugees. Certainly, large sudden shifts in migrant flows, due to natural disasters or wars, bring critical societal issues into play for domestic policy consideration. But larger questions have been raised about the downsides of regional integration and globalization in general and the role that deeper integration initiatives have played as a driver in the rise of populism (see, for example, Rodrik 2018).

Thus far, the skepticism has not led to a widespread retreat from integration among ECA countries. The institutions and policies that promote regional and global connectivity remain largely intact, with most countries continuing to benefit. However, ECA integration has been slowing, and the challenges and questions call for a better understanding of ECA connectivity and its economic impacts. Analyzing the evolution of ECA's regional and global connectivity calls for paying particular attention to how the various types of connections have interacted with one another and why connectivity in the region and in the larger global network has played a key role in boosting growth and living standards. While recognizing the benefits of greater connectivity, it is important to acknowledge the potential downside risks through the transmission of economic shocks as well as the choices countries face regarding which types of connections to strengthen with various partner countries.

> While recognizing the benefits of greater connectivity, it is important to acknowledge the potential downside risks through the transmission of economic shocks.

This Overview summarizes the main findings of the World Bank flagship study *Critical Connections*.[2] The flagship's primary purpose is to offer a deep analysis of ECA connectivity and how it has evolved over the past two decades. The framework and logical flow of chapters for this report is shown in figure O.2. In a key innovation of the study, a network analysis measure of *multidimensional connectivity* captures the relationship between different forms of connectivity and their joint impacts on growth and the transmission of shocks (chapter 1). The next step is to examine how knowledge flows through trade and investment channels from the ECA's frontier firms to less technically advanced companies, improving productivity at the firm level (chapter 2). In the ECA region, firm connectivity does not just exert its influence through foreign investment; it also works through enhancing

FIGURE O.2 Framework and logical flow of chapters for this report

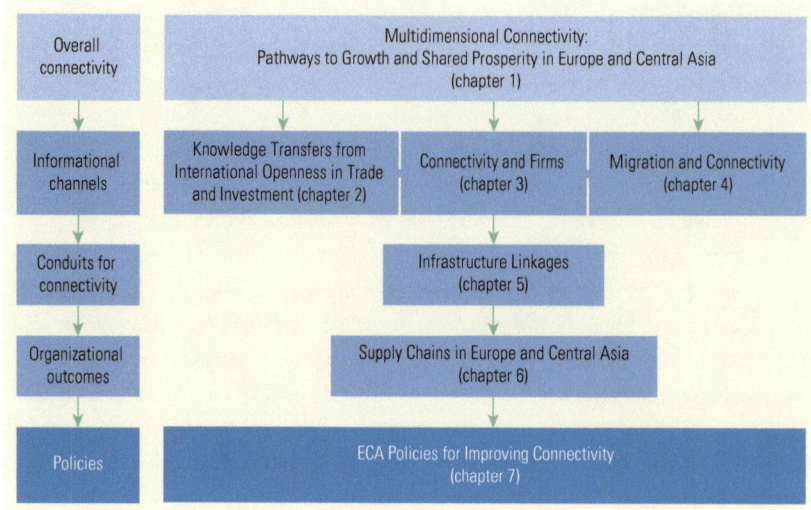

management practices. Ties between firms are associated with better outcomes in foreign-owned or -managed firms as well as with spillover effects that improve outcomes in locally owned and managed firms (chapter 3). Another complementary channel of ECA connectivity is migration (chapter 4). A new methodology for filling in large gaps in our knowledge of ECA migration, particularly regarding skills and gender, provides insights into the trends and determinants of migration and migration's economic impact on the region.

Facilitating the movement of people and goods across the ECA region is the focus of the next layer of connectivity: infrastructure linkages (chapter 5). Another key innovation looks at the time and cost involved in moving goods and people across the region, rather than the kilometers and density of roads and rail links. This network analysis yields a richer perspective on the ECA's transport links. The development of supply chains has been a key organizational outcome of the depth of ECA informational channels and conduits for connectivity (chapter 6). The development of Europe's supply chains ("Factory Europe"), and the efficiency gains they provide, reflects the successes of narrowing policy barriers to trade, investment, migration, information and communication technology (ICT), and transport. Finally, ECA countries' policy progress in supporting international connectivity over time and relative to other countries is evaluated to guide future policy actions (chapter 7).

Multidimensional Connectivity Is a Key to Europe and Central Asia's Development and Growth

International connections include trade, FDI, migration, ICT, and transport links. Most studies measure the impact of each of these channels individually. This study takes a different approach, creating an indicator that combines all channels (networks) in a functional form that recognizes their complementarity—the *multidimensional connectivity index* (represented in figure O.3 as the MDC network). The measure reflects both the depth of each channel between each

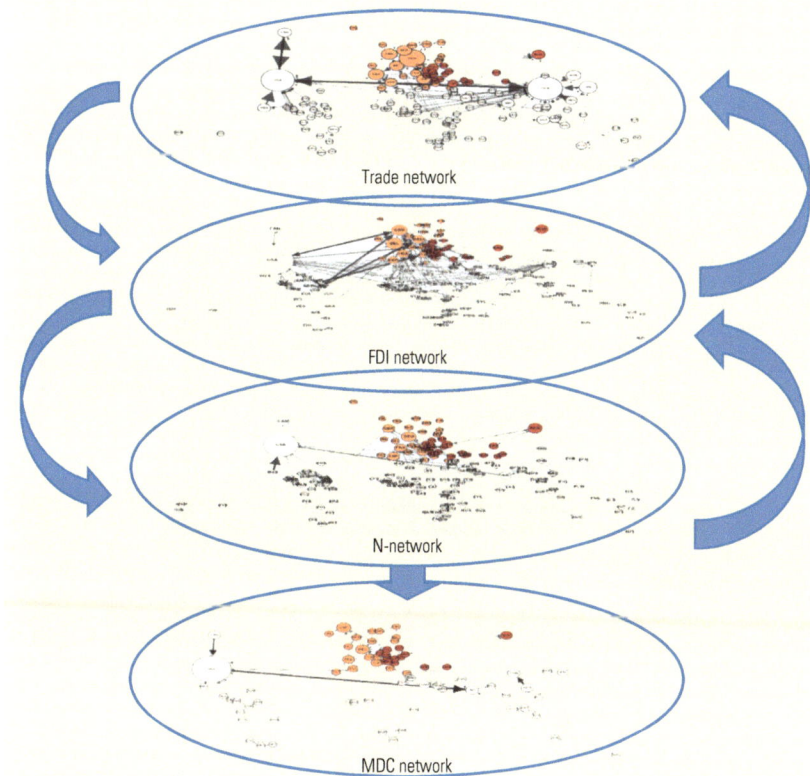

FIGURE O.3 **Multidimensional connectivity combines many channels of connectivity**

Note: This figure presents an indicative representation of the multidimensional connectivity (MDC) network that incorporates the relationship between all networks—trade, FDI, and other measured global networks (N)—into a single collapsed network. A modified form of PageRank centrality for each country (node) is developed based on this collapsed network and used as an indicator of how overall connectivity influences growth overall and growth of the bottom 40 percent of the income distribution. FDI = foreign direct investment.

pair of countries (e.g., the size of bilateral trade relative to each country's GDP) and the benefits a country may reap from being connected to another well-connected country (e.g., Croatia's trade with Germany is likely to boost knowledge spillovers more than Croatia's trade with Albania owing to Germany's wider global connections in addition to its higher level of technology).

Compared with traditional approaches, this method more accurately measures a country's exposure to knowledge flows via direct and indirect international connections. The analysis presented in this study emphasizes the importance of complementary and balanced connectivity across the various channels. The impact on growth of any single connectivity channel is expected to decline as additional knowledge gains from the channel diminish—unless other channels of connectivity grow as well. In other words, policies to improve trade without complementary policies to improve investment and transport will have diminishing returns. Thus, promoting balanced connectivity across trade, transport, foreign investment, and other channels is likely to be more beneficial than focusing on enhancing only one channel.

TABLE O.1 Multidimensional Connectivity Varies by ECA Subregion, with the Highest Connectivity in the Western Part of the Region and the Lowest in the Eastern Part

ECA subregions	Multidimensional connectivity	Trade	FDI	Migration	ICT	Airline	Portfolio flows
High connectivity							
Western Europe	6	6	6	9	9	15	19
Northern Europe	12	12	17	26	21	23	22
of which Baltics	*30*	*28*	*36*	*38*	*50*	*28*	*21*
Southern Europe	25	24	26	21	28	23	22
Central Europe	31	27	34	36	41	46	46
Medium connectivity							
Russian Federation	55	53	61	28	63	64	83
Turkey	57	51	67	33	73	79	40
Eastern Europe	62	59	60	81	54	57	76
Low connectivity							
Western Balkans	88	75	97	45	88	86	99
Central Asia	94	99	93	101	101	103	101
South Caucasus	104	104	102	64	104	104	93

Note: The table shows global rankings, from best to worst, in combined per capita connectivity, with lower values indicating better connectivity. Subregion indicators are median values of the subregion's countries ECA = Europe and Central Asia; FDI = foreign direct investment; ICT = information and communication technology.

The various channels exhibit some degree of substitutability, but complementarity dominates. In some contexts, for example, trade may substitute for FDI because firms can either export a product to a foreign market or invest in the foreign market to produce there. However, the information flows from trade tend to complement those from FDI. Firms may discover opportunities to export to a foreign market because of their exposure through investing there. Thus, improving connectivity in one dimension improves connectivity through other channels.

In terms of per capita levels in ECA subregional multidimensional connectivity (table O.1), Western Europe has the highest global ranking, followed by Northern, Central, and Southern Europe, while Russia, Turkey, and Eastern Europe are in the middle range, and the Western Balkans, Central Asia, and the South Caucasus have the lowest levels of overall connectivity. Not surprisingly, higher per capita levels of connectivity are associated with higher levels of development, reflecting both the number and depth of connections a country has. Tables OA.1 and OA.2 show individual country rankings of multidimensional connectivity on an absolute and a per capita basis, respectively. Central Asia and the South Caucasus rank low on overall connectivity, but because they started from a low base, they also saw the greatest improvement from 2000 to 2014 (figure O.4). The South Caucasus saw connectivity increase by nearly 75 percent, while Central Asia saw connectivity increase by more than 40 percent. Eastern Europe and the Western Balkans, although also starting from relatively low levels, have not seen increases as rapid, with connectivity increasing only 20 percent and 10 percent, respectively. The key challenge for these regions is to find ways to improve balanced

FIGURE O.4 Europe and Central Asia's connectivity has grown, but there are wide variations across subregions

Growth in connectivity, percent, 2000–14

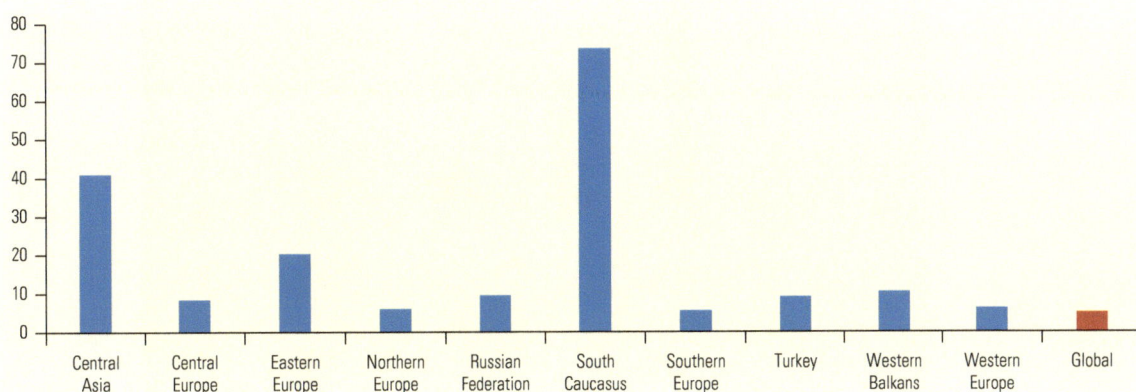

Note: Subregional and global indicators are median growth rates.

connectivity, particularly through easing domestic constraints on doing business and facilitating trade, FDI, airline, and ICT connectivity. For the ECA region as a whole, while improvements in connectivity have slowed since 2008, it still has grown faster than global connectivity since 2000, reflecting the EU integration process as well as strides taken in transition economies.

Using this study's new MDC measure, we find a closer association with growth than when considering individual connectivity indexes separately. In the ECA region, the depth of a country's international connections in 2000 contributed to growth over the subsequent 16 years, after accounting for other fundamental determinants of growth typically used in cross-country studies (such as initial GDP, education, size of government, inflation, investment rate, and quality of governance). This is because a deepening of each channel tends to increase the growth impact of other channels. The association between MDC and growth is shown in figure O.5, along with each individual component connectivity channel. The level of trade connectivity has the most significant individual impact on growth, followed by measures of connectivity through FDI, migration, and airline flights. Trade connectivity is statistically significant and associated with more rapid income growth of the bottom 40 percent of the income distribution, but the other connectivity indicators are not, perhaps because the bottom 40 percent benefit more directly from trade and less so from other forms of connectivity.

The increase in international connectivity over the past decade has occurred in tandem with severe disruptions to the international economy, most notably the global financial crisis. Greater connectivity may have increased ECA countries' exposure to such shocks, but it may also have increased countries' ability to cope with them. Least vulnerable to shocks are countries with very high levels of connectivity *and* countries with very low levels of connectivity. The former can more easily find alternative export markets or sources of finance, and the latter are more insulated from the global economy. Countries in the middle of the range tend to be the most vulnerable to shocks for lack of easy alternatives to compensate for declines

FIGURE O.5 Connectivity's effects on overall and bottom-40 growth

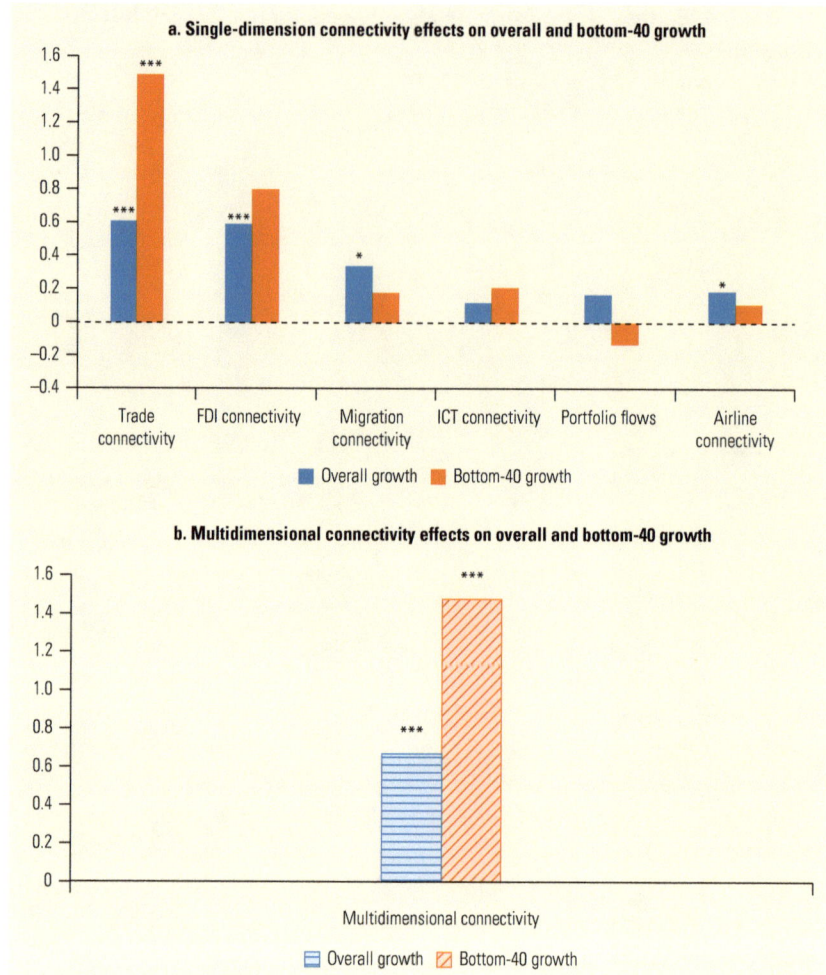

a. Single-dimension connectivity effects on overall and bottom-40 growth

b. Multidimensional connectivity effects on overall and bottom-40 growth

Note: All coefficients (except those on multidimensional connectivity) are estimated with ordinary least squares regression; multidimensional connectivity is estimated using a maximum likelihood procedure. The connectivity variables, including multidimensional connectivity, are normalized using the standard normal distribution; therefore, the size of the coefficient represents the annual growth impact of a one-standard-deviation change. FDI = foreign direct investment; ICT = information and communication technology.
Significance level: * = 10 percent, ** = 5 percent, *** = 1 percent.

in connectivity. One example is countries highly dependent on a well-connected country—as shown in figure O.6 in the case of a shock originating in Germany.

Using multidimensional connectivity to better understand the transmission of shocks also indicates that ripples radiate across countries indirectly connected to places experiencing hard times. The impacts are not always obvious. Take, for example, the potential impact of Brexit. In this example, a 20 percent drop in all connections between the United Kingdom and the 27 remaining EU countries (EU27) is simulated. As expected, the United Kingdom suffers the greatest harm, followed by small countries of the EU27, such as Malta and Ireland, that get most of their global connectivity through the UK. However, other countries outside the EU that are not directly affected by Brexit, such as Norway, Senegal, Libya, and Fiji, are nonetheless indirectly affected through

FIGURE O.6 **A shock originating in Germany has the largest impact on countries that gain their global connectivity through Germany**

Shock: 10 percent fall in all types of connectivity

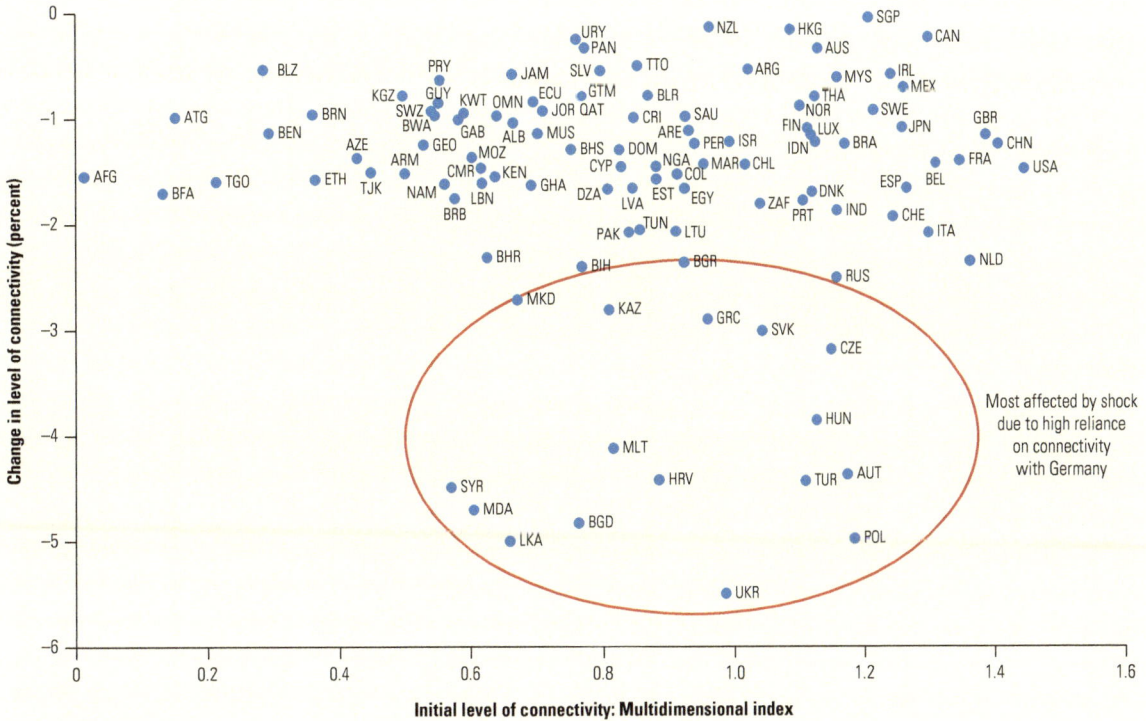

TABLE O.2 **EU and Non-EU Countries Most Affected by Brexit**

1. United Kingdom	15. Italy
2. Malta	16. Poland
3. Ireland	17. Germany
4. Cyprus	18. Latvia
5. Netherlands	19. Finland
6. Denmark	20. Hungary
7. Luxembourg	21. Czech Republic
8. Sweden	22. Senegal
9. France	23. Libya
10. Spain	24. Suriname
11. Norway	25. Slovenia
12. Greece	26. Fiji
13. Portugal	27. Iceland
14. Belgium	28. Austria

Note: The table ranks countries according to the impact on the countries from Brexit, with a ranking of 1 indicating the greatest impact. EU = European Union.

the connections of connections (table O.2). Interestingly, these countries are more affected by Brexit than some EU countries, such as Austria, Estonia, Lithuania, Romania, and Bulgaria.

How connectivity transmits shocks is relevant to the past decade's shift in public sentiment away from openness and toward a more inward-looking stance.

At the same time, the new mood increases the need to better understand how connectivity works to improve economic performance. The next few sections describe the ECA region's recent experiences with the key channels of greater connectivity: knowledge transfers, foreign ownership and management, migration, infrastructure, and supply chains.

Europe and Central Asia Connectivity Is a Critical Source of Knowledge Transfers

ECA connections with other countries through trade, investment, and production sharing are important because they increase access to technology and ideas critical to growth. Importing firms learn from exposure to more diverse and sophisticated inputs to their production, and exporters learn through opportunities to achieve economies of scale, upgrade workers' skills, and improve products to compete in foreign markets. Local firms involved in FDI learn through technology transfers and exposure to high-skilled workers. Moreover, local firms not involved in trade or FDI also may learn through exposure to, or competition from, more internationally connected firms. All of this emphasizes the critical importance of openness to international transactions for gaining access to the knowledge essential for growth and productivity enhancements. Romania's greater openness after it joined the EU led a Belgian logistics provider and an American software company to extend global value chains (GVCs) into the country, creating spillovers that benefited the local economy (box O.1).

BOX O.1 Global Value Chain Spillovers in Romania

H. Essers and Oracle are two examples of foreign companies investing in Romania that illustrate benefits from foreign investments.

H. Essers is a leading European logistics firm with headquarters in Belgium, focusing on chemicals, pharmaceuticals, health care, and high-quality products. After its integration with a Dutch company already doing business in Romania, the Belgian firm increased its presence in Romania, with an eye on Eastern Europe and Central Asia. Knowledge and know-how coming from traditional logistics hubs like the Netherlands and Belgium subsequently improved Romania's logistics performance. Logistics is the backbone of supply chains, making production fragmentation and the smooth coordination of its stages possible. Knowledge spillovers occur through clients' learning good practices in quality norms, information technology, and cold chains.

Oracle is a major multinational company headquartered in the United States, specializing in developing and marketing database software and technology, cloud-engineered systems, and enterprise software products. In the mid-2000s, it opened a branch in Bucharest and began to hire local engineers for routine software development. In addition to short-term spillovers, Oracle's entry has spurred a new generation of entrepreneurs who got their start at the company's operations in Bucharest and went on to create their own businesses. One of them is Softelligence, a Romanian software company that designs tailored mobile applications for financial institutions. The low cost of entry for new entrepreneurs in this industry—coupled with competitive wages, a qualified workforce, and excellent internet connectivity—has boosted this sector and diversified the economy.

Europe compares well to the global frontier in manufacturing productivity, but it lags behind the global frontier in services and in some innovation-based growth industries. Technology creation in European manufacturing is very similar to that in other advanced economies, as measured by the gap in labor productivity growth between frontier firms in Europe and the Organisation for Economic Co-operation and Development (OECD) countries (figure O.7).[3] However, labor productivity growth is lower in European services firms than in firms at the OECD frontier. The numbers suggest that the continent could be served well by pursuing better connectivity to the global frontier firms in the services sector. Similar sectoral differences between the most advanced European and global firms can be seen in the intensity of investment in research and development (R&D).

FDI inflows, FDI outflows, and imports are all important to productivity growth across the world; as such, they are conduits for the transmission of both tacit and explicit knowledge. Empirical evidence suggests that when a pair of countries are linked through FDI or trade, an increase in R&D investment in one is associated with an increase in total factor productivity (TFP) in the other. In other words, FDI and trade help international R&D spillovers materialize.[4] When the focus is trade as a conduit of R&D spillovers, evidence reveals that the quality of domestic institutions is an important factor that facilitates spillovers. Better business environments, the quality of tertiary education systems, and stronger patent protection are associated with stronger R&D spillovers.

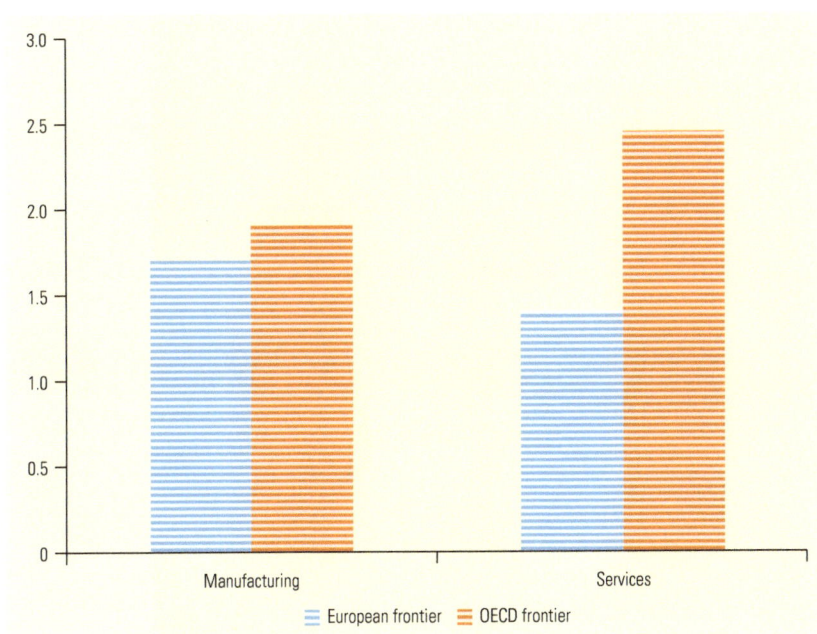

FIGURE O.7 Europe lags behind the frontier in services
Average annual labor productivity growth, percent, 2010–13

Source: Calculations based on data from the Organisation for Economic Co-operation and Development (OECD) and Amadeus.
Note: Sample is based on firms with more than 20 employees. The European frontier is among the EU15 (that is, the original core countries of the European Union). The technology gap is proxied by the difference in productivity growth between frontier firms and other firms (laggards) in the same sector and year.

Productivity increases in most firms are generated by the absorption of knowledge from other sources, rather than through their own investment in creating new knowledge. A firm's potential to learn from existing knowledge can be measured by the difference between the firm's TFP (or its TFP growth rate) and that of the most advanced firms in the sector. In Europe, advanced firms tend to be larger, have higher levels of capital relative to labor, invest more in intangibles (such as marketing practices), and have more-educated workers than other firms, although some of these differences vary by sector.

The transfer of knowledge from international sources tends to follow a two-stage process (figure O.8). First, the most advanced domestic firms absorb knowledge from the most advanced firms globally, often through participation in GVCs that involve production sharing through trade, investment ties, and contractual agreements. Second, less advanced domestic firms absorb this knowledge through their exposure to the most advanced domestic firms. By contrast, the direct technology transfer between the most advanced global firms and the less advanced domestic firms tends to be limited. Econometric evidence for the ECA region confirms that a rise in TFP growth among advanced domestic firms (defined as the top 20 percent of domestic firms by TFP in each sector) leads to a similar increase in TFP among other domestic firms, but an increase in TFP among the most advanced global firms has little direct impact on the less advanced domestic firms.

This analysis sheds light on the productivity slowdown in many ECA countries after the global economic crisis. Productivity growth in Central and Eastern European EU members fell by 8.2 percentage points in 2008–14, compared to 2000–07 (figure O.9). The crisis was transmitted through global supply chains and sharply reduced domestic firms' engagement in these chains, which serve advanced markets in Europe and the United States. This decreased opportunities for firms in Central and Eastern Europe to learn, led to a fall in their R&D spending as a share of GDP, and lowered their propensity to introduce new

FIGURE O.8 How technology flows from European frontier firms (global value chain lead firms) to the remaining European firms

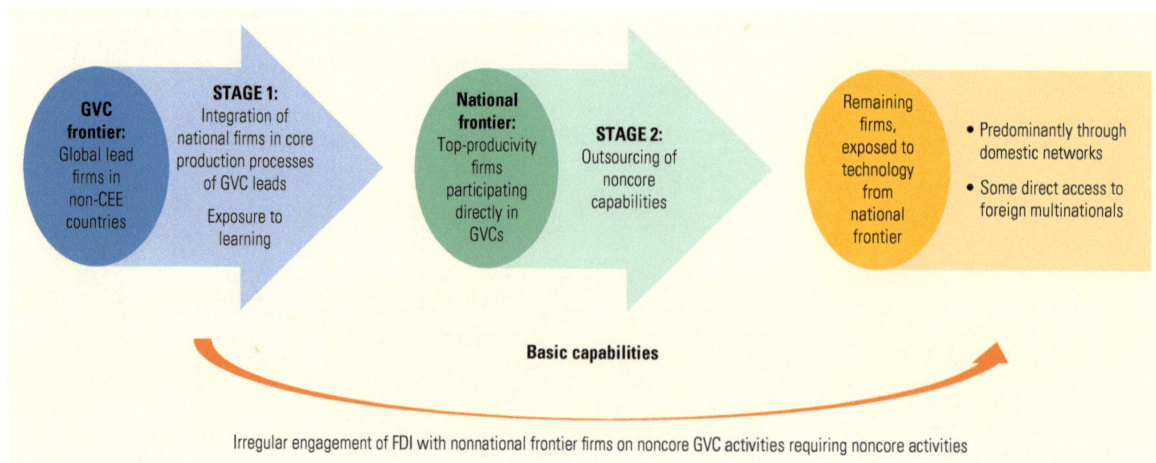

Note: CEE = Central and Eastern Europe; FDI = foreign direct investment; GVC = global value chain.

FIGURE O.9 Productivity growth was lower in Central and Eastern Europe during the crisis

Difference between labor productivity growth in Central European EU countries and that in Eastern European EU countries, 2000–07 versus 2008–14

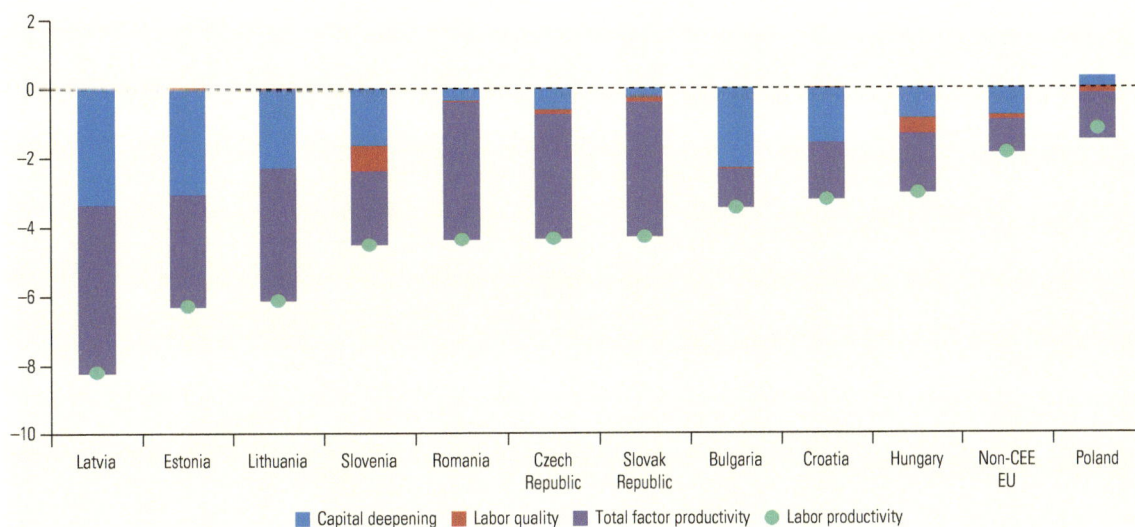

■ Capital deepening   ■ Labor quality   ■ Total factor productivity   ● Labor productivity

Source: Calculations based on Conference Board data.
Note: Overall macroeconomic data may reflect both sectoral changes and within-firm productivity growth. "Non-CEE EU" refers to the unweighted average for Austria, Belgium, Cyprus, Denmark, Finland, France, Germany, Ireland, Italy, Luxembourg, Malta, the Netherlands, Portugal, Spain, Sweden, and the United Kingdom. CEE = Central and Eastern Europe; EU = European Union.

products or processes—as shown in the World Bank's Enterprise Surveys. In this instance, exposure to international volatility was a major driver of slower growth following the crisis. However, the "cure" of reducing firms' exposure to international volatility through restrictions on trade or FDI would be worse than the disease, because such policies would diminish firms' opportunities to learn through participation in global supply chains and other international transactions. This would particularly depress growth in less advanced countries, where firms are further from the productivity frontier and thus have greater opportunities to learn through connections with foreign markets.

International knowledge flows and their productivity impacts take place within companies—so their internal operating characteristics are likely to be important in determining whether connectivity gains are large or small. A critical factor is management. Looking at micro data, the next section focuses on how foreign management, regardless of ownership, can influence firm outcomes.

Foreign-Owned and -Managed Firms Tend to Perform Better and Contribute to Local Firms' Productivity

The share of ECA firms owned by foreigners (excluding firms owned by parent companies located in tax havens) ranges from negligible, in countries such as Belgium, Bulgaria, Hungary, Russia, Ukraine, and most Southern European countries, to 5 percent or more in most of Central Europe, Latvia, Lithuania, and the Western Balkans, to more than 32 percent in Ireland and the United Kingdom. More than half of foreign-owned firms in ECA also have predominantly foreign management (figure O.10). Across the ECA, foreign-owned firms tend to be larger than domestic firms, although the age of foreign-owned firms is not, on average, significantly different from that of local firms (figures O.11 and O.12). Many ECA firms are owned by people or firms in large, rich economies, such as Germany or the United States. However, geographic proximity, common language, cultural heritage, trade ties, and immigration from the source country are also important determinants of foreign ownership (table O.3).

Firms that are foreign owned or foreign managed tend to achieve higher growth in operating revenues, employment, and average wages than other firms (figure O.13). Foreign-owned firms with foreign management have 28.3 percent higher growth in operating revenue, 19.6 percent higher job growth, and 16.8 percent higher wage growth than local firms.

Foreign affiliates with local managers also perform better than local firms, although less so than foreign firms with foreign management. However, it is unclear whether the foreign firms' better performance reflects the impact of foreign ownership or management or foreign companies' tendency to invest in the most productive regions, sectors, or firms.

FIGURE O.10 Foreign-owned and foreign-managed firms in ECA, 2013

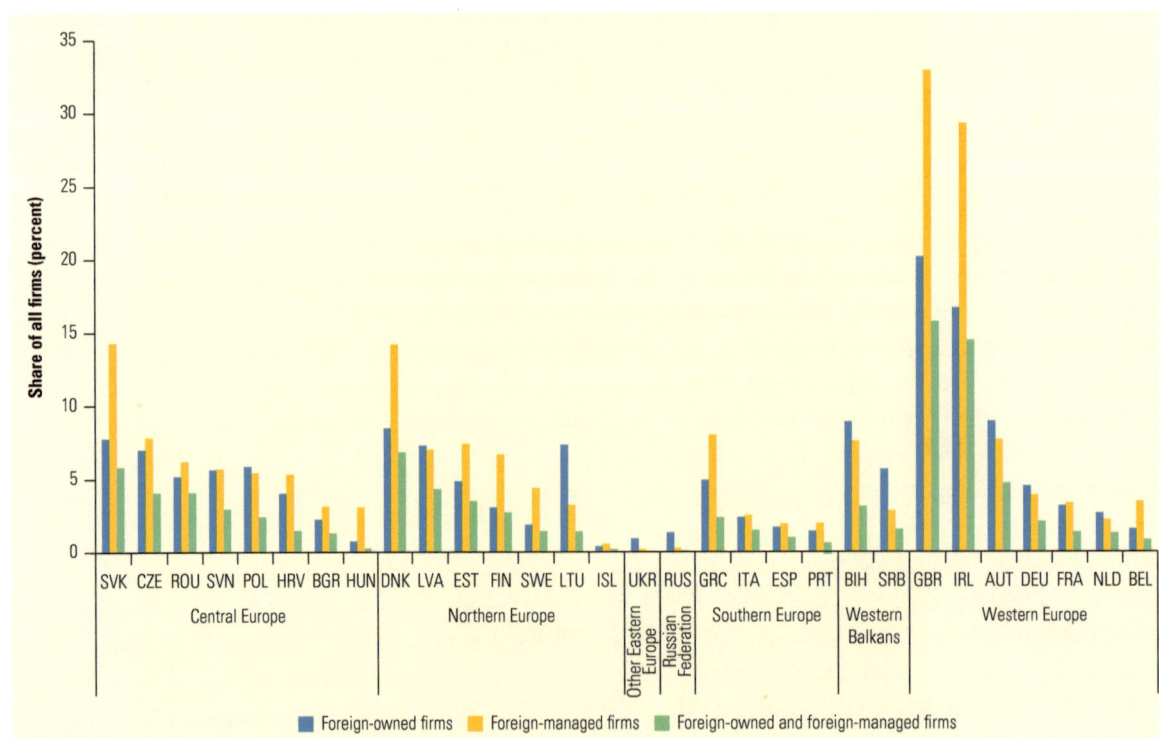

Source: Calculations using Orbis data.
Note: Sample excludes firms with owners in tax haven countries. ECA = Europe and Central Asia.

FIGURE O.11 Large firms are more likely to be foreign owned in ECA

Share of foreign-owned firms by number of employees, 2013

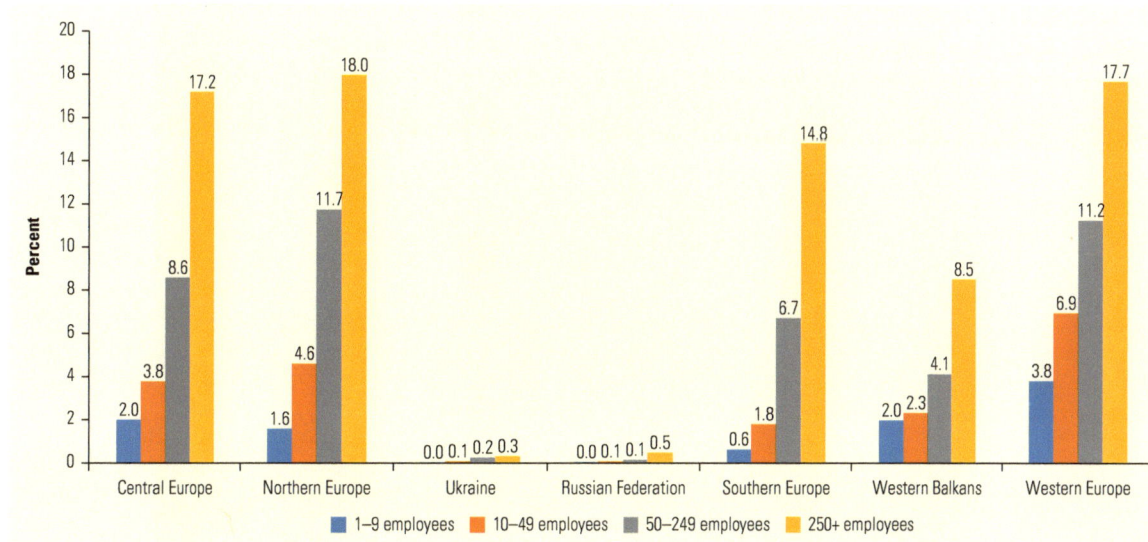

Source: Calculations using Orbis data.
Note: Sample excludes firms with owners in tax haven countries. ECA = Europe and Central Asia.

FIGURE O.12 There is no clear relationship between a firm's age and the likelihood of its being foreign owned

Share of foreign-owned firms by age of firm, 2013

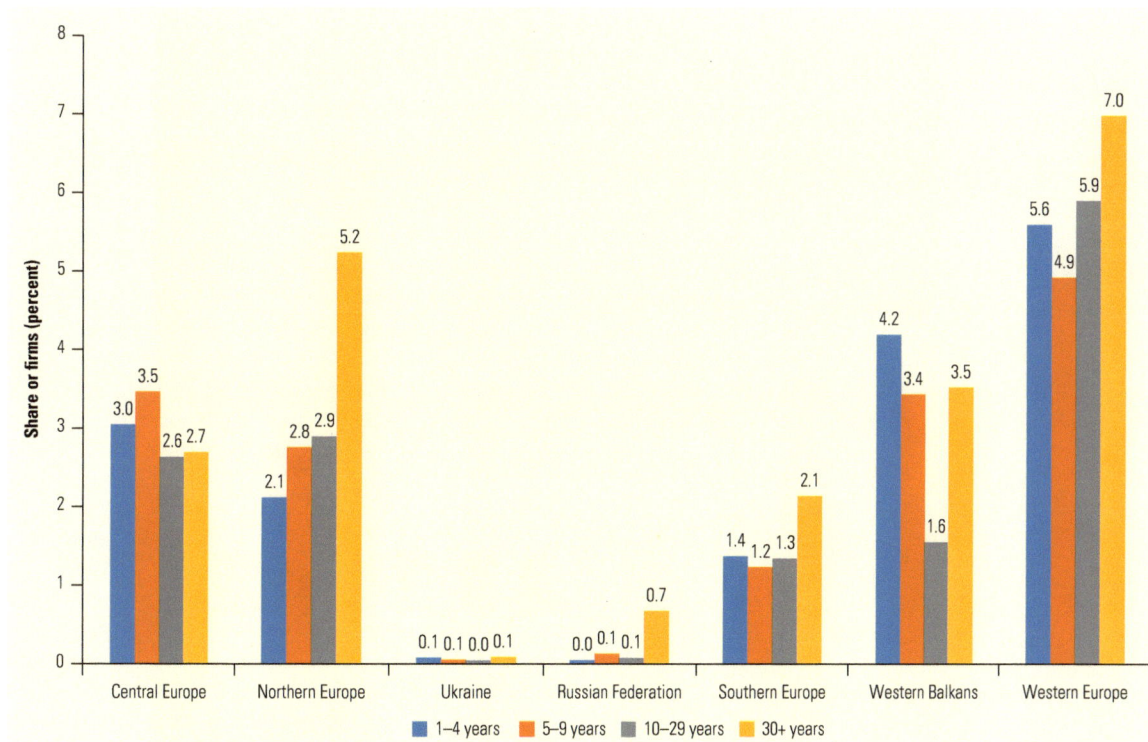

Source: Calculations using Orbis data.
Note: Data for 2013. Sample excludes firms with owners in tax haven countries.

TABLE O.3 Most Foreign Firms in ECA Are Owned by German and US Firms

Region	Most common global ultimate owner									
	Germany	United States	United Kingdom	Netherlands	Austria	France	Italy	Finland	Sweden	Others (from left to right, top to bottom): Denmark, Norway, Russian Federation, Belgium, Croatia, Slovenia, and Japan
Central Europe	Germany	United States	United Kingdom		Austria					Norway
Northern Europe	Germany	United States	United Kingdom					Finland	Sweden	Denmark
Ukraine	Germany	United States	United Kingdom	Netherlands						Russian Federation
Russian Federation	Germany	United States	United Kingdom	Netherlands	Austria			Finland		
Southern Europe	Germany	United States	United Kingdom	Netherlands		France	Italy			
Western Balkans	Germany	United States	United Kingdom		Austria	France	Italy			Belgium, Croatia
Western Europe	Germany	United States	United Kingdom	Netherlands		France	Italy		Sweden	Slovenia, Japan

Note: Sample excludes firms owned by tax haven countries. Each row in the table shows the five (or more, if there is a tie) most common countries of ownership. For each country or region at left. For the Russian Federation and Ukraine, the rows show the five countries with the largest ownership shares. ECA = Europe and Central Asia.

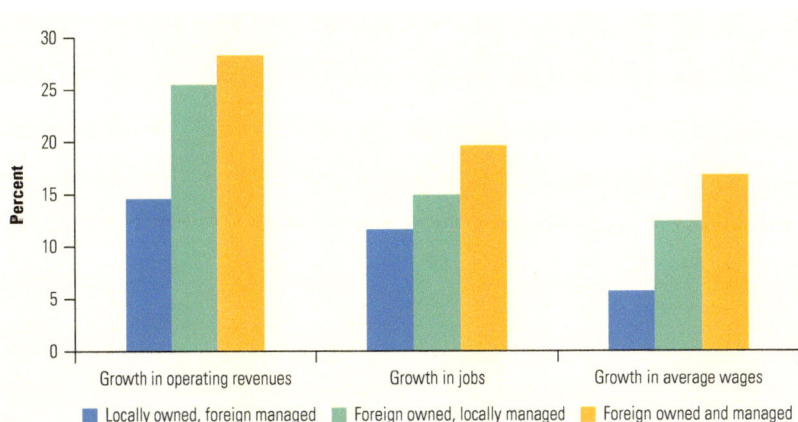

FIGURE O.13 Foreign-owned and -managed firms perform better than local firms

Note: Each bar in the figure represents the difference in growth (of the type labeled) between the type of firm depicted in that bar and that of firms that are both locally managed and locally owned. All underlying coefficients are statistically significant.

Transfer of management practices from the source country is likely an important reason for the better performance of foreign firms. For example, US-owned firms in Europe have management practices that place more emphasis on merit in determining career success, which is associated with greater use of ICT, than do domestic firms or firms owned by other countries (Bloom et al. 2018). On average in the ECA region, but not in the most advanced ECA economies, foreign-owned firms tend to have better management practices than local firms (figure O.14). The source country's management quality is significantly related to the performance of its foreign affiliates: foreign affiliates from countries with better management practices perform better than other foreign affiliates, even after differences between the source countries' income levels, financial development, population, and stock of immigrants are taken into account.

Local firms without foreign ownership or management can also benefit from the presence of foreign-owned firms (figure O.15). Local firms can learn from observing management practices and technology in foreign affiliates, or through hiring workers trained in foreign affiliates. However, evidence of such effects across industries is mixed. Better-performing foreign affiliates also may affect local firms through competition—by forcing them either to improve or to exit the market. Local firms tend to achieve significantly higher growth in operating revenues and wages in regions or sectors in ECA countries with higher shares of foreign firms than in sectors in which foreign affiliates are less prevalent.

For small and young firms, there is no statistically significant relationship between the share of foreign firms in a sector and local firms' employment growth. A possible interpretation of this result is that the presence of foreign firms forces some successful small and young local firms to become more efficient by increasing capital relative to labor, slowing job creation. In addition, other firms that cannot compete shed labor (to more efficient firms) or close. Again, these relationships may in part reflect foreign owners' decisions to invest in better-performing sectors or regions.

FIGURE O.14 Foreign affiliates tend to have better management practices than local firms

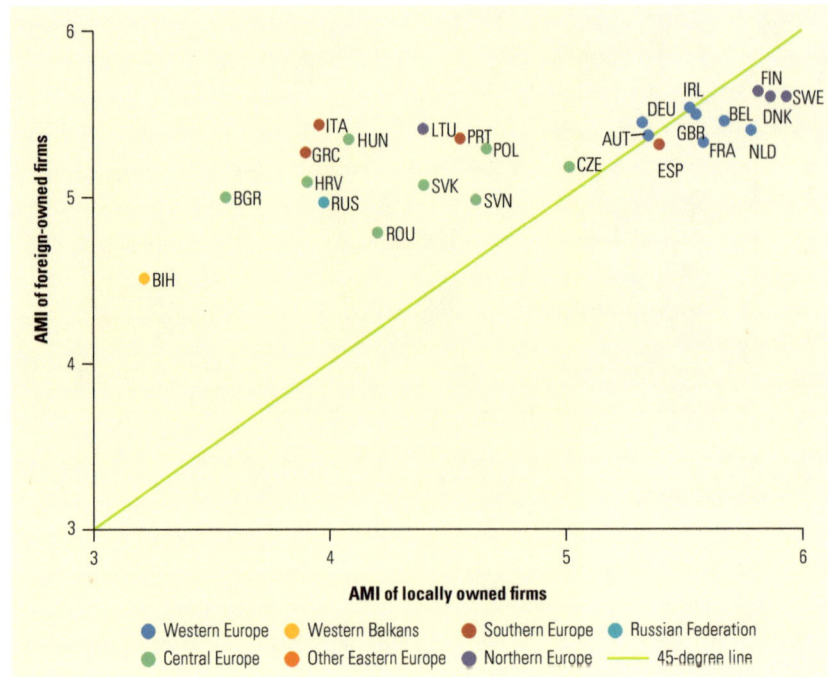

Source: Calculations using data from the World Economic Forum (WEF) Global Competitiveness Survey and Orbis.
Note: A country's Average Management Index (AMI) is based on the WEF Global Competitiveness survey that measures the quality of national business schools and the reliance of professional management. This index is also highly correlated with the World Management Survey, which is more comprehensive, but not as widely available.

Because of competition from better-managed companies, larger and older firms are more likely to upgrade and adjust compared with younger and smaller firms. Increases in the quality of management in foreign affiliates are associated with faster growth in operating revenues, wages, and employment in local firms more than four years old and having more than 50 employees, but lower growth in these performance indicators in younger and smaller firms.

Foreign ownership of firms tends to reduce the level of employment volatility in a country's domestic economy. Interestingly, once a number of variables that influence firm performance are controlled for, the performance of an average foreign firm in the ECA region is not statistically correlated with local economic growth. Foreign firms are less responsive to local economic conditions than local firms, regardless of whether foreign and local economies have the same business cycle. This could reflect better access to finance during an economic upswing in the parent country or a search for opportunities abroad when the parent company's profits at home are limited relative to the destination country. Regardless of the economic conditions in the parent country, foreign companies' employment decisions seem to be less procyclical with respect to the domestic economy than domestic companies: the former tend to create fewer jobs when the local (host) economy expands (figure O.16). Likewise, this also means that foreign companies tend to destroy fewer jobs than domestic firms when the local economy experiences a recession, possibly reflecting access to external factors that allow foreign companies to buffer

FIGURE O.15 The positive spillovers of well-managed foreign firms seem weaker for small and young firms

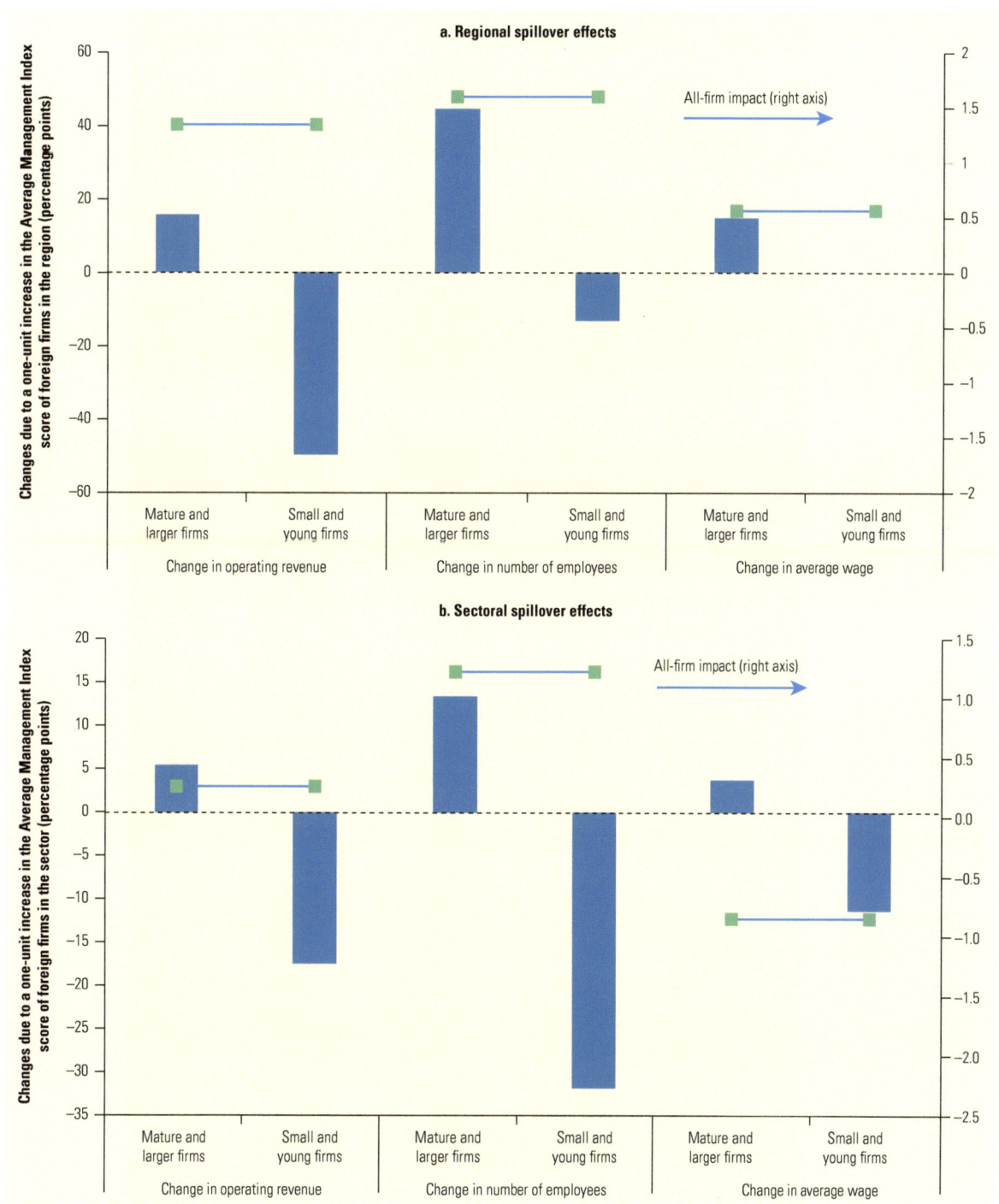

a. Regional spillover effects

b. Sectoral spillover effects

Note: Small firms are those with 49 employees or fewer; young firms are those four years old or younger. Each bar represents the effect of increasing by one point the Average Management Index scores of foreign firms. The bars in each panel show the baseline effect (mature and larger firms), the baseline effect plus the interaction term associated with size, and the baseline effect plus the interaction terms associated with size and age simultaneously.

FIGURE O.16 Foreign firms' employment decisions are less procyclical than those of their domestic peers

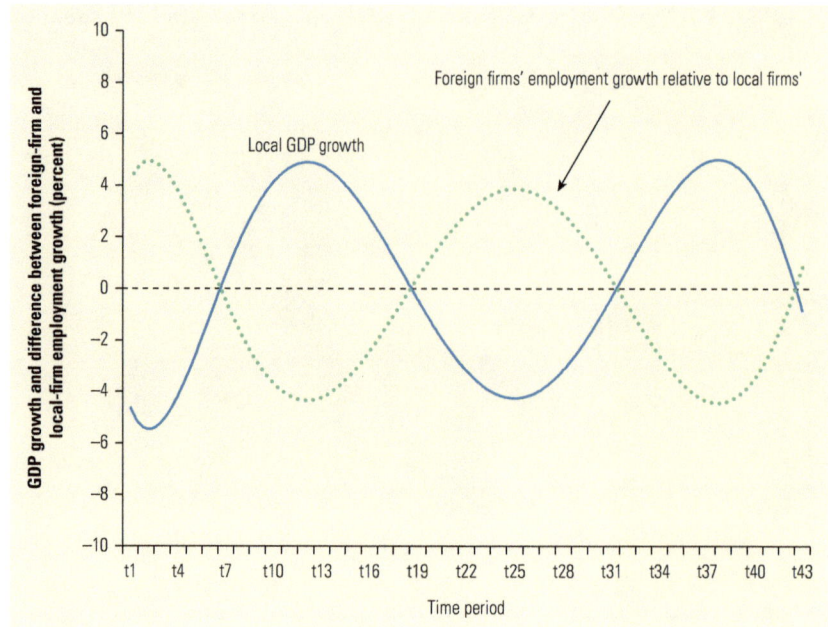

the impact of the decline in economic activity. In other words, while foreign firms seem to contribute less to job creation than their local counterparts when the local economy is growing, they seem to bring more stability to the labor market during a downturn in economic activity because they lay off workers to a lesser extent than local companies do.

It is just a short step from foreign owners and managers to the broader topic of migration, a hot-button issue in recent years. The next section focuses on how the ECA region's increasing migration facilitates trade, knowledge transfers, and other benefits associated with greater connectivity.

Economic Migration Has Been Beneficial to Europe and Central Asia

In general, openness to migration, including that by foreign managers, helps many countries gain the skills, technology, and resources required to improve efficiency and compete in an increasingly complex, globalized world. In destination countries, workers who are close substitutes for immigrants (e.g., they have similar skills) may lose as a result of lower wages or diminishing job opportunities. At the same time, workers with skills complementary to those of immigrants may benefit. While the net economic effect for the country overall is positive, income distribution impacts may be positive or negative depending on the skill mix of the native and immigrant populations. Outside of economic considerations, large sudden shifts in migrant flows as a result of natural disasters or wars, such as the recent Syrian refugee crisis, bring humanitarian and local social impacts into play for the host country. These are critical societal issues for domestic policy consideration but are outside the purview of this analysis.

Both emigration and immigration rates in many ECA countries are higher than the global average (map O.1), mostly driven by the removal of barriers to mobility within the EU and large migration flows following the opening up of Eastern-bloc countries. High levels of ECA migration have encouraged greater cross-border investment and trade (for example, by helping firms learn about foreign markets) and have facilitated the sharing of technology and knowledge between countries (for example, through schooling and language skills attained abroad).

A large diaspora can generate substantial economic benefits for many origin countries in the ECA region. Remittances are an important source of income, have a positive impact on long-term economic growth and poverty reduction, and can improve access to capital markets. Diasporas are also a significant source of investment, export demand, and knowledge transfers for ECA economies, particularly given the disproportionately high flows of skilled emigrants from regional countries (see box O.2). Finally, the increasing share of migrants going to the United States and Northern, Western, and Southern Europe may have contributed to improving institutions in ECA transition economies by increasing their populations' exposure to the norms of competitive democratic countries.

What determines migration connectivity? To answer this question, this report develops a global bilateral migration matrix showing the number of migrants between all country pairs. Constructing the matrix requires estimating migration flows for the many countries missing such data and then estimating the global relationship between population flows and various drivers of migration (figure O.17). Most migrants move to countries with similar or higher levels of per capita income. Migration tends to increase as the distance between countries decreases. A large share of low-skilled migrants move to neighboring countries, but high-skilled migrants are more likely to move to nonneighboring countries, reflecting the tendency for high-skilled emigrants from developing countries to move to high-income OECD countries (especially English-speaking countries). Sharing a similar language also has a positive effect on migration flows, particularly for skilled migrants, whose jobs often require strong language skills. Finally, the existence of a diaspora tends to increase the flow of migrants (particularly for unskilled workers) by reducing the costs of information, financing movements, and perhaps reducing the risks involved in migration.

Some characteristics of ECA migration differ from these global patterns. Migrants from ECA countries (other than the advanced European economies), regardless of education level or gender, tend to move to other countries within the region. By contrast, migrants in other regions are no more likely to move within the region, once distance between countries and common borders are taken into account. High-skilled (but not low-skilled) migrants from former Soviet Union countries tend to go to other former Soviet Union countries, where they find similar institutions (a legacy of the Soviet Union) and close economic integration. Differences in the size of the working-age population (those 25–65 years of age) are also important determinants of migration flows. Countries with larger and younger working-age populations tend to have larger emigration to countries with smaller and older working-age populations. Because of aging populations in Central and Eastern European countries, a smaller working-age population emigrates from those countries. Central Asia, however, remains a

MAP O.1 Emigration and immigration shares have seen the highest increase in Europe and Central Asia

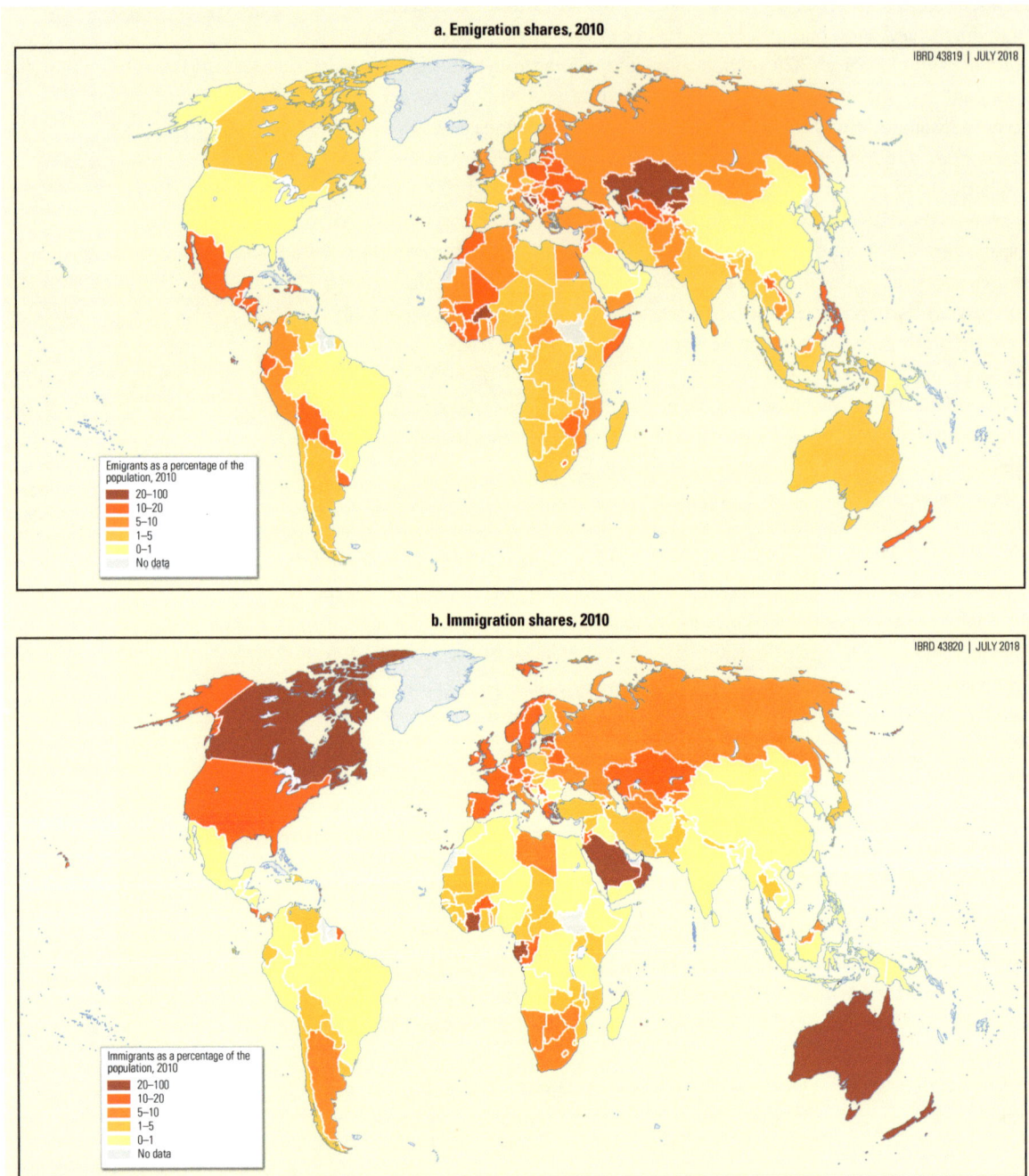

a. Emigration shares, 2010

IBRD 43819 | JULY 2018

Emigrants as a percentage of the
population, 2010
- 20–100
- 10–20
- 5–10
- 1–5
- 0–1
- No data

b. Immigration shares, 2010

IBRD 43820 | JULY 2018

Immigrants as a percentage of the
population, 2010
- 20–100
- 10–20
- 5–10
- 1–5
- 0–1
- No data

Source: World Bank 2018.
Note: Reported data for Central Asia for 2010 are particularly spotty; therefore these maps rely heavily on an estimation methodology developed by the World Bank staff.

BOX O.2 Marius Stefan of Autonom Romania: Knowledge transfers through travel and studies abroad

Marius Stefan, a Romanian national, graduated with an MBA from the University of Maryland in 2004.[a] His proud parents flew in from Romania for the ceremony, and Marius decided to show them around the US East Coast on a short road trip. Marius did it the way he learned from friends: he rented a car.

His father was amazed that a private individual—from a foreign country, no less—could rent a car so easily. Such businesses were unknown in Romania. Marius had a good understanding of the car rental market from one of the case studies from his MBA program, and he explained the business model to his father.

After seeing how it was done and listening to his son, Marius's father made an unexpected proposal: that they would open a car rental business in Romania. Marius's family was from Piatra Neamt, a small town in one of the poorest regions in northeast Romania. It had almost no tourism and little economic activity at the time. While starting a business was exciting, Marius thought there was no potential and quickly forgot the conversation.

Marius returned to Romania and worked in several small businesses in Bucharest, the country's capital. But his father kept reminding him about his proposal to start a car rental business in his home town. Marius finally relented and agreed to ship three vehicles to Piatra Neamt to gauge the potential for car rentals. To his surprise, the rent-a-car business became an overnight success. Within a few weeks, employees at the business were calling Marius in Bucharest, asking why the company had just three cars. There were always more people wanting to rent, but too few cars to satisfy the demand.

Marius traveled from Bucharest to Piatra Neamt to investigate and found a simple explanation. When the country joined the European Union, more than three million Romanians emigrated—most moving from the economically depressed region around Piatra Neamt to Spain and Italy. Many of the migrants returned to Romania frequently, and they were glad to have the opportunity to rent a car. When Marius realized the potential, he decided to act on a lesson from business school: after a pilot project is successful, focus all your efforts on scaling up as rapidly as possible.

Marius's brother had been educated in France and had been working in Paris as an international consultant. After a year of successful business development, Marius added his brother's experience and knowledge to the business, and they have been working together as the enterprise has expanded beyond anyone's dreams.

Autonom now operates in 46 locations, employs 300 workers, and offers more than 5,000 cars for rent. The company is going through a stage of accelerated growth. It is developing a division for long-term rentals (operating leases) both organically and through acquisitions. It recently acquired the operational leasing division of Banca Transilvania, the largest bank in Romania, and the plan is to double the company's turnover and assets in 2018. While developing the business across Romania, the company started to expand abroad. It started Autonom Hungary three years ago and Autonom Serbia in May 2018—in effect, transitioning from a national champion to a regional player.

None of this would have happened had the Stefan brothers not migrated abroad. An idea sparked by a routine car rental in another country, combined with the knowledge gained by studying abroad, helped Marius and his brother build a successful company that testifies to the power of connectivity and its knowledge transfers.

a. This box was based on discussions with Marius Stefan in 2018. The author thanks Mr. Stefan for being so generous with his time.

FIGURE O.17 **ECA migration is driven by geography, language, historical ties, and past migration**

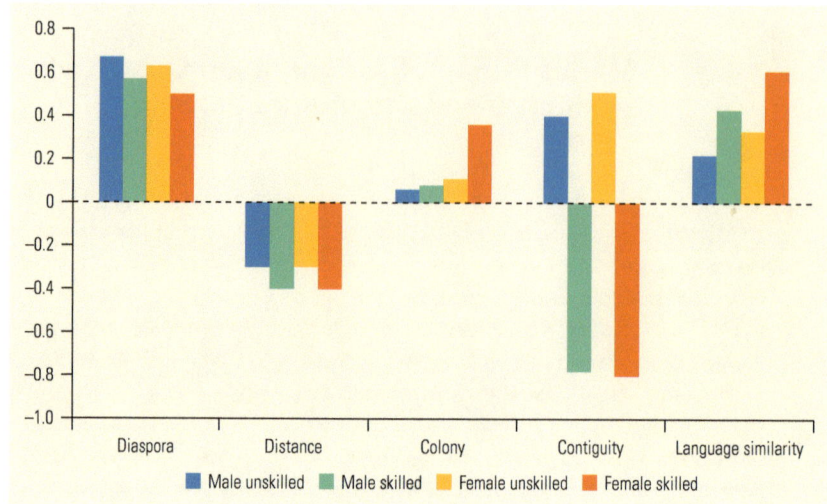

Note: Calculations are for 2010. "Skilled" migrants are those completing tertiary education. The size of the bars in the figure represents the coefficient of a regression equation and the percentage point impact on migration from a percentage point change in the migrant and home/host country attributes. Regressions also include regional dummies, such as migration within Europe and Central Asia (ECA) subregions and within the rest of the world.

subregion with a relatively young working-age population and has relatively large emigration. In addition, while women make up slightly less than half of global emigrants, they are the majority of ECA emigrants, possibly because of their higher skill levels relative to the global pool of emigrants.

Migration and the other connectivity components discussed in previous sections require highways, railroads, air links, and cargo transport to reach their full potential. The next section examines the role infrastructure plays in enhancing the ECA region's connectivity. While all forms of transportation are important in this regard, this research project focuses on the differences in cost and time needed to move goods and people among various countries.

Strong Infrastructure Transport Links Provide Important Support for Connectivity

Transport infrastructure forms the bedrock for international (and domestic) connectivity. This is obvious in the cases of trade in goods and migration, but services trade and investment flows also require supportive logistics, travel-related services, and infrastructure and may be linked to goods trade. Measuring the extent to which a country's transport infrastructure facilitates connectivity through the channels mentioned is complicated. Many traditional infrastructure indicators—such as kilometers of roads and rail, their condition, or the density of connections—provide only limited information on the economic value of transport connections. To get an alternative view, this study looks at new data on transport services and network analysis tools to measure the economic value of ECA countries' connections through roads, railroads, and to a lesser extent maritime transport.

The economic value of connections is measured here by the cost of transport, the time required, and the importance of the destination country in the overall transport network. Time is a particularly important consideration when the type of product (for example, perishable goods or parts and components traded within supply chains) or the nature of the passenger trip (for example, urgent business) requires rapid and reliable transport. Information on these dimensions is therefore essential for evaluating infrastructure investments' real impact on growth and welfare.

With some exceptions, domestic travel in the most advanced economies tends to take less time and be more affordable for residents (given the high incomes in these countries) than travel in other countries (figure O.18). By contrast, the time required to deliver a container from one main city to another within a country differs little across ECA subregions, except in the case of Russia, for which distance between major cities plays a large role. However, time required for cargo shipments between countries is quite high in a few countries that serve as gateways to their neighbors (e.g., Belgium, Luxembourg, and the Netherlands), likely owing to the high level of congestion in their highway systems.

The cost and time required for passengers to connect with neighboring countries varies greatly within ECA, from the highest levels in Central Asia to the lowest in the Western Balkans. Advanced Europe's high-level road and rail infrastructure also delivers fast travel times at relatively low cost for residents, given their high incomes. Transport takes up a larger share of income in poorer ECA

FIGURE O.18 Transport connectivity (cost and time) between and within ECA countries
Regional averages

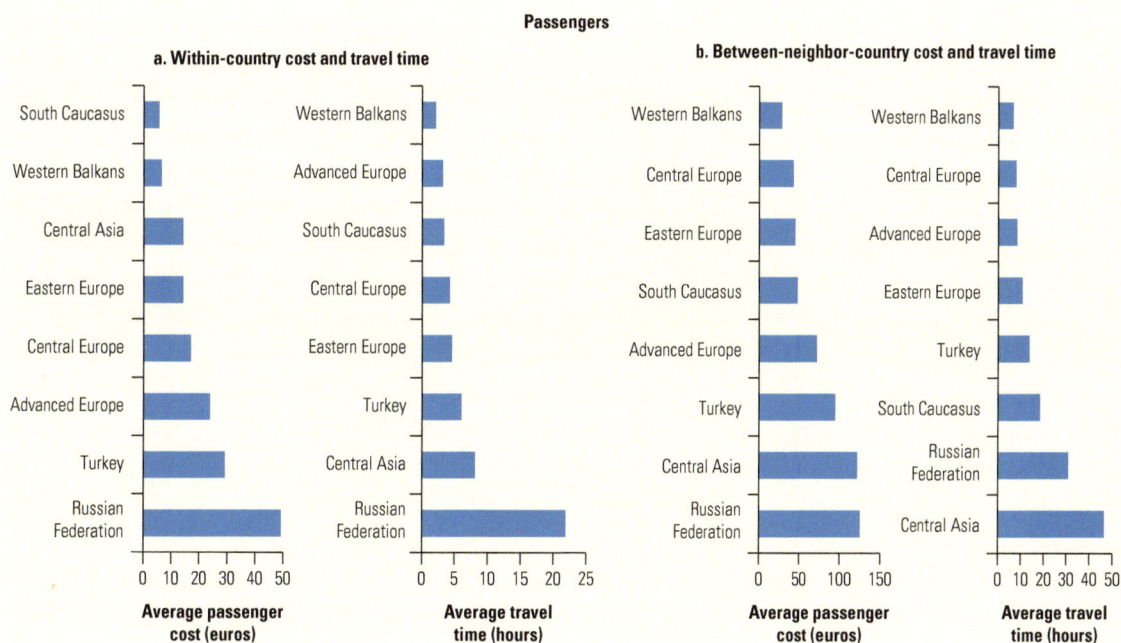

Passengers

a. Within-country cost and travel time

b. Between-neighbor-country cost and travel time

continued

FIGURE O.18 *continued*

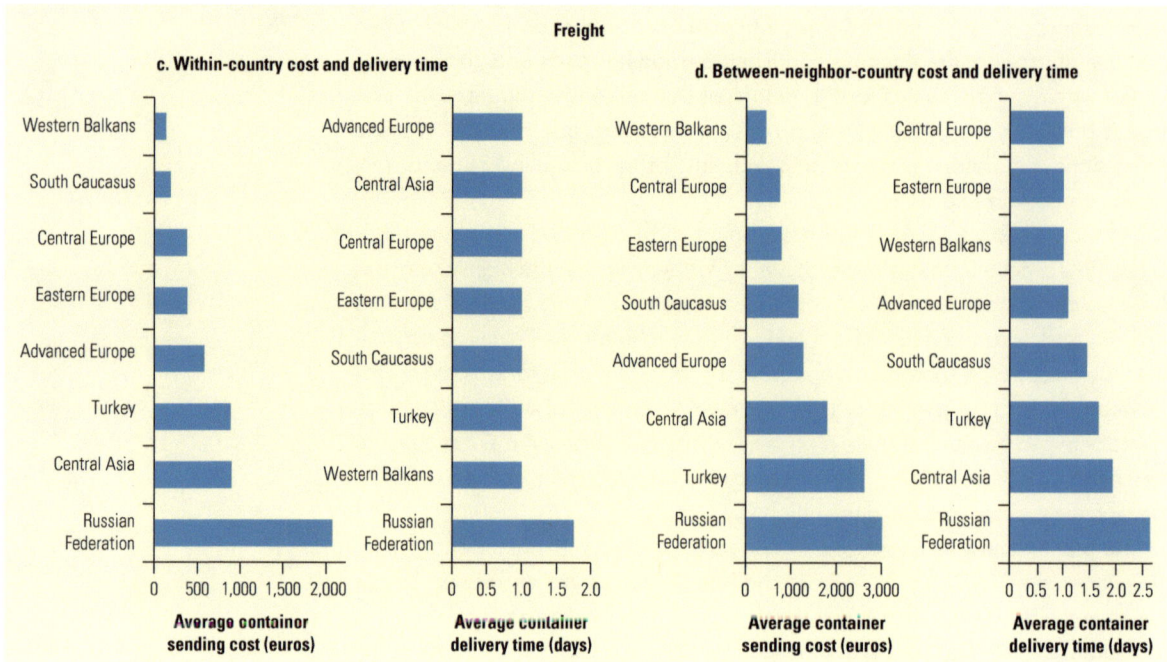

Freight

c. Within-country cost and delivery time

d. Between-neighbor-country cost and delivery time

Note: Within-country transport connectivity as measured here is multimodal, averaging across road, rail, and bus modes the price that must be paid to travel to a representative main city in the country. Transport connectivity between neighboring countries as measured here is multimodal between a country's capital city and main cities of neighboring countries. Only countries with complete data for time and cost for all modes (road, bus, and rail) are included. Within-country freight transport connectivity for a given city is measured as the average price to send a container from that city to the other main cities within a country. Between-neighbor-country freight transport connectivity is measured as the average price to send a container from a country's capital city to the main cities of neighboring countries. "Advanced Europe" includes countries in Western, Southern, and Northern Europe that signed the Maastricht Treaty or joined the European Union before 1995. ECA = Europe and Central Asia.

countries, with most Central European and Baltic countries in the middle of the pack. The average cost and time required to ship a container from a country's capital city to the main city of neighboring countries varies little among most subregions, except for higher costs and time in Central Asia, Russia, and Turkey.

Central Asian countries have much higher travel costs for both road and container transport and much longer travel times than other ECA regions. These countries might get help in integrating and improving their connectivity through recent or expected infrastructure projects gathered under the Belt and Road Initiative, a long-term project designed to reduce the cost of transport from China to Europe. Along with Portugal and Spain, the island countries Cyprus, Ireland, and Malta are also among the countries with the highest costs and longest time to reach the rest of the ECA network. South Caucasus performs better in terms of costs compared to time, whereas in Western Europe the opposite is the case. Central and Eastern European countries have relatively cheaper and faster connections to the rest of the network. The similarity in these rankings largely reflects road transport costs, which are determined in part by infrastructure quality and its impact on average speeds. The cost of moving containers is another matter. Unlike passenger road costs, this cost reflects other parameters, such as logistics costs, the presence of rent seekers, and the degree of competitiveness among service providers. As a result, countries' cost versus time performance is more diverse when looking at the cost of moving containers rather than people. Countries like Armenia, Greece, Kosovo, the former Yugoslav Republic of Macedonia, and Turkey have relatively better connectivity in terms of container costs than they do in terms of time. Montenegro, Norway, Slovenia, and others have relatively better time connectivity than cost connectivity. Understanding country specificities requires a deeper look into institutional factors, the quality of logistics, and the competitiveness of the transport sector.

In addition to cost and time, determining the economic value of connections requires considering destination countries' place in the network. The availability of close connections varies greatly within the ECA region: the total number of a country's neighbors (or neighbors of neighbors) ranges from 2 to 22, and the level of aggregate GDP in the countries adjacent to a country varies significantly from country to country. Thus, some connections have a higher value than others in terms of access to a larger market. So in planning transport investments, a country should consider whether a particular investment improves access to a relatively isolated country or to a country with connections to a wider network.

Transportation infrastructure channels the movement of goods and people along major cross-country networks and, within networks, corridors. The comprehensive nature of the economic benefits that accrue to countries from being on a particular corridor, or at a specific crossroads of a network, remains an open question. A key question is whether roads or rail that pass though countries provide economic benefits if ancillary businesses associated with the corridor fail to materialize. If a country's economic and business environment is sufficiently attractive for investment, however, transit flows may increase export and import opportunities for firms along these routes (or corridors), develop new sectors such as logistics services, and generate nonmaterial benefits (flows of ideas and knowledge) to boost productivity. Firms located in transport hub countries may benefit from lower production costs and an improved ability to deliver on time. Higher transport network connectivity might be desirable for increasing a country's participation in regional and GVCs, attracting FDI, or increasing its participation in development corridors.

It is important to identify the most *critical* countries in transport networks. Doing so reveals which countries have more control over transportation networks' operability and what shocks in these countries imply for other connected countries. Measuring critical transport networks can help countries target investments to reduce their vulnerability to specific country shocks that might impede access to markets or other areas of the network. More generally, critical countries in the transport network are those where disruption would have a major impact on subnetworks or countries that can be de facto disconnected. For container costs, Russia is the most critical country in the network in Eurasia (figure O.19). A country's cost-driven criticality reflects the increase in costs that a shipper (in the case of containers) would incur if it had to avoid that

FIGURE O.19 Cost-driven criticality in container network for Europe and Central Asia

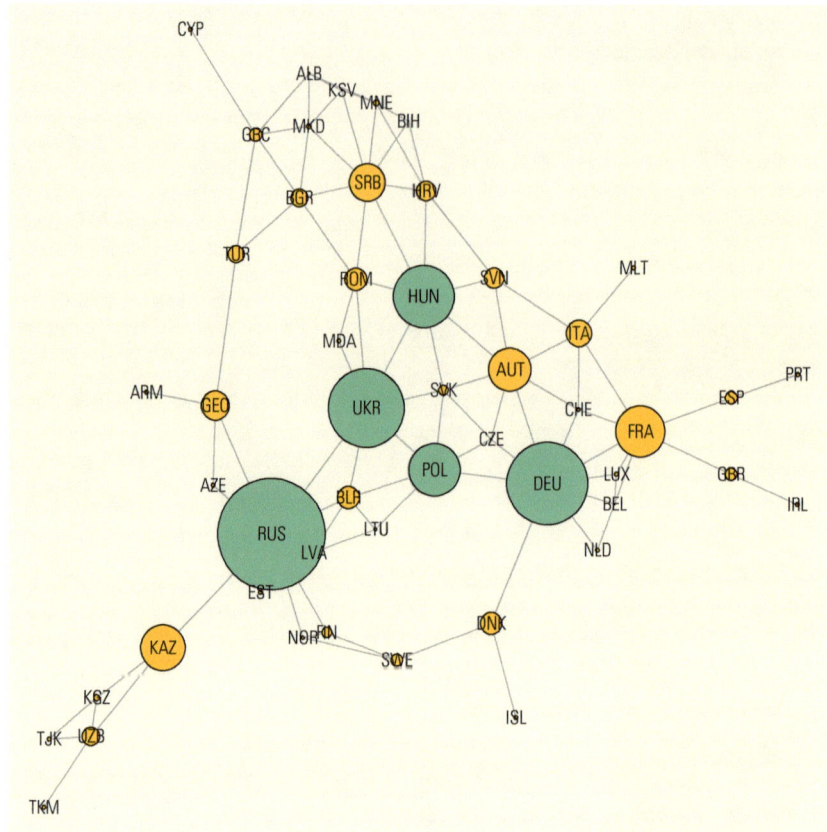

Note: The results shown in the figure capture only the Europe and Central Asia (ECA) transport network and do not include connectivity to countries outside ECA. Consequently, large ports (e.g., Rotterdam) that are connected to the United States or China will not appear as critical, although they are in the larger global context. Circle size indicates level of criticality (larger diameter = greater criticality). For illustrative purposes, the circles representing the top five countries in criticality are colored in green. Lines between nodes indicate the presence in the physical network of an optimal corridor connecting countries. Locations of circles and countries are not linked to geography in any way. Results for time-driven criticality are not presented, as the results are very similar to those presented.

country in shipping cargo. Germany, Ukraine, Hungary, and Poland are among the five most network-critical countries. As expected, islands or isolated countries have a very low criticality. While France is not a top-five country in terms of network criticality, disruptions in the French transport network would affect connectivity to the rest of the ECA region for Spain, Portugal, the United Kingdom, and Ireland: Portugal's connection to the European network is contingent upon Spain's, and so forth.

Different goals for transport networks may imply quite different investment priorities:

• Countries may choose to strengthen partnerships—for example, to reach large markets, participate in supply chains, or connect to countries with high levels of technology (so the potential for learning is greater). As revealed by the cost and time of freight transport, ECA countries can be grouped into three categories in terms of partnerships: (a) the Western Balkans and Central Europe incur lower costs to reach the largest economies of Europe; (b) countries in

Central Asia and South Caucasus together with Russia incur lower costs to reach countries with similar technology levels; and (c) countries in Advanced and Eastern Europe, as well as Turkey, incur lower costs to reach either the largest ECA economies or countries with more sophisticated technology.

- Another possible goal among countries is to maximize the size of the market made accessible by their transport systems. Advanced Europe captures the largest amount of GDP per unit cost of transport (a container, private car, or railway ticket) among ECA subregions, followed by Eastern and Central Europe (85–90 percent of Advanced Europe's market potential), South Caucasus and Turkey (50 percent), and Central Asia (40 percent). While the size of investments and the quality of services are important, many countries' ability to increase their market connectivity by improving transport is limited by long distances from markets and difficult terrain.

- Countries also may choose their investments to maximize their integration within the ECA transport network. Some connections contribute more to a country's overall connectivity with the region than others. The Czech Republic, the Slovak Republic, and Austria are the three most integrated countries in the ECA network, while Central Asia remains poorly integrated. Factors over which a country has no control, such as the number of neighboring countries it has, are also key elements in determining its degree of integration, but its transportation network is more important.

More cooperation among countries, especially along corridors, could increase the global benefits of transport investments. When it comes to the Belt and Road Initiative, for example, the benefit of investments for the network as a whole varies by individual segment. Reducing the cost of shipping a container in the Kazakhstan-China segment would have the largest impact on Kazakhstan's ability to reach foreign markets, but Russia and Germany also would benefit significantly. Improving the Belarus-Russia segment would mostly benefit Belarus. A cost reduction on the Poland-Belarus segment would have the smallest impact on the network as a whole.

Although it would provide broad support for all aspects of ECA connectivity, better infrastructure has particular relevance for cross-border supply chains. Today's businesses, rather than being concentrated in a single country, find their production of goods is now divided among plants in different countries, with each assigned production of particular components or the assembly of components from other plants. The final consumer product may thus reflect inputs from a number of countries.

The Growth of Supply Chains Reflects Greater Connectivity and Has Facilitated Increased International Knowledge Flows

Regional supply chains are deepening around the world and are focused in three clusters—Asia, Europe, and North America. Europe's supply chain is largely focused on Germany, particularly in motor vehicles, retail, and machinery and equipment. Despite enormous reductions in the prices of transport and communication, geographic proximity continues to be important in coordinating production throughout supply chains. In fact, the importance of regional supply chains increased somewhat faster than that of global supply chains from 1995 to 2011.

Proximity remains important for several reasons. Suppliers often need complex information (tacit knowledge) that cannot easily be codified in blueprints or instruction manuals (explicit knowledge), requiring frequent, face-to-face communications with lead firms that are difficult and costly to achieve when plants are separated by thousands of kilometers. Proximity is associated with similarities in culture and language as well as migration networks—both of which facilitate these detailed information transfers. On-time delivery and reliable quality are critical in supply chains, where the lack of an intermediate input can slow production all along the chain. Therefore, lead firms may place greater emphasis on allocating production to close-by firms they know, rather than seeking cheaper locations at greater distance. Locating plants in proximity to one another can help improve the allocation of workers and machines across firms, facilitate the transfer of knowledge across plants, and enable more efficient use of infrastructure and other public services. Finally, regional integration agreements such as the EU encourage supply chain production through regional partners by lowering costs at the border, establishing similar legal and regulatory frameworks, and providing confidence in the stability of integration frameworks over time.

The growth of supply chains has generated substantial benefits. Participation in supply chains can expand the range of goods produced in developing countries. For example, a poor country that finds it difficult to compete with more sophisticated firms in the production of complex electronic products may be able to exploit its advantage of low-cost labor to assemble such products from components produced elsewhere. The transfer of knowledge is heightened in supply chains, which often involve intensive contacts with more sophisticated firms through trade, investment, and the movement of technicians and managers. Exposure to such knowledge can improve productivity. The growth of supply chains can also increase productivity through more intense competition, greater specialization (which can improve worker performance through learning by doing), and access to increased diversity of inputs. In OECD countries, growth in a country's participation in supply chains is associated with growth in its real labor productivity (figure O.20), although this association may partly reflect the fact that more productive countries are more likely to participate in supply chains.

Increased participation in European (and Asian) supply chains has been associated with rising revenues from exports of both goods and services, even after subtracting the value of associated imports. To be more precise, participation in supply chains boosts the gross exports recorded in the balance of payments statistics. However, a substantial share of these export revenues must be devoted to paying for imported inputs used in the production of the goods, so the funds channeled to domestic profits and wages (i.e., domestic value added) may be a small fraction of gross export revenues. ECA countries that have increased their participation in supply chains tend to achieve a more rapid increase than other countries in the domestic value added generated by exports. From 2000 to 2011, for example, Turkey and Poland experienced some of the largest

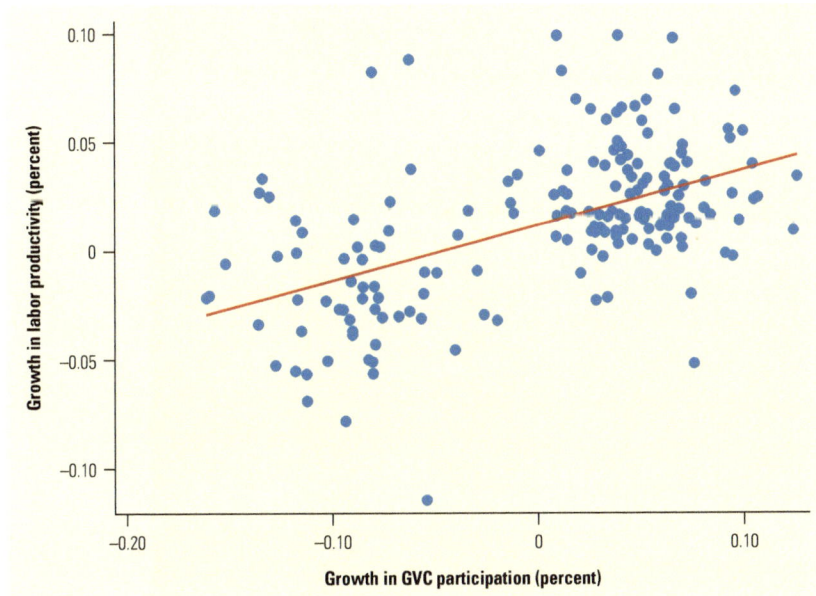

FIGURE O.20 Participation in global value chains is correlated with higher labor productivity

Source: World Bank labor productivity data and country global value chain participation index for member countries of the Organisation for Economic Co-operation and Development over the period 2009–11.
Note: Each dot in the figure represents one country for one year. GVC = global value chain.

percentage increases in the share of exports through supply chains among transition countries (figure O.21, panel a) as well as the highest growth rate of exports of value added (figure O.21, panel b). By contrast, Slovenia, Russia, and Hungary saw decreases in the share of exports through supply chains over the same period and only modest growth of value-added exports.

Greater participation in supply chains also tends to increase a country's dependence on other countries, potentially raising economic volatility in some segments of the country's economy. For example, a natural disaster in Indonesia that interrupts the production of an intermediate good may idle workers in the Czech Republic and reduce the profits of German retailers.

Finding the central sectors and the major cross-border links is important to understanding how positive or adverse shocks spread through production networks in the ECA region. A country or a sector that is central might be able to spread ideas to the rest of the network, but it might also more frequently receive shocks from the rest of the network.

The ECA production network is organized around several clusters that include sectors (for example, retail trade and motor vehicles) from different parts of the region. Having sectors from different regions in the same production cluster illustrates the interdependence of country-sectors across most ECA countries through input-output linkages. By evaluating which countries and sector clusters are most critical for production in ECA, it becomes clear that motor vehicles in Germany are the most central sector in the ECA production network. This sector largely relies on wide-reaching regional value chains to organize its production. The retail sectors in Italy, France, Germany, and Russia are all

FIGURE O.21 Among the transition countries, greater production fragmentation is associated with a more rapid increase in the flows of value added in exports

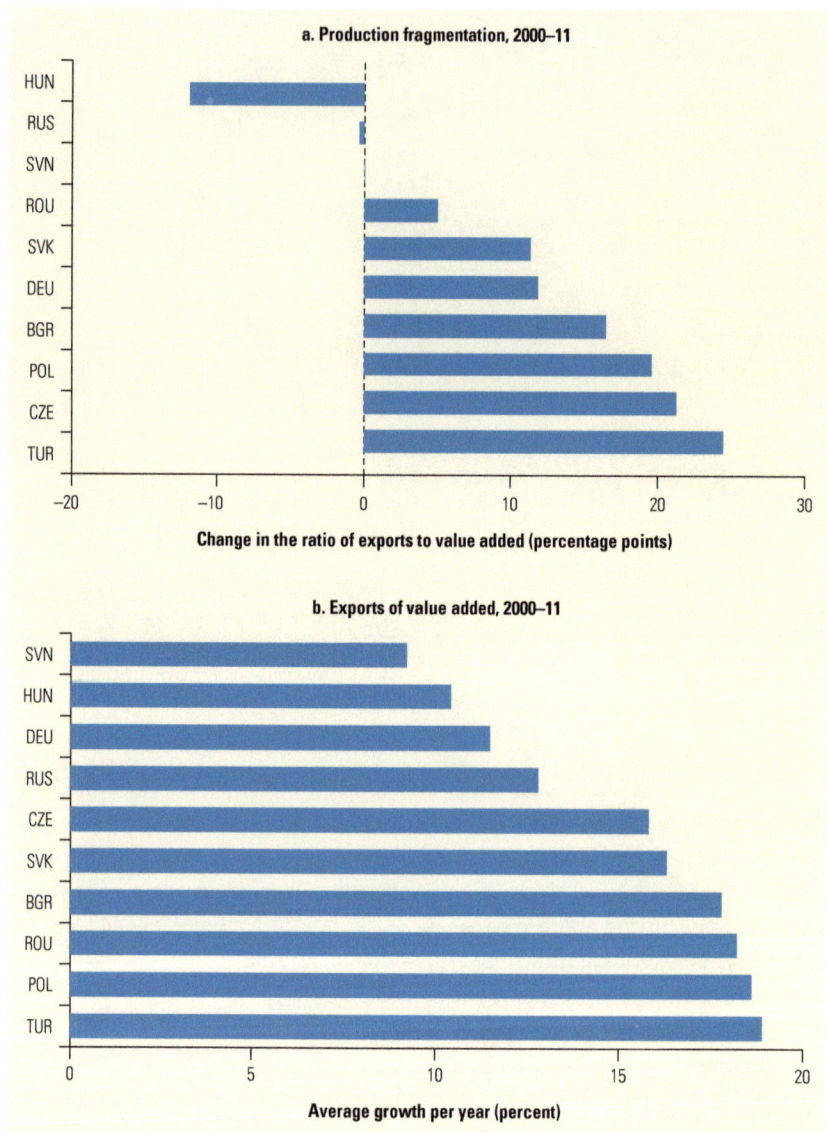

a. Production fragmentation, 2000–11

Change in the ratio of exports to value added (percentage points)

(Countries from top to bottom: HUN, RUS, SVN, ROU, SVK, DEU, BGR, POL, CZE, TUR)

b. Exports of value added, 2000–11

Average growth per year (percent)

(Countries from top to bottom: SVN, HUN, DEU, RUS, CZE, SVK, BGR, ROU, POL, TUR)

Source: Calculations based on Organisation for Economic Co-Operation and Development Trade in Value Added database.

important as well, but Germany's machinery and equipment sector is among the most critical value chain sectors. Outside of the mature EU countries, manufacturing clusters in Poland, Russia, and Turkey play a secondary role. By far, France, Germany, and Italy are the most important centers for the ECA trade production network, followed by Russia and Turkey. The least central countries are the Baltic countries, the Eastern European countries, and Portugal.

To this point, *Critical Connections* has focused on important aspects of connectivity in the ECA region. The phenomenon is multidimensional, with its various components working together to increase productivity. The gains, not shared equally among or within countries, are spurred by foreign ownership and management, migration, vital infrastructure, and supply chains.

Connectivity, however, carries risks and ignites changes in national economies. The remaining task for the study centers on ECA policies: first, the ECA region's recent record on promoting connectivity, and second, the challenges and opportunities that remain.

European and Central Asian Countries Have Moved toward More Open Policies

While most economic policies can affect international connectivity in some way, this study's evaluation of ECA policy progress focuses on a set of areas that have important implications for openness to international connections. These include policies governing import tariffs, preferential trade agreements (PTAs), inward FDI, bilateral investment treaties (BITs) that protect investors from expropriation and adverse changes in investment policies, product market regulations, sectoral domestic regulations, visa regimes, and integration of migrants.

ECA countries have made important progress on policies to boost international connectivity. In part, this has reflected individual countries' efforts to open themselves up to the global economy, particularly following the collapse of the Soviet Union. However, regional agreements have also played a critical role, including the increasing sectoral coverage and depth of agreements within the EU, the expansion of the EU membership, and the formation of the Eurasian Economic Union, composed of Armenia, Belarus, Kazakhstan, and Russia.

The EU also has entered into more than 50 PTAs with countries in and around Europe. Over time, these agreements have shifted their primary focus away from reducing trade barriers, expanding to include liberalizing trade in services, public procurement markets, and cross-border investment. In addition, they have added provisions governing how the agreements are implemented through national regulatory regimes (figure O.22). This broader agenda requires more complex decisions than negotiations over tariff levels. For example, regulations designed to achieve such objectives as safeguarding the health and safety of consumers (which are consistent with a trade agreement) have a greater scope than regulatory measures that serve only to protect domestic producers (which are inconsistent with the market integration goals of a trade agreement). Studies have found that participation in deeper and more comprehensive trade agreements is related to a country's ability to attract FDI. Each provision added to an agreement between a pair of countries (particularly in the areas of competition policies, investment, movement of capital, and intellectual property rights) is associated with an average 3 percent increase in FDI flows between the agreement partners.

ECA countries have, on average, made considerable progress in reducing barriers to trade and investment:

- Tariff levels applying to countries outside of preferential agreements have fallen steadily in ECA countries—from an average of 7 percent in 1988–96 to 5 percent in 2006–15. ECA's average tariff in the latter period was lower than that in all other regions except North America (Canada and the United States).

FIGURE O.22 ECA ranks among the top regions in regard to the number of trade agreements and investment treaties

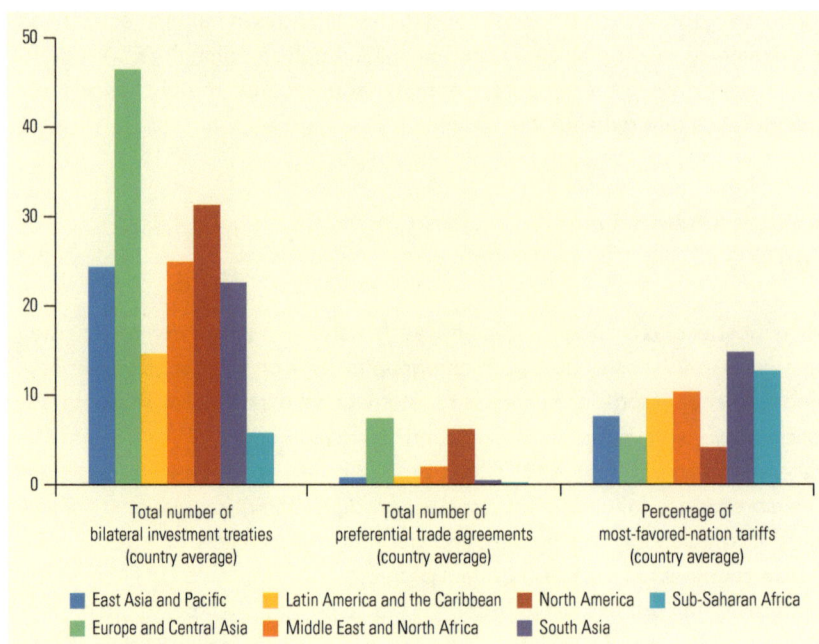

Note: ECA = Europe and Central Asia.

Although tariff rates were reduced in all ECA subregions over this period, they were particularly low in high-income countries.

- ECA countries are among the least restrictive globally toward inward FDI, according to the OECD's FDI Regulatory Restrictiveness Index (although data are not available for the Western Balkans and the South Caucasus subregions). EU countries are the least restrictive, but all ECA subregions achieved some reduction in restrictions from 1997 to 2015.

- ECA's average score on an index of the intensity of use of PTAs dwarfs those of all other regions, driven by regional integration among EU member states and—to a lesser extent—an expansion of PTAs by Turkey and Russia.

- The average ECA country has entered into more BITs—almost 50 from 2000 to 2016—than the average country in other global regions. Almost 60 percent of all BITs signed by the average ECA country involve a partner in the ECA region.

ECA countries have also made progress in reducing product market restrictions that hamper international connectivity, but the advances have slowed in recent years. A measurement of product market restrictions that includes barriers to entrepreneurship, trade, and investment, as well as the impact of the scope and nature of state control of the economy, shows that the restrictiveness of the average European country has declined since 1998—but progress has stalled since 2008. Similarly, an index of the degree of policy restrictiveness in the ECA region implied by domestic regulatory regimes for energy, transport, and communications has improved since the mid-1980s (though the country coverage of this index is limited)—but progress has been negligible over the past 10 years. According to both indicators, the ECA region has more restrictive policies, on average, than Canada and the United States.

The transition countries (mostly not covered in the two regulation indicators discussed in the previous paragraph) have made significant progress in improving market-friendly regulations, as measured by the Transition Indicator Database developed and managed by the European Bank for Reconstruction and Development. The market openness indicators in formerly centrally planned economies in the Baltic countries and Central Europe improved markedly from 1989 to 2000, although the pace of reform slowed in the subsequent decade. Other subregions also made significant progress, but scores on these indicators of open markets vary considerably. For example, the gap between scores for the average country in Central Asia and the OECD benchmark is four times larger than the gap between the average country in the Baltics and Central Europe and the OECD standard.

Barriers to cross-border movement of people in high-income ECA countries—as measured by visa requirements, visa-issuing practices, and consular services—declined moderately from 2006 to 2012, and they remain substantially less than those imposed by the United States. However, obtaining a formal sector job is more difficult for immigrants in high-income ECA countries than in the United States. The decline in visa restrictions in both the ECA and the United States has applied mostly to nationals of high- and upper-middle-income countries, while nationals from poorer countries have seen little decline in restrictions on moving to high-income countries.

> Barriers to cross-border movement of people in high-income ECA countries—as measured by visa requirements, visa-issuing practices, and consular services— declined moderately from 2006 to 2012.

In many of the region's countries, limited integration of immigrants has impaired their contributions to host economies. For example, unemployment rates in the region tend to be higher among the foreign-born than the native-born population. Support for integration is even more important for refugees, who tend to take longer after entry to participate in the labor force. Although scores vary within the region, the ECA fares poorly on average when compared with other regions regarding policies supporting migrant integration (as measured by the Migrant Integration Policy Index). The average ECA country has had less success in integrating migrants than three of the four comparator countries selected for this exercise: Canada, the Republic of Korea, and New Zealand. (The ECA region has had more success than the fourth comparator country, Japan). The Central Europe subregion and Turkey have the worst performance, and while average scores in Western, Southern, and Northern Europe are closer to those of the best performers outside ECA, no ECA subregion has a score above the best-performing regions.

In summary, ECA countries have been global leaders in cooperation through PTAs and BITs and are comparable to high-income countries in terms of policies toward immigration. However, the average ECA country is more restrictive than countries in non-ECA regions regarding domestic regulations and migrant integration policies. The trend toward more open policies has slowed significantly, however, particularly since the first decade of this century. Little progress has been made in tariff liberalization (as of the beginning of the 2000s), the use of BITs (as of the end of the 2000s), or reductions in FDI regulatory restrictions and product market liberalization (as of 2010).

Considerable Scope Remains for Improving Policies to Increase Connectivity in Europe and Central Asia

Over the past few decades, steps toward increasing connectivity have brought economic growth and greater productivity to most countries in the ECA region. It would be beneficial to develop these connections more broadly and deeply to support broad-based growth. This conclusion rests firmly on *Critical Connections'* primary innovation: a multidimensional approach that examines the depth and breadth of ECA countries' connections, both within the region and globally. It explicitly recognizes the complementarity of the individual channels of connectivity: trade, FDI, migration, ICT, portfolio flows, and transport. The principal message is that diversity in country connections and balance in all channels of international connectivity are critical for achieving the highest impact on growth and economic resilience. It is not enough to focus on a few countries for connectivity or on one or two channels. The deepening of one channel can boost the impact of the other channels on growth.

In addition to recognizing that channels are mutually supportive, multidimensional connectivity provides the following lessons:

- ECA policies that build *regional* and *global* connectivity will stimulate robust growth. Being well connected in the global network of countries is important for long-run inclusive economic growth.
- Multidimensional connectivity puts a spotlight on cross-border transfers of knowledge and ideas as the wellspring of sustained growth. An ongoing improvement in the stock of knowledge leads to increases in TFP that allow countries to get more output from the same amount of inputs. Knowledge flows that occur though connectivity are mostly "tacit"—that is, "learning by doing"—and not transmitted via books or blueprints.
- As a result of the complementarity of the channels that link countries together, a balanced connectivity profile may be more important for knowledge spillovers and growth than being well connected in a single connectivity dimension. Deep and comprehensive FTAs are a way to achieve this.
- The number of connections a country's economic partner has might be just as important as the type of connections. Not all partner countries are the same in this regard. Some partner countries have more connections than others, which makes them potentially better conduits for knowledge transfers.
- In some cases, a country will be better off completing all channels of connectivity to a poorly connected partner than building a single channel of connectivity to a well-connected country.
- Connectivity's being multidimensional implies that shocks in one dimension (say, migration) can have adverse effects in other dimensions (say, FDI and trade) as well. However, countries with the greatest connectivity are among those with the most resilience to shocks.

The ECA region is a great laboratory for observing the role of multidimensional connectivity in action. Regional supply chains are strong, and links between countries across the various forms of connectivity allow observation of how connectivity opens doors for the knowledge transfers that support sustained growth. The variation in connectivity between countries can be exploited empirically to explore which forms of connectivity matter the most.

Although the ECA region as a whole has moved toward greater connectivity, progress has been uneven across countries. Lower trade barriers have not always been associated with fewer restrictions on immigration or product markets, and some countries still rely heavily on other ECA partners for global connectivity. Most higher-income countries have pursued complementary policies in most areas of connectivity, but complementary policies have been less prevalent in lower-middle-income countries (e.g., lower tariffs are not uniform across partner countries and lose effectiveness because of more restrictive domestic regulatory regimes). Moreover, infrastructure linkages remain quite poor in some parts of ECA, particularly Central Asia.

ECA is a diverse region, and the appropriate policy mix to promote multidimensional connectivity will vary from one country to the next. This study supports some general observations about the direction of policy, however. Most obviously, countries can maximize their exposure to international knowledge flows and their ability to exploit their comparative advantages by maintaining low barriers to international transactions, including low tariff rates, minimal constraints on inward or outward FDI, and efficient procedures for border transactions. Multidimensional connectivity suggests countries should not try to rely on one or two types of connections; rather, they should develop a wide variety of mutually supportive outside links, including migration. In addition, participation in deep multilateral trade agreements that support integration of services markets and the reduction of differences in rules governing product markets would increase the impact of low barriers to international transactions on connectivity.

> ECA is a diverse region, and the appropriate policy mix to promote multidimensional connectivity will vary from one country to the next.

Broad improvements to the domestic business climate can make opening up an economy to the outside world more beneficial. A host of policies, desirable in themselves because they increase domestic economic efficiency, offer improved connectivity as a bonus: strengthening institutions, boosting financial sector development, and ensuring flexible labor markets. Adopting international best practice for standards governing product markets, worker protections, and the environment also tends to encourage international connectivity, particularly by making it easier to participate in global and regional supply chains.

Infrastructure investments that focus on improving the efficiency of logistics services are critical for most forms of international connectivity. Recognizing how some connections are more meaningful can give countries a framework to help evaluate the costs and benefits of infrastructure projects. In most economies, trade in final goods relative to trade in services is not as dominant as it once was. So improvements in telecommunications, including reducing the cost and increasing the efficiency of internet connections, would support international commercial transactions and improve contacts with diasporas and other foreign sources of knowledge.

Greater connectivity has two sides: the sending and the receiving countries. A lack of pertinent market information could keep the two from building business connections. Countries seeking to improve connectivity—in particular, those without a history of involvement with trade and FDI—may benefit from proactive policies that can help increase foreign investment and contacts with foreign firms. Investment promotion activities may be useful to encourage investors who lack sufficient information on domestic business opportunities or the policy regime and to reduce unnecessary or burdensome procedures for investment approvals.

Policies should aim to boost the positive effects of connectivity at the firm level, which are associated with better performance. Encouraging skilled immigration may facilitate the introduction of the foreign management practices that increase productivity. Promoting linkages with foreign affiliates, both within ECA and outside it, increases the kind of learning that improves the operation of local firms. Policies to help local firms acquire and absorb efficient global best practices could include increasing access to finance, management training, and supporting labor force mobility.

Migration is a key element of multidimensional connectivity. Improving its benefits within the ECA will require policy reforms to better integrate migrants into the labor force and increased investment in education for all workers to cope with the ongoing transformation of work driven by technological change. From 2000 to 2010, the share of temporary migration rose in more than two-thirds of high-income ECA host countries. Temporary work has also been a more prevalent feature of the labor market, reflecting greater connectivity and faster technological change. Helping all workers benefit from a rapidly changing global economy involves moving away from social safety nets tied to long-term employment toward general safety nets, allowing for more flexible contracts, investments in education, and the removal of constraints on workers' ability to move to find employment.

Improvements in various types of connectivity are perhaps most critical for the lower-middle-income countries, particularly those in the South Caucasus and Central Asia. Because of both their geographic position and limited infrastructure, many of these countries are only weakly connected to other ECA countries and the global economy. The vast distances between Central Asia and Europe will remain an obstacle to connectivity. However, infrastructure investments and policies to improve integration through freer trade, infrastructure, and investment policies are likely to provide large growth benefits in Central Asia.

The more diversified upper-middle-income countries, on the other hand, have a broader set of opportunities to improve connectivity. Participation in supply chains is strong in most of these countries, but balancing the currently uneven supply chain linkages, particularly low levels of imports of intermediate goods, versus already-high levels of exports of these goods, would support greater benefits from connectivity. A large set of policies—from removing barriers to trade and FDI to strengthening intellectual property protection and competitiveness reforms—are needed to improve participation in value chains and make the most of cross-border production opportunities.

The high-income countries that recently entered the EU have established relatively open economies and strong domestic business climates in the context of deep integration within the EU. Nevertheless, further efforts are required to bring their domestic business climates to the level of the most advanced European countries. Most of the transition EU economies would benefit from reducing the excessive economy-wide restrictiveness in product markets that are relevant from a connectivity dimension. This calls for a review of the state's role in the economy and the extent to which regulatory regimes impede new firms' entry into sectors. If a country has relatively closed markets internally, its external connectivity will be affected by the reduction in its attractiveness for inward FDI and participation in global supply chains.

The ECA region's once-confident march toward greater connectivity has for the most part stalled in the past decade. Voices are currently casting doubt on the wisdom of opening to the outside world. The economic benefits of deeper and more diverse connectivity, however, are strong—most notably, the knowledge transfers from trade, FDI, and migration that deepen participation in multinational supply chains and lead to faster growth. By exploring multidimensional connectivity and its impact, *Critical Connections* provides a framework for understanding the benefits of and concerns about globalization and helps provide information for policy discussions and actions that recognize how the various aspects of connectivity might work together to deliver resilient and faster growth.

Annex OA. Selected Indicators

TABLE OA.1 Multidimensional Connectivity Indexes (on an Absolute Basis)

Global ranking, from best to worst, in combined connectivity (lower rankings indicate better connectivity)

Country	Multidimensional connectivity	Trade	FDI	Migration	ICT	Airlines	Portfolio flows
ECA							
Germany	2	1	5	3	4	3	3
United Kingdom	4	6	2	4	2	1	4
Netherlands	5	10	3	14	12	8	14
France	6	5	6	5	5	4	5
Belgium	7	7	7	18	9	13	18
Italy	8	8	13	7	6	7	6
Spain	10	12	12	10	7	6	9
Switzerland	13	15	10	17	8	10	17
Ireland	14	16	11	29	14	14	31
Sweden	15	17	14	19	13	12	19
Poland	17	28	25	20	27	28	23
Austria	18	18	22	21	18	15	20
Russian Federation	22	19	37	13	23	30	13
Czech Republic	23	21	28	39	35	25	38
Hungary	25	25	26	43	37	33	42
Denmark	28	26	23	25	20	11	24
Luxembourg	29	38	4	61	39	37	57
Finland	30	22	24	31	30	21	30
Turkey	31	32	39	16	33	27	16
Portugal	32	31	29	28	25	20	29
Norway	33	33	21	22	22	16	21
Slovak Republic	35	34	41	52	53	68	51
Ukraine	40	42	64	48	67	66	47
Greece	42	39	40	26	26	22	27
Bulgaria	48	47	59	62	58	62	62
Lithuania	50	49	58	68	80	49	65
Croatia	51	53	54	56	49	57	54
Estonia	52	50	57	84	59	61	78
Belarus	54	65	101	67	100	100	63
Latvia	58	55	63	79	73	54	76
Cyprus	60	71	52	74	45	51	70
Malta	62	64	60	94	70	63	95
Kazakhstan	63	62	83	53	95	88	53
Bosnia and Herzegovina	68	68	76	65	64	80	82
Macedonia, FYR	77	69	74	95	79	79	96
Albania	78	80	87	76	72	75	90
Moldova	86	89	100	102	89	92	102
Georgia	97	103	102	99	102	104	97
Armenia	98	105	103	103	103	103	101
Kyrgyz Republic	99	96	95	106	101	101	104
Tajikistan	100	106	106	107	105	106	105
Azerbaijan	101	102	107	87	104	102	84
Other countries							
United States	1	2	1	1	1	2	1
China	3	3	8	6	15	19	7
Canada	9	9	9	9	3	5	8
Mexico	11	11	20	8	10	9	11
Japan	12	4	17	2	19	18	2
Singapore	16	14	19	42	29	29	40
Brazil	19	29	18	11	24	32	10
Malaysia	20	13	31	36	31	38	37

continued

TABLE OA.1 *continued*

Country	Multidimensional connectivity	Trade	FDI	Migration	ICT	Airlines	Portfolio flows
India	21	24	38	12	17	24	12
Indonesia	26	23	35	24	48	36	25
Thailand	27	20	34	32	43	31	32
Hong Kong SAR, China	34	27	16	33	16	26	33
South Africa	36	35	30	27	38	50	26
Argentina	37	37	27	30	42	48	28
Chile	38	41	33	40	50	59	39
Israel	39	36	46	37	28	56	35
New Zealand	41	45	32	41	21	35	41
Morocco	43	46	51	45	46	40	52
Peru	44	52	45	49	52	60	48
United Arab Emirates	45	43	53	34	47	42	34
Saudi Arabia	46	40	43	23	36	53	22
Egypt, Arab Rep.	47	57	49	47	55	52	46
Colombia	49	58	44	35	41	45	36
Nigeria	53	67	48	46	32	73	45
Tunisia	55	44	71	59	51	44	60
Trinidad and Tobago	56	59	61	70	62	69	77
Costa Rica	57	54	65	72	63	43	68
Pakistan	59	48	66	44	66	76	43
Dominican Republic	61	51	67	54	40	34	58
Algeria	64	56	81	38	56	55	44
El Salvador	65	60	73	57	34	46	72
Panama	66	77	50	75	77	64	74
Guatemala	67	61	77	58	44	58	64
Qatar	69	70	56	60	57	47	56
Bangladesh	70	63	92	51	97	94	50
Uruguay	71	73	55	77	71	77	71
Bahamas, The	72	84	42	92	65	17	89
Jordan	73	66	68	82	61	67	80
Mauritius	74	74	47	93	83	83	94
Ecuador	75	85	70	55	60	65	55
Ghana	76	78	82	83	78	85	83
Jamaica	79	87	62	63	68	39	79
Sri Lanka	80	76	91	69	93	93	66
Oman	81	72	84	64	54	41	59
Kenya	82	93	72	71	84	71	69
Bahrain	83	91	85	80	99	82	75
Lebanon	84	79	78	73	76	78	67
Cameroon	85	90	79	78	92	87	73
Mozambique	87	97	69	89	90	98	91
Kuwait	88	81	89	50	69	95	49
Gabon	89	94	75	88	88	97	86
Barbados	90	99	36	97	75	70	100
Syrian Arab Republic	91	75	88	66	74	81	61
Namibia	92	86	90	96	86	89	92
Paraguay	93	95	80	86	85	86	88
Guyana	94	92	86	85	81	84	108
Botswana	95	83	94	90	91	96	85
Swaziland	96	82	93	104	94	99	103
Ethiopia	102	100	99	81	98	90	81
Brunei Darussalam	103	88	96	91	96	91	87
Benin	104	98	104	101	107	105	99
Belize	105	101	97	105	87	74	106
Antigua and Barbuda	106	104	98	108	82	72	107
Burkina Faso	107	108	108	100	108	108	98
Afghanistan	108	107	105	98	106	107	93

Note: ECA = Europe and Central Asia; FDI = foreign direct investment; ICT = information and communication technology.

TABLE OA.2 **Multidimensional Connectivity Indexes (on a Per Capita Basis)**

Global ranking, from best to worst, in combined connectivity (lower rankings indicate better connectivity)

Country	Multidimensional connectivity	Trade	FDI	Migration	ICT	Airlines	Portfolio flows
ECA							
Luxembourg	1	2	1	1	1	3	32
Ireland	2	3	6	4	3	5	28
Netherlands	3	6	5	21	15	13	9
Belgium	4	4	4	6	7	19	79
Switzerland	6	5	8	2	2	7	7
Malta	7	23	7	35	23	6	53
Sweden	9	8	13	8	10	12	84
Norway	11	13	12	10	13	8	15
Cyprus	12	37	3	16	6	11	14
United Kingdom	13	19	15	11	9	17	5
Denmark	14	11	17	15	12	4	11
Finland	15	9	16	31	25	16	16
Austria	16	7	19	9	17	14	70
Germany	18	10	20	12	19	26	19
France	19	17	18	13	22	30	18
Czech Republic	21	12	28	29	34	34	30
Hungary	22	18	25	51	37	36	26
Spain	23	25	24	17	29	23	48
Estonia	24	20	30	23	27	22	1
Portugal	26	27	29	24	30	24	21
Slovak Republic	27	14	32	41	43	56	66
Italy	31	22	31	32	32	33	12
Lithuania	35	28	40	45	77	35	2
Latvia	37	32	41	20	55	21	60
Poland	38	34	36	47	45	49	34
Croatia	41	44	37	59	38	39	56
Greece	42	45	42	26	31	31	20
Bulgaria	45	43	45	71	51	50	62
Turkey	56	55	57	39	76	62	85
Belarus	58	48	73	30	83	100	98
Bosnia and Herzegovina	60	60	63	88	49	63	82
Macedonia, FYR	61	52	58	83	65	58	69
Russian Federation	63	49	67	43	73	80	40
Ukraine	71	62	76	27	87	81	104
Albania	75	79	75	37	60	48	75
Kazakhstan	76	68	83	25	99	90	99
Georgia	84	102	65	63	98	99	90
Moldova	86	81	94	48	62	68	80
Armenia	87	90	70	77	89	79	81
Kyrgyz Republic	95	99	97	50	100	95	94
Tajikistan	102	109	101	67	107	98	103
Azerbaijan	106	106	107	87	103	93	106
Other countries							
Singapore	5	1	11	14	11	20	10
Hong Kong SAR China	8	15	10	22	5	29	4
Bahamas, The	10	41	9	36	14	1	8
Canada	17	16	22	7	4	18	22
Barbados	20	85	2	49	28	10	63
Australia	25	35	23	3	21	44	17
Qatar	28	33	21	42	18	9	23
New Zealand	29	39	26	5	8	27	13
United States	30	30	27	18	26	46	64
Mauritius	32	57	14	52	66	52	6
Trinidad and Tobago	33	31	33	66	33	28	72

continued

TABLE OA.2 *continued*

Country	Multidimensional connectivity	Trade	FDI	Migration	ICT	Airlines	Portfolio flows
United Arab Emirates	34	29	34	55	39	37	77
Malaysia	36	21	43	54	40	60	65
Israel	39	24	46	19	24	51	61
Chile	40	46	35	58	63	66	29
Japan	43	26	50	75	57	71	24
Panama	44	59	38	53	52	40	73
Bahrain	46	42	49	72	70	42	37
Uruguay	47	73	39	40	56	59	3
Mexico	48	40	51	56	42	53	107
Thailand	49	38	55	78	82	69	36
Costa Rica	50	36	60	70	54	38	83
Argentina	51	66	44	34	61	74	27
Saudi Arabia	52	51	54	44	41	65	42
Oman	53	56	56	61	35	32	41
South Africa	54	53	53	64	68	82	39
Brazil	55	69	48	69	85	87	49
Gabon	57	80	47	46	81	75	33
Brunei Darussalam	59	50	71	60	67	43	78
China	62	54	62	113	88	96	89
Peru	64	74	59	85	72	77	71
El Salvador	65	63	61	80	16	45	86
Jamaica	66	83	52	68	46	25	88
Morocco	67	75	66	106	79	61	44
Dominican Republic	68	61	64	62	36	41	91
Tunisia	69	47	79	90	59	55	25
Jordan	70	65	68	33	44	54	51
Indonesia	72	71	77	99	97	89	43
Guyana	73	64	80	81	53	47	76
Philippines	74	58	84	79	80	86	45
Colombia	77	84	72	86	74	78	50
Swaziland	78	67	89	82	91	83	93
Antigua and Barbuda	79	92	69	28	20	2	58
Lebanon	80	77	74	103	64	57	31
Namibia	81	70	93	74	75	67	92
Kuwait	82	76	86	104	48	73	55
Botswana	83	72	92	109	92	76	87
Egypt, Arab Rep.	85	86	78	97	95	85	67
Guatemala	88	78	88	84	58	64	96
Belize	89	93	87	38	47	15	74
Ecuador	90	96	85	65	69	70	101
Algeria	91	82	98	107	93	72	52
Ghana	92	87	95	100	50	94	105
Paraguay	93	100	96	57	94	84	46
Nigeria	94	101	90	101	71	104	68
Cameroon	96	105	91	91	102	97	35
India	97	88	99	95	84	101	47
Zimbabwe	98	89	100	76	90	91	54
Sri Lanka	99	91	102	92	105	102	59
Mozambique	100	107	82	73	104	103	108
Kenya	101	103	81	94	86	88	95
Pakistan	103	97	103	111	78	106	57
Sudan	104	98	105	105	112	113	113
Syrian Arab Republic	105	94	104	108	96	92	102
Bangladesh	107	95	108	96	101	109	38
Benin	108	108	109	89	111	111	100
Togo	109	104	113	93	108	105	97
Ethiopia	110	111	110	112	109	107	112
Afghanistan	111	113	106	110	106	110	110
Niger	112	112	111	98	113	112	111

Notes

1. Transmission of shocks is not new. The bubonic plague of 542 CE, which decimated the Byzantine Empire, is thought to have arrived in Constantinople (today's Istanbul) by way of the Silk Road. The spice trade was also accompanied by struggles for economic dominance as wars were fought, lands were colonized, and fortunes were made and lost.
2. This study is available electronically at http://www.worldbank.org/en/region/eca /publication/critical-connections.
3. Note that the OECD average includes the European Union countries.
4. In a seminal contribution, Coe, Helpman, and Hoffmaister (1997) identify that by trading with industrial countries with a large "stock of knowledge" accumulated through R&D activities, developing countries boosted their productivity by importing intermediates and capital goods that embodied knowledge and information. Van Pottelsberghe de la Potterie and Lichtenberg (2001) identify that FDI, and in particular outward FDI, has also been a conduit for R&D spillovers for 13 industrial countries (including 11 EU member countries).

References

Bernstein, William J. 2008. *A Splendid Exchange: How Trade Shaped the World*. New York: Grove.

Bloom, Nicholas, Kalina Manova, John Van Reenen, Stephen Teng Sun, and Zhihong Yu. 2018. "*Managing Trade: Evidence from China and the US.*" NBER Working Paper 24718, National Bureau of Economic Research, Cambridge, MA. http://www.nber.org /papers/w24718.

Coe, David T., Elhanan Helpman, and Alexander W. Hoffmaister. 1997. "North–South R&D Spillovers." *Economic Journal* 107: 134–49.

Parthesius, Robert. 2010. *Dutch Ships in Tropical Waters: The Development of the Dutch East India Company (VOC) Shipping Network in Asia 1595–1660*. Amsterdam: Amsterdam University Press.

Rodrik, Dani. 2018. "Populism and the Economics of Globalization." *Journal of International Business Policy* 1 (1–2): 12–33. https://link.springer.com/article/10.1057/s42214 -018-0001-4.

Romer, Paul. M. 1990. "Endogenous Technological Change." *Journal of Political Economy* 98: S71–S102.

Starr, S. Frederick. 2015. *Lost Enlightenment: Central Asia's Golden Age from the Arab Conquest to Tamerlane*. Princeton, NJ: Princeton University Press.

van Pottelsberghe de la Potterie, Bruno, and Frank Lichtenberg, 2001. "Does Foreign Direct Investment Transfer Technology across Borders?" *Review of Economics and Statistics* 83 (3): 490–97.

World Bank. 2012. *Golden Growth: Restoring the Lustre of the European Economic Model*. Washington, DC: World Bank.

———. 2018. *Moving for Prosperity: Global Migration and Labor Markets*. Policy Research Report. Washington, DC: World Bank.

Multidimensional Connectivity: Pathways to Growth and Shared Prosperity in Europe and Central Asia

International connections through trade, foreign direct investment (FDI), migration, the internet, and other channels are critical for the transmission of knowledge and growth. But how much knowledge is transmitted to a country is not only the result of the overall level of connectivity, but also to whom a country is connected and how the connections complement each other. For example, being well connected to an economy with wide-reaching global connections is likely to be a stronger conduit for knowledge transfers than being connected to an isolated economy. Likewise, connections are likely to complement each other. For example, e-commerce is often seen as a benefit of internet connectivity, but without transport connectivity, e-commerce may not amount to much. This broader definition of connectivity, referred to as *multidimensional connectivity,* is explored in this chapter for Europe and Central Asia (ECA) and forms the basis for examining connectivity in various channels in subsequent chapters of this flagship report.

ECA's international multidimensional connectivity has expanded sharply over the past three decades, owing to greater global integration driven by lowering of costs to economic transactions, the breakup of the Soviet Union, and increasing integration within, and expansion of, the European Union (EU). Enhanced international connectivity generally has been associated with growth, through the transmission of technologies across borders. This transmission is most effective when deep connections exist across different channels, and when countries are connected to other,

47

well-connected countries. This chapter discusses the multidimensional character of connectivity. It assesses the impact of improved connectivity on income and income distribution, and it addresses the question of whether the region is optimally connected to other economic poles in the world. The report will summarize the related policy options.

Main Messages

- Regional connections through trade, FDI, migration, telecommunications, and other channels over the past two decades have risen more rapidly than ECA's connections outside the region, in part reflecting policies geared toward increasing regional integration and the rising importance of regional value chains. However, countries in ECA that are linked to strong globally connected ECA countries, for example, Germany or the United Kingdom, may nevertheless have experienced substantial increases in global connectivity as well. Among connectivity channels, ECA's intraregional trade links are stronger than its FDI links, while airline connections and labor market integration have increased sharply among European countries.

- Network connectivity measures for trade, FDI, migration, information and communication technology, airline flights, and portfolio flows are all positively related to growth, and each is associated with higher growth over and above the influence of standard growth determinants. However, not all channels play an equally important role. Trade connectivity is perhaps the most important and is related to overall growth and the income growth of the bottom 40 percent of the income distribution. Increasing linkages in each form of connectivity are complements to one another, suggesting that a balanced connectivity profile along all dimensions of connectivity is more important than a large increase in one channel only. The growth impact of multidimensional connectivity is higher than the impact of each of the individual network indexes, suggesting that overall connectivity is more important than each of the individual channels separately. Thus, policies to promote connectivity across trade, migration, and FDI are likely more beneficial than focusing on enhancing only one channel, and reducing connectivity in one dimension may reduce the impact of growth from other channels.

- Greater international connectivity can increase a country's exposure to international shocks, but may also mitigate shocks by enabling a country to increase its reliance on other links in its network. Both countries with low and countries with high levels of connectivity tend to be more resilient to shocks in the global network, the first because of the limited number of partners that may become a source of shocks, the second because well-diversified connections may provide alternative sources of, for example, finance or export demand. In contrast, countries in the "middle" of the connectivity spectrum, that is, countries that are highly dependent on a few well-connected countries, appear to be most susceptible to shocks that originate from, or affect, these countries.

Introduction

Globalization often means different things to different people. For some, it is the large number of imported goods seen on store shelves. To others it is a social phenomenon that includes everyday exposure to a wide variety of cultures, peoples, foods, products, and spoken languages. In major cities throughout ECA the change is perhaps most apparent, while in smaller towns or villages it may be less so. In Central Europe the look and feel of major cities is very different now than before the transition to market economies in the early 1990s. But even in the small towns in Northern, Western, and Southern Europe, integration brought by the European Union and greater global connectivity has changed the look and feel of everyday life and economic opportunities. Regardless of where one is physically located, or how one observes globalization, the interconnectedness of the world is increasingly touching us either directly by the people we encounter or indirectly through the items we purchase or foreign firms that employ us.

Since the early 1990s, the countries of ECA have been radically transformed, as borders were opened and many hurdles impeding cross-border connectivity were lowered. The move toward the common market in the European Union and the fall of the Iron Curtain had impacts well beyond trade—including positive impacts on income and income distribution. This trend toward income convergence with developed countries occurred despite intermittent external shocks, suggesting, in turn, that economic connectivity to regional and global markets has likely been an important driver of growth and improved standards of living. Since 2008–09, the global financial crisis, deepening geopolitical tensions, the refugee influx, and sharp commodity price fluctuations have posed new challenges for the region, pointing, among other things, to the need to more fully understand the role that economic connectivity can play in preserving economic growth and incomes in times of political and economic flux.

Much of the empirical work done to date has recognized the importance of openness for economic growth, including through trade, FDI, the internet (information and communication technology—ICT), migration, and other forms of connectivity (Dollar 1992; Ben-David 1993; Sachs and Warner 1995; Edwards 1998; Frankel and Romer 1999; and Javorcik 2004, among others). While there are many nuances to the empirical findings, and questions remain regarding causality between outcomes and policies (Rodriguez and Rodrik 2000), the association appears to be strong and intuitively appealing. Technologies embodied in goods, investments, and people are likely to be transmitted across borders, as long as the source and host countries are open and have the capacity to absorb these innovations. In other words, in addition to the gains from specialization that openness brings through each layer of connectivity, knowledge spillovers are also likely created. This leads not only to one-time increases in output, but also, in the context of endogenous growth theory, long-term increases in economic growth because the cost of acquiring new knowledge falls with an increasing stock of knowledge (Romer 1990; Helpman 2004).

To date, economic research has only examined one dimension at a time of partner connectivity and the relationship to economic growth. Empirical research is available on the relationship between various types of trade and economic growth, FDI and growth, the internet and growth, and migration and growth (Mountford 1997; Borensztein, De Gregorio, and Lee 1998; Alfaro et al. 2004; Czernich, Falck, and Kretschmer 2011). But empirical and theoretical work has yet to examine how the *interplay* between these various layers of connectivity complement each other. For example, internet connectivity has various direct avenues for influencing economic growth, including providing individuals the ability to quickly research products available in foreign countries, take online courses, and transact in services remotely, as well as serving as the backbone for facilitating greater deepening of cross-border global supply chains. E-commerce has been greatly enhanced by the availability of broadband internet. Nonetheless, without transport connectivity through roads, rail, shipping, and air transport, the effects of broadband connectivity as a channel to stimulate growth via e-commerce would be greatly diminished. (See Spotlight 3, "Reaping Digital Dividends through Complementary Investments.").

More telling regarding the interplay between various forms of connectivity is the role of migration and international travel, be it for permanent migration, foreign study, or tourism. While Gould (1994) first identified the complementary relationship between migration and trade between the home and host countries of migrants, subsequent research has also identified migration's importance in influencing FDI and its direct influence on growth through knowledge transfers (Onodera 2008). Consequently, migration may not only be important for growth by directly transferring knowledge between the host and home countries, but also by facilitating knowledge embodied in trade and FDI flows through bridging market information gaps.

The Importance of Identifying Partners in Connectivity

A fundamental prerequisite for identifying the complementarity between various forms of connectivity is the ability to identify the specific country links in the connectivity chain. For example, matching migration and trade flows between country partners is essential to identify the complementarity between migration and trade in enhancing economic growth. Knowing the size of overall trade and migration flows for a country is not sufficient to identify that trade from specific countries is facilitated by migration from those same countries.

Mapping these direct connections between countries also brings to light the potential importance of indirect connections. While two similar countries may have the same number and size of connections, they may be connected to very different countries. Being connected to "well-connected" countries may provide greater opportunities for knowledge transfers from partners of partner countries (Duernecker, Meyer, and Vega-Redondo 2014). For example, a dollar of trade between Algeria and Germany may provide greater knowledge spillovers than a dollar of trade between Algeria and Morocco, because Germany is much more connected to the global economy and is likely to be a source of advanced knowledge as well as a conduit for technology and knowledge from other countries it is connected to.

> Being connected to "well-connected" countries may provide greater opportunities for knowledge transfers from partners of partner countries.

The importance of direct and indirect connections between countries, as well as the complementarity between various types of connections for knowledge transfers and economic growth, lends itself to the use of *multilayer network analysis*. Network analysis is simply a tool for studying the direct and indirect connections between countries. Multilayer networks (Kivela et al. 2014) go beyond the notion of a single, one-dimensional isolated network, and provide a description of the interactions between various types of connections (layers) in a larger network.

This chapter finds that being connected to well-connected countries matters for economic growth, but there is complementarity in the various types of connections that enhances growth as well. Countries can benefit from (a) multiple types of economic links (such as trade, investment, migration, modern telecommunications, and transport) that underpin the movement of technologies and ideas, but also (b) the quality of connections in terms of knowledge spillovers and the indirect connections made through partners that are well connected. These are both aspects of interconnectedness that affect growth and growth spillovers.

Trends in Economic Connectivity

Economic links facilitate trade and the transfer of factors of production (capital, labor, and so on) and therefore has an impact on the overall level of production. However, these links are also likely to facilitate the flow of ideas and innovation, and, hence, long-run growth. But the strength of information flows is likely different for different economic connections. For example, the knowledge spillovers associated with merchandise trade are likely centered around the information embodied in the products traded (knowledge spillovers related to trade in processed food, for example, may be different from those related to trade in semiconductors) (Hidalgo and Hausmann 2009). FDI links are associated with a transfer of managerial, organizational, and corporate governance expertise (see chapter 2). And migration flows can facilitate the transfer of knowledge directly, but also support less tangible cultural exchange, increase exposure to foreign languages, and bridge gaps in trust in business dealings that cannot always be narrowed through explicit contracting, particularly with differences in governance and legal systems (see chapter 5).

As mentioned earlier, country and regional connectivity has typically been viewed as the size of trade relative to gross domestic product (GDP) or global trade. ECA's share of global trade has declined since the early 2000s (figure 1.1, panel a). Moreover, although intra- and extraregional trade have grown, intraregional trade has grown more rapidly (figure 1.1, panel b). Increased trade within ECA may reflect greater cooperation across institutional and regulatory dimensions with important implications for regional integration and convergence. Similar aggregate measures of connectivity (total FDI, migration, telecommunications, and others) suggest that while regional integration has increased substantially, growth of global connections may not have kept up.

While past studies find evidence that greater trade openness and integration improves growth, these aggregate measures of integration may obscure the

FIGURE 1.1

Trends in intraregional trade in ECA

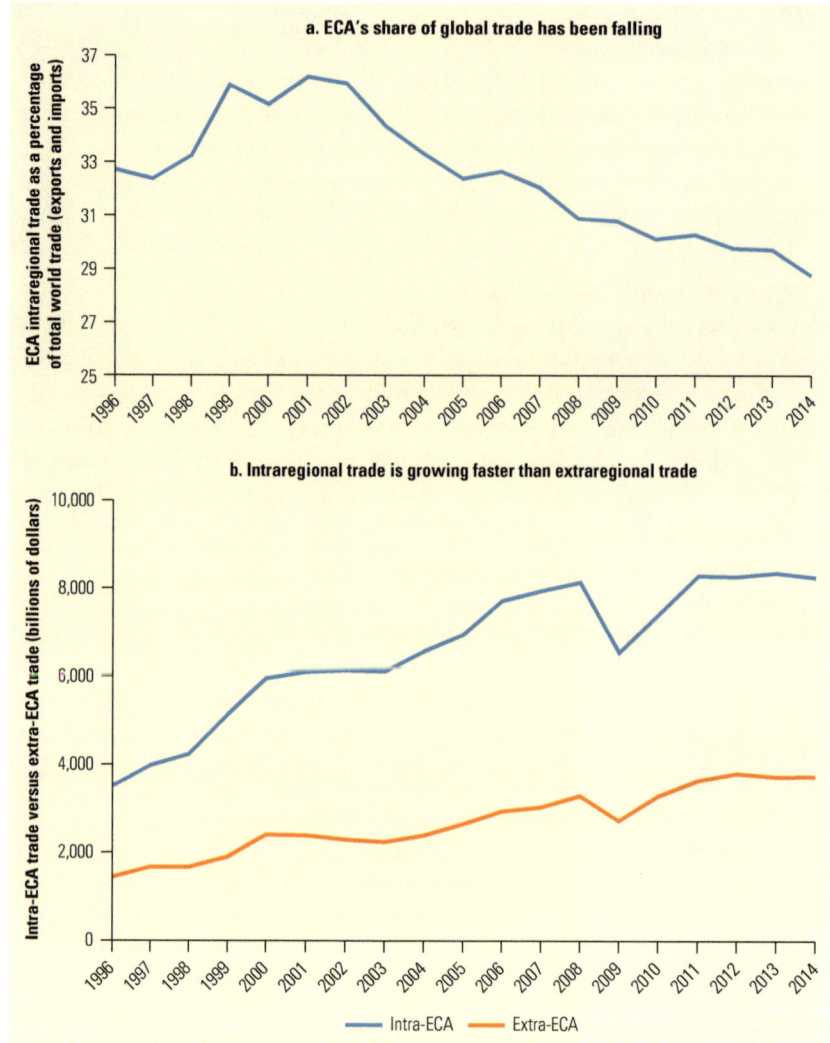

a. ECA's share of global trade has been falling

ECA intraregional trade as a percentage of total world trade (exports and imports)

b. Intraregional trade is growing faster than extraregional trade

Intra-ECA trade versus extra-ECA trade (billions of dollars)

Intra-ECA   Extra-ECA

Source: Calculations based on data from the United Nations Conference on Trade and Development (UNCTAD) and World Bank, *World Development Indicators.*
Note: ECA = Europe and Central Asia.

underlying bilateral connections and the importance of partner country connections. In other words, while ECA's intraregional connectivity may be growing faster in the aggregate than extraregional connectivity, it is difficult to determine how well ECA countries are connecting to other ECA countries that are well connected globally. ECA global connectivity may actually be increasing for the average ECA country, if countries in ECA are linking to strong globally connected ECA countries. The following section examines the pattern of connections between countries and how countries are connected to the broader network of countries. Subsequently, the chapter uses this wider network of connectivity information to analyze types of connectivity, how the various layers of connectivity interact, and how connectivity might be associated with economic growth and shared prosperity.

Examining ECA Connectivity in the Global Context

While there are potentially hundreds of ways countries can connect, with varying implications for the transfer of ideas, this chapter focuses on six types of economic connections: trade, FDI, migration, information and communication technologies (ICT), air transport, and portfolio financial flows. While other forms of connectivity may also be important for how knowledge transfers between countries and for economic growth, these data are the only ones available on a global and country-to-country basis. Subsequent chapters will drill down into additional layers of connectivity (for example, transport in ECA in chapter 5) as well as unique aspects of the layers of connectivity (such as firm foreign management in chapter 4). This chapter takes a broad macro view of the many layers of connectivity as a means to observe general trends in the strength of connections, how ECA countries are connected to each other and the rest of the world, and how these connections influence growth.

As an initial overview of ECA connectivity in the global context, we show graphically how countries in ECA and the rest of the world are connected in each layer of connectivity. We show data for the initial year and the last period available to see how connectivity in a particular dimension has changed over time.

In figures 1.2–1.7, ECA countries are highlighted in shades of blue, and the rest of the world is shown in shades of orange. The size of each country node is proportional to the size of its total connectivity in each layer of connectivity described. Outward arrows point to the two strongest bilateral partners. The methodology for plotting the countries attempts to show clearly the connections between countries in the global network of countries.[1] The largest country nodes are pulled to the outer boundaries of the graph, but the pull is counterbalanced by the number and strength of connections with partner countries. Consequently, country nodes will tend to be grouped together if they share common connections with well-connected countries.

Trade

Figure 1.2 is based on trade of manufactured goods between all the countries in the world in 2000 and 2014. The size of each country node reflects the total volume of trade (exports and imports) for each country, and the two outward arrows are pointed to each country's two top export destinations. One of the most dramatic developments in global trade has been the emergence of China (CHN) since 2000, which has not only grown to one of the three largest traders, along with the United States (USA) and Germany (DEU), but also is pulled toward the center of the graph, with numerous connections to regional hubs in Europe, the Americas, and Asia. ECA's relative dominance in trade has declined, along with other regions, as China and other Asian countries' share of global trade has increased. Interestingly, however, ECA country nodes are much closer to each other in recent years than in the past, reflecting the higher degree of regional integration and value chain development in Europe. Germany is the primary hub for ECA's manufacturing integration. The United Kingdom (GBR) is pulled equally between Europe and the United States, and, hence, is located almost equidistant between these two poles.

FIGURE 1.2 Exports of manufactured goods

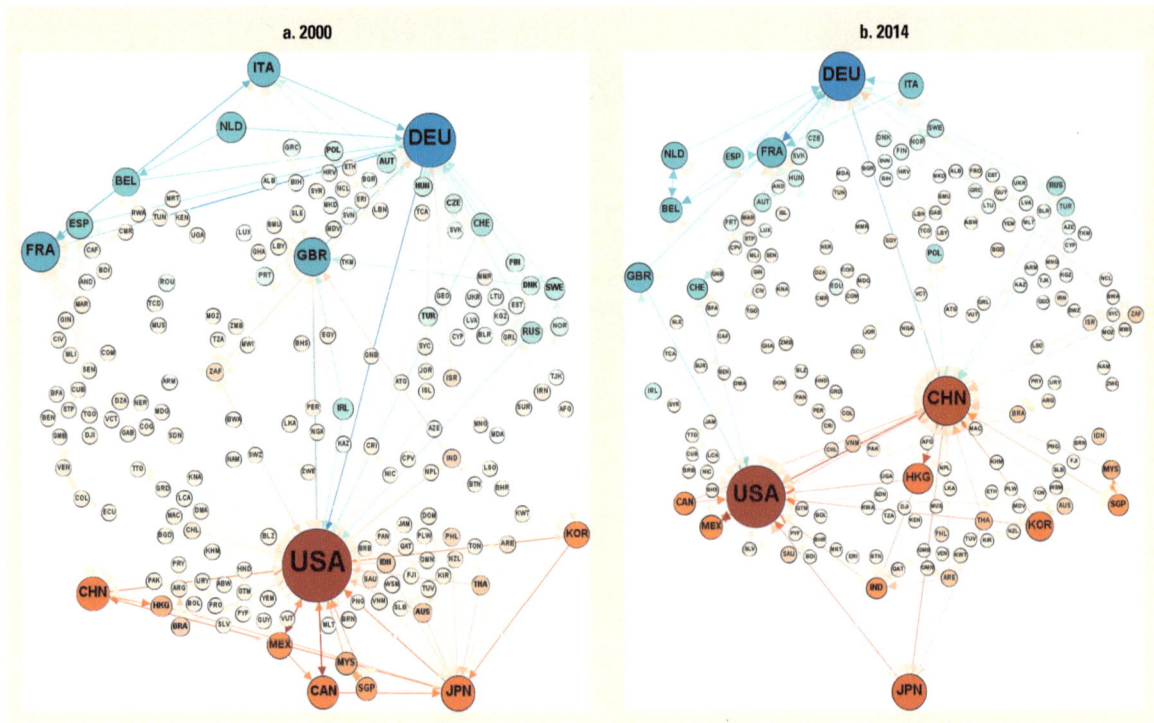

a. 2000   b. 2014

Source: Calculations based on data from the United Nations Conference on Trade and Development.
Note: The size of each country node reflects the total volume of trade. Each node has two outgoing links, which point to the country's two top export partners. Europe and Central Asia countries are shown in shades of blue.

Foreign Direct Investment

Figure 1.3 is based on total stocks of FDI (inward and outward) for all the countries in the world. Each country node shows two outward arrows that are pointed to each country's two top FDI destinations. Unlike the international trade network, global FDI remains dominated by the developed countries in Europe and the United States, although developing countries have seen some modest increase. Much FDI moves between countries of similar levels of development, with relatively modest investments going from developed to developing countries and vice versa. China and the rest of Asia were the beneficiaries of significant incoming investment flows between 2000 and 2012. China, on the other hand, has focused its outgoing investments toward the United States and neighboring countries.

For ECA, the distribution of FDI is also less regionally focused than trade. FDI appears to be connected to language and historical colonial linkages (for example, francophone African countries largely share in FDI flows with France and Belgium) as well as driven by corporate acquisitions for technology, transport, access to markets, and natural resource endowments. Financial centers (e.g., the United Kingdom and Switzerland) have also become increasingly important for attracting FDI. Interestingly, compared to trade, Germany's and China's participation in global FDI is small, but while China's share has grown, Germany's relative FDI stocks have fallen. Nonetheless, ECA's overall participation in global FDI increased from 2002 to 2012, and has

FIGURE 1.3 Foreign direct investment

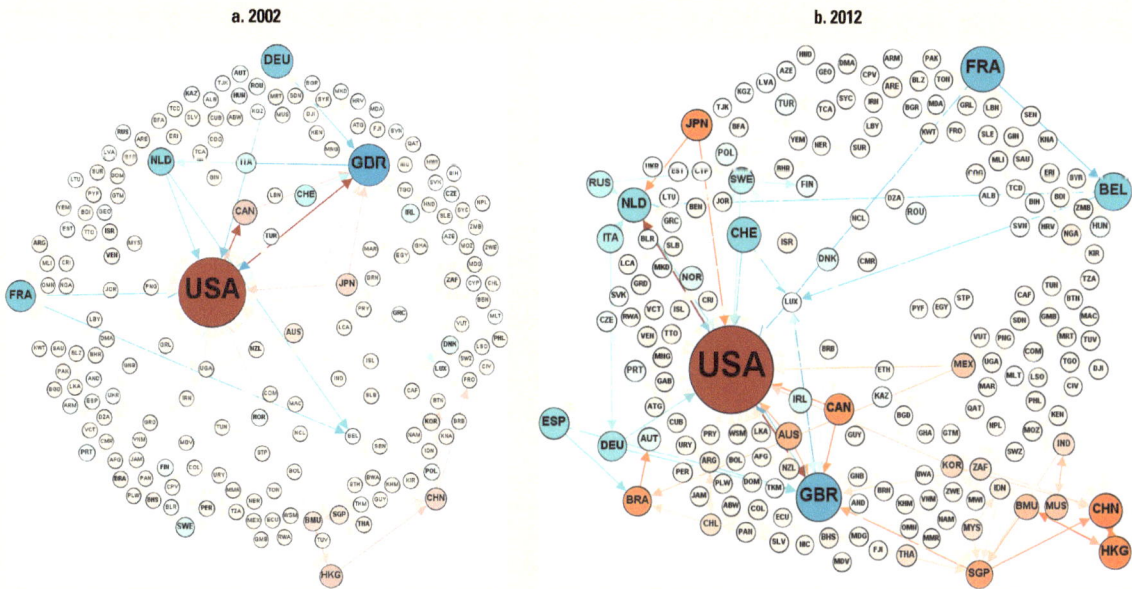

a. 2002

b. 2012

Source: Calculations based on data from the Organisation for Economic Co-operation and Development and fDiMarkets.com.
Note: The size of each country node reflects the country's total foreign direct investment (FDI) stocks (incoming and outgoing). Each country has two outgoing links that point to its two main FDI destinations. Europe and Central Asia countries are shown in shades of blue.

become more equally distributed as Spain (ESP), Belgium (BEL), the Russian Federation (RUS), and Sweden (SWE) have seen relative increases.

International Migration

Perhaps more than any other connectivity layer, international migration is dominated by the United States, which is the main recipient of migrants in the world (figure 1.4). Although the importance of China in this network increased between 2000 and 2010, China's migration connectivity in the global network is significantly lower than its other connections. Russia is a particularly large center of migration in ECA, but this is primarily a legacy of the breakup of the Soviet Union. Individuals that were born in former Soviet Republics living in Russia are classified as foreign born, although at the time of birth they were nationals of the same country as Russian natives. Nonetheless, Russia remains an important destination for migrants from Central Asian countries, such as Tajikistan (TJK) and Uzbekistan (UZB). Remittance flows generated by these migrant workers living in Russia account for a substantial share of income for many Central Asia economies (in some cases, more than 30 percent, see chapter 4).

The share of immigrant populations among European countries appears to have increased from 2000 to 2010. The region is more integrated in its labor market, as evidenced by the somewhat higher clustering of European countries in the last year, reflecting easing of immigration rules in the EU under the Schengen Agreement. It is interesting to note that Germany was a large recipient of migration flows from Russia and other communist bloc countries during the first decade after the breakup of the Soviet Union; however, in the figure for 2010 Germany is

FIGURE 1.4 Migration

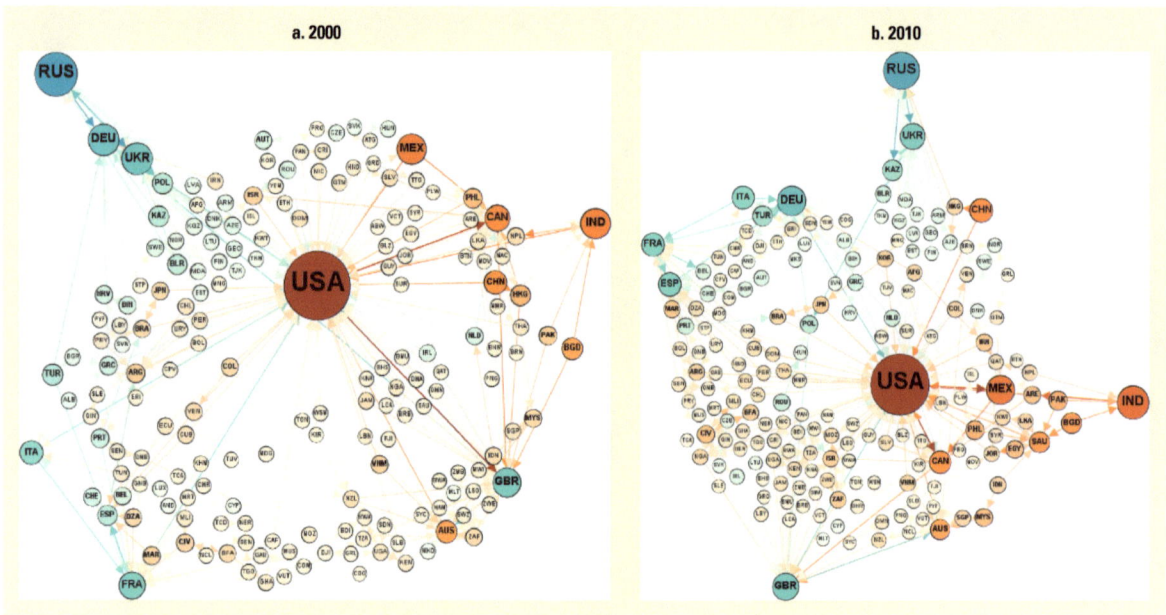

Source: Calculations based on data from the Organisation for Economic Co-operation and Development.
Note: The size of each country node represents the total number of foreign-born individuals residing in the country plus the total number of native-born citizens living outside the country. Each country node has two outgoing links that represent the country's two largest emigration destinations. Europe and Central Asia countries are shown in shades of blue.

pulled much closer to the center of EU countries. Likewise, Poland after joining the EU has closer migration linkages to Germany and the United Kingdom, compared to its connections to Russia and the United States.

In general, migration flows are strongly influenced by language similarities (e.g., Romanians living in Italy and Spain), proximity (e.g., the United States, Canada, and Mexico), and historical colonial ties (e.g., France and North Africa; the United Kingdom and Australia).

Passenger Airline Connectivity

The bilateral airline connectivity shown in figure 1.5 represents not simply the number of flights between countries, but the origin and final destination of passengers, which requires information on passenger itineraries. Oftentimes passengers utilize hubs and transfer to other flights and airlines before reaching their destination, which, without data on itineraries, can overweight hubs as being the final passenger destination and underweight countries that connect to the global network of countries through hubs. These data were painstakingly estimated by the International Civil Aviation Organization, using flight and itinerary information to build a data set for passenger flight origins and final destinations. However, despite these efforts, private flights are not always included in available data and hubs may still be overrepresented as the final destination for air passengers.

What appears from the data is that, similar to the migration network, the links among European countries increased substantially between 2000 and 2012 as shown by the increased clustering of ECA countries in the later period. Moreover,

FIGURE 1.5 Airline connectivity

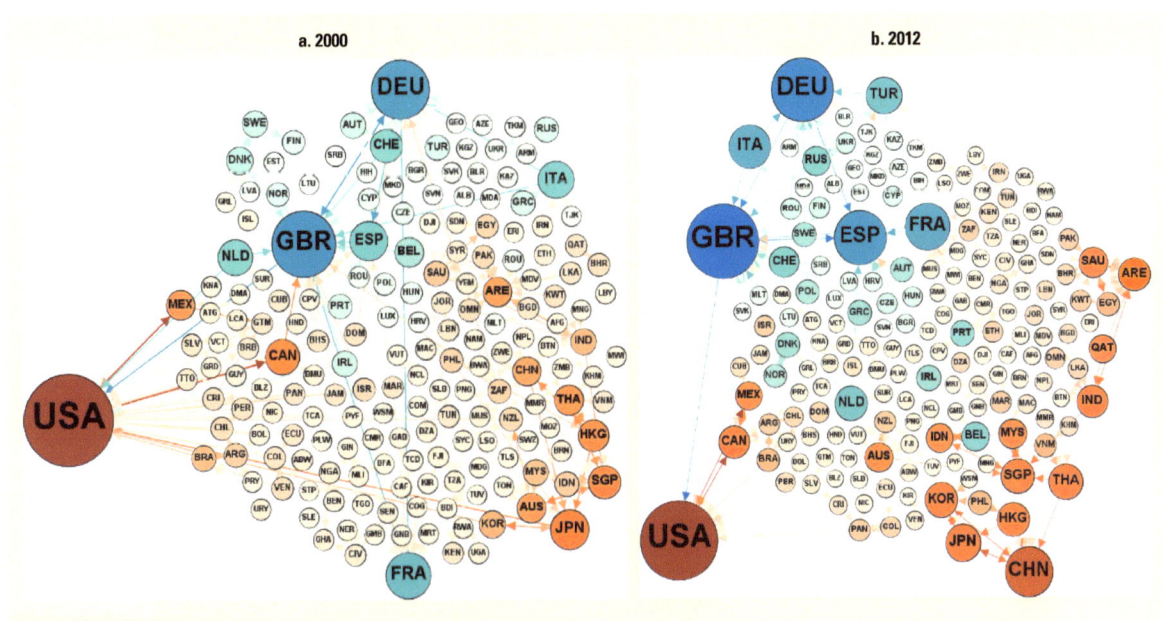

Source: Calculations based on International Civil Aviation Organization data.
Note: The size of each country node represents the estimated total number of air passengers. Each country node has two outgoing links that point to the country's two largest passenger flight destination countries. Europe and Central Asia countries are shown in shades of blue.

ECA high-income countries, particularly Germany, the United Kingdom, France, Spain, Italy, and Turkey, have increased in importance in airline passenger origin and destination countries.

Since 2007, Europe's direct connectivity gains within the region have been driven by regional integration policies and the subsequent expansion of regional short-haul low-cost carriers. Meanwhile, full-service carriers have seen their regional direct connectivity drop with the greater competition. Low-cost carriers now account for nearly a third of Europe's direct connectivity and are focused on linking airports within the intra-European market. The lion's share of Europe's direct connectivity to other world regions is still held by full-service carriers.

Outside of ECA, rapid economic development made China an attractive destination for international flyers; China overtook Japan's role as the top airline flight destination in Asia in 2012. The development of popular Middle East Gulf carriers (e.g., Qatar and Emirate Airlines) may indicate a country bias in the data due to their importance as regional hubs, but it is also reasonable that they are attracting greater final destination air traffic due to broader investments to diversify their economies away from oil.

International Internet and Communications Technology

The international ICT global flows network is shown in figure 1.6. The data are constructed by using total country internet bandwidth (bilateral country data are not available) and allocating bilateral traffic in proportion to bilateral telephone calls for each country. ICT flows appear to be clustered in three groups: Europe,

FIGURE 1.6 Internet and communication technologies

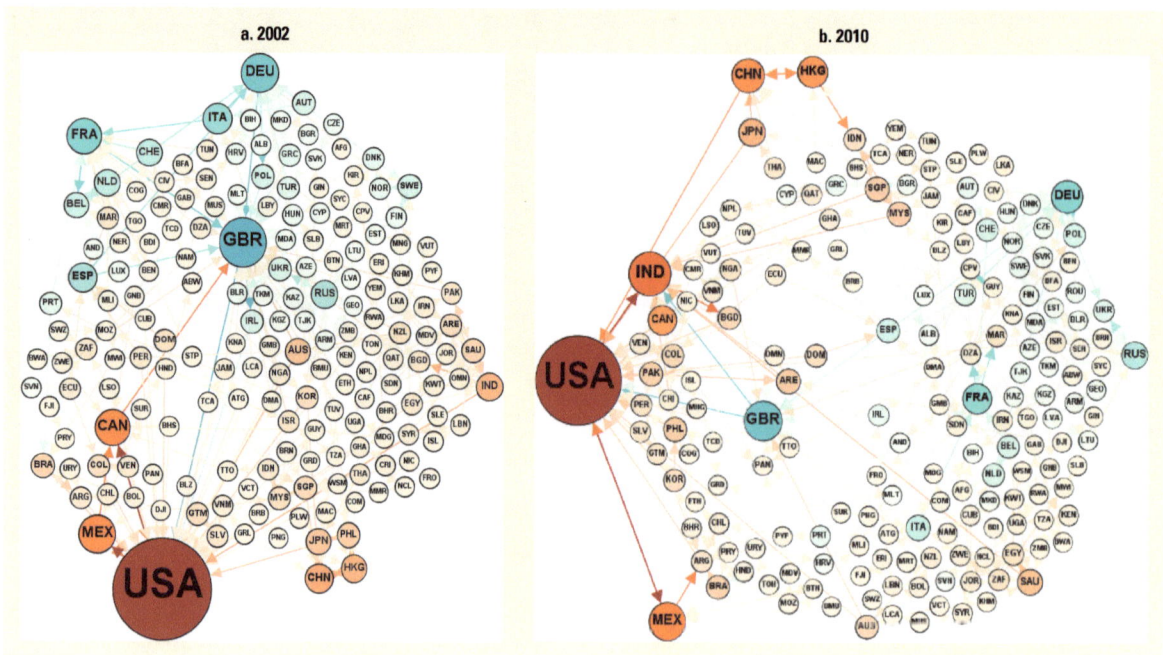

Source: Calculations based on TeleGeography data.
Note: Each country node represents the combined value of the estimated incoming and outgoing information and communication technology communication and has two outgoing links that point to the country's two main outgoing communication partners. Europe and Central Asia countries are shown in shades of blue.

North America, and Asia. The United States and the United Kingdom are the major hubs in this network, with a notable increase in the importance of India in 2010 due to the back-office outsourcing of service jobs and call centers. It should be noted, however, that data on the network in the latter period are not as complete as in the early period and should be interpreted skeptically. Nonetheless, intuitive regional patterns persist with connections driven by language, supply-chain linkages, and economic activity.

Portfolio Financial Flows

The portfolio financial flows are derived from the Bank for International Settlements Consolidated Banking Statistics.[2] The Consolidated Banking Statistics capture the worldwide consolidated positions of internationally active banking groups headquartered in the Bank for International Settlements reporting countries. Portfolio financial flows appear to be driven by the largest financial centers, without a strong relationship to underlying trade or other economic relationships (figure 1.7). The six top centers include Germany, the United Kingdom, Japan, France, the United States, and Switzerland. Some relationships are economically intuitive, with many ECA countries having at least one top portfolio flow connection in the ECA region and the second in the United States. In 2010 Spain's two top connections included Germany and the United States, reflecting integration within ECA and outside, while in 2000 it was Mexico and the United States. In other words, ECA ties became relatively stronger. Nonetheless, even within ECA, because of the agglomeration benefits of financial sectors and the practice of many companies to issue many companies' practice of

FIGURE 1.7 Portfolio financial flows

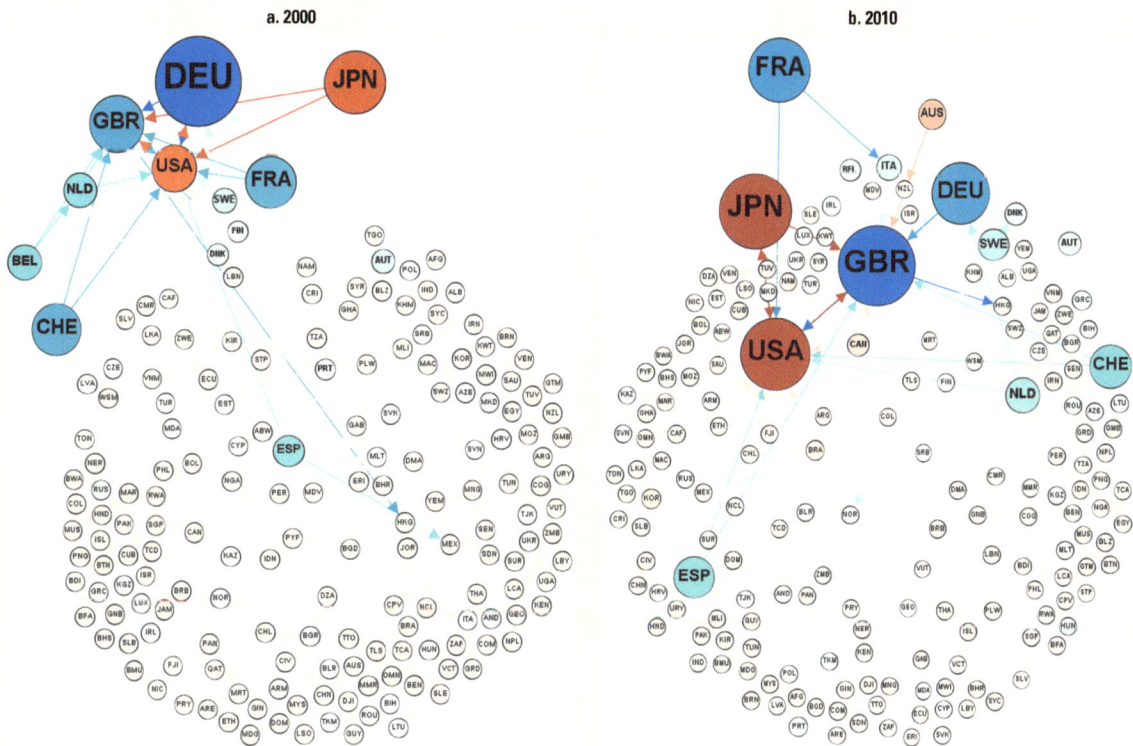

Source: Calculations based on Bank for International Settlements Consolidated Banking Statistics.
Note: Each country node represents the combined value of portfolio inflows and outflows and has two outgoing links that point to the country's two main recipients of portfolio financial flows. Europe and Central Asia countries are shown in shades of blue.

issuing portfolio financial bond or equity instruments in well-established markets where market size and transparency help to stimulate supply and demand, financial flows do not particularly match the level of real economic relationships. The concentration of portfolio flows centered in a few country nodes, however, provides some insight into how vulnerable portfolio flows may be to shocks in the central nodes.

In summary, Europe's integration policies have had a positive impact on internal European connectivity through most economic relationships, especially in trade, migration, and air passenger transport, but less so in FDI, ICT, and portfolio financial flows. In the early 2000s, there were strong migration patterns between the transition economies and Northern, Western, and Southern Europe (particularly Russia and Germany), which then diverged into two regional blocks, one centered around Russia and the other the EU, with Germany as the primary country node. Transitional European countries trade and migrate intensively within Europe, but are increasingly creating linkages with the rest of the world. Established (advanced) European countries have had wider global connections with the United States and Asian countries, but regional connections are deepening. Overall, ECA's relative importance as a central node for connectivity with the rest of the world has fallen as emerging economies (especially China) are growing and account for a larger share of global economic activity. This is true for most advanced countries, including the United States, as emerging economies are increasing in economic size and wealth. Perhaps not surprisingly, airline and ICT connectivity have changed the most over the past decade because of deregulation and innovation, while portfolio financial flows have tended to be concentrated in a few dominant financial sectors that have changed only slightly.

Multidimensional connectivity network analysis adds to the previous research on economic relationships and their influence on growth by not looking at one network layer independently of others, but by examining the many layers of connectivity together. Not only do individual connections matter but so do their interdependence in economic relationships. Connectivity should be seen as a multidimensional concept including trade, migration, finance, transport, communications, and other factors. Greater connectivity in one area may be a complement to or substitute for connectivity in another area.

Connectivity and Income Growth

According to traditional growth models, an increase in trade or other forms of connectivity will have no impact on long-run income growth. The *level* of income will increase due to gains from specialization, but this will not lead to sustained increases in growth unless it has an impact on improving technological accumulation over time (i.e., the endogenous growth model, Romer 1990). Thus, the main mechanism through which connections affect growth is the transfer of knowledge and innovative ideas and technologies. Innovations are continuously generated globally, and they travel the world through the network of countries. Greater multidimensional connectivity increases the probability that an economy will absorb these new ideas and increase long-run growth.

The empirical strategy we use for understanding how a country's international connections and the interplay of these connections influence economic growth is threefold. First, we simply estimate a baseline growth model that includes standard explanatory variables, including the initial GDP per capita level, schooling, size of government, inflation, quality of governance, and investment rates. Second, we include the traditional measure of connectivity, trade/GDP, that is used in the economic literature on openness. Our interest is not so much replicating previous research, but rather determining a benchmark against which to compare network effects of connectivity.

Third, we develop network centrality measures for each type of connection indicator (for example, trade and FDI) based on a modified Google PageRank algorithm (Page et al. 1999). This algorithm gives a higher ranking to countries that have a larger number of connections to well-connected countries as well as connections to countries with a high "intrinsic value." Intrinsic value in our context means a high propensity to generate and disseminate knowledge. We use the size of the country's population and GDP per capita as proxies for this intrinsic value.

We modify and expand the analysis in Duernecker, Meyer, and Vega-Redondo (2014) of the relationship between a network measure of trade and economic growth to other measures of connectivity (trade, FDI, migration, airline transport, portfolio flows, and ICT). We compare our six individual network centrality results with the relationship between traditional measures of connectivity (for example, overall trade to GDP) and growth to determine whether network centrality measures are any better at describing long-run growth than the standard, nonnetwork, measures.

Finally, we develop a comprehensive measure of overall network centrality, referred to as multidimensional connectivity, that combines all six types of connectivity into a single network measure. This indicator takes into consideration the complementarity of the various forms of connectivity, as described in the introduction. Multidimensional connectivity is found to be significantly related to long-run growth, and provides a better explanation of long-run growth than the individual connectivity channels. In other words, the whole is greater than the sum of its parts. As a robustness check, we develop an alternative index of network centrality, multiplex connectivity, that describes the complete network but does not impose the restriction that each layer of the network is a complement to other layers. This indicator has a similar, albeit less strong, relationship with growth than the multidimensional connectivity indicator.

> Multidimensional connectivity . . . provides a better explanation of long-run growth than the individual connectivity channels. In other words, the whole is greater than the sum of its parts.

Network Centrality

This section introduces a measure of centrality, or influence, based on the well-known Google PageRank algorithm, which was used to rank websites based on their links in the network. The algorithm was initially developed to rank websites in terms of their "importance" and "relevance" to a search query. Network analysis was a natural starting point for this problem because websites with more hyperlinks pointing at them were thought of as being of higher quality. In addition to the number of the incoming links, having more links from higher-quality websites is yet another indicator of website quality. The innovation by Page et al. (1999) consisted in modifying the popular network eigenvector centrality measure so that the centrality value of a website was proportional to the probability that a person clicking randomly on hyperlinks would land on that page.[3] Or more precisely, the PageRank value reflects the share of visits to the website by a random web surfer over some period of time.

We modified the PageRank algorithm so that its initial idea—capturing the probability that a random traveler in the network will arrive at a certain node—remains in place. In the economic network discussed in this chapter, the connectivity index is proportional to the probability that a random economic or technological innovation will reach the country. This probability reflects the likelihood that an innovation will be transmitted to that country through each form of connectivity (trade, FDI, and so on), based on the country's links to other countries, those countries' links to other countries, and so on (the value of connections is progressively reduced by 15 percent at each link in the chain).[4] The index also reflects the intrinsic probability that each connection (country) will innovate and disseminate knowledge independently (proxied by population and GDP per capita).[5] The formulation of the centrality measure is shown in annex 1D.

Network Centrality Measures and Growth

In this section, we estimate the importance for growth of the connectivity measures described in the previous section. We first estimate a standard cross-country, long-run model over 2000–16, where growth depends on the initial levels of GDP per capita, education, investment rate, governance, government size, and inflation. We then add trade/GDP, the traditional measurement of openness, as an additional explanatory variable. Finally, we add each of our network measures of connectivity to determine whether network centrality measures are any better at describing long-run growth than the standard, nonnetwork measure.

Two adjustments are required to the network connectivity measures described above before including them in the model. First, we scale the value by population to account for the fact that more populous countries are expected to depend less on being connected to the rest of the world for innovations and growth than smaller countries, which, due to their size, naturally rely more on connectivity (e.g., China vs. Singapore). This has the effect of transforming connectivity into per capita terms. Second, because the network connectivity measure includes the country's own level of GDP per capita (as well as GDP per capita of partner countries), we subtract the country's own level of GDP per capita from the connectivity measure because it is already included as an explanatory variable in describing country growth. This, in effect, eliminates double counting. The intrinsic value of partner countries' GDP per capita is still included in the network connectivity measure.

The estimation of the relationship between growth and the variables typically used in the empirical literature (and included here) faces several key challenges. Perhaps the most difficult concerns *endogeneity*, often reflecting reverse causality, or the influence of the dependent variable (growth) on some of the independent variables (e.g., government size). Our main goal is to measure the contribution of our network connectivity measures to growth, after controlling for other variables (inflation and so) on thought important to growth. However, both our connectivity measures and these other variables may themselves be determined, in part, by growth (they may not be *exogenous*, as assumed in our estimation procedure). Thus, most researchers using cross-sections are only able to capture partial correlations instead of causality.

Our identification strategy attempts to reduce problems from endogeneity, although it does not eliminate them. First, we calculate the right-hand side variables by taking the earliest observation available in the data at the start of the growth period. This of course does not correct all potential endogeneity problems, but it is indicative of a lack of reverse causality. Second, our measures of connectivity build on direct and indirect links for the various types of connectivity in the global network, and countries are only able to impact direct links and not indirect ones. By taking into consideration higher-order indirect links, our connectivity measures are at least to some extent exogenous, or unaffected by growth of the country being measured. Moreover, for robustness we also include geographic distance between countries as a separate layer of connectivity to account for geographic proximity that may affect growth and the strength of connectivity channels simultaneously.[6] For a deeper treatment of endogenous relationships in economic growth we refer the reader to the rich literature (see Frankel and Romer 1999; Rodriquez and Rodrik 2000; Beck 2008; Helpman 2004; Feyrer 2009; and Panizza and Presbitero 2013).

This kind of estimation also may suffer from the existence of unobserved country effects (which are potentially correlated with the independent variables used in the empirical model). Furthermore, most variables are measured with considerable error. Since developing countries represent a large fraction of our sample, results depend on the reliability of the data. Hence, measurement error can be a source for inconsistent coefficient estimates.

We examine the growth effects of connectivity along each network layer separately (trade, FDI, migration, ICT, airline connectivity and portfolio flows) in table 1.1.

Compared to the base model and the standard measure of openness (trade/GDP), nearly every network connectivity measure manages to increase the explanatory power (Adj-R^2) of the standard growth equation, although not every network layer is statistically significant at the minimum 10 percent level. Deeper integration along each individual dimension is associated with stronger per capita GDP growth over the subsequent 16-year period. Unlike the traditional measure of openness and connectivity (trade/GDP), the PageRank-based index, which was designed to capture the knowledge spillovers from connections, is associated with higher long-term growth in the case of international trade, FDI, migration, and airline connectivity. A one-standard-deviation increase in the trade connectivity of a country is associated with more than half a percentage point (0.6 percent) higher annual economic growth over the long term. The effect of FDI connectivity is similar (0.59 percent), and the effects of migration and airline connectivity are markedly lower (0.34 percent and 0.19 percent, respectively).

TABLE 1.1 Connectivity Effects on Overall Income Growth

	(1)	(2)	(3)	(4)	(5)	(6)	(7)	(8)
GDP per capita$_{t=0}$	−0.91***	−1.10***	−1.31***	−1.29***	−1.15***	−1.06***	−1.11***	−1.11**
Years of schooling$_{t=0}$	2.46***	2.4***	1.7***	1.87***	1.60***	2.06***	1.99***	2.04***
Government size$_{t=0}$	−9.24**	−8.64**	−5.81	−5.24	−4.91	−5.44	−5.21	−5.79
Inflation$_{t=0}$	1.02	0.99	2.92	2.75	2.54	2.1	1.82	1.73
Governance$_{t=0}$	1.18	2.13	1.2	0.99	1.04	1.43	1.32	1.63*
Investment rate$_{t=0}$	0.160**	0.170***	0.190***	0.21***	0.20***	0.20***	0.20***	0.20***
Baseline Standard Connectivity model								
Trade/GDP$_{t=0}$		0.28						
Network effects (PageRank)								
Trade Connectivity per capita$_{t=0}$				0.61***				
FDI Connectivity per capita$_{t=0}$					0.59***			
Migration Connectivity per capita$_{t=0}$						0.34*		
ICT Connectivity per capita$_{t=0}$							0.12	
Portfolio Flows per capita$_{t=0}$								0.17
Airline Connectivity per capita$_{t=0}$								0.19*
Adjusted R^2	0.54	0.53	0.59	0.58	0.56	0.54	0.55	0.56

Note: The dependent variable in each model is the annualized income growth (in percent) between 2000 and 2016. All right-hand-side variables are transformed in logs, and the first available observation for the growth period is taken. There are 111 countries for which each version of the model can be estimated. The connectivity variables/PageRank are normalized using the standard normal distribution. Therefore, the size of the coefficient represents the growth impact of a one-standard-deviation change. All model specifications include an intercept, which is not reported in the table. All coefficients are estimated with ordinary least squares regression.
Significance level: * = 10 percent, ** = 5 percent, *** = 1 percent.

> Connectivity can also boost shared prosperity. . . . The poor and bottom 40 percent may directly benefit from greater connectivity.

Connectivity can also boost shared prosperity. Economic channels by which the poor and bottom 40 percent may directly benefit from greater connectivity include improved access to finance and markets, changes in the return to capital or labor, exposure to technology and better governance, and changes in the relative prices of goods and services. Trade, for example, may enhance resource allocation across countries leading to improved opportunities for asset use by the bottom 40 percent of the income distribution. Investment flows may generate new returns for the bottom 40 percent. As production becomes more competitive, the poor may also experience a mix of welfare gains and losses from relative price changes. Migration may open new opportunities, but also has implications for the labor market. Connectivity influences commerce and investment, but it also is a means for transferring ideas, technology, and institutional arrangements, which are all potential sources for spillovers to growth and may indirectly influence shared prosperity.

Table 1.2 summarizes the estimated impact of connectivity on the income growth of the poorest 40 percent of the income distribution in each country. Trade connectivity has the largest impact. In fact, the knowledge spillover effects from trade appear to be more important for the bottom 40 percent than for the top 60 percent. However, the other measures of connectivity do not appear to play a statistically significant role in bottom-40 growth.

Multidimensional Connectivity: Interplay of Network Connections and Growth

In this section, we develop two unique methods for combining each individual network layer (trade, FDI, migration, ICT, airline transport, and portfolio flows) into

TABLE 1.2 Connectivity Effects on Bottom-40 Income Growth

	(1)	(2)	(3)	(4)	(5)	(6)	(7)	(8)
GDP per capita$_{t=0}$	−0.77**	−0.69*	−1.19***	−1.08***	−0.69***	−0.71*	−0.75**	−1.77***
Years of schooling$_{t=0}$	2.1***	2.1***	2.32***	2.39***	2.15***	1.91**	2.65***	2.51***
Government size$_{t=0}$	−7.37	−7.38	−3.61	−9.05	−10.38	−6.4	−8.05	−5.72
Inflation$_{t=0}$	2.61	2.62	5.69	6.21	5.08	5.23	4.01	0.96
Governance$_{t=0}$	1.13	1.14	−0.74	0.75	1.37	1.5	2.18	0.3
Investment rate$_{t=0}$	0.09*	0.08*	0.08*	0.13**	0.09*	0.12**	0.09*	0.09*
Baseline Standard Connectivity model								
Trade/GDP$_{t=0}$		0.02						
Network Effects (PageRank)								
Trade Connectivity per capita$_{t=0}$			1.49**					
FDI Connectivity per capita$_{t=0}$				0.8				
Migration Connectivity per capita$_{t=0}$					0.18			
ICT Connectivity per capita$_{t=0}$						0.21		
Portfolio Flows per capita$_{t=0}$							−0.13	
Airline Connectivity per capita$_{t=0}$								0.11
Adjusted R^2	0.24	0.24	0.28	0.26	0.25	0.23	0.23	0.23

Note: The dependent variable in each model is the annualized bottom-40 income growth (in percent) between 2000 and 2016. All right-hand-side variables are transformed in logs, and the first available observation for the growth period is taken. There are 88 countries for which each version of the model can be estimated. The connectivity variables/PageRank are normalized using the standard normal distribution. The size of the coefficient therefore represents the growth impact of a one-standard-deviation change. All model specifications include an intercept, which is not reported in the table. FDI = foreign direct investment; ICT = information and communication technology.
Significance level: * = 10 percent, ** = 5 percent, *** = 1 percent.

TABLE 1.3 **Correlation between Connectivity Layers Is High, Except in the Case of Portfolio Financial Flows**

	Trade	FDI	Migration	ICT	Airline	Portfolio flows
Trade	1					
FDI	0.9295*	1				
Migration	0.7173*	0.7092*	1			
ICT	0.7107*	0.7882*	0.6789*	1		
Airline	0.8515*	0.9090*	0.6200*	0.8348*	1	
Portfolio flows	0.2560*	0.2751*	0.2624*	0.2286*	0.2697*	1

Note: FDI = foreign direct investment; ICT = information and communication technology.
Significance level: * = 10 percent or higher.

a single total network measure of connectivity to address the complementarity between connectivity measures and their relationship to growth. Indeed, there appears to be a strong correlation between all measures of connectivity, with perhaps the exception of portfolio financial flows (table 1.3). FDI and trade are the most correlated across connectivity layers, airline transport and migration less so, while portfolio flows is highly idiosyncratic. Intuitively, interplay between various forms of connectivity can be seen most clearly in migration and international travel.

Much research has found that migration and trade tend to be complements (greater migration between two countries is associated with greater trade between them), and subsequent research has also identified migration's importance in influencing FDI and its direct influence on growth through knowledge transfers (see, for example, Gould 1994 and Onodera 2008). Thus, people-to-people contact may be important for growth by directly transferring knowledge between the host and home countries, as well as indirectly by facilitating knowledge embodied in trade and FDI flows through bridging market information gaps.

The six network connectivity measures could be aggregated in a simple, ad hoc way (for example, taking averages of the network centrality measures). However, this is likely to result in a loss of important information and would not account for the interaction of various network layers and their effect on economic growth. For example, vastly different bilateral connectivity patterns in each dimension can result in similar average values (box 1.1).

We therefore adopt a somewhat more intuitively appealing procedure for aggregating the connectivity measures. This includes calculating the weighted multiplicative average of the separate connectivity measures.[7] Essentially, the six networks are collapsed into one network where each bilateral link is a function of each of the layers, as shown in figure 1.8. The functional form used has several desirable features that have been well documented in other economic contexts. First, it imposes decreasing returns to scale, that is, having a large amount of one type of connection provides the country with decreasing informational returns, with other forms of connectivity held constant. A balanced increase in connectivity along each dimension would have a stronger impact on the bilateral informational link than a rapid increase in the connectivity along one layer only. It is very likely that these different channels complement each other in terms of the information they transmit. For example, a foreign investor is likely to be more successful in transferring know-how in the host country if there already are deep links through migration and trade that can complement the information flows embedded in FDI.

BOX 1.1 A Better Way of Measuring Network Connectivity

Figure B1.1.1 provides two examples of network connectivity and the modified PageRank of country A.

In the left and right panels of figure B1.1.1, country A has the same centrality index calculated using simple averages of modified PageRank centrality across three types of networks, represented by the three types of arrows (line, dash, and dot). It is clear, however, that the patterns of connections and the overall network for country A are vastly different between the two cases. It is easy to show that using aggregation at the country level, the modified PageRank used in this study produces a higher centrality for country A in the case in the right panel compared to the one in the left panel. This is an intuitively more appealing method than simple averaging.

FIGURE B1.1.1 **Examples of network connectivity and the modified PageRank**

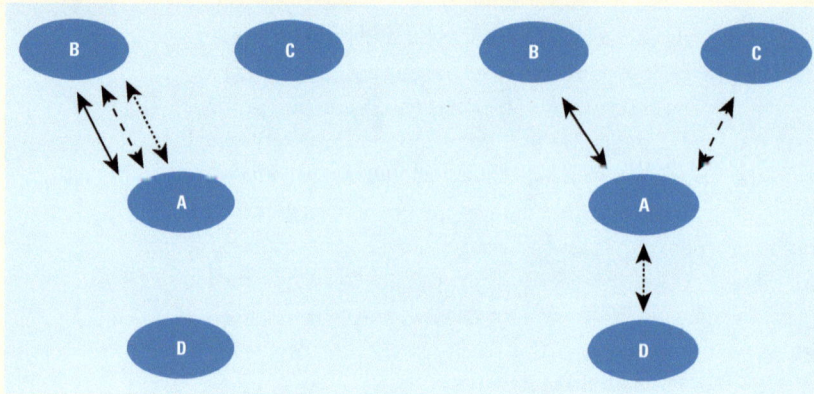

Furthermore, the estimated weights on each of the network layers can be interpreted as the efficiency or importance of each channel in transmitting information that facilitates long-term income growth. Each country's aggregate connectivity index, representing the likelihood of a country adopting an innovation, is then calculated in a fashion similar to that used in calculating the individual connectivity indexes. That is, the aggregate index of connectivity is summed across partner countries and added to the likelihood of the country generating an innovation independently (represented by GDP).[8]

The impact of multidimensional centrality on growth and the indicator's component weights for each network layer are estimated simultaneously using a maximum likelihood procedure. The estimated weights for each layer of the multidimensional connectivity indicator and the indicator's impact on growth are shown in table 1.4. The growth impact of the multidimensional connectivity indicator is higher than each of the individual network indexes (shown in table 1.1). A one-standard-deviation increase in the multidimensional connectivity indicator is associated with 0.67 percent higher annualized growth. These results suggest that the overall connectivity profile of the country (one that combines all network layers) is more important than each of the individual layers separately. Moreover, in the combined network, trade has the highest importance, followed by FDI,

FIGURE 1.8
**Multidimensional
connectivity network**

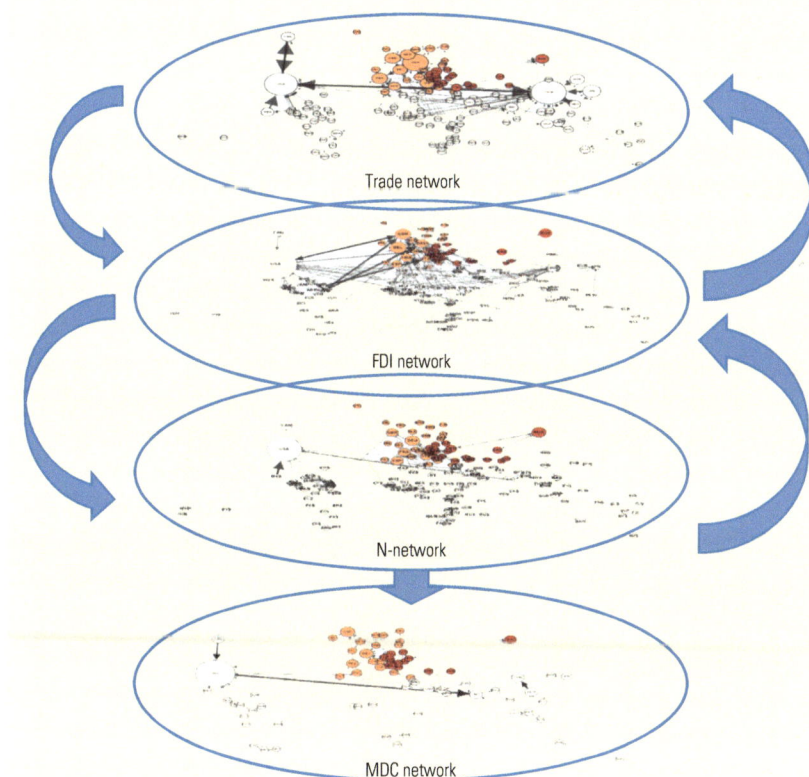

Trade network

FDI network

N-network

MDC network

Note: FDI = foreign direct investment; MDC = multidimensional connectivity; N-network = other measured global networks.

TABLE 1.4 **Multidimensional Connectivity**

	Overall growth	B40 growth
Multidimensional connectivity impact	0.67***	1.49***
Efficiency exponents/weights of connectivity channels		
Trade channel efficiency	0.532	1
FDI channel efficiency	0.37	0
Migration channel efficiency	0.1	0
ICT channel efficiency	0	0
Airline channel efficiency	0	0
Portfolio flows	0	0
Adjusted R^2	0.61	0.28

Note: The dependent variable in each model is annual income growth (in percent). All right-hand-side variables are transformed in logs. The PageRank coefficient is standardized to represent the effect of a change of one standard deviation. The values of the exponent parameters (efficiency exponents/weights) α, β, γ, and δ were estimated using the maximum likelihood procedure where the objective function was to maximize the goodness-of-fit measure (adjusted R^2). B40 = bottom 40 percent of the income distribution. FDI = foreign direct investment; ICT = information and communication technology.
Significance level: *** = 1 percent in an ordinary least squares regression.

and then migration. Neither ICT, airline transport, nor portfolio flows add additional information above these three connectivity channels. By contrast, the multidimensional measure does not add new information above the single network measure of trade connectivity in explaining changes in the growth of the incomes of the bottom 40 percent of the distribution.

Figure 1.9 is based on the values of each country's multidimensional connectivity index in the overall growth model. As the figure indicates, multidimensional connectivity shows a much stronger cohesion between ECA countries than any single network connection and these connections grew from 2000 to 2014. Of all the ECA countries, the United Kingdom shows the strongest overall linkages within ECA and non-ECA countries. In contrast, Germany is the strongest overall connector between ECA countries, but has few strong links outside of ECA. Interestingly, while China has increased network linkages with the world, it is much smaller and less connected compared to only the trade network as indicated in figure 1.1; as a result, its importance to the global network is about the same as Germany's, but less than Japan's.

In terms of per capita levels in ECA subregional multidimensional connectivity (table 1.5), Western Europe has the highest global ranking, followed by Northern, Central, and Southern Europe, while Russia, Turkey, and Eastern Europe are in the middle range, and the Western Balkans, Central Asia, and the South Caucasus have the lowest levels of overall connectivity. Not surprisingly, levels of connectivity are associated with higher levels of development.

Interestingly, although Central Asia and the South Caucasus rank relatively low on overall connectivity, they also saw the greatest improvement from 2000 to 2014 (figure 1.10). The South Caucasus has seen connectivity increase by nearly 75 percent, while Central Asia has seen connectivity increase by more than 40 percent. Eastern Europe and the Western Balkans, although also starting from relatively low levels, have not seen as rapid an increase, with connectivity increasing only 20 and 10

FIGURE 1.9 Multidimensional network connectivity

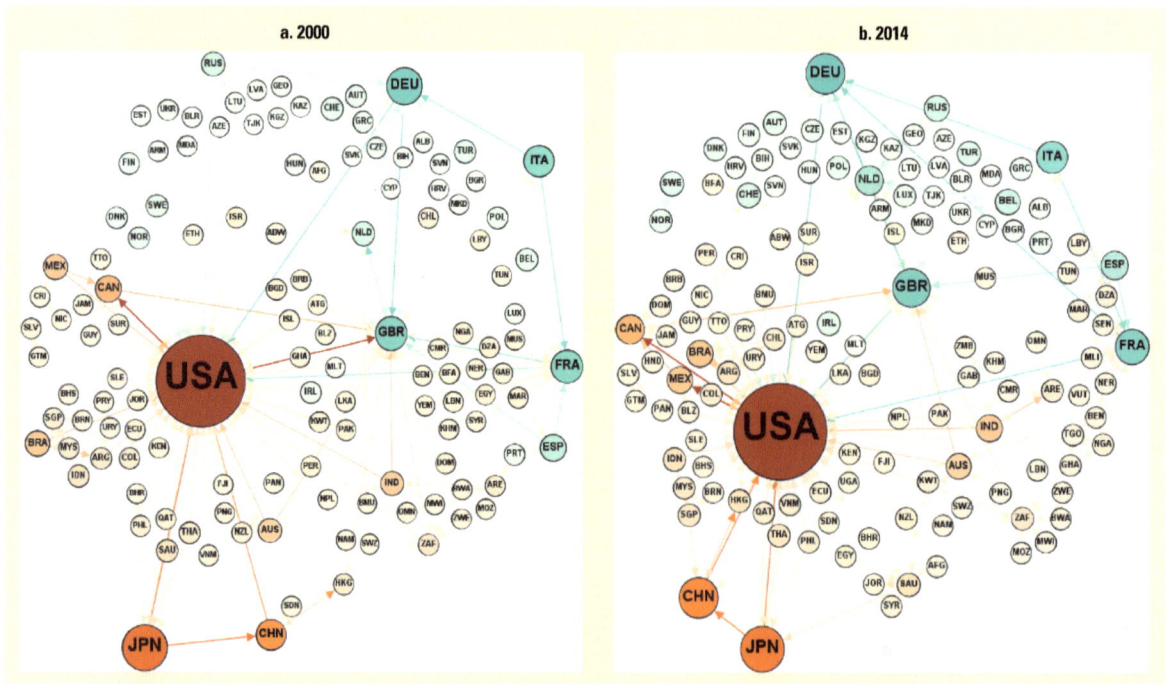

Note: The size of the node represents the multidimensional connectivity index of each country. Each node has two outgoing links that point to the strongest two connections in the multidimensional network according to the overall growth model (table 1.4, column 1). Europe and Central Asia countries are shown in shades of blue.

percent, respectively. The key challenge for these regions is to find ways to improve balanced connectivity, particularly easing constraints and facilitating trade, FDI, and airline and ICT connectivity. For the ECA region as a whole, connectivity has improved more than global connectivity, reflecting the integration process of the EU as well as strides taken in transition economies.

The analysis of multidimensional connectivity and its relationship to economic growth can be useful in evaluating where countries can benefit the most in terms

TABLE 1.5 Multidimensional Connectivity Varies by ECA Subregion, with the Highest Connectivity in the Western Part of the Region and the Lowest in the Eastern Part

ECA subregions	Multidimensional connectivity	Trade	FDI	Migration	ICT	Airline	Portfolio flows
High connectivity							
Western Europe	6	6	6	9	9	15	19
Northern Europe	12	12	17	26	21	23	22
of which Baltics	*30*	*28*	*36*	*38*	*50*	*28*	*21*
Southern Europe	25	24	26	21	28	23	22
Central Europe	31	27	34	36	41	46	46
Medium connectivity							
Russian Federation	55	53	61	28	63	64	83
Turkey	57	51	67	33	73	79	40
Eastern Europe	62	59	60	81	54	57	76
Low connectivity							
Western Balkans	88	75	97	45	88	86	99
Central Asia	94	99	93	101	101	103	101
South Caucasus	104	104	102	64	104	104	93

Note: The table shows global rankings, from best to worst, in combined per capita connectivity, with lower values indicating better connectivity. Subregion indicators are median values of the subregion's countries ECA = Europe and Central Asia; FDI = foreign direct investment; ICT = information and communication technology.

FIGURE 1.10 Europe and Central Asia's connectivity has grown, but there are wide variations across subregions
Growth in connectivity, percent, 2000–14

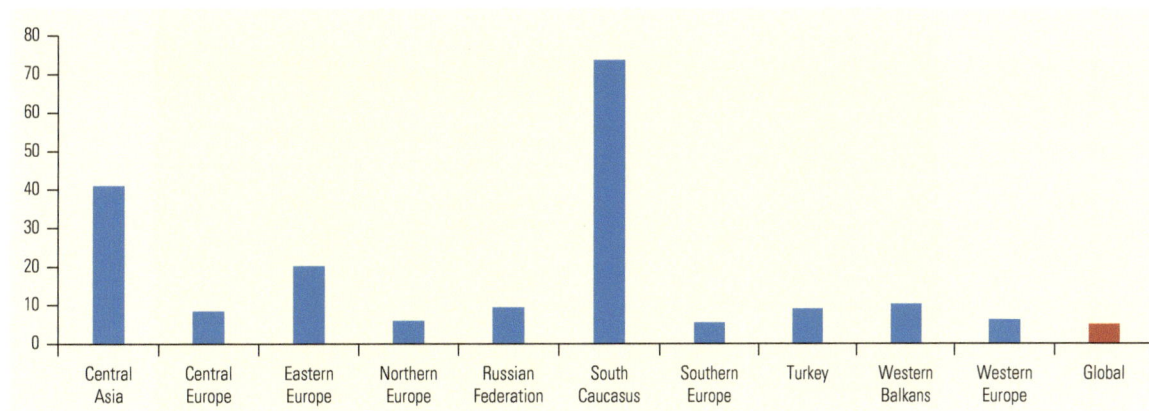

Note: Subregional and global indicators are median regional averages.

of reducing barriers to entry and facilitating linkages with well-connected countries. It can also help identify which connections are likely to have the largest impact on growth. For example, in China's case, while the trade network is strong, the migration and FDI networks are weak in comparison. Likewise, taking the case of Kazakhstan, increasing FDI in Bulgaria would bring a higher increase in multidimensional connectivity than increasing FDI in Poland, despite Poland's greater overall connectivity. This is due to the higher complementarity of Kazakhstan's FDI with other preexisting connections with Bulgaria compared to Poland (see box 1.2).

BOX 1.2 Example of Using Connectivity Measures for Investment Decisions

Assume that a country like Kazakhstan would like to use its national sovereign wealth fund to invest US$100 million of its income from natural resources in Central Europe. Assume also that the risk adjusted rate of return in the region has been equalized by the market. Consequently, the government decides to choose a strategic destination for its investment, which would create future knowledge spillovers and innovation transfers. Table B1.2.1 lists the potential markets and their connectivity indexes.

Not surprisingly the country with the highest connectivity index is Poland. Poland is well integrated in European global value chains, and in particular into Germany's manufacturing industries. By virtue of its strong ties with the Western European economies, Poland has one of the highest overall connectivity indexes in ECA, and the benefits of connecting with it are significant (table B1.2.2).

Somewhat counterintuitively, Kazakhstan achieves the highest connectivity increase by investing in Bulgaria and not in countries with better integration in the global network such as Poland and Hungary.

There are two reasons for this result. First, having a balanced connectivity portfolio is superior,

TABLE B1.2.1 Potential Markets and Their Connectivity Indexes

Potential country in which to place investment	Multidimensional Connectivity Index
Poland	0.29
Hungary	0.27
Czech Republic	0.26
Romania	0.25
Bulgaria	0.21
Slovenia	0.20

TABLE B1.2.2 Kazakhstan's New Multidimensional Connectivity Index after Investing $100 Million Each in Various Markets

Country	Change in Kazakhstan's Multidimensional Connectivity Index (percent)
Bulgaria	.00735
Poland	.00525
Czech Republic	.00523
Hungary	.00519
Slovenia	.00515
Romania	.00510

continued

BOX 1.2   Example of Using Connectivity Measures for Investment Decisions *continued*

in terms of knowledge spillovers, to being well connected in only one dimension at the expense of the others. For example, migration may bridge information between countries and stimulate other types of economic connections, such as external investment, trade, and communications linkages. Kazakhstan has relatively stronger ties to Bulgaria in terms of trade and migration but less so in terms of FDI. Therefore, increasing its FDI generates more benefits because of the complementarity of the channels.

Second, although richer countries have more knowledge than poorer ones, that knowledge is more difficult to reach. A moderate investment in a small economy can tap into a greater share of the potential of that economy than the same investment in a large one.

Choosing Bulgaria over Poland would generate over the long term 0.0021 percent greater

economic growth. This translates into US$1.07 million higher annual income. Although this amount is negligible in terms of overall income growth, it is an additional 1.07 percent spillover return on the original investment from better connectivity.

Examining this from another direction, figure B1.2.1 summarizes the improvement in Kazakhstan's connectivity rank under several different scenarios. In the first scenario Kazakhstan increases each of its connections in trade, FDI, and migration by 20 percent with every country in the world and improves its centrality by four places in the global ranking. However, if the same amount of increased trade, FDI, and migration is focused on bilateral connections with Germany, for example, Kazakhstan's overall connectivity ranking improves by eight places. Likewise, its ranking increases with a focus on greater connectivity with China and the Russian Federation as well, but by slightly less.

FIGURE B1.2.1 Kazakhstan's connectivity ranking change

Ranking change resulting from 20 percent increase in connectivity vis-à-vis the world and selected countries

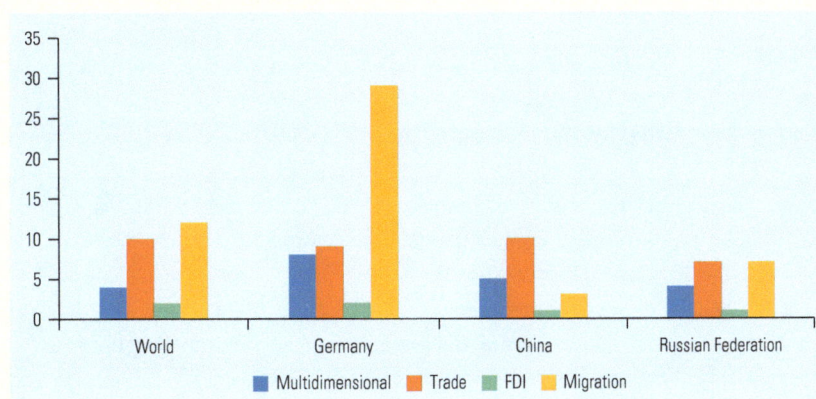

Note: FDI = foreign direct investment.

As a robustness test of the multidimensional connectivity indicator used above, a second approach to calculating multidimensional connectivity is evaluated using the recent techniques in the study of multiplex networks, where the functional form of the relationships is unknown. These multiplex networks do not rely on collapsing the network into a single layer and do not restrict the functional form (i.e., they do not rely on the Cobb-Douglas functional form as used earlier). A benefit is that the functional form need not be assumed; the cost is that if economic theory suggests a particular relationship (i.e., complementarity between network layers), this information is not used.

Multiplex networks are observed in all types of complex systems, including economic, social, biological, infrastructure, and socio-technical systems. For example, the air transportation system is a socio-technical system that exhibits many layers, all of them contributing to and essential for the overall functioning of the system. Interdependence among different layers of the air transportation system arises naturally because different airlines use the same airports. As a consequence, if an airport is closed, all the flights coming into and out of it stop for all the airlines. Another aspect of interdependence arises because for a flight to take off, it needs both a crew and a plane. Similarly, banks are also connected (in often very complex ways) by their derivatives positions, by overlap of portfolio composition, by joint exposure to the same creditors, and so on. In other words, a multi-layer network model of each system is essential to estimate the degree of resilience of the entire system to random events or attacks against some of its parts. The aim, then, would be to study potential contagion effects via multiple channels in first attempts at modeling multidimensional network structures. For example, a description of the financial system as a three-layer multilayer network, composed of layers representing financial activities for funding, collateral, and assets, has been recently proposed by Bookstaber and Kenett (2016).

Similar to the measure of multidimensional connectivity described above, we consider the multilayer network of the individual flow networks. In this approach, we examine the multilayer network as a whole, and do not collapse the different flow layers one on another. Instead, we follow the approach developed by Rahmede et al. (2017) to calculate the Multiplex PageRank centrality (see annex 1C). This approach assigns a measure of centrality to each country based on its connectivity across all the layers put together. A country's centrality is measured by assigning a score based on its connectivity in one flow-defined layer, and by assigning a score to the overall importance of a given economic flow-defined layer. These two scores are calculated simultaneously and are codependent.

Following the approach described above, we repeat the regression analysis using the same dependent and independent variables in the standard growth model, but instead use the standardized Multiplex PageRank centrality measure. This results in a statistically significant (albeit smaller) coefficient of the multiplex connectivity measure of 0.39 (p-value = 0.02, adj. R^2 = 0.534). This alternative methodology confirms the importance of combining the multiple ways countries can connect, rather than simply focusing on one connection layer at a time, particularly for overall growth.

Trade-Offs and Resilience to Shocks

Although the long-run effects of connectivity on growth appear to be positive, connectivity can also expose an economy to shocks and exacerbate crises. For example, Kaminsky and Reinhart (2000), Kaminsky, Reinhart, and Végh (2003), and Bae, Karolyi, and Stulz (2003) show that financial sector linkages play an important role in propagating shocks. The 2005 commodity food price shock and the 2008 global financial crisis also demonstrated the cascade effects that shocks in one market can have in other markets.

Connectivity, however, may also mitigate shocks that originate in some country nodes in the network. For example, if a given country is well integrated in the network, then a shock to one of its partners can be ameliorated by leveraging its other links to the remainder of the network.

This analysis provides supporting evidence for both of these phenomena. Countries with low levels of connectivity are more resilient to shocks in the global network because they have few partners and fewer connections that would transmit shocks. On the other hand, countries with high levels of connectivity also appear to be less affected by shocks to the network. This is likely due to well-diversified connections that can mitigate the severity of the shock. Countries in the "middle" of the connectivity spectrum appear to be most susceptible to international shocks, that is, they have low levels of diversified connectivity and are highly dependent on a few well-connected countries and connections (which boosts their overall connectivity). They are particularly susceptible to shocks affecting one of the well-connected countries where they derive access to global markets and connectivity.

Figure 1.11 shows this pattern. A 10 percent simultaneous, negative shock is simulated to three connections (trade, migration, and FDI) in each of three "central" and well-connected countries (Germany, the United States, and Russia). The countries with the largest declines in their initial connectivity are those that are strongly connected to the country experiencing the shock and do not have strong connections to other partner countries. These countries tend to be in the middle range of centrality and receive their connectivity through a few well-connected countries. A shock to one of these well-connected countries would do the largest damage to their global connectivity.

As figure 1.11 shows, a 10 percent adverse shock to German trade, migration, and FDI has an important impact on most countries in the world because of Germany's high centrality. (The vertical axis shows the change in connectivity and the horizontal axis shows the initial level of connectivity.) However, not surprisingly, the most affected countries are the smaller countries for which Germany is the main partner country, including countries in ECA, the Middle East, and parts of Asia. The largest decrease in connectivity, caused by a 10 percent decline in German connectivity, is in Poland, Ukraine, and Sri Lanka, followed by Bangladesh, the former Yugoslav Republic of Macedonia, Croatia, and Turkey. However, because of the importance of German in the ECA network, even well-connected countries such as Switzerland and the Netherlands experience a significant decline in their centralities. The least affected countries are the small Latin American countries and well-connected Asian economies, like Singapore.

An adverse shock to US connectivity has an even stronger impact on most countries in the world because of the high centrality of the United States (compare the range of the left axes in all the graphs). However, not surprisingly, the most affected countries are the smaller countries for which the United States is the main partner country. The largest decreases in connectivity, caused by a 10 percent decline in US connectivity, are in Jamaica and Belize, followed by Guatemala and the Dominican Republic. Because of the importance of the United States in the international global network, even well-connected large countries such as Japan, Mexico, and Canada experience a significant decline in their centralities. The least affected countries are the small European countries whose main trading partners are Germany, the United Kingdom, or Russia. Thus, Luxembourg, Estonia, the Slovak Republic, and Lithuania barely experience any decline in their overall connectivity.

A 10 percent shock originating in Russia would have a modest impact on global connectivity (left axis). The shock would most affect countries that are closely tied to Russia, such as the former Soviet Republics that are, in general, less connected to the global economy as a whole. In other words, they are highly reliant on Russia for connectivity to the world.

FIGURE 1.11

Simulated impact on individual countries' connectivity measure (modified PageRank) of a 10 percent decline in trade, foreign direct investment, and migration in Germany, the Russian Federation, and the United States

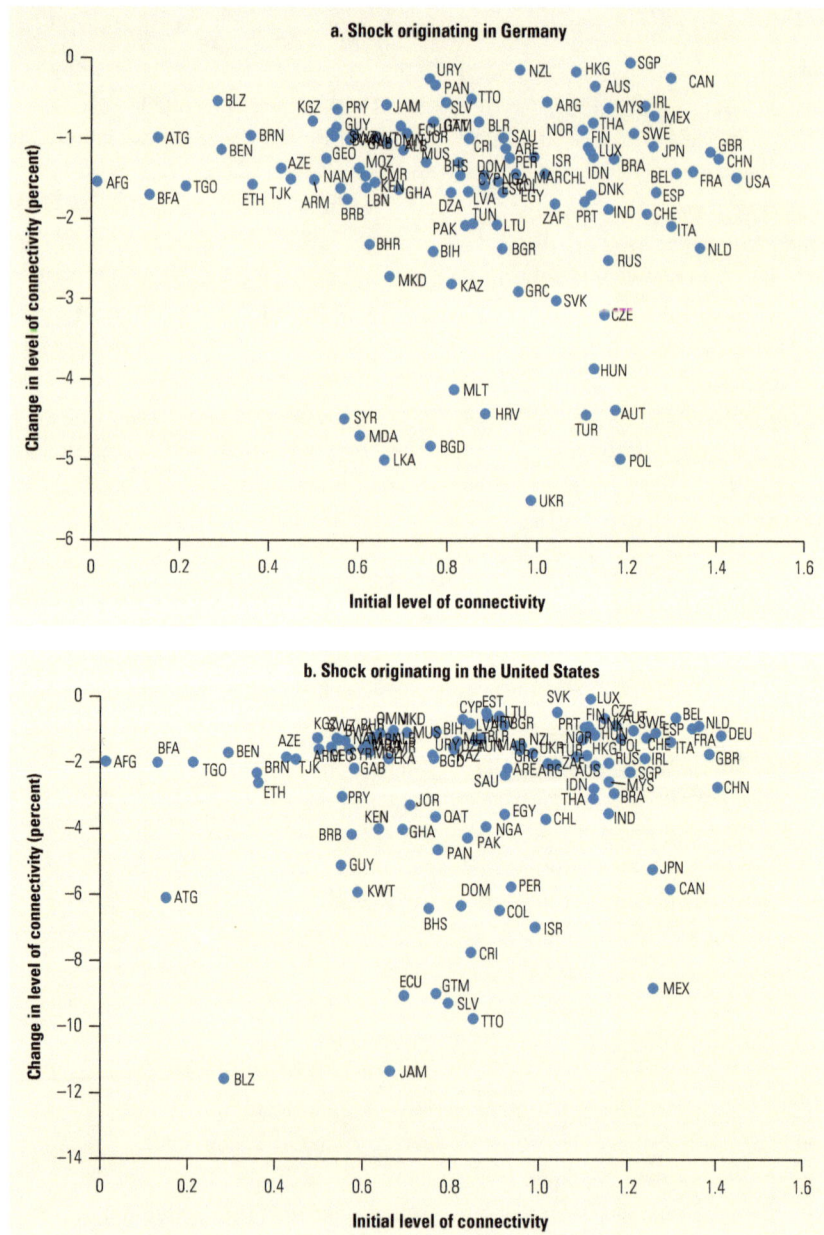

a. Shock originating in Germany

b. Shock originating in the United States

continued

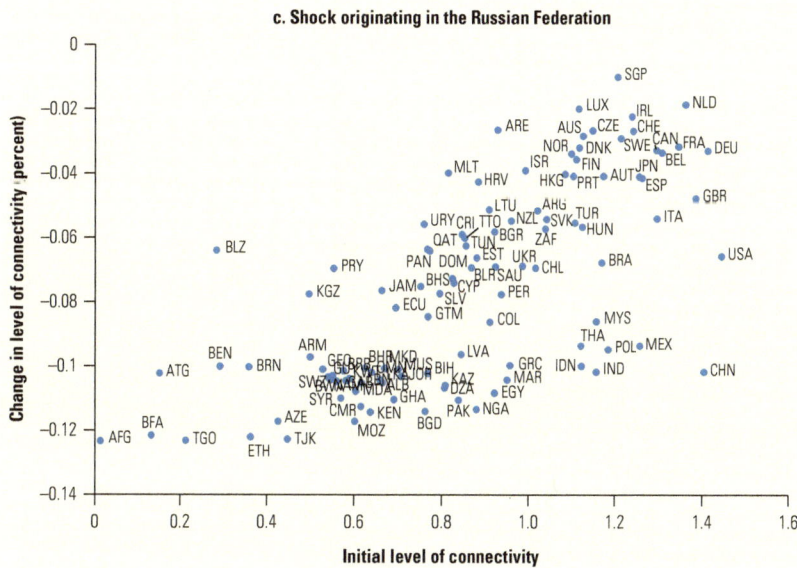

c. Shock originating in the Russian Federation

FIGURE 1.11
continued

This framework allows for a multitude of scenarios, including impacts to just one dimension and country (say, trade from China), or several dimensions across a subset of countries. However, a particularly pertinent one in recent times is a shock to the United Kingdom's ties to the rest of the EU, the "Brexit" scenario.

Brexit would affect the connectivity of ECA countries. Table 1.6 shows the effect on ECA's overall connectivity index from a 10 percent reduction in all flows from the United Kingdom to other EU27 countries. Even though the other EU27 countries are those affected directly by the shock, all of ECA is impacted by Brexit because of their indirect links to the United Kingdom and EU countries. Smaller, well-connected nations such as Malta, Ireland, Cyprus, and Luxembourg would be the most affected countries from this assumed Brexit scenario. Alternatively, the countries in Central Asia and the South Caucasus would be the least affected.

Different regions in ECA have different exposures to types of connectivity shocks (trade, migration, FDI). For example, Western Europe is the most exposed to shocks in other Western European economies. Table 1.7 shows the largest two contributors to the decline in overall connectivity of each ECA subregion in response to a 10 percent shock in three network layers (trade, FDI, migration). Not surprisingly, the overall connectivity of Central Asia in terms of shocks to trade, FDI, and migration is affected most by Russia (trade, FDI, migration), but also by China (trade and FDI), and Germany (migration). The rest of ECA appears to be more sensitive to trade shocks in other ECA countries, particularly Germany, as well as the United States. Belgium and the Netherlands have the greatest impact on overall connectivity for the ECA region due to shocks to FDI, because of their large role in trade logistics and finance. Migration shocks are transmitted to various ECA subregions via countries in close proximity and with language similarities and historic ties.

TABLE 1.6 ECA Countries Most and Least Affected by Brexit

Percent decrease in multidimensional connectivity

Most affected		Least affected	
United Kingdom	–3.46864	Georgia	–0.00105
Malta	–1.35494	Kazakhstan	–0.00109
Ireland	–1.05116	Azerbaijan	–0.00141
Cyprus	–0.76504	Armenia	–0.00153
Luxembourg	–0.70449	Tajikistan	–0.00194
Netherlands	–0.65897	Kyrgyz Republic	–0.00234
Belgium	–0.57851	Albania	–0.00456
Sweden	–0.30127	Bulgaria	–0.00459
Spain	–0.30023	Macedonia, FYR	–0.00623
Denmark	–0.28094	Latvia	–0.00796

Note: ECA = Europe and Central Asia.

TABLE 1.7 Transmission of Trade, Migration, and FDI Shocks to ECA Subregions

	Largest origin countries of shocks due to a 10 percent shock in		
ECA region affected	Trade	FDI	Migration
Central Asia	Russian Federation and China	Russian Federation and China	Russian Federation and Germany
Central Europe	Germany and Netherlands	Germany and Austria	Germany and Austria
Western Balkans	Italy and Germany	Austria and Hungary	Italy and Germany
South Caucasus	Turkey and United States	Russian Federation and Kazakhstan	Russian Federation and Ukraine
Eastern Europe	Russian Federation and Germany	Russian Federation and Germany	Russian Federation and Poland
Russian Federation	Germany and United States	Germany and Switzerland	Germany and Ukraine
Turkey	Germany and Italy	Belgium and Netherlands	Germany and Netherlands
Southern Europe	Germany and France	Belgium and Netherlands	United Kingdom and Poland
Northern Europe	Germany and Netherlands	Belgium and Netherlands	Finland and Norway
Western Europe	Germany and Netherlands	Belgium and Netherlands	Italy and United Kingdom

Note: ECA = Europe and Central Asia; FDI = foreign direct investment.

Conclusion

While it has been well documented that globalization has long-term growth benefits through the technology and knowledge transferred via international connections, this is the first analysis to examine how the connections of the connections of partner countries matter for growth and how various types of connections interact with each other to influence economic growth. Economic interactions, aside from their direct benefits, also have indirect effects that can have lasting influence. Trade, migration, and FDI move the flow of ideas and innovation across borders. Each of these channels individually appears to be an important source of economic growth by facilitating the transmission of knowledge. Moreover, multidimensional connectivity is more important for growth than any individual type of connectivity by itself. The whole of the connectivity network is greater than the sum of its parts. Although there is certainly some level of substitutability between the various layers, when it comes to information flows, complementarity dominates. In fact, there might be a high degree of complementarity of the information flows that contribute to growth. Therefore, policies to promote balanced connectivity in many dimensions—those that focus on trade, migration, and FDI—are more beneficial than focusing on a policy to enhance only one. Indeed, reducing connectivity in one dimension may have adverse impacts on growth derived from other dimensions. Proposals to reduce migrations flows, for example, may have adverse consequences for the growth-enhancing benefits of trade and FDI flows.

Annex 1A. Data

TABLE 1A.1 Long-Term Growth Determinants

Indicator	Description	Coverage
Initial GDP per capita	Logarithm of initial value of GDP per capita for growth period in question (2000–16). Source: World Bank, *World Development Indicators* (WDI).	2000–16
Governance	Index of quality of governance that takes into account corruption, rule of law, and quality of institutions. Source: WDI.	2000–16
Inflation	Measure of consumer price index change. Source: WDI.	2000–16
Government size	Total government expenditure as a share of GDP. Source: WDI.	2000–16
Years of schooling	Average number of years of schooling. Source: www.barrolee.com.	2000–10

TABLE 1A.2 Network Country Data

Indicator	Description	Coverage
FDI	Total bilateral FDI stocks. Source: Organisation for Economic Co-operation and Development (OECD).	2002–13
Trade	Bilateral total trade flows for manufacturing goods. Source: United Nations Conference on Trade and Development.	2000–15
Migration	Total migration stocks. Source: Individual countries' census data; OECD and World Bank estimates (see Artuc et al. 2017).	2000, 2010
ICT	Proxy for ICT flows; estimated by combining bilateral duration of phone conversations and bandwidth capacity between countries. Source: Derived from TeleGeography data.	2003–11
Airlines	Estimated bilateral number of flights (end destination). Source: International Civil Aviation Organization.	2002–12
Portfolio flows	Total bilateral portfolio flows. Source: Bank for International Settlements, Consolidated Banking Statistics.	2000–14

Note: FDI = foreign direct investment; ICT = information and communication technology.

Annex 1B. Network Graph Methodology

Country node placement utilizes Barnes-Hut algorithm (http://arborjs.org/docs /barnes-hut). The algorithm attempts to place large country nodes closer to the edges of the graph as a means of more clearly showing their numerous connections to smaller country nodes. The repulsion of the country nodes away from the center of the graph is proportional to their size. The repulsion away from the center of the graph is counterbalanced by the attraction forces caused by how strongly each pair of countries are connected to one another.

Once the forces of repulsion and attraction on the country nodes have been defined, the behavior of the entire graph under these forces may then be simulated as if it were a physical system. In such a simulation, the forces are applied to the country nodes, pulling them closer together or pushing them further apart. This is repeated iteratively until the system comes to a mechanical equilibrium state; that is, their relative positions do not change from one iteration to the next. The positions of the country nodes in this equilibrium generate the graphical depiction of the network.

Annex 1C. Multiplex PageRank Centrality

Given the surge of interest in multiplex networks, methodologies have recently been proposed to assess the centrality of nodes in multiplex, and more generally multilayer, structures (Halu et al. 2013; Sola et al. 2013; Kenett, Perc, and Boccaletti 2015; De Domenico et al. 2015; Rahmede et al. 2017). Halu et al. (2013) and Iacovacci and Bianconi (2016) propose an algorithm that captures how the centrality of the nodes in a given layer of the multiplex can affect the centrality of the nodes in other layers. This effect is modeled by considering a PageRank algorithm based on the centrality of the nodes in the master layer. De Domenico et al. (2015) propose instead to rank simultaneously nodes and layers of the multiplex network based on any previous measure of centrality established for single-layer networks, including random walk processes that hop between nodes of the same layer and between nodes of different layers as well. The resulting centrality, called "versatility," strongly awards nodes active (connected) in many layers; however, the description was not intended to weight layers in any specific way.

Recently, Rahmede et al. (2017) proposed a different approach, in which they consider a random walk hopping through links of different layers with different probabilities determined by the centrality of the layers (influences). This is following the work of Sola et al. (2013) in which different measures for the centrality of the nodes given a set of influences of the layers have been proposed. Rahmede et al. (2017) propose a ranking algorithm, called MultiRank, that is specified by a coupled set of equations that simultaneously determine the centrality of the nodes and the influences of the layers of a multiplex network. The MultiRank algorithm applies to any type of multiplex network, including weighted and directed multiplex network structures. Very generally, this algorithm proposes an extension to the classical PageRank centrality calculation by coupling the centrality of the node to the influence of the layer in which it is active. This is done by considering the node-layer interaction as a bipartite network. Such a coupling provides new insights into the centrality of a node across different connectivity dimensions.

Annex 1D. Centrality Indicator

More formally, the centrality value Θ_i is proportional to the probability that an innovation will be transmitted to a country:

$$\Theta_i = \lambda \sum_k A_{ki} \Theta_k + (y_i * P_i).$$

The value A_{ki} is a function of the links between countries k and i, λ is an exogenous parameter that captures the weight of decay placed on connections (set to 0.85), y_i is GDP per capita, and P_i is the population (the last two terms together equal aggregate GDP).

The intrinsic value, proxied by GDP, plays an important part in determining the value of the index. For example, even a completely isolated country has a positive probability of innovating and growing based on its domestic resources only. Our choice of proxy for the intrinsic (internal) likelihood to innovate is based on two simple considerations. First, the greater the number of people in a country, the greater the knowledge (or new ideas) that could potentially be generated. Second, we assume that higher-income countries are closer to the technological frontier and thus have a higher probability of producing new knowledge. If a country does not produce the knowledge intrinsically, it can learn from others through its connections. This mechanism is captured by the term $\lambda \sum_k A_{ki} \Theta_k$.

Thus, the probability that an economy has the knowledge to innovate is a sum of the likelihood of its intrinsic innovation (proxied by GDP) and a weighted average of the connectivity of its partners where the weights (A) are a function of the connections. These weights reflect the strength of the informational link and ultimately the probability of successful transmission of ideas.

A_{ki} takes on the following set of values:

$$\left\{ \frac{Trade_{ki}}{GDP_k} ; \frac{FDI\,stock_{ki}}{GDP_k} ; \frac{Migration\,stock_{ki}}{POP_k} ; \frac{ICT\,flow_{ki}}{POP_k} ; \frac{Flights_{ki}}{GDP_k} ; \frac{Portfolio\,flows_{ki}}{GDP_k} \right\}.$$

Each connection (total bilateral trade, total FDI stock, bilateral migration stocks, ICT, airline transport, and portfolio flows) is divided by a proxy for the size of the country (GDP or population). In the original PageRank algorithm, this feature is introduced by dividing by the total number of outgoing links of the partners. Therefore, the probability of getting from website A to website B by a random web surfer decreases as the number of outgoing links in A increases (there are more sites on which the surfer can land). In the case at hand, the probability of an idea reaching a specific country decreases with the population of the sending country.

Similar adjustments are necessary when one considers information flows between countries along the various networks. For example, conditional on an innovation being present in country A, the probability that a single migrant from A to B will carry this idea decreases with the size of the population of A. Although large countries are more likely to generate ideas domestically, they need greater flows and deeper links to transmit those ideas to their partners. This chapter argues that this measure is a good proxy for the probability of growth-relevant knowledge generation by each country (either through learning from its connections or developing knowledge domestically).

Notes

1. The data and graphing methodology are described in annexes 1A and 1B.
2. https://www.bis.org/statistics/consstats.htm.

3. Eigenvector centrality is a measure of the influence of a node in a network. A high eigenvector score means that a node (country in our case) is connected to many nodes that themselves have high scores.

4. This is the standard value of similar parameters used in most network analyses.

5. In the original search engine applications of PageRank this value captured the likelihood that the random surfer can type the URL of the website without relying on hyperlinks to get to it.

6. Including a layer of network connectivity that was determined solely by geographic (capital to capital) distance between countries was not a significant determinant of growth, nor did it change the empirical results related to our empirical inferences related to the multidimensional connectivity index described later in the discussion.

7. The equation is $I_{ki} = x_{ki}^{\alpha} f_{ki}^{\beta} m_{ki}^{\gamma} i_{ki}^{\delta} a_{ki}^{\nu} p_{ki}^{\eta}$, in which I_{ki} is the network information function and $\alpha,\beta,\gamma,\delta,\nu,\eta$. are the estimated weights for each connectivity layer. The weights are calculated using the maximum likelihood procedure where the objective function was to maximize the goodness of fit of the growth equation (adjusted R-squared).

8. The functional form being $\Theta_i^{\mu} = \lambda \sum_k I_{ki} \Theta_k^{\mu} + \left(y_i * P_i \right)$.

References

Alfaro, Laura, Areendam Chanda, Sebnem Kalemli Özcan, and Selin Sayek. 2004. "FDI and Economic Growth: The Role of Local Financial Markets." *Journal of International Economics* 64 (1): 89–112.

Artuc, Erhan, Frederic Docquier, Caglar Ozden, and Chris Parsons. 2017. "Global Skilled Migration: Structural Estimation of 2000–2010 Patterns." Unpublished manuscript, Development Research Group, World Bank, Washington, DC.

Bae, Kee-Hong, G. Andrew Karolyi, and Reneé M. Stulz. 2003. "A New Approach to Measuring Financial Contagion." *Review of Financial Studies* 16 (3): 717–63.

Beck, Thorsten. 2008. *The Econometrics of Finance and Growth.* Washington, DC: World Bank.

Ben-David, Dan. 1993. "Equalizing Exchange: Trade Liberalization and Income Convergence." *Quarterly Journal of Economics* 108 (3): 653–79.

Bookstaber, R., and D. Y. Kenett. 2016. "Looking Deeper, Seeing More: A Multilayer Map of the Financial System." Office of Financial Research Brief 16-06, US Department of the Treasury, Washington, DC. https://www.financialresearch.gov/briefs/files /OFRbr_2016-06_Multilayer-Map.pdf.

Borensztein, Eduardo, Jose De Gregorio, and Jong-Wha Lee. 1998. "How Does Foreign Direct Investment Affect Economic Growth?" *Journal of International Economics* 45 (1): 115–35.

Czernich, Nina, Oliver Falck, and Tobias Kretschmer. 2011. "Broadband Infrastructure and Economic Growth." *Economic Journal* 121 (552): 505–32.

De Domenico, M., A. Sole-Ribalta, E. Omodei, S. Gomez, and A. Arenas. 2015. "Ranking in Interconnected Multilayer Networks Reveals Versatile Nodes." *Nature Communications* 6: 6868.

Dollar, David. 1992. "Outward-Oriented Developing Economies Really Do Grow More Rapidly: Evidence from 95 LDCs, 1976–1985." *Economic Development and Cultural Change* 40 (3): 523–44.

Duernecker, Georg, Moritz Meyer, and Fernando Vega-Redondo. 2014. "The Network Origins of Economic Growth." No. 14–06, Working Paper Series, Department of Economics, University of Mannheim, Mannheim, Germany.

Edwards, Sebastian. 1998. "Openness, Productivity and Growth: What Do We Really Know?" *Economic Journal* 108 (447): 383–98.

Feyrer, J. 2009. "Trade and Income—Exploiting Time Series in Geography." Working Paper 14910, National Bureau of Economic Research, Cambridge, MA. http://www .nber.org/papers/w14910.

Frankel, Jeffrey A., and David Romer. 1999. "Does Trade Cause Growth?" *American Economic Review* 89 (3): 379–99.

Gould, David M. 1994. "Immigrant Links to the Home Country: Empirical Implications for US Bilateral Trade Flows." *Review of Economics and Statistics* 76 (2): 302–16.

Halu, A., R. J. Mondragon, P. Panzarasa, and G. Bianconi. 2013. "Multiplex Pagerank." *PLoS One* 8: e78293.

Helpman, E. 2004. *The Mystery of Economic Growth.* Cambridge, MA: Harvard University Press.

Hidalgo, C., and R. Hausmann. 2009. "The Building Blocks of Economic Complexity." *Proceedings of the National Academy of Sciences* 106: 10570–75.

Iacovacci, J., and G. Bianconi. 2016. "Extracting Information from Multiplex Networks." *Chaos* 26: 065306.

Javorcik, Beata Smarzynska. 2004, "Does Foreign Direct Investment Increase the Productivity of Domestic Firms? In Search of Spillovers through Backward Linkages." *American Economic Review* 94 (3): 605–27.

Kaminsky, Graciela, and Carmen Reinhart. 2000. "On Crises, Contagion, and Confusion." *Journal of International Economics* 51 (1): 145–68.

Kaminsky, Graciela, Carmen Reinhart, and Carlos A. Végh. 2003. "The Unholy Trinity of Financial Contagion." *Journal of Economic Perspectives* 17 (4): 51–74.

Kenett, Dror Y., Matjaž Perc, and Stefano Boccaletti. 2015. "Networks of Networks–An Introduction." *Chaos, Solitons & Fractals* 80: 1–6.

Kivelä, Mikko, Alex Arenas, Marc Barthelemy, James P. Gleeson, Yamir Moreno, and Mason A. Porter. 2014. "Multilayer Networks." *Journal of Complex Networks* 2 (3): 203–71.

Mountford, Andrew. 1997. "Can a Brain Drain Be Good for Growth in the Source Economy?" *Journal of Development Economics* 53 (2): 287–303.

Onodera, Osamu. 2008. "Trade and Innovation Project: A Synthesis Paper." OECD Trade Policy Papers, No. 72, Organisation for Economic Co-operation and Development, Paris.

Page, Lawrence, Sergey Brin, Rajeev Motwani, and Terry Winograd. 1999. *The PageRank Citation Ranking: Bringing Order to the Web.* Technical Report. Stanford, CA: Stanford InfoLab, Stanford University.

Panizza, Ugo, and Andrea Filippo Presbitero. 2013. "Public Debt and Economic Growth in Advanced Economies: A Survey." *Swiss Journal of Economics and Statistics* 149 (2): 175–204.

Rahmede, Christoph, Jacopo Iacovacci, Alex Arenas, and Ginestra Bianconi. 2017. "Centralities of Nodes and Influences of Layers in Large Multiplex Networks." *Journal of Complex Networks.* https://doi.org/10.1093/comnet/cnx050.

Rodriguez, Francisco, and Dani Rodrik. 2000. "Trade Policy and Economic Growth: A Skeptic's Guide to the Cross-National Evidence." In *NBER Macroeconomics Annual,* vol. 15, ed. Ben S. Bernanke and Kenneth Rogoff, 261–38. Cambridge, MA: MIT Press.

Romer, P. M. 1990. "Endogenous Technological Change." *Journal of Political Economy* 98: S71–102.

Sachs, Jeffrey D., and Andrew Warner. 1995. "Economic Reform and the Process of Global Integration." *Brookings Papers on Economic Activity* 1995 (1): 1–118.

Sola, L., M. Romance, R. Criado, J. Flores, A. Garca del Amo, and S. Boccaletti. 2013. "Eigenvector Centrality of Nodes in Multiplex Networks." *Chaos* 23: 033131.

SPOTLIGHT 1

Trends in Foreign Direct Investment in Europe and Central Asia

Foreign direct investment (FDI) flows have made an important contribution to the level of the Europe and Central Asia (ECA) region's multidimensional connectivity. This spotlight highlights the trends and composition of FDI in ECA countries.[1]

ECA has been a key player both as a destination and as a source of FDI. Accounting for about 45 percent of world's GDP, the ECA region hosted, on average, about 28 percent of the world's inward FDI. At the same time, it was the source of 40 percent of outward FDI.[2] Focusing on FDI announcements, during 2014, US$155 billion in FDI projects had ECA countries as destinations, while FDI projects for US$256 billion were originated in ECA countries. Between 2003 and 2014 FDI

outflows from the ECA region were consistently higher than FDI inflows, in terms both of values and of shares of world FDI flows (see figure S1.1).

EU15 countries have been both the main source and main destination of FDI announcements. Accounting for 80 percent of the region's GDP, advanced EU15 countries (Western, Northern, and Southern Europe) have generated more than 80 percent of FDI outflows from the region to the world and have received more than 40 percent of total FDI inflows from the world. The share of EU13 member countries and non-EU ECA countries of FDI inflows from the world is 10 times larger than their share of FDI outflows to the world (see figure S1.2).

All ECA countries, apart from the original core of the EU (EU15), receive FDI well above what would

FIGURE S1.1 **The relevance of ECA as both a destination and an origin of FDI has fallen since 2008**
ECA FDI patterns over time: Share of world FDI flows, 2003–14

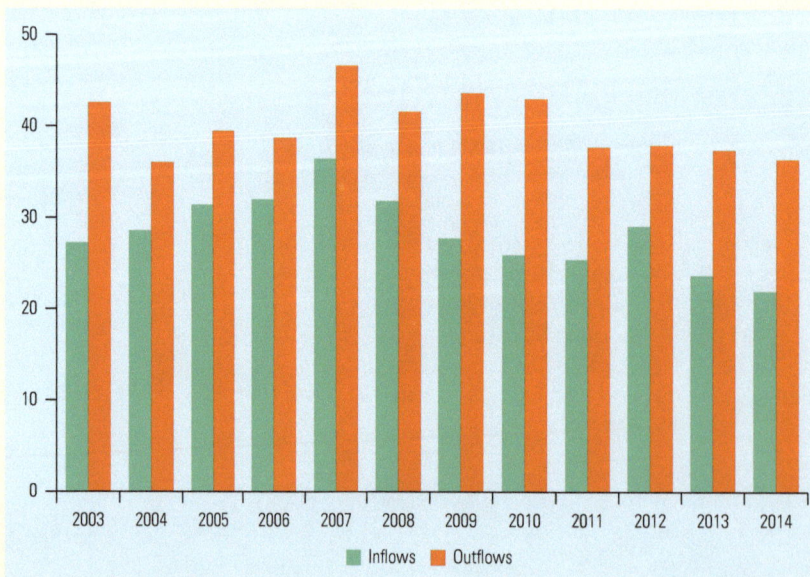

Source: Calculations based on fDiMarkets.com data set.
Note: ECA = Europe and Central Asia; FDI = foreign direct investment.

FIGURE S1.2 World FDI inflows into ECA are relatively more diversified by ECA destination than ECA FDI outflows to the world

World FDI flows over time, by subgroup of countries

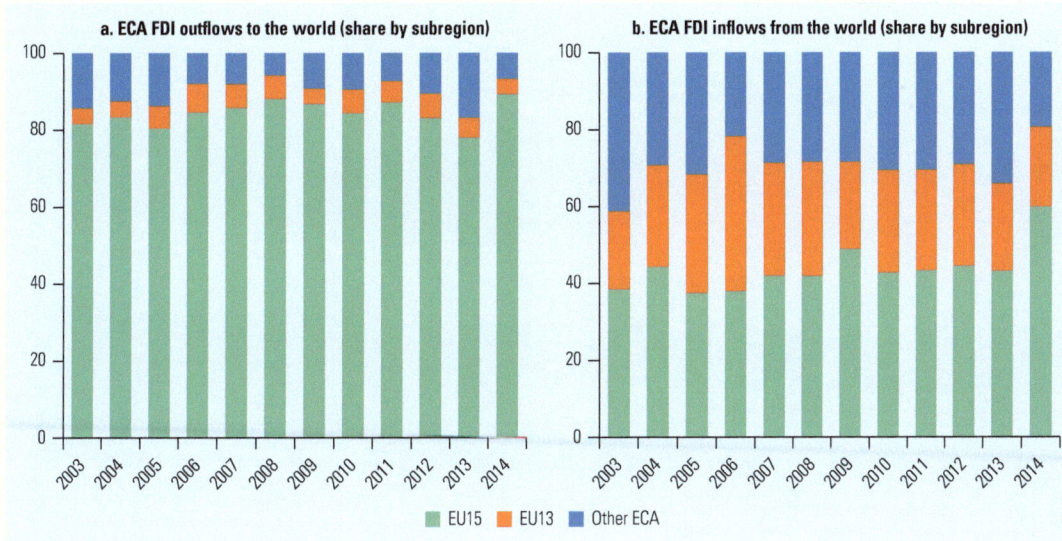

a. ECA FDI outflows to the world (share by subregion)

b. ECA FDI inflows from the world (share by subregion)

■ EU15   ■ EU13   ■ Other ECA

Source: Calculations based on fDiMarkets.com data set.
Note: ECA = Europe and Central Asia; EU = European Union; FDI = foreign direct investment.

be expected given their size. The share of global FDI flows received by the core EU countries is less than their contribution to global GDP—that is, the FDI intensity index was well below 1 during the period 2003–14 (figure S1.3). By contrast, the 13 EU member states that joined the EU in or after 2004 (EU13) and the rest of ECA have been important recipients of FDI, given their size. An intuition behind this pattern is that capital should flow from capital-abundant economies (EU15), where returns are expected to be relatively low, to capital-scarce countries (rest of ECA), where returns are expected to be high.

Patterns of FDI inflows vary substantially across countries. Figure S1.4 shows the average level of FDI inflows as a percentage of GDP per capita for all countries between 2003 and 2014. It essentially confirms the results described above by country group (unconditional on size): on average, FDI inflows have been the greatest among EU13 countries, followed by EU15, and then by the rest of ECA. The fact that the intensity is greater for EU13 than for other ECA

countries reflects the importance of deep international agreements as determinants of FDI attraction (see spotlight 2). However, FDI levels differed within each of these groups. Resource-rich countries, such as Azerbaijan (or even Kazakhstan), have secured particularly high levels of FDI. Similarly, countries that are attractive for financial investments, such as Montenegro, show high levels of FDI, particularly because of low tax regimes. In addition to these exceptions, other countries have managed to attract high levels of FDI within ECA. These include Hungary, Bulgaria, and Estonia among the EU13 group; Georgia, Moldova, Turkmenistan, Serbia, and Albania have also attracted above-average levels of FDI inflows—Albania and Serbia on the back of high integration into European global value chains (see chapter 6).[3]

FDI in natural resources is more prevalent in non-EU ECA members. While almost 90 percent of FDI inflows to EU (EU13 and EU15) countries goes to manufacturing and services sectors, this share is

SPOTLIGHT 1 *continued*

FIGURE S1.3 **ECA's share of world FDI inflows is greater than its share of world GDP**
FDI intensity index (share of FDI/share of GDP), 2003–14

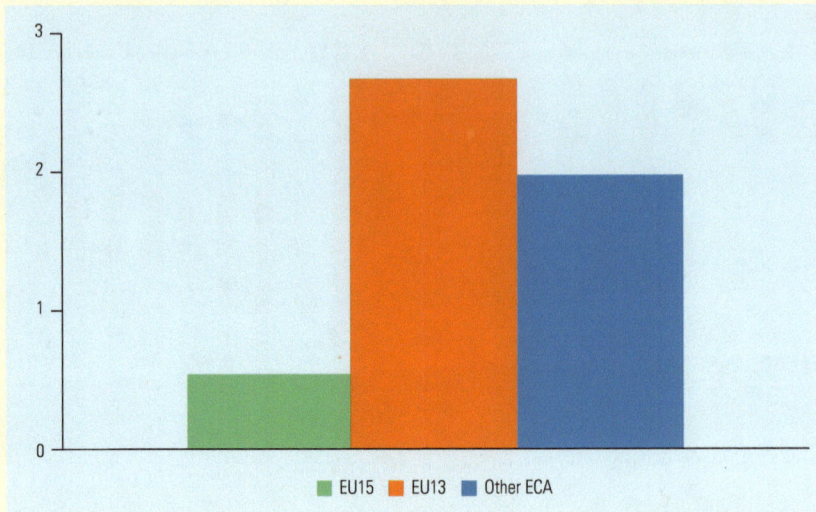

Source: Calculations based on fDiMarkets.com data set.
Note: ECA = Europe and Central Asia; EU = European Union; FDI = foreign direct investment.

FIGURE S1.4 **FDI attraction patterns increase with development levels but vary by country**
Average FDI inflows as a percentage of GDP per capita, 2003–14

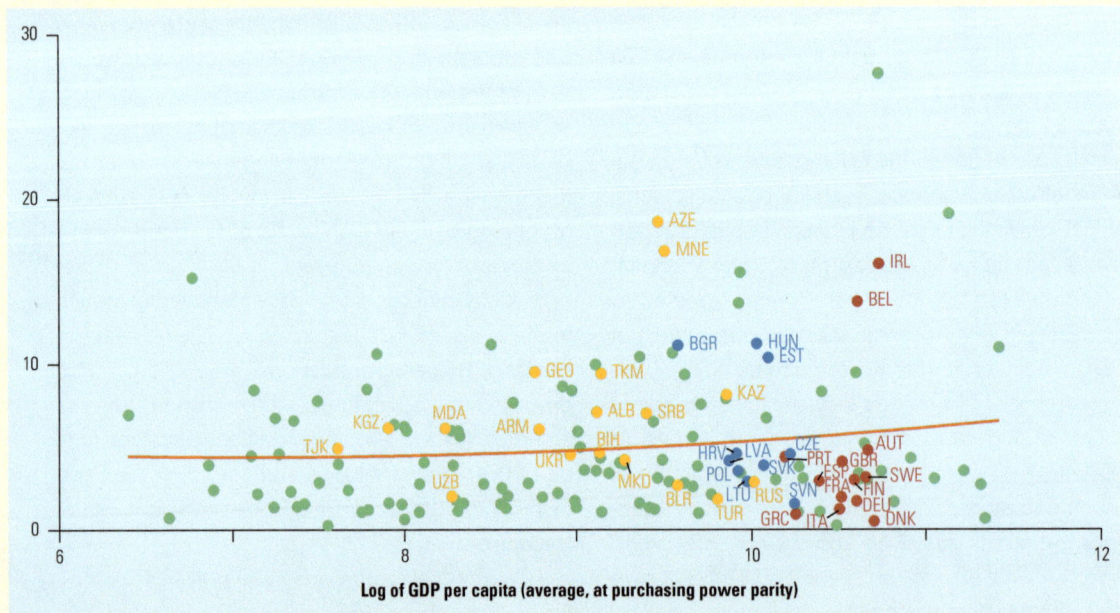

Source: Calculations based on fDiMarkets.com data set.
Note: Countries shown in red are in the EU15, those in blue are in the EU13 group, those in yellow are in the rest of ECA, and those in green are outside of ECA. ECA = Europe and Central Asia; EU = European Union; FDI = foreign direct investment.

closer to 80 percent for other ECA countries (non-EU), with natural resources playing a more important role (see figure S1.5).

Increasingly, the rest of the world is becoming a crucial source of FDI into ECA. The share of FDI inflows into ECA that originated in the region fell from 63 percent in 2003 to 48.6 percent in 2014. This approximately 14 percentage point decline over the period was compensated for by increases in FDI from East Asia and Pacific, the Middle East and North Africa, and other regions (see table S1.1).

FIGURE S1.5 Services and manufacturing dominate FDI inflow patterns across ECA
Average percentage of FDI inflows by sector, 2003–14

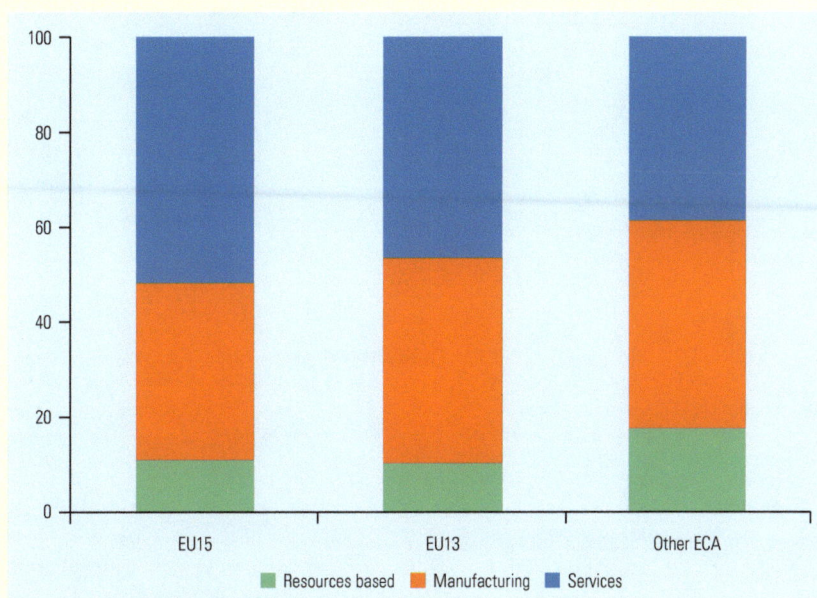

Source: Calculations based on fDiMarkets.com data set.
Note: ECA = Europe and Central Asia; EU = European Union; FDI = foreign direct investment.

TABLE S1.1 ECA Is the Main Investor in ECA
Source of announced ECA foreign direct investment

	Share (percent)		Investment (US$ million)
Region	2003	2014	2014
Europe and Central Asia	63.0	48.6	75,102
North America	25.2	23.4	36,140
East Asia and Pacific	6.9	18.8	29,053
European Free Trade Association	2.1	3.7	5,648
Middle East and North Africa	0.9	3.5	5,483
Other	1.8	2.1	3,215
Total			**154,642**

Source: Calculations based on fDiMarkets.com data set.
Note: ECA = Europe and Central Asia.

SPOTLIGHT 1 *continued*

FIGURE S1.6 Germany and the United States dominate EU investment; France and China lead elsewhere
Main investors in ECA, by subregion, 2014

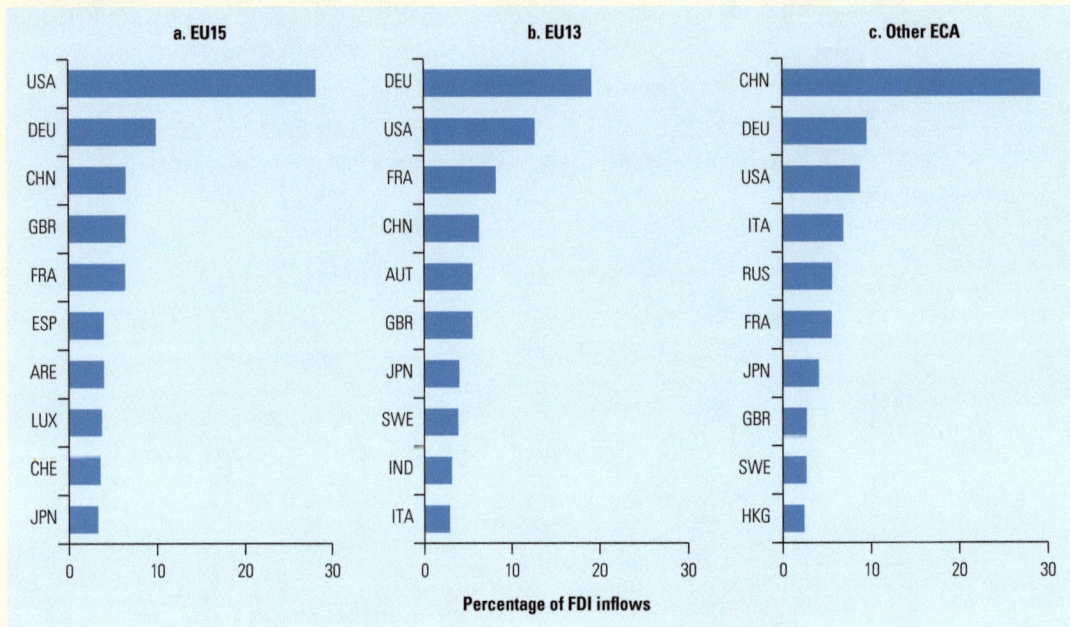

Source: Calculations based on fDiMarkets.com data set.
Note: ECA = Europe and Central Asia; EU = European Union; FDI = foreign direct investment.

The country source of FDI inflows is similar across ECA subregions. The United States, Germany, and China are the principal investors in EU15, EU13, and other ECA countries, representing 44 percent of total FDI inflows into the ECA region. The United States represents almost 30 percent of EU15 FDI inflows, while Germany accounts for 19 percent of EU13 FDI inflows. However, China is the main source of foreign investment in other ECA countries such as Russia and Turkey (see figure S1.6).

3. Serbia is integrated as a first-tier supplier in the automotive value chain. Albania is, for example, closely integrated with Italy in garments and footwear.

Reference

Laget, E., N. Rocha, and G. Varela. 2018. "FDI and Deep Preferential Trade Agreements: An Empirical Investigation." Unpublished, World Bank, Washington, DC.

Notes

1. This spotlight draws from Laget, Rocha, and Varela (2018).
2. Both the share of ECA in the world's GDP and the share of ECA's inward and outward FDI are calculated as an average for the period 2003–14.

2

Knowledge Transfers from International Openness in Trade and Investment: The European Case

This chapter reviews the role of international trade, foreign investment, and global value chains (GVCs) in transferring knowledge that helps to improve productivity in Europe and Central Asia (ECA) countries. This discussion complements the microanalysis in chapter 3 on the impact on domestic firms of foreign ownership and management. This discussion is particularly relevant for the European continent, where connectivity through trade, investment, and production sharing is high and has greatly increased in the past two decades. Two main questions are considered: what type of knowledge and innovation are being created in Europe and how knowledge diffusion takes place across the continent and to what extent firm-to-firm connectivity within Europe contributes to productivity growth through learning and knowledge transfer. The first section discusses knowledge creation in Europe, and the second section reviews the literature on the link between openness and learning, and how importing, exporting, exposure to foreign firms, and participation in GVCs leads to technological catchup across borders. The third section investigates technology diffusion across and within national borders. The fourth section concludes.

Main Messages

- Learning is the principal source of productivity growth for most countries, largely through the absorption of existing innovations rather than own research.

The most advanced firms in Europe tend to be larger and more capital intensive, have greater investment in intangibles, and have a greater level of human capital than other firms. Europe compares well to the global frontier in manufacturing, but lags behind the global frontier in services and in some innovation-based growth industries.

- Firms can learn through importing as a result of exposure to more diverse and sophisticated inputs; through exporting from opportunities to achieve economies of scale, upgrade workers' skills, and learn techniques to improve product appeal; and from foreign direct investment (FDI) through technology transfers and exposure to high-skilled workers. These effects are significant, for countries in general and in ECA in particular, once the impact of cultural or geographical distance, level of development, and the quality of domestic and international institutions is taken into account.

- The typical channel of technology transfer is from the most advanced global firms to the most advanced national firms (which tend to be strongly involved in GVCs), and then to other domestic firms. This process is confirmed by econometric evidence for Europe, where a rise in total factor productivity (TFP) growth of national frontier firms leads to a similar increase in TFP by other domestic firms, but an increase in TFP by GVC frontier firms has little direct impact on other domestic firms.

- The reduction in trade from the global economic crisis reduced firms' propensity to expand participation in GVCs, leading to a sharp drop in productivity growth compared to the precrisis period. Calls to limit exposure to foreign volatility in light of the deep global recession following the crisis would limit firms' ability to benefit from foreign technology, particularly depressing growth in less advanced economies where firms are further away from the productivity frontier.

Knowledge Creation in Europe

TFP Growth and Knowledge Flows

Learning is the main source of productivity gains for most firms. Increases in knowledge are typically ascribed to two main sources: investment in new knowledge (e.g., through research and development [R&D]) and use of existing knowledge (past discoveries and knowledge sharing) (Griliches 1979). However, only a small set of companies invest in R&D and patents or introduce any radically new products or processes (Cirera and Maloney 2017).[1] Most firms opt instead for learning from existing knowledge, which originates from many possible sources: universities, clients, suppliers, competitors, or other entities within the same corporation. In the United Kingdom, out of a sample of 804 firms surveyed through the UK Community Innovation Survey,[2] 51 percent reported learning from competitors, 65 percent from suppliers, 68 percent from clients, 49 percent from other entities in the same corporation, and only 19 percent from universities (Crespi et al. 2008). Controlling for the impact of other factors, a UK firm learning from competitors, suppliers, and other entities in the same group enjoys a 4.7 percent faster growth in TFP than a firm without such learning (Crespi et al. 2008). This differential explains nearly 50 percent of the productivity gap between the top and the bottom performers (i.e., the firms in the top productivity quartile and the firms in the bottom quartile, respectively).

It is very hard to measure knowledge flows. Direct measurement based on patent citations has two shortcomings. First, research on both US companies (Jaffe and Trajtenberg 2005) and European companies (Criscuolo and Verspagen 2008) shows that patents are a very noisy measure of information flows. As much as 91 percent of patent citations in Europe and 50 percent in the United States are entered by examining officers rather than the inventors themselves. More importantly, only a small share of knowledge is patentable or patented. Most knowledge flows involve nonpatenting firms. For example, knowledge that is transferred between multinational enterprises and their affiliates or between suppliers and customers is usually not patented.

An indirect method of measuring knowledge flows is based on TFP. By looking at the relationship between TFP growth and factors thought to be potentially causing information flows, a number of papers have established a statistically robust relationship between TFP differences and information flows (e.g., Crespi et al. 2008). The distance-to-frontier literature (e.g., Griffith, Redding, and Van Reenen 2004) postulates that knowledge from inside the firm can be measured by TFP levels (or TFP growth rates) in the firm itself, while learning from the frontier can be measured by differences in TFP levels (or in TFP growth rates) between the firm and a nominated frontier firm or set of firms. The indirect method of measuring knowledge flows as gaps in TFP growth between frontier and non-frontier firms has the advantage of implicitly looking at nonpatentable innovations and makes it easier to draw links with policies.

The Innovators in Europe

How do the most productive firms differ from less productive firms? Having established that there is a relationship between TFP differences and differences in information flows, the first step of the analysis is to assess the key characteristics of European Union (EU) innovators. Following the distance-to-frontier literature, we assume that the frontier in Europe consists of the top 100 productive firms in each two-digit industry/year, for 13 countries in the Amadeus (BvD) database over the period 2010–13.[3] The frontier firms in each narrowly defined sector (across Europe) have several differences with the other, less productive firms that may be related to their higher productivity.

Frontier firms stand out in terms of size, capital intensity, investment in intangibles, and human capital, but the importance of these characteristics differs by sector (figure 2.1). In information technology (IT)–intensive manufacturing, frontier firms are 130 percent larger, 50 percent more capital intensive, and invest 49 percent more in intangibles. They pay a 31 percent wage premium to their workers compared to less productive peers in the same two-digit industry, suggesting that the quality of human capital in these firms is also higher. The size premium is even higher for traditional manufacturing (270 percent). In IT-intensive services, frontier firms are twice as capital intensive (102 percent) than laggards, invest 74 percent more in intangibles, and offer a wage premium of 49 percent, but their size is no different from other firms. Non-IT-intensive service firms also pay a high wage premium, but capital intensity and investment in intangibles are not outsized.

FIGURE 2.1 **Differences between frontier and laggard firms vary across sectors**
Frontier firms as a percentage of laggard firms, average, 2010–13

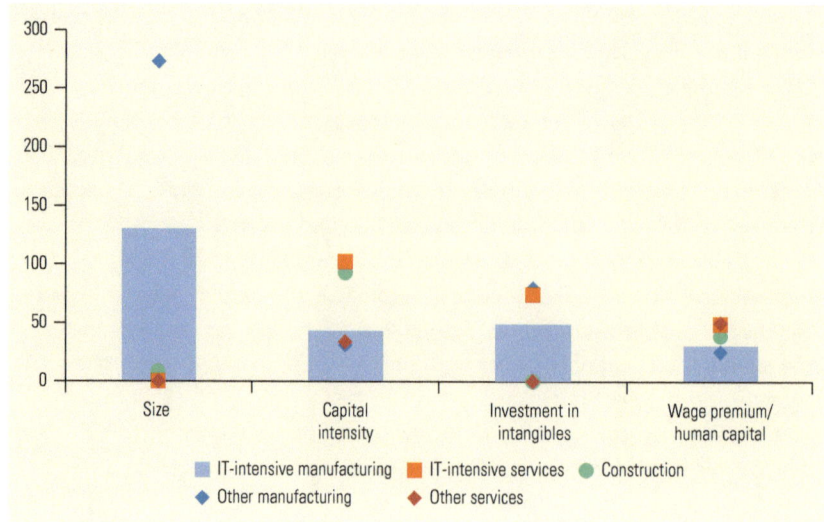

Source: Calculations based on Amadeus data.
Note: Regression at the two-digit industry level in which each variable is regressed on a dummy that equals 1 (frontier firm) or 0 (laggard). Country, year, and sector fixed effects are controlled for. IT = information technology.

Finally, frontier firms in construction post a premium in capital intensity, while intangibles and size do not play a significant role.

The European Versus the Global Frontier

Europe compares well to the global frontier in manufacturing, but lags behind the global frontier in services and in some innovation-based growth industries. Technology creation in European manufacturing is very similar to that in other advanced economies, as measured by the TFP growth gap between frontier firms in Europe and in the Organisation for Economic Co-operation and Development (OECD) (figure 2.2).[4] However, labor productivity growth in European services firms is lower than in firms at the OECD frontier. These numbers suggest that the continent could be served well by pursuing better connectivity to the global frontiers in the services sector.

Direct measures of innovation based on R&D investment confirm that European technology is strong in key manufacturing industries, but lags behind in services and high-growth technology areas. The Innovation Union Scoreboard for the EU is an instrument developed by the European Commission under the Lisbon Strategy to compare the innovation performance of the EU member states. It indicates that the EU is almost as innovative as the United States, overall. Yet there is a gap in services sectors and in some strategically important manufacturing industries, where R&D intensity is above the overall manufacturing average and where leading innovators are predominantly young companies. Compared with the United States, Europe posts a gap in the so-called Revealed Technology Advantage in the internet industries, computer hardware and services, and biotechnology, as well as in semiconductors, software, and health care equipment and services (table 2.1). By contrast, the European Revealed Technology Advantage is strongest in industries including industrial machinery, electrical components and equipment, fixed

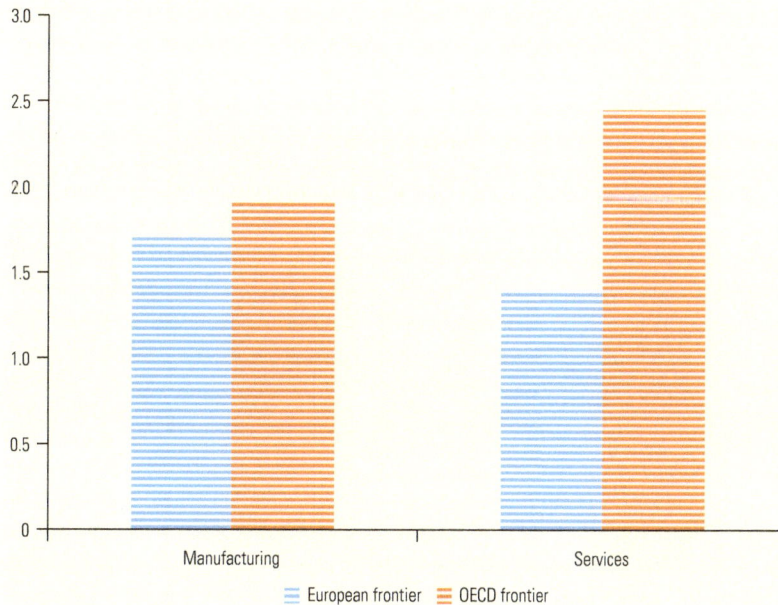

FIGURE 2.2 Europe lags behind the frontier in services
Average annual labor productivity growth, in percent, 2010–13

Source: Calculations based on data from the Organisation for Economic Co operation and Development (OECD) and Amadeus.
Note: Sample is based on firms with more than 20 employees. The European frontier is among the EU15 (that is, the original core countries of the European Union). The technology gap is proxied by the difference in productivity growth between frontier firms and other firms (laggards) in the same sector and year.

TABLE 2.1 Europe Specializes in Several Sectors with Below-Average R&D Intensity and Growth
Revealed technology advantage, European Union and United States

	RTA	
	European Union	**United States**
Industrial machinery	1.84	0.24
Electrical components and equipment	1.56	0.18
Fixed and mobile telecommunications	1.53	0.20
Aerospace and defense	1.50	1.13
Telecommunication equipment	1.38	1.09
Chemicals	1.31	0.64
Pharmaceuticals	1.27	1.16
Auto and parts	1.26	0.58
Industrial metals	1.00	0.30
Health care equipment and services	0.70	1.86
Software	0.51	2.05
Semiconductors	0.50	1.72
Biotechnology	0.32	2.20
Computer hardware and computer services	0.08	1.39
Internet	0	2.54

Sources: Bruegel and the World Bank, based on the Institute for Prospective Technological Studies R&D Scoreboard.
Note: Table depicts the revealed technology advantage (RTA) for the period from 2010 to 2015. The RTA is calculated as a region's share in total sectoral research and development (R&D) relative to its share in total R&D. An RTA greater than 1 reflects a region's specialization in a given sector.

and mobile telecom, aerospace and defense, telecommunications equipment, chemicals, pharmaceuticals, and autos and auto parts.

Knowledge and Learning from Trade, Investment, and GVCs: Insights from the Economic Literature

Neo-Schumpeterian models assume that a country-sector's productivity growth depends on exposure to the global frontier and distance to the frontier (Aghion and Howitt 2006; Saia, Andrews, and Albrizio 2015). Having assessed that European technology is close to the global frontier in manufacturing but a bit more removed in services sectors, we next focus on how technology flows within the continent and the role played by firm-to-firm connectivity in helping technology spread. The mechanism we track in this chapter is predominantly cross-border in nature and focuses on productivity convergence as a measure of technology convergence: variations in productivity growth differentials between different groups of firms are used to gain insights into how technology is transferred from the European frontier to firms located within the domestic economies of the countries in the rest of the continent.

Openness facilitates learning, upgrading, and innovation through various channels. In the next paragraphs we focus on how different types of openness enable firms to acquire knowledge and valuable capabilities.[5] We define capabilities as in Cirera and Maloney (2017): "firm features that are mainly internal to the firm, firm specific, knowledge-based, and not easily replicable … and that manifest themselves in routines, management practices, and assets that are adopted or acquired by the firm, internally or externally, that can be measured, and that are the result of learning and accumulation over time."

Imports: Direct and Indirect Knowledge Spillovers from International Suppliers of Inputs

Importers are larger and more productive than firms that do not trade, with productivity gains generated mostly from access to more differentiated imported inputs. Earlier studies for developed countries conclude that importers are larger and more productive, a finding recently confirmed for developing countries as well (Şeker 2012). Importing is found to raise productivity (Amiti and Konings 2007), with the largest productivity gains due, not to a competition effect, but rather to improved access to inputs. Access to a more differentiated variety of inputs (Goldberg et al. 2010; Halpern, Koren, and Szeidl 2015) seems to matter more than the direct benefits from lower prices or higher-quality foreign inputs. For example, Goldberg et al. (2010) find that the increase in product scope by Indian firms following India's comprehensive trade reforms in the 1990s was due to an increase in the number of imported varieties rather than a decrease in prices. Likewise, Halpern, Koren, and Szeidl (2015) find that Hungarian firms enjoyed a 22 percent rise in productivity from importing inputs over 1993–2002, with about half of the effect due to imperfect substitution between foreign and domestic inputs. The firms that benefit most from importing are multinational firms: they use imports more effectively and benefit from scale economies that reduce the fixed costs of importing. Importing by these firms is also found to have beneficial effects on other domestic firms via supply chain linkages.

Imports also trigger learning effects and feedback loops. Importing gives rise to tacit knowledge, which materializes in intangible assets (MacGarvie 2006; Koren and Csillag 2011). Sophisticated machinery and capital goods imports require highly trained operators. Using data from Hungary for the period 1994–2004, Koren and Csillag (2011) construct a measure of exposure to imported machines, combining data on workers' occupations with information on imported products. They find that, other things equal, the average wage of workers increases by about 3 percent after a firm acquires the imported machinery. MacGarvie (2006) finds a positive association between the nature of technology imported and the subsequent patents by French firms, based on propensity score matching[6] applied to patent citations.

> Imports also trigger learning effects and feedback loops. Importing gives rise to tacit knowledge, which materializes in intangible assets.

Importing better inputs or connecting to better (more productive) firms also leads to upgrading for direct importers and other firms indirectly connected via supply chains. Javorcik (2004) shows that the presence of multinational corporations in a country and industry increases the productivity of firms in industries that are their suppliers. Kee (2015) highlights through interviews and empirically that firm-level connections induce productivity improvements in domestic suppliers. Kee (2015) further shows, using a sample of Bangladeshi garment firms, that local intermediate inputs may also enhance performance of other domestic firms through what she calls the "shared supplier spillovers" of FDI firms. She finds that after EU firms expanded FDI in Bangladesh, domestic firms that shared the same suppliers with the foreign investors expanded their product scope by 25 percent and enjoyed productivity gains of 33 percent.

Finally, there are complementarities in capabilities, with the return to importing and innovation activities increasing in the intensity of one another. For example, Bøler, Moxnes, and Ulltveit-Moe (2015) find that firms involved in foreign sourcing are more innovative, and innovation increases the profitability from the international sourcing. Specifically, they find that returns to lowering R&D costs are higher for importers. Cost complementarities between R&D and international sourcing are crucial to explaining productivity gains: 25 percent of the productivity gains are due to international sourcing and 75 percent to the complementary R&D investments.

Exports: Knowledge Spillovers from Competitors and Clients

Exporting generates opportunities for learning for firms and its workers (De Loecker 2013). Bustos (2011) finds that Argentinean firms increased their demand for skills after the creation of Mercosur (Bustos 2011).[7] Evidence from Taiwanese firms shows that there is complementarity between exporting, R&D, and workers' training (Aw, Roberts, and Winston 2007). Exporting requires firms to acquire new capabilities to perform a complex set of activities, including manufacturing tasks, marketing, distribution, foreign trade finance activities, and exporting services, even when the product exported is non-skill-intensive (Feenstra and Hanson 1996;

Matsuyama 2007; Grossman and Rossi-Hansberg 2008; Verhoogen 2008). Moreover, exporters tend to be larger and more productive and pay higher wages, inducing a greater need for more complex management structures, which in turn increases the demand for skills.[8] Management is a key factor regulating complexity in firms' operations. Systematic, large-scale evidence from data on management practices, balance sheets, and comprehensive trading activity for the United States and China establishes a clear link between managerial competence and export performance (Bloom et al. 2018).

Demand factors also play an important role in inducing positive knowledge spillovers from exporting. Exporting enables firms to learn about more sophisticated consumers and more competitive markets. Investments in capability building to improve product appeal and demand is an important reason for the phenomenal success of Chinese manufacturing firms in world trade over the past two decades (Sutton 2007; Brandt, Rawski, and Sutton 2008; Schott 2008). Searching for consumers is tightly linked to marketing (Eslava et al. 2015), investments in the customer base (Fitzgerald, Haller, and Yedid-Levi 2015), and branding as a way to signal quality by building reputation, as buyers often do not observe quality directly (Cagé and Rouzet 2015). Coe and Helpman (1995) show that the extent to which a country benefits from other countries' R&D efforts depends on how much it trades with them.

The characteristics of destination markets affect the impact of exporting on learning. Features such as income, quality valuation, distance, and transport costs affect firms' decisions on upgrading, and hence on both the propensity to undergo the costs of acquiring new knowledge and the type of knowledge acquired (Hummels and Skiba 2004; Verhoogen 2008; Bastos and Silva 2010; Manova and Zhang 2012; Martin 2012). Firms that export to high-income countries more intensely use higher levels of skills and pay higher wages than domestic firms or exporters that are specialized in middle- or low-income countries (Brambilla et al. 2012). Mexican companies exporting to the US market upgrade quality, as measured by ISO 9000 certification, and raise the wages of white- and blue-collar workers more than do firms that export to lower-income countries or that do not export (Verhoogen 2008).

Complex Engagements through GVCs: Learning from Import-to-Export Activity and Engagement with Multinational Corporations

Exporters that import their intermediate inputs are more productive than companies that only import or only export (Kasahara and Lapham 2013). Firms' productivity affects their decisions to be in international markets, and importing inputs affects productivity. An implication of the complementarities between importing and exporting is that imposing import restrictions can reduce exports and affect most negatively the domestic frontier firms.

The productivity of firms at the domestic technology frontier matters since these firms tend to induce their suppliers to also upgrade technology and innovate. Producing higher-technology goods tends to require more skill-intensive and higher-technology inputs. The innovating firm will demand better inputs, thus inducing its suppliers to adopt newer technologies. Also, with economies of scale, the price of advanced inputs produced by the innovating firm will decline, increasing the incentives for other firms to use the same inputs to upgrade their own technology (see Kee 2015 for Bangladesh and Fieler, Eslava, and Xu 2018 for Colombia). Thus, if production exhibits internal or external economies of scale, increased demand for higher-technology goods will increase technology adoption in the aggregate.

Innovation tends to flow faster and more easily within GVCs. Such production arrangements link together multiple firms, usually located in different countries, in ways similar to intragroup investment and trade. In so doing, they offer a high degree of exposure to, and learning from, the fast-evolving, technology-enabled business models that characterize GVCs, even without the need for participating firms to engage in ownership arrangements.[9]

At the same time, countries and firms with weaker connections to GVCs may reduce their innovation because of competition from countries and firms more strongly embedded in GVCs. For example, Mexican suppliers to US companies reduced their investment in innovation as demand fell because of their buyers' increased GVC integration with third parties in China. And other buyers (e.g., German buyers) of the same Chinese suppliers also experienced adverse effects because their production costs in China rose as a consequence of the increased demand from the United States (Arkolakis and Muendler 2010).

The power relationship between companies in GVCs also matters for innovation. Some suppliers within GVCs are heavily dependent on the buyer's decisions, private standards, and technological requirements for production (referred to as a "captive" relationship). Success for these suppliers is largely determined by the ability to assimilate new and improved technologies developed and transferred by the large global buyers.

FDI and Technology Spillovers

Foreign direct investment (FDI) and multinational corporations can provide important learning opportunities. The cost of transferring technology is reduced within integrated companies, and foreign-owned companies tend to be better managed. Moreover, these companies are responsible for the largest share of trade and investment globally (Bernard, Jensen, and Schott 2005; Yeaple 2013). The cost of transferring technology to subsidiaries encourages multinationals to acquire the most productive (or domestic frontier) firms (Arnold and Javorcik 2009; Criscuolo and Martin 2009; Ramondo 2009). A foreign-acquired firm appears to be 57 percent more likely to have undertaken a process of innovation while foreign owned, relative to a firm that stays domestic (Guadalupe, Kuzmina, and Thomas 2012).

FDI can influence the domestic productivity of firms in the same sector as the investment, upstream sectors, and downstream sectors. Empirical studies that examine the impact of FDI on domestic firms' productivity identify three types of spillovers. Horizontal spillovers—the effect of FDI in a given sector on the productivity of domestic (or other foreign) firms operating in the same sector—can materialize through increased competition, technology and knowledge transfers, and workers' circulation.[10] Vertical spillovers through forward linkages—the effect of FDI in upstream

FDI can influence the domestic productivity of firms in the same sector as the investment, upstream sectors, and downstream sectors.

(inputs) sectors on the productivity of domestic (or other foreign) firms operating in downstream sectors (final product)—can materialize through improved provision of inputs (more varied, cheaper, or better quality), and through technology and knowledge transfers via, for example, training of clients (Arnold et al. 2010; Fernandes and Paunov 2012; Duggan, Rahardja, and Varela 2013). Finally, vertical spillovers through backward linkages—the effect of FDI in downstream (final product) sectors on the productivity of domestic (or other foreign) firms operating in upstream (input) sectors—can materialize through training of suppliers and through the sophistication of inputs demanded (Javorcik 2004).

Both inward and outward FDI can act as channels of spillovers. Most of the firm-level research on spillovers has focused on *inward* FDI.[11] However, as van Pottelsberghe de la Potterie and Lichtenberg (2001) argue, foreign investment outflows can also result in transfers of knowledge and technology leading to productivity increases. If foreign firms imitate domestic counterparts, or if they source the domestic knowledge base, their country of origin may also benefit from potential spillovers. The authors make an analogy with language learners. One can learn a foreign language by bringing home a speaker of the foreign language, or by fully immersing oneself in the foreign country. While learning can happen in both cases, it is likely that the "full immersion" strategy provides greater scope for it. Indeed, there is evidence that firms engage in "technology sourcing" practices, targeting countries with substantial technological and scientific capabilities.[12] Van Pottelsberghe de la Potterie and Lichtenberg (2001) consider three alternative channels for international technology (or R&D) spillovers: (a) trade, (b) inward FDI, and (c) outward FDI. Their findings suggest that there are technology transfers only through outward FDI.

However, evidence on the existence, magnitude, and channels of knowledge spillovers is mixed. In their meta-analysis of the literature, Iršová and Havránek (2013) conclude that horizontal spillovers are on average zero, and that the sign and size of these spillovers depend on both the characteristics of the domestic firms and domestic environment and the characteristics of the foreign investors as well.[13] By contrast, the evidence on vertical spillovers (through both backward and forward linkages) tends to be more conclusive, suggesting a positive effect of FDI.[14] Yet overall these studies suggest these positive spillover effects are neither inevitable nor automatic. Domestic technology investments, and in general, the building up of absorptive capabilities are necessary. One explanation for this lack of conclusive evidence is that the ability of countries and firms to benefit from spillovers from foreign firms may depend on other mediating factors. Indeed, one strand of literature identifies three factors that may be necessary for knowledge spillovers to materialize: distance, the level of economic development of partners, and the quality of domestic and international institutions.

First, distance between partners may matter. A well-established body of work has shown that spatial proximity to the source of knowledge is an important condition allowing spillovers to take place (Jaffe, Trajtenberg, and Henderson 1993; Audretsch and Feldman 1996). Take exposure through FDI. Geographic distance can be a deterrent for circulation of experts between the parent and subsidiary company, which tends to be a mechanism that facilitates knowledge transfers (Girma and Wakelin 2007). Although new technologies have reduced the cost of moving ideas across distant locations, the costs of moving people remain high, and they could reduce the scope of spillovers (Javorcik, Saggi, and Spatareanu 2004). Alternative measures of distance that take into account language barriers or cultural differences may also play a role by increasing the costs of communicating ideas.

Second, the level of development of both partners plays a role in international spillovers. Firm-level empirical evidence that looks at FDI spillovers, for example, demonstrates that absorptive capabilities matter for the extent of the spillovers (Griffith, Redding, and Simpson 2002; Blalock and Gertler 2008; Benli 2016). At the country level, this argument means that for international spillovers to materialize, it may not be enough to trade or invest in a country that actively invests in R&D. Capabilities at home matter too, and these are linked to a country's level of development. Thus, for example, the scope and scale of FDI knowledge spillovers may differ between industrial and industrializing countries, showing the importance of host country characteristics in exploiting benefits from FDI (Silajdzic and Mehic 2015). In addition, the capabilities of the partner are likely to matter too, given its level of investment in R&D, if these capabilities affect the effectiveness of that investment.[15]

Third, the quality of institutions can reduce the costs of transferring knowledge. Institutions have been identified as key determinants of economic growth. They could potentially also affect the degree to which domestic and foreign R&D investment affects TFP. Countries with better institutions may be more efficient at investing in R&D (Coe, Dicken, and Hess 2008). A better doing business environment, for example, may encourage more entrepreneurial R&D that results in larger quality improvements for a given R&D effort. Also, better infrastructure of international agreements—another dimension of institutional quality—could improve intellectual property protection and stimulate the circulation of proprietary information between parent and subsidiary companies.

Summary of Lessons from the Literature

Imports and exports between firms generate learning and technology transfer through a rich variety of push and pull factors. Importing activity induces technology transfer through four main channels. First, access to more diversified varieties and complementarities between imported inputs and domestic products generate gains in product scope and in productivity. Second, using more sophisticated imported technology leads to learning effects and feedback loops in tacit knowledge for workers. Third, self-reinforcing complementarities between importing and innovation capabilities generate greater returns to both activities. Finally, domestic linkages of GVCs ensure that the positive effects are not limited to direct importers but spread to other domestic firms through shared supplier networks. Exporting activity is also associated with learning and innovation, but spillovers from exports are lower than the effect induced by imports, which propagate to other domestic companies via shared supplier networks. The link between exporting and absorbing new technologies rests on competition and both supply and demand factors. On the supply side, the main effect of exports is on skill upgrading. This is induced by learning from competitors as well as from the activity of exporting: exporting in itself is complex and skill intensive and leads to the need to expand the organizational structure and the organizational capital of the company, as a result of the fact that exporters tend to become

> The positive effects are not limited to direct importers, but spread to other domestic firms through shared supplier networks.

larger. On the demand side, learning originates from a push to improve product appeal, including through better marketing, branding, and customer search and retention. Finally, destination market characteristics matter: exports to more sophisticated markets induce greater product and process upgrading.

FDI can improve productivity through learning and exposure to competition. FDI can influence the domestic productivity of firms in the same sector as the investment and in upstream sectors and downstream sectors through the transfer of technology and knowledge (e.g., training of clients or suppliers or exposure to more sophisticated workers), through competition, which forces some firms to improve and weak firms to exit, and through improved availability of inputs. Evidence of the size of these spillovers is mixed, however, perhaps because the ability of countries and firms depends on other characteristics, referred to as *mediating factors*, including the geographic distance between investing and receiving countries, the level of development of each country, and the quality of domestic and international institutions, that can facilitate or impede knowledge transfer.

Knowledge Diffusion in Europe: The Two-Stage Process of Technology Transfer

The impacts of trade, foreign investment, and GVC participation on innovation discussed in the literature review indicate a two-stage process of technology transfer between firms. Technology spreads first from global frontier firms to national frontier firms through trade and investment linkages, and then to the rest of the firms in the domestic economy through domestic linkages.[16] Sources of learning and innovation focus differ across firm types, as exemplified in figure 2.3, which shows sources of learning for different types of firms (left column) and

FIGURE 2.3 Technology transfer tends to follow a typical sequence

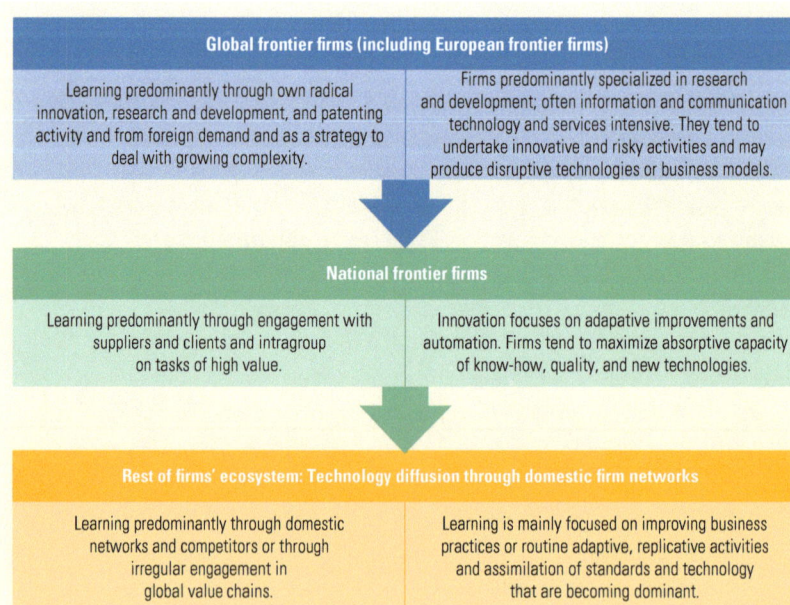

Global frontier firms (including European frontier firms)

| Learning predominantly through own radical innovation, research and development, and patenting activity and from foreign demand and as a strategy to deal with growing complexity. | Firms predominantly specialized in research and development; often information and communication technology and services intensive. They tend to undertake innovative and risky activities and may produce disruptive technologies or business models. |

National frontier firms

| Learning predominantly through engagement with suppliers and clients and intragroup on tasks of high value. | Innovation focuses on adapative improvements and automation. Firms tend to maximize absorptive capacity of know-how, quality, and new technologies. |

Rest of firms' ecosystem: Technology diffusion through domestic firm networks

| Learning predominantly through domestic networks and competitors or through irregular engagement in global value chains. | Learning is mainly focused on improving business practices or routine adaptive, replicative activities and assimilation of standards and technology that are becoming dominant. |

innovation focus (right column). Firms at the global frontier of innovation learn predominantly through own radical innovation, R&D, and patenting activity, and from addressing untapped needs of sophisticated customers, usually at a global scale. These firms tend to specialize in R&D and high-value information and communication technology and service activities. They undertake risky activity and may produce disruptive technologies or business models. National frontier firms tend to be the most connected to global frontier firms through complex trade and investment arrangements, as discussed in the subsection "Complex Engagements through GVCs." Openness to trade and investment is critical to acquiring new technology, learning new processes, and achieving technological upgrading. The innovation in national frontier firms focuses predominantly on adapting own processes and products to the quality, scale, and efficiency required by the international markets, including through automating production. Learning for these firms is mostly focused on creating the mechanisms for absorbing foreign buyers' know-how and of world-class standards and technology. Finally, the remainder of firms (i.e., firms with productivity, technology, and skills below the national frontier) tend to learn predominantly through domestic channels, including domestic supplier networks and competitors. Their direct engagement with global frontier firms is either nonexistent or irregular, and the learning content of the exposure to international counterparts limited (more on this in the next paragraph). Learning for the average nonfrontier firm is mainly focused on improving their business practices and routine adaptive and replicative activities, and through assimilation of standards and technology that are already widespread or dominant.

The two-stage process of technology transmission within Europe can be measured. Using CompNet Data,[17] we consider that national frontier firms in a given macrosector[18] are those in the top 20 percent in terms of TFP. The middle firms are those between the 30th and the 70th percentiles in the productivity distribution. And laggards are the bottom 20 percent of firms in terms of TFP. In line with the discussion in the earlier sections of this chapter, we test the assumption that technology flows from European frontier firms with GVC links with the countries of Central and Eastern Europe (CEE) to the CEE firms following a two-stage process of technology transmission (figure 2.4).[19] At stage 1, knowledge flows from European technology frontier firms, which we assume are the GVC lead firms, to the national frontier firms. National frontier firms are suppliers that are deeply integrated in the production process of the GVC lead: they carry out core production processes for the lead firm. At stage 2, knowledge flows from the national frontier firms to the rest of the domestic firms, predominantly through domestic firm-to-firm and firm-to-worker linkages. Domestic networks are fueled by the outsourcing of noncore activities of the value chain.

There is also a direct channel from foreign companies to the medium-to-low productivity firms in peripheral economies, which, however, grants lower technology transfer. The engagement most likely involves noncore functions, requires capabilities that are basic in nature, and is based on arm's length trade relationships. This is a critically different type of engagement from the one the GVC lead entertains with the national frontier firms, which is based on deep relationships that involve ownership or licensing, franchising, joint ventures, strategic alliances, or other forms of nonequity modes of investment. It is the deep nature of

FIGURE 2.4 How technology flows from European frontier firms (global value chain lead firms) to the remaining European firms

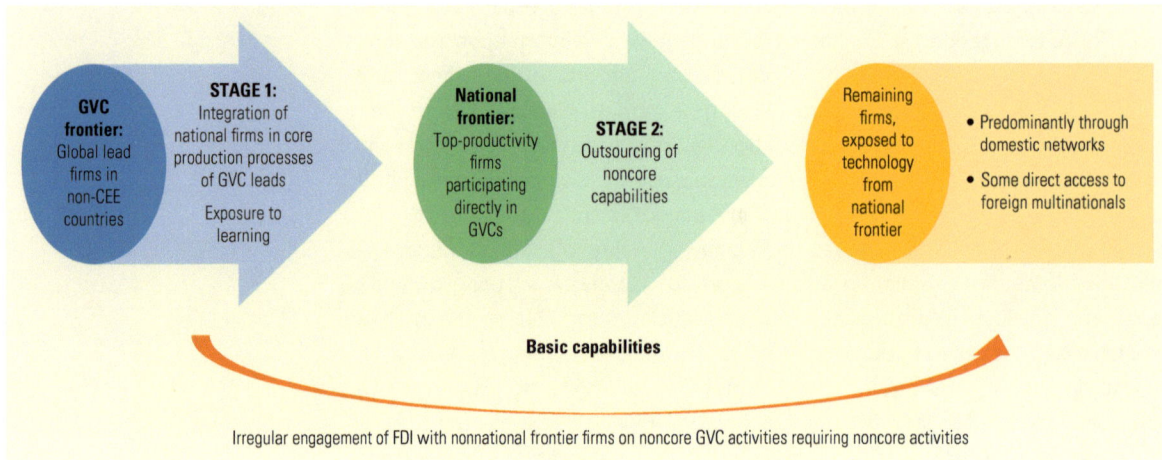

Note: CEE = Central and Eastern Europe; FDI = foreign direct investment; GVC = global value chain.

engagement that allows the faster, more sizable, and knowledge-intensive transfer of capabilities between countries.

Convergence to the technological frontier and participation in GVCs are correlated. Technology transfers are more intense in the context of complex firm engagements, and both the degree of connectivity of firms at the receiving end of technology transfer and the degree of sophistication of the trade partner matter. The pecking order is summarized in figure 2.5. Firms far away from the technology frontier tend to have no engagement with GVCs or intermittent engagement through executing noncore, often low-value-added activities using basic capabilities requirements. Engaging in GVCs for these firms requires facing entry costs to align their goals and processes with those of the buyer. These firms tend to be most active in domestic production and sales, and they mainly compete on price. More dynamic domestic firms, both in terms of productivity and learning, tend to have a more stable engagement in GVCs. These firms need to manage greater size and complexity, and pay greater attention to the quality of their products. The more technologically sophisticated they are, the more likely they are to have a strong interdependence with their parent firms, as such collaboration requires sharing valuable, proprietary intellectual property. For such firms learning and absorbing know-how becomes fundamental. They also benefit from feedback loops from exposure to new technologies, skills, and processes. As companies upgrade toward the technological frontier (national, regional, or global) they increasingly focus on organizational capital, innovation, and high-value-added activities as core competences. This, and a strong focus on R&D and quality, allows these firms to create disruptive technologies and to achieve intersectoral upgrading.

GVC participation is high in the EU, and particularly high in CEE countries (figure 2.6). A similar indicator shows that import intensity is exceptionally high for this region. The intensity of imports is measured as the ratio of all GVC-related imports to the value of final products, weighted by final output.

FIGURE 2.5 Firms' international connectivity and technology transfer follow three stages

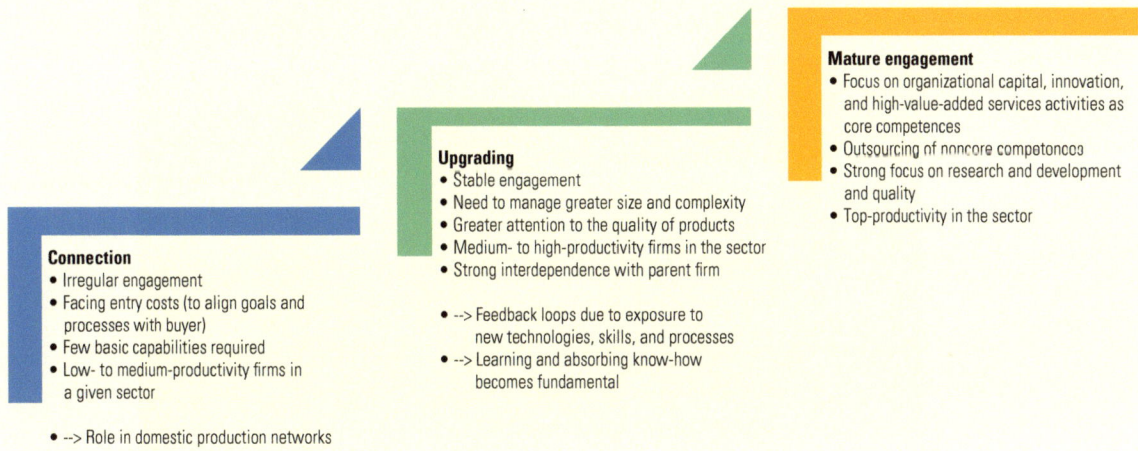

Mature engagement
- Focus on organizational capital, innovation, and high-value-added services activities as core competences
- Outsourcing of noncore competences
- Strong focus on research and development and quality
- Top-productivity in the sector

Upgrading
- Stable engagement
- Need to manage greater size and complexity
- Greater attention to the quality of products
- Medium- to high-productivity firms in the sector
- Strong interdependence with parent firm

- --> Feedback loops due to exposure to new technologies, skills, and processes
- --> Learning and absorbing know-how becomes fundamental

Connection
- Irregular engagement
- Facing entry costs (to align goals and processes with buyer)
- Few basic capabilities required
- Low- to medium-productivity firms in a given sector

- --> Role in domestic production networks

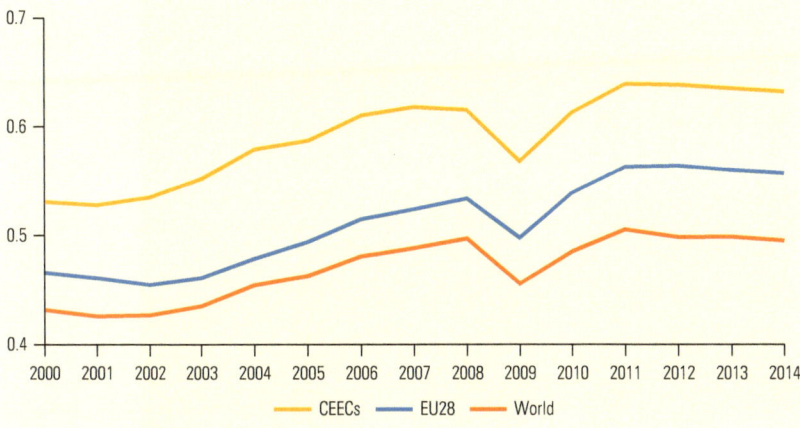

FIGURE 2.6 GVC participation is particularly high in Central and Eastern Europe
GVC participation, 2000–14

Source: World Input-Output Database (WIOD).
Note: Central and Eastern European countries (CEECs) include those for which data are available from the WIOD, including Bulgaria, Croatia, the Czech Republic, Estonia, Hungary, Latvia, Lithuania, Poland, Romania, the Slovak Republic, and Slovenia. Global value chain (GVC) participation is measured as the share (not in percent) in gross exports of the sum of two measures: domestic value added in third-country exports (forward GVC participation) and foreign value added in own exports (backward GVC participation). EU28 includes all EU member countries.

While import intensity flattened out in 2008 at the global level, it continued growing in the EU until 2012. Import intensity of production in CEE countries has also stagnated since 2012, but overall it has increased dramatically (figure 2.7).

The decline in trade with the global economic crisis may have contributed to the slowdown in productivity growth by reducing firms' opportunities to learn through engagement with GVCs. Total factor productivity growth in the CEE members of the EU was 8.2 percentage points lower during 2008–14 compared to 2000–07 (figure 2.8). As documented in Chiacchio, Gradeva, and Lopez-Garcia (2018), econometric estimates of TFP growth in these countries, controlling for country-sector fixed effects, confirm that TFP growth was lower

FIGURE 2.7 **Import intensity varies over time for Central and Eastern European EU countries**
Import intensity growth relative to 2000

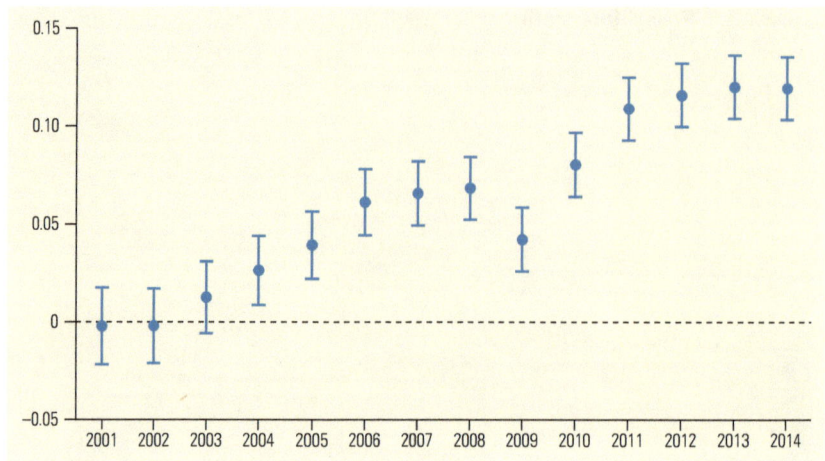

Source: World Input-Output Database (WIOD).
Note: Central and Eastern European countries (CEECs) include those for which data are available from the WIOD, including Bulgaria, Croatia, the Czech Republic, Estonia, Hungary, Latvia, Lithuania, Poland, Romania, the Slovak Republic, and Slovenia. Import intensity is measured by coefficients of variation, relative to 2000, calculated on the basis of regressions that control for country-sector fixed effects, in which sectors are relative to the end product. The data points represent the estimated coefficients for the year dummies, and the bars represent the 95 percent confidence intervals for the year dummy regression coefficients. EU = European Union.

FIGURE 2.8 **Productivity growth was lower in Central and Eastern Europe during the crisis**
Difference between labor productivity growth in Central European EU countries and that in Eastern European EU countries, 2000–07 versus 2008–14

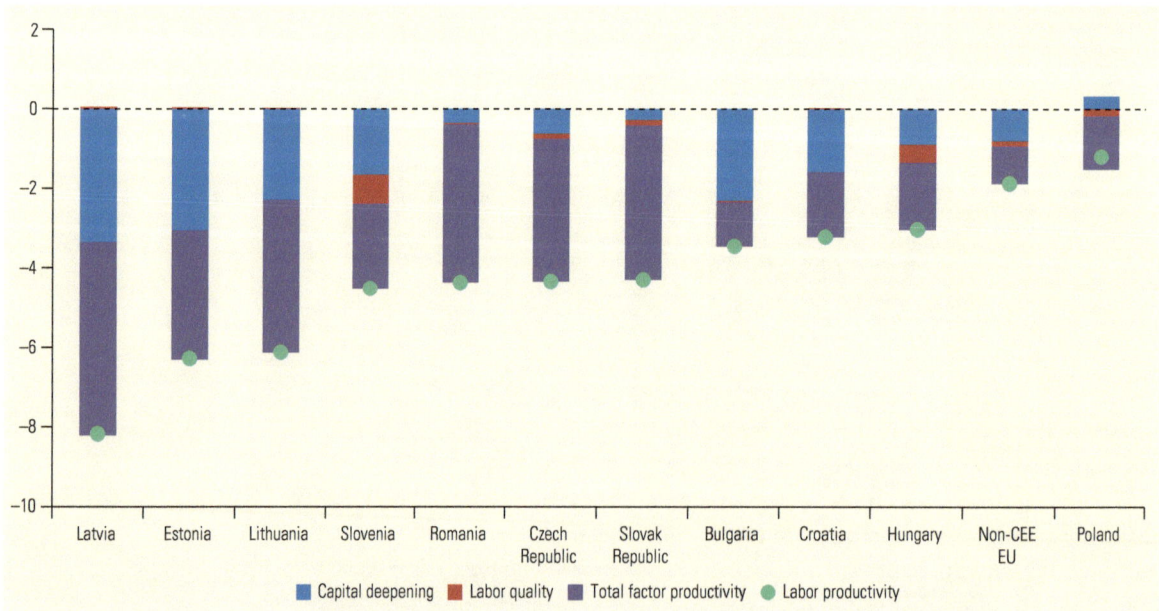

Source: Calculations based on Conference Board data.
Note: "Non-CEE EU" refers to the unweighted average for Austria, Belgium, Cyprus, Denmark, Finland, France, Germany, Ireland, Italy, Luxembourg, Malta, the Netherlands, Portugal, Spain, Sweden, and the United Kingdom. CEE = Central and Eastern Europe; EU = European Union.

during the crisis (2008–10) and postcrisis period (2010–12) compared to the period 2000–07 by 8.2 percentage points and 2.3 percentage points, on average. The assumption explored in that paper, which is the basis for the current analysis, is that the slowdown in integration through global production networks may have slowed the transmission of technology diffusion within the EU, thus slowing productivity growth, particularly in the less-advanced EU countries.

TFP growth in the CEE members of the EU is strongly correlated with GVC activity. TFP growth at the sectoral level in CEE-EU countries over the period 2000–12 is explained by technology creation at the GVC frontier and by the lagged gap in TFP with the frontier, consistently with neo-Schumpeterian models. A 10 percent increase in TFP growth at the EU GVC frontier increases TFP growth of national frontier firms by 4.8 percent, and a 10 percent gap in TFP explains another 5.2 percent of overall sectoral TFP growth (Chiacchio, Gradeva, and Lopez-Garcia 2018).[20] Estimates of the determinants of TFP growth by national frontier firms confirm these more aggregate results. Furthermore, the capacity to learn from parent firms, that is, the absorptive capacity of host firms, decreased by about 10 percent in the crisis period (2008–10) and postcrisis period (2010–12). The slowdown in TFP growth at the GVC frontier affected growth of national frontier firms only after 2010, but it did so severely, with half of the precrisis impact lost. Sectors with higher GVC growth were more resilient to the crisis and postcrisis slowdown. This indicates that strengthening GVC connectivity may have important growth and economic convergence effects.

Econometric evidence also confirms the two-stage process of knowledge transmission (see above). TFP growth by laggard firms is affected much more by their exposure to national frontier firms than by exposure to GVCs. A 10 percent increase in TFP growth of national frontier firms leads to a 9.2 percent increase in TFP growth of laggards, while a 10 percent increase in TFP growth for GVC frontier firms only generates 1.5 percent additional growth in TFP for laggard firms. This latter effect is additional to the indirect effect that GVC frontier TFP growth has on laggards through boosting productivity growth of national frontier firms. Qualitatively similar results hold for middle-productivity firms. All results are robust to a battery of tests on the presence of specific year outliers, base effects linked to the GVC level, or the choice of the GVC indicator.

What is driving the decline in productivity growth in the Central and Eastern part of the EU since 2008? Firms' ability to innovate depends on their own investment in innovation, R&D, and human capital (Cohen and Levinthal 1989, 1990, 1994; Griffith, Redding, and Van Reenen 2004; Lopez-Garcia and Montero 2012). The decline in connections with GVCs as a result of the crisis reduced the return on such investment in intangibles by CEE-EU frontier firms. This led to a fall in R&D spending as a share of GDP and in firms' propensity to introduce new products or processes, as shown in the World Bank's Enterprise Surveys. Econometric evidence at the sectoral level confirms this hypothesis, finding that the drop in investment in intangibles is limited to R&D-intensive sectors only.

Conclusion

Trade and FDI offer significant opportunities for firms to increase their productivity through technology transfers. The economic literature provides an extensive discussion of the theoretical benefits for developing-country firms of international interactions. The empirical evidence on such effects is mixed, in part because technology transfers from partner countries may depend on distance, the level of development, and the quality of institutions. Our empirical results suggest, both globally and for ECA, that trade with, and FDI from, countries that do more R&D are associated with increased productivity. However, the impact can be reduced by the extent of geographical or cultural distance between the two countries, and developing countries benefit from spillovers only from FDI originating in developed countries.

An important technology-diffusion channel in the EU is through production sharing through GVCs, which can encompass both trade and FDI. Frontier and laggard firms in host countries benefit from GVC participation in different ways. Frontier firms benefit from learning that ranges from managerial practices to organization of the supply chain to access to advanced cutting-edge research. Laggards benefit from contact with national frontier firms and also, to a lesser extent, from direct contact with parent companies. Learning focuses more on efficient identification of the firm's own niche, efficient use of inputs, and adaptation of own product and processes to fit more smoothly in advanced production.

The global economic crisis reduced international trade, thus slowing down EU firms' engagement in GVCs. The benefit EU firms derived from cross-border knowledge flows therefore fell, which made an important contribution to the decline in productivity growth in the region. This underlines the importance of maintaining open policies toward foreign trade and investment to support the productivity growth of firms.

Notes

1. In most developing countries well below 5 percent of firms do any patenting (Cirera and Maloney 2017). While the number grows as we approach the technological frontier, it remains below 25 percent for most countries, with the exception of Japan and Germany, where more than 40 percent of firms sampled report patenting. Even Australia, Singapore, the United Kingdom, and the United States appear to have relatively few firms patenting (about 10 percent). Bloom and Van Reenen (2002) report that 72 percent of all patents originated from as few as 12 firms, out of their sample of 59,919 UK firms.
2. The UK Community Innovation Survey is an official survey of businesses on innovation outputs, innovation inputs, and sources of knowledge for innovation efforts.
3. Sample of firms with at least 20 employees.
4. Note that the OECD average includes the European Union countries.
5. Openness as a source of knowledge spillovers and growth has long been acknowledged in the literature. Grossman and Helpman (1991) study the growth performance of a small country in which scientific and technological knowledge flows from abroad and these flows are related to its extent of foreign trade. In this environment, trade generates an externality that coexists with the externality of domestic innovation. They show that domestic innovation produces both positive and negative externalities, and

the existence of negative externalities leads to an undersupply of innovation overall. Policies that reduce the extent of international trade contribute to the undersupply of innovation. By contrast, some trade-promoting policies accelerate growth and raise national welfare because they offset some of the harmful negative externalities from domestic innovation.

6. Propensity score matching is a popular approach to estimating causal treatment effects. It applies for all situations in which one has a treatment, a group of treated individuals, and a group of untreated individuals. This technique attempts to estimate the effect of a treatment, policy, or other intervention by accounting for the covariates that predict receiving the treatment.

7. The paper provides an explanation for the relationship between trade opening, exporting, and the increased demand for skills. Exporters have higher innovation and skill intensity for both production and nonproduction occupations. New technologies reduce the variable costs of production but induce higher fixed costs. As a consequence, a parsing between firms takes place: the more skill-intensive new technologies are adopted by the more productive producers who also tend to export. On the other hand, middle-productivity firms export but do not adopt the advanced technologies. Meanwhile, market reallocation effects induce the least productive firms to downgrade skills.

8. A firm's productivity depends on how production is organized (Caliendo and Rossi-Hansberg 2012). Heterogeneity in demand, which is likely to increase when one firm serves more than one market, leads to heterogeneity in productivity and expanding skill composition. Moreover, a larger firm uses more than one layer of managers: the higher they are in the hierarchy, the less-common problems they tackle, and the higher their skills. Adding an extra layer can be thought of as reducing the marginal cost of the firm in exchange for increasing the fixed cost of acquiring and communicating knowledge.

9. Despite the opportunities and incentives, in many cases spillovers do not occur because domestic firms lack the complementary capabilities that would allow them to accumulate knowledge.

10. While studies focusing on developing countries produce mixed results concerning the presence of positive spillovers (e.g., Djankov and Hoekman 2000; Konings 2001), a more optimistic picture emerges from studies on industrial nations (e.g., Haskel, Pereira, and Slaughter 2002; Keller and Yeaple 2003). For a review of this literature, see Lipsey (2004).

11. There are exceptions to this. One example is Tang and Altshuler (2015), who examine home effects of outward FDI from the United States and find evidence of positive and significant spillovers flowing from multinational customers to their domestic suppliers.

12. Kogut and Chang (1991) and Yamawaki (1993), for example, show that Japanese firms tend to enter the United States and European markets by acquiring domestic firms when Japanese parent companies are at a technological disadvantage relative to US and European firms.

13. They find that spillovers are higher when foreign investors form joint ventures, and when the technological gap of the investor with respect to the host economy is relatively narrow (suggesting that domestic firms will have the absorptive capabilities to learn from the multinationals) (see Iršová and Havránek 2013).

14. In the context of Indonesia, for example, Blalock and Gertler (2008) find evidence of positive vertical spillovers from increased FDI in downstream activities of the manufacturing sector. Focusing on Lithuania, Javorcik (2004) provides evidence of positive productivity spillovers from FDI taking place through interactions between foreign affiliates and their local suppliers in upstream sectors. Most recent literature on vertical spillovers through forward linkages has concentrated on how FDI in upstream services sectors affects the productivity of downstream manufacturers. In the Czech Republic, for example, Arnold, Javorcik, and Mattoo (2007) find sizable effects on productivity of increased foreign entry into upstream services.

15. Amann and Virmani (2014), for example, show that developing countries benefit more when technology-rich countries invest in them than the other way around.

16. Such sequencing is in line with neo-Schumpeterian models (Aghion and Howitt 2006; Saia, Andrews, and Albrizio 2015) and models of technology diffusion in multiple stages (Bartelsman, Haltiwanger, and Scarpetta 2013; van der Wiel et al. 2008; Iacovone and Crespi 2010).

17. CompNet is a research network originally created in 2012 within the European System of Central Banks and is devoted to the analysis of competitiveness from a multidimensional perspective. The CompNet database is based mainly on administrative data from firm registries and is constructed following a micro-distributed approach due to the confidential nature of firm-level information in most countries (Bartelsman, Haltiwanger, and Scarpetta 2004). The database provides harmonized cross-country information on all deciles of the distribution of a number of variables related to firm performance and competitiveness, including productivity, in a given country, sector, and year. In total, CompNet covers about 18 EU countries, 9 macrosectors including manufacturing and construction, and 7 service sectors for the period 2001–13. For more information on the data set and coverage, please refer to Lopez-Garcia, di Mauro, and the CompNet Taskforce (2015).

18. Defined roughly as one-digit sectors according to the NACE (Nomenclature des Activités Économiques dans la Communauté Européenne, the European Classification of Economic Activities) rev. 2 classification system.

19. The mapping between non-CEE EU countries and CEE countries is done according to the relative importance of each non-CEE EU country in total intermediate imports of CEE countries by sector and year.

20. See Chiacchio, Gradeva, and Lopez-Garcia (2018) for the detailed results.

References

Aghion, P., and P. Howitt. 2006. "Joseph Schumpeter Lecture: Appropriate Growth Policy; A Unifying Framework." *Journal of the European Economic Association* 4 (2–3): 269–314.

Amann, E., and S. Virmani. 2014. "Foreign Direct Investment and Reverse Technology Spillovers: The Effect on Total Factor Productivity." *OECD Journal: Economic Studies* 2014: 129–53.

Amiti, M., and J. Konings. 2007. "Trade Liberalization, Intermediate Inputs, and Productivity: Evidence from Indonesia." *American Economic Review* 97 (5): 1611–38.

Arkolakis, C., and M. Muendler. 2010. "The Extensive Margin of Exporting Products: A Firm-Level Analysis." NBER Working Paper 16641, National Bureau of Economic Research, Cambridge, MA. http://aida.econ.yale.edu/~ka265/research/MultiProduct/Arkolakis_Muendler_products.pdf.

Arnold, M. J., and B. S. Javorcik. 2009. "Gifted Kids or Pushy Parents? Foreign Direct Investment and Plant Productivity in Indonesia." *Journal of International Economics* 79 (1): 42–53.

Arnold, J. M., B. S. Javorcik, M. Lipscomb, and A. Mattoo. 2010. "Services Reform and Manufacturing Performance: Evidence from India." Discussion Paper DP8011, Centre for Economic Policy Research, London.

Arnold, M. J., B. S. Javorcik, and A. Mattoo. 2007. "Does Services Liberalization Benefit Manufacturing Firms? Evidence from the Czech Republic." Policy Research Working Paper 4109, World Bank, Washington, DC. https://openknowledge.worldbank.org/handle/10986/6882.

Audretsch, D., and M. P. Feldman. 1996. "R&D Spillovers and the Geography of Innovation and Production." *American Economic Review* 86 (3): 630–40.

Aw, B. Y., M. J. Roberts, and T. Winston. 2007. "Export Market Participation, Investments in R&D and Worker Training, and the Evolution of Firm Productivity." *World Economy* 30 (1): 83–104. http://doi.wiley.com/10.1111/j.1467-9701.2007.00873.x.

Bartelsman, E. J., J. Haltiwanger, and S. Scarpetta. 2004. "Microeconomic Evidence of Creative Destruction in Industrial and Developing Countries." Discussion Paper 1374, Institute of Labor Economics (IZA), Bonn, Germany.

———. 2013. "Cross-Country Differences in Productivity: The Role of Allocation and Selection." *American Economic Review* 103 (1): 305–34.

Bastos, P., and J. Silva. 2010. "The Quality of a Firm's Exports: Where You Export to Matters." *Journal of International Economics* 82 (2): 99–111.

Benli, M. 2016. "Productivity Spillovers from FDI in Turkey: Evidence from Quantile Regressions." *Theoretical and Applied Economics* 3 (608): 177–96.

Bernard, A. B., J. B. Jensen, and P. K. Schott. 2005. "Importers, Exporters, and Multinationals: A Portrait of Firms in the U.S. that Trade Goods." NBER Working Paper 11404, National Bureau of Economic Research, Cambridge, MA. http://www.nber.org/papers/w11404.

Blalock, G., and P. J. Gertler. 2008. "Welfare Gains from Foreign Direct Investment through Technology Transfer to Local Suppliers." *Journal of International Economics* 74 (2): 402–21.

Bloom, N., K. Manova, J. Van Reenen, S. Sun, and Z. Yu. 2018. "Managing Trade: Evidence from China and the US." NBER Working Paper 24718, National Bureau of Economic Research, Cambridge, MA.

Bloom, N. and J. Van Reenen. 2002. "Patents, Real Options and Firm Performance." *Economic Journal* 112: C97–C116.

Bøler, E. A., A. Moxnes, and K. H. Ulltveit-Moe. 2015. "R&D, International Sourcing and the Joint Impact on Firm Performance." *American Economic Review* 105 (12): 3660–703.

Brambilla, I., R. Dix-Carneiro, D. Lederman, and G. Porto. 2012. "Skills, Exports and the Wages of Seven Million Latin American Workers." *World Bank Economic Review* 26 (1): 36–60.

Brandt, L., G. T. Rawski, and J. Sutton. 2008. "China's Industrial Development." In *China's Great Economic Transformation*, ed. L. Brandt and G. T. Rawski, 593–604. Cambridge, UK: Cambridge University Press. http://kczx.xhu.edu.cn/G2S/eWebEditor/uploadfile/20120427135908_684449439144.pdf.

Bustos, P. 2011. "Trade Liberalization, Exports, and Technology Upgrading: Evidence on the Impact of MERCOSUR on Argentinian Firms." *American Economic Review* 101 (1): 304–40.

Cagé, J., and D. Rouzet. 2015. "Improving 'National Brands': Reputation for Quality and Export Promotion Strategies." *Journal of International Economics* 95 (2): 274–90.

Caliendo, L., F. Monte, and E. Rossi-Hansberg. 2015. "The Anatomy of French Production Hierarchies." *Journal of Political Economy* 123 (4): 809–52.

Caliendo, L., and E. Rossi-Hansberg. 2012. "The Impact of Trade on Organization and Productivity." *Quarterly Journal of Economics* 127 (3): 1393–1467. http://qje.oxford journals.org/content/early/2012/04/13/qje.qjs016.abstract.

Chiacchio, F., K. Gradeva, and P. Lopez-Garcia. 2018. "The Post-crisis TFP Growth Slowdown in CEE Countries: Exploring the Role of Global Value Chains." Working Paper 2143, European Central Bank, Frankfurt, Germany.

Cirera, Xavier, and William F. Maloney. 2017. *The Innovation Paradox: Developing-Country Capabilities and the Unrealized Promise of Technological Catch-Up*. Washington, DC: World Bank.

Coe, N. M., P. Dicken, and M. Hess. 2008. "Global Production Networks: Realizing the Potential." *Journal of Economic Geography* 8 (3): 271–95.

Coe, D. T., and E. Helpman. 1995. "International R&D Spillovers." *European Economic Review* 39 (5): 859–87.

Cohen, W. M., and D. A. Levinthal. 1989. "Innovation and Learning: The Two Faces of R&D." *Economic Journal* 99: 569–96.

———. 1990. "Absorptive Capacity: A New Perspective on Learning and Innovation." *Administrative Science Quarterly* 35: 128–52.

———. 1994. "Innovation Fortune Favours the Prepared Firm." *Management Science* 40 (2): 227–51.

Crespi, Gustavo, Chiara Criscuolo, Jonathan E. Haskel, and Matthew Slaughter. 2008. "Productivity Growth, Knowledge Flows, and Spillovers." NBER Working Paper 13959, National Bureau of Economic Research, Cambridge, MA.

Criscuolo, C., and R. Martin. 2009. "Multinationals and U.S. Productivity Leadership: Evidence from Great Britain." *Review of Economics and Statistics* 91 (2): 263–81.

Criscuolo, Paola, and Bart Verspagen. 2008. "Does It Matter Where Patent Citations Come From? Inventor vs. Examiner Citations in European Patents." *Research Policy* 37 (10): 1892–908.

De Loecker, J. 2013. "A Note on Detecting Learning by Exporting." *American Economic Journal: Microeconomics* 5 (3): 1–21. https://www.aeaweb.org/articles.php?doi =10.1257/mic.5.3.1.

Djankov, S., and B. Hoekman. 2000. "Foreign Investment and Productivity Growth in Czech Enterprises." *World Bank Economic Review* 14 (1): 49–64.

Duggan, V., S. Rahardja, and G. Varela. 2013. "Service Sector Reform and Manufacturing Productivity: Evidence from Indonesia." Policy Research Working Paper 6349, World Bank, Washington, DC. https://ssrn.com/abstract=2210300.

Eslava, M., J. Tybout, D. Jinkins, C. Krizan, and J. Eaton. 2015. "A Search and Learning Model of Export Dynamics." Paper presented at 2015 Annual Meeting, Society for Economic Dynamics, Warsaw, June 25–27.

Feenstra, R. C., and G. H. Hanson. 1996. "Globalization, Outsourcing, and Wage Inequality." *American Economic Review* 86 (2): 240–45.

Fernandes, A., and C. Paunov. 2012. "Foreign Direct Investment in Services and Manufacturing Productivity: Evidence for Chile." *Journal of Development Economics* 97 (2): 305–21.

Fieler, A., M. Eslava, and D. Y. Xu. 2018. "Trade, Technology and Input Linkages: A Theory with Evidence from Colombia." *American Economic Review*. 108 (1): 109–46

Fitzgerald, D., S. Haller, and Y. Yedid-Levi. 2015. *How Exporters Grow*. Staff Report 524, Federal Reserve Bank of Minneapolis, Minneapolis, MN.

Girma, S., and K. Wakelin. 2007. "Local Productivity Spillovers from Foreign Direct Investment in the U.K. Electronics Industry." *Regional Science and Urban Economics* 37 (3): 399–412.

Goldberg, P., A. M. Khandelwal, N. Pavcnikh, and P. Topalova. 2010. "Imported Intermediate Inputs and Domestic Product Growth: Evidence from India." *Quarterly Journal of Economics* 125 (4): 1727–67.

Griffith, R., S. J. Redding, and H. Simpson. 2002. "Productivity Convergence and Foreign Ownership at the Establishment Level." Discussion Paper 3765, Centre for Economic Policy Research, London. https://ssrn.com/abstract=388802.

Griffith, R., S. J. Redding, and J. Van Reenen. 2004. "Mapping the Two Faces of R&D: Productivity Growth in a Panel of OECD Countries." *Review of Economics and Statistics* 86 (4): 883–95.

Griliches, Zvi. 1979. "Issues in Assessing the Contribution of Research and Development to Productivity Growth." *Bell Journal of Economics* 10 (1): 92–116.

Grossman, Gene M., and Elhanan Helpman. 1991. "Trade, Knowledge Spillovers, and Growth." *European Economic Review* 35 (2–3): 517–26.

Grossman, Gene M., and E. Rossi-Hansberg. 2008. "Trading Tasks: A Simple Theory of Offshoring." *American Economic Review* 98 (5): 1978–97.

Guadalupe, M., O. Kuzmina, and C. Thomas. 2012. "Innovation and Foreign Ownership." *American Economic Review* 102 (7): 3594–27. http://ideas.repec.org/a/aea/aecrev /v102y2012i7p3594-3627.html [Accessed November 14, 2015].

Halpern, L., M. Koren, and A. Szeidl. 2015. "Imported Inputs and Productivity." *American Economic Review* 105 (12): 3660–703.

Haskel, J., S. Pereira, and M. J. Slaughter. 2007. "Does Inward Foreign Direct Investment Boost the Productivity of Domestic Firms?" *Review of Economics and Statistics* 89 (3): 482–96.

Hummels, D., and A. Skiba. 2004. "Shipping the Good Apples Out? An Empirical Confirmation of the Alchian-Allen Conjecture." *Journal of Political Economy* 112 (6): 1384–402.

Iacovone, L., and G. A. Crespi. 2010. "Catching Up with the Technological Frontier: Micro-level Evidence on Growth and Convergence." *Industrial and Corporate Change* 19 (6): 2073–96.

Iršová, Z., and T. Havránek. 2013. "Determinants of Horizontal Spillovers from FDI: Evidence from a Large Meta-analysis." *World Development* 42 (C): 1–15.

Jaffe, Adam B., and M. Trajtenberg. 2005. *Patents, Citations, and Innovations: A Window on the Knowledge Economy.* Cambridge, MA: MIT Press.

Jaffe, A., M. Trajtenberg, and R. Henderson. 1993. "Geographic Localization of Knowledge Spillovers as Evidenced by Patent Citations." *Quarterly Journal of Economics* 108 (3): 577–98.

Javorcik, B. S. 2004. "Does Foreign Direct Investment Increase the Productivity of Domestic Firms? In Search of Spillovers through Backward Linkages." *American Economic Review* 94 (3): 605–27.

Javorcik, B. S., K. Saggi, and M. Spatareanu. 2004. "Does It Matter Where You Come From? Vertical Spillovers from Foreign Direct Investment and the Nationality of Investors." Policy Research Working Paper 3449, World Bank, Washington, DC. https:// ssrn.com/abstract=625327.

Kasahara, H., and B. Lapham. 2013. "Productivity and the Decision to Import and Export: Theory and Evidence." *Journal of International Economics* 89 (2): 297–316.

Kee, H. L. 2015. "Local Intermediate Inputs and the Shared Supplier Spillovers of Foreign Direct Investment." *Journal of Development Economics* 112 (C): 56–71.

Keller, W., and S. R. Yeaple. 2009. "Multinational Enterprises, International Trade, and Productivity Growth: Firm-Level Evidence from the United States." *Review of Economics and Statistics* 91 (4): 821–31.

Kogut, B., and S. J. Chang. 1991. "Technological Capabilities and Japanese Foreign Direct Investment in the United States." *Review of Economics and Statistics* 73 (3): 401–13.

Konings, J. 2001. "The Effects of Foreign Direct Investment on Domestic Firms." *Economics of Transition* 9 (3): 619–33.

Koren, M., and M. Csillag. 2011. "Machines and Machinists: Capital-Skill Complementarity from an International Trade Perspective." IEHAS Discussion Paper MT-DP - 2011/14. Institute of Economics, Hungarian Academy of Sciences. http://ideas.repec.org/p/has /discpr/1114.html.

Lipsey, R. E. 2004. "Home and Host Country Effects of FDI." In *Challenges to Globalization*, ed. Robert E. Baldwin and L. Alan Winters. Chicago: University of Chicago Press.

Lopez-Garcia, P., F. di Mauro, and the CompNet Taskforce. 2015. "Assessing European Competitiveness: The New CompNet Microbased Database." Working Paper 1764, European Central Bank, Frankfurt.

Lopez-Garcia, P., and J. M. Montero. 2012. "Spillovers and Absorptive Capacity in the Decision to Innovate of Spanish Firms: The Role of Human Capital." *Economics of Innovation and New Technology* 21 (7): 589–612.

MacGarvie, M. 2006. "Do Firms Learn from International Trade?" *Review of Economics and Statistics* 88 (1): 46–60.

Manova, K., and Z. Zhang. 2012. "Export Prices across Firms and Destinations." *Quarterly Journal of Economics* 127 (1): 379–436.

Martin, J. 2012. "Markups, Quality, and Transport Costs." *European Economic Review* 56 (4): 777–91.

Matsuyama, K. 2007. "Beyond Icebergs: Towards a Theory of Biased Globalization." *Review of Economic Studies* 74 (1): 237–53.

Ramondo, N. 2009. "Foreign Plants and Industry Productivity: Evidence from Chile." *Scandinavian Journal of Economics* 111 (4): 789–809.

Saia, A., D. Andrews, and S. Albrizio. 2015. "Productivity Spillovers from the Global Frontier and Public Policy: Industry-Level Evidence." Economics Department Working Paper 1238, Organisation for Economic Co-operation and Development, Paris.

Schott, P. K. 2008. "The Relative Sophistication of Chinese Exports." *Economic Policy* 23: 5–49.

Şeker, M. 2012. "Importing, Exporting, and Innovation in Developing Countries." *Review of International Economics* 20 (2): 299–314.

Silajdzic, S., and E. Mehic. 2015. "Knowledge Spillovers, Absorptive Capacities and the Impact of FDI on Economic Growth: Empirical Evidence from Transition Economies." *Procedia—Social and Behavioral Sciences* 195 (3): 614–23.

Sutton, J. 2007. "Quality, Trade and the Moving Window: The Globalisation Process." *Economic Journal* 117 (524): F469–98.

Tang, J., and R. Altshuler. 2015. "The Spillover Effects of Outward Foreign Direct Investment on Home Countries: Evidence from the United States." Working Paper 1503, Oxford University Centre for Business Taxation. http://dx.doi.org/10.2139/ssrn.2545129.

van der Wiel, H., H. Creusen, G. van Leeuwen, and E. van der Pijll. 2008. "Cross Your Border and Look Around." Paper presented at the Dynamics, Economic Growth, and International Trade (DEGIT) Conference, Manila.

van Pottelsberghe de la Potterie, B., and F. Lichtenberg. 2001. "Does Foreign Direct Investment Transfer Technology across Borders?" *Review of Economics and Statistics* 83 (3): 490–97.

Verhoogen, E. A. 2008. "Trade, Quality Upgrading, and Wage Inequality in the Mexican Manufacturing Sector." *Quarterly Journal of Economics* 123 (2): 489–530.

Yamawaki, H. 1993. "Location Decisions of Japanese Multinational Firms in European Manufacturing Industries." In *European Competitiveness*, ed. K. Hughes. Cambridge, UK: Cambridge University Press.

Yeaple, S. R. 2013. "The Multinational Firm." *Annual Review of Economics* 5 (1): 193–217.

Attracting Foreign Direct Investment: The Role of Deep Preferential Trade Agreements

International trade agreements can be an important means of encouraging foreign direct investment (FDI) flows.[1] Chapter 2 shows that FDI is often associated with transfers of knowledge that contribute to growth, underlining the importance of policies that attract FDI flows. This spotlight provides an empirical analysis of how *deep* preferential trade agreements (PTAs)—those that go beyond the reduction of border restrictions to trade to reduce behind-the-border barriers as well as harmonize regulations and standards—encourage greater FDI flows. This is an important illustration of how policies that encourage one connectivity channel (trade) can affect another channel (FDI).

The main results suggest that PTAs going beyond tariff liberalization and including disciplines in the area of trade, investment, and the business environment, among others, are important for FDI attraction. Each provision added to an agreement between a pair of countries is associated with an average 3 percent increase in FDI flows between that pair, underlining the importance of participation in PTAs (participation in PTAs is discussed in chapter 7). This positive impact is mainly driven by policies governing competition, investment, movement of capital, and intellectual property rights, which are key drivers of FDI flows. The impact of deep agreements on FDI matters for manufacturing and services, but not for natural resources. Deep agreements seem to be more helpful in attracting FDI from more culturally distant destinations within the manufacturing sector, emphasizing the role of agreements in facilitating learning. For the ECA region, the relevance of deep agreements in stimulating FDI depends on the origin and the destination of the flows: for FDI originating in EU15 countries, agreements matter more for investments in more distant regions that are otherwise less connected with the EU15 than for investments in its immediate vicinity.

Deep PTAs in ECA: A Snapshot

PTAs signed by countries in Europe and Central Asia (ECA) represent 40 percent of total active agreements. Countries around the world have increased their participation in PTAs, especially in the past two decades. From the 1950s onward, the number of active PTAs increased more or less continuously to almost 70 in 1990. Thereafter, PTA activity accelerated noticeably, with the number of PTAs more than doubling over the next five years and more than quadrupling until 2010 to reach close to 280 PTAs presently in force. ECA countries are considered the most integrated in terms of the number of agreements signed. A total of 111 agreements have been signed by ECA members, either between them or with other countries (see map S2.1).

ECA agreements have become deeper over time. Agreements signed before 1991 included on average 9 provisions, whereas agreements signed between 2005 and 2015 included on average 15 provisions. Analysis based on the new World Bank data set on the content of PTAs (see annex S2A) shows that the treaty establishing the European Community and the EU enlargements are the deepest agreements that have been signed and incorporate a total of 44 legally enforceable provisions, including all provisions that fall under the current mandate of the World Trade Organization (WTO) (we refer to these provisions as "WTO") and 30 disciplines that go beyond the current WTO mandate (referred to as "WTO+"). PTAs signed by non-EU

SPOTLIGHT 2 *continued*

MAP S2.1 **The European Union and North America show the deepest forms of integration**
Number of agreements by country, 2015

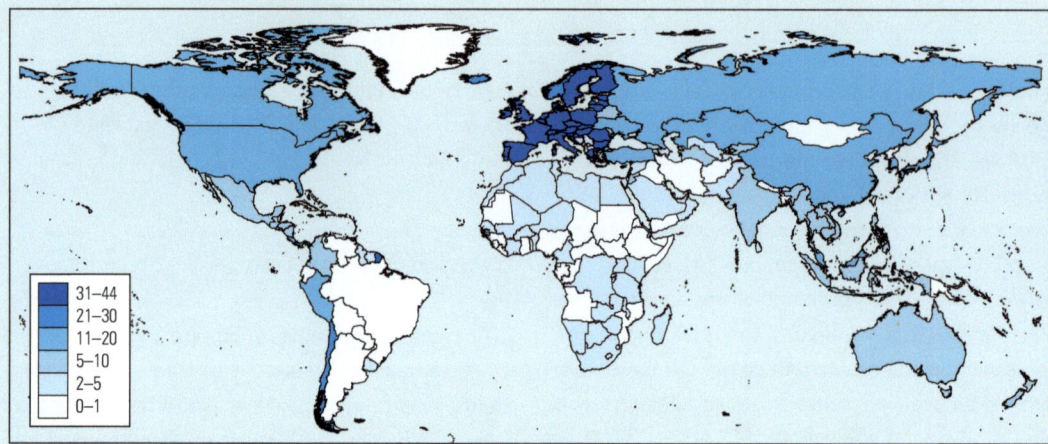

Source: Calculations based on World Trade Organization, Regional Trade Agreement data set.

FIGURE S2.1 **The European Union shows the greatest depth of agreements among ECA country groups**
PTA coverage, by subgroups

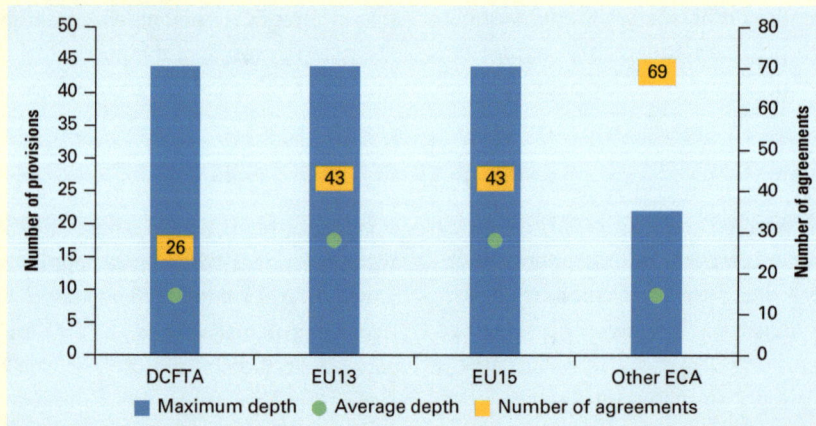

Source: Calculations based on World Bank data set on the content of PTAs. For definitions of the subgroups, see annex S2A.
Note: DCFTA = deep and comprehensive free trade agreement; ECA = Europe and Central Asia; EU = European Union;
PTA = preferential trade agreement.

members tend to be shallower, and include on average 9 provisions. Within non-EU members, the deepest agreement has been signed with EU countries and includes 44 disciplines. Deep and comprehensive free trade agreements with the EU (DCFTAs) have been very important in attracting FDI and facilitating technology transfers across countries (see results below). In the case of non-EU non-DCFTA countries, the maximum number of disciplines that has been included in an agreement is 22

FIGURE S2.2 **Sectoral and customs-related provisions are the most frequent WTO provisions in ECA PTAs**
Percentage of ECA PTAs including WTO provisions

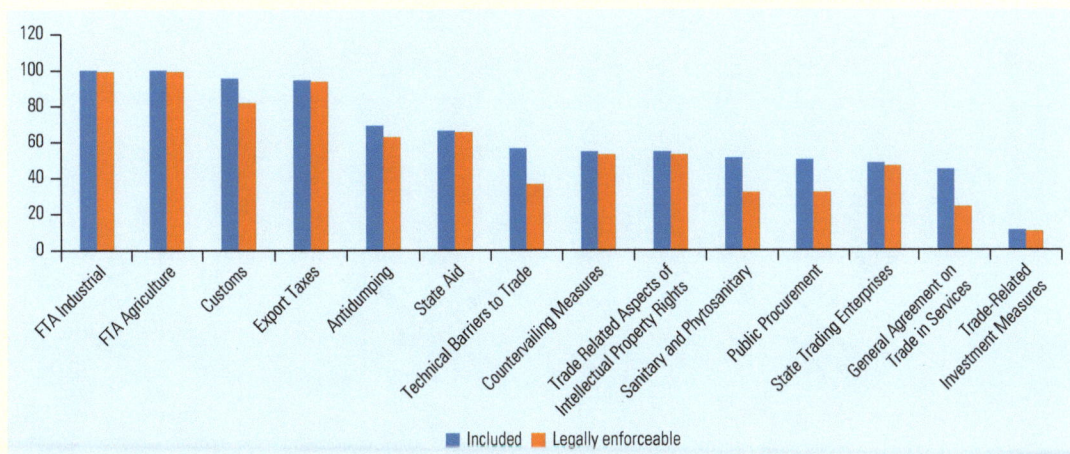

Source: Calculations based on World Bank data set on PTA content.
Note: ECA = Europe and Central Asia; FTA = free trade agreement; PTA = preferential trade agreement; WTO = World Trade Organization.

(see figure S2.1 and table S2A.1 for the country classification).

PTAs signed by ECA countries cover policy areas that fall under the current mandate of the WTO and go beyond tariff reductions. More than 50 percent of the agreements signed by ECA countries include WTO provisions such as export taxes, customs, state-owned enterprises, antidumping, countervailing measures, and Trade-Related Aspects of Intellectual Property Rights. Disciplines such as the General Agreement on Trade in Services, public procurement, Technical Barriers to Trade, and Sanitary and Phytosanitary are included in only 20–40 percent of the agreements (see figure S2.2). The coverage of WTO provisions is in general larger in PTAs signed by EU members compared with non-EU members. While more than 40 percent of agreements signed by EU members include all WTO disciplines except for Trade Related Investment Measures (TRIMS), only 10 percent of the

agreements signed by non-EU members include them (see table S2A.2).

Only a few WTO+ provisions, such as competition policy, movement of capital, and intellectual property rights are included and legally enforceable in a relevant number of ECA trade agreements (see table S2A.3 for a list of WTO and WTO+ policy areas in PTAs). Competition policy is covered and enforceable in more than 80 percent of ECA agreements, followed by movement of capital and intellectual property rights, which are covered in 40 percent of ECA agreements (see figure S2.3). However, while these two provisions are included in more than half of the agreements that are signed by EU members, they are only covered by less than 30 percent of the agreements signed by non-EU members (see table S2A.4). Other provisions such as labor market regulation and investment, which are present in almost 20 percent of ECA agreements, are legally enforceable in, respectively, 17 percent and 15 percent of agreements, on average.

SPOTLIGHT 2 *continued*

FIGURE S2.3 **Among WTO+ provisions, Competition Policy, Movement of Capital, and Intellectual Property Rights are the most frequent WTO+ provisions included in ECA PTAs**
Percentage of ECA PTAs including WTO+ provisions

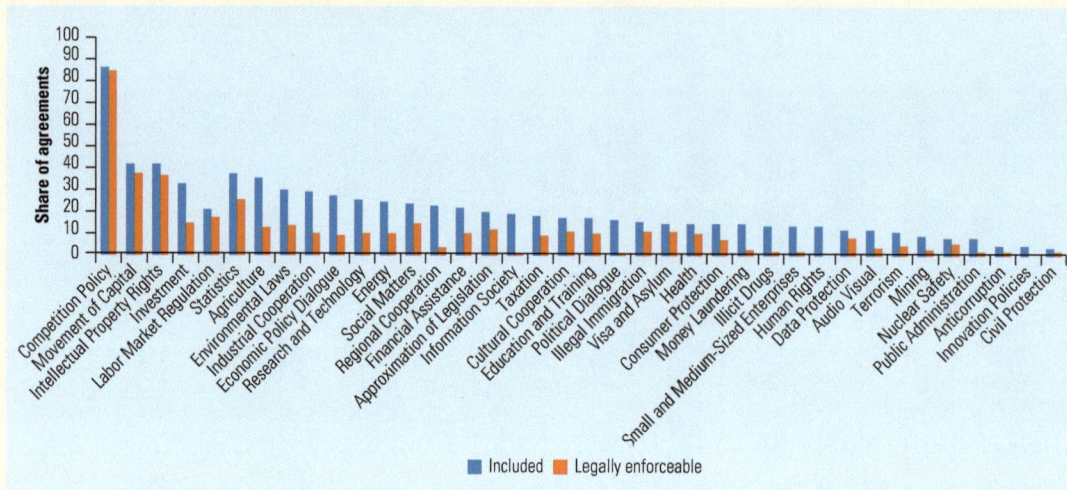

Source: Calculations based on World Bank data set on PTA content.
Note: ECA = Europe and Central Asia; PTA = preferential trade agreement; WTO = World Trade Organization.

Linking Deep Agreements with FDI: Empirical Strategy

The relationship between deep agreements and FDI flows is estimated using a structural gravity equation. An augmented gravity equation is estimated for 170 countries, using data from 2003 to 2014 (table S2.5), to investigate the relationship between the depth of an agreement and FDI (see the discussion of methodology in box S2A.1). The depth of an agreement is captured by the number of legally enforceable provisions that it includes. This methodology has been extensively used by economists to test empirically the determinants of trade flows and to estimate the effect of preferential trade opening on trade flows. The results should be viewed as conditional correlations rather than causal effects, as causation likely runs both ways: deep PTAs can encourage FDI by reducing the costs involved, while pressure from firms involved in FDI is one reason that countries enter into deeper trade agreements.

Linking Deep Agreements with FDI: Results

The empirical results show that deeper agreements tend to encourage higher FDI flows:

- Pairs of countries that have signed deeper agreements—that is, incorporating additional legally enforceable provisions—have higher FDI flows than those that have not signed them. In particular, each provision added to an agreement between a pair of countries is associated with an average 3 percent increase in FDI flows between that pair[2] (see figure S2.4, panel a, and table S2A.6, column 1).[3]
- The effect of deep PTAs on FDI attraction from ECA countries is not different than the average global effect (see table S2A.7).[4]
- The impact of deep agreements on FDI flows is significant for both the manufacturing and services sectors, but not for natural resources (see figure S2.4, panel a, and table S2A.6, columns 2–4).

FIGURE S2.4 **The impact of deep agreements on FDI**

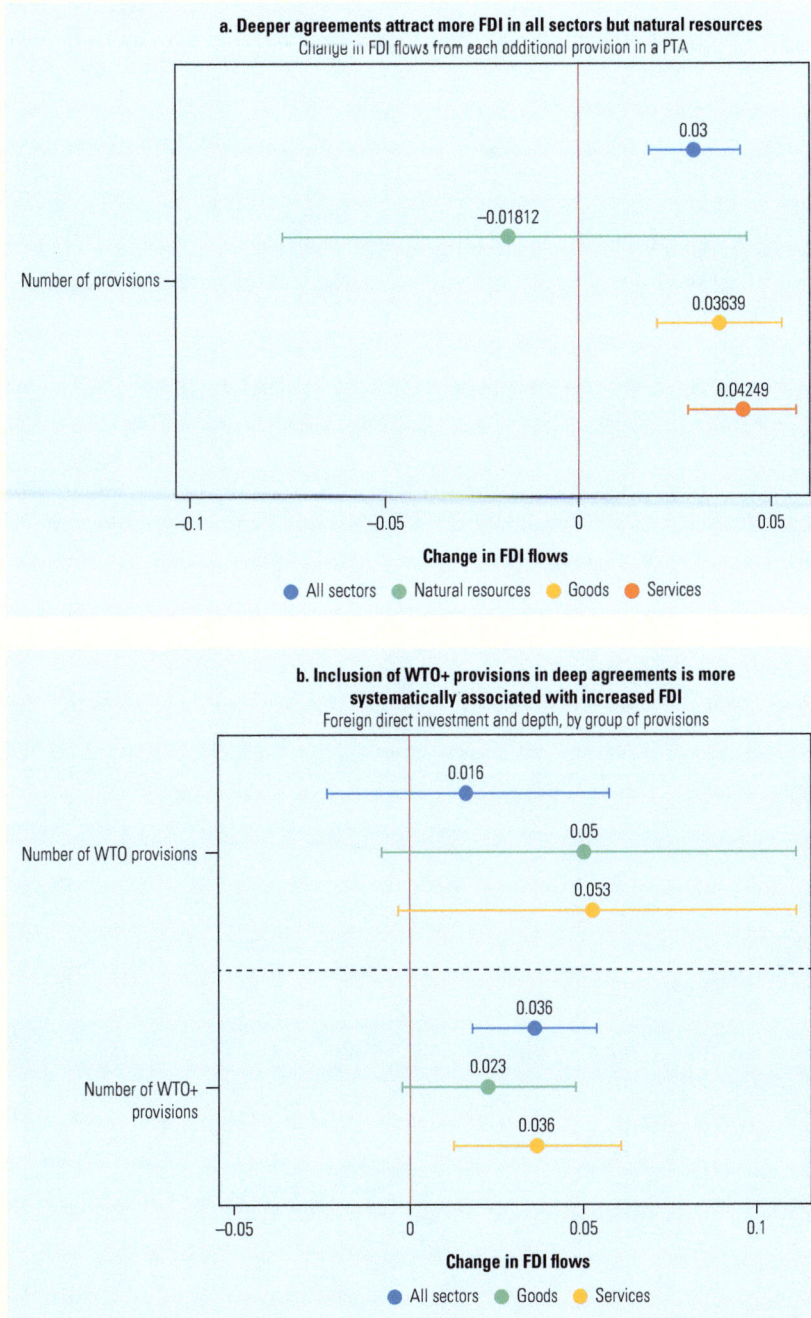

a. Deeper agreements attract more FDI in all sectors but natural resources
Change in FDI flows from each additional provision in a PTA

Number of provisions

0.03

−0.01812

0.03639

0.04249

−0.1   −0.05   0   0.05

Change in FDI flows

● All sectors   ● Natural resources   ● Goods   ● Services

b. Inclusion of WTO+ provisions in deep agreements is more systematically associated with increased FDI
Foreign direct investment and depth, by group of provisions

Number of WTO provisions

0.016

0.05

0.053

Number of WTO+ provisions

0.036

0.023

0.036

−0.05   0   0.05   0.1

Change in FDI flows

● All sectors   ● Goods   ● Services

Note: The bullets in the figure represent the estimated coefficients from the regressions, and the lines represent the 90 percent confidence intervals, which in turn represent the range of values that describe the uncertainty surrounding an estimate. Confidence intervals are one way to represent how "good" an estimate is. The larger a confidence interval for an estimate, the more caution required when using the estimate. FDI = foreign direct investment; PTA = preferential trade agreement; WTO = World Trade Organization.

SPOTLIGHT 2 *continued*

The average impact of deep agreements is slightly larger for manufacturing sectors with lower levels of technological intensity, although the difference is not statistically significant (see table S2A.9).[5]

- While the inclusion of one additional WTO+ provision is associated with a 3.6 percent increase in FDI flows, the impact of WTO provisions is not statistically different from zero (see figure S2.4, panel b, and table S2A.8). WTO+ provisions can encourage FDI in different ways: competition policy, by preventing the abuse of market power, enables multinational firms to optimally fragment production internationally to take full advantage of cross-country cost differentials; and provisions governing investment or intellectual property protect firm-specific assets such as human capital and intellectual property in which international firms may have a competitive advantage.

One of the reasons deep agreements stimulate FDI is because they mitigate the costs of cultural distance, thus facilitating learning. Distance—be it geographic, cultural, or institutional—reduces home effects associated with outward FDI (Driffield, Love, and Yang 2016). Indeed, cultural distance has been identified by multinationals as a key obstacle for knowledge transfers. Signing bilateral investment treaties, by providing clearer rules, reduces the costs of investing in markets that are unfamiliar to investors (Gomez-Mera et al. 2014). However, deep agreements seem to be more helpful in facilitating FDI in manufacturing in more culturally distant destinations, while the opposite is shown for services[6] (see figure S2.5 and table S2A.10).

The relevance of deep agreements in stimulating FDI depends on the origin and the

FIGURE S2.5 **Deep agreements are more helpful in facilitating FDI in culturally distant destinations for manufacturing, while the opposite is true for services**
Foreign direct investment and cultural distance

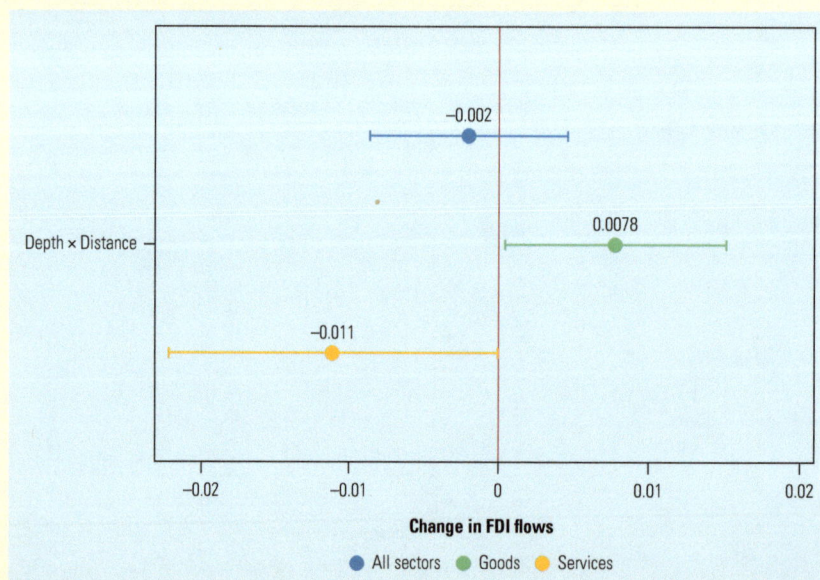

Note: Cultural distance is measured by comparing country pairs on four "cultural dimensions." According to Hofstede (2011), these dimensions describe typical characteristics of cultures: power distance index, individualism versus collectivism, masculinity versus femininity, and uncertainty avoidance. The bullets in the figure represent the estimated coefficients from the regressions, and the lines represent the 90 percent confidence intervals, which in turn represent the range of values that describe the uncertainty surrounding an estimate. Confidence intervals are one way to represent how "good" an estimate is. The larger a confidence interval for an estimate, the more caution required when using the estimate. FDI = foreign direct investment.

destination of the flows. Agreements matter more for FDI from EU15 countries to more distant regions that are otherwise less connected with the EU15 than for FDI to countries in its immediate vicinity. For example, the depth of agreements matters for cross-border investments of EU15 companies in the world, but it does not matter for those investments in ECA countries (table S2A.11, column 1). In fact, the effect of depth on the investment of EU15 in non-ECA countries is about twice the size of the average effect of depth on all cross-border investments (table S2A.11, column 2). Interestingly, results also differ across ECA countries. Depth does not matter for investments from the EU15 into the EU28, while it does matter for investments from the EU15 into non-EU ECA countries (table S2A.11, columns 3 and 4). These results further point to the role of cultural and institutional distance in facilitating FDI, beyond the effect of agreements.

Annex S2A. Definition of Country Groups and Methodology

This spotlight covers a total of 47 countries referred to as Europe and Central Asia (ECA). These countries are divided into four groups: EU15, EU13, DCFTA, and other ECA, as shown in table S2A.1.

EU15 includes the 15 EU member states that joined before 2004; these countries are also referred to as "EU core." EU13 includes the 13 EU member states that joined in or after 2004; they can also be referred to as "EU noncore." The non-EU members are separated into two subgroups: DCFTA, which includes the 3 countries with DCFTA with the EU, and Other ECA, which refers to the 16 countries that do not have a DCFTA with the EU.

PTA Content Data Set

The new World Bank data set on content of PTAs is an extension of Horn, Mavroidis, and Sapir (2010) and WTO (2011) data sets and contains 280 PTAs signed by 180 countries between 1980 and 2015 (Hofmann, Osnago, and Ruta 2017).

The methodology of Horn, Mavroidis, and Sapir (2010) is followed to define the content and the legal enforceability of PTAs (see box S2A.1). As a first step, a set of 51 policy areas covered in PTAs is identified. These areas can be classified into two different groups. The first group is represented by WTO provisions that fall under the current mandate of the WTO and are already subject to some form of commitment in WTO agreements. The second group of policy areas, which is denoted as WTO+ provisions, includes those obligations that are outside the current mandate

TABLE S2A.1 Country Groups and Subgroups

ECA					
EU28				Non-EU	
EU15		EU13		DCFTA	non-DCFTA (Other ECA)
Austria	Italy	Bulgaria	Lithuania	Georgia	Albania	FYR Macedonia
Belgium	Luxembourg	Croatia	Poland	Moldova	Armenia	Montenegro
Denmark	Netherlands	Cyprus	Romania	Ukraine	Azerbaijan	Russian Federation
Finland	Portugal	Czech	Slovak Republic		Belarus	Serbia
France	Spain	Republic	Slovenia		Bosnia and Herzegovina	Tajikistan
Germany	Sweden	Estonia	Malta		Kazakhstan	Turkey
Greece	United Kingdom	Hungary			Kosovo	Turkmenistan
Ireland		Latvia			Kyrgyz Republic	Uzbekistan

Note: DCFTA = deep and comprehensive free trade agreement; ECA = Europe and Central Asia; EU = European Union.

BOX S2A.1 Methodology for the Estimation of the Impact of Deep Integration on FDI Flows

Gravity equations are derived from models that seek to explain or predict the relationship between a (dependent) variable (in this case bilateral foreign direct investment [FDI]) and a set of other independent or explanatory variables whose values can be estimated (in this case, elements of deep integration).

Endogeneity occurs when both the variable being explained (the left-hand-side variable in the equation) and the explanatory variable (the right-hand-side variable in the equation) may be determined by a third factor not in the model. For example, firms that want to invest in a country may also lobby for free trade agreements. Consequently, a free trade agreement may not increase FDI, but both FDI and free trade agreements may come about as a result of perceived economic benefits of firms and their political lobbying efforts.

The following structural gravity regression is estimated for a set of 160 countries[a] using Poisson pseudo–maximum likelihood (see Piermartini and Yotov 2016):

$$FDI_{ijt} = exp \{\beta_1 Depth_{ijt} + \delta_{ij} + \delta_{it} + \delta_{jt}\} + \varepsilon_{ijt},$$

in which FDI_{ijt} is a measure of FDI between country i and j at time t. $Depth_{ijt}$ is a measure of the depth of preferential trade agreements. A statistically significant and positive coefficient β_1 implies that signing a deeper agreement is associated with greater FDI. This variable is calculated as the number of enforceable provisions that are included in a certain agreement. The δ_s are a series of fixed effects: i for importer, j for exporter, and t is year from 2003 to 2014. Finally, ε_{ijt} is the error term.

a. See table S2A.5 for the list of countries that are included in the regression.

TABLE S2A.2 Percentage of ECA PTAs Including WTO Provisions, by Subgroup

	EU15	EU13	DCFTA	Other ECA
Number of agreements	43	43	27	70
FTA Industrial	100	100	100	99
FTA Agriculture	100	100	100	99
Export Taxes	93	93	100	93
Customs	95	95	59	76
Antidumping	98	98	26	46
State Aid	79	79	37	60
Countervailing Measures	86	86	22	37
Trade-Related Aspects of Intellectual Property Rights	72	72	30	44
State Trading Enterprises	67	67	19	39
Public Procurement	49	49	22	21
Technical Barriers to Trade	40	40	22	34
Sanitary and Phytosanitary	40	40	15	26
General Agreement on Trade in Services	42	42	22	10
Trade-Related Investment Measures	19	19	7	3

Source: Calculations based on World Bank data set on PTA content.
Note: ECA = Europe and Central Asia; FTA = free trade agreement; PTA = preferential trade agreement; WTO = World Trade Organization.

TABLE S2A.3 WTO and WTO+ Policy Areas in PTAs

Areas covered by the WTO	Areas beyond the WTO (WTO+)	
Tariffs. Industrial Goods	Anticorruption	Health
Tariffs: Agricultural Goods	Competition Policy	Human Rights
Customs Administration	Environmental Laws	Illegal Immigration
Export Taxes	Intellectual Property Rights	Illicit Drugs
Sanitary and Phytosanitary Measures	Investment Measures	Industrial Cooperation
State Trading Enterprises	Labor Market Regulation	Information Society
Technical Barriers to Trade Measures	Movement of Capital	Mining
Countervailing Measures	Consumer Protection	Money Laundering
Antidumping	Data Protection	Nuclear Safety
State Aid	Approximation of Legislation	Political Dialogue
Public Procurement	Agriculture	Public Administration
Trade-Related Investment Measures	Audiovisual	Regional Cooperation
General Agreement on Trade in Services	Civil Protection	Research and Technology
Trade-Related Aspects of Intellectual	Innovation Policies	Small and Medium-Sized Enterprises
Property Rights	Cultural Cooperation	Social Matters
	Economic Policy Dialogue	Statistics
	Education and Training	Taxation
	Energy	Terrorism
	Financial Assistance	Visa and Asylum

Source: World Bank data set on PTA content.
Note: PTA = preferential trade agreement; WTO = World Trade Organization.

TABLE S2A.4 Percentage of ECA PTAs Including WTO+ Provisions, by Subgroup

	EU15	EU13	DCFTA (non-EU)	Other ECA (non-EU)
Number of agreements	43	43	27	70
Competition Policy	84	84	93	86
Movement of Capital	63	63	19	21
Intellectual Property Rights	58	58	19	29
Statistics	19	19	48	27
Social Matters	37	37	4	3
Labor Market Regulation	30	30	4	9
Investment	28	28	7	7
Approximation of Legislation	28	28	7	4
Environmental Laws	30	30	4	3
Illegal Immigration	28	28	4	3
Visa and Asylum	26	26	7	1
Cultural Cooperation	28	28	4	0
Financial Assistance	26	26	7	0
Health	26	26	4	0
Energy	21	21	7	3
Industrial Cooperation	23	23	4	1
Education and Training	23	23	4	1
Research and Technology	23	23	4	1
Data Protection	21	21	7	1
Economic Policy Dialogue	23	23	4	0
Agriculture	19	19	4	9

continued

SPOTLIGHT 2 *continued*

TABLE S2A.4 *continued*

Number of agreements	EU15	EU13	DCFTA (non-EU)	Other ECA (non-EU)
	43	43	27	70
Terrorism	21	21	4	1
Consumer Protection	14	14	4	3
Nuclear Safety	14	14	0	0
Regional Cooperation	9	9	4	0
Audiovisual	9	9	4	0
Taxation	7	7	4	3
Mining	7	7	4	0
Anticorruption	5	5	4	0
Civil Protection	5	5	4	0
Public Administration	5	5	4	0
Money Laundering	2	2	4	3
Illicit Drugs	2	2	4	1
Small and Medium-Sized Enterprises	5	5	0	0
Information Society	2	2	4	0
Political Dialogue	2	2	4	0
Innovation Policies	0	0	0	0
Human Rights	0	0	0	0

Source: Calculations based on World Bank data set on PTA content.
Note: ECA = Europe and Central Asia; PTA = preferential trade agreement; WTO = World Trade Organization.

TABLE S2A.5 Countries and Economies Included in the Estimations

Albania	Cambodia	France	Korea, Rep.
Algeria	Cameroon	Gabon	Kuwait
Andorra	Canada	Gambia, The	Kyrgyz Republic
Angola	Chile	Georgia	Lao PDR
Antigua and Barbuda	China	Germany	Latvia
Argentina	Colombia	Ghana	Lebanon
Armenia	Congo, Dem. Rep.	Greece	Libya
Australia	Congo, Rep.	Guatemala	Liechtenstein
Austria	Costa Rica	Guyana	Lithuania
Azerbaijan	Côte d'Ivoire	Haiti	Luxembourg
Bahamas, The	Croatia	Honduras	Macao SAR, China
Bahrain	Cyprus	Hong Kong SAR, China	Macedonia, FYR
Bangladesh	Czech Republic	Hungary	Madagascar
Barbados	Denmark	Iceland	Malawi
Belarus	Djibouti	India	Malaysia
Belgium	Dominican Republic	Indonesia	Mali
Belize	Ecuador	Iraq	Malta
Bolivia	Egypt, Arab Rep.	Ireland	Mauritius
Bosnia and Herzegovina	El Salvador	Israel	Mexico
Botswana	Equatorial Guinea	Italy	Micronesia, Fed. Sts.
Brazil	Eritrea	Jamaica	Moldova
Brunei	Estonia	Japan	Montenegro
Bulgaria	Ethiopia	Jordan	Morocco
Burkina Faso	Fiji	Kazakhstan	Mozambique
Burundi	Finland	Kenya	Myanmar

continued

TABLE S2A.5 *continued*

Namibia	Romania	Sri Lanka	Ukraine
Nepal	Russian Federation	St. Lucia	United Arab Emirates
Netherlands	Rwanda	Sudan	United Kingdom
New Zealand	Samoa	Sweden	United States
Nicaragua	San Marino	Switzerland	Uruguay
Nigeria	Saudi Arabia	Syrian Arab Republic	Uzbekistan
Norway	Senegal	Taiwan, China	Vanuatu
Oman	Serbia	Tajikistan	Venezuela, RB
Pakistan	Seychelles	Tanzania	Vietnam
Panama	Sierra Leone	Thailand	Yemen, Rep.
Papua New Guinea	Singapore	Togo	Zambia
Peru	Slovak Republic	Trinidad and Tobago	Zimbabwe
Philippines	Slovenia	Tunisia	
Poland	Solomon Islands	Turkey	
Portugal	South Africa	Turkmenistan	
Qatar	Spain	Uganda	

Note: All countries in the list are included in the estimations on the impact of deep agreements on foreign direct investment (FDI) flows. The countries in blue are included in the estimation on FDI spillovers.

TABLE S2A.6 **Regression Results: Deep Agreements and Foreign Direct Investment**

	(1)	(2)	(3)	(4)
	Total	Natural resources	Goods	Services
Depth	0.0296***	−0.0183	0.0357***	0.0416***
	(0.00699)	(0.0371)	(0.00956)	(0.00822)
Number of observations	106,635	16,214	57,351	66,020
R^2	0.835	0.784	0.839	0.818

Note: Poisson pseudo–maximum likelihood estimations. All specifications include bilateral fixed effects and country-time fixed effects. Robust standard errors, clustered by country pair, are in parentheses. Significance level: *** = 1 percent.

TABLE S2A.7 **Foreign Direct Investment and Depth: Interactions with ECA**

	(1)
	Total
Depth	0.0314***
	(0.00794)
Depth × ECA receiving	−0.00287
	(0.00522)
Number of observations	85,271
R^2	0.795

Note: Poisson pseudo–maximum likelihood estimations. All specifications include bilateral fixed effects and country-time fixed effects. Robust standard errors, clustered by country pair, are in parentheses. ECA = Europe and Central Asia. Significance level: *** = 1 percent.

SPOTLIGHT 2 *continued*

TABLE S2A.8 Foreign Direct Investment and Depth, by Group of Provisions

	(1)	(2)	(3)
	Total	Goods	Services
WTO	0.0162	0.0490	0.0513
	(0.0242)	(0.0347)	(0.0333)
WTO+	0.0352***	0.0223	0.0357**
	(0.0105)	(0.0149)	(0.0141)
Number of observations	106,635	43,871	50,261
R^2	0.835	0.851	0.849

Note: Poisson pseudo–maximum likelihood estimations. All specifications include bilateral fixed effects and country-time fixed effects. Robust standard errors, clustered by country pair, are in parentheses. WTO = World Trade Organization.
Significance level: ** = 5 percent, *** = 1 percent.

TABLE S2A.9 Foreign Direct Investment and Depth, by Technology Level (OECD Rev. 3)

	(1)	(2)	(3)	(4)	(5)	(6)
	Total goods		Low technology		High technology	
Depth	0.0295***		0.0347***		0.0296**	
	(0.00998)		(0.0126)		(0.0148)	
WTO		0.0490		0.0305		0.025
		(0.0347)		(0.0499)		(0.0464)
WTO+		0.0223		0.0364*		0.022
		(0.0149)		(0.0216)		(0.0185)
Number of observations	43,871	43,871	34,004	34,004	28,674	28,674
R^2	0.851	0.851	0.782	0.782	0.864	0.863

Note: Poisson pseudo–maximum likelihood estimations. All specifications include bilateral fixed effects and country-time fixed effects. Robust standard errors, clustered by country pair, are in parentheses. WTO = World Trade Organization.
Significance level: * = 10 percent, ** = 5 percent, *** = 1 percent.

TABLE S2A.10 Foreign Direct Investment, Depth, and Distance

	(1)	(2)	(3)	(4)	(5)	(6)
	Total	Goods	Services	Total	Goods	Services
Depth	0.0461**	0.0522*	0.0209	0.0419**	−0.00706	0.0844***
	(0.0229)	(0.0305)	(0.0351)	(0.0186)	(0.0210)	(0.0305)
Depth × Geographical	−0.00115	−0.00275	0.00283			
	−0.00312	(0.00389)	(0.00474)			
Depth × Cultural				−0.00201	0.00778*	−0.0111*
				(0.00402)	(0.00447)	(0.00673)
Number of observations	91,881	42,693	49,188	65,567	31,225	34,342
R^2	0.849	0.851	0.850	0.840	0.858	0.818

Note: Poisson pseudo–maximum likelihood estimations. All specifications include bilateral fixed effects, country-time fixed effects, and industry-country-time fixed effects. Robust standard errors, clustered by country pair, are in parentheses.
Significance level: * = 10 percent, ** = 5 percent, *** = 1 percent.

TABLE S2A.11 Foreign Direct Investment and Depth: Triple Interactions

Variables	(1) Investment	(2) Investment	(3) Investment	(4) Investment
Depth	0.0363***	0.0254***	0.0361***	0.0253***
	(0.00935)	(0.00835)	(0.00940)	(0.00834)
Depth × ECA destination	−0.0109			
	(0.00857)			
Depth × EU15 source	0.0217	−0.0214*	0.0221	−0.0214*
	(0.0169)	(0.0121)	(0.0169)	(0.0121)
Depth × EU15 source × ECA destination	−0.0431**			
	(0.0197)			
Depth × non-ECA destination		0.0109		0.0106
		(0.00857)		(0.00863)
Depth × EU15 source × non-ECA destination		0.0431**		0.0432**
		(0.0197)		(0.0197)
Depth × EU28 destination			−0.0104	
			(0.00859)	
Depth × EU15 source × EU28 destination			−0.0439**	
			(0.0196)	
Depth × ECA non-EU destination				−0.0155
				(0.0336)
Depth × EU15 source × ECA non-EU destination				0.154
				(0.116)
Number of observations	65,118	65,118	65,118	65,118
R^2	0.813	0.813	0.813	0.813

Note: Poisson pseudo–maximum likelihood estimations. All specifications include bilateral fixed effects, country-time fixed effects, and industry-country-time fixed effects. Robust standard errors, clustered by country pair, are in parentheses. ECA = Europe and Central Asia; EU = European Union.
Significance level: * = 10 percent, ** = 5 percent, *** = 1 percent.

of the WTO. Table S2A.3 lists the 51 policy areas that are identified.

The legal enforceability of the PTA obligations is established according to the language used in the text of the agreements. In other words, it is assumed that commitments expressed with clear, specific, and imperative legal language can more successfully be invoked by a complainant in a dispute settlement proceeding, and therefore are more likely to be legally enforceable. In contrast, unclear legal language might be related to policy areas that are covered but that might not be legally enforceable.

Notes

1. This spotlight draws on Laget, Rocha, and Varela (2018).
2. For simplicity, the variable depth that is used in this analysis considers that all the provisions included in an agreement have the same weight, and therefore are equally important for FDI. Analysis not presented in this spotlight and that uses alternative measures to capture the depth of an agreement (e.g., depth constructed using principal component analysis) also confirms a positive relationship between deeper agreements and FDI flows (Osnago, Rocha, and Ruta 2015a, 2015b).

SPOTLIGHT 2 *continued*

3. These results are in line with the results from Osnago, Rocha, and Ruta (2015a, 2015b) showing that an additional provision in deep PTAs increases vertical FDI flows by approximately 2 percent.

4. The existence of a differential effect is tested by augmenting the cross-country gravity equation with an interaction of depth with a dummy that identifies observations for ECA countries as destinations of FDI flows. ECA countries and subgroup definitions can be found in table S2A.1.

5. Adding one extra provision in an agreement is associated with increases in FDI flows of low- and high-intensity products of approximately 3.5 and 3 percent, respectively. Only the WTO+ provisions, and not the WTO provisions, are significant for sectors with lower levels of technological intensity (see table S2A.9). The classification of sectors by technology intensity is taken from the OECD Rev.3 classification. This classification is only available for the manufacturing sector.

6. The interaction between physical distance and depth is not significant, suggesting that the impact of deep agreements is the same in distant countries as in non-distant ones (see annex S2A).

References

Driffield, Nigel, James Love, and Yong Yang. 2016. "Reverse International Knowledge Transfer in the MNE: (Where) Does Affiliate Performance Boost Parent Performance?" *Research Policy* 45 (2): 491–506.

Gomez-Mera, L., T. Kenyon, J. G. Reis, and G. Varela. 2014. *New Voices in Investment: A Survey of Investors from Emerging Economies.* Washington, DC: World Bank Group.

Hofmann, Claudia, Alberto Osnago, and Michele Ruta. 2017. "Horizontal Depth: A New Database on the Content of Preferential Trade Agreements." Policy Research Working Paper 65837, World Bank, Washington, DC.

Hofstede, Geert. 2011. "Dimensionalizing Cultures: The Hofstede Model in Context." *Online Readings in Psychology and Culture* 2 (1):1–26.

Horn, H., P. C. Mavroidis, and A. Sapir. 2010. "Beyond the WTO? An Anatomy of EU and US Preferential Trade Agreements." *World Economy* 33 (11): 1565–88.

Laget, E., N. Rocha, and G. Varela. 2018. "FDI and Deep Preferential Trade Agreements: An Empirical Investigation." Unpublished, World Bank, Washington, DC.

Osnago, Alberto, Nadia Rocha, and Michele Ruta. 2015a. "Deep Trade Agreements and Vertical FDI: The Devil Is in the Details." Policy Research Working Paper 7464, World Bank, Washington, DC.

———. 2015b. "Do Deep Trade Agreements Boost Vertical FDI?" *World Bank Economic Review* 30 (1): 119–25.

Piermartini, Roberta, and Yoto Yotov. 2016. "Estimating Trade Policy Effects with Structural Gravity." School of Economics Working Paper Series 2016-10, LeBow College of Business, Drexel University, Philadelphia.

WTO (World Trade Organization). 2011. *The WTO and Preferential Trade Agreements: From Coexistence to Coherence.* Geneva: WTO.

3

Connectivity and Firms

Ownership and management links with foreign firms enable domestic firms to perform better than firms lacking such connections. This chapter first examines the prevalence of firm connectivity in Europe and Central Asia (ECA) through ownership or management ties, and then discusses why these connections are important. Then evidence of the spillover benefits of foreign firms on local firms is reviewed, followed by a discussion of policy recommendations.

Main Messages

- Many firms in ECA have foreign connections, although the extent of foreign ownership varies greatly across the region. More than half of foreign-owned firms in ECA also have a predominantly foreign management. Firms that are foreign owned and foreign managed have higher growth in operating revenues, jobs, and average wages than firms lacking these connections, due to technology transfers and better management practices. Employment in foreign-connected firms is less procyclical, likely because of access to finance and resources from the parent firm economy.
- Domestic firms without foreign connections also benefit from the presence of foreign-owned firms. Competition from connected firms can force domestic firms to become more efficient, although competition from better-performing

foreign-connected firms also may force domestic firms to downsize or leave the market. In ECA, small and young domestic firms are particularly at risk.

- Governments can implement policies to boost the positive effects of connectivity while minimizing the risks:
  - General improvements to the business environment
  - Removing barriers to foreign direct investment (FDI) and carrying out investment-promotion activities to reduce information asymmetries and burdensome regulatory procedures
  - Promotion of skilled migration
  - Efforts to strengthen firm linkages (for example, to encourage innovation transfers between domestic and foreign firms)
  - Steps to help domestic firms compete (e.g., improved access to finance for small and young firms, educational programs to help strengthen local management, and the easing of labor market regulations that restrict the ability of firms to manage workers efficiently)
  - Efforts to smooth workers' adjustment to unemployment (e.g., facilitating geographic mobility, improving education and training, and providing social insurance in ways that do not distort labor market decisions).

Firm Connectivity in ECA

Characteristics of Firm Connectivity in ECA

There is a high incidence of connections between firms in ECA and foreign owners, especially among larger firms. This section analyzes the extent of foreign ownership in ECA (a discussion of overall trends in FDI in ECA countries from a macro perspective can be found in spotlight 1). We exclude firms owned by individuals or companies located in countries considered to be tax havens, as the country of ownership may be a result of tax incentives and regime and not actually capture the economic impacts typically associated with FDI. In addition, firms that are owned by tax haven countries may not truly represent the characteristics of their source country as the parent company may be located in the tax haven country for tax purposes but the operational headquarters, where management decisions are made, are in a third country. Annex 3A presents the coverage of the firm-level data used in the descriptive statistics and analysis throughout this chapter.

Many firms in ECA are owned by foreigners (see figure 3.1). At one extreme, more than 32 percent of all firms in the United Kingdom and Ireland are owned by people or firms in another country. Foreign ownership is also present in other ECA countries to a lesser extent. On average, about 5 percent or more of firms in most of Central Europe, the Western Balkans, Latvia, and Lithuania are foreign owned. At the other extreme, foreign ownership is negligible in Hungary, Bulgaria, Ukraine, the Russian Federation, Belgium and most Southern European countries. The shares of foreign ownership exclude firms owned by parent companies located in tax havens, which is discussed below. A restrictive FDI regime may explain the low presence of foreign companies in some of these economies, such as Ukraine,

FIGURE 3.1 **The presence of foreign firms varies substantially across ECA countries**
Foreign-owned and foreign-managed firms in ECA, 2013

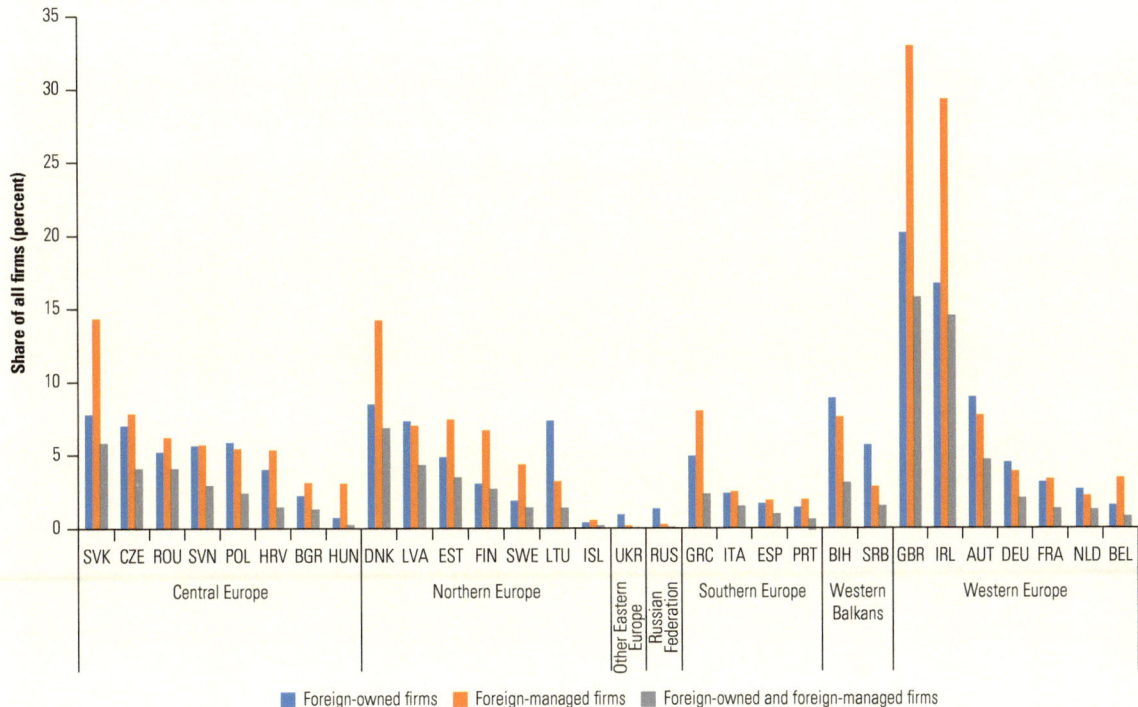

Source: Calculations using Orbis data.
Note: Sample excludes firms with owners in tax haven countries. ECA = Europe and Central Asia.

Belgium, and Italy, which rank poorly in the Services Trade Restrictiveness Index (Borchert, Gootiiz, and Mattoo 2012).

Some of the efficiency effects of foreign companies take place through the transfer of soft technologies, such as management skills, since their capital investment is often accompanied by the hiring of foreign managers (Djankov and Hoekman 2000; Blalock and Gertler 2008). In ECA, hard and soft investments from abroad are highly correlated, as countries with a higher share of foreign-owned firms also tend to have a high share of foreign managers. Indeed, a significant share of the foreign-owned firms in ECA are also managed by foreigners. On average, more than half of foreign companies in ECA also have foreign managers.

Large firms in ECA are more likely than their smaller peers to be foreign owned. As seen in figure 3.2, while at least 15 percent of firms with 250 employees or more are foreign owned in Central, Northern, Southern, and Western Europe, that figure is less than 4 percent for small firms. While the extent of foreign ownership differs across the region, the ratios of the shares of small and large foreign firms are similar: for every firm in the country there are three times more large foreign firms than small ones. As discussed in the following sections, these patterns could be partially explained by foreign-owned firms exhibiting higher growth than those with domestic owners. However, it may also reflect the fact that foreign investors are more likely to invest in firms that have achieved a large enough size.

FIGURE 3.2 Large firms are more likely to be foreign owned in ECA
Share of foreign-owned firms by number of employees, 2013

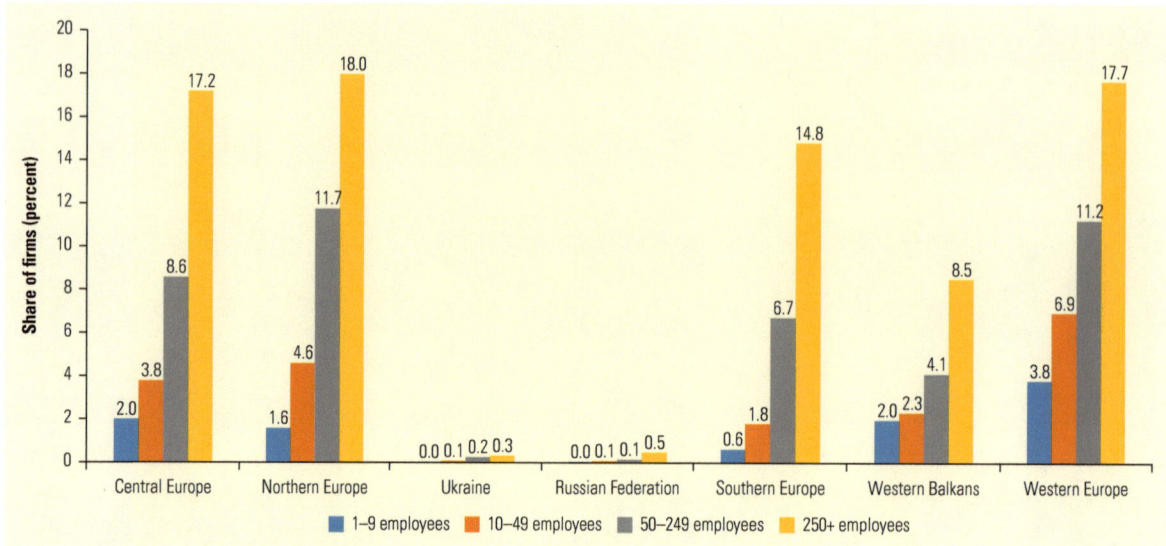

Source: Calculations using Orbis data.
Note: Sample excludes firms with owners in tax haven countries. ECA = Europe and Central Asia.

In most subregions, older firms are not significantly more likely than younger ones to be foreign owned (figure 3.3). For instance, old and young firms in Central Europe, Ukraine, and the Western Balkans are equally likely to be foreign owned. This is an interesting finding considering that firms age 30 years or older in 2013 were founded before the transition among the former socialist economies. In contrast, older firms in Northern, Western, and Southern Europe as well as Russia are slightly more likely to be foreign owned than their younger peers. This may indicate that for this group of countries, FDI tends to be attracted by firms with a longer presence in the market, or that foreign firms are more likely to survive. The comparison between the age of foreign-owned firms in former socialist economies suggests that there are fewer entry barriers to foreign startups in the Western Balkans and Central Europe. In these countries, there are equal shares of young and old foreign-owned firms compared with Russia, where foreign-owned firms are older.

Most foreign owners of firms in ECA are persons or companies in Germany and the United States (see table 3.1). Given the size of these two economies and their level of economic development, it is expected that both countries would have a strong presence in the arena of multinational companies. However, in addition to the characteristics of the investor country, other factors such as geographic proximity, common language, and cultural heritage seem to be important determinants of owning a company in another nation. This is consistent, for example, with Nordic countries being among the most common foreign owners of companies in Northern Europe; or with Croatia and Slovenia being among the most common owners of foreign companies in the Western Balkans.

FIGURE 3.3 There is no clear relationship between a firm's age and the likelihood of its being foreign owned

Share of foreign-owned firms by age of firm, 2013

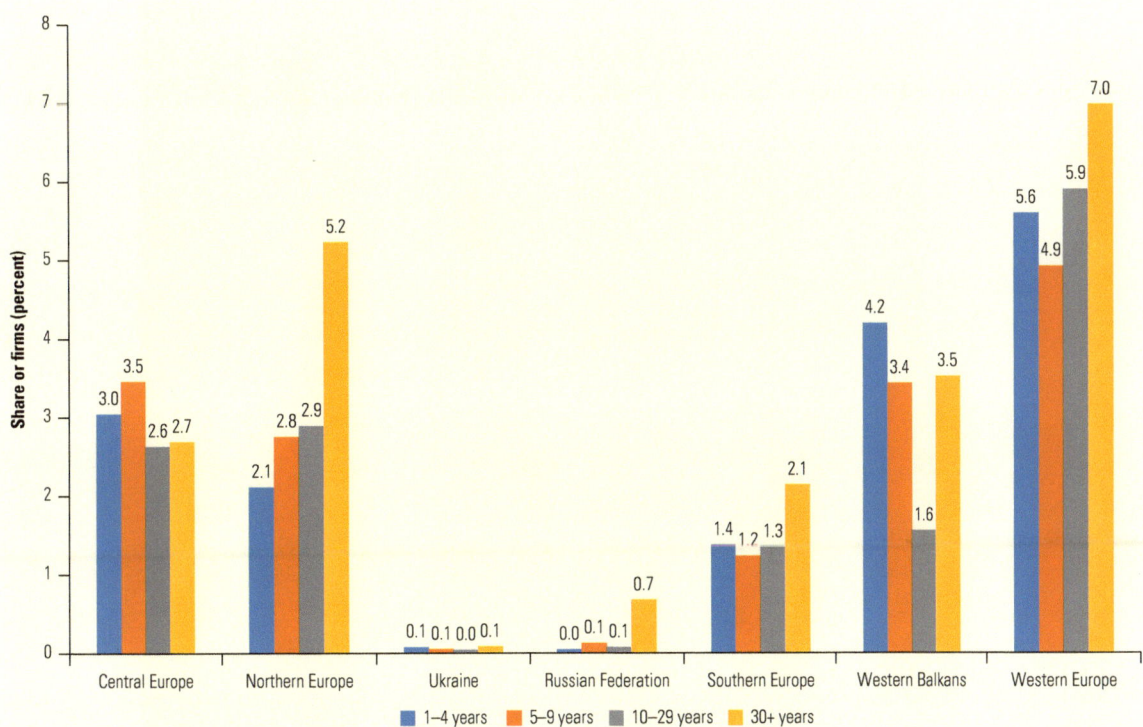

Source: Calculations using Orbis data.
Note: Sample excludes firms with owners in tax haven countries.

Determinants of Firm Connectivity in ECA

We shed light on the drivers of foreign ownership by estimating a gravity model that examines the bilateral relationships between the source country, which owns the foreign affiliates or sends foreign managers, and the host country, where the foreign affiliate is located. The share of foreign ownership and management are measured in three ways: (a) the number of foreign affiliates owned by the source country and the number of firms primarily managed by foreigners from the source country as a share of all firms; (b) the sales of; and (c) the operating revenue of the foreign affiliate owned by and companies primarily managed by the source country as a share of all firms.[1] Foreign ownership and management are likely to be driven by the usual patterns observed in FDI and international trade flows. Table 3.2 explores how foreign ownership and management are determined by linkages between the source and host country through a shared cultural and historical heritage, political relationships or union, and geographic proximity or shared borders.[2]

Geographic and economic linkages, and to a lesser extent historical and cultural linkages, are important determinants of foreign ownership and management.

TABLE 3.1 Most Foreign-Owned Firms in ECA Are Owned by Germany and the United States

Region	Most common global ultimate owner									Others (from left to right, top to bottom): Denmark, Norway, Russian Federation, Belgium, Croatia, Slovenia, and Japan
	Germany	United States	United Kingdom	Netherlands	Austria	France	Finland	Italy	Sweden	
Central Europe	🇩🇪	🇺🇸			Austria					Norway
Northern Europe	🇩🇪	🇺🇸	🇬🇧				Finland		Sweden	Denmark
Ukraine	🇩🇪	🇺🇸	🇬🇧		Austria					Russian Federation
Russian Federation	🇩🇪	🇺🇸	🇬🇧	Netherlands			Finland			
Southern Europe	🇩🇪	🇺🇸	🇬🇧	Netherlands		France				Belgium
Western Balkans	🇩🇪	🇺🇸	🇬🇧	Netherlands	Austria	France		Italy		Croatia
Western Europe	🇩🇪	🇺🇸		Netherlands		France		Italy	Sweden	Slovenia, Japan

Source: Calculations using Orbis data.

Note: Sample excludes firms with owners in tax haven countries. Each row in the table shows the five (or more, if there is a tie) most common countries of ownership, among the top ten countries of ownership, for each country or region at left. For the Russian Federation and Ukraine, the rows show the five countries with the largest ownership shares. ECA = Europe and Central Asia.

TABLE 3.2 Determinants of Foreign Ownership and Management

	Log (Foreign firms, simple count)	Log (Foreign firms, sales)	Log (Foreign firms, operating revenue)	Log (Foreign manager, simple count)	Log (Foreign manager, sales)	Log (Foreign manager, operating revenue)
Log (Distance)	−0.369***	−0.766**	−0.717**	−0.505***	−1.689***	−1.483***
	(0.0771)	(0.307)	(0.291)	(0.0732)	(0.327)	(0.303)
Log (Immigrants)	0.105***	0.188***	0.165***	0.147***	0.132**	0.0990**
	(0.0120)	(0.0557)	(0.0457)	(0.0116)	(0.0574)	(0.0483)
= 1 if countries were or are same country	0.536***	0.749	1.425**	0.429***	0.580	1.173*
	(0.180)	(0.652)	(0.669)	(0.165)	(0.689)	(0.673)
= 1 if contiguous	0.416***	0.699	0.543	0.413***	0.240	0.589
	(0.121)	(0.473)	(0.451)	(0.113)	(0.501)	(0.464)
= 1 if common language	0.243**	0.367	0.0269	0.580***	2.404***	2.169***
	(0.115)	(0.523)	(0.432)	(0.111)	(0.580)	(0.463)
Log (Exports)	0.271***	0.597***	0.680***	0.228***	0.683***	0.694***
	(0.0291)	(0.130)	(0.110)	(0.0283)	(0.135)	(0.119)
Log (Imports)	0.0969***	0.293***	0.168*	0.112***	0.151	0.145*
	(0.0225)	(0.0914)	(0.0869)	(0.0206)	(0.0926)	(0.0873)
Tax haven	2.994***	2.504	10.93**	0.356	2.402	1.106
	(1.128)	(3.659)	(4.816)	(0.667)	(3.563)	(2.681)
Number of observations	1,747	1,362	1,637	1,880	1,457	1,748
R^2	0.853	0.730	0.716	0.831	0.737	0.727

Note: The regressions are ordinary least squares regressions using 2013 data and including source and host country fixed effects. Robust standard errors are in parentheses.
Significance level: * = 10 percent, ** = 5 percent, *** = 1 percent.

Geographically proximate countries and countries that share borders are more likely to have higher shares of foreign affiliates and foreign managers. A 10 percent decrease in the bilateral distance between source and host country is correlated with a 3.7 percent increase in the share of foreign affiliates and a 5.1 percent increase in the share of foreign managers in the host country. Economic linkages matter too: when the host country exports more to and imports more from the source country, the share of foreign ownership and management from the source country is higher. Similarly, when there are more immigrants from the source country, foreign ownership and management by that country increases. Sharing a common colonial history and language is correlated with a higher share of foreign ownership and management but only in terms of the number of foreign affiliates and not the sales and revenue share of these foreign affiliates. These effects of historical and cultural linkages may be absorbed by including bilateral imports and exports in the econometric model.

Firms in Tax Havens

Some foreign affiliates are owned by persons or companies located in tax havens, which are countries with low tax regimes.[3] Examining the linkages between these foreign affiliates and their ownership may be misleading as the owners are located in the tax haven country but the actual headquarters that has control and gives operational directions may be in another country. The incidence of foreign affiliates with owners in a tax haven country is low in many ECA countries, where fewer than 20 percent of the foreign affiliates have owners in a tax haven country (figure 3.4).

FIGURE 3.4 Foreign affiliates owned by tax haven countries are small and medium sized

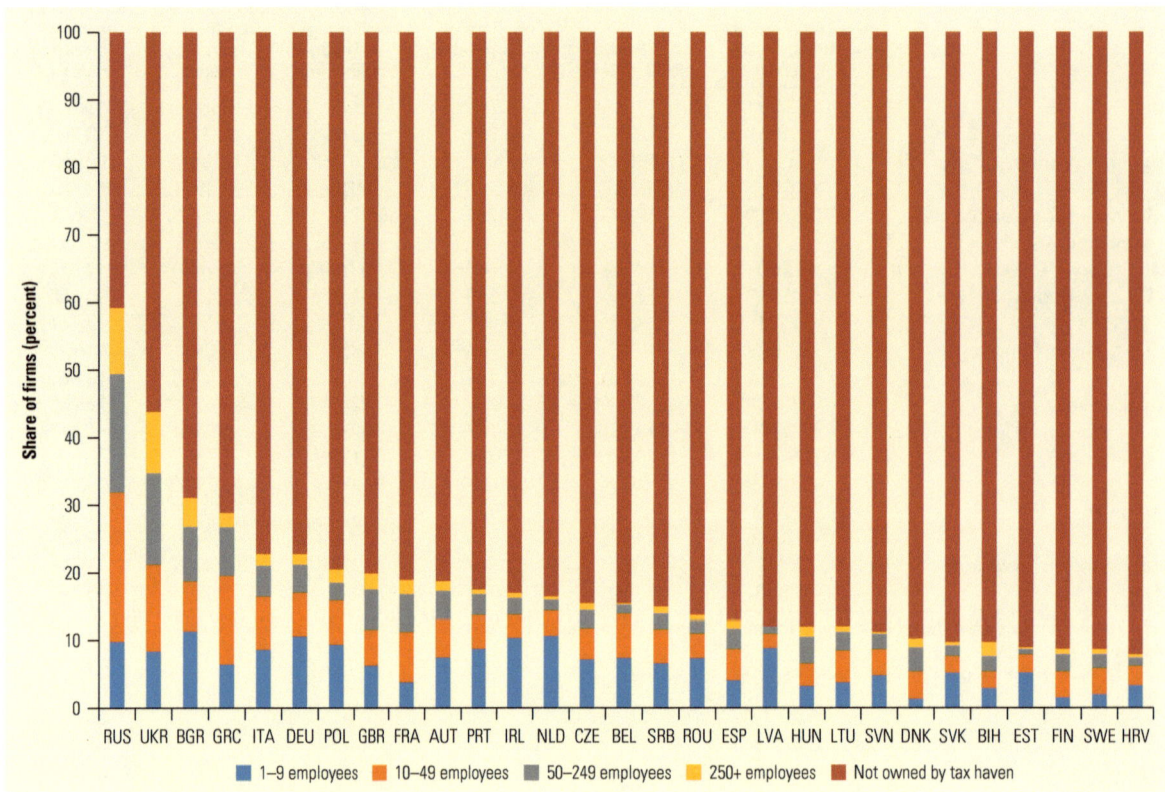

Source: Calculations using Orbis data.
Note: Foreign affiliates are further disaggregated by firm size: micro-sized firms with 1 to 9 employees, small-sized firms with 10 to 49 employees, medium-sized firms with 50 to 249 employees, and large-sized firms with more than 250 employees.

However, two countries stand out: 59 percent of foreign affiliates in Russia and 44 percent in Ukraine are owned by an individual or company located in a tax haven country. One important detail is that many foreign affiliates with owners in a tax haven country are micro- and small-sized with fewer than 50 employees, suggesting that these foreign affiliates may not benefit as much from their foreign connections. Profits and assets in these foreign companies may be transferred to the parent companies located in the tax haven to take advantage of the low tax rate. As a result, these firms remain small as they are not retaining their profits for investment to expand their operations.

Importance of Firm Connectivity

FDI and Transfer of Technology

Multinational enterprises (MNEs) bring technology and know-how that can benefit local firms. The linkages between MNEs and the companies they own in the foreign market, or foreign affiliates, are usually established through direct investments in existing local companies or greenfield investments. These MNEs are often the most productive firms in their domestic market and can transplant intangible inputs, such as know-how and management practices, as well as capital and technology to their foreign affiliates. Atalay, Hortaçsu, and Syverson (2014) show that the vertical ownership structures between US firms and their subsidiaries do not constitute input-output linkages; in fact, there is very little shipment of physical goods from upstream firms to downstream firms. Instead, the ownership structures are in place to transfer intangible inputs efficiently between firms.

MNEs can contribute significantly to ECA countries, and most empirical studies find that foreign-owned firms tend to be larger (Haddad and Harrison 1993) and more productive (Girma, Greenaway, and Wakelin 2001; Conyon et al. 2002; Vahter and Masso 2007)[4] and pay higher wages (Girma, Greenaway, and Wakelin 2001; Lipsey and Sjöholm 2004; Conyon et al. 2002) than their local counterparts. The performance gap between foreign-and domestically-owned firms can be explained by a selection effect,[5] but multinational firms may also benefit from knowledge assets such as technological, managerial, and foreign-market-related knowledge that domestic firms do not have. The existence of such knowledge assets is supported by studies finding that multinational firms invest more in new technologies and training of their employees (Djankov and Hoekman 2000; Görg, Strobl, and Walsh 2007),[6] are better managed (Bloom and Van Reenen 2010), and export more (Aitken, Hanson, and Harrison 1997).

Knowledge transfers to foreign affiliates not only benefit the affiliates but the presence of foreign firms can also benefit domestic firms indirectly through knowledge spillovers. Competition from foreign-owned firms may also induce domestic firms to increase productivity to maintain their market shares. Empirical studies support, to some extent, the suggested positive spillovers from knowledge transfers and competition. Firm- and plant-level studies by Keller and Yeaple (2009) for the United States, Dries and Swinnen (2004) for Poland,[7] and Haskel, Pereira, and Slaughter (2007)[8] for the United Kingdom are examples of the studies that find evidence of productivity spillovers from multinational firms. Keller and Yeaple (2009) argue that the spillovers stem from technological transfers, and Javorcik (2004) likewise shows that contacts between partially foreign-owned firms and their local suppliers in Lithuania facilitate positive productivity spillovers. Moreover, Kokko, Tansini, and Zejan (2001) for Uruguay and Aitken, Hanson, and Harrison (1997) for Mexico find that the presence of foreign firms increases the likelihood that domestic firms will export. These results may suggest that some foreign-market-related knowledge is being transferred to domestic firms. Although the effect from knowledge spillovers is difficult to distinguish from the potential positive effects from foreign competition, a paper by Bao and Chen (2016) presents evidence of the latter. They show that merely the prospect of foreign firms entering the local market induces local firms to be more productive in various countries.

Although these studies provide empirical support of positive spillovers, the overall empirical evidence on spillovers from multinational to domestic firms is ambiguous (Görg and Greenaway 2004). For example, studies by Haddad and Harrison (1993) on Morocco, Aitken and Harrison (1999) on República Bolivariana de Venezuela, Djankov and Hoekman (2000) on the Czech Republic, and Konings (2001) on three Central and Eastern European countries question the findings of positive productivity spillovers. Konings (2001), for instance, uses firm-level data for the mid-1990s and finds evidence of negative productivity spillovers to domestic firms in Bulgaria and Romania and no spillovers in Poland. The same ambiguous picture emerges for wage spillovers. Lipsey and Sjöholm (2001) find evidence of positive wage spillovers in Indonesia; Girma, Greenaway, and Wakelin (2001) find no evidence of wage spillovers in the United Kingdom; and the findings of Aitken, Harrison, and Lipsey (1996) suggest no or negative effects in Mexico and República Bolivariana de Venezuela and positive wage spillovers in the United States.[9] Although the evidence of positive spillovers from multinational to domestic firms is inconclusive, it seems to be stronger in developed countries. If spillovers stem from knowledge transfers, it is plausible that the estimated effect of spillovers is influenced by the absorptive capacity of the domestic firms (Görg and Greenaway 2004). Kokko, Tansini, and Zejan (1996), for instance, examine intra-industry spillovers in Uruguay in 1988 and find positive spillovers only to domestic firms with a moderate technology gap with respect to foreign firms. They interpret their findings as evidence of the importance of the absorptive nature of domestic firms.

The presence of positive knowledge spillovers is supported theoretically and to some extent empirically. However, the findings of nonpositive spillovers may suggest that other opposing effects from multinational firms are in play. The displacement of production, jobs, and tax revenue can be a concern when it comes to FDI, and while increased competition from foreign firms may raise the productivity of some firms, other firms may lose market share or be pushed out of the market (Aitken and Harrison 1999). These crowding-out effects are documented empirically by Kosová (2010), who finds that initial foreign entry in the Czech Republic market increases the exit rates of domestic firms. Accordingly, Aitken and Harrison (1999) find stronger negative productivity spillovers from multinational to small domestic firms in República Bolivariana de Venezuela[10] and suggest that small firms were less able to compete with multinational firms. Aitken, Harrison, and Lipsey (1996) also suggests that the observed negative wage spillovers in República Bolivariana de Venezuela may partly be due to increased competition for workers resulting in foreign firms attracting the best workers. So while foreign firms contribute to a productivity increase for some firms, empirical evidence also suggests that less competitive incumbent firms are at risk of losing market share and being driven out of business. While these negative effects may create some tensions in the short term, they also contribute to the process of creative destruction, where old and traditional sectors shrink and new and more productive ones emerge. As less productive firms exit the market, resources are shifted to more productive incumbents and the foreign entrants. As a result, the aggregate productivity of the country increases. The speed by which factors of production move from the former to the latter is crucial to maximize efficiency gains (Hollweg et al. 2014).

Transfer of Management Practices

One channel by which MNEs can increase the productivity and performance of their foreign affiliates is through the transfer of management practices. Similar to the discussions on information and communication technology (ICT) and the internet, management practices can be thought of as a technology (Bloom et al. 2016) that can be transplanted from headquarters to foreign affiliates. Different quality of management practices from headquarters can account for large differences in the productivity of firms. Heyman, Norback, and Hammarberg (2014) show that about 30 percent of the difference in the labor productivity of foreign firms in Sweden can be explained by variations in management practices at headquarters. The management practices adopted by foreign affiliates can also determine their adoption and use of technology. The US-owned firms in the UK have more ICT capital and higher ICT intensity than domestic firms and firms with owners in other countries (Bloom, Sadun, and Van Reenen 2012). The main reason for the difference in ICT capital stock and intensity of use is that the US-owned firms have management practices that are centered on merit-based promotion, reward, and hiring and firing, which are management practices prevalent in US-owned firms in Europe.

The transmission of management practices between MNEs and their foreign affiliates provides an avenue for countries to improve their aggregate productivity.[11] Studies show that management practices can account for the heterogeneity in total factor productivity (TFP), among firms. Even within narrowly defined sectors, Syverson (2004) estimates that a plant is four times more productive at the 90th percentile than at the 10th percentile of the productivity distribution. Bloom, Sadun, and Van Reenen (2016) find that management practices can account for, on average, 30 percent of the differences in cross-country TFP. Better management practices are also beneficial to workers: using employer-employee-linked data, Bender et al. (2016) show that better-managed German firms pay higher wages. Understanding the determinants of firm productivity is key to promoting economic growth and reducing income inequality between countries.

> The transmission of management practices between MNEs and their foreign affiliates provides an avenue for countries to improve their aggregate productivity.

Examining how management practices affect firm performance and productivity requires some measure of management practices. The measurement of management practices, especially across a large set of countries, is still a nascent area of research. Bloom, Sadun, and Van Reenen (2016) have created a data set of management practices—the World Management Survey (WMS)—by surveying companies in operations management, performance monitoring and talent management, and target setting and leadership management. The WMS contains the most comprehensive measures of management practices. Because it is a resource-intensive task, the data set is currently available for only 34 countries and it does not cover all the countries of foreign owners and managers in the Orbis database.

A proxy for management practices can be created from the World Economic Forum (WEF) Global Competitiveness survey, which measures the quality of national business schools and the reliance on professional management. A management index is calculated from the average scores of the two measures, or Average Management Index (AMI). There is a strong positive correlation between the WMS and the AMI, which is presented in figure 3.5.[12] Unlike the WMS, which has the management scores of individual firms, the AMI is available at the country level and is used in this chapter as a proxy for the management quality of the average owner and manager from that country.

Foreign affiliates tend to be from countries that have better management practices than the host country. The average AMI of the foreign affiliates is higher

FIGURE 3.5 The Average Management Index is strongly correlated with the WMS Management Index

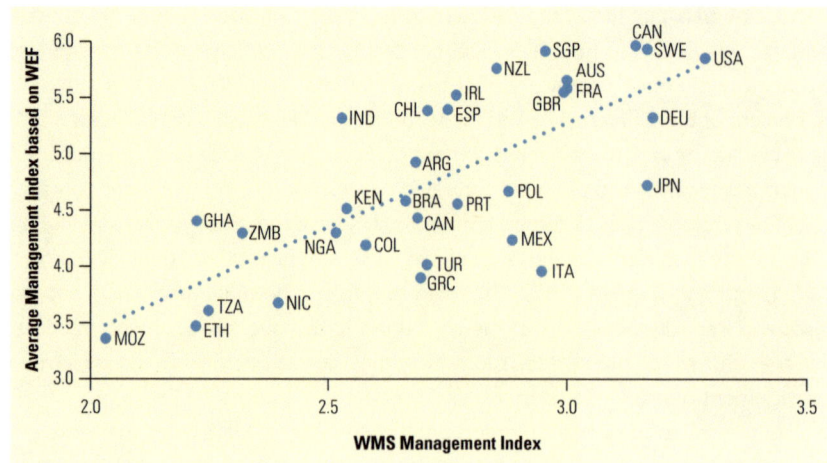

Source: Calculations using data from the World Economic Forum (WEF) Global Competitiveness Survey and the World Management Survey (WMS) (Bloom et al. 2016).

than the AMI of local firms in Bosnia and Herzegovina, Central Europe, and many Southern European countries (figure 3.6). In contrast, the foreign affiliates in Western European and Northern European countries tend to have slightly lower AMI than the local firms. The difference may reflect FDI patterns where Western European firms (such as German, French, and British firms) with better management practices invest in Eastern European countries while American firms with higher AMI invest in Western and Northern Europe. Similar patterns emerge when analyzing the percentage of foreign firms with better AMI than local firms (see figure 3.7). The differences are stark for some ECA countries: almost 100 percent of foreign affiliates in Bosnia and Herzegovina, Bulgaria, Greece, Italy, and Ukraine are owned by companies in countries that have a higher AMI than the local AMI (figure 3.7). In contrast, given the highly rated management practices in Sweden and Denmark, only 4 percent of foreign affiliates in Sweden and 26 percent in Denmark are owned by countries with better AMI.

Transmission of Economic Volatility: Do Foreign Firms Import Volatility in ECA?

Foreign-owned firms may also affect the domestic economy by allowing shocks to be transmitted across countries. On the one hand, if foreign-owned companies are more affected by the unpredictability of international finance or are subject to policy changes from the parent country, they may bring volatility to their country of location. At the same time, by being more connected to the other country, they may be less exposed to local shocks if, for example, they have better access to finance or talent in the parent country or if they rely more on demand from abroad. The extent to which foreign companies attenuate or exacerbate the effect of the volatility of the local economy also depends on the extent to which local shocks are correlated with those experienced by the parent country.

Trade is one channel through which the presence of multinational firms may affect the host economy. While FDI and exports can be alternative ways to enter

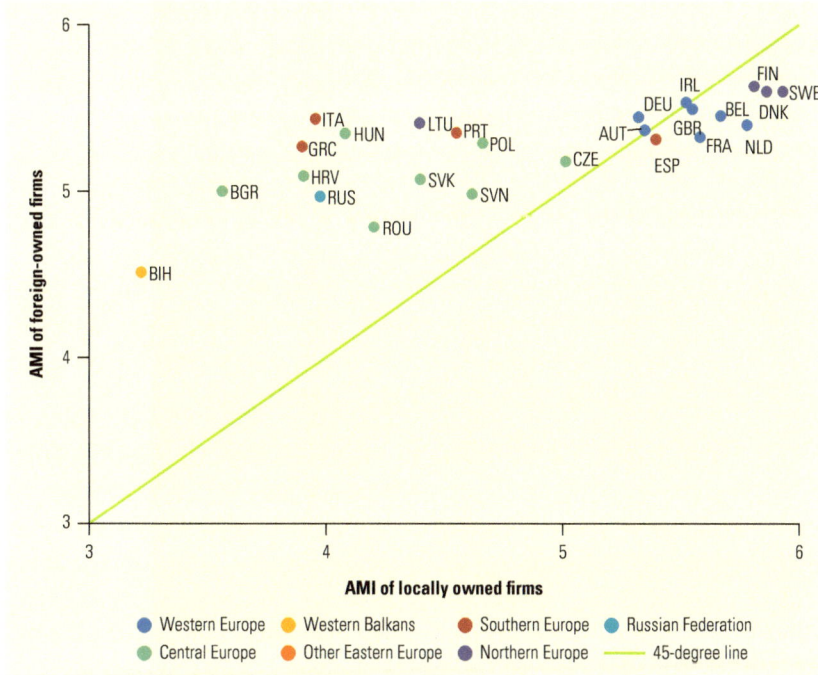

FIGURE 3.6 Foreign affiliates tend to have better management practices than local firms

Source: Calculations using data from the World Economic Forum Global Competitiveness Survey and Orbis.
Note: AMI = Average Management Index (see chapter text for construction).

FIGURE 3.7 More foreign affiliates are owned by countries with better management indexes

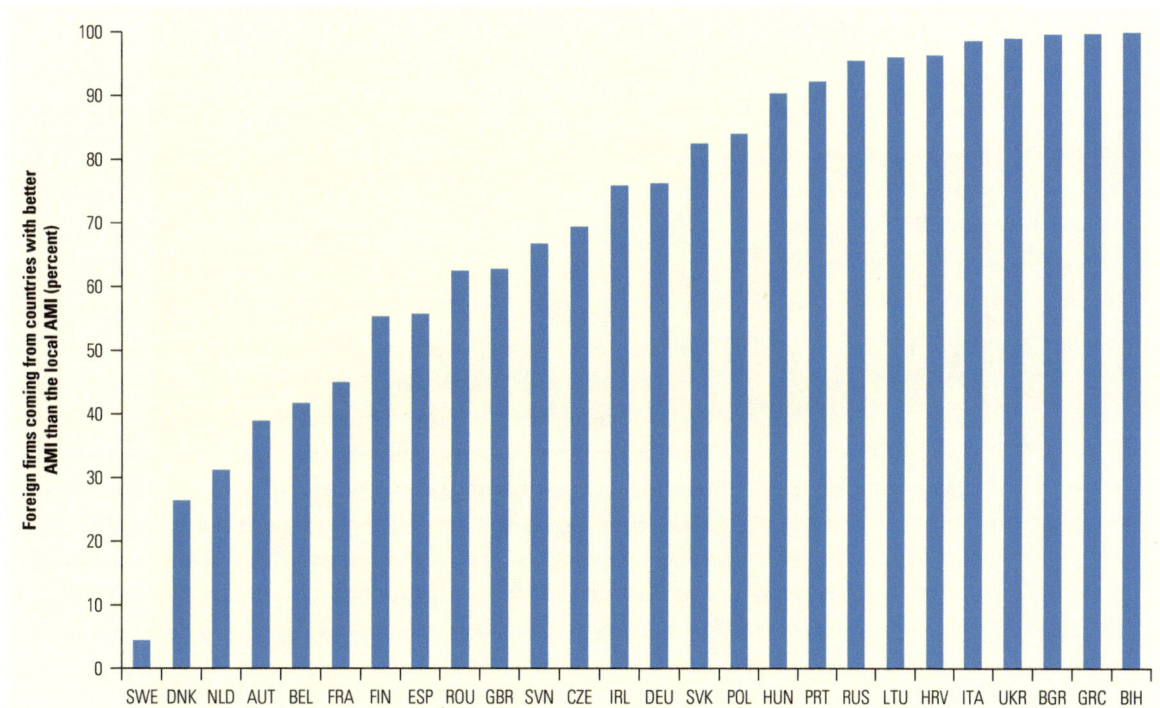

Source: Calculations using data from the World Economic Forum Global Competitiveness Survey, the World Management Survey (Bloom et al. 2016b), and Orbis.
Note: AMI = Average Management Index (see chapter text for construction).

a market, FDI can also spur imports if foreign affiliates tend to import intermediate goods from their country of origin. Most empirical work finds a positive relationship between exports and FDI (Blomström, Lipsey and Kulchycky 1988;[13] Clausing 2000; Head and Ries 2001), and studies suggest that this relationship is partly driven by increased demand for intermediate goods from the country of origin (Lipsey and Weiss 1984; Head and Ries 2001). The possible increase in trade induced by multinational firms may, as mentioned, raise concerns about the volatility of the connected economies, and empirical evidence suggests that countries connected through trade and FDI are indeed more exposed to demand and supply shocks of their partnering countries. For example, an early study by Frankel and Rose (1998) examining a panel of 20 industrial countries shows that bilateral trade intensity is strongly associated with correlated business cycles. Kleinert, Martin, and Toubal (2015) examine the prevalence of comovements of gross domestic product (GDP) growth in France and connected countries. They find that the regional share of foreign affiliates' employment is associated with significantly stronger comovements in regional GDP growth and GDP growth of the ownership country. Using the Orbis database Cravino and Levchenko (2016) likewise show that there is strong comovement in sales growth of the headquarters and sales growth of the affiliate. They also find that shocks in the source country are transmitted to the host country and estimate that the combined shock of all multinationals accounts for 10 percent of the aggregate productivity shock. Another recent study by Boehm, Flaaen, and Pandalai-Nayar (2016) finds that international production networks of multinational firms affect aggregate volatility of an economy. More specifically they show that multinational firms and affiliates in Japan transmitted the shock of the 2011 Tohoku earthquake to their US parent firms because of low short-run input substitution of multinational firms. Other studies also suggest that rent sharing between parent and affiliate firms takes place. Budd, Konings, and Slaughter (2005), for instance, show that affiliate wages of multinationals respond to both parent and affiliate profitability and that parent firms' profit may explain more than 20 percent of observed variation in affiliate wages. In summary, the empirical evidence seems to be in favor of bilateral firm connections imposing an increased exposure to supply and demand shocks of the partnering countries.

The volatility of the domestic economy and labor market may also be affected by the potential footloose nature of multinational firms.

The volatility of the domestic economy and labor market may also be affected by the potential footloose nature of multinational firms. Navaretti, Checchi, and Turrini (2003) examine employment adjustments of firms in 11 Northern and Western European countries and find that multinational affiliates adjust employment significantly faster to shocks than do their domestic counterparts. However, they also find that the extent of the adjustment is more limited and that for a given wage increase, multinational affiliates decrease employment by less than domestic firms. Buch and Lipponer (2010) find that multinational affiliates in Germany do not adjust employment systematically more in response to wages and output than do domestic firms.

Table 3B.4 shows how sales, employment, and average wages of firms in ECA respond to local and foreign business cycles. Interestingly, once a number of variables are controlled for, the performance of an average firm in ECA is not

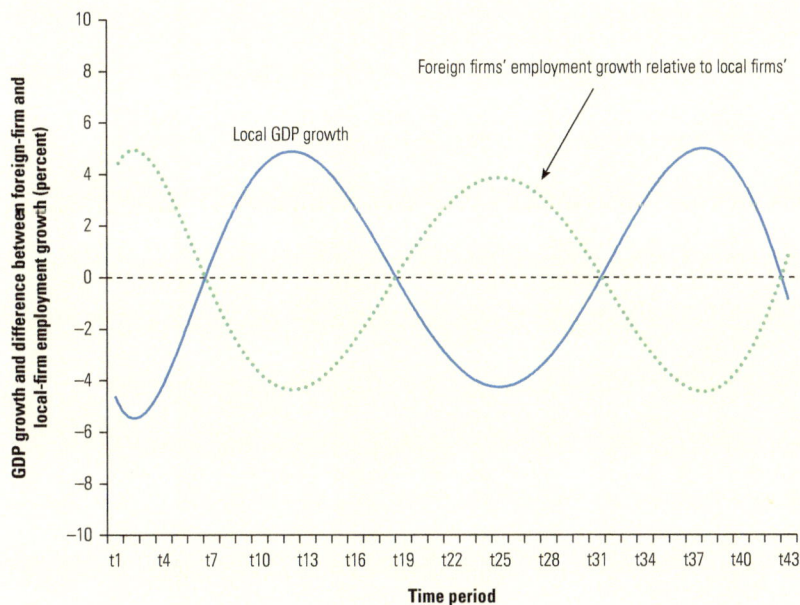

FIGURE 3.8 Foreign firms' employment decisions are less procyclical than those of their domestic peers

Note: See table 3B.4 for full regression results.

significantly correlated with local economic growth. In contrast, foreign firms are much more responsive to aggregate economic conditions. As seen in the second column of the table, foreign firms create more jobs when the foreign country of ownership is growing. This could reflect increasing demand for exports or better access to finance during an economic upswing in the parent country. In contrast, foreign companies' employment decisions seem to be more countercyclical with respect to the domestic economy than those of domestic companies, as the former tend to create fewer jobs when the local economy expands (see figure 3.8). Likewise, this also means that foreign companies tend to destroy fewer jobs than do domestic firms when the domestic economy experiences a recession, possibly reflecting access to external factors that allow them to buffer the impact of the decline in local economic activity. In other words, while foreign firms in ECA seem to contribute less to job creation than their local counterparts when the local economy is growing, they seem to bring more stability to the labor market during a downturn in economic activity because they lay off workers to a lesser extent than local companies do.

Effects of Foreign Firms on Local Economy

Performance of Foreign Firms Versus Local Firms

If MNEs transplant their management practices to foreign affiliates, the better management practices will enable foreign affiliates to perform better than local firms. Figure 3.9 explores whether foreign-owned and foreign-managed firms perform better than local firms. The figure depicts the estimation results that are presented in table 3B.1 and the estimation distinguishes between the combinations of foreign ownership and foreign management. Firms included in

FIGURE 3.9 Foreign-owned and -managed firms perform better than local firms

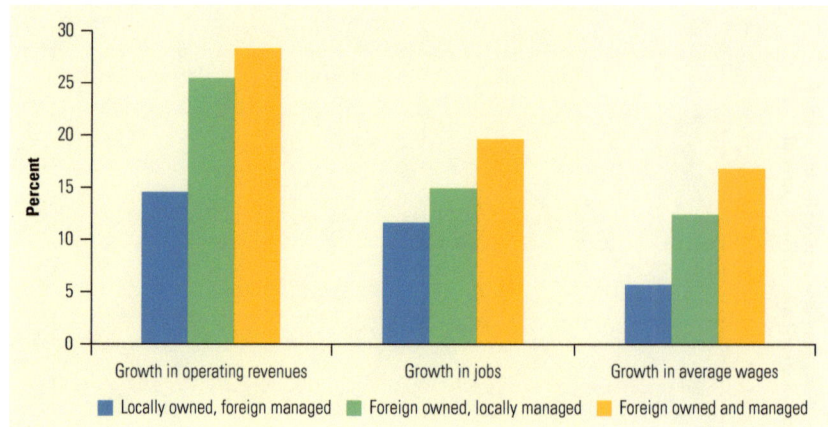

Note: Each bar in the figure represents the difference in growth (of the type labeled) between the type of firm depicted in that bar and that of firms that are both locally managed and locally owned. Table 3B.1 presents full regression results. All underlying coefficients are statistically significant.

the estimation can be firms owned and managed by a local firm or person, foreign affiliates managed by a local national, a local firm managed by a foreigner, and a foreign affiliate managed by a foreigner. The estimation examines the different performance of firms owned, managed, or both owned and managed by foreigners and does not consider the different quality of management practices.

Compared with local firms, foreign affiliates perform better and the benefits of foreign ownership are present even with local management. Foreign affiliates with local managers have 25.5 percent higher growth in operating revenue, 14.9 percent higher job growth, and 12.4 percent higher growth in wages over the 2010–13 period. Foreign managers have a smaller but still positive effect on firm performance. Importantly, it is the combination of being foreign owned and having a foreign manager that has the largest effect on firm performance. These firms have 28.3 percent higher growth in operating revenue, 19.6 percent higher job growth, and 16.8 percent higher wage growth than local firms.

The performance of foreign firms is heterogeneous and can depend on the quality of management practices that are transmitted from headquarters. Table 3.3 examines how better management practices affect the growth of operating revenue, jobs, and average wages. The econometric model examines how firm performance is affected by the quality of management practices controlling for factors in the parent country that can affect firm performance through more exports (per capita income and population), better financial access (market capitalization), and cultural links (immigrant stock). Factors in the source country that may affect firm performance such as governance and the business environment are captured by country fixed effects.

Foreign affiliates that are owned by countries with better management practices perform better than other foreign affiliates, even after controlling for income levels, financial development, population, and immigrant stock in the source country. Source countries that are classified as tax havens may not

TABLE 3.3 Better-Managed Foreign Affiliates Perform Better

	Log (Operating revenue), change, 2010–13	Log (Number of employees), change, 2010–13	Log (Average wage), change, 2010–13
Log management index	0.232***	0.121***	0.0242
	(0.0473)	(0.0441)	(0.0307)
Log GDP per capita	0.0573***	0.0452***	0.00458
	(0.0169)	(0.00865)	(0.00455)
Log market capitalization of GDP	−0.0243**	−0.00713	−0.00375
	(0.0110)	(0.00732)	(0.00485)
Log population	0.0108**	0.0132***	0.00669***
	(0.00541)	(0.00338)	(0.00165)
Log immigrant stock	−0.00476	−0.00414**	−0.00282
	(0.00311)	(0.00204)	(0.00189)
Number of observations	92,320	114,837	74,858
R^2	0.055	0.114	0.067

Note: The estimation is restricted to foreign affiliates. The independent variables in the regression capture the characteristics of the country of ownership. The regression includes the initial values of the dependent variables to account for mean reversion, and country, sector, size, and age fixed effects. The sector is equivalent to the 1-digit NACE rev. 2 code. Age is grouped into intervals of 0–4 years, 5–14 years, 15–30 years, and 30+ years, and size is grouped into intervals of 1–2 employees, 3–7 employees, 8–49 employees, 50–249 employees, and 250+ employees. Robust standard errors (in parentheses) are clustered around country of ownership.
Significance level: ** = 5 percent, *** = 1 percent.

transplant their management practices to the foreign affiliates so the relationship between management practices and firm performance for these firms may not hold. Excluding these firms from the estimation does not change the relationships, and indeed the effects of better management practices on firm performance are slightly stronger.

Better management practices in the source country are related to better firm performance. A higher AMI in the source country is correlated with higher growth of operating revenue and number of employees between 2010 and 2013. This reinforces the findings in Bloom, Sadun, and Van Reenen (2016) that better-managed firms perform better than poorly managed firms. The economic size of the source country, measured by income levels and population size, is also positively related to growth in operating revenue and number of employees. While information about firms' export activities is not available, it is likely that foreign affiliates will export to their source country so it is not surprising that foreign affiliates owned by large countries will perform better. The quality of management practices is, however, not related to growth in average wages in foreign affiliates. While workers in foreign firms generally have higher wage growth, better firm performance from better management practices is not accompanied by higher wage growth. Similar relationships are present between better management practices and firms managed by foreign managers, and the results are presented in annex 3B.

Selection bias makes it difficult to establish a causal relationship between the management advantages of foreign ownership and the performance of foreign affiliates. Foreign companies can choose the most productive region and sector in a country for greenfield investments or the best local firms to directly invest in. As a result, better firm performance may not be a result of foreign owners' management practices.

Indeed, many foreign affiliates are located in regions and sectors with well-functioning local firms that have higher operating revenues and more employees and pay higher wages (table 3.4). More foreign affiliates with better management practices are located in regions with good local firms, but fewer foreign affiliates are located in the well-functioning sectors. Selection bias is a persistent issue in many studies of FDI and it is difficult to resolve (Javorcik 2015). This issue is even more difficult to tackle with the data set used in this section, as foreign ownership and management are recorded only for the latest year. In other words, it is not possible to identify changes in ownership or management for a company over time with the present data.

Spillover Effects of Foreign Firms on Local Firms

The location of foreign affiliates may have spillover effects on local firms. Local firms can learn from foreign affiliates through demonstration effects, where they obtain new information about management practices and knowledge through observation, and labor mobility where local firms hire workers that are trained in foreign affiliates. Evidence of spillovers across industries is mixed but some studies do show positive spillover effects.[14] For example, Haskel, Pereira, and Slaughter (2007) find that there is a positive correlation between the TFP of domestic firms in the UK and the share of foreign firms in the industry. A 10 percentage point increase in foreign presence in the industry raises the TFP of domestic plants by 0.5 percent.

A higher presence of foreign firms with good management practices in ECA could have both displacement effects, driving local firms out of the market, and spillover effects, if increased competitive pressures create incentives for local firms to become more efficient. Disentangling these effects is difficult since, as shown in the previous section, foreign firms do not choose where to locate randomly within ECA, and in fact they are more likely to locate in regions or sectors with firms that

TABLE 3.4 Foreign Firms Locate in Regions and Sectors with Larger Local Firms

	Share of foreign firms in region	AMI of foreign firms in region	Share of foreign firms in sector	AMI of foreign firms in sector
Mean operating revenue of local firms in region	0.00348***	0.0237**		
	(0.000550)	(0.00964)		
Mean number of employees of local firms in region	0.0191***	0.268***		
	(0.00408)	(0.0997)		
Mean average wages of local firms in region	0.00420***	0.0356**		
	(0.00117)	(0.0168)		
Mean operating revenue of local firms in sector			0.00153***	−0.0123
			(0.000575)	(0.0102)
Mean number of employees of local firms in sector			0.0150***	−0.00814
			(0.00327)	(0.0516)
Mean average wages of local firms in sector			0.00144	−5.26E-05
			(0.00152)	(0.0203)
Country fixed effects	Yes	Yes	Yes	Yes
Sector fixed effects			Yes	Yes
Cluster standard errors	Region	Region	Sector	Sector

Note: The estimation is performed between each dependent variable and independent variable separately. For example, the share of foreign firms in a region is regressed on the mean operating revenue of local firms in the region. The sector is equivalent to the 1-digit NACE rev. 2 code. The region is defined at the NUTS-3 level of aggregation, or at a more aggregated level if NUTS-3 is not available. Robust standard errors are in parentheses.
Significance level: ** = 5 percent, *** = 1 percent.

either have higher sales or employment or pay higher wages. In other words, foreign firms may locate in regions with better access to public services or infrastructure or a skilled labor force. Accordingly, foreign investors may choose to own firms in sectors that are growing for reasons such as better relative prices or technological change. Thereby, a positive correlation between a higher presence of foreign firms and domestic firms' performance may capture not only an effect of the former on the latter, but also the impact of a host of other factors.

With these caveats in mind, table 3.5 explores how a higher presence of foreign-owned firms may affect the performance of firms with local owners. The first two rows indicate that domestic firms perform better, in terms of sales growth, in regions and sectors with a higher presence of foreign firms. Accordingly, domestic firms in regions or sectors with a higher fraction of foreign firms experience a higher rate of average wage growth. In contrast, a higher presence of foreign firms in a region is not significantly correlated with higher employment growth of domestic firms. In other words, if these coefficients are biased upward, these results may suggest that while a higher presence of foreign firms in an area may generate some displacement effects (in the sense that domestic firms lay off employees), some domestic firms are able to become more efficient and thereby increase their sales and wages paid.[15]

Not only the presence of foreign firms matters, but also the quality of their management practices. As seen in the third row of table 3.5, domestic firms grow faster in terms of sales, employment, and wages when foreign firms in the region are from countries with better management practices. For instance, domestic firms' sales and employment grow by approximately an additional 3 percentage points in regions where the AMI score of the foreign firms in the region is 6 (a score almost as high as Finland's) instead of 4 (a score slightly lower than Bosnia and Herzegovina's). In contrast, better-managed foreign firms in the same sector seem to be associated with lower wage growth among domestic firms. Since changes in the measure of

TABLE 3.5 Domestic Firms in ECA Grow Faster in Regions with Well-Managed Foreign Firms

	Log(Operating revenue), change, 2010–13	Log(Number of employees), change, 2010–13	Log(Average wage), change, 2010–13
Share of foreign firms in the region	0.500***	0.0405	0.466***
	(0.112)	(0.0593)	(0.0685)
Share of foreign firms in the sector	0.762***	0.271***	0.728***
	(0.181)	(0.100)	(0.180)
AMI score of foreign firms in the region	0.0133***	0.0158***	0.00557**
	(0.00396)	(0.00308)	(0.00233)
AMI score of foreign firms in the sector	0.00263	0.0122	−0.00850*
	(0.00930)	(0.00772)	(0.00499)
Number of observations	2,273,884	2,891,026	1,741,141
R^2	0.062	0.177	0.122
Log of dependent variable in level, 2010	Included	Included	Included
Country fixed effects	Yes	Yes	Yes
Sector fixed effects	Yes	Yes	Yes
Size fixed effects	Yes	Yes	Yes
Age fixed effects	Yes	Yes	Yes

Note: Sample includes firms with local owners. The region is defined at the NUTS-3 level of aggregation, or at a more aggregated level if NUTS-3 is not available. The sector is equivalent to the 1-digit NACE rev. 2 code. The Average Management Index (AMI) score is that of the foreign country of ownership, from 1 (worst) to 7 (best). The log of the dependent variable in level in 2010 is included to control for regression toward the mean. Robust standard errors are in parentheses. ECA = Europe and Central Asia.
Significance level: * = 10 percent, ** = 5 percent, *** = 1 percent.

wage growth used here are driven by both changes in the level of wages and the composition of employment, this result is consistent with foreign firms in the sector attracting high-wage employees from domestic firms. The horizontal lines in figure 3.10 show the spillover effects by region and sector (from table 3.5) for the three indicators of firm performance.

Bigger and older firms seem to capture the positive spillover effects of having well-managed foreign firms in their sector or region to a larger extent than small and young ones do. As seen in figure 3.10, the total spillover effects for small and young firms (i.e., those four years old or younger and with fewer than 50 employees in 2007) are negative, whether we consider the regional or sectoral dimensions, suggesting that small and young firms are more likely to suffer the displacement effects of an increased prevalence of well-managed foreign companies. In contrast, the correlation between performance and the presence of foreign companies is positive and large for big and older domestic companies (i.e., those with 50 employees or more, or older than four years), suggesting that they may actually be better able to cope with the additional competition and thereby experience a larger increase in sales, average size, and wages than their smaller counterparts.

How does a higher presence of foreign companies translate into shared prosperity? While the data do not allow providing a definitive answer to this question, the estimated relationships between the share and the performance of foreign companies, and the performance of domestic ones provide some guidance. On the one hand, the results from the previous section suggest that foreign companies' size (their number of employees) and average wages grow faster than those of their domestic counterparts. At the same time, the presence of foreign companies from countries with good management practices is positively correlated with the performance of domestic firms, especially bigger and older ones. On the other hand, the results suggest the existence of some displacement effects of well-managed foreign companies for smaller and younger domestic firms. The sign of the net effects will depend on the extent to which the displaced workers from small and young companies can be absorbed by other domestic firms or by foreign companies.

Connected Firms: A Bridge to Economic Development?

The international connections of firms in ECA have historical origins based on language and geographic proximity, but they were also shaped by evolving economic forces. Countries that have strong ties through international trade or migration are also more likely to have businesses that are owned or managed by citizens from their partner countries. A virtuous circle exists in which one type of connection reaffirms and even magnifies the other ones. When firms in ECA have owners or managers from more advanced economies, they tend to grow faster than the rest. Part of this successful performance may be due to technology transfers but also to the transfer of soft technologies, as foreign companies can transplant their more efficient management practices to developing countries where business skills are scarcer. In ECA, even local businesses may benefit from the presence of well-managed foreign companies, as competitive pressures may force them to become more efficient to stay in the market. Another advantage of having connected firms is that they may be more resilient to negative shocks in the country of location. In ECA, foreign firms tend to smooth the impact of the local business

FIGURE 3.10 The positive spillovers of well-managed foreign firms seem weaker for small and young firms

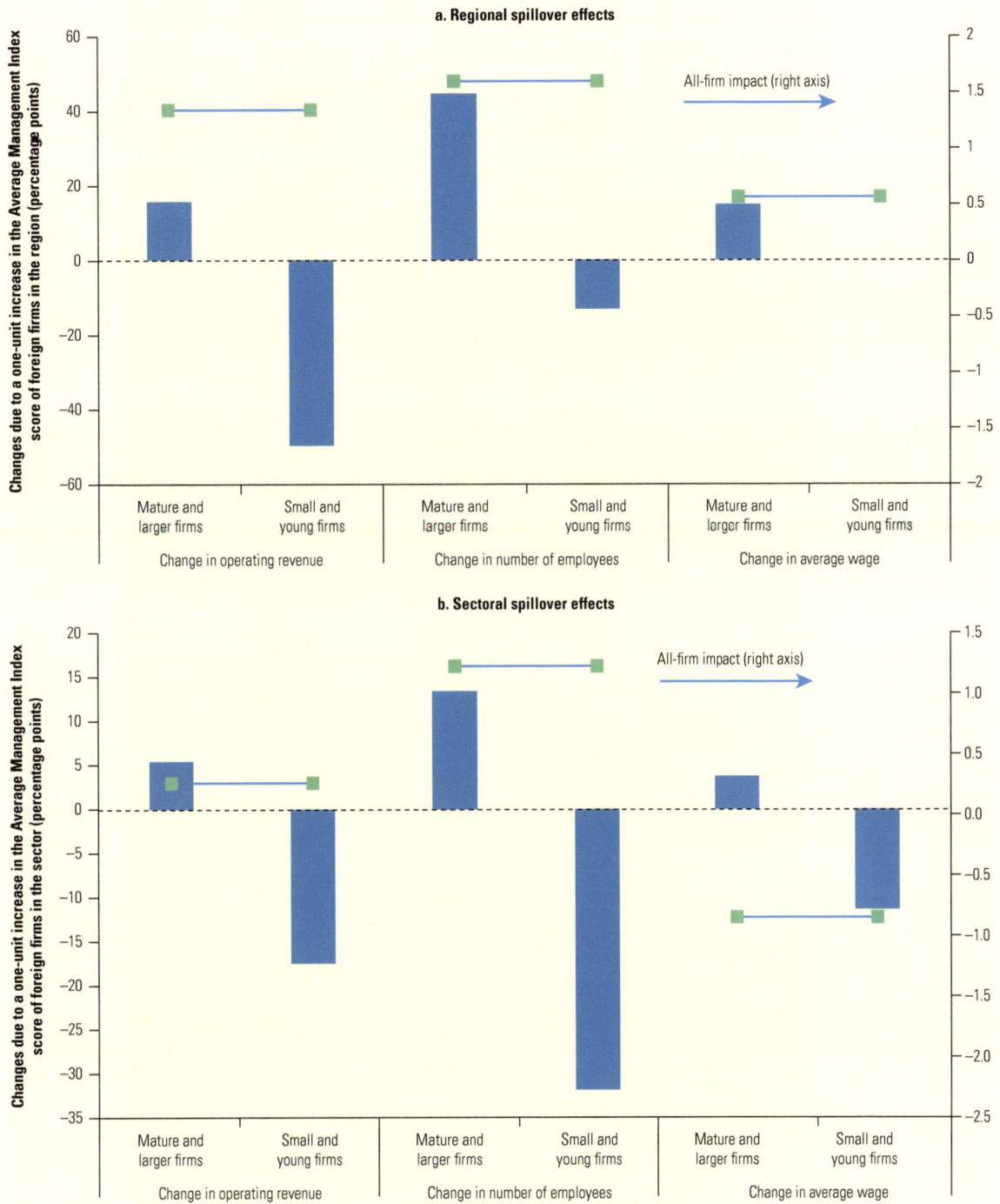

a. Regional spillover effects

b. Sectoral spillover effects

Note: Table 3B.3 presents full regression results. Small firms are those with 49 employees or fewer; young firms are those four years old or younger. Each bar represents the effect of increasing by one point the Average Management Index scores of foreign firms. The bars in each panel show the baseline effect (mature and larger firms), the baseline effect plus the interaction term associated with size, and the baseline effect plus the interaction terms associated with size and age simultaneously, according to table 3B.3. The horizontal lines show these spillover effects for all local firms as a benchmark, by region and sector (from table 3.5), for the three indicators of firm performance.

cycle, by creating more employment than local firms during a downturn and growing more slowly during a boom.

However, improving firms' connection to the outside world also comes with risks. Domestic firms that are unable to compete with their more efficient foreign counterparts may have no choice but to downsize or leave the market. In ECA, small and young firms seem the most at risk when they have to compete against foreign firms in the region. The associated job destruction could have a negative impact on households' welfare and shared prosperity, since jobs and labor income are a crucial component of households' total income. Accordingly, while foreign firms are more resilient to local shocks, they can also make the local economy more exposed to external shocks, as the performance of foreign firms in ECA is highly linked to the level of economic activity of the owners' and managers' country of origin.

> Improving the connection of firms to the outside world also comes with risks. Domestic firms that are unable to compete with their more efficient foreign counterparts may have no choice but to downsize or leave the market.

Given this evidence, policies should aim to boost the positive effects of connectivity while minimizing the risks. Improving the business environment and removing barriers to FDI and trade would strengthen the incentives for foreign investors to invest in new or existing local firms (see, for example, Antras, Desai, and Foley 2009). Investment promotion has also been an effective tool for fostering FDI by reducing information asymmetries and unnecessary procedures in developing countries,[16] which can be a significant obstacle to capital flows across borders (Harding and Javorcik 2011).[17] Policies to promote skilled migration may also be an effective tool for fostering the transfer of management practices from abroad. Finally, governments should also employ policies to promote firm linkages, especially those between foreign affiliates and domestic firms, to increase the spillover benefits of foreign ownership. These policies can focus on more innovation transfers between foreign and domestic firms.[18]

Policies to level the playing field among firms can help local businesses catch up with their more efficient foreign competitors. For example, improving access to finance for small and young firms can facilitate productive investments and expansion. Policies to improve the quality of local management are also crucial. More business education could contribute to improving management, especially in developing economies (Bloom and Van Reenen 2010). Labor market regulations that make it difficult to hire, lay off, pay, and promote employees may also restrict the ability of firms to manage workers efficiently.

When foreign firms lead their local counterparts to downsize or go out of business, the final impacts on workers will depend on the extent to which they can cope with the shock of losing their jobs. On the one hand, the extent to which workers can adjust to the shock by moving to another location, or find a job in another sector or occupation, will be crucial to mitigating the final economic impact. If workers can easily relocate, or have skills that are transferable to a job in another sector or occupation, the impact of displacement on their well-being will likely be smaller than in a case in which workers cannot quickly find another job. Policies to facilitate geographic mobility or to improve education (in terms of quality, but also in terms of fostering lifelong learning) can contribute to smoothing the impact of displacement. At the same time, a social insurance system that protects workers in the short term and does not distort the decision to work or to look for a job could mitigate the negative short-term impacts of unemployment.

Multinational firms could serve as a bridge to economic development by facilitating the cross-border transfer of factors that are key to explaining the success of richer countries. However, higher connectivity also entails more exposure to new risks from abroad. Policies to promote capital and skilled labor inflows can set countries on the path of long-term economic growth. Policies to smooth the short-term disruptive impacts of higher connectivity are also crucial, not only to protect vulnerable workers but also for the political economy of implementing long-term economic reforms.

Annex 3A. Coverage of Orbis Data

The data for this analysis come from the Orbis database, which covers 170 million private (99 percent) and public firms from around the world. The data are collected by Bureau van Dijk (BvD), which also maintains the quality and the accuracy of the database and ensures standardized formats, making cross-border comparisons possible (http://www.bvdinfo.com/). The database contains detailed firm-level information on balance sheet accounts, profit and loss accounts, sectors, location, ownership structures, and management, and relies on firms' legal obligation to file accounts. The coverage varies substantially across countries, and for many countries, information for only a few firms is usable. The data are processed per the recommendations by Kalemli-Özcan et al. (2015) to ensure national representativeness. In the estimation on foreign versus local and the management regressions (table 3B.1 and table 3B.2), we look at 30 European countries,[19] and in the estimation on spillovers (table 3B.3 and table 3B.4), we include 26 out of the 30 countries.[20]

The most recent data are from 2013 and while the balance sheet information is available at a yearly frequency, information such as ownership and management is available only for the most recent year. Ownership and management are therefore approximated in all years by information in 2013. Moreover, as opposed to the global ultimate owner, there may be many people with different nationalities listed as management personnel and the primary nationality of the management personnel is used to classify the nationality of the managers in each firm.[21]

The data sets used for the analysis include only unconsolidated financial statements to avoid double counting of firms,[22] and all financial variables are adjusted to 2010 prices. Observations lacking information essential to the analysis or obviously incorrect registrations are also dropped from the sample. This includes firms with no record of an opening or a closing date, balance sheet information prior to the registered opening date of the firm (negative age), or no industry specification. Observations are also dropped from the sample if information on total assets, operating turnover, sales, and number of employees is missing; the currency of the financial variables is misstated;[23] or material costs, operating revenue, and total assets are either missing or negative. Moreover, all firm observations are dropped from the sample if total assets, sales, or tangible fixed assets are negative in any year or if the number of employees is negative or larger than 2 million in any year. Some firms have registered multiple financial accounts within the same year. This may be explained by quarterly reports (Kalemli-Özcan et al. 2015), and to prevent double counting, only the observation with the highest operating revenue is kept in each year. Moreover, firms reporting their financial variables in different units over time are dropped from the sample if the change in unit is accompanied by a change in total assets of more than 70 percent. Firms registered with zero employees are also dropped, thereby making the sample more comparable across countries as well as in an attempt to exclude dormant firms.

The classification levels of sectors and regions across countries are largely the same when constructing the spillover variables (NACE Rev. 2). However, the level of detail in the registration of the regional location of firms varies considerably across countries. Therefore, firms are classified according to the NUTS-3 classification if possible. When this level of disaggregation is not feasible, the NUTS-2 level is used.

Annex 3B. Additional Tables

TABLE 3B.1 Foreign-Owned and Foreign-Managed Firms Perform Better Than Local Firms

	Log (Operating revenue), change, 2010–13	Log (Number of employees), change, 2010–13	Log (Average wage), change, 2010–13
Foreign owned, locally managed	0.227***	0.139***	0.117***
	(0.0459)	(0.0435)	(0.0375)
Foreign managed, locally owned	0.136***	0.110***	0.0551***
	(0.0213)	(0.0306)	(0.0191)
Foreign owned *and* managed	0.249***	0.179***	0.155***
	(0.0353)	(0.0576)	(0.0307)
Number of observations	2,482,453	3,131,653	1,886,679
R^2	0.063	0.171	0.111

Note: The independent variables in the regression are dummy variables that equal 1 if the firm is foreign owned, foreign managed, or both. As the dependent variable is in logs, the coefficients of the dummy variables have to be calculated according to the formula: 100 × [exp(b)−1]. The regression includes the initial values of the dependent variables to account for mean reversion and country, sector, size, and age fixed effects. The sector is equivalent to the 1-digit NACE rev. 2 code. Age is grouped into intervals of 0–4 years, 5–14 years, 15–30 years, and 30+ years, and size is grouped into intervals of 1–2 employees, 3–7 employees, 8–49 employees, 50–249 employees, and 250+ employees. Robust standard errors (in parentheses) are clustered around country of ownership.
Significance level: *** = 1 percent.

TABLE 3B.2 Firms with Better Foreign Managers Perform Better

	Log (Operating revenue), change, 2010–13	Log (Number of employees), change, 2010–13	Log (Average wage), change, 2010–13
Log management index	0.192***	0.166***	−0.0427
	(0.0541)	(0.0323)	(0.0683)
Log GDP per capita	0.0313***	0.0195***	0.00732
	(0.0114)	(0.00451)	(0.00580)
Log market capitalization of GDP	−0.0147	−0.00984*	0.00391
	(0.00889)	(0.00513)	(0.0117)
Log population	0.00878**	0.0104***	0.00693***
	(0.00423)	(0.00226)	(0.00230)
Log immigrant stock	−0.00583**	−0.00402***	−0.000567
	(0.00229)	(0.00143)	(0.00211)
Number of observations	98,208	120,305	89,521
R^2	0.046	0.073	0.065

Note: The estimation is restricted to foreign affiliates. The independent variables in the regression capture the characteristics of the country of ownership. The regression includes the initial values of the dependent variables to account for mean reversion and country, sector, size, and age fixed effects. The sector is equivalent to the 1-digit NACE rev. 2 code. Age is grouped into intervals of 0–4 years, 5–14 years, 15–30 years, and 30+ years; and size is grouped into intervals of 1–2 employees, 3–7 employees, 8–49 employees, 50–249 employees, and 250+ employees. Robust standard errors (in parentheses) are clustered around country of ownership.
Significance level: * = 10 percent, ** = 5 percent, *** = 1 percent.

TABLE 3B.3 Spillover Effects of Foreign-Owned Firms on Domestic Firms

Variables	Log(Operating revenue), change, 2010–13	Log(Number of employees), change, 2010–13	Log(Average wage), change, 2010–13
Share of foreign firms in the region	1.158***	0.576***	1.707***
	(0.184)	(0.137)	(0.202)
Share of foreign firms in the sector	0.806***	0.437***	1.052***
	(0.195)	(0.167)	(0.222)
AMI score of foreign firms in the region	0.145***	0.368***	0.138***
	(0.0221)	(0.0464)	(0.0224)
AMI score of foreign firms in the sector	0.0531**	0.126**	0.0368*
	(0.0250)	(0.0506)	(0.0221)
AMI score of foreign firms in the region × Small firm	−0.696***	−0.555***	−1.297***
	(0.160)	(0.135)	(0.199)
Share of foreign firms in the region × Small firm	−0.0921	−0.211	−0.529***
	(0.142)	(0.151)	(0.149)
AMI score of foreign firms in the sector × Small firm	−0.120***	−0.350***	−0.133***
	(0.0213)	(0.0445)	(0.0228)
Share of foreign firms in the sector × Small firm	−0.0503**	−0.116**	−0.0448**
	(0.0246)	(0.0502)	(0.0224)
AMI score of foreign firms in the region × Young firm	−0.135	−0.0715	−0.346**
	(0.145)	(0.115)	(0.167)
Share of foreign firms in the region × Young firm	−0.191	−0.315	−0.150
	(0.186)	(0.220)	(0.149)
AMI score of foreign firms in the sector × Young firm	−0.125***	−0.159***	−0.0242***
	(0.0185)	(0.0337)	(0.00917)
Share of foreign firms in the sector × Young firm	−0.0147	−0.0237*	−0.0117
	(0.0190)	(0.0126)	(0.00796)
	2.933***	0.350***	3.321***
	(0.214)	(0.0923)	(0.311)
Number of observations	2,273,882	2,891,023	1,741,140
R^2	0.063	0.182	0.124
Initial value	Included	Included	Included
Country fixed effects	Yes	Yes	Yes
Sector fixed effects	Yes	Yes	Yes
Size fixed effects	Yes	Yes	Yes
Age fixed effects	Yes	Yes	Yes
Cluster	Sector country	Sector country	Sector country
Outliers	Included	Included	Included

Note: Sample includes firms with local owners. The region is defined at the NUTS-3 level of aggregation or at a more aggregated level if NUTS-3 is not available. The sector is equivalent to the 1-digit NACE rev. 2 code. The Average Management Index (AMI) score is that of the foreign country of ownership, from 1 (worst) to 7 (best). The log of the dependent variable in level in 2010 is included to control for regression toward the mean. Large firms are those with 50 employees or more; young firms are those four years old or younger.
Significance level: * = 10 percent, ** = 5 percent, *** = 1 percent.

TABLE 3B.4 **Firm Growth over the Business Cycle**

	Log(Operating revenue), annual change	Log(Number of employees), annual change	Log(Average wage), annual change
Foreign owned, Locally managed	0.0669***	0.0410***	0.0369***
	(0.0148)	(0.0116)	(0.0117)
Foreign managed, Locally owned	0.0422***	0.0366***	0.0175***
	(0.00700)	(0.0102)	(0.00613)
Interaction between Foreign managed and Foreign owned	0.0823***	0.0678***	0.0470***
	(0.0120)	(0.0219)	(0.0120)
Local GDP growth	2.435	−0.0576	−1.151
	(1.551)	(0.405)	(0.824)
GDP growth of country of ownership	0.150	0.272**	−0.0147
	(0.106)	(0.102)	(0.0782)
Foreign-owned × Local GDP growth	−0.851**	−1.170**	0.0223
	(0.390)	(0.512)	(0.473)
Number of observations	7,097,750	9,108,130	5,421,604
R^2	0.019	0.073	0.024
Initial value	Included	Included	Included
Country fixed effects	Yes	Yes	Yes
Sector fixed effects	Yes	Yes	Yes
Size fixed effects	Yes	Yes	Yes
Age fixed effects	Yes	Yes	Yes
Cluster	Country	Country	Country
Year fixed effects	Yes	Yes	Yes

Note: Sample includes all firms with annual data between 2010 and 2013. Robust standard errors are in parentheses.
Significance level: ** = 5 percent, *** = 1 percent.

Notes

1. As the dependent variable is in logs, the results do not change if the foreign firms are taken as a share of all firms or all foreign firms in the country.
2. The estimation of the gravity model follows Anderson and van Wincoop (2003). As with most trade and FDI data, there are source countries that do not have any foreign affiliates or foreign managers in the host country. These zero shares may represent either a true absence of a linkage or missing data, which can bias the results. The results in table 3.2 presents the ordinary least squares (OLS) coefficients. To account for the bias, a Poisson pseudo–maximum likelihood (PPML) estimation is also performed following Silva and Tenreyro (2006). The results from the PPML estimation are not presented but are similar to the OLS results.
3. There are lists of tax haven countries from different sources (for example, OECD 2000; Dharmapala and Hines 2009). We use a combined list produced by Gravelle (2015), which combines the various lists and classifies these countries as tax havens: Andorra; Anguilla; Antigua and Barbuda; Aruba; The Bahamas; Bahrain; Barbados; Belize; Bermuda; British Virgin Islands; Cayman Islands; Cook Islands; Costa Rica; Cyprus; Dominica; Gibraltar; Grenada; Guernsey; Hong Kong SAR, China; Ireland; Isle of Man; Jersey; Jordan; Lebanon; Liberia; Liechtenstein; Luxembourg; Macau SAR, China; Maldives; Malta; Marshall Islands; Mauritius; Monaco; Montserrat; Nauru; the Netherlands Antilles; Niue; Panama; Samoa; San Marino; Seychelles; Singapore; St. Kitts and Nevis; St. Lucia; St. Vincent and the Grenadines; Switzerland; Tonga; Turks and Caicos; US Virgin Islands; and Vanuatu.
4. Konings (2001), on the other hand, looks at firm performance in Bulgaria, Romania, and Poland and find that only in Poland do foreign firms on average perform better than domestic firms.

5. Where foreign firms acquire firms that are more productive or more promising than the average firm on the market as well as locate in more productive sectors and regions (Aitken and Harrison 1999).

6. More specifically, the findings of Görg, Strobl, and Walsh (2007) suggest that the training of employees provided in foreign-owned firms is more productive than that in domestically owned firms.

7. Dries and Swinnen (2004) examine the Polish dairy sector.

8. Haskel, Pereira, and Slaughter (2007) find evidence of intra-industry spillovers but not regional spillovers.

9. Görg and Greenaway (2004) note that the two analyses supporting the idea of positive wage spillovers should be treated with caution because they are based on cross-sectional data.

10. The analysis is conducted with data from between 1976 and 1989.

11. Management practices can also be improved through business training programs. Bloom et al. (2013) provided management training to Indian textile firms, and firms that received free consulting services and adopted the new management practices increased their productivity by 17 percent. These firms were also able to grow faster, compared with firms that did not receive the consulting services.

12. The correlation between the WMS management index and the WEF management index is 0.73.

13. Blomström, Lipsey, and Kulchycky (1988) look at the relationship for both Sweden and the United States. In the case of Sweden, they find a positive relationship whereas the evidence is mixed for the United States.

14. See Gorg and Greenaway (2004) and Smeets (2008) for a discussion.

15. Given that the omitted factors seem to be positively correlated with both the presence of foreign firms and the performance of domestic ones, the estimated OLS coefficients would be biased upward.

16. The authors find a positive effect of investment promotion on FDI only for developing countries, not industrial economies.

17. Harding and Javorcik (2012) also find that higher-quality investment promotion agencies (measured by more professional service standards and better websites) are able to attract more FDI.

18. Sánchez-Martín et al. (2015) find that foreign firms have more backward linkages with (i.e., purchase inputs from) domestic firms if (a) these foreign firms entered the country to serve the market ("market-seeking") compared with those that are producing locally and exporting their goods back to the home country ("export oriented"); (b) the foreign firms are not using foreign-licensed technology.

19. Austria, Belgium, Bosnia and Herzegovina, Bulgaria, Croatia, the Czech Republic, Denmark, Estonia, Finland, France, Germany, Greece, Hungary, Iceland, Ireland, Italy, Latvia, Lithuania, the Netherlands, Poland, Portugal, Romania, Russia, Serbia, the Slovak Republic, Slovenia, Spain, Sweden, Ukraine, and the United Kingdom.

20. Austria, Belgium, Bosnia and Herzegovina, Bulgaria, Croatia, the Czech Republic, Denmark, Finland, France, Germany, Greece, Hungary, Ireland, Italy, Lithuania, the Netherlands, Poland, Portugal, Romania, Russia, the Slovak Republic, Slovenia, Spain, Sweden, Ukraine, and the United Kingdom.

21. If there are an equal number of local managers and managers from the same foreign country, then the foreign country is assigned as the primary nationality of the management personnel in the firm. If there are an equal number of managers from different foreign countries, then the primary nationality of the management personnel of the firm is chosen randomly.

22. We do not include firms with limited financial variables in the samples. Information on firms with limited financial variables is often based on rounded figures or class levels officially available. For most of these firms only information on the number of employees and the operating revenue is available (BvD online, Orbis—User Guide).

23. We assume that the currency is misstated if it is not the local currency, former local currencies, the US dollar, the euro, the British pound, the Chinese yuan, or the Japanese yen.

References

Aitken, B. J., G. H. Hanson, and A. E. Harrison. 1997. "Spillovers, Foreign Investment, and Export Behavior." *Journal of International Economics* 43 (1): 103–32.

Aitken, B. J. and A. E. Harrison. 1999. "Do Domestic Firms Benefit from Direct Foreign Investment? Evidence from Venezuela." *American Economic Review* 89 (3): 605–18.

Anderson, J. E. and E. Van Wincoop. 2003. "Gravity with Gravitas: A Solution to the Border Puzzle." *American Economic Review* 93 (1): 170–92.

Antras, Pol, Mihir A. Desai, and C. Fritz Foley. 2009. "Multinational Firms, FDI Flows, and Imperfect Capital Markets." *Quarterly Journal of Economics* 124 (3): 1171–219.

Atalay, E., A. Hortaçsu, and C. Syverson. 2014. "Vertical Integration and Input Flows." *American Economic Review* 104 (4): 1120–48.

Bao, Cathy Ge, and Maggie X. Chen. 2016. "Foreign Rivals Are Coming to Town: Responding to the Threat of Foreign Multinational Entry." Working Paper 2016-22, Institute for International Economic Policy, George Washington University, Washington, DC.

Bender, S., N. Bloom, D. Card, J. Van Reenen, and S. Wolter. 2016. "Management Practices, Workforce Selection and Productivity." Working Paper 22101, National Bureau of Economic Research, Cambridge, MA.

Blalock, Garrick, and Paul J. Gertler. 2008. "Welfare Gains from Foreign Direct Investment through Technology Transfer to Local Suppliers." *Journal of International Economics* 74 (2). 402–21.

Blomström, M., R. Lipsey, and K. Kulchycky. 1988. "U.S. and Swedish Direct Investment and Exporters." In *Trade Policy Issues and Empirical Analysis*, edited by R. E. Baldwin, 259–97. Chicago, IL: University of Chicago Press.

Bloom, N., E. Brynjolfsson, L. Foster, R. Jarmin, M. Patnaik, I. Saporta-Eksten, and J. Van Reenen. 2016. "What Drives Differences in Management?" Unpublished manuscript, Stanford University, Stanford, CA.

Bloom, N., B. Eifert, A. Mahajan, D. McKenzie, and J. Roberts. 2013. "Does Management Matter? Evidence from India." *Quarterly Journal of Economics* 128 (1): 1–51.

Bloom, N., R. Sadun, and J. Van Reenen. 2012. "Americans Do IT Better: US Multinationals and the Productivity Miracle." *American Economic Review* 102 (1): 167–201.

———. 2016. "Management as a Technology?" Working Paper 22327, National Bureau of Economic Research, Cambridge, MA.

Bloom, N., and J. Van Reenen. 2010. "Why Do Management Practices Differ across Firms and Countries?" *Journal of Economic Perspectives* 24 (1): 203–24.

Boehm, C. E., A. Flaaen, and N. Pandalai-Nayar. 2016. *The Role of Global Supply Chains in the Transmission of Shocks: Firm-Level Evidence from the 2011 Tōhoku Earthquake.* Washington, DC: Board of Governors of the Federal Reserve System.

Borchert, I., B. Gootiiz, and A. Mattoo. 2012. "Guide to the Services Trade Restrictions Database." Policy Research Working Paper 6108, World Bank, Washington, DC.

———. 2014. "Policy Barriers to International Trade in Services: Evidence from a New Database." *World Bank Economic Review* 28 (1): 162–88.

Buch, C. M., and A. Lipponer. 2010. "Volatile Multinationals? Evidence from the Labor Demand of German Firms." *Labour Economics* 17 (2): 345–53.

Budd, J. W., J. Konings, and M. J. Slaughter. 2005. "Wages and International Rent Sharing in Multinational Firms." *Review of Economics and Statistics* 87 (1): 73–84.

Clausing, K. A. 2000. "Does Multinational Activity Displace Trade?" *Economic Inquiry* 38 (2): 190–205.

Conyon, M. J., S. Girma, S. Thompson, and P. W. Wright. 2002. "The Productivity and Wage Effects of Foreign Acquisition in the United Kingdom." *Journal of Industrial Economics* 50 (1): 85–102.

Cravino, J., and A. A. Levchenko. 2016. "Multinational Firms and International Business Cycle Transmission." *Quarterly Journal of Economics* 132 (2): 921–62.

Dharmapala, D., and J. R. Hines. 2009. "Which Countries Become Tax Havens?" *Journal of Public Economics* 93: 1058–68.

Djankov, Simeon, and Bernard Hoekman. 2000. "Foreign Investment and Productivity Growth in Czech Enterprises." *World Bank Economic Review* 14 (1): 49–64.

Dries, L., and J. F. M. Swinnen. 2004. "Foreign Direct Investment, Vertical Integration, and Local Suppliers: Evidence from the Polish Dairy Sector." *World Development* 32 (9): 1525–44.

Frankel, J., and A. Rose. 1998. "The Endogeneity of the Optimum Currency Area Criteria." *Economic Journal* 108: 1009–25.

Girma, S., D. Greenaway, and K. Wakelin. 2001. "Who Benefits from Foreign Direct Investment in the UK?" *Scottish Journal of Political Economy* 48 (2): 119–33.

Görg, H., and D. Greenaway. 2004. "Much Ado about Nothing? Do Domestic Firms Really Benefit from Foreign Direct Investment?" *World Bank Research Observer* 19 (2): 171–97.

Görg, H., E. Strobl, and F. Walsh. 2007. "Why Do Foreign-Owned Firms Pay More? The Role of On-the-Job Training." *Review of World Economics* 143 (3): 464–82.

Gravelle, Jane G. 2015. "Tax Havens: International Tax Avoidance and Evasion." Washington, DC: Congressional Research Service.

Haddad, M., and A. Harrison. 1993. "Are There Positive Spillovers from Direct Foreign Investment? Evidence from Panel Data for Morocco." *Journal of Development Economics* 42: 51–74.

Harding, Torfinn, and Beata S. Javorcik. 2011. "Roll Out the Red Carpet and They Will Come: Investment Promotion and FDI Inflows." *Economic Journal* 121 (557): 1445–76.

———. 2012. "Investment Promotion and FDI Inflows: Quality Matters." *CESifo Economic Studies* 59 (2): 337–59.

Haskel, J. E., S. C. Pereira, and M. J. Slaughter. 2007. "Does Inward Foreign Direct Investment Boost the Productivity of Domestic Firms?" *Review of Economics and Statistics* 89 (3): 482–96.

Head, K., and J. Ries. 2001. "Overseas Investment and Firm Exports." *Review of International Economics* 9 (1): 108–22.

Heyman, F., P. J. Norback, and R. Hammarberg. 2014. "Foreign Direct Investment, Source Country Heterogeneity and Management Practices." Working Paper 1041, Research Institute of Industrial Economics (IFN), Stockholm.

Hollweg, C. H., D. Lederman, D. Rojas, and E. R. Bulmer. 2014. *Sticky Feet: How Labor Market Frictions Shape the Impact of International Trade on Jobs and Wages.* Washington, DC: World Bank.

Javorcik, B. S. 2004. "Does Foreign Direct Investment Increase the Productivity of Domestic Firms? In Search of Spillovers through Backward Linkages." *American Economic Review* 94 (3): 605–27.

———. 2015. "Does FDI Bring Good Jobs to Host Countries?" *World Bank Research Observer* 30 (1): 74–94.

Kalemli-Özcan, S., B. Sorensen, C. Villegas-Sanchez, V. Volosovych, and S. Yesiltas. 2015. "How to Construct Nationally Representative Firm Level Data from the ORBIS Global Database." Working Paper 21558, National Bureau of Economic Research, Cambridge, MA.

Keller, W., and S. R. Yeaple. 2009. "Multinational Enterprises, International Trade, and Productivity Growth: Firm-Level Evidence from the United States." *Review of Economics and Statistics* 91 (4): 821–31.

Kleinert, J., J. Martin, and F. Toubal. 2015. "The Few Leading the Many: Foreign Affiliates and Business Cycle Comovement." *American Economic Journal: Macroeconomics* 7 (4): 134–59.

Kokko, A., R. Tansini, and M. C. Zejan. 1996. "Local Technological Capability and Productivity Spillovers from FDI in the Uruguayan Manufacturing Sector." *Journal of Development Studies* 32: 602–11.

———. 2001. "Trade Regimes and Spillover Effects of FDI: Evidence from Uruguay." *Review of World Economics* 137 (1): 124–49.

Konings, J. 2001. "The Effects of Foreign Direct Investment on Domestic Firms: Evidence from Firm Level Panel Data in Emerging Economies." *Economics of Transition* 9 (3): 619–33.

Kosová, R. 2010. "Do Foreign Firms Crowd Out Domestic Firms? The Evidence from the Czech Republic." *Review of Economics and Statistics* 92 (4): 861–81.

Lipsey, R. E., and F. Sjöholm. 2001. "Foreign Direct Investment and Wages in Indonesian Manufacturing." Working Paper 8299, National Bureau of Economic Research, Cambridge, MA.

———. 2004. "Foreign Direct Investment, Education and Wages in Indonesian Manufacturing." *Journal of Development Economics* 73 (1): 415–22.

Lipsey, R. E., and M. Y. Weiss. 1984. "Foreign Production and Exports of Individual Firms." *Review of Economics and Statistics* 66 (2): 304–8.

Navaretti, G. B., D. Checchi, and A. Turrini. 2003. "Adjusting Labor Demand: Multinational Versus National Firms: A Cross-European Analysis." *Journal of the European Economic Association* 1 (2–3): 708–19.

OECD (Organisation for Economic Co-operation and Development). 2000. *Towards Global Tax Competition*. Paris: OECD.

Sánchez-Martín, Miguel Eduardo, Jaime De Piniés, and Kássia Antoine. 2015. "Measuring the Determinants of Backward Linkages from FDI in Developing Economies: Is It a Matter of Size?" Policy Research Working Paper 7185, World Bank, Washington, DC.

Silva, J. S., and S. Tenreyro. 2006. "The Log of Gravity." *Review of Economics and Statistics* 88 (4): 641–58.

Smeets, R. 2008. "Collecting the Pieces of the FDI Knowledge Spillovers Puzzle." *World Bank Research Observer* 23 (2): 107–38.

Syverson, C. 2004. "Product Substitutability and Productivity Dispersion." *Review of Economics and Statistics* 86 (2): 534–50.

Vahter, P., and J. Masso. 2007. "Home versus Host Country Effects of FDI: Searching for New Evidence of Productivity Spillovers." *Applied Economics Quarterly* 53: 165–96.

SPOTLIGHT 3
Reaping Digital Dividends through Complementary Investments

The growth of supply chains, which has been driven by improvements in both telecommunications and transport infrastructure, is one example of the interdependence of different connectivity channels in contributing to growth.[1] Similarly, internet technology has tremendous potential to transform economic systems in Europe and Central Asa (ECA). But in addition to establishing the necessary infrastructure and regulatory environment for the internet, reaping the full benefits from internet connectivity requires a host of complementary activities. Efficient transport infrastructure, financial systems, education, and institutions that support market competition are all important to enable individuals to exploit internet technology and avoid potentially undesirable consequences from this technology.

Successful e-commerce requires strong trade infrastructure to guarantee timely and reliable delivery of goods. Improvements in trade facilitation, particularly streamlining procedures and investing in the infrastructure required to speedily transit imports through ports, could greatly expand the potential for e-commerce in many ECA countries. For example, eBay introduced a global shipping program that facilitates shipping and customs clearance for its sellers. Sellers selected for the program had 2.7 percent more exports than those not selected. Conversely, countries can leverage information and communication technology (ICT) to modernize customs agencies and procedures. For example, Albania reduced its customs clearance time and increased trade significantly from 2007 to 2012 by implementing the Automated System for Customs Data to improve its risk management and inspection processes. Efficient logistics and internet use can reinforce each other. A study examining the entry of foreign products into the US market finds that the probability of product entry increases 0.65 percent when there are 10 additional internet users per 100 people in the foreign country, but the probability increases 1.18 percent when these 10 additional internet users are in a country with highly efficient export logistics (Riker 2015). Finally, an efficient postal system can reduce the costs for e-commerce companies to make the last-mile parcel delivery to their consumers.

E-commerce also requires the availability of electronic payment instruments, such as debit or credit cards. For example, one reason that e-commerce is more limited in the European Union (EU) than in Japan or the United States, despite the EU's greater affordability and quality of internet access, is that the EU is well behind these countries in the use of credit cards. Similarly, countries in Central and Eastern Europe underperform the economies of East Asia in this regard. In Central Asia, the South Caucasus, and the Western Balkans, the use of credit cards is almost negligible. On average, only 15 percent of individuals in many ECA countries have credit cards, compared with about 50 percent in Western Europe.[2] Together, the quality of payment systems and logistics systems is strongly associated with the share of firms with online sales (figure S3.1).

Adequate levels of education are necessary for individuals and firms to use the internet effectively. For instance, more than 50 percent of 15-year-olds in Central Asia are functionally illiterate (that is, they know how to read and write, but cannot make inferences or understand forms of indirect meaning).[3] Given this deficit, better internet provision may not necessarily complement their skills and translate them into wage gains. At the same time,

SPOTLIGHT 3 *continued*

FIGURE S3.1 Firms' online sales rise with more efficient logistics and payment systems

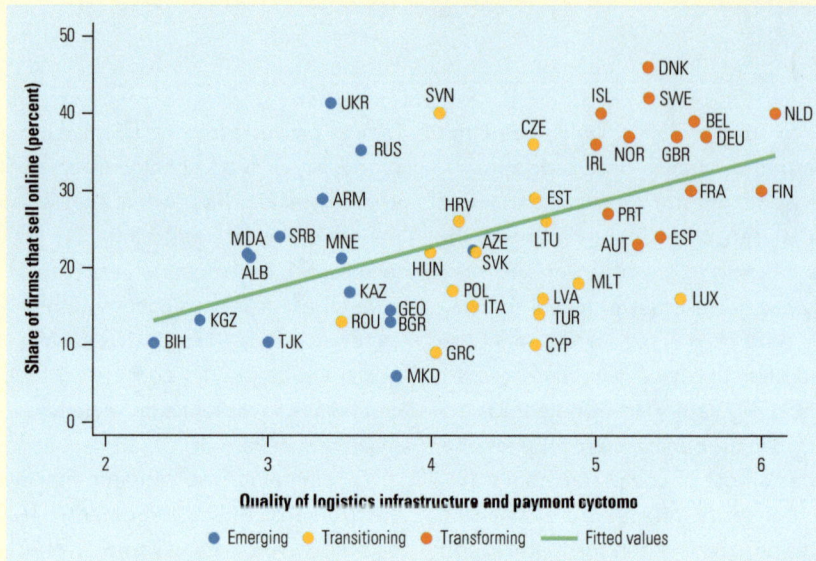

Source: Calculations based on data from the World Bank Enterprise Surveys, Eurostat, and World Economic Forum 2015.
Note: Data for firms selling are calculated from the Enterprise Survey and Eurostat and obtained for the latest available years. The quality of logistics infrastructure and payment systems is calculated as an average of the response from executives in the World Economic Forum (WEF) Competitiveness Survey. The questions concern the quality of roads, railroad infrastructure, port infrastructure, and air transport infrastructure and the affordability and availability of financial services, with the answers ranging from 1 (worst) to 7 (best). For each country, the year of the data from the WEF Competitiveness Survey corresponds to the year of the data on firms selling online.

educational and training systems need to provide the skills needed for the new economy, such as socioemotional or high cognitive skills. If not, firms interested in technological upgrades may have difficulty recruiting workers with the skills that complement the new technologies.

A World Bank assessment of skills shortages in the region finds that the quality of upper-secondary and tertiary education in many countries is not keeping up with the changing demand for skills (Sondergaard et al. 2012). For instance, the highly specialized and compartmentalized nature of tertiary education in the Russian Federation, often closely affiliated with specific sectors of the economy, fails to deliver the flexibility needed by workers in the internet economy (OECD 2013). In many ECA countries, improving

fluency in languages that are widely used on the internet would increase the benefits of more widespread internet access.

The shortage of advanced computer skills in ECA, reflected in the high level of vacancies in computer jobs, also constrains internet adoption. These shortages could intensify in the older, rapidly aging ECA economies. In many countries, the lower level of skills in older workers appears to be driven by a mixture of cohort effects and a deterioration of skills with age. While the share of ICT specialists in total employment has increased in most countries with adequate data, most studies find that a shortage of ICT specialists creates bottlenecks even in the developed European economies (Falk 2002). A study by the European Commission (Attström et al. 2014) finds that ICT specialists are one of the top three occupations with the largest skills bottle-necks in Europe.

The more developed countries also can satisfy their demand for ICT specialists through immigration and encouraging greater participation by women in science, technology, engineering, and mathematics specialties. For instance, immigrant workers in Canada are overrepresented among information technology occupations in Canada when compared with their share of total employment (OECD 2004). And in most European countries, only about a third or less of ICT specialists are women, and the gender gap has risen in almost every country during the past 10 years.[4] These gender gaps start early in life, as girls perform worse than boys in mathematics (OECD 2015). Encouraging parents and teachers to become more aware of these gender gaps could increase the participation of women in the internet economy and reduce bottlenecks in ICT skills.

Competitive, well-regulated markets are required to encourage internet adoption and to exploit the resulting gains. Poor competition policies can mean that firms fail to have the incentives to incorporate the internet into their production processes. Countries with poor competitive frameworks in ECA often have lower-than-average shares of firms that use websites (figure S3.2). For example, import tariffs or subsidies may reduce the competitive pressures necessary to force firms to adopt new technology. Reducing tariffs on ICT equipment can improve firms' ability to use the internet. Many ECA countries have committed to removing tariffs on ICT equipment (under the International Technology Agreement of the World Trade Organization), but eight ECA countries still have import tariffs on ICT products. The lack of consumer protection legislation can make consumers particularly reluctant to purchase from foreign sellers, as it may be difficult to obtain refunds or protection

FIGURE S3.2 Internet use by firms is associated with the intensity of local competition

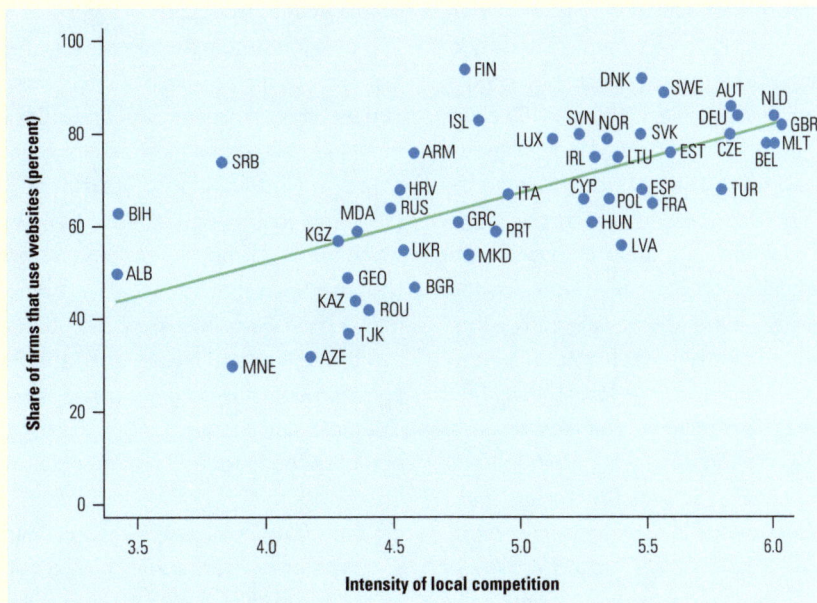

Source: Calculations based on data from the World Bank Enterprise Surveys, Eurostat, and World Economic Forum 2015.
Note: Data for most countries are from 2013; exceptions are the Russian Federation, for which Internet use data are from 2012, and Tajikistan, for which competition data are from 2014.

SPOTLIGHT 3 *continued*

against fraud. And absent regulation to ensure competition, the economies of scale generated by digital technologies can lead to market concentration and the reemergence of monopolies, and thus to less future innovation.

Improvements in regulation in the more advanced economies are necessary to adapt competition policies to the new market structures that the internet is creating, such as multisided markets. These markets or platforms are different from the usual markets, as there are often two (or more) distinct groups of customers, network effects within and across these groups, and an intermediary that brings these two customer groups together (such as eBay). In standard economic models, if prices are higher than marginal costs, firms have some form of market power. With a multisided market, prices do not necessarily equal marginal costs, as it may be efficient (to maximize the size of the market) for the platform to charge certain customer groups higher prices and others lower prices or even to offer the product for free. Thereby, the competition agency cannot consider price without considering the effects on the other parts of the market (OECD 2009).

Appropriate institutions also are necessary to avoid undesirable labor market effects of the widespread adoption of internet technologies. By allowing traditional tasks to be broken into smaller and more specialized tasks, the internet is driving the rise of the "gig" economy, in which traditional employment—defined as a full-time, permanent salaried job—shrinks, and alternative work arrangements grow. In fact, countries that were early adopters of telecommunications reforms aimed at improving the availability and affordability of the internet have experienced more dramatic increases in the incidence of alternative work arrangements among ICT-intensive sectors. Moreover, many online freelancers operate in the informal economy. For example, in a sample composed mostly of Russians and Ukrainians, only about 12 percent of online freelancers had a full legal contract with their clients, while 34 percent relied on fully informal and

52 percent relied on mixed agreements.[5] Freelancers often face barriers in participating in social protection systems—pensions, health insurance, unemployment insurance—that are often provided as part of permanent employment. This new mode of employment will require that social protection benefits become increasingly attached to the worker and not to the job.

Without appropriate incentives to be in the formal economy and access to insurance against job loss, sickness, and disability, the rise of digital technologies will not improve inclusion, and might increase inequality. The rise in the informal economy facilitated by digital technologies could also reduce tax receipts, undermine pension systems, and increase the burden on the budget. For example, if online freelancers do not make pension contributions, they are at risk of falling into poverty in old age and becoming eligible for social assistance. Cooperation between governments and online platforms to facilitate tax and social contribution payments would nudge workers out of the shadow economy and provide them with some employment protection.

Some of the complementary activities required to capitalize on the adoption of internet technology are largely under the control of firms. Strong management can ensure that new technologies are incorporated effectively into business processes. Organizational change, as well as a new strategy and vision for the company, is often needed. A study of UK firms finds that information technology investments have a positive impact on firm productivity, but the effects are larger when this investment is complemented by organizational change (Crespi, Criscuolo, and Haskel 2007). Similarly, the combination of skilled labor and firm reorganization explains the returns to ICT investment in Italian manufacturing firms (Bugamelli and Pagano 2004). The extent and type of organizational change will depend on what type of technology the firm is implementing. For example, introducing a website to provide customer service might require modifying the existing customer service functions, while introducing more collaboration through cloud-based office software requires large changes to processes, procedures, and workflows. A study of French firms shows that adopting an enterprise resource planning system requires redesigning the organization to focus on core competencies, quality improvements, and a decentralized decision-making structure (Bocquet, Brossard, and Sabatier 2007).

Governments also can help firms improve their ability to adopt new technologies. Programs that provide free consulting services to improve management practices have been shown to improve productivity and quality among firms. A study that randomly assigned Indian firms to receive consulting services shows that such programs can increase firm productivity 17 percent and that these firms grow faster than firms in the control group (Bloom, Sadun, and Van Reenen 2013). But management programs need to be tailored for each firm and can be expensive to implement.

Notes

1. This spotlight is based on findings from Kelly et al. (2017).
2. This is based on 2014 data from the World Bank's Findex database
3. Based on data from PISA, latest available data points (2015, 2012, and 2009). Available at http://www.oecd.org/pisa/data/.
4. The data are from Community Statistics for Information Society (CSIS) Eurostat.
5. The source is Shevchuk and Strebkov (2012), based on a sample of online freelancers from Russia (70 percent), Ukraine (11 percent), Belarus (3 percent), and other countries (16 percent).

References

Attström, K., S. Niedlich, K. Sandvliet, H.-M. Kuhn, and E. Beavor. 2014. "Mapping and Analysing Bottleneck Vacancies on the EU Labour Markets." European Commission, Brussels.

Bloom, N., R. Sadun, and J. Van Reenen. 2013. "Management as a Technology." Unpublished, London School of Economics, London.

Bocquet, R., O. Brossard, and M. Sabatier. 2007. "Complementarities in Organizational Design and the Diffusion of Information Technologies: An Empirical Analysis." Research Policy 36 (3): 367–86.

Bugamelli, M., and P. Pagano. 2004. "Barriers to Investment in ICT." Applied Economics 36 (20): 2275–86.

Crespi, G., C. Criscuolo, and J. Haskel. 2007. "Information Technology, Organisational Change, and Productivity Growth: Evidence from UK Firms." Discussion Paper 783, Centre for Economic Performance, London School of Economics.

Falk, M. 2002. "What Drives the Vacancy Rate for Information Technology Workers?" Jahrbucher fur Nationalokonomie und Statistik 222 (4): 401–20.

Kelly, Tim, Aleksandra Liaplina, Shawn W. Tan, and Hernan Winkler. 2017. Reaping Digital Dividends: Leveraging the Internet for Development in Europe and Central Asia. Washington, DC: World Bank.

OECD (Organisation for Economic Co-operation and Development). 2004. Information Technology Outlook, 2004. Paris: OECD.

———. 2009. Two-Sided Markets: Policy Roundtable. Paris: OECD.

———. 2013. "Russia: Modernising the Economy." Better Policies Series, OECD, Paris.

———. 2015. "The ABC of Gender Equality in Education: Aptitude, Behavior, and Confidence." OECD, Paris.

Riker, D. 2015. "The Internet and Product-Level Entry into the U.S. Market." Research Note 2015-05B, Office of Economics, U.S. International Trade Commission, Washington, DC.

Shevchuk, A., and D. Strebkov. 2012. "Freelance Contracting in the Digital Age: Informality, Virtuality, and Social Ties." Research Paper BRP 12, Higher School of Economics, National Research University, Moscow.

Sondergaard, L., M. Murthi, D. Abu-Ghaida, C. Bodewig, and J. Rutkowski. 2012. Skills, Not Just Diplomas: Managing Education for Results in Eastern Europe and Central Asia. Washington, DC: World Bank

World Economic Forum. 2015. Global Competitiveness Report 2015–2016. Geneva: World Economic Forum.

4

Migration and Connectivity

Migration is an integral part of supporting connectivity between countries. Migration facilitates connectivity by narrowing market information gaps between countries and can lead to greater cross-border investments and trade between the migrant host and origin countries. Migration also directly increases sharing of technology and knowledge between countries through schooling and language skills attained abroad. Migrants, whether by returning home and swaying policies based on experiences gained abroad, or by influencing their friends and family at home, can also have an impact on home and host country institutions as they shape perspectives on governance and influence expectations of what type of government works best. While migration has often been thought of as simply an increase in the supply of labor, with consequent distributional wage impacts, openness to migration also helps many countries gain the skills, technology, and resources required to improve efficiency and compete in an increasingly complex globalized world.

Main Messages

- Migration has, on balance, benefited Europe and Central Asia (ECA). Both emigration and immigration rates in many ECA countries continue to be higher than the global average, mostly driven by European Union (EU) integration and flows after the opening up of Eastern bloc countries. There is considerable empirical and anecdotal evidence that diaspora investments and trade and knowledge transfer have benefited ECA economies. The region's

disproportionately high flows of skilled workers have provided a conduit for the transfer of technology between countries. And the increasing share of migrants going to the United States and Northern, Western, and Southern Europe may have contributed to improving institutions in ECA transition economies.

- But some ECA countries have failed to reap all of the potential gains from migration. Problems affecting the institutional and policy environment have reduced the attractiveness of some ECA countries for immigration. Countries in Central Europe, Eastern Europe, and Central Asia attract relatively few immigrants from outside the region. The lack of adequate programs to facilitate the integration of immigrants has increased concerns about the economic benefits of migration, but policy actions to improve economic participation may alleviate potential problems. High-income ECA countries tend to have relatively liberal visa regimes compared with the United States, but the policy environment to facilitate access to labor markets is more burdensome.

- Work and migration patterns are changing, and ECA countries need to evolve in response. To fully reap the benefits from cross-border mobility of people, policy reforms should help both migrants and native-born residents cope with increased and unavoidable challenges in the new and dynamic economy, in which lifetime employment is rare and the rate of technological change has increased. Successful reforms would include increased portability of benefits, greater income security for workers with flexible contracts, investments in education to ensure that workers can compete in this globalized environment, and better integration of migrants in host countries. Policies in origin countries could strengthen ongoing engagement with the diaspora and reduce challenges to return migration by improving the institutional and economic environment at home.

Migration Patterns in Europe and Central Asia

Emigration plays an important role in ECA. While emigration rates for most countries in the world are low (map 4.1), many countries in the ECA region have higher emigration rates than the global average. This is partly due to mobility within the EU. In addition, there is significant mobility between former Soviet Republics, particularly from Central Asia to the Russian Federation. However, some of these migrants are people who moved within the former Soviet Union and technically became international migrants after the breakup of the country following 1989. Overall, the level of emigration from ECA countries (excluding the EU15+)[1] slightly increased from 2000 to 2010.[2] This is partly due to the financial crisis, which reduced demand in labor markets across Europe. The largest growth in emigration between 2000 and 2010 is observed for Romania (129 percent) and Bulgaria (66 percent), countries that entered the EU in 2007. By contrast, some of the 2004 EU accession countries experienced substantial declines in emigration from 2000 to 2010 (the Czech Republic by 52 percent and Poland by 30 percent), and others experienced small declines (except Slovenia's increase of 32 percent).

Immigration rates are also high in ECA. Immigration rates in Central and Eastern European countries tend to be above the global average, and are on par with some

MAP 4.1 Emigration shares have seen the highest increase in ECA

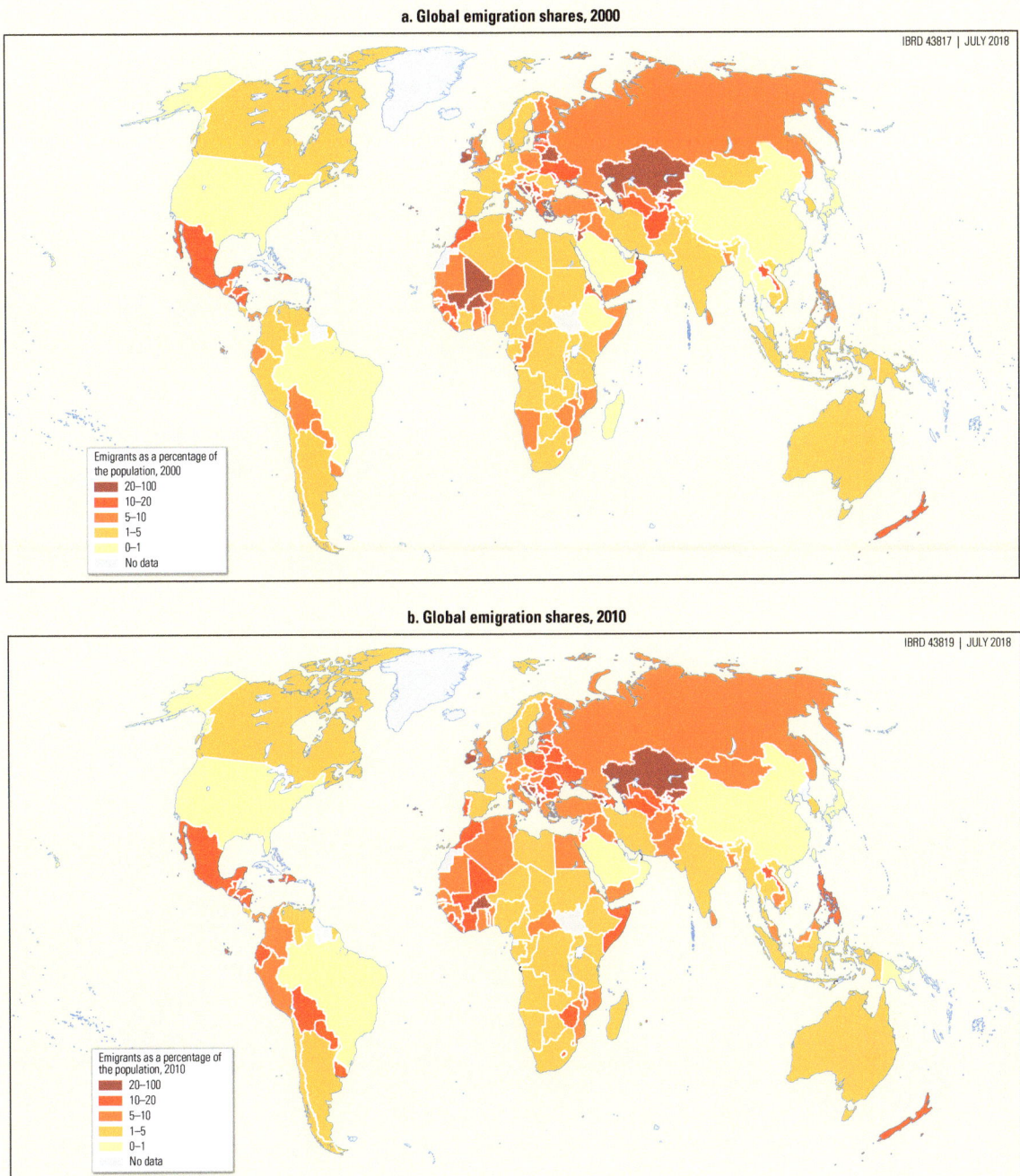

a. Global emigration shares, 2000

IBRD 43817 | JULY 2018

Emigrants as a percentage of
the population, 2000
- 20–100
- 10–20
- 5–10
- 1–5
- 0–1
- No data

b. Global emigration shares, 2010

IBRD 43819 | JULY 2018

Emigrants as a percentage of
the population, 2010
- 20–100
- 10–20
- 5–10
- 1–5
- 0–1
- No data

Source: World Bank 2018.

of the EU15+ countries (map 4.2). The number of emigrants from Central and Eastern Europe exceeded that of immigrants by about 14 million people in both 2000 and 2010 (including estimates for countries with missing data—see annex 4A for methodology).[3] Thus, a significant share of these countries' emigrants go either to the EU15+ countries or outside the region. (Their lack of attractiveness for

MAP 4.2 Immigration shares are significant in many ECA countries

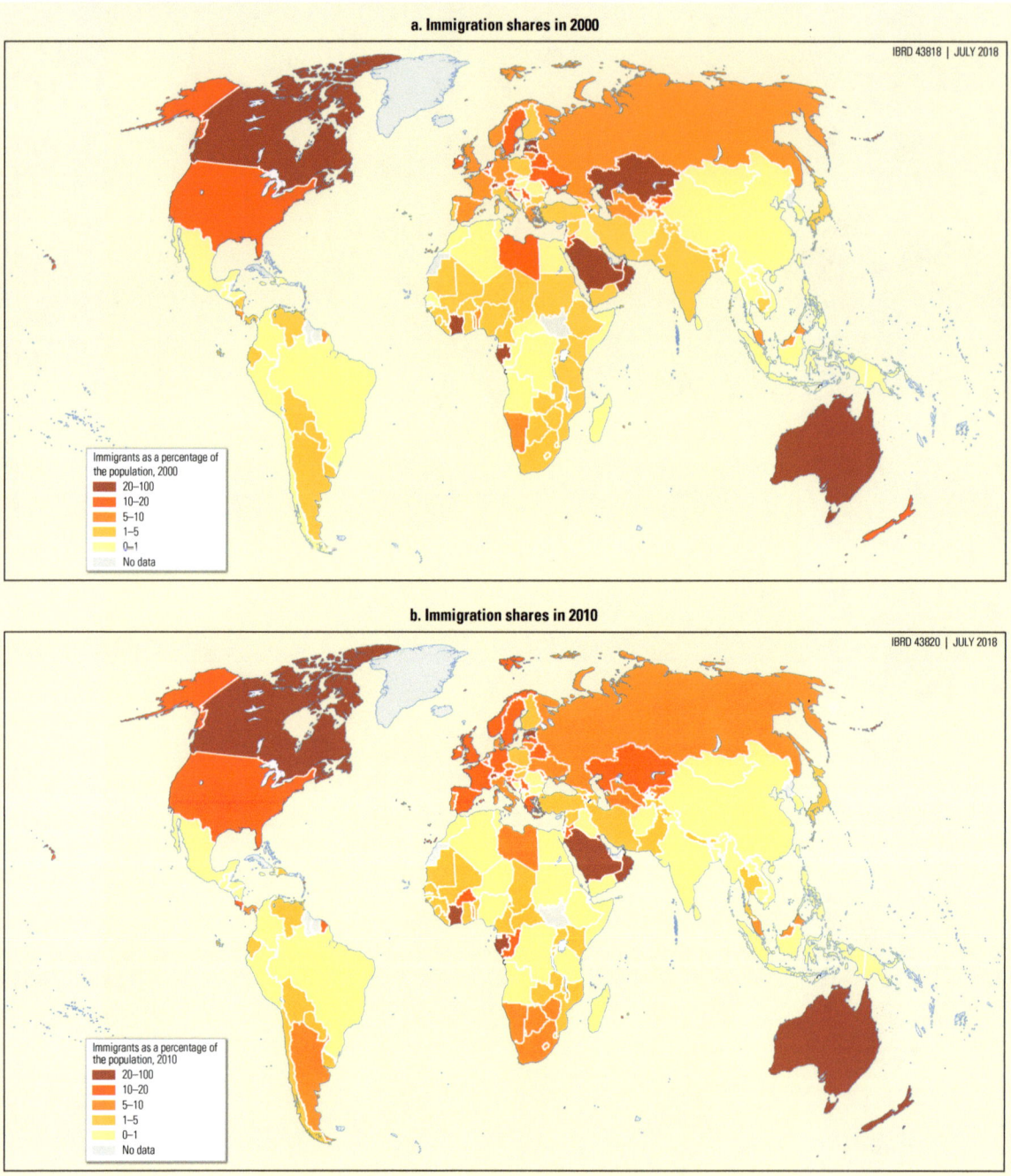

a. Immigration shares in 2000

IBRD 43818 | JULY 2018

Immigrants as a percentage of
the population, 2000
- 20–100
- 10–20
- 5–10
- 1–5
- 0–1
- No data

b. Immigration shares in 2010

IBRD 43820 | JULY 2018

Immigrants as a percentage of
the population, 2010
- 20–100
- 10–20
- 5–10
- 1–5
- 0–1
- No data

Source: World Bank 2018.

immigration from outside the region is discussed in Artuc et al. 2015, and the OECD DIOC-E data set provides available data.) The only major exception is Russia, which hosts large flows of migrants from Central Asian countries.

Per capita income, proximity, and regional integration are major determinants of emigrant patterns from ECA. Emigrants from the EU15+ countries go largely to other high-income countries (figure 4.1, panel a). Since income differences are the main determinants of migration flows, migrants from high-income countries are unlikely to migrate to lower-income countries. Seven of the top ten destinations are in Europe, indicating the important role of physical proximity as well as the removal of mobility barriers within the European Union. Six of the top ten destinations for emigrants from Eastern and Central Europe are also high-income countries—Germany, Italy, Spain, the United Kingdom, the United States, and Israel (figure 4.1, panel b). The United States is the largest destination country in the world, and Israel has special status because of Jewish migration, especially after

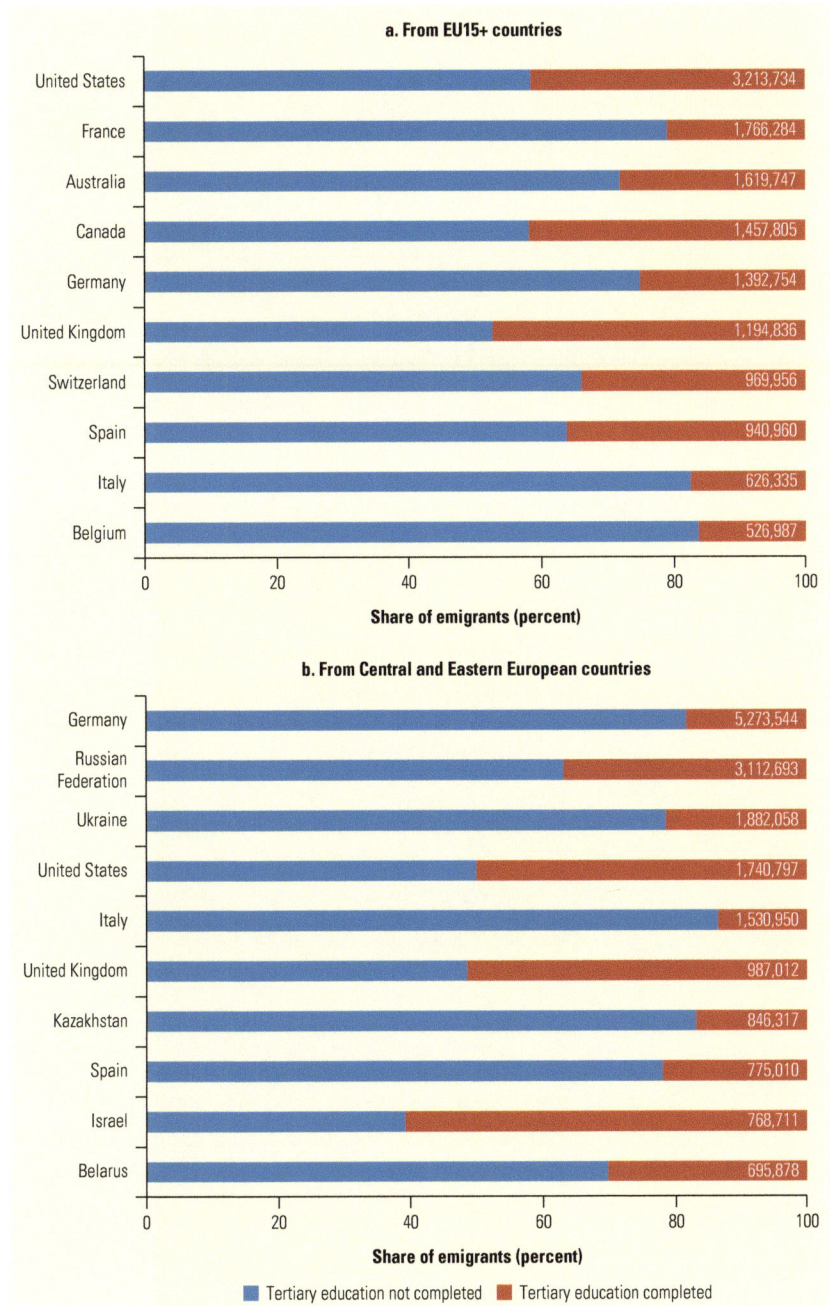

FIGURE 4.1 Top destinations of emigrants and share of total who have completed tertiary education, 2010

a. From EU15+ countries

Country	Value
United States	3,213,734
France	1,766,284
Australia	1,619,747
Canada	1,457,805
Germany	1,392,754
United Kingdom	1,194,836
Switzerland	969,956
Spain	940,960
Italy	626,335
Belgium	526,987

Share of emigrants (percent)

b. From Central and Eastern European countries

Country	Value
Germany	5,273,544
Russian Federation	3,112,693
Ukraine	1,882,058
United States	1,740,797
Italy	1,530,950
United Kingdom	987,012
Kazakhstan	846,317
Spain	775,010
Israel	768,711
Belarus	695,878

Share of emigrants (percent)

■ Tertiary education not completed ■ Tertiary education completed

continued

FIGURE 4.1 *continued*

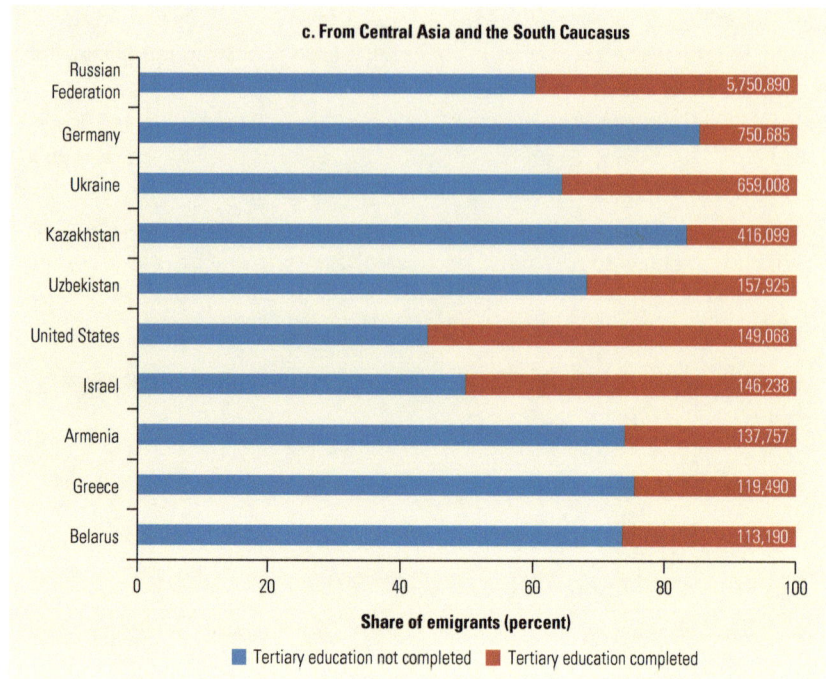

c. From Central Asia and the South Caucasus

Destination	Total migrants
Russian Federation	5,750,890
Germany	750,685
Ukraine	659,008
Kazakhstan	416,099
Uzbekistan	157,925
United States	149,068
Israel	146,238
Armenia	137,757
Greece	119,490
Belarus	113,190

Share of emigrants (percent)

■ Tertiary education not completed ■ Tertiary education completed

Note: The numbers on the bars are the total number of migrants in each destination country.

the collapse of the Soviet Union where emigration was restricted. Finally, four countries—Belarus, Kazakhstan, Russia, and Ukraine—are on the list as leading examples of intraregional migration flows, again, mainly after the breakup of the Soviet Union. The role of regional ties and distance are more prominent in shaping emigration patterns from Central Asian countries (figure 4.1, panel b). There are two Western and Southern European destinations among the top ten—Germany and Greece—and only two non-European destinations—the United States and Israel. All the other destinations—Armenia, Belarus, Kazakhstan, Russia, Ukraine, and Uzbekistan—reflect regional mobility flows, distance, and cultural and political ties.

The destination of highly educated emigrants reflects income levels, policies, distance, and language.[4] The share of the highly educated among emigrants from the EU15+ countries reaches more than 40 percent in several high-income destinations, such as the United States, the United Kingdom, and Canada. This is due to immigration policies in these destination countries that favor the high-skilled, the skill premium in these labor markets, the ability of the tertiary educated to migrate further distances than the less educated, and perhaps the use of English, which many educated people learn as a second language (language fluency is an important determinant of the returns to migration for highly skilled workers). Similarly, more than 50 percent of emigrants from Eastern and Central Europe to the United States, the United Kingdom, and Israel are highly educated, while emigrants to other regional destinations have tertiary-educated ratios of less than 25 percent (figure 4.1, panel b). And emigrants from Central Asia to the United States and Israel tend to be highly

> The destination of highly educated emigrants reflects income levels, policies, distance, and language.

educated, with emigrants to regional destinations significantly less educated (figure 4.1, panel c).

The share of tertiary-educated individuals among emigrants varies considerably within subregions. For Northern and Western European countries, the share of the high skilled among emigrants exceeds 40 percent in Sweden, Norway, Iceland, Denmark, France, Belgium, and the United Kingdom, but is only slightly more than 20 percent among the Mediterranean and Southern European countries such as Spain, Greece, Italy, and Portugal. Patterns are even more diverse among Eastern European countries. The share of the tertiary educated is near or more than 40 percent in Ukraine, Latvia, Lithuania, Hungary, Belarus, and Estonia. On the other hand, in countries with lower levels of income and education, such as Turkey, Albania, the Former Yugoslav Republic of Macedonia and Bosnia, the level is about 15 percent. Similarly, in Central Asian countries the share of the tertiary educated in 2010 ranges from 19 percent in Kazakhstan to more than 50 percent in Turkmenistan (figure 4B.3). While the share of the tertiary educated among emigrants from the EU15+ declined from 2000 to 2010, this share rose from Central and Eastern Europe. One potential explanation is that Central and Eastern Europe's rapid increase in education levels and integration into the global economy increased the pool of younger and better-educated workers with globally marketable skills.

Differences in the age distribution between sending and receiving countries play a limited role in migration in some ECA subregions. Globally, differences in the relative sizes of the working-age populations (25–65 age group) are important determinants of migration flows (see World Bank 2018). Working-age individuals may move from developing countries with young and rapidly growing populations, often suffering from youth unemployment and underemployment and related social problems, to high-income countries that have completed their demographic transitions and have aging populations. Thus, the 25–64 age group comprises slightly more than 60 percent of the native-born population of the EU15+ but 75 percent of the foreign-born population, while immigrants' share among the elderly (older than age 65) is only half that of the native born (figure 4.2, panel a). However, many Central and Eastern European countries have relatively old and rapidly aging populations. Thus, differences in the age composition of populations are less important in shaping immigration to Central and Eastern Europe, where the share of working-age individuals is slightly less among immigrants than among natives. The role of demography in regional migration flows can be seen more clearly when comparing the age composition of native-born and emigrant populations from sending countries (figure 4.2, panel b). Emigrants from each region are concentrated in the 25–64 age group, especially in Central Asia, where their share in this group is 11 percentage points higher than that of those who did not emigrate. These data confirm that labor market concerns are important motivations for migration, and are consistent with the view that most migrants leave their countries after they complete their education (and enter the 25–64 age group).

Women make up the majority of emigrants from ECA. Female migrants made up about 48 percent of the global migrant stock in 2015 (World Bank 2018), about the same level in 2000 and slightly lower than the share of 50 percent in 1980.

FIGURE 4.2 Age composition of native-born and immigrant populations, 2010

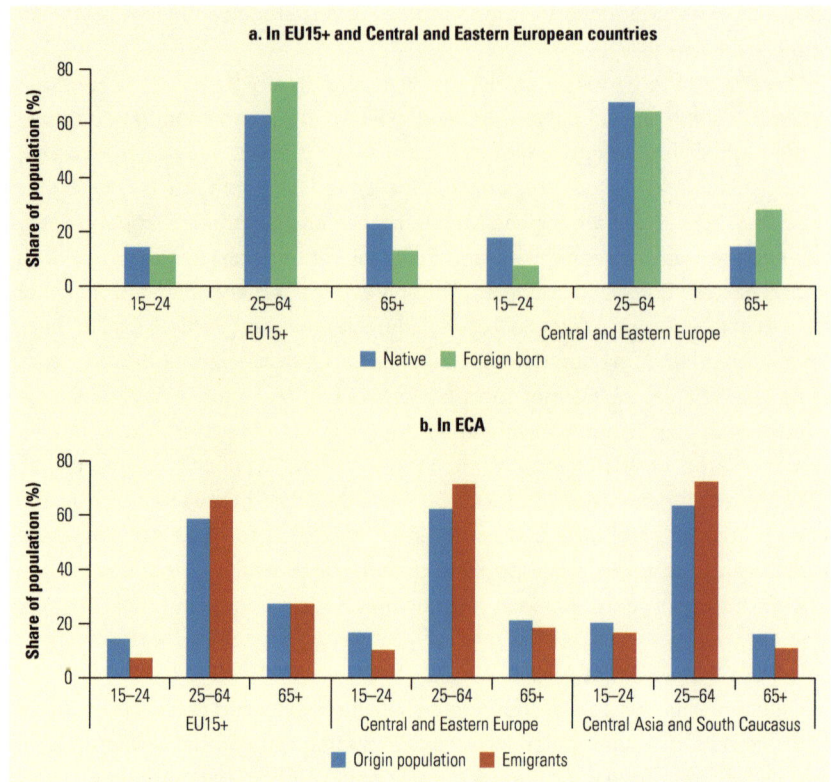

a. In EU15+ and Central and Eastern European countries

b. In ECA

However, women accounted for more than 50 percent of emigrants from almost every country in Northern, Western, and Southern Europe, except for Greece, Italy, the Netherlands, and Portugal. In Sweden and Finland women make up about 60 percent of emigration (figure 4.3, panel a). Similarly, more than 50 percent of emigrants from Central and Eastern Europe (figure 4.3, panel b) and Central Asia and the South Caucasus (figure 4.3, panel c) are women. Despite the common perception that most migrants from Central Asian countries, especially to Russia, are men, the majority of emigrants in most of the countries are women, reaching 60 percent among many of the largest sending countries, such as Russia, Ukraine and Moldova. The main exceptions are the lower-income countries such as Albania and Turkey, but there is significant increase over time in these cases as well.

The reasons for the overrepresentation of women in emigration are unclear. One potential explanation is that women in many low- or middle-income countries make up at least half of the tertiary educated, but face various forms of discrimination and restrictions in the labor market. Thus, they prefer to migrate to higher-income countries where potential career opportunities tend to be superior and discrimination lower.

Many of these empirical observations on migration in ECA are confirmed by an analysis based on global migration patterns. A gravity model is used to estimate the global relationship between several variables and migration for 2000 and 2010 (annex 4B and table 4B.1 provide a description of the model and estimation results), which is then applied to the ECA context (see Anderson 2011 and Beine, Bertoli, and Moraga 2014 for a review of gravity models and estimation). Migration

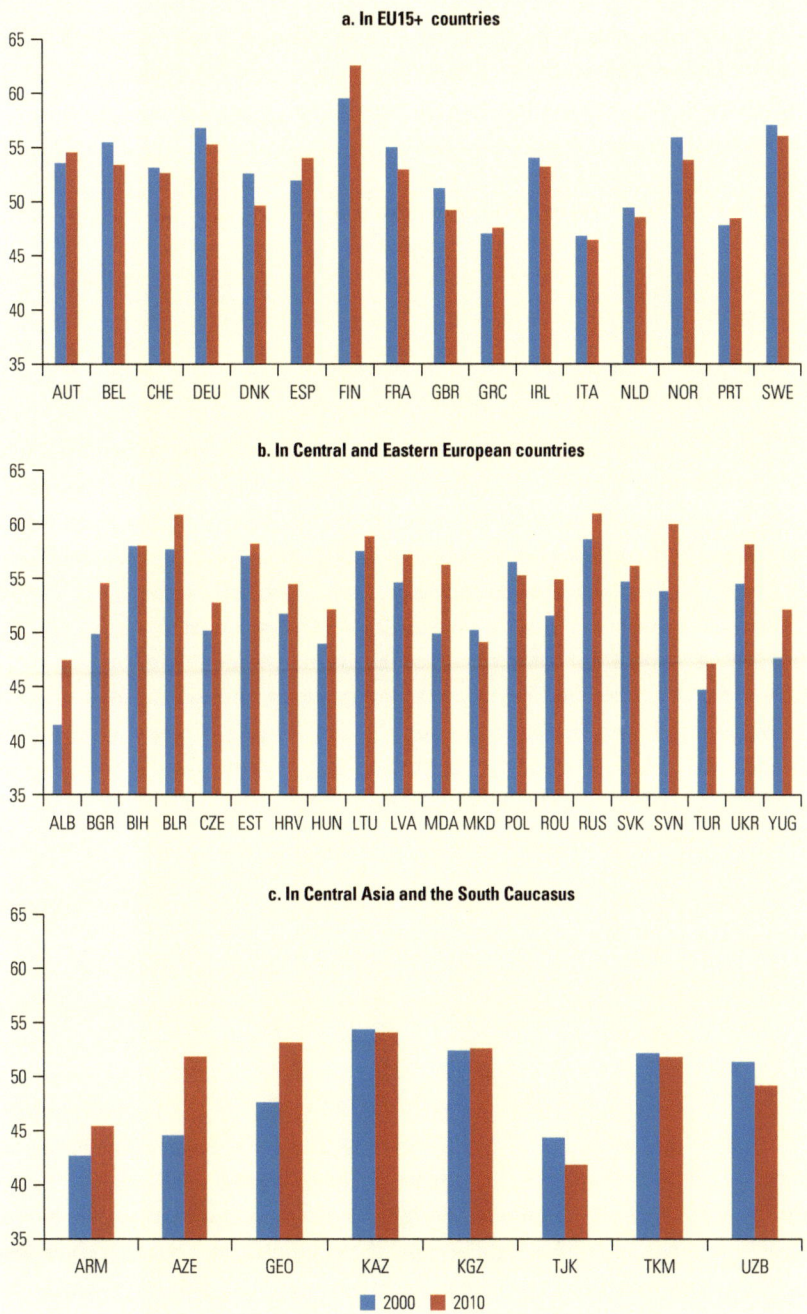

FIGURE 4.3 Percentage of women among emigrants, 2010

Note: The figure presents the number of female emigrants as a percentage of the total number of emigrants. YUG = Serbia and Montenegro.

tends to be higher the smaller the distance between countries. This effect is marginally stronger for the unskilled (relative to the skilled) and men (relative to women). At the extreme, sharing a border has a strong positive effect on migration. Almost half of all unskilled migrants in the world and 20 percent of skilled migrants move to a neighboring country (World Bank 2018). The stock of unskilled migrants almost doubles for both men and women in both years if two countries are neighbors (assuming all other bilateral relationships are kept identical). The effect on high-skilled migrants, on the other hand, is negative, especially in 2010. In other words, high-skilled migrants prefer to move to nonneighboring countries. This is consistent with the fact that most high-skilled migrants move to high-income Organisation for Economic Co-operation and Development (OECD) member countries, especially the English-speaking countries.

Migrants from Central Europe, Eastern Europe, and Central Asia (that is, all ECA countries except the EU15+) are likely to go to other countries within this region.[5] The effect is very similar regardless of the education level or the gender of the migrants. This is in stark contrast to other pairs of countries in other regions where the effect is almost zero (since this analysis controls for distance and contiguity). In 2010, any pair of non-EU15+ ECA countries (except the cases where both are former Soviet Union countries) have between 450 and 800 percent more migration between them compared with other country pairs. Furthermore, the effect has increased since 2000 when it was between 300 and 400 percent. The preference for moving within this group of countries likely reflects remaining ties (business, transport, language, and personal) from when most were members of the Communist bloc. The regional effect for EU15+ countries is positive for the high skilled but negative for the low skilled. This implies that low skilled EU15+ migrants are more likely to leave the region, while the high skilled tend to stay. However, the likelihood of Central and Eastern Europe and Central Asia and the South Caucasus migrants moving to EU15+ is also very strong, especially in 2010. The migration from Central and Eastern Europe and Central Asia and the South Caucasus to EU15+ is about 200 percent (for skilled females) to 275 percent (for unskilled men and women) higher than that of between other country pairs. The lowest is for skilled men, at about 140 percent.

Mobility between former Soviet Union countries is also high for skilled migrants. In addition to many similar economic and academic institutions that are the legacy of the Soviet Union, the economies of these countries are closely integrated. These effects are very high and positive for the high skilled but almost zero for the low skilled. In 2010, high-skilled migrants from former Soviet Union countries are almost 400 percent more likely to move to other former Soviet Union countries, compared with a random pair of countries. This figure is less than those for the Central and Eastern Europe and Central Asia and the South Caucasus countries, but much higher than that estimated for migration to Northern, Western, and Southern Europe.

Mobility between former Soviet Union countries is high for skilled migrants...

The existence of a diaspora tends to increase the stock of migrants, as it reduces a number of costs associated with migration. Diasporas provide valuable information to migrants regarding labor markets, housing, education, and various other social norms. They can help with the financing of migration costs and may be a source of insurance in case of negative shocks. In an extensive econometric analysis of the role of diasporas in shaping migration patterns, Beine, Docquier, and Özden (2011) find that the elasticity of a diaspora with respect to migrant stocks is slightly less than 0.5 for the unskilled in 2010 and 0.2 for the skilled for both gender groups. These levels are lower than those in 2000, especially for skilled migrants.

Sharing a similar language also has a positive effect on migration patterns, particularly for skilled migrants. The effect is large and positive for the high skilled, slightly positive for unskilled women, and insignificant for unskilled men. More specifically, if two countries share a similar language, skilled migration for both men and women increases by almost 175 percent in 2010. The almost-zero effect for the unskilled reflects the lesser importance of strong language skills in their work compared with that of skilled migrants, where facility with the local language interacts with skills to boost returns to human capital (see Borjas 1995 for overall impacts of migration).

Migration Patterns in ECA Are Likely to Change

Migration will continue to play an important, but changing, role in the economic and social development of the region. Differences in income and unemployment rates, as well as demand for skilled labor from the region's economic power-houses, will remain key drivers of voluntary migration. While near-term political debate about benefits of migration may slow more open polices toward migration, the trend toward regional economic integration is expected to continue. Improvements in transport and communications have greatly increased the integration of labor markets, in part through the rise of global value chains, and general technological improvements have intensified global competition for high-skilled workers. These developments will boost cross-border connectivity in many dimensions, which will facilitate migration. Some aspects of technological progress, for example, ECA's significant participation in internet-based platforms that connect workers and employers across the world,[6] increase services trade rather than migration. However, in general, technological advancement is complementary to global movements of skilled workers (Kerr et al. 2016). Indeed, the level of high-skilled migration to ECA countries that are OECD members increased more than that of less-skilled migration during 2000–10 (figure 4.4), and ECA countries are increasingly trying to raise the number of high-skilled immigrants (see Castles, de Haas, and Miller 2013 for global migration patterns and their future).

Technological progress and global integration are also reducing the duration of migration. More than two-thirds of OECD host countries for which migration data are available witnessed a rise in the share of temporary migration between 2000 and 2010. In part this reflects the weakening of skilled workers' ties to a location or national identity and increased global perspectives and connections, which also promotes more circular migration. It also reflects the rise in the share of temporary employment in most ECA subregions from 2002 to 2016 (figure 4.5), in part driven by technological progress, as countries with larger shares of temporary employment tend to have larger shares of temporary immigration (figure 4.6).[7]

Higher education is increasingly globalized (box 4.1), which generates significant benefits. International students gain wider access to education and employment opportunities abroad, while the receiving countries capture a broader range

FIGURE 4.4 The share of high-skilled immigrants to high-income ECA OECD member countries increased between 2000 and 2010

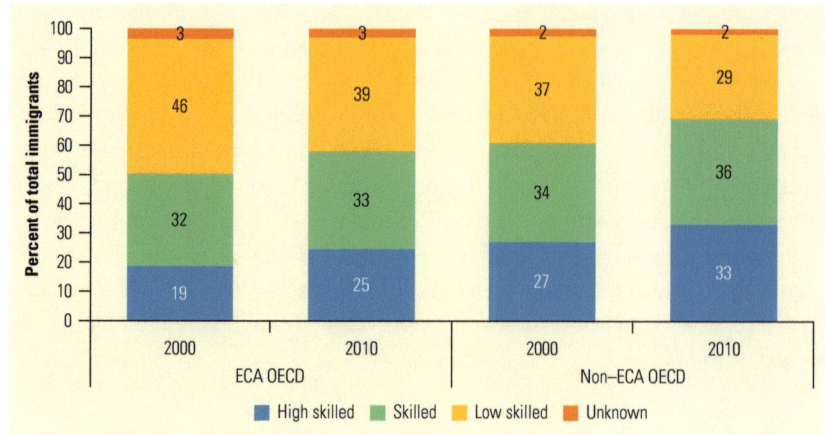

Source: Organisation for Economic Co-operation and Development (OECD), Database on Immigrants in OECD Countries.
Note: "Low skilled" refers to people with no more than lower-secondary education; "Skilled" refers to people with upper-secondary to postsecondary nontertiary education; "High skilled" refers to people with tertiary education. "ECA OECD" includes Austria, Belgium, the Czech Republic, Denmark, Finland, France, Germany, Greece, Hungary, Ireland, Italy, Luxembourg, the Netherlands, Poland, Portugal, the Slovak Republic, Spain, Sweden, Turkey, and the United Kingdom. "Non-ECA OECD" includes Australia, Canada, Japan, Mexico, New Zealand, Norway, Switzerland, and the United States. ECA = Europe and Central Asia.

FIGURE 4.5 The share of temporary employment increased in Europe and Central Asia between 2002 and 2016

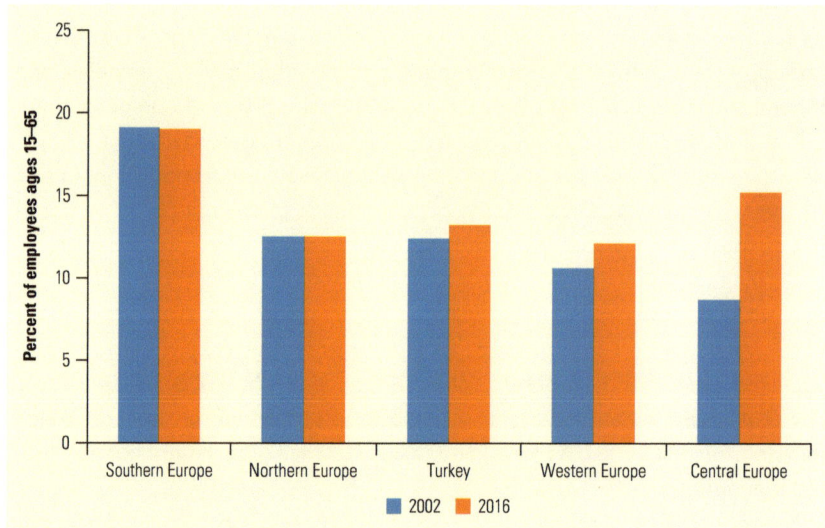

Source: World Bank 2016b.
Note: Shares for Turkey are based on 2006 and 2016 data.

of skills (Tse 2012). Student mobility can be an important source of longer-term immigration. Globally, between 1970 and 2000, a 10 percent increase in international students (including ECA students) increased the stock of tertiary-educated workers in host countries by 0.9 percent (Felbermayr and Reczkowski 2012). Foreign students who join the host country workforce have a positive impact on host countries. An internationally diverse workforce tends to improve the performance of research and development (see Chellaraj, Maskus, and Mattoo 2008 and Kerr and Lincoln 2010 for the United States and Niebuhr 2010 for Germany).

FIGURE 4.6 The share of temporary migration is positively related to the share of temporary employment

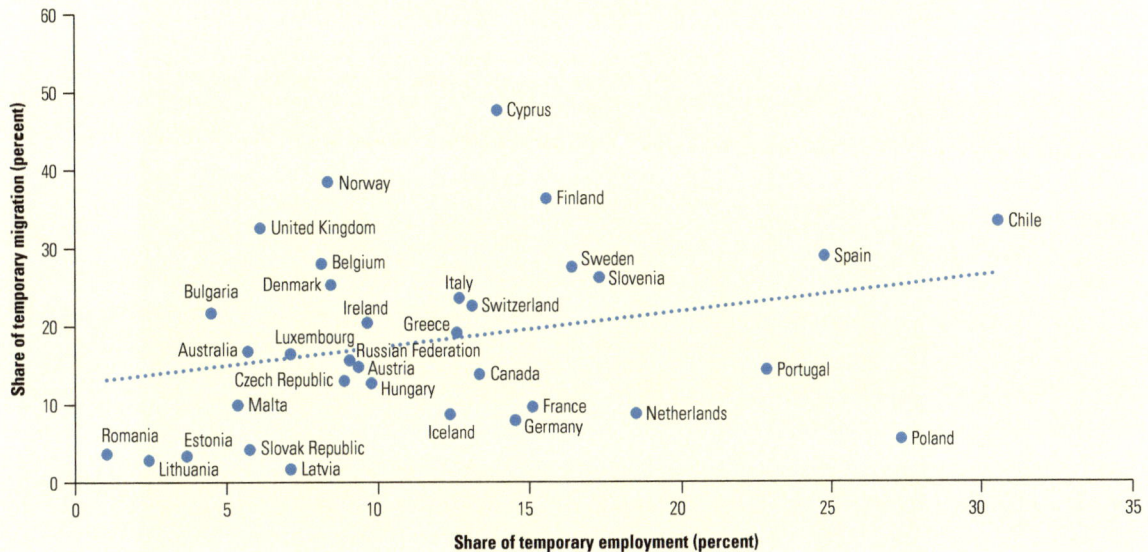

Source: Organisation for Economic Co-operation and Development (OECD) data for 2010.

BOX 4.1 **The Globalization of Education**

While students coming to study in foreign countries have been an important channel for knowledge transfer within Europe and Central Asia (ECA) since the ancient Greeks, the movement of students within ECA and between ECA and other regions increased following the collapse of the Soviet Union (Ackers and Gill 2008). ECA has experienced a further rise in the number of international students over the past decade, facilitated by technological progress and rising incomes in source countries. The number of international students hosted by the top 10 ECA destination countries increased significantly between 2004 and 2014, except in Germany (figure B4.1.1). In 2014, apart from China and India, most of the top 10 sources of foreign students in ECA were other ECA countries (figure B4.1.2).

ECA countries hosted about half of all foreign students globally (figure B4.1.3). Among the top 10 corridors of international tertiary student flows, China–United Kingdom and Kazakhstan–Russian

Federation witnessed remarkable increases in the number of international undergraduate and graduate students, of 80 percent and 145 percent, respectively (figure B4.1.4).

During a meeting in Bologna in 1999, European officials proposed harmonizing their postsecondary educational systems and offering programs in English, with the aim of increasing interest in and recognition of their degrees globally. This harmonization has resulted in a common three-cycle system for tertiary education (the bachelor's, master's, and doctorate degrees). The European Higher Education Area and Bologna Process has 48 full members. The Commonwealth of Independent States (CIS) signed an agreement on the mutual recognition of education credentials for secondary and vocational education in 2004, effective beginning in September 2005. Russia also has bilateral agreements on mutual recognition with other CIS countries, including Azerbaijan, Moldova, Turkmenistan, and Ukraine.

continued

BOX **4.1**   **The Globalization of Education** *continued*

FIGURE B4.1.1 **Most top ECA destinations attracted more international tertiary students in 2014 than in 2004**

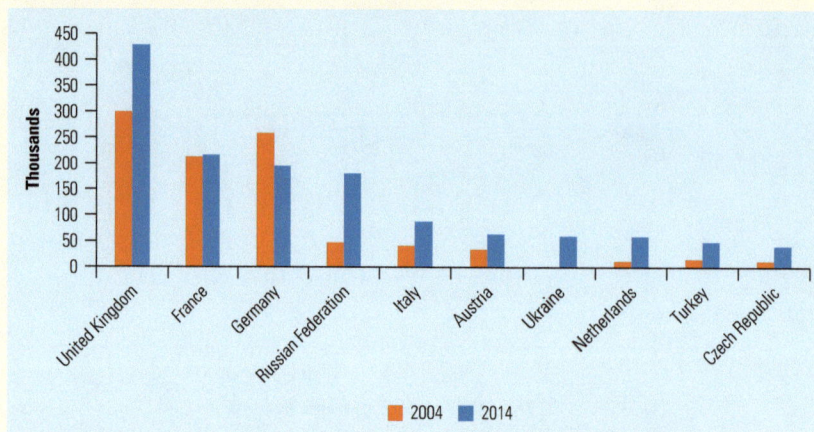

Source: United Nations Educational, Scientific, and Cultural Organization (UNESCO) Institute for Statistics data set on international student mobility in tertiary education, available at http://data.uis .unesco.org/.

FIGURE B4.1.2 **Most source countries of international tertiary students are in ECA**

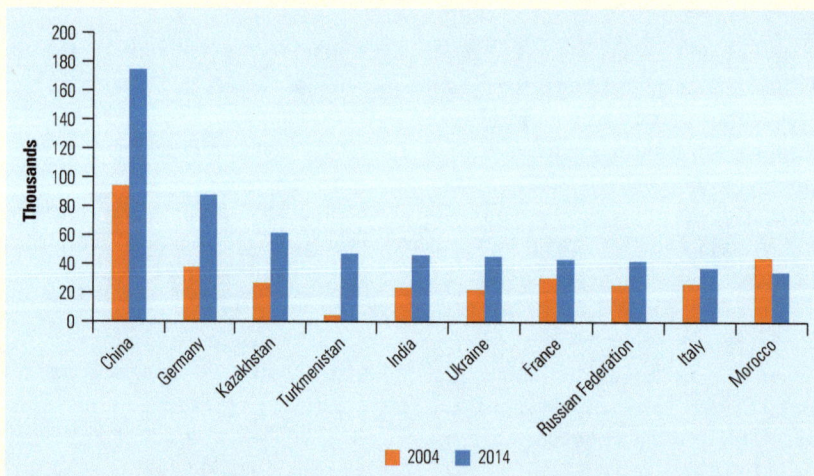

Source: United Nations Educational, Scientific, and Cultural Organization (UNESCO) Institute for Statistics data set on international student mobility in tertiary education, available at http://data.uis .unesco.org/.
Note: Data for 2014 are not available for Georgia, Greece, and Spain. Data for 2004 are not available for Azerbaijan, Bosnia and Herzegovina, Croatia, Luxembourg, Serbia, Turkmenistan, Ukraine, and Uzbekistan.

continued

BOX 4.1 **The Globalization of Education** *continued*

FIGURE B4.1.3 ECA hosted half of the world's tertiary students in 2014

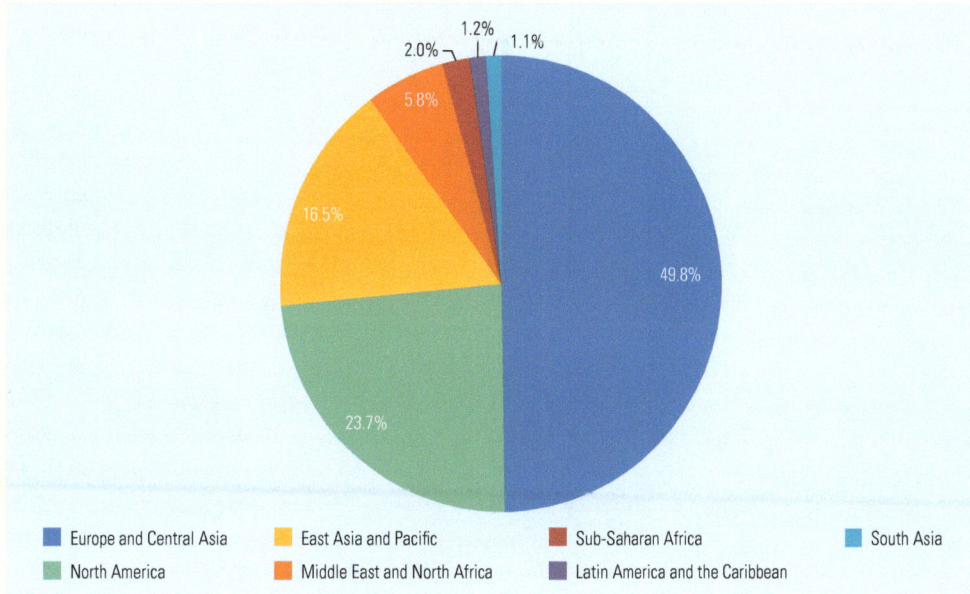

■ Europe and Central Asia	■ East Asia and Pacific	■ Sub-Saharan Africa	■ South Asia
■ North America	■ Middle East and North Africa	■ Latin America and the Caribbean	

Source: United Nations Educational, Scientific, and Cultural Organization (UNESCO) Institute for Statistics data set on international student mobility in tertiary education, available at http://data.uis.unesco.org/.
Note: Regional groupings follow the World Bank classification, with the following exceptions: (a) Europe and Central Asia (ECA) is adjusted to include the countries monitored by the World Bank's ECA regional office; (b) countries not included in the World Bank list are classified using the UN Population Division's regional grouping; and (c) countries not included in either list are assigned to a region on the basis of geographic location, using World Bank region names. Table 4B.6 lists the countries for which data are available.

FIGURE B4.1.4 Top 10 corridors of international tertiary students with ECA hosts
Number of tertiary students (thousands)

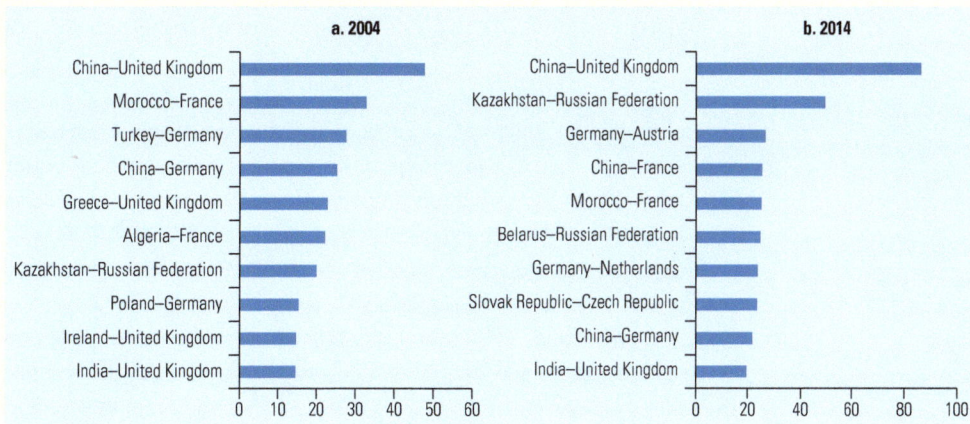

Source: United Nations Educational, Scientific, and Cultural Organization (UNESCO) Institute for Statistics data set on international student mobility in tertiary education, available at http://data.uis.unesco.org/.

In general, students who stay contribute to the cultural enrichment of host countries (Van Mol 2014). Collaboration between academics also is an important example of the benefits of connectivity. For example, scientists from Western European countries have played a key role in stimulating international academic collaboration by engaging in research projects with Eastern European scholars (Teodorescu and Andrei 2011).

Support for migration should be an integral part of the growth agenda for countries in ECA. Individuals, employers, and countries may be more successful if they can find out how best to navigate these new, more integrated global labor markets, considering their own regulatory constraints. Seizing the opportunities of new technologies will require an institutional and policy framework that welcomes workers, encourages circular migration, and reaps the benefits of the diaspora community. As markets become increasingly integrated, countries should help people, migrants and native born alike, navigate new competitive forces and try to prevent growing inequalities. One aspect of these efforts, which could benefit both individual workers and countries, should involve increased investment in education, so that a country's citizens can better participate in the global labor market.

Increased competition from immigrants is not a major threat to natives' employment prospects. Competition for high-quality jobs is largely driven by the broader rise in connectivity, rather than direct migration. Competition occurs almost irrespective of where competing workers are located. Indeed, empirical evidence suggests that migration has only a small and temporary impact on average domestic workers' wages and employment (see, for instance, Longhi, Nijkamp, and Poot 2005; National Academies of Sciences, Engineering, and Medicine 2017), although close substitutes may lose, and complements win, especially in the short run. Both the positive and negative effects of increased connectivity depend on the flexibility of labor markets and the complementarity between the skills of native-born workers and migrants. The workers who lose out are often migrants who arrived previously.

> **Both the positive and negative effects of increased connectivity depend on the flexibility of labor markets and the complementarity between the skills of native-born workers and migrants.**

Policies Should Aim to Improve the Integration of Migrants

Improving the integration of migrants in ECA host countries would help maximize the gains from international migration for both origin and host countries (see Eurostat 2017). In most countries in ECA, unemployment rates are higher among the foreign-born than the native-born population (figure 4.7). In part, this is because when jobs are scarce, many native-born workers may leave the labor force and rely on their assets, while foreign-born workers are less likely to have such resources to fall back on and thus continue to search for work. While natives tend to have higher secondary education rates than immigrants, tertiary education rates are nearly the same between natives and nonnatives (figure 4.8). A lack of integration of migrants into the employed workforce weakens the economic benefits of migration and its contribution to host countries' economies.

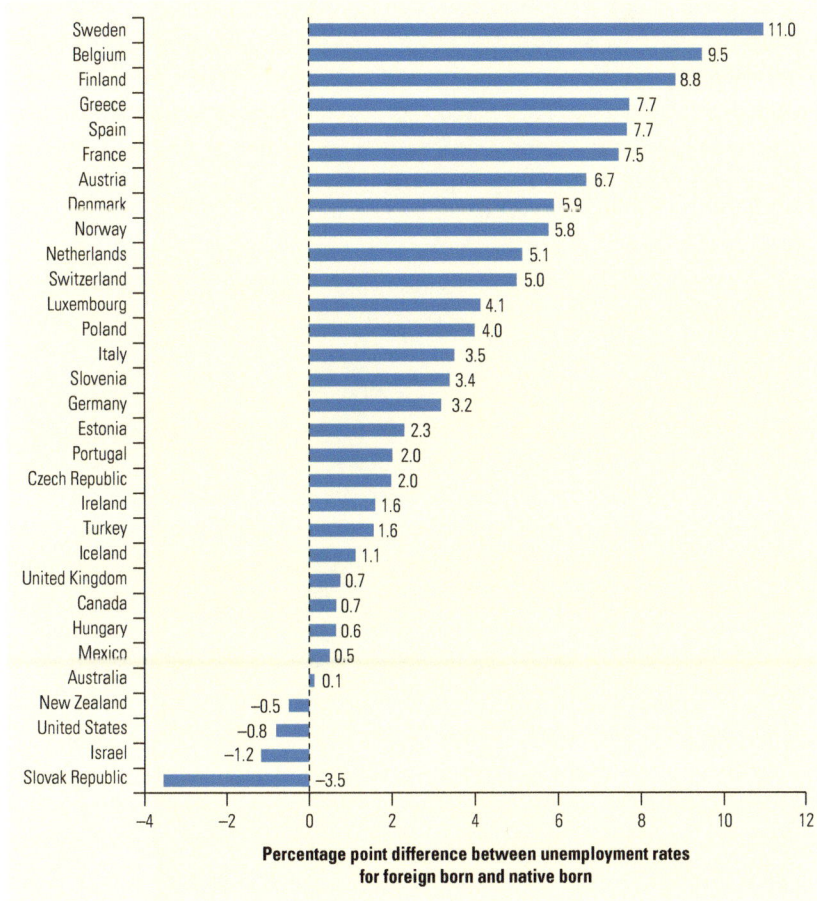

FIGURE 4.7 Unemployment rates are higher for foreign-born than for native-born workers in most countries in Europe and Central Asia

Source: Organisation for Economic Co-operation and Development, available at http://www.oecd.org/els/mig/keystat.htm.
Note: Data are for 2016.

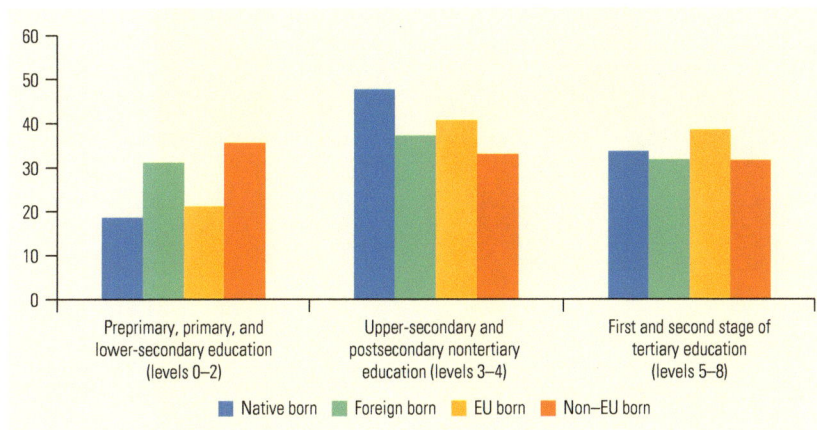

FIGURE 4.8 Tertiary education rates in the European Union are about the same among native- and foreign-born working-age populations (ages 25–54)

Source: Eurostat.
Note: Data are for 2017. "EU born" does not include the reporting country. EU = European Union.

Immigration is most likely to be complementary to native workers in host countries, but this depends on the labor market response. Bussolo, Koettl, and Sinnott (2015) show that people who immigrated to Northern, Western, and Southern Europe between 1990 and 2000 had complementary skills to natives and contributed to increasing wages and reducing inequality among natives. The effect of immigration also depends on the work responses of natives. Cattaneo, Fiorio, and Peri (2015) find that native workers in Europe are more likely to move to occupations associated with higher skills and status when they are faced with a large inflow of migrants into the labor market. Foged and Peri (2015) find that in Denmark the presence of low-skilled migrants was associated with upward wage and skill mobility of low-skilled native workers.

ECA policies could be more supportive of efforts to integrate migrants. The Migrant Integration Policy Index (MIPEX), which measures policies that affect integration of immigrants into host economies (the scale is 0–100, and higher values denote more favorable integration policies), indicates that the average ECA country has a lower degree of migrant integration for labor markets than other regions (Huddleston et al. 2015).[8] Comparing ECA to benchmark countries (Canada, Japan, New Zealand, the Republic of Korea, and the United States), ECA has the lowest degree of overall integration except for Japan and the lowest degree of integration for labor market mobility. Moreover, ECA has made little or no policy progress in either labor integration or political participation over time (both are components of the overall MIPEX and have a range of 0–100; figure 4.9). The labor market dimension captures the ease of access to public or private sector as well as self-employment. It also accounts for access to general and targeted support for the worker (state facilitation of recognition of workers' qualifications) and for workers' rights. The political participation dimension instead captures electoral rights and political liberties such as the right to association.

FIGURE 4.9 Migrant Integration Policy Index overall, labor market integration, and political participation scores in ECA and selected countries
0–100 scale

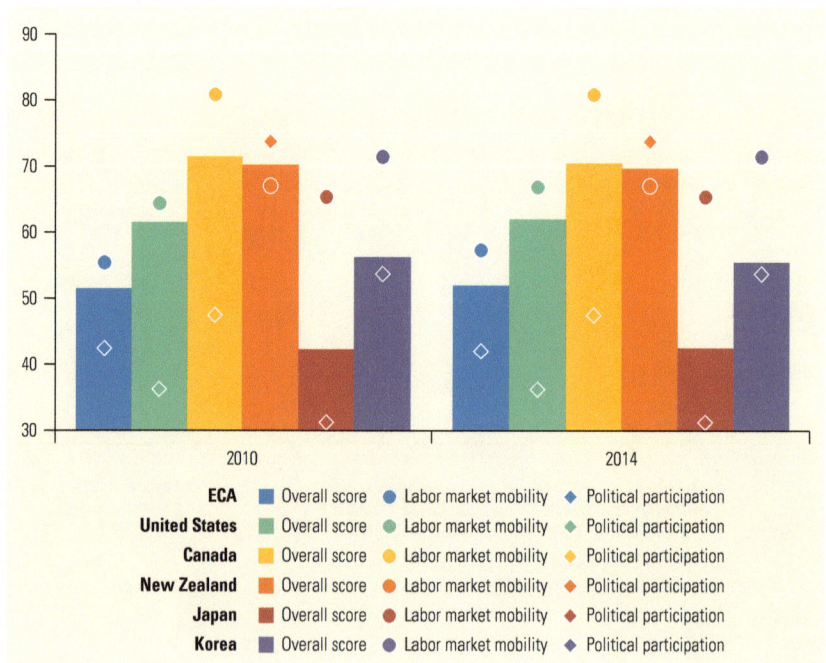

Policy efforts to support the integration of migrants in the labor market vary considerably across countries. More comprehensive programs are more common in the EU15 countries than in the rest of the region (table 4.1). Integration policies are weak in Turkey and Central Europe. Western, Southern, and Northern Europe perform almost as well as the best performers outside ECA. Progress is apparent only in Northern and Central Europe (see also Bamieh, Fiorini, and Hoekman 2017).

TABLE 4.1 The Availability of Programs Designed to Integrate Migrants Varied in ECA, 2015

		Policy on migrant integration, 2015		
		Language skills training	Transfer of professional credentials	Protection against discrimination
EU15	Austria	Yes	Yes	Yes
	Belgium	Yes	Yes	Yes
	Denmark	Yes	Yes	No
	Finland	Yes	Yes	Yes
	France	Yes	Yes	Yes
	Germany	Yes	Yes	Yes
	Greece	Yes	Yes	Yes
	Ireland	Yes	Yes	Yes
	Italy	Yes	Yes	Yes
	Luxembourg	Yes	Yes	Yes
	Netherlands	Yes	Yes	No
	Portugal	Yes	Yes	Yes
	Spain	Yes	Yes	Yes
	Sweden	Yes	Yes	Yes
	United Kingdom	Yes	Yes	Yes
EU13	Bulgaria	Yes	Yes	Yes
	Croatia	Yes	Yes	Yes
	Cyprus	Yes	Yes	Yes
	Czech Republic	Yes	No	Yes
	Estonia	Yes	Yes	Yes
	Hungary	Yes	Yes	Yes
	Latvia	Yes	No	No
	Lithuania	No	Yes	Yes
	Malta	Yes	Yes	Yes
	Poland	Yes	No	Yes
	Romania	Yes	Yes	Yes
	Slovak Republic	Yes	Yes	Yes
	Slovenia	Yes	Yes	Yes
Western Balkans	Albania	No	No	No
	Bosnia and Herzegovina	No	No	No
	Montenegro	No	No	No
	Serbia	No	No	No
South Caucasus	Armenia	Yes	Yes	Yes
	Azerbaijan	No	No	Yes
	Georgia	No	Yes	Yes
Central Asia	Kazakhstan	No	No	Yes
	Tajikistan	No	No	Yes
	Turkmenistan	No	No	No
	Uzbekistan	n.a.	n.a.	n.a.
Russian Federation		Yes	No	Yes
Turkey		No	No	Yes
Other Eastern Europe	Belarus	Yes	No	Yes
	Ukraine	Yes	Yes	Yes

Source: United Nations Department of Economic and Social Affairs (UNDESA) Population Division, World Population Policies Database.
Note: The table shows official responses about policies or combinations of policies aimed at integrating immigrants into the host society. ECA = Europe and Central Asia; n.a. = not available.

Support for integration is even more important in the context of refugees. Evidence from the 2008 EU Labor Force Survey shows that refugees take six years to achieve the labor force participation rates of migrants who moved for family reasons and more than 15 years to catch up with migrants who came for work or education (OECD 2016). The recent influx of refugees accentuates the need for strong integration programs.

Emigration Generates Net Benefits in ECA Origin Countries

While emigration does have distributional impacts in origin countries, with losers and winners, emigration is often a safety valve for jobs during economic downturns or crises, with net positive economic effects. Emigrants themselves benefit, as the choice to migrate is made based on weighing the expected benefits and costs to moving relative to those from staying. Workers in the origin countries that stay and who are close substitutes are likely to benefit, while people with complementary skills may not benefit or may even lose (see Elsner 2013 for Lithuania; Bouton, Paul, and Tiongson 2011 for Moldova; and Dustmann, Frattini, and Rosso 2015 for Poland). For some ECA countries, remittances from workers living aboard are large relative to gross domestic product (GDP) and an important source of income in the region (figure 4.10). They have a mildly positive impact on long-term economic growth in emigration countries in ECA and a positive impact on poverty reduction for the poorest households (Mansoor and Quillin 2006). They can also improve access to international capital markets.

There is considerable anecdotal evidence on diaspora investments and the promotion of trade and knowledge transfer. The return of migrants to their home country can support economic development, particularly when they bring capital and knowledge with them and the origin country provides the framework conditions to help them make use of their skills and investments. The development of the wine industry in Argentina provides a striking example of the impact of technology transfer as a result of migration (box 4.2). The return of Albanian migrants

FIGURE 4.10 Many countries in Europe and Central Asia depend on remittances

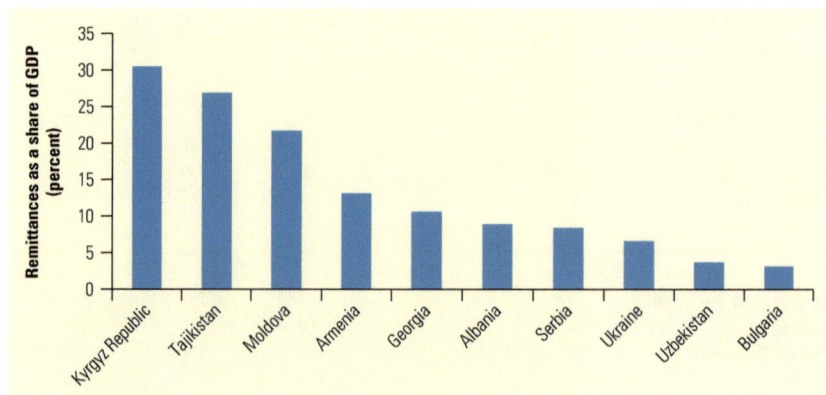

Source: World Bank, World Development Indicators database.
Note: Data are for 2016.

BOX 4.2   Nicolas Catena Zapata and the Malbec: Technology Transfer through Migration

Nicolas Catena Zapata, one of the most important innovators in the international wine industry, developed an entire new industry of quality wine in Argentina based on technology learned abroad.[a] Catena's approach to wine making illustrates what Galenson (2007) refers to as an experimental innovation, which develops by a process of trial and error. Experimental innovators proceed tentatively, building their skills gradually, and tend to make their greatest contributions late in their careers. By contrast, conceptual innovations tend to be dramatic, often something completely different that breaks the conventional rules of a discipline or activity. Generally, conceptual innovators have precise goals, which allows them to plan their work and execute it decisively. Their most radical new ideas, and consequently their greatest innovations, tend to occur early in their careers. While the breakthrough ideas of conceptual innovators are easy to communicate among people in the same field, experimental innovations are hard to communicate and have to be experienced to understand.

Catena's presence in Napa Valley during the early 1980s was critical for importing the new California winemaking technique to Argentina. He was born into a family of Argentinean wine producers, but became an economics professor. While a visiting professor at UC Berkeley in the early 1980s, he discovered that the techniques used to achieve international-level quality in California were far in advance of those used in Argentina. He subsequently began a project to use the California methodology, adapted to Argentina, to achieve international quality levels.

Catena resurrected the Malbec as a varietal in the 1995 harvest. The new Malbec was produced in traditional areas of Mendoza, but was produced with what Catena calls his Californian-French style or methodology. This was a significant change from what Catena calls the "ancient Italian" style traditionally used in Argentina. Catena's Malbec had unique characteristics, and its appearance was a milestone in the world of wine.

Despite his success, Catena found that his wines, particularly the Cabernet Sauvignon, were of a lower quality than European and Californian wines. He believed that the problem was the high temperature in the vineyards, and began planting in locations at higher altitudes and in the south, with lower temperatures. This was a risky experiment, because colder areas can be subject to an early and a late frost, and there was some potential that the grapes would not ripen.

The results were excellent. Catena undertook trials with Chardonnay, Cabernet Sauvignon, Malbec, and Pinot Noir. Surprisingly, the Malbec not only behaved better with the cold, but produced something original. These experiments led to the birth of the high-altitude Malbec, Catena's second experimental innovation.

Without Catena's incidental exposure to foreign wine technology through his temporary emigration to California, the wine industry in Argentina likely would have been substantially less productive.

a. This box was written by Julio Elias based on an interview with Nicolas Catena in 2016. The author thanks Mr. Catena for his great generosity with his time.

with the Greek crisis—which increased Albania's labor force by 5 percent between 2011 and 2014 alone—had positive effects on the wages of low-skilled nonmigrants and overall positive effects on employment of those who stayed (Hausmann and Nedelkoska 2017). Return migrants are also more often self-employed than workers who never left, potentially contributing to employment generation and economic growth. The majority of ECA countries have developed policies to encourage the return of their nationals. Between 2000 and 2015, the number of EU13 countries with return policies increased significantly (table 4.2).

TABLE 4.2 Nearly All EU13 Countries Have Developed Policies to Encourage the Return of Their Citizens

		Policy to encourage the return of citizens?	
		2005	2015
EU15	Austria	Yes	Yes
	Belgium	No	No
	Denmark	No	No
	Finland	No	Yes
	France	No	No
	Germany	No	No
	Greece	Yes	Yes
	Ireland	Yes	Yes
	Italy	No	Yes
	Portugal	No	Yes
	Spain	Yes	Yes
	Sweden	No	No
	United Kingdom	No	No
EU13	Bulgaria	n.a.	Yes
	Croatia	Yes	Yes
	Cyprus	Yes	n.a.
	Czech Republic	No	Yes
	Estonia	Yes	Yes
	Hungary	No	Yes
	Latvia	Yes	Yes
	Lithuania	No	Yes
	Malta	No	No
	Romania	No	Yes
	Slovenia	Yes	Yes
Western Balkans	Albania	Yes	Yes
	Bosnia and Herzegovina	Yes	Yes
	Montenegro	n.a.	Yes
	Serbia	n.a.	Yes
South Caucasus	Armenia	Yes	Yes
	Azerbaijan	Yes	Yes
	Georgia	n.a.	Yes
Central Asia	Kazakhstan	Yes	Yes
	Tajikistan	Yes	No
	Turkmenistan	n.a.	n.a.
	Uzbekistan	n.a.	n.a.
Russian Federation		n.a.	Yes
Turkey		No	No
Other Eastern Europe	Belarus	Yes	Yes
	Ukraine	No	Yes

Source: United Nations Department of Economic and Social Affairs (UNDESA) Population Division, World Population Policies Database.
Note: Table shows official responses regarding whether the government has adopted any policies or programs to encourage the return of its citizens living abroad. n.a. = not available.

Emigration can help improve institutions in the origin country, although the destination matters. Emigration can improve institutions by increasing the home country population's exposure to the values and norms of the host countries. For example, Docquier et al. (2010) present cross-country evidence that unskilled emigration from a large sample of developing countries to OECD countries over 1975–2000 improved institutional quality in origin countries, as measured by the value of political rights, civil liberties, and openness of political institutions.[9] Beine and Sekkat (2014) find, however, that emigration to economically or politically powerful countries has a positive impact on the quality of home country institutions, but no effect is found when the destination is former colonizers. Emigration also may lead to worse institutions and values if dissatisfied people with the motivation to change them leave. There is evidence indicating that emigration helped relax domestic pressure to reform autocratic regimes in Mexico (Hansen 1988), Cuba (Colomer 2000; Hoffman 2005), and Haiti (Ferguson 2003). Furthermore, remittance inflows may relieve the governments of public finance accountability, similar to the effect of large natural resource flows, and have adverse effects on domestic institutional quality (Abdih et al. 2012). Econometric estimates show that emigration to more democratic countries has a positive impact on political institutions, but emigration to less democratic countries does not (box 4.3).

BOX 4.3 Emigration Can Improve Political Institutions in the Home Country

Econometrics can identify the effect of the diaspora on the institutional quality of the sending country through the following model:

$$I_{i,t} = \alpha + \beta Emigrant_{i,j,t-1} + \gamma I_{i,t-1} + \Phi X_{i,t} + \partial year_t + \varepsilon_{i,j,t}$$

(B4.3.1)

where I_{it} is the institutional quality of origin country i in time t, $Emigrant_{i,j,t-1}$ is the lagged number of individuals born in country i and living in country j as a share of the origin country's population, and $X_{i,j}$ is a vector of control variables. The regression over the pooled cross-section also includes a year dummy $year_t$ to control for the time period. The control variables include time-varying confounders that likely have an effect on institutional quality, including GDP per capita (in purchasing parity terms), the share of tertiary-educated population among the population age 25 and older, and age composition of the population (the share of population age 0–14 and share of population age 65 and older). The inclusion of the lagged value of institutional quality enables us to control for time-invariant characteristics of the origin country linked to the quality of institutions.

Migration stock data (from World Bank 2016b, which includes new bilateral data on migration stocks; the Global Bilateral Migration Database 2013 by the World Bank; Özden et al. 2011; and the 2010 OECD International Migration Database

and its extension, which also includes non-OECD receiving countries) are only available for most countries for every 10 years (from 1960 to 2010). To allow for the effect of emigration, the lag period chosen is 5–10 years. For example, the average institutional value of 1995–2000 is regressed against the emigrant stock of 1990, and so on. Values of institutional quality come from Polity IV, a global data set that consists of multiple dimensions of governance and political systems. Education data are derived from the World Bank's World Development Indicators (WDI) database, the Barro and Lee (2001) database, and the ILOStats database of the International Labour Organization. Population and GDP data come from the WDI. Since GDP in purchasing parity terms is only available since the 1980s, the data are limited to four rounds of cross-section: 1980, 1990, 2000, and 2010.

To examine the impact of the host country's values on the home country, the regressions distinguish three destinations: all countries, countries with higher institutional quality (according to the composite measure polity2 by the Polity IV project), and those with worse institutional quality.

The results are summarized in table B4.3.1. The quality of fit is high (60–70 percent). When all destinations are considered, the size of the diaspora (as a share of the population of the home country) has no relationship with institutional quality. However, emigration to more democratic

continued

BOX 4.3 Emigration Can Improve Political Institutions in the Home Country *continued*

TABLE B4.3.1 Impact of Emigration on Institutions of Origin Countries, by Type of Destination

	Institutionalized democracy	Institutionalized autocracy	Executive recruitment	Executive constraints	Political competition	Polity
a. All emigration						
Emigrants (% of home population)	0.005 (0.009)	−0.003 (0.008)	0.005 (0.006)	0.004 (0.006)	0.000 (0.008)	0.007 (0.015)
Lagged institution value	0.736 (0.002)**	0.684 (0.002)**	0.731 (0.002)**	0.654 (0.002)**	0.712 (0.002)**	0.726 (0.002)**
R^2	0.77	0.71	0.72	0.70	0.74	0.76
Number of observations	99,189	99,189	99,189	99,189	99,189	100,522
b. Emigration to more democratic countries						
Emigrants (% of home population)	0.056 (0.015)**	-0.030 (0.012)*	0.032 (0.009)**	0.032 (0.009)**	0.030 (0.011)**	0.080 (0.024)**
Lagged institution value	0.734 (0.005)**	0.718 (0.004)**	0.768 (0.004)**	0.650 (0.005)**	0.716 (0.005)**	0.740 (0.004)**
R^2	0.62	0.71	0.70	0.58	0.65	0.69
Number of observations	28,275	28,275	28,275	28,275	28,275	28,882
c. Emigration to similar or less democratic countries						
Emigrants (% of home population)	−0.090 (0.020)**	0.068 (0.017)**	−0.064 (0.014)**	−0.044 (0.012)**	−0.050 (0.020)*	−0.147 (0.032)**
Lagged institution value	0.556 (0.005)**	0.425 (0.005)**	0.499 (0.006)**	0.470 (0.005)**	0.528 (0.005)**	0.510 (0.005)**
R^2	0.69	0.50	0.54	0.60	0.64	0.65
Number of observations	35,598	35,598	35,598	35,598	35,598	35,931

Note: Robust standard errors are in parentheses.
*Significant at 5 percent level, **significant at 1 percent level.

countries is significantly associated with improvements in institutionalized democracy, as well as associated aspects such as open political competition, regulated executive recruitment, and constraints on executive power. The reverse is true for emigration to countries that are equally or less democratic.

Institutionalized Democracy is an additive 11-point scale (0–10) indicator derived from coding of the competitiveness of political participation, the openness and competitiveness of executive recruitment, and the existence of institutionalized constraints on the exercise of power by the executive.

Institutionalized Autocracy is an additive 11-point scale (0–10) indicator derived from coding of the competitiveness of political participation, the regulation of participation, the openness and competitiveness of executive recruitment, and the existence of institutionalized constraints on the exercise of power by the executive.

Executive Recruitment combines information presented in three component variables: Regulation of Chief Executive Recruitment (whether there are any established modes at all by which chief executives are selected); Competitiveness of Executive Recruitment (the extent that prevailing modes of advancement give subordinates equal opportunities

continued

BOX 4.3   Emigration Can Improve Political Institutions in the Home Country *continued*

to rise in the firm hierarchy); and Openness of Executive Recruitment (the extent to which all the politically active population has an opportunity, in principle, to attain the position through a regularized process). It uses an 8-point scale (1–8).

Executive Constraints (using a 7-point scale) refers to the extent of institutionalized constraints on the decision-making powers of chief executives, whether individuals or collectivities.

Political Competition combines information presented in two components: the competitiveness of participation (the extent to which alternative preferences for policy and leadership can be pursued in the political arena) and the regulation of participation (participation is regulated to the extent that there are binding rules on when, whether, and how political preferences are expressed). It uses a 10-point scale (1–10).

The polity score is computed by subtracting the autocracy score from the democracy score; the resulting unified polity scale ranges from +10 (strongly democratic) to −10 (strongly autocratic).

Source: Adapted from Nguyen 2017.

Former Warsaw pact countries may have benefited from increased emigration to countries with more democratic institutions. The breakup of the Soviet Union led to an increase in the share of ECA emigration going to the United States and Northern, Western, and Southern Europe as opposed to Russia, resulting in a steady rise in the stock of emigrants from ECA to countries that rank higher on various indicators of political institutions by the Polity IV project (Center for Systemic Peace 2015).[10] In Moldova, for example, communities with higher prevalence of emigration to Northern, Western, and Southern Europe are more likely to vote for western-style democratic parties than those with higher migration to Russia, and westward migration significantly contributed to putting an end to the Communists' rule in the 2009 election (Barsbai et al. 2017).

The significant benefits from international migration in ECA are reflected in high-income countries' relatively low restrictions on mobility. For example, the restrictiveness of visa regimes in ECA high-income countries declined moderately from 2006 to 2012, and remains well below that of the United States (figure 4.11, panel a). These lower restrictions in part reflect intra-EU mobility, but much of the difference is driven by fewer mobility barriers imposed on middle- and low-income countries. The United States is stricter than ECA high-income countries toward all countries, particularly countries in Latin America and the Caribbean (figure 4.11, panel b). Both the United States and high-income ECA apply no visa restrictions on North American nationals, which includes the United States, but the United States still applies restrictions on nationals of high-income ECA countries.

FIGURE 4.11 High-income ECA countries are much more permissive toward international mobility than the United States

Mobility restrictions imposed by high-income ECA countries and the United States

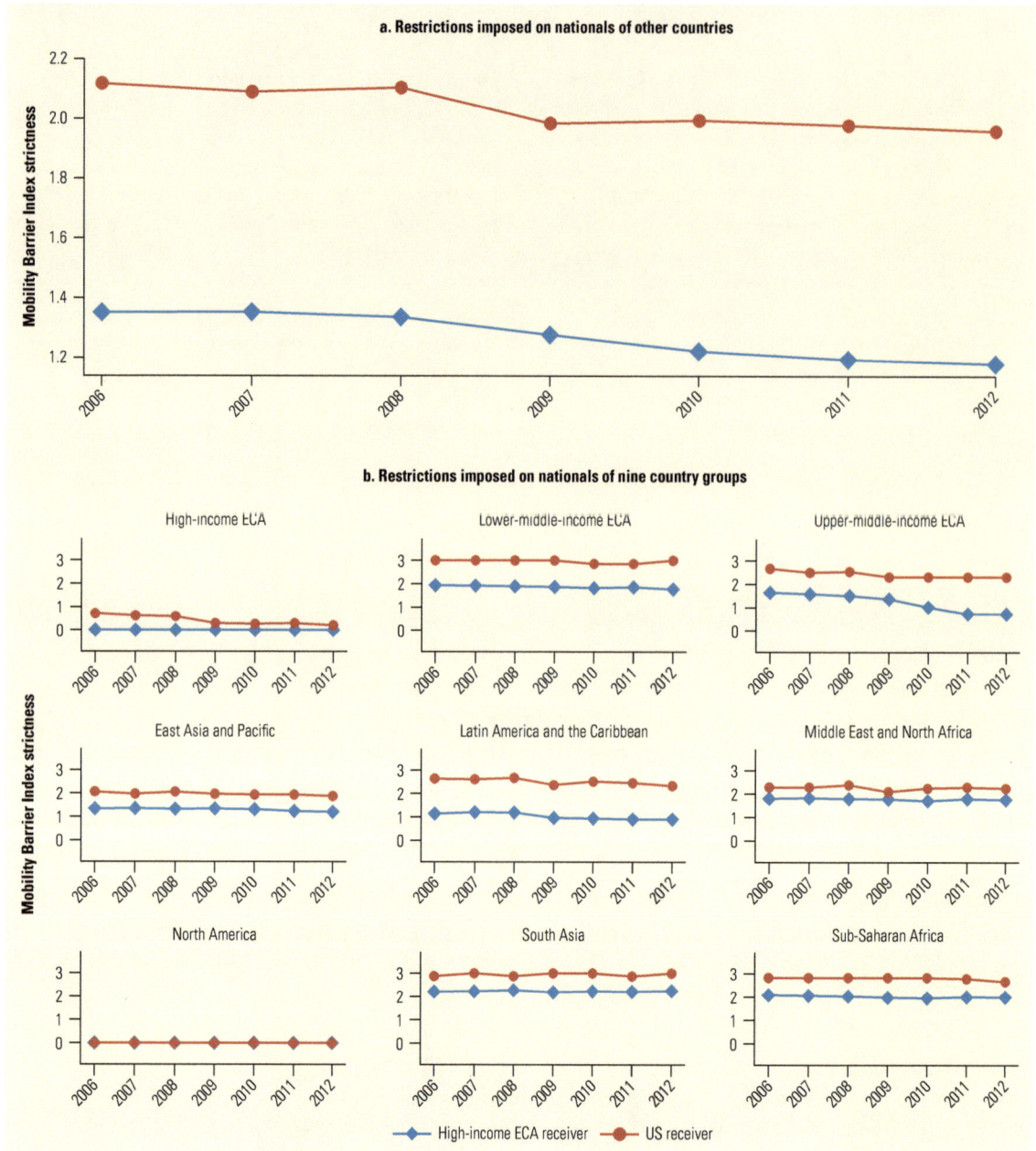

Source: Bamieh, Fiorini, and Hoekman 2017.
Note: The figure presents data covering 199 countries. The Mobility Barrier Index, compiled as part of The European Visa Database project, measures visa requirements, visa-issuing practices, and consular services (for more information see http://www.mogenshobolth.dk). It has an ordinal scale from 0 to 3 (0 = no barriers, 1 = low barriers, 2 = medium barriers, 3 = high barriers) and is constructed as follows: if no visa requirement is in force, a score of 0 is assigned. If a receiving state does not provide visa-related consular services in a sending state, a score of 2 is assigned. If a receiving state relies on the consular services of another for visa issuance, the two states are assumed to have similar practices. If the visa refusal rate is below 3 percent, a score of 1 is assigned; between 3 percent and 20 percent, a score of 2; and above 20 percent, a score of 3. This grouping is based on a quantitative analysis of the total data set: group 1 is approximately the first interquartile range, group 2 the second and third, and group 3 the fourth and last. If the number of visa applications is low (below 20 percent of a modeling estimate) compared with the population of the sending and receiving country—and the travel distance between them—the score is increased by 1 to take into consideration that receiving states can put into place barriers that prevent people from lodging applications (see http://www .lse.ac.uk/government/research/resgroups/MSU/documents/workingPapers/WP_2012_03.pdf). ECA = Europe and Central Asia.

Conclusion

Migration has played a key role in enhancing connectivity and improving economies and institutions in the ECA region for centuries. Maintaining supportive policies toward migration would make a critical contribution to prosperity in the region. Although the recent flows of refugees have certainly dominated the news and are a concern to policy makers in the region, a broader, longer-term perspective is critical to appreciating the economic gains from migration. Measures to increase the integration of migrants in destination countries and greater support for migrant education would improve productivity in the host and home countries. Increasing the flexibility of labor market institutions and improving skills would help promote employment; increasing the portability of benefits and improving income security could reduce fears over the economic impact of immigrants on native workers as well as facilitate circular migration. Reaching international agreement on migration in a multilateral framework could enhance the benefits of migration for both origin and destination countries.

Annex 4A. Gravity Model

The standard gravity equation for migration $m_{k,t}^{ij}$ from origin i to destination j is expressed as

$$m_{k,t}^{ij} = exp\left(c_{k,t}^{i} + d_{k,t}^{j} + B_{k,t} X^{ij} \right) + e_{t}^{ij},$$

where $c_{k,t}^{i}$ is the origin fixed effect (the push variable) for origin country i and education group k at time t, $d_{k,t}^{j}$ is the destination fixed effect (the pull variable) for destination country j, X^{ij} is the set of bilateral variables between i and j, $B_{k,t}$ is the coefficient of the bilateral variables, and e_{t}^{ij} is the regression residual. The bilateral variables include language similarity, diaspora size in 1960, colonial links, distance, and regional dummies, such as migration within ECA, migration from Eastern and Central Europe to Northern, Western, and Southern Europe, and so on.

Since we do not have detailed data on skilled and unskilled migration for many destination countries, we cannot include skill-specific destination fixed effects in the gravity regressions. We assume that we can express the skill-specific destination fixed effect in terms of a general (not specific to skill) destination fixed effect plus some explanatory variables, such as education level, GDP, military service, and female labor force participation. Then the skill-specific destination fixed effect becomes

$$d_{k,t}^{j} = d_{t}^{j} + A_{k,t} Y_{t}^{j},$$

where d_{t}^{j} is the general destination fixed effect (the pull variable) for country j, Y_{t}^{ij} is the set of bilateral explanatory variables, $A_{k,t}$ is the coefficient of the explanatory variables. Then we can combine the two equations to get the final gravity regression equation

$$m_{k,t}^{ij} = exp\left(c_{k,t}^{i} + d_{t}^{j} + A_{k,t} Y_{t}^{j} + B_{k,t} X^{ij} \right) + e_{t}^{ij}.$$

The gravity model must be estimated on a global scale using a full set of origin and destination countries to identify push, pull, and gravity forces correctly.

Omitting a destination or an origin country can affect the multilateral resistance terms and bias the estimates as pointed out by Anderson and van Wincoop (2003). However, unlike the bilateral international trade data, there are no comprehensive bilateral migration data sets with different skill and education levels available. In other words, we lack the full square data matrix to estimate the migration model on a global scale using a traditional gravity model.

One approach to solve the missing data problem is presented in a recent paper by Artuc et al. (2015). This paper is based on this novel approach that obtains unbiased estimates of the gravity parameters in the case of missing corridors. The estimation strategy is based on two statistical algorithms: (a) Poisson pseudo–maximum likelihood to estimate gravity parameters introduced by Santos Silva and Tenreyro (2006) and (b) an Expectation Maximization algorithm, which was originally used in the genetics literature by Dempster, Laird, and Rubin (1977), followed by economics research such as Hamilton (1990) and Arcidiacono and Bailey (2003). The estimation strategy consists of two recursive steps: (a) Maximization step: This step estimates determinants of migration using a detailed gravity model that includes both skilled and unskilled migrants, with origin fixed effects, destination fixed effects, and connectivity parameters such as existing diaspora links, distance, and common language; (b) Expectation step: Using the estimated gravity parameters, the procedure predicts and fills in missing migration data. After the expectation step, the algorithm returns to the maximization step, and continues going back and forth between the steps recursively until it converges to a solution.

The estimation procedure is based on the Expectation-Maximization algorithm and consists of two iterative steps, similar to Arcidiacono and Bailey (2003). The first, "Expectation," step fills in the missing cells based on the theoretical gravity model. The second, "Maximization," step updates the coefficient estimates using the actual and simulated data. Then these two steps are repeated back and forth a few hundred times until the coefficients converge.

Expectation Step

For a moment, let us assume that we have estimates of $m_{k,t}^{ij}$, expressed as $\hat{m}_{k,t}^{ij}$ for every skill level k. Then we can use the aggregate data, m_t^{ij}, (which is not skill specific) to impute the number of type k migrants, because the aggerate data should be equal to the sum of different skill groups. For example, we observe the total number of Polish immigrants in Russia, but we do not know the number of college graduate Polish immigrants in Russia. However, if we add college graduate Polish immigrants in Russia and non-college-graduate Polish immigrants in Russia we should get the total Polish immigrants in Russia. Thus, we can use this restriction and the data on aggregate migration for identification. Therefore,

$$m_t^{ij} = \sum_k m_{k,t}^{ij}.$$

The expectation step equation is

$$\widetilde{m}_{k,t}^{ij} = \frac{\hat{m}_{k,t}^{ij}}{\sum_l \hat{m}_{l,t}^{ij}} m_t^{ij},$$

where $\widetilde{m}_{k,t}^{ij}$ is the "imputed" migration data that goes into the *maximization* step.

After imputing the number of skilled and unskilled immigrants for each corridor using estimates of skilled and unskilled immigrants and the data on total immigrants, we move on to the maximization step.

Maximization Step

We estimate the gravity equation using the imputed migration data, $\tilde{m}^{ij}_{k,t}$, when the migration corridor is missing with the following gravity regression

$$\bar{m}^{ij}_{k,t} = \exp\left(c^i_{k,t} + d^j_t + A_{k,t}Y^j_t + B_{k,t}X^{ij} \right) + e^{ij}_t,$$

where $\bar{m}^{ij}_{k,t}$ is equal to $m^{ij}_{k,t}$ when the skill-specific migration data are available, and equal to $\tilde{m}^{ij}_{k,t}$ when skill-specific migration data are not available. After the gravity regression, we calculate the migrant estimates using the regression equation and estimates of the coefficients, $\hat{c}^i_{k,t}$, $\hat{d}^j_t$, $\hat{A}_{k,t}$ and $\hat{B}_{k,t}$:
$\hat{m}^{ij}_{k,t} = \exp\left(\hat{c}^i_{k,t} + \hat{d}^j_t + \hat{A}_{k,t}Y^j_t + \hat{B}_{k,t}X^{ij} \right).$
Then we go back to the expectation step and continue moving between the expectation and maximization steps recursively until the estimates converge.

Annex 4B. Additional Tables and Figures

TABLE 4B.1 Gravity Regression Results

	Male		Female	
	Unskilled	Skilled	Unskilled	Skilled
a. 2010				
Diaspora	0.67	0.57	0.63	0.50
	(72.86)	(49.50)	(71.48)	(41.46)
Distance	−0.30	−0.40	−0.30	−0.40
	(−11.18)	(−10.71)	(−11.41)	(−10.38)
Colony	0.06	0.08	0.11	0.36
	(1.22)	(1.20)	(2.36)	(5.85)
Contiguity	0.40	−0.78	0.51	−0.80
	(8.33)	(−10.64)	(10.93)	(−10.61)
Language similarity	0.22	0.43	0.33	0.61
	(4.71)	(7.19)	(6.97)	(9.49)
Within EU15+	−0.11	0.27	−0.18	0.45
	(−1.11)	(2.12)	(−1.92)	(3.53)
Within non-EU15+	0.56	1.32	0.79	1.63
	(3.09)	(5.83)	(4.52)	(7.41)
Non-EU15+ to EU15+	1.05	0.60	1.10	0.86
	(9.40)	(4.51)	(10.61)	(7.05)
EU15+ to non-EU15+	0.16	0.79	0.11	1.28
	(0.69)	(2.28)	(0.49)	(3.74)
Rest of world within regions	−0.17	−0.98	0.05	−0.55
	(−2.68)	(−11.33)	(0.74)	(−6.11)
Former Soviet Union	−1.19	0.58	−1.09	0.63
	(−7.49)	(2.74)	(−7.38)	(3.17)
b. 2000				
Diaspora	0.53	0.44	0.52	0.38
	(70.03)	(37.06)	(67.53)	(30.03)
Distance	−0.26	−0.05	−0.22	−0.10
	(−10.55)	(−1.38)	(−9.50)	(−2.59)

continued

TABLE 4B.1 *continued*

	Male		Female	
	Unskilled	**Skilled**	**Unskilled**	**Skilled**
Colony	0.27	−0.06	0.17	0.01
	(5.45)	(−0.86)	(3.65)	(0.15)
Contiguity	0.81	0.14	0.83	−0.10
	(19.28)	(1.80)	(20.01)	(−1.29)
Language Similarity	0.05	0.83	0.35	0.89
	(1.12)	(11.62)	(8.04)	(10.97)
Within EU15+	0.09	0.34	0.01	0.44
	(1.09)	(2.66)	(0.10)	(3.39)
Within non-EU15+	1.55	1.42	1.80	1.59
	(9.88)	(6.92)	(11.61)	(7.47)
Non-EU15+ to EU15+	0.72	0.15	0.60	0.22
	(7.16)	(1.01)	(6.38)	(1.57)
EU15+ to non-EU15+	0.41	1.12	0.67	1.25
	(2.01)	(4.08)	(3.51)	(4.40)
Rest of world within regions	0.47	−0.14	0.51	0.06
	(8.28)	(−1.56)	(8.99)	(0.57)
Former Soviet Union	0.08	1.02	−0.02	1.37
	(0.55)	(5.26)	(−0.13)	(7.25)

Note: Estimation using Poisson pseudo–maximum likelihood methodology. *t*-statistics are in parentheses. All *t*-statistics greater than 2 are significant at the 5 percent level or higher.

TABLE 4B.2 **Emigration in ECA Countries (excluding EU15+), 2000**

	Male			Female		
	Total	**Unskilled**	**Skilled**	**Total**	**Unskilled**	**Skilled**
Albania	553,074	172,993	14,664	472,082	104,386	11,338
Armenia	460,824	224,521	72,749	383,759	161,846	58,998
Azerbaijan	728,953	336,907	105,207	776,845	343,218	115,961
Belarus	760,391	447,020	185,458	1,105,949	749,091	222,883
Bosnia and Herzegovina	807,098	576,014	95,336	863,830	668,324	63,213
Bulgaria	376,007	211,479	58,526	403,931	232,267	41,307
Croatia	462,978	352,168	64,958	501,449	396,553	58,627
Czech Republic	435,443	61,911	46,715	505,619	100,658	49,419
Estonia	102,553	23,109	18,837	133,550	35,144	27,780
Georgia	520,417	210,683	110,741	603,456	251,875	120,511
Hungary	220,989	85,309	74,643	251,699	108,198	72,097
Kazakhstan	1,451,504	752,767	228,507	1,911,536	1,027,953	346,063
Kyrgyz Republic	317,079	117,318	151,764	376,412	90,279	243,139
Latvia	158,502	37,222	33,372	193,339	51,805	47,821
Lithuania	256,909	69,472	40,771	317,752	120,129	50,375
Moldova	290,522	154,216	47,154	367,904	184,459	63,064
Poland	2,443,641	337,078	269,635	2,733,042	504,030	338,718
Romania	632,140	183,424	90,652	694,834	217,507	100,846
Russian Federation	4,587,448	1,717,500	1,323,930	6,223,586	2,882,230	1,488,465
Serbia and Montenegro	989,318	302,838	101,023	927,636	302,611	59,040
Slovak Republic	267,240	156,897	30,947	309,978	202,288	27,452
Slovenia	63,424	43,217	14,991	74,310	59,002	10,242
Tajikistan	276,557	148,773	87,153	277,286	80,834	152,889
Turkey	1,687,246	1,004,105	102,098	1,414,001	789,980	47,649
Turkmenistan	162,461	64,904	47,428	173,258	64,671	64,184
Ukraine	2,532,632	1,277,681	719,933	3,690,195	2,088,707	947,751
Uzbekistan	782,593	346,369	130,359	875,333	370,056	183,670

TABLE 4B.3 Emigration in ECA Countries (excluding EU15+), 2010

	Male			Female		
	Total	Unskilled	Skilled	Total	Unskilled	Skilled
Albania	686,254	489,005	26,744	580,727	306,411	48,507
Armenia	433,146	59,005	358,475	359,428	69,830	249,374
Azerbaijan	697,067	109,370	313,891	601,591	215,612	49,915
Belarus	698,438	211,611	202,025	936,088	413,037	259,463
Bosnia and Herzegovina	811,913	494,037	122,814	844,606	579,000	82,800
Bulgaria	628,499	266,694	81,222	653,981	291,891	101,381
Croatia	423,617	207,428	70,405	487,444	362,669	51,400
Czech Republic	186,061	67,503	64,776	259,596	138,559	73,115
Estonia	79,545	32,633	22,808	97,178	32,117	26,069
Georgia	414,859	139,993	233,122	396,486	237,164	90,953
Hungary	244,367	101,364	89,033	265,290	144,362	91,940
Kazakhstan	1,823,123	1,019,518	776,016	2,084,622	1,764,949	271,431
Kyrgyz Republic	374,380	8,080	357,691	402,790	60,532	316,507
Latvia	145,379	65,245	56,265	165,765	61,726	60,879
Lithuania	226,364	117,139	75,759	285,839	124,438	100,884
Macedonia, FYR	262,770	156,234	22,685	263,437	176,375	20,673
Moldova	412,838	161,159	179,818	445,820	204,669	155,733
Poland	1,639,333	976,854	571,161	1,880,192	976,757	743,278
Romania	1,432,015	1,072,317	218,177	1,617,985	895,175	319,485
Russian Federation	4,833,306	1,444,919	1,280,908	6,103,269	2,334,833	1,232,999
Serbia and Montenegro	766,434	384,644	60,569	713,213	279,555	52,486
Slovak Republic	235,286	155,537	46,104	291,857	201,430	65,385
Slovenia	75,508	27,000	13,969	110,160	73,444	15,593
Tajikistan	351,935	2,749	336,162	258,065	18,623	189,075
Turkey	1,622,419	1,259,307	192,738	1,472,566	1,130,708	142,303
Turkmenistan	172,289	51,872	109,178	181,282	126,979	47,318
Ukraine	2,537,323	944,572	918,172	3,111,315	1,539,198	1,015,666
Uzbekistan	1,048,511	281,092	740,620	939,362	441,072	441,231

TABLE 4B.4 Immigration in ECA Countries (excluding EU15+), 2000

	Male			Female		
	Total	Unskilled	Skilled	Total	Unskilled	Skilled
Albania	34,929	21,052	1,877	39,507	27,800	975
Armenia	121,835	54,361	17,395	177,492	84,668	25,787
Azerbaijan	102,159	51,247	20,371	134,417	69,522	28,435
Belarus	570,469	247,946	157,737	662,863	339,789	175,335
Bosnia and Herzegovina	21,166	6,279	2,710	22,647	9,051	2,955
Bulgaria	54,645	26,211	8,299	66,682	33,956	10,668
Croatia	292,472	227,649	33,716	329,881	280,473	20,229
Czech Republic	206,350	132,093	24,580	245,551	174,097	21,799
Estonia	101,027	48,303	23,772	148,804	73,693	35,721
Georgia	107,619	49,966	21,284	121,723	63,173	24,636
Hungary	136,400	73,328	13,150	174,012	98,106	12,705
Kazakhstan	1,313,270	513,796	496,568	1,540,344	773,235	461,300
Kyrgyz Republic	151,446	59,928	46,892	211,444	92,642	62,550
Latvia	241,596	132,802	51,697	364,690	218,375	78,790
Lithuania	92,038	50,256	20,190	120,029	69,249	27,606
Macedonia, FYR	45,414	19,622	6,823	63,563	31,332	7,811

continued

TABLE 4B.4 *continued*

	Male			Female		
	Total	Unskilled	Skilled	Total	Unskilled	Skilled
Moldova	208,461	92,191	47,463	265,901	137,377	61,207
Poland	336,829	156,444	38,635	485,144	291,692	38,260
Romania	93,493	48,061	11,534	76,278	47,985	6,169
Russian Federation	5,356,263	2,921,347	1,236,481	6,916,092	3,852,371	1,641,808
Serbia and Montenegro	462,001	285,747	51,065	590,930	424,932	43,262
Slovak Republic	51,947	22,836	9,976	66,007	37,422	9,787
Slovenia	91,621	65,158	12,823	80,082	59,842	8,983
Tajikistan	138,039	48,706	44,480	182,308	70,315	51,675
Turkey	600,760	289,293	82,763	648,474	300,052	39,512
Turkmenistan	96,811	31,699	39,191	127,863	41,091	51,338
Ukraine	2,362,068	1,119,696	512,934	3,151,215	1,769,083	586,758
Uzbekistan	580,500	198,380	224,781	766,716	276,013	279,472

TABLE 4B.5 **Immigration in ECA Countries (excluding EU15+), 2010**

	Male			Female		
	Total	Unskilled	Skilled	Total	Unskilled	Skilled
Albania	42,170	11,620	2,218	46,939	16,702	2,229
Armenia	142,812	31,817	5,895	176,430	55,825	9,055
Azerbaijan	134,549	32,280	24,171	155,524	47,485	27,377
Belarus	519,123	133,307	114,168	606,195	208,895	160,349
Bosnia and Herzegovina	12,821	3,499	352	12,930	5,843	382
Bulgaria	33,830	13,075	3,815	42,617	21,810	7,547
Croatia	346,346	214,112	22,873	387,281	264,718	20,092
Czech Republic	340,920	192,963	67,938	309,463	208,124	55,425
Estonia	89,989	17,970	30,874	131,098	31,203	43,425
Georgia	87,595	20,385	16,871	100,369	29,558	18,427
Hungary	208,835	100,789	31,446	230,718	124,933	34,879
Kazakhstan	1,753,698	520,151	294,058	1,847,960	666,760	318,856
Kyrgyz Republic	106,038	27,052	31,556	131,612	40,487	43,316
Latvia	140,009	33,450	37,497	203,169	64,132	52,549
Lithuania	89,522	20,183	22,356	116,085	34,214	29,441
Macedonia, FYR	54,814	19,279	5,313	76,533	34,472	6,607
Moldova	184,216	61,629	36,865	212,611	89,634	41,195
Poland	278,302	150,322	30,226	399,062	255,551	38,254
Romania	80,043	37,056	3,748	83,233	51,938	3,882
Russian Federation	5,513,127	2,517,076	1,717,419	5,679,115	2,958,227	1,739,533
Serbia and Montenegro	314,766	90,028	4,814	410,972	224,430	6,871
Slovak Republic	76,309	24,263	11,218	87,577	42,186	15,143
Slovenia	131,073	73,887	31,985	97,714	59,696	21,219
Tajikistan	122,586	27,898	27,648	167,666	43,960	37,109
Turkey	879,406	278,401	115,422	869,667	269,961	120,188
Turkmenistan	99,888	19,943	55,318	118,715	23,834	68,911
Ukraine	2,123,859	721,228	303,278	2,590,436	1,180,337	336,223
Uzbekistan	532,901	155,159	202,368	638,141	207,455	245,718

TABLE 4B.6 Economies Included in Figure B4.1.3

Region	Economies
East Asia and Pacific	Australia; Brunei Darussalam; China; Hong Kong SAR, China; Japan; Korea, Rep.; Lao PDR; Macao SAR, China; Malaysia; Mongolia; New Zealand; Thailand; Vietnam
Europe and Central Asia	Albania; Armenia; Austria; Azerbaijan; Belarus; Belgium; Bosnia and Herzegovina; Bulgaria; Croatia; Cyprus; Czech Republic; Denmark; Estonia; Finland; France; Germany; Hungary; Ireland; Italy; Kazakhstan; Kyrgyz Republic; Latvia; Liechtenstein; Lithuania; Luxembourg; former Yugoslav Republic of Macedonia; Malta; Netherlands; Norway; Poland; Portugal; Moldova; Romania; Russian Federation; Serbia; Slovak Republic; Slovenia; Sweden; Switzerland; Tajikistan
Latin America and the Caribbean	Aruba; Brazil; Chile; Colombia; Dominican Republic; Ecuador; El Salvador; Honduras; St. Kitts and Nevis; St. Lucia; Sint Maarten (Dutch part)
Middle East and North Africa	Bahrain; Egypt, Arab Rep.; Iran, Islamic Rep.; Israel; Morocco; Oman; Qatar; Saudi Arabia; United Arab Emirates
North America	Bermuda; United States
Sub-Saharan Africa	Botswana; Burundi; Cabo Verde; Côte d'Ivoire; Ghana; Lesotho; Madagascar; Mauritius; Mozambique; Namibia; Rwanda; South Africa
South Asia	India; Sri Lanka

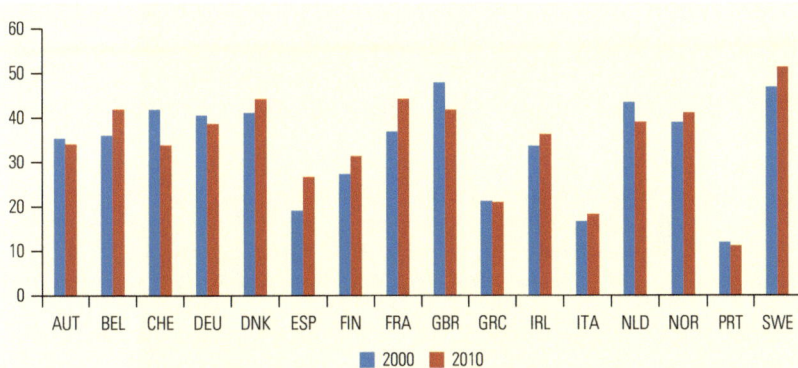

FIGURE 4B.1 Share of tertiary educated among emigrants from EU15+ countries, 2000 and 2010

Note: Share is calculated as the number of tertiary-educated emigrants as a percentage of the total number of emigrants. "Tertiary" is defined, for 2000, as at least some tertiary and for 2010, as completed tertiary.

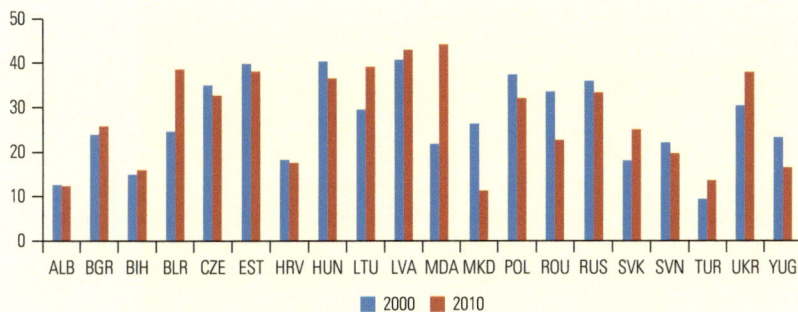

FIGURE 4B.2 Share of tertiary educated among emigrants from Central and Eastern European countries, 2000 and 2010

Note: Share is calculated as the number of tertiary-educated emigrants as a percentage of the total number of emigrants. "Tertiary" is defined, for 2000, as at least some tertiary and for 2010, as completed tertiary. YUG = Serbia and Montenegro.

FIGURE 4B.3 **Share of tertiary educated among emigrants in Central Asia and the South Caucasus, 2000 and 2010**

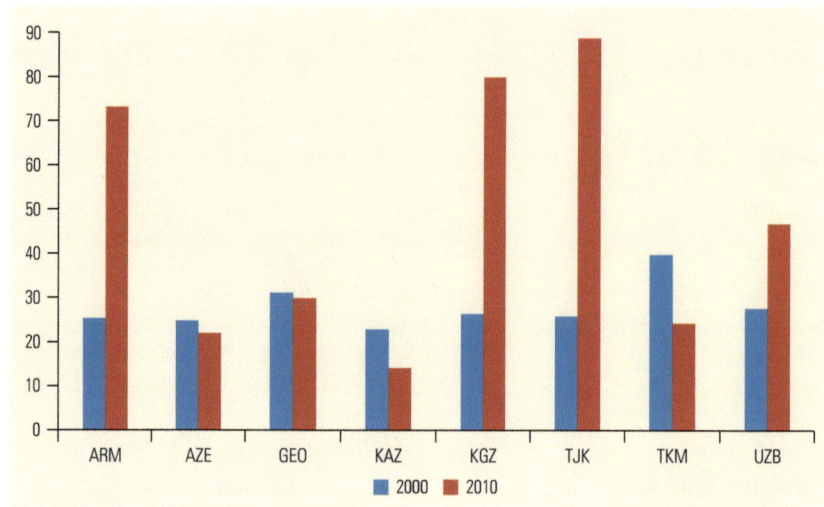

Note: Share is calculated as the number of tertiary-educated emigrants as a percentage of the total number of emigrants. "Tertiary" is defined, for 2000, as at least some tertiary and for 2010, as completed tertiary.

Notes

1. This group includes the 15 countries that were members of the EU before the 2004 accession countries joined, plus Norway and Switzerland.
2. These figures include predicted migration stocks for the missing corridors so that the data can be compared over time. See annex 4A for methodology and data.
3. Reported data for Central Asia for 2000 or 2010 are particularly spotty and, hence, we rely heavily on the estimation methodology.
4. In the migration context, the most widely used proxy for human capital and skills is the education level of the workers. Even though there are numerous complications, this is the most widely and consistently available metric in most countries. Thus, "high skilled" and "tertiary educated" are used interchangeably here.
5. This analysis uses dummy variables for the following intraregional migration corridors: (a) within Central and Eastern Europe and Central Asia and the South Caucasus: takes the value of 1 if both countries (origin and destination) are in the ECA region (except EU15+); (b) within EU15+: takes the value of 1 if both countries are in Western Europe; (c) Central and Eastern Europe and Central Asia and the South Caucasus to EU15+: takes the value of 1 if the origin country is in Central and Eastern Europe and Central Asia and the South Caucasus and destination in EU15+; (d) EU15+ to Central and Eastern Europe and Central Asia and the South Caucasus: takes the value of 1 if the origin country is in EU15+ and destination is in Central and Eastern Europe and Central Asia and the South Caucasus; (e) rest of world within regions: takes the value of 1 if both countries are in the same World Bank regions (except ECA); and (f) former Soviet Union: takes the value of 1 if both countries are former Soviet Union countries. These six variables capture all regional relationships; the excluded relationship is if two countries are not in the same region.
6. Russia and Ukraine are the fifth- and sixth-largest suppliers, respectively, of contract labor to the US market, and Ukraine had the third-largest cumulative online worker wage bill through 2014 (Horton, Kerr, and Stanton 2017).
7. Temporary migrants are defined as foreign-born residents who have been in the host country for less than five years. They could stay longer.

8. MIPEX is sourced from the MIPEX database of CIDOB (Barcelona) and MPG (Brussels); see http://www.mipex.eu/. For the definitions of MIPEX indicators, see http://www.mipex.eu/sites/default/files/downloads/Definitions_of_Who_Benefits_Outcome_and_Beneficiaries_Indicators.pdf.

9. Skilled emigrants, however, had an ambiguous effect. A positive relationship between international emigration and the demand for political accountability is found by Batista and Vicente (2011) for Cape Verde, and between emigration and political stability and voice and accountability by Li and McHale (2009) based on cross-country data. Spilimbergo (2009) shows that foreign education acquired in democratic countries seems to promote democracy in home countries. Li, McHale, and Zhou (2013) find that skilled migrants have positive effects on the home country's political institutions, measured by voice and accountability, political stability and absence of violence, government effectiveness, regulatory quality, rule of law, and control of corruption. There is evidence for Mexico (Pérez-Armendáriz and Crow 2010) and Mali (Chauvet and Mercier 2013) that individuals in migrant households are more likely to vote.

10. On the scale from +10 (strongly democratic) to −10 (strongly autocratic) per the Polity IV project, Russia's rank has fluctuated between 3.5 and 4.7 over the years while the United States, Great Britain, France, Germany, Italy, and Spain have been ranked consistently at 10 since 1980.

References

Abdih, Yasser, Ralph Chami, Jihad Daghe, and Peter Montiel. 2012. "Remittances and Institutions: Are Remittances a Curse?" *World Development* 40 (4): 657–66.

Ackers, Louise, and Bryony Gill. 2008. *Moving People and Knowledge: Scientific Mobility in an Enlarging European Union.* Northampton, MA: Elgar.

Anderson, James E. 2011. "The Gravity Model." *Annual Review of Economics* 3 (1): 133–60.

Anderson, James E., and Eric van Wincoop. 2003 "Gravity with Gravitas: A Solution to the Border Puzzle." *American Economic Review* 93 (1): 170–92.

Arcidiacono, Peter, and John Bailey. 2003. "Finite Mixture Distributions, Sequential Likelihood and the EM Algorithm." *Econometrica* 71 (3): 933–46.

Artuc, Erhan, Frederic Docquier, Çağlar Özden, and Christoper Parsons. 2015. "A Global Assessment of Human Capital Mobility: The Role of non-OECD Destinations." *World Development* 65 (1): 6–26

Bamieh, Omar, Matteo Fiorini, and Bernard Hoekman. 2017. "Trends in Selected Connectivity-Related Policy Indicators for Europe and Central Asia." Unpublished, European University Institute, Florence, Italy.

Barro, R. J., and J. W. Lee. 2001. "International Data on Educational Attainment: Updates and Implications. *Oxford Economic Papers* 53: 541–63.

Barsbai, Toman, Hillel Rapoport, Andreas Steinmayr, and Christoph Trebesch. 2017. "The Effect of Labor Migration on the Diffusion of Democracy: Evidence from a Former Soviet Republic." *American Economic Journal: Applied Economics* 9 (3): 36–69.

Batista, Catia, and Pedro C. Vicente. 2011. "Do Migrants Improve Governance at Home? Evidence from a Voting Experiment." *World Bank Economic Review* 25 (1): 77–104.

Beine, Michel, Simone Bertoli, and Jesús Fernández-Huertas Moraga. 2014. "A Practitioners' Guide to Gravity Models of International Migration." Working Papers 2014-03, FEDEA.

Beine, Michel, Frédéric Docquier, and Çağlar Özden. 2011. "Diasporas." *Journal of Development Economics* 95 (1): 30–41.

Beine, Michel, and Khalid Sekkat. 2014. "Emigration and Origin Country's Institutions: Does the Destination Country Matter?" *Middle East Development Journal* 6 (1): 20–44.

Borjas, George J. 1995. "The Economic Benefits from Immigration." *Journal of Economic Perspectives* 9 (2): 3–22.

Bouton, Lawrence, Saumik Paul, and Erwin R. Tiongson. 2011. "The Impact of Emigration on Source Country Wages: Evidence from the Republic of Moldova." Policy Research Working Paper 5764, World Bank, Washington, DC.

Bussolo, Maurizio, Johannes Koettl, and Emily Sinnott. 2015. *Golden Aging: Prospects for Healthy, Active, and Prosperous Aging in Europe and Central Asia*. Washington, DC: World Bank.

Castles, S., H. de Haas, and M. J. Miller. 2013. *The Age of Migration: International Population Movements in the Modern World*. London: Palgrave Macmillan.

Cattaneo, Cristina, Carlo V. Fiorio, and Giovanni Peri. 2015. "What Happens to the Careers of European Workers When Immigrants 'Take Their Jobs'?" *Journal of Human Resources* 50 (3): 655–93.

Center for Systemic Peace. 2015. *Polity IV Project, Political Regime Characteristics and Transitions, 1800–2015.*

Chauvet, L., and M. Mercier. 2013. "Migration and Elections in Mali. Does Migration Promote Democratization in Africa?" Unpublished, Paris School of Economics, Paris.

Chellaraj, Gnanaraj, Keith E. Maskus, and Aaditya Mattoo. 2008. "The Contribution of International Graduate Students to US Innovation." *Review of International Economics* 16 (3): 444–62.

Colomer, J. M. 2000. "Exit, Voice, and Hostility in Cuba." *International Migration Review* 34 (2): 423–42.

Dempster, A. P., N. M. Laird, and D. B. Rubin. 1977. "Maximum Likelihood from Incomplete Data via the EM Algorithm." *Journal of the Royal Statistical Society, Series B* 39 (1): 1–38.

Docquier, Frédéric, Elisabetta Lodigiani, Hillel Rapoport, and Maurice Schiff. 2010. "Emigration and the Quality of Home Country Institutions." Discussion Paper 2010-35, Université catholique de Louvain, Institut de Recherches Economiques et Sociales (IRES), Louvain, Belgium.

Dustmann, Christian, Tommaso Frattini, and Anna Rosso. 2015. "The Effect of Emigration from Poland on Polish Wages." *Scandinavian Journal of Economics* 117 (2): 522–64.

Elsner, Benjamin. 2013. "Emigration and Wages: The EU Enlargement Experiment." *Journal of International Economics* 91 (1): 154–63.

Eurostat. 2017. *Migrant Integration Statistical Book*. http://ec.europa.eu/eurostat /documents/3217494/8081569/KS-01-17-539-EN-N.pdf/3eba7121-91fd-4512 -aeb5-b820a55517e2.

Felbermayr, Gabriel, and Isabella Reczkowski. 2012. "International Student Mobility and High-skilled Migration: The Evidence." Working Paper 132, IFO Institute, Munich. https://www.econstor.eu/handle/10419/73806.

Ferguson, J. 2003. "Migration in the Caribbean: Haiti, the Dominican Republic and Beyond." Minority Rights Group International, London.

Foged, Mette, and Giovanni Peri. 2015. "Immigrants' Effect on Native Workers: New Analysis on Longitudinal Data." IZA Discussion Paper 8961, Institute for the Study of Labor, Bonn. http://ftp.iza.org/dp8961.pdf.

Galenson, David W. 2007. *Old Masters and Young Geniuses: The Two Life Cycles of Artistic Creativity*. Princeton, NJ: Princeton University Press.

Hamilton, James D. 1990. "Analysis of Time Series Subject to Changes in Regime." *Journal of Econometrics* 45 (1–2): 39–70.

Hansen, L. O. 1988. "The Political and Socio-economic Context of Legal and Illegal Mexican Migration to the U.S. (1942-1984)." *International Migration* 26 (1): 95–107.

Hausmann, R., and L. Nedelkoska. 2017. "Welcome Home in a Crisis: Effects of Return Migration on the Non-migrants' Wages and Employment." CID Faculty Working Paper 330, Center for International Development at Harvard University, Cambridge, MA. https://albania.growthlab.cid.harvard.edu/files/albaniagrowthlab/files/return _migration_cidwp_330.pdf.

Hoffman, B. 2005. "Emigration and Regime Stability: Explaining the Persistence of Cuban Socialism." *Journal of Communist Studies and Transition Politics* 21 (4): 436–61.

Horton, John, William R. Kerr, and Christopher Stanton. 2017. "Digital Labor Markets and Global Talent Flows." NBER Working Paper 23398, National Bureau of Economic Research, Cambridge, MA.

Huddleston, Thomas, Özge Bilgili, Anne-Linde Joki, and Zvezda Vankova. 2015. *Migrant Integration Policy Index 2015*. Barcelona/Brussels: CIDOB (Barcelona Center for International Affairs) and MPG (Migration Policy Group).

Kerr, Sari Pekkala, William Kerr, Çağlar Özden, and Christopher Parsons. 2016. "Global Talent Flows." *Journal of Economic Perspectives* 30 (4): 83–106.

Kerr, William, and William Lincoln. 2010. "The Supply Side of Innovation: H-1B Visa Reforms and US Ethnic Invention." *Journal of Labor Economics* 28: 473–508.

Li, Xiaoyang, and John McHale. 2009. "Emigrants and Institutions." Unpublished, University of Michigan, Ann Arbor, and National University of Ireland, Galway.

Li, Xiaoyang, John McHale, and Xuan Zhou. 2013. "Does Brain Drain Lead to Institutional Gain? A Cross Country Empirical Investigation." Unpublished, Sauder School of Business, University of British Columbia, and Queen's School of Business, Queen's University, Kingston, Ontario, Canada.

Longhi, Simonetta, Peter Nijkamp, and Jacques Poot. 2005. "A Meta-analytic Assessment of the Effect of Immigration on Wages." *Journal of Economic Surveys* 19 (3): 451–77.

Mansoor, Ali, and Bryce Quillin. 2006. *Migration and Remittances: Eastern Europe and the Former Soviet Union*. Washington, DC: World Bank. http://documents.worldbank .org/curated/en/183131468024337798/pdf/384260Migratio101OFFICIAL0USE0O NLY1.pdf.

National Academies of Sciences, Engineering, and Medicine. 2017. *The Economic and Fiscal Consequences of Immigration*. Washington, DC: National Academies Press.

Nguyen, Tu Chi. 2017. "Leveraging Emigration for Institutional Strengthening." Unpublished, World Bank, Washington, DC.

Niebuhr, Annekatrin. 2010. "Migration and Innovation: Does Cultural Diversity Matter for Regional R&D Activity?" *Papers in Regional Science* 89 (3): 563–85. https://doi .org/10.1111/j.1435-5957.2009.00271.x.

OECD (Organisation for Economic Co-operation and Development). 2010. "Public Opinions and Immigration: Individual Attitudes, Interest Groups and the Media." In *International Migration Outlook 2010*. Paris: OECD Publishing. http://dx.doi.org/10.1787/migr _outlook-2010-6-en.

———. 2016. *Making Integration Work: Refugees and Others in Need of Protection*. Paris: OECD Publishing.

Özden, C., C. Parsons, M. Schiff, and T. L. Walmsley. 2011. "Where on Earth Is Everybody? The Evolution of Global Bilateral Migration, 1960-2000." *World Bank Economic Review* 25 (1): 12–56.

Pérez-Armendáriz, C., and D. Crow. 2010. "Do Migrants Remit Democracy? International Migration, Political Beliefs, and Behavior in Mexico." *Comparative Political Studies* 43 (1): 119–48.

Santos Silva, J. M. C., and Silvana Tenreyro. 2006. "The Log of Gravity." *Review of Economics and Statistics* 88 (4): 641–58.

Spilimbergo, Antonio. 2009. "Foreign Students and Democracy." *American Economic Review* 99 (1): 528–43.

Teodorescu, Daniel, and Tudorel Andrei. 2011. "The Growth of International Collaboration in East European Scholarly Communities: A Bibliometric Analysis of Journal Articles Published between 1989 and 2009." *Scientometrics* 89 (2): 711–22.

Tse, Emily. 2012. "Approaches to International Degree Recognition: A Comparative Study." Working Paper, International Education Research Foundation, Culver City, CA.

Van Mol, C. 2014. "The Reconstruction of a Social Network Abroad." In *Intra-European Student Mobility in International Higher Education Circuits: Europe on the Move* (Palgrave Studies in Global Higher Education), 66–90. London: Palgrave Macmillan. https://doi.org/10.1057/9781137355447_4.

World Bank. 2016a. *Migration and Development: A Role for the World Bank Group.* Washington, DC: World Bank.

———. 2016b. *The Migration and Remittances Factbook.* Washington, DC: World Bank. www.worldbank.org/prospects/migrationandremittances.

———. 2018. *Moving for Prosperity: Global Migration and Labor Markets.* Policy Research Report. Washington, DC: World Bank.

5

Infrastructure Linkages: Cost, Time, and Networks

The benefits of connectivity in transport infrastructure cannot be simply measured by kilometers of roads and rail, their condition, or density of connections. Evaluating transport connectivity in this way could lead to building too many roads or rail connections that do not pay back economic dividends in the long run. The Russian Federation might decide to build a six-lane road in Siberia, but unless it is connecting two important economic centers, or is providing access to natural resources that were previously unreachable, it may make little economic sense. A preferable approach is to measure the quality and importance of transport services in terms of availability, speed, cost, timeliness, and the economic value to what is being connected. Is it a road to nowhere, or a bridge between two important economic hubs? This chapter uses new transport service data and network analysis tools to measure the degree of transport service connectivity through roads, railroads, and to lesser extent, maritime transport of Europe and Central Asia (ECA) countries.

A clear understanding of the benefits of within-country transport connectivity and how a country links to the broader regional transport network is critical to evaluating transport investment. Measuring the quality and value of transport service connectivity should allow for the design of strategies aimed at improving the economic benefits of transport investment to countries or regions and help assess which interventions a country or region should focus on to achieve a strategic policy or economic objective (for example, attract traffic or increase the economic benefits to being in a network of countries). Taking such an approach can help us understand, for example, benefits from the proposed corridor development projects such as the Belt and Road Initiative (BRI)[1] and the Trans-European Transport Network[2] as well as sustainable financing schemes.

Main Messages

- Countries face various strategic choices in deciding on transport investments, including the target markets (e.g., domestic, neighbor countries, or strategic partners) and underlying goals (e.g., maximizing the economic activities reached by transport infrastructure, strengthening regional partnerships, or increasing resilience and improving the integration of networks). A country's investment program may be judged a success in meeting some of these goals but not others; thus, the flexibility of the proposed methodology for evaluating transport investment is critical.
- Transport investments may improve the probability that a transport flow will pass through a country or increase the importance of the country to the overall network. The former may generate gains from transit traffic and the opportunities from trade, foreign direct investment (FDI), knowledge sharing, and migration. By contrast, the latter implies that transport disruptions would have a more negative impact on other countries. Such network-based evaluations could facilitate regional agreements supporting mutually beneficial investment that reflects the impact of domestic transport on improving access in other countries.
- With respect to reaching neighboring countries, the cost and time required for passenger travel varies greatly in ECA, while the cost and time for delivering a container varies little, except it is much higher for the Russian Federation, Turkey, and Central Asia. Countries with high costs for connecting to neighbors but low costs for connecting to ECA as a whole (e.g., Russia) could focus transport resources on improving connections with neighbors, while countries with low costs to connect to neighbors but high costs to connect to the ECA network (e.g., Central Asia) could focus on improving connections to the region as a whole, or to countries outside ECA. For freight transport, ECA is increasingly an integrated market. Thus, compared with passenger transport, the competitiveness of traders is more influenced by the logistics cost structure than by affordability.

Connecting Cities and Neighbors: A Vicinity View of Transport Services in ECA

To understand overall transport connectivity in ECA, we begin the analysis by evaluating connectivity within each country and between countries and their neighbors. ECA countries' connectivity is based on direct measures of cost and time of travel or shipment for both passenger and freight transport for (a) domestic connectivity or connectivity among the five main cities within a country, or (b) neighbor connectivity or connectivity from the capital city of a given country to capital cities of each neighboring country.[3]

Connecting Cities within a Country

Domestic connectivity is largely determined by geography and demographic factors. As an element of geography, the size of a country plays an important role in determining the cost and time of transport services. For example, it would take an average Russian passenger 8–10 times longer to visit the country's key cities than it would take an average passenger in the much smaller Balkan countries to visit the key cities within each Balkan country. Similarly, a Russian passenger would pay a staggering 50 euros on average to visit a main city from Moscow, while a person in the South Caucasus or in the Western Balkans would pay less than 10 euros to travel from the capital to another large city (figure 5.1, panel a). Distance also goes a long way toward explaining the long travel times in the big and sparsely populated countries of Central Asia. Natural elements, such as the location of forests, mountains, deserts, and raw materials (such as minerals), also affect the level and type of domestic connectivity. Considerations affected by individual choices, such as where people live, businesses locate, and services are provided, as well as population density, also help define the type of connectivity that is optimal for a country. Normalized metrics of speed and unit costs adjusted by purchasing power provide a first proxy for the transport user experience with transport infrastructure and service quality.[4]

Income level is a good predictor of both the quality (speed) and affordability (unit cost adjusted for purchasing power) of *domestic* transport services for passengers in ECA. For example, Austria, Denmark, France, Sweden, Switzerland, and Germany, all among the richest countries in ECA, fare very well in terms of service performance (speed) and also in terms how their domestic passengers can afford the services (figure 5.1, panel b, top-right quadrant). By contrast, poorer countries such as Moldova, Kosovo, Armenia, and Bosnia rank very low in both speed and affordability of their internal transport connections (figure 5.1, panel b, bottom-left quadrant).

There are a few exceptions. Turkey, Ukraine, and Uzbekistan provide fast services that are not particularly affordable for the average domestic passenger. At the other extreme, passenger services in Azerbaijan, Norway, and Turkmenistan are affordable but the speed is low, likely because of their challenging geography and low population density. The market structure of the transport sector, taxes, fees, subsidies, and the level of government regulation can be sources of domestic cost differentials. Technology selection, geography, and network design (for instance, the number of transition points built into the system given by feeder road or track infrastructure and terminals) can be sources of domestic speed differentials.[5]

Cargo owners and freight forwarders have a different view of domestic connectivity. Except in Russia, where it takes close to two days to deliver a container from one main city to another, there is no significant difference in time to deliver a container within a country in all the subregions of ECA, which on average takes one day (figure 5.1, panel c).

Some countries that serve as gateways to their neighbors perform poorly according to speed indicators. Belgium and the Netherlands have a surprisingly poor ranking for speed (figure 5.1, panel d) given their income levels. This is likely due to the high level of congestion in their highway systems; both countries feature as the top congestion hotspots in Europe according to the INRIX traffic scorecard.[6] Another clear outlier on speed performance is Luxembourg, which suffers not so much from its own traffic but from transit flows through its territory. These countries face tension between the burden on internal infrastructure of increased transit traffic and the benefits of providing transportation services to the region.

FIGURE 5.1 Domestic connectivity

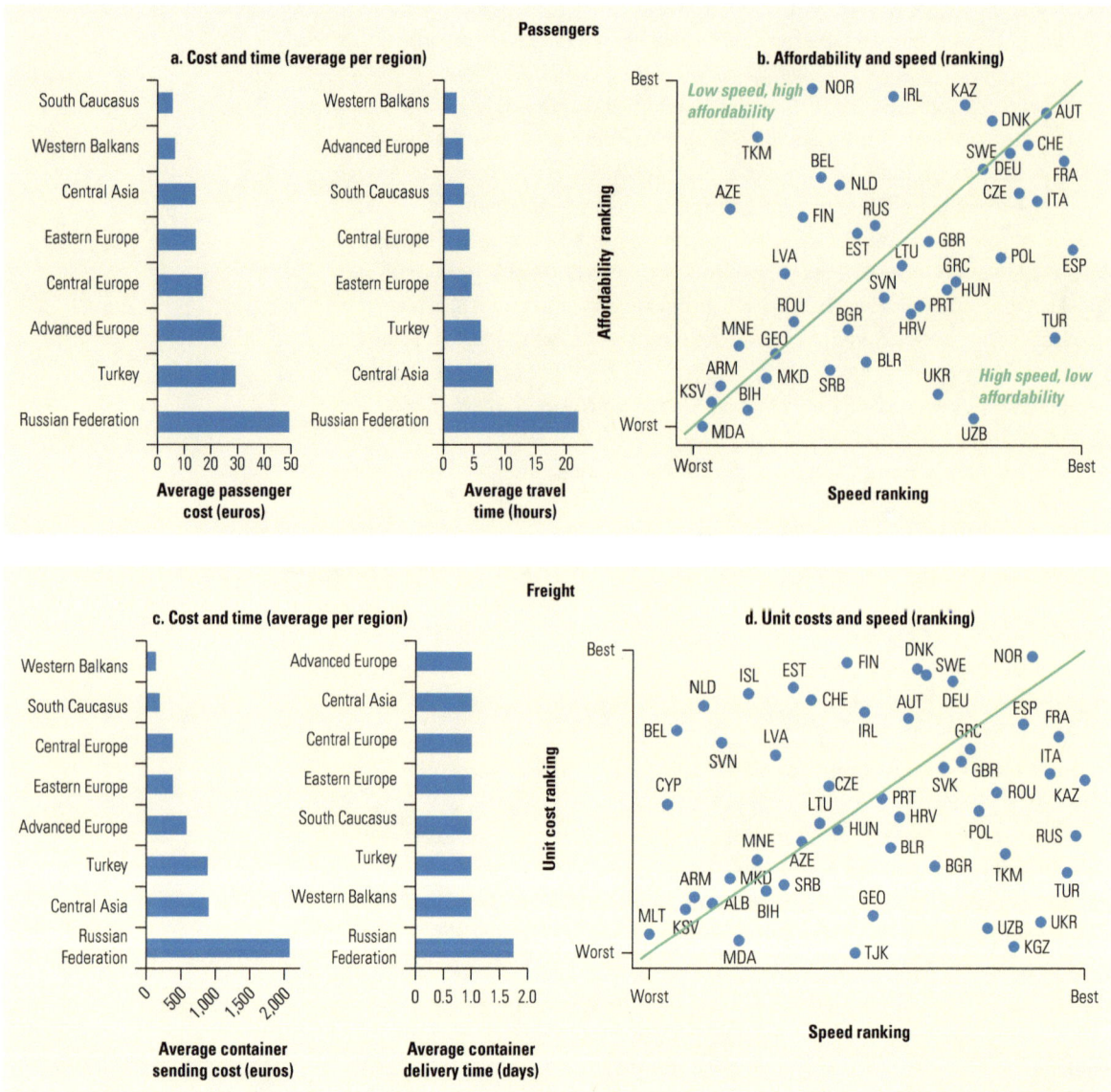

Passengers

a. Cost and time (average per region)

b. Affordability and speed (ranking)

Freight

c. Cost and time (average per region)

d. Unit costs and speed (ranking)

Note: Passenger transport connectivity as measured here is multimodal, averaging across road, rail, and bus modes the price that must be paid to travel to a representative main city in the country. Only countries with complete data for time and cost for all modes (road, bus, and rail) are included. Affordability is estimated using the unit cost of services adjusted for purchasing power. Freight transport connectivity for a given city is measured as the average price to send a container from that city to the other main cities within a country. Luxembourg is not included in the analysis of affordability and speed because of data concerns. "Advanced Europe" includes countries in Western, Southern, and Northern Europe that signed the Maastricht Treaty or joined the European Union before 1995.

Individuals in wealthier countries, such as the Scandinavian countries, France, the Netherlands, Austria, Italy, and Germany, may have a higher opportunity cost of time and thus are willing to accept higher absolute costs to achieve faster transport (figure 5.1, panel d, top-right quadrant). Countries with lower gross domestic product (GDP) per capita, such as Armenia, Moldova, and Azerbaijan, seem to prefer to sacrifice speed (quality) and make freight connectivity more affordable within the country (figure 5.1, panel d, bottom-left quadrant).

Connecting with Neighbors (Regional Angle)

The cost and time required to connect with neighboring countries vary greatly within ECA. The average passenger in a Central Asian country pays close to 125 euros and travels close to two days (47 hours) to reach main cities in neighboring countries (figure 5.2, panel a), despite strong economic potential and the need for connections as a result of being landlocked. Connectivity to neighbors is low. The average cost faced by a Russian passenger is similar to that of an average Central Asian passenger, though, surprisingly, the average travel time to neighbors is lower (about 30 hours). By contrast, countries in the Western Balkans show the lowest average cost to connect with neighbors, primarily because of the proximity among the main cities in the region. Similarly, average travel times to connect with neighbors for passengers in the Western Balkans and Central Europe are less than 10 hours. Advanced Europe's high-level road and rail infrastructure also delivers low travel times, but at somewhat higher cost. However, advanced Europe's high incomes mean that affordability of passenger transport to neighboring countries is among the highest in ECA (figure 5.2, panel b, top-right quadrant) as transport is a small share of their total income. Poorer parts of ECA fare worse in terms of affordability (figure 5.2, panel b, bottom-left quadrant), with transport taking up a larger share of their relatively low income. Most Central European and Baltic countries remain in the middle of the pack, which is reasonable given their infrastructure stock and their cost of living.[7]

For freight transport, ECA is increasingly an integrated market. Thus, compared with passenger transport, the competitiveness of traders is more influenced by the logistics cost structure than by affordability. Freight transport costs are determined by prices in both the origin and destination countries, and transport costs might not be symmetric because of load factors and market structures of the trucking and shipping industry. Relatively low unit transport costs might help countries like Albania, Armenia, Kazakhstan, and the Kyrgyz Republic, which export products with lower value added.

The average cost and time required to ship a container from the capital city to the main city of neighboring countries varies little among most regions, except for Russia, Turkey, and Central Asia. Russia faces the highest shipment cost and time to its neighbors' main cities (figure 5.2, panel c). This is not surprising, given that Russia has 11 neighbors including China in the Far East and Norway in Scandinavia.[8] Turkey is the second most expensive place to send a container, followed by Central Asia. It takes twice as long to ship a container in some Central Asian countries and Russia compared with the best-performing regions.

While not shown in the figures, the average cost to ship a container in landlocked ECA countries is lower than for coastal and island countries, although landlocked countries face slightly higher shipment times. Costal and island countries would likely register better performance if the comparison were made based on the transport of bulk commodities as opposed to containers. This is due to the greater role of sea transport (a natural advantage of coastal and island countries) for such commodities.[9] This implies that a geographic advantage does not necessarily translate into a cost advantage. Conceivably, landlocked

FIGURE 5.2 Neighbor connectivity

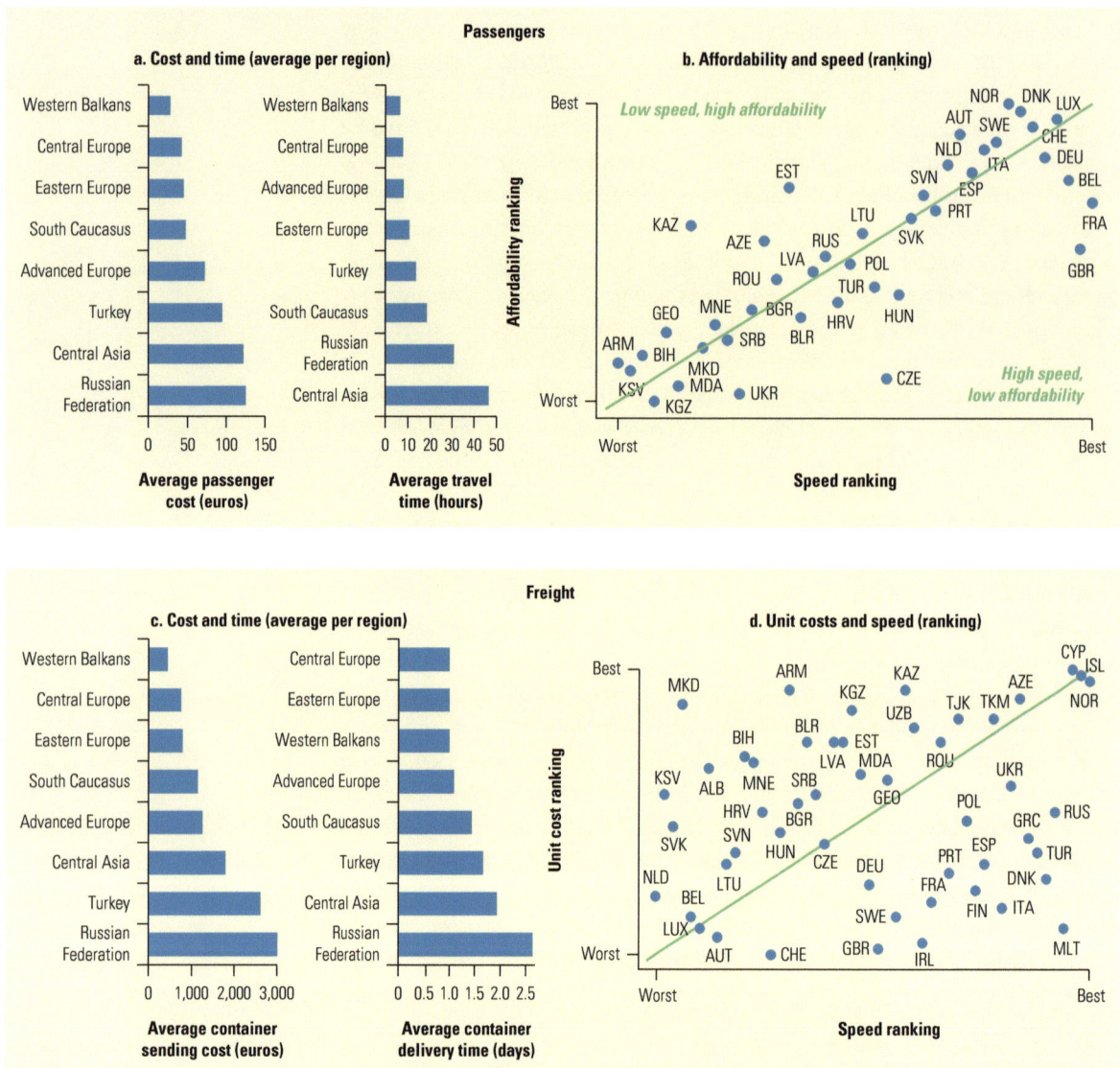

Note: Passenger transport connectivity for each country is measured as the average (over rail and road transport options) travel time and travel cost passengers incur to reach the main cities in neighboring countries, starting from the capital city. Only countries with complete data for travel time and cost for all modes (road and rail) are included. Freight transport connectivity for a given country is measured as the average price to send a container from its capital city to the main cities of neighboring countries. "Advanced Europe" includes countries in Western, Southern, and Northern Europe that signed the Maastricht Treaty or joined the European Union before 1995.

countries can outperform coastal countries if they have good road and rail connections to their neighbors' main cities, but it is costly. Landlocked countries have strong economic payoffs for good transit networks to connect with key trade outlets.[10]

Like what was observed for domestic freight connectivity, shippers and traders in Belgium and the Netherlands face the slowest speed to send containers to main cities in their neighboring countries. Again, the high level of congestion in the highway systems of these countries is likely the main the culprit.

From First Neighbors to Transport Networks: Connectivity as a Policy Objective

An approach to connectivity that exploits the opportunities presented by the entire network, rather than just by neighboring countries, can increase the benefit from the movement of goods, services, capital, people, and ideas across countries. Comparing the number of neighbors of the neighbors of a country, versus the number of direct neighbors, illustrates the importance of thinking in terms of transport networks. For individual countries of ECA, the aggregate number of countries that are neighbors or neighbors of neighbors varies from 2 to 22. Ukraine, Russia, Hungary, and Germany have the highest number of neighbors plus neighbor of neighbor countries, while Ireland, Portugal, and Iceland have the lowest number (figure 5.3, panel a).

Similarly, the level of aggregate GDP next to a country varies significantly for each country, and it is not directly proportional to the number of neighbors (or neighbors of neighbors). Germany, France, Switzerland, Belgium, and Luxembourg have adjacent access to large economic centers (higher GDP), while Romania, Belarus, FYR Macedonia, Kazakhstan, and Georgia—with similar numbers of neighbors (or neighbors of neighbors)—have adjacent access to much lower aggregate GDP levels (figure 5.3, panel b). These basic examples underscore the importance for a country of incorporating a wider network (or the whole ECA network) in its decisions.

A comparison of the costs faced by countries when only connecting with neighbors compared with when connecting with ECA as a whole reveals country-specific challenges or opportunities. For example, Russia has the highest average cost to connect to its neighbors but the lowest average cost to connect to the whole of ECA (figure 5.4). Thus, improving access to the rest of the ECA countries may not represent a big cost-saving opportunity, while targeting next-door neighbors could bring more benefits. By contrast, Central Asian countries have low average costs to connect to neighbors but a high average cost to connect to the rest of the ECA network. South Caucasus and Western Balkan countries, which are small and centrally located, have very low costs to reach their neighbors and lower average costs to reach the whole ECA region compared with Central Asian or advanced European countries. Because of their centrality in ECA, countries in Eastern and Central Europe face relatively low costs to reach all ECA countries.

As shown earlier, it also is important to assess connectivity in terms of *time*, particularly when products or the nature of the passenger trip require reliability and predictability. Perishable products might need cuts in time even at the expense of using more costly transport alternatives, thus shipping products by air rather than by land (e.g., as in the flower export business). Similarly, a business traveler may pay a premium for more rapid transportation, likely in proportion to the opportunity cost of the traveler's time. Exporters optimally choose between modes and routes depending on their preference for a cheaper solution that might take longer or be less reliable, versus a more expensive one that is faster or more reliable. Hummels and Schaur (2013) find that delays can impose high costs (each day in transit is equivalent to an ad valorem tariff of 0.6 to 2.1 percent), and that the

FIGURE 5.3 Nonlinear impact of connecting with neighbors of neighbors

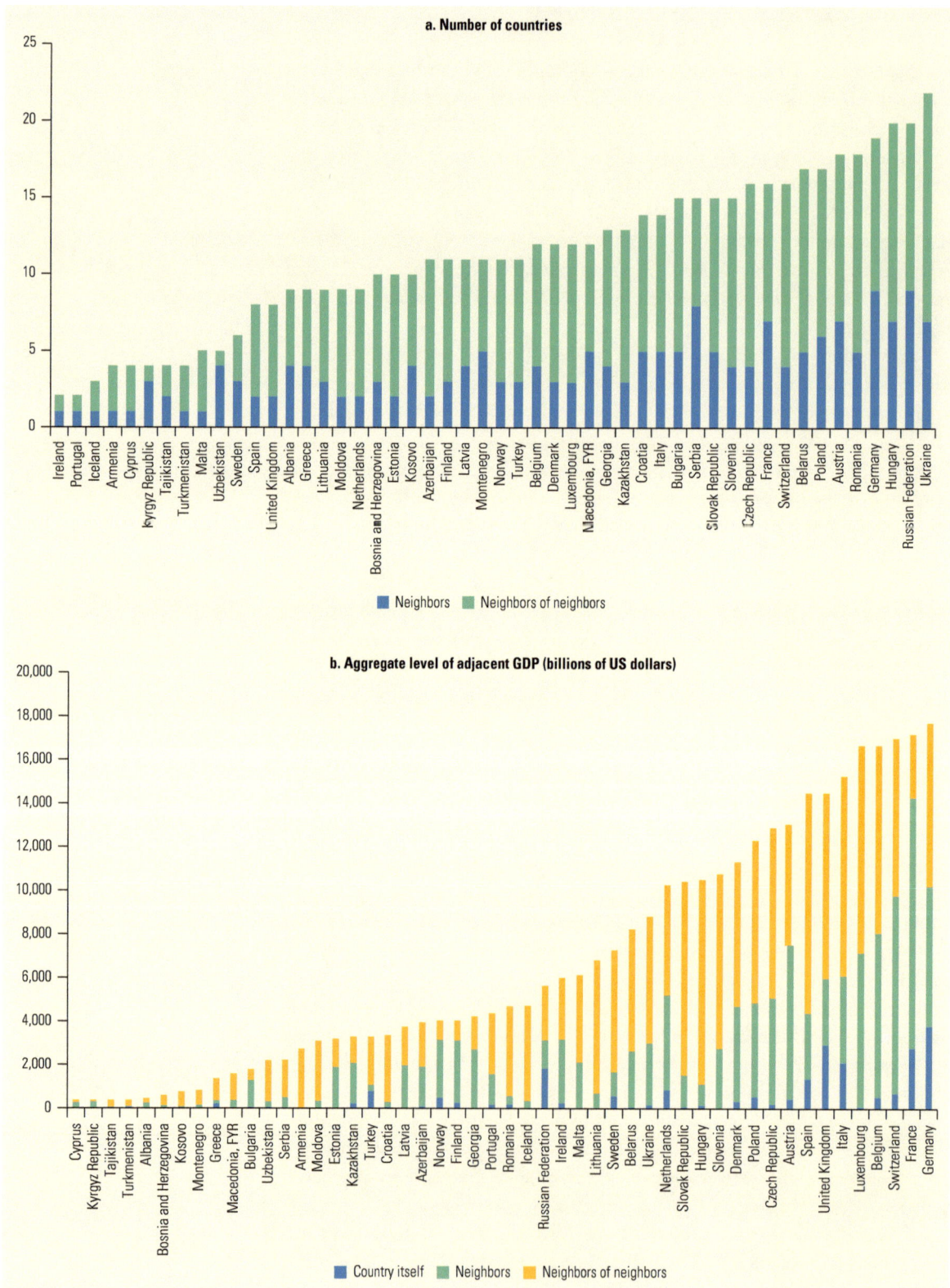

a. Number of countries

Neighbors ■ Neighbors of neighbors ■

b. Aggregate level of adjacent GDP (billions of US dollars)

Country itself ■ Neighbors ■ Neighbors of neighbors ■

FIGURE 5.4 **Cost-based connectivity of the ECA road transport network, by region**

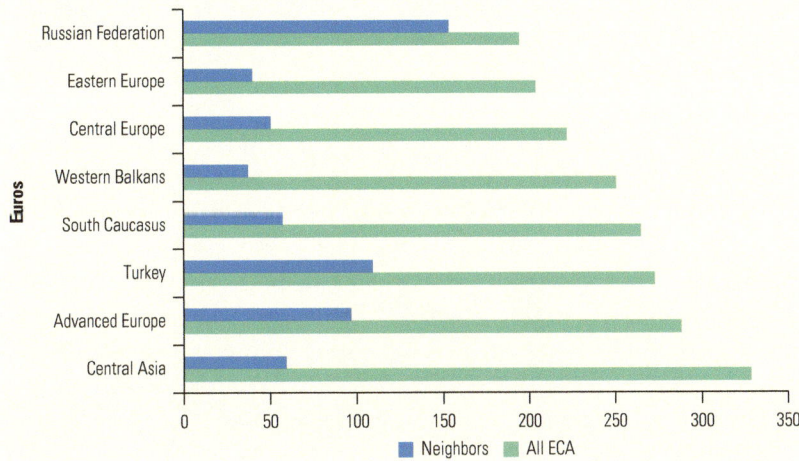

Note: Regions are sorted with respect to the costs incurred to reach all Europe and Central Asia (ECA) countries. The figure shows average weighted road costs for each ECA region for two cases: (a) costs to connect to neighbor countries and (b) costs to connect to all ECA countries. Road costs are measured using the average speed on the road and the fuel costs in each country. Average costs are estimated as follows:

$$Cost_c^m = \frac{\sum_{d \in \Delta(c)} dist_{c \to d}^m \times cost_{c \to d}^m}{\sum_{d \in \Delta(c)} dist_{c \to d}^m},$$

in which $\Delta(c)$ is the set of countries of interest to be reached starting from the main city of country c, $dist_{c \to d}^m$ is the distance in kilometers, and $cost_{c \to d}^m$ is the cost (in euros) between the main cities of countries c and d via modality m.

most time-sensitive trade flows involve parts and components trade, which may be one reason for the large and growing share of world trade shipped by air.

Rankings of ECA countries by cost and time of transport (across transport modes) differ little. Central Asian countries have much higher costs (for both road and container transport) and much longer times than other ECA regions (Figure 5.5). Recent or expected infrastructure projects, gathered under the Belt and Road Initiative, might help integrate these countries and improve their connectivity. The islands Cyprus, Malta, and Ireland, as well as Spain and Portugal, are also among the countries with the highest costs and time to reach the rest of the ECA network. The South Caucasus performs better in terms of costs compared to time, whereas Western Europe is the opposite. Eastern and Central European countries have relatively cheaper and faster connections to the rest of the network. The similarity in these rankings largely reflects road transport costs, which are determined in part by average speeds—reflecting the quality of infrastructure—and are thus more correlated with time than are container prices, which reflect other parameters, such as logistics costs, the presence of rent-seekers, and the degree of competitiveness among service providers. Thus, cost versus time performances of countries are more diverse when looking at container prices (figure 5.5, panel b). Some countries, like Armenia, Kosovo, Turkey, Macedonia, FYR, and Greece, have relatively better connectivity in terms of container costs than for time. Others, like Montenegro, Slovenia, and Norway, have instead relatively better time connectivity than cost connectivity. Understanding country specifics requires a deeper look into institutional factors, the quality of logistics, and the competitiveness of the transport sector.

The rest of this section discusses three strategies that countries might choose in improving connectivity. Some countries could embrace a transport network development strategy based on targeted agreements, for instance, connecting to central hubs rather than engaging in bilateral connections, or emphasizing transport connectivity to key economic centers or political allies (strengthening partnerships). Other countries might aim to maximize the regional GDP that their transport networks unleash (maximizing potential). A final possible strategy can be rooted in strengthening existing transport corridors by increasing their resilience or just emphasizing the integration of transport networks by shortening distances (fostering redundancy and integration). This is not an exhaustive list of options, and certainly they are not mutually exclusive policy targets.

Strengthening Partnerships: Connectivity through the Lens of Alliances

There is a trade-off between slightly improving all connections and significantly improving a few well-chosen ones, which means going from a focus on the whole network to a few strategic partners. The choice of partnerships to strengthen through better connectivity may depend on many factors beyond distance and geographic constraints. Countries may wish to improve connections with large and sophisticated markets, which can offer large trade opportunities. The opportunity to participate in cross-border supply chains might push countries to focus on improving their connectivity to headquarters economies like Germany. A similar reasoning can be applied for the benefits from knowledge transfers. Learning from markets that are closer to the actual technological frontier might allow a country to leapfrog in productivity, or make incremental productivity gains, depending on its initial conditions.

Comparing travel time and cost performance for the main three strategic poles in ECA (the European Union [EU], Russia, and Turkey) can help countries assess their geopolitical connectivity in ECA.[11] Focusing on costs and time reveals complementary patterns of connectivity and provides a better picture of transport services than just looking at geographic connectivity. Disaggregating the previous results into connectivity toward the three main ECA poles helps countries position themselves with respect to the main poles. Western Balkans and Central Europe have high costs to reach Russia relative to the average cost of reaching all EU countries, whereas the South Caucasus has higher costs to reach all EU countries compared to reaching Russia. Turkey can be reached at a relatively low cost from Western Balkans, South Caucasus, and Central Asian countries. Being well connected to one or several of these poles matters for ECA countries in terms of economic and political opportunities.

Comparing travel time and cost performances for different sets of intended markets can help countries assess the probability of success of various improvements to transport connections. For simplicity,

Focusing on costs and time reveals complementary patterns of connectivity and provides a better picture of transport services than just looking at geographic connectivity.

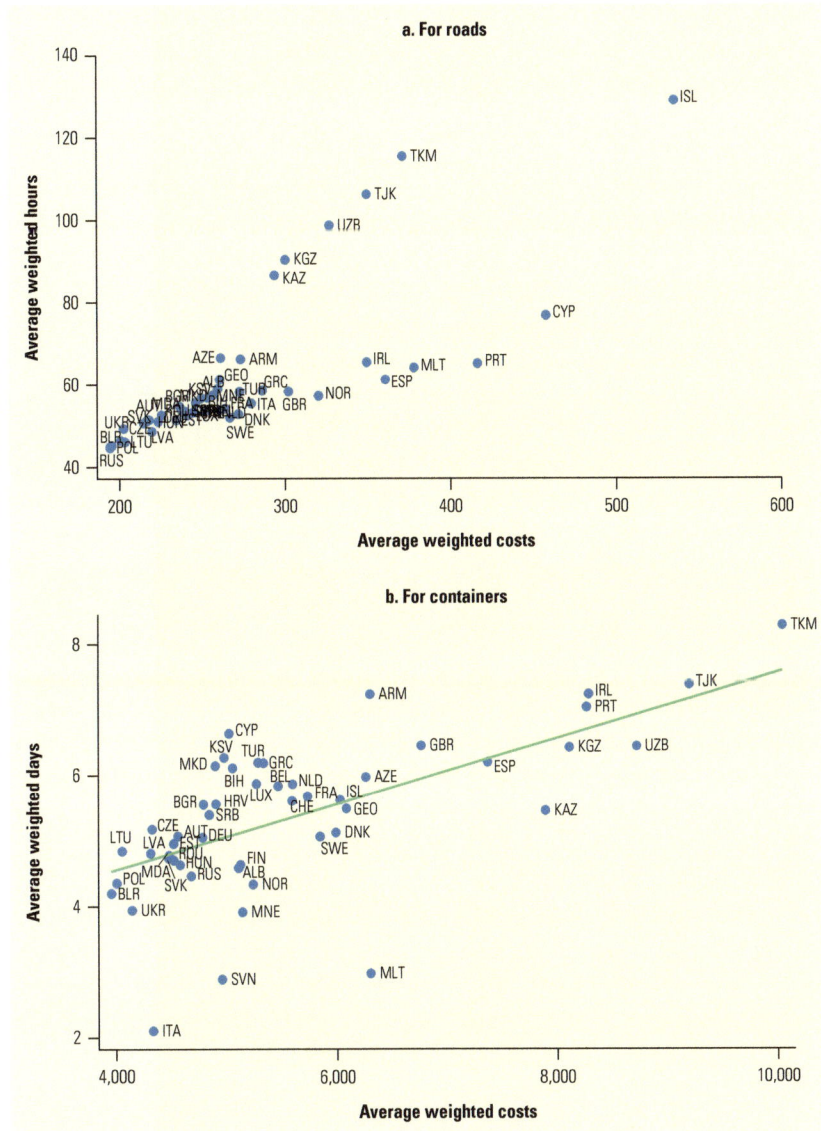

FIGURE 5.5 Cost and time connectivity in the ECA network

Note: Weighted cost indexes are computed by summing the costs for countries weighted and normalized by the distance between the two countries. Country-weighted costs are then averaged across regions using a simple average method. The green line in panel b shows the linear prediction. Average costs and times are estimated as follows:

$$Cost_c^m = \frac{\sum_{d \in \Delta(c)} dist_{c \to d}^m \times cost_{c \to d}^m}{\sum_{d \in \Delta(c)} dist_{c \to d}^m},$$

$$Time_c^m = \frac{\sum_{d \in \Delta(c)} dist_{c \to d}^m \times time_{c \to d}^m}{\sum_{d \in \Delta(c)} dist_{c \to d}^m},$$

in which $\Delta(c)$ is the set of countries of interest to be reached starting from the main city of country c, $dist_{c \to d}^m$ is the distance in kilometers, and $cost_{c \to d}^m$ and $time_{c \to d}^m$ are the cost (in euros) and the time (in hours or days) between the main cities of countries c and d via modality m.

only five types of scenarios are compared. First is connecting only to neighbors. Trade or capital flows tend to increase with proximity, partly because of the importance of factors other than transport costs, such as migration diasporas and language or cultural proximity. Proximity is associated with knowledge transfers (Arrow 1969; Bahar, Hausmann, and Hidalgo 2014). Second is connectivity to the whole network of countries as a means to assess trade potential and knowledge transfers without any assumptions concerning the value of different connections. Third is connecting to just the largest economies in terms of GDP to target markets with the highest potential for trade opportunities and knowledge spillovers.[12] Fourth is increasing connections to economies with the highest levels of technological sophistication, which may help maximize trade and knowledge spillover opportunities if initial conditions are sufficiently strong (i.e., strong business and governance environment).[13] And finally, increasing connections to economies with similar levels of complexity captures opportunities with the highest potential for firms that would not be competitive in the largest or most complex economies.

According to the proposed measure of cost connectivity (for simplicity and to capture the trade dimension, we focus on freight costs only), ECA countries can be grouped into three categories based on the strategies mentioned above. First, countries in the Western Balkans or Central Europe face lower costs and greater connectivity with the largest economies of Europe. Second, countries in Central Asia and the South Caucasus, together with Russia, face lower costs and higher connectivity toward countries with similar levels of production sophistication. Finally, countries in advanced Europe, Eastern Europe, and Turkey face similar costs to reach either the largest ECA economies or countries with higher production sophistication (figure 5.6).

Countries with high costs to connect with ECA's largest markets may decide whether to focus on improving the connectivity to those markets. For instance, they could alternatively decide to target markets that are currently accessible, improve connections to strategically selected partners, or develop and improve connectivity to different economic gravity centers.

A comparison of Central Asia and Western Balkans illustrates the usefulness of this approach. Central Asian countries face an average cost to send a container to the largest ECA economies of 10,000 euros, more than double that of countries in Central Europe, Western Balkans, and even Turkey. Thus, large and expensive investments, and an unlikely leapfrog in technology (given initial conditions), would be required to enable Central Asian countries to gain economically in investing in greater connectivity to European markets. For Central Asia, aiming at strengthening ties with neighbors as a means to building corridors to the larger ECA network seems a more cost-effective strategy.[14] By contrast, Western Balkan countries are in a very different position than Central Asia, with very advantageous connectivity to the main economic gravity center of ECA.

Clearly, variables other than transport interventions, such as characteristics of the business environment, level and type of technology available, amount of resources the country has available for investment, and other critical dimensions, also will determine which connections a country wants to prioritize.

FIGURE 5.6 Container cost connectivity

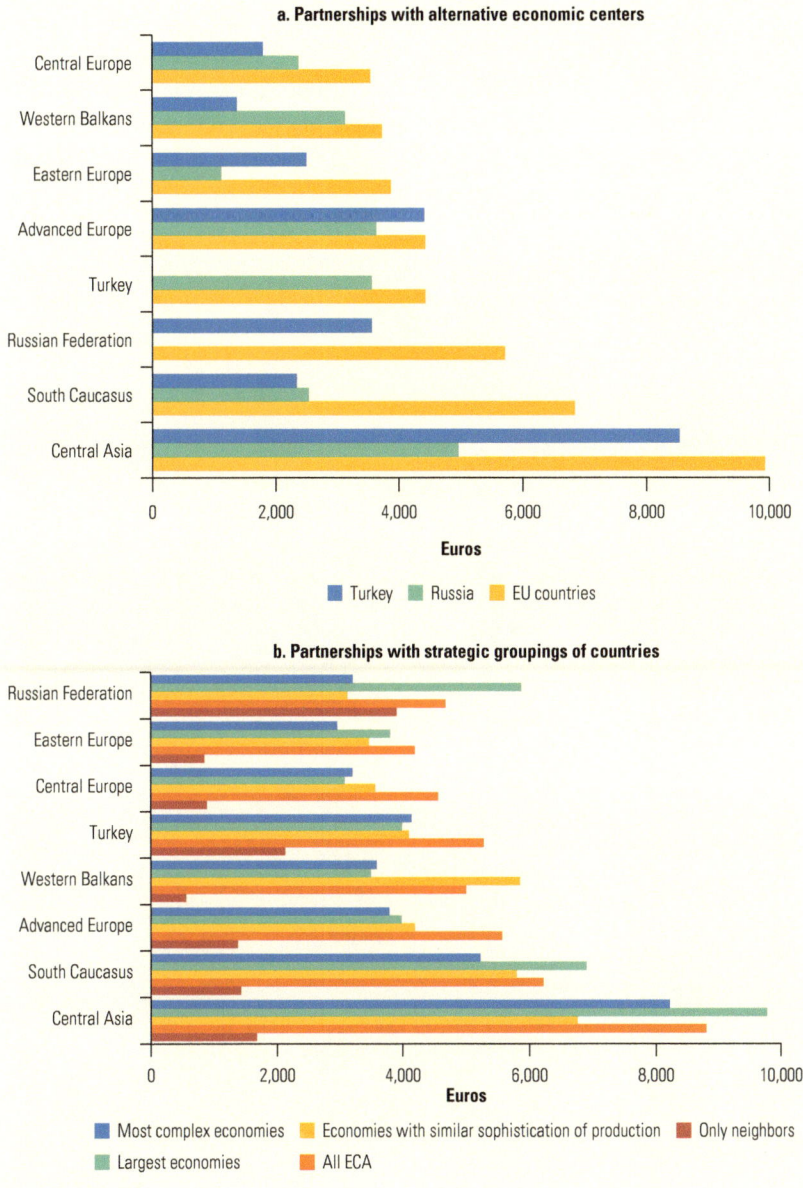

a. Partnerships with alternative economic centers

Legend: Turkey · Russia · EU countries

b. Partnerships with strategic groupings of countries

Legend: Most complex economies · Economies with similar sophistication of production · Only neighbors · Largest economies · All ECA

Note: Weighted costs (in euros) are computed as follows:

$$Cost_c^m = \frac{\sum_{d \in \Delta(c)} dist_{c \to d}^m \times cost_{c \to d}^m}{\sum_{d \in \Delta(c)} dist_{c \to d}^m},$$

in which $\Delta(c)$ is the set of countries of interest to be reached starting from the main city of country c, $dist_{c \to d}^m$ is the distance in kilometers, and $cost_{c \to d}^m$ is the cost (in euros) between the main cities of countries c and d via modality m. The resulting costs are averaged across regions. ECA = Europe and Central Asia; EU = European Union.

Maximizing Potential: Connectivity through the Lens of Market Access

An efficient transport network allows firms to reach foreign markets and serve both final producers buying intermediate inputs and consumers buying final products. One policy goal when designing a road or railway network is to maximize the GDP footprint of the ECA region made accessible by that transport system. This type of approach demands that the connectivity assessment incorporate the size of the reachable markets together with the cost of connectivity (box 5.1).

Advanced Europe scores the highest realized potential for both road and rail networks in terms of out-of-pocket cost, and therefore is the best-performing region for market access connectivity (figure 5.7). That sets the yardstick for the other regions. Eastern and Central Europe also perform very well, accessing 85–90 percent of the market potential with their road networks.

The Central Asia road network opens roughly 40 percent of the GDP attainable by the road network of advanced Europe, which implies that Central Asia would need to more than double its road connectivity by reducing costs to have the same market access as the advanced Europe benchmark. Similarly, the South Caucasus and Turkey, which reach only 50 percent of the ECA market frontier, would need to cut their road transport costs in half to be at the connectivity performance of road networks in advanced Europe. Many countries' ability to increase their market connectivity by improving efficiency is limited by

---

BOX 5.1   Measuring Market Access

The potential index using costs is estimated for each country according to the following equation:

$$Potential_c^m = \sum_d \frac{GDP_d}{cost_{c \to d}^m},$$

in which

 c is the country analyzed and of origin
 d is each country of destination in the targeted market including c
 m is the transport modality
 $cost_{c \to d}^m$ is the cost from c to d using a specific transport mode m with $cost_{c \to c}^m$ the cost of reaching main cities within a country

Potential captures the amount of GDP a country can reach with a unit of transport cost (one container, one private car, or one individual using the railway). It is unit-less. It also includes the domestic potential for each country, defined as the domestic GDP divided by the average cost of reaching the main domestic cities.

Realized Potential is defined as the potential attained by a country with respect to the maximum realized potential achieved by any country in the sample for that transport mode or network in the geographic area considered:

$$Realized\ Potential_c^m = \frac{Potential_c^m}{\max\left(Potential^m\right)}.$$

Potentials are computed for each country and the unrealized potential is then estimated with respect to the best-performing country (or region) of ECA.

The term $cost_{c \to d}^m$ when c and d are not adjacent countries is estimated by finding the optimal route between c and d in a virtual network that concatenates all collected data between neighboring countries. For this, the Dijkstra algorithm considers all possible paths between countries and determines the shortest or cheapest route between any pair of nonneighbor countries.

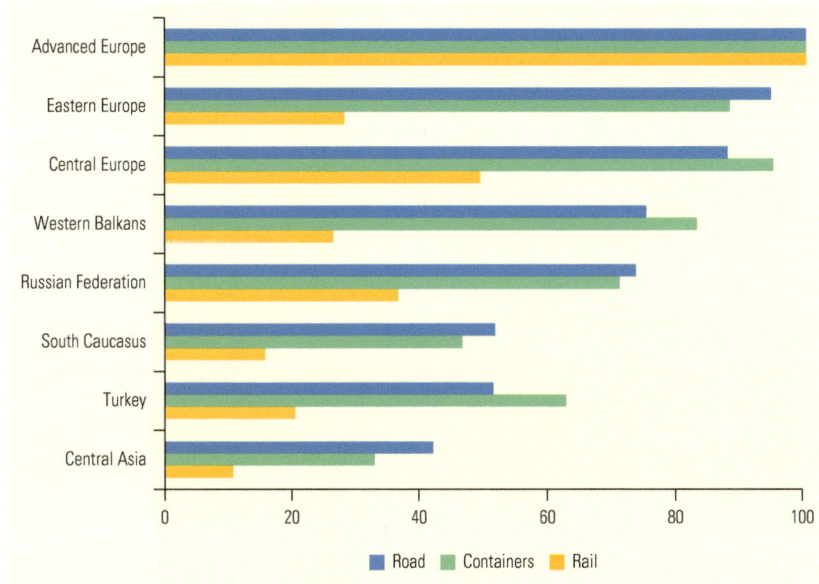

FIGURE 5.7 Realized potential of connectivity to ECA markets relative to advanced Europe
Benchmark: Roads, railways, and containers

Note: The targeted market is defined as all countries in Europe and Central Asia (ECA). Potentials are averaged per region and then normalized by the highest potential. Albania, Cyprus, Iceland, Malta, and Tajikistan are removed from the measure of rail connectivity either because of their lack of rail connections with neighbor countries or because of limited data availability.

long distances from markets and difficult terrain (figure 5.8, panel a, provides country data).

Differences in realized potentials across ECA regions are greater for rail transport networks (figure 5.7). The second-best region after advanced Europe in accessing economic opportunities by railroads is Central Europe, achieving about half of the maximum potential attainable. Eastern Europe performs relatively well for roads but poorly for the rail network.

Central Asia also remains well behind all regions in its railroad and container networks. Central Asia would have to increase its container connectivity (reduce costs) by a factor of three to have the same potential as advanced European countries. Its rail connections barely capture 10 percent of the economic potential of advanced European countries, which is consistent with previous results and implies that Central Asian firms face huge obstacles to reaching markets in ECA. While Central Asian countries could improve their railroad connectivity by reducing prices, the long distances and costs inherent in reaching the largest ECA markets makes it unlikely that they could match the economic potential of other regions (figure 5.8, panel b).[15]

Fostering Linkages and Overall Integration: Connectivity through the Lens of Robustness

Countries should be strategic in choosing which connections to focus on in improving their connectivity in the overall transport network. Some linkages to countries might become redundant, in the sense of not improving the overall integration of a country in the ECA network. Linkages and integration indexes characterize the relationship between having linkages to many neighboring countries and being well integrated in the whole ECA network (box 5.2). The Czech Republic, the Slovak Republic, and Austria are the three most integrated countries in the whole ECA region. Central Asian countries remain poorly integrated in the whole network.

Interestingly, some countries are well integrated despite having few linkages to neighbors (Lithuania, FYR Macedonia, the Czech Republic, Luxembourg, Estonia,

FIGURE 5.8 **Realized potential of connectivity to markets by country, 2016**
Percent of benchmark (100 = best)

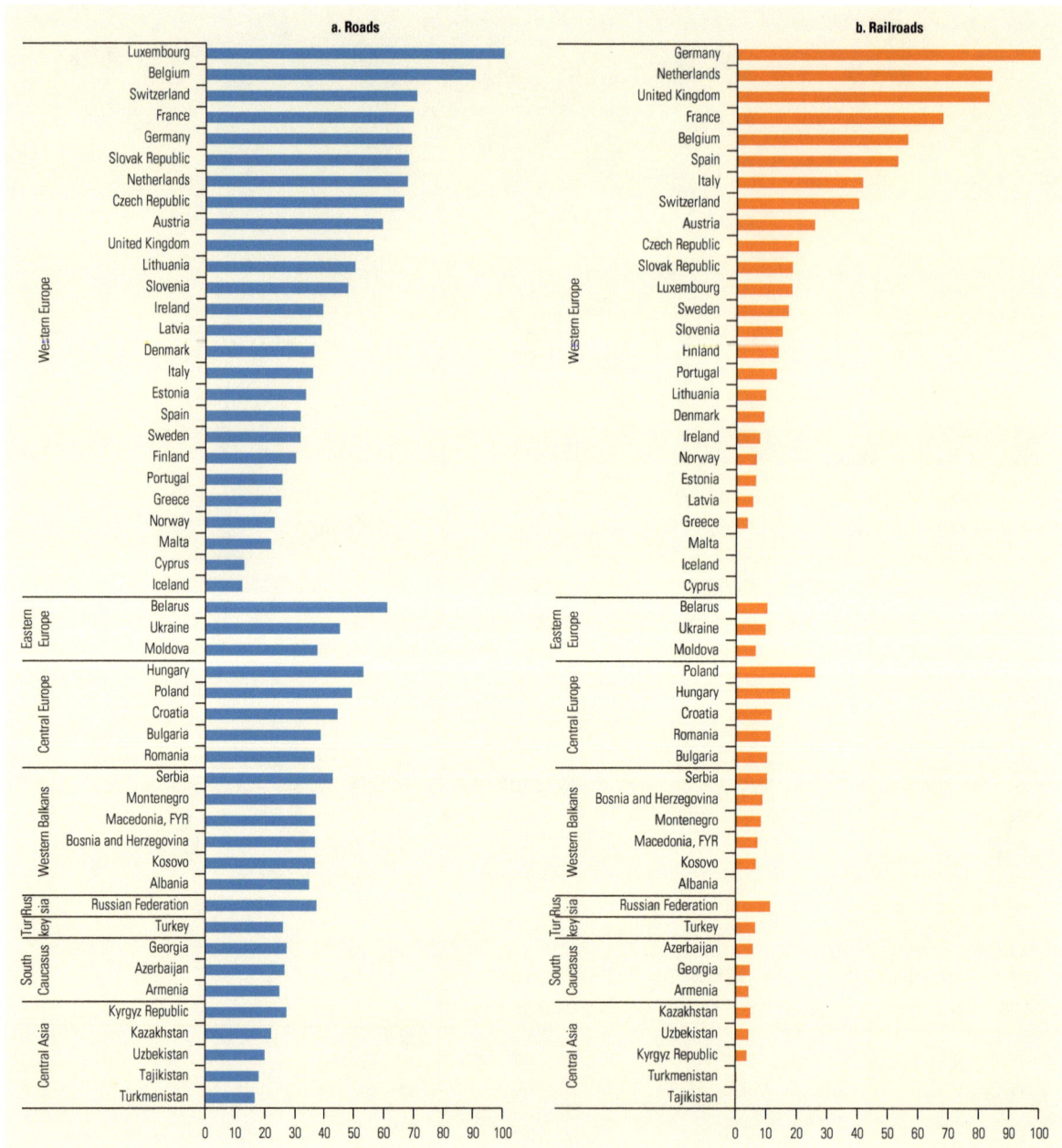

continued

FIGURE 5.8 *continued*

c. Containers

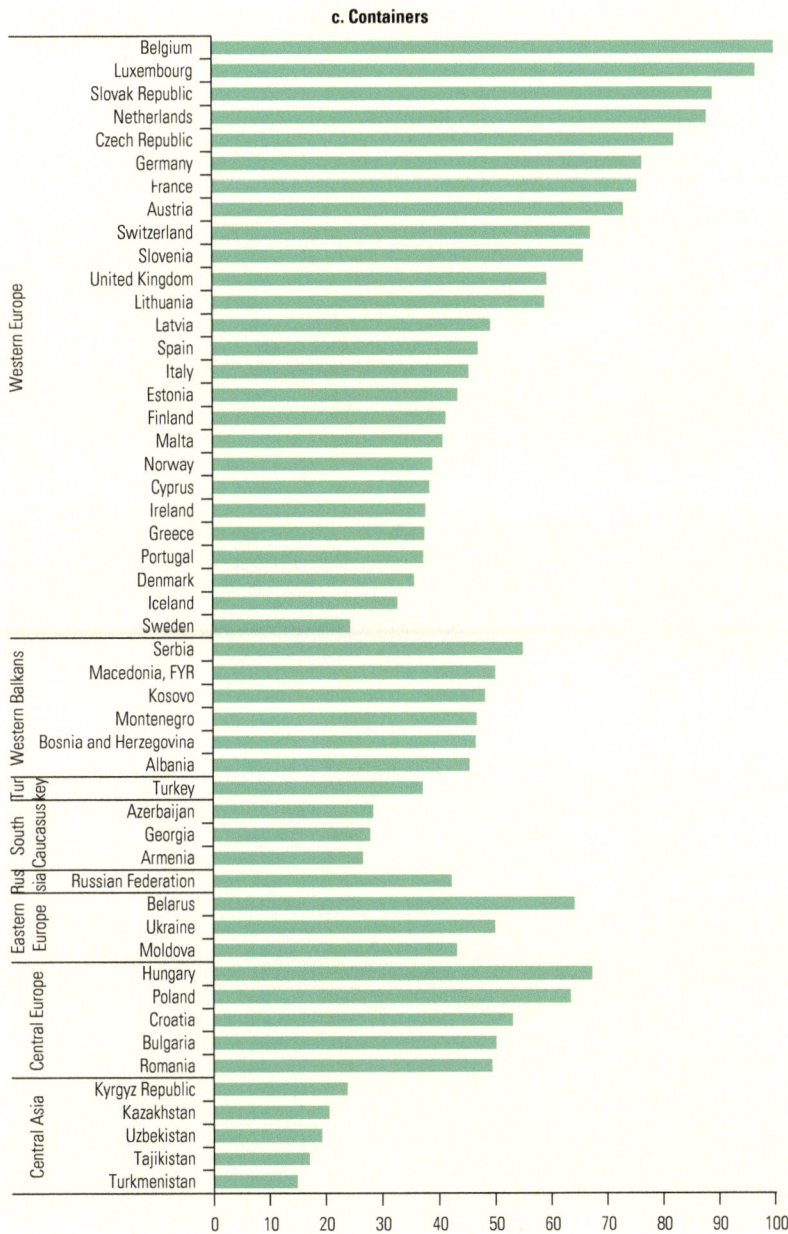

Note: The targeted market is defined as all countries in Europe and Central Asia.

the Netherlands (figure 5.9). Some countries are relatively poorly integrated despite having many linkages to neighboring countries (Uzbekistan, Greece, Italy, France, and Georgia). Exogenous constraints, such as the number of neighboring countries, are important in determining the degree of integration, but other factors such as the state of the transportation network are more crucial in determining how well integrated a country is.

BOX 5.2   Linkages and Integration

Being well integrated in the transport network depends on the number of connected neighbors but also on the nature of the neighbors. After factoring in the risks of being more vulnerable to shocks, a country might benefit from having low transport costs to a hub country instead of having several connections to nonhub countries. Two measures help to understand the position of a country in a network: (a) linkages and (b) overall integration. Linkages are given by the number of connected neighbors (degree centrality) that a country has. Overall integration is measured as the average shortest paths between one country and the rest of the network (closeness centrality).

FIGURE 5.9   Linkages and overall integration

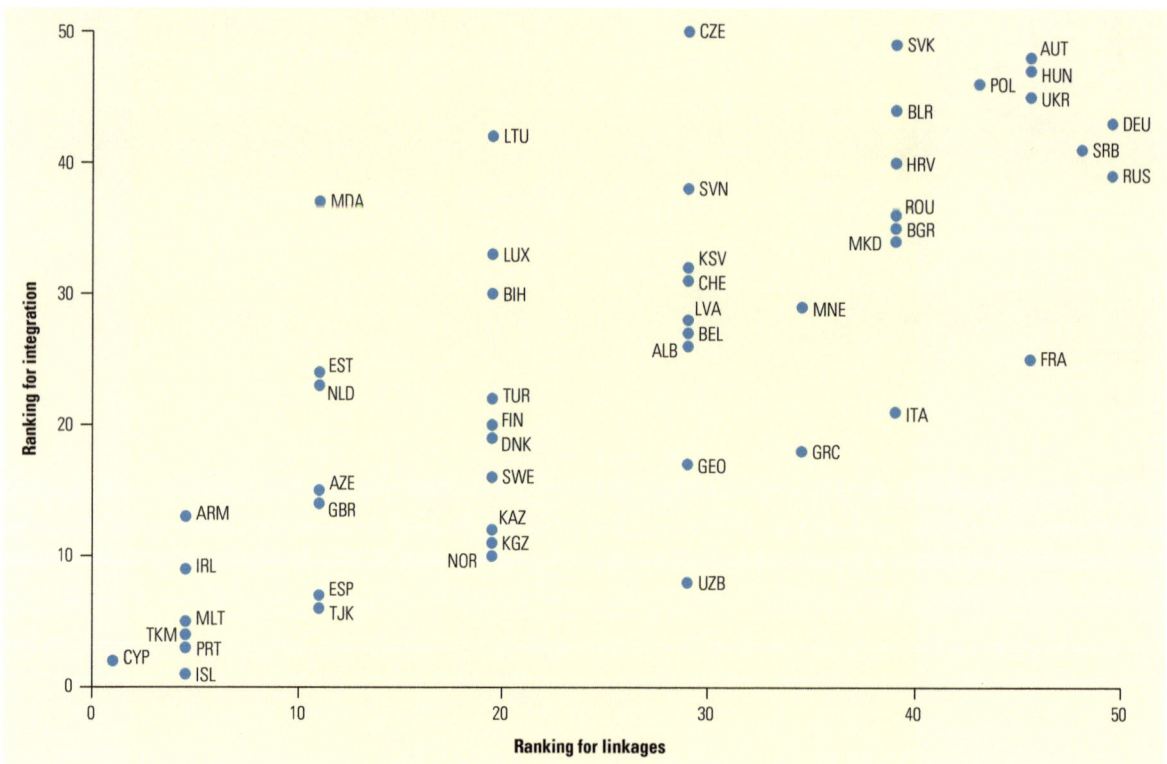

Note: Measures of linkages (unweighted degree centrality) and integration (closeness centrality) are used to rank countries. High ranks mean high centrality indexes. Countries with a similar rank for linkages have the same number of connected neighboring countries.

Connectivity as a Collective Challenge: Centrality and Criticality

Improving one segment of the whole transport network creates positive externalities for all other countries. Improving the quality of a road or reducing transport services costs between two countries not only improves the connectivity and the potential of the directly affected countries, but also many other countries and links belonging to the same transport network or system. Such externalities are usually not fully reflected in the returns to transport investments, especially when they happen between countries. The EU allows for some cross-country coordination of interventions that, by design, internalizes many of these network externalities. The concrete instruments used are coordinated planning, budgets, and policies governing infrastructure investments. The Trans-European Transport Network corridors investments, a flagship EU program, aim at improving transport infrastructure, mostly in segments located in emerging European markets. However, the improved connections will also greatly benefit advanced European economies, which have better access to Eastern and Asian markets and to important gateways.

Considering the whole transport network, rather than the network of an individual country, helps to provide an understanding of the dynamic of transport systems. Some policies might be optimal from a country perspective but not optimal from the perspective of the whole network. Network measures characterizing the position of countries in the network provide stylized tools for understanding which countries might benefit from corridor paths between countries or which countries might get the most from their central or critical position.

The network "positioning" indexes provide complementary information to understand the structure of the transport networks in ECA, but also which countries benefit, or potentially could benefit, the most from corridors and trade routes (box 5.3). Solving the coordination problem among all ECA countries would facilitate targeting of efficient investment that could benefit the region as a whole. It is also interesting to assess potential benefits and choose complementary policies that would help firms and workers fully reap the benefits of better connectivity with other countries.

How important a country is in a transport network depends on its centrality and on its criticality. Higher transport *centrality* may bring benefits such as direct gains from transit traffic and increase potential opportunities from trade, FDI, knowledge sharing, and migration.[16] Higher *criticality* implies that disruptions affecting the country's transport infrastructure will have a more negative impact on the rest of the countries (or some countries) that connect to the country.

Centrality and Criticality in the ECA Network

Transportation infrastructure channels the movement of goods or people along major cross-country networks and, within networks, corridors. The comprehensive nature of the economic benefits for countries of being on a corridor or

---

BOX 5.3 Centrality and Criticality

Being in a central position to benefit from corridor routes depends on two criteria: (a) centrality and (b) criticality. Centrality is given by the probability for a transport flow to pass through this country given the transport network (PageRank centrality). Criticality is given by the number of optimal routes between all pairs of countries that pass through the country (betweenness centrality).

specific crossroads of a network remains an open question. For example, do roads or rail that pass though countries provide economic benefits if ancillary businesses associated with the corridor fail to materialize? However, transit flows may increase the export and import opportunities of firms along these routes or corridors, develop new sectors such as logistics services, and generate nonmaterial benefits (flows of ideas and knowledge) to boost productivity if the economic and business environment is sufficiently attractive for investment. Firms located in transit countries may benefit from lower production costs and an improved ability to deliver on time. Higher transport *centrality* might be desirable for a country to increase participation in regional and global value chains or attract FDI or participate in development corridors (chapter 7 discusses the importance of participation in supply chains for developing countries).

Centrality is a proxy for the ability to attract traffic and potential corridor spillovers. However, the level of centrality of a country or city varies depending on the metrics used, which are defined by, among other things, the product, value chain, and services transported. The five most *central* countries in the ECA network differ, depending on whether cost or time is considered. In terms of transport cost, Austria, the Slovak Republic, and FYR Macedonia are in the top five of the most *central* countries for the network (figure 5.10, panel a) whereas in terms of time, Serbia, Ukraine and Russia are in the top five for the network (figure 5.10, panel b). France and Germany are among the top five measured in *both time and cost* (figure 5.10). As discussed, whether traders focus on cost or time depends on several factors that are not considered here, including the nature of the goods or

FIGURE 5.10 Centrality in the ECA network for container transport

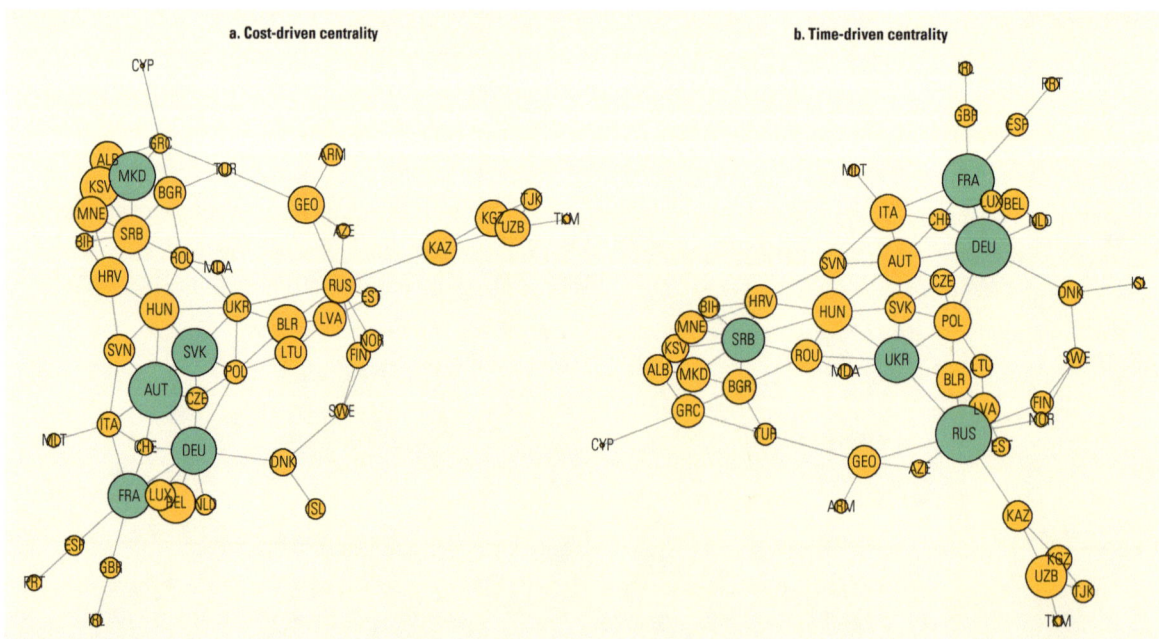

Note: Circle size indicates level of centrality (larger diameter = greater centrality). For illustrative purposes, the circles representing the top five countries in centrality are colored in green. Lines between nodes indicate the presence in the physical network of an optimal corridor connecting countries. Locations of circles and countries are not linked to geography in any way. ECA = Europe and Central Asia.

services, whether the goods traded are part of a supply chain, and the presence of border costs.[17]

Identifying the most *critical* countries in transport networks reveals which countries have more control over transportation network operability and if these countries suffer a shock, what the implications for other connected countries would be (figure 5.11). This measure can help countries target investments to reduce their vulnerability to specific country shocks in accessing markets or other areas of the network. More generally, critical countries in the transport network are those where disruption would have a major impact on subnetworks or countries that can be, de facto, disconnected. Russia is the most critical country in the network of container costs in Eurasia (figure 5.11). Germany, Ukraine, Hungary, and Poland are among the five most critical countries. Islands or isolated countries have a very low criticality, as would be expected.

As shown, while not a top-five country in terms of criticality, disruptions in the French transport network would affect the connectivity of Spain, Portugal, the United Kingdom, and Ireland to the rest of ECA. Portugal's connection to the European network is contingent upon Spain, and so forth.

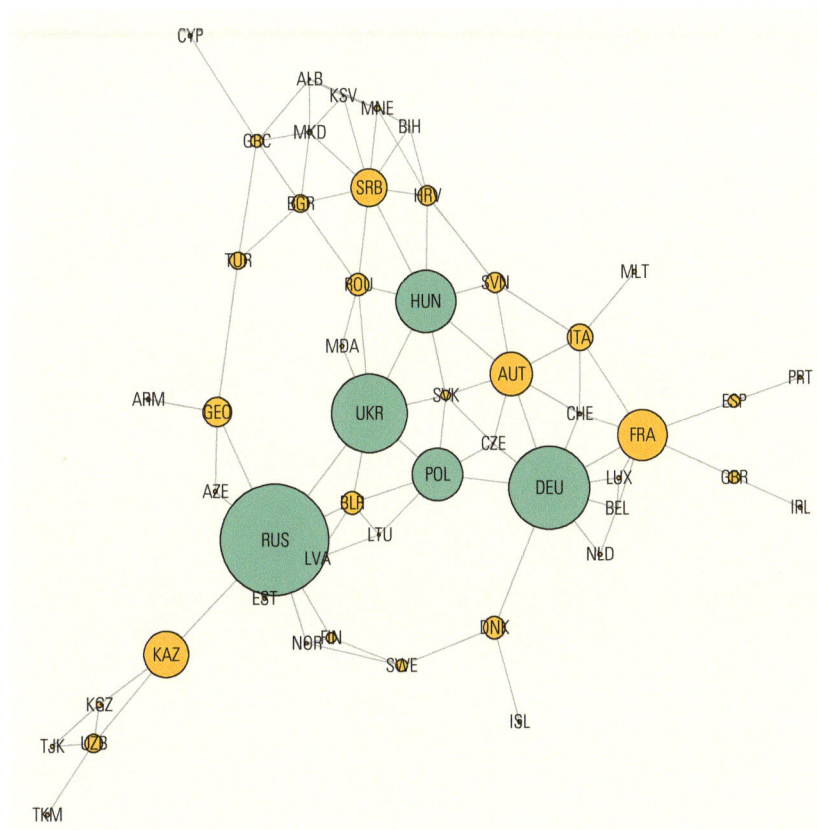

FIGURE 5.11 Cost-driven criticality in the ECA network for container transport

Note: Circle size indicates level of criticality (larger diameter = greater criticality). For illustrative purposes, the circles representing the top five countries in criticality are colored in green. Lines between nodes indicate the presence in the physical network of an optimal corridor connecting countries. Locations of circles and countries are not linked to geography in any way. Results for time-driven criticality are not presented, as the results are very similar to those presented.

Centrality as a Strategic Target

Improving connectivity can change the centrality of a country in the transport network in many ways and will be accompanied by economic benefits. Increased centrality in a network, subnetwork, or corridor, when properly managed, is a desirable objective for a country to benefit from a prospective or existing corridor.[18] Looking at centrality indexes is a first attempt at understanding the broader benefits from transport connectivity at the country level, and can complement measurements of the direct user benefits provided in most cost-benefit analyses of projects and corridors.

The centrality of a country (or node) in a network can be affected by the efficiency, and therefore, the transport costs of its network. A key question for policy makers is the distribution and level of benefits from alternative interventions, that is, the impact of reducing transport costs in a specific segment (as opposed to randomly chosen links). This information can help in making strategic decisions about which segment to invest in to increase the potential benefits from a network or corridor, and how to structure a project's financing to make it sustainable and linked to the stream of benefits.

This analysis can be illustrated by the case of Romanian investment choices. A one-third decrease in the costs of transporting a container traveling between Bulgaria and Romania would increase Romania's *centrality* in the corridor by 14 percent, meaning that Romania's probability of attracting cargo flows would increase by 14 percent. At the same time, Bulgaria would increase its centrality by 9 percent. Romania, however, could instead invest in reducing container transport costs in its trade with Ukraine. If the cost of moving a container in the Romania–Ukraine corridor were reduced by a third, Romania's centrality would increase by 6 percent. Thus, investing in Romania's connection with Bulgaria would have a larger impact on Romania's *centrality* (table 5.1).

Similarly, one can compare a decrease in the costs of shipping goods from Poland toward Germany, the Slovak Republic, or Ukraine. The resulting estimates suggest that gains in centrality are slightly higher when the segment Poland–Ukraine is improved. Kazakhstan would increase its centrality the most by reducing the cost of shipping goods to the Kyrgyz Republic. Interestingly, a decrease in costs between Russia and Kazakhstan does not increase the centrality of either country. This can be explained by Kazakhstan's degree of isolation and the very high costs of such connections.

Criticality and Market Access as Strategic Targets

Alternatively, a policy maker might want to decrease transport costs in a specific segment to increase the criticality of its networks in a broader context or, in other words, the importance of its role as a country in supporting the reliability and stability of the wider transport system. Increasing criticality can position a country as a transit country that "sells" or exports transport services to other countries. Similarly, when capturing network effects, decreasing container costs for a country would affect each country and link differently.

In the case of Romania, transport costs for containers between Bucharest and the main cities of neighboring countries (Belgrade, Budapest, Chisinau, Kiev,

TABLE 5.1 Changes in Centrality Due to a Decrease in Container Transport Costs

Percent

Affected segment	First beneficiary	Second beneficiary
Bulgaria–Romania	Romania: 14	Bulgaria: 9
Poland–Germany	Poland: 4	Germany: 2
Poland–Slovak Republic	Poland: 5	Slovak Republic: 3
Kazakhstan–Russian Federation	Russian Federation: 2	Kazakhstan: 0
Kazakhstan–Kyrgyz Republic	Kazakhstan: 13	Kyrgyz Republic: 12
Kazakhstan–Uzbekistan	Kazakhstan: 6	Uzbekistan: 4
Bosnia and Herzegovina–Serbia	Bosnia and Herzegovina: 19	Serbia: 6
Bosnia and Herzegovina–Croatia	Bosnia and Herzegovina: 15	Croatia: 4
Ukraine–Romania	Romania: 6	Ukraine: 4
Ukraine–Slovak Republic	Slovak Republic: 2	Ukraine: 1
Ukraine–Poland	Poland: 7	Ukraine: 5
Armenia–Georgia	Armenia: 28	Georgia: 8

Note: Changes in centrality are calculated as the normalized centrality PageRank index in which $Centrality_{n,i}$ is defined by

$$Centrality_{n,\,i} = \frac{Centrality_i - min\left(Centrality_{j \in ECA}\right)}{max\left(Centrality_{j \in ECA}\right) - min\left(Centrality_{j \in ECA}\right)},$$

in which $centrality_i$ is the PageRank index for a given country i, $min(Centrality_{j=ECA})$ is the minimum for all countries, and $max(Centrality_{j=ECA})$ is the maximum for all ECA countries. Simulations consist in assuming a 30 percent decrease in transport costs in the listed links. Criticality is estimated before and after the cost shock. Percentage point changes are as reported.

and Sofia) are assumed to be reduced by a third. The decrease in costs for the links out of Romania to reach its neighbors affects those direct costs but also, as expected, the costs of shipping goods from Romania to all ECA countries (figure 5.12, panel a). Criticality increases for Romania and, simultaneously, for the Czech Republic and Ukraine. However, it decreases for Bulgaria, France, Poland, Hungary and the Slovak Republic (figure 5.12, panel b).

Cost reductions in the links going out of Romania would also increase its market access potential. However, *the change in costs would also increase market potential for all countries in Central Europe* (figure 5.12, panel c). Admittedly, the largest increase is for Romania, but Croatia and Bulgaria would also accrue important increases in realized potential.

If Kazakhstan's transport costs for containers are reduced by one-half between Almaty and the main cities of neighboring countries (Bishkek, Moscow, and Tashkent) the centrality of neighboring countries and the network as a whole would increase significantly as a result of connections with Russia and Russia's connections to the rest of ECA. The analysis shows that Kazakhstan, as a Central Asian country, is very isolated from the rest of ECA and would benefit highly, as would the other Central Asian countries, from lower-cost connections to other ECA countries. Interestingly, the Kyrgyz Republic would see the largest increase in realized potential market access (figure 5.13).

Collective Benefits of Improved Connectivity along a Corridor

What happens if a broader, corridor-wide, improvement in connectivity is achieved? Consider the case of a one-third reduction in container costs in the West-East

FIGURE 5.12 Romania: Impact of a 30 percent decrease in container transport costs

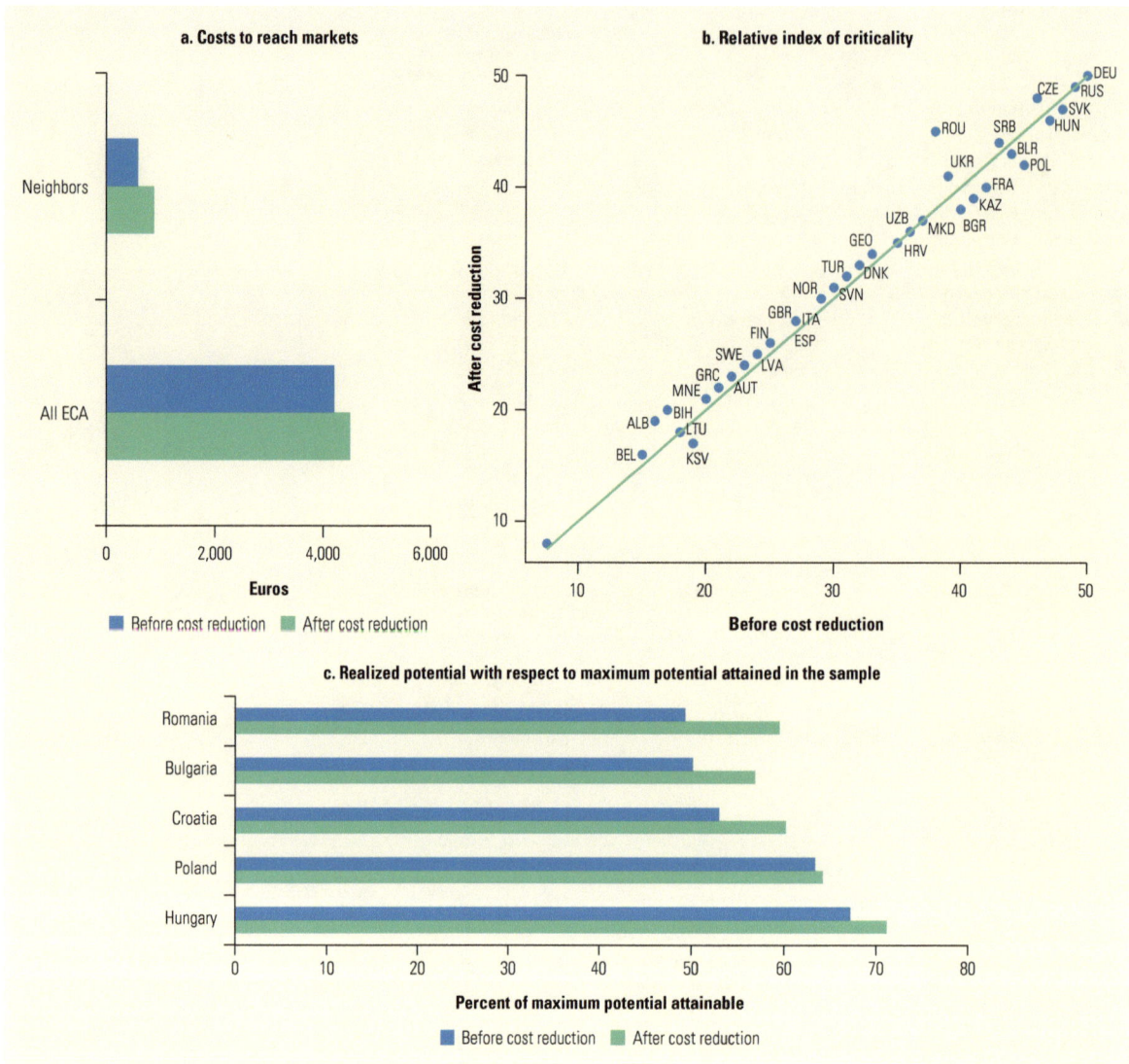

a. Costs to reach markets

b. Relative index of criticality

c. Realized potential with respect to maximum potential attained in the sample

Note: Realized potential is estimated based on Europe and Central Asia as a whole. Market access along the corridor is proxied by the potential indexes for markets located along the corridor:

$$Potential_{c,\,corridor} = \sum_{p \in Corridor} \frac{GDP_p}{cost_{c \to p}}.$$

corridor that starts in China (Shanghai) and goes to Germany through Kazakhstan, Russia, Belorussia, and Poland. This corridor contains segments that are central to the whole BRI. Market access potential (or GDP made accessible per unit of transport used) for each country along the corridor would increase on each of the segments of interest defined, broadly speaking, by each pair of country/capital cities. Measuring the impact of cost reductions for containers on market access potential would enable us to better understand the location and size of the impact of some targeted investments of the BRI.

FIGURE 5.13 Kazakhstan: Costs and potential indexes before and after decrease in costs

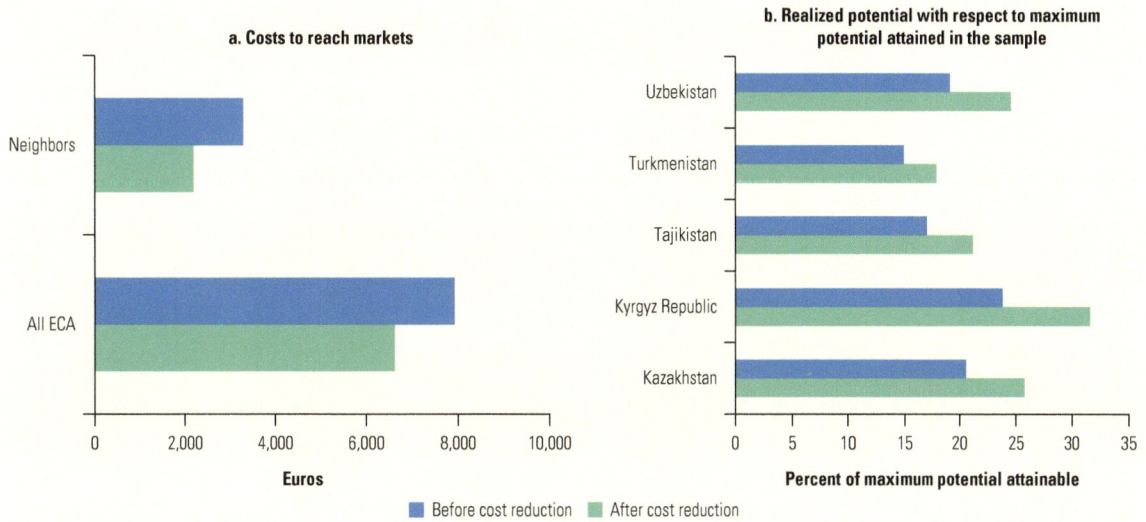

a. Costs to reach markets

b. Realized potential with respect to maximum potential attained in the sample

■ Before cost reduction   ■ After cost reduction

Note: Realized potential is estimated based on Europe and Central Asia as a whole. Market access along the corridor is proxied by the potential indexes for markets located along the corridor:

$$Potential_{c, corridor} = \sum_{p \in Corridor} \frac{GDP_p}{cost_{c \to p}}.$$

TABLE 5.2 Segments Affected by 33 Percent Cost Reduction in Container Transport

Percent

Recipient of changes in market access potential	Germany–Poland	Poland–Belarus	Belarus–Russia	Russia–Kazakhstan	Kazakhstan–China
Germany	21	3	2	7	16
Poland	25	8	6	3	8
Belarus	7	3	26	7	8
Russian Federation	8	6	9	9	21
Kazakhstan	1	1	1	12	44

Note: Market access potential along the corridor is proxied by the potential indexes for markets located along the corridor:

$$Potential_{c, corridor} = \sum_{p \in Corridor} \frac{GDP_p}{cost_{c \to p}}.$$

A cost reduction of one-third for the Kazakhstan–China segment would have the largest impact on market potentials: Kazakhstan's potential would increase by 44 percent because of cheaper access to China's large GDP. Russia and Germany would also benefit substantially from this cost reduction. Improving the Belarus–Russia segment would mostly benefit Belarus. A cost reduction on the Germany–Poland segment would greatly improve the potential of both Germany and Poland, as well as increase Kazakhstan's potential by 1 percent. The cost reduction on the Poland–Belarus segment has the smallest impact (table 5.2).

Reducing container costs increases the market potential of each country along the corridor and illustrates the extent to which transport infrastructure investment is a collective problem. Improving a segment of a corridor generates positive externalities and boosts the economic opportunities of all countries along the corridor. However, these results do not consider costs or other potential effects of transport improvements. Relocation of activities and people might offset some of the positive impacts of investing in these corridors, and the trade-offs between potential positive and negative effects should be further studied.

Conclusion

This chapter offers several insights into transport connectivity in ECA, from both methodological and strategic decision-making viewpoints.

From a methodological standpoint, this chapter uses data on ECA transport costs to study transport services rather than just focusing on transport infrastructure (e.g., kilometers of roads). It relies on a simplified collection of prices (or out-pocket costs) for different modes and purposes (passengers and cargo) for all ECA countries. The cost and time data collected focus on transport connectivity (a) within countries and (b) from a country and its immediate neighboring countries. As a means to generate estimates of cost and time connectivity for the whole network, network analysis is used to re-create paths from one country to any given country. This two-step approach enormously simplifies the data collection and facilitates connectivity analysis that can be adapted to the level of granularity desired and resources available.

The introduction of a geographic attribute as part of the definition of connectivity is essential to the analysis. Connectivity and other measures of accessibility to markets use diverse definitions of geographic spaces and markets, including regional—for example, coverage of the ECA space—the largest economies or economic gravity centers, countries with similar levels of production sophistication, and so forth. This allows practitioners and policy makers to assess the trade-offs, opportunities, and limitations of various connectivity strategies.

From a strategic standpoint, decisions to improve connectivity of specific transport network segments, corridors, or subnetworks are linked to the potential economic and trade strategies of a country. This approach nuances any possible performance evaluation of connectivity. Connectivity of a specific country will be better or worse depending on what market the transport system aims to cover: domestic connectivity, connectivity to the ECA transport network, to neighbors only, to strategic partners, and so forth. Some countries might wish to develop connectivity to maximize their own GDP unleashed by their transport networks (maximizing potential). Other countries could embrace a transport network development strategy based on regional cooperation agreements, for instance, connecting to central hubs rather than engaging in bilateral connections, or underscoring transport connectivity to key economic centers or political allies (strengthening partnerships). A third strategy can be rooted in strengthening existing transport corridors by increasing their resilience or just emphasizing the integration of transport networks by shortening distances (fostering linkages and integration). A country can be highly successful in achieving one policy goal, and not that successful in achieving another. One policy goal could be feasible given the country's geography and geopolitics, and another one might not be affordable given the fiscal space available. Thus, the flexibility of the methodology proposed is not trivial.

Adopting a network perspective on the whole transport network, rather than focusing on an individual country, helps provide an understanding of the dynamics of transport systems. Network measures characterizing the position of countries in the network provide stylized tools for understanding which countries would benefit from corridor paths between countries or which countries would get the most from their central or critical position.

Transport investments can generate positive externalities for other countries in a corridor. Solving the coordination problem among all ECA countries would help policy makers target efficient investment that would maximize the benefits for all countries in the region. The inability of the country making the investment to capture these benefits can lead to general underinvestment. More cooperation between countries, especially along corridors, could therefore increase the global benefits of transport investments.

> Solving the coordination problem among all ECA countries would help policy makers target efficient investment that would maximize the benefits for all countries in the region.

For ECA, the cost and time required for passenger travel, both within countries and to neighboring countries, varies greatly, with richer countries tending to have both higher quality and affordability of domestic transport services for passengers. By contrast, the cost and time required to deliver a container within the domestic market or to the capital city of neighboring countries varies little across ECA regions, except for Russia, Turkey, and Central Asia. It takes twice as long to ship a container in some Central Asian countries and Russia as it does in the best-performing regions.

Countries with high costs for connecting to neighbors but low costs for connecting to ECA as a whole (e.g., Russia) could focus transport resources on improving connections with neighbors, while countries with low costs to connect to neighbors but high costs to connect to the ECA network (e.g., Central Asia) could focus on improving connections to the region as a whole, or to extraregional countries. It also is important to assess connectivity in terms of time, particularly when products (e.g., those traded through supply chains) or the nature of the passenger trip (e.g., for businesspeople with a high opportunity cost of time) require reliability and predictability. Cost and time rankings differ more for container transport compared to passenger travel, as container prices depend on various parameters, such as logistics costs and the degree of competitiveness among service providers.

A comparison of time and cost performance for different intended markets can help countries better assess the probability of success of transport interventions. For example, the very high costs faced by Central Asia makes it difficult to enter new markets with competitive prices, so a focus on an East-West corridor, building on access to neighbors and their access to global markets might be more productive. A second option is to maximize the regional GDP reached by transport networks. Advanced, Central, and Eastern European countries have the greatest market access, and Central Asia the lowest. Finally, countries should consider the value of targeted markets in the whole network. For example, strengthening connections with neighbors that are well connected may contribute most to the overall integration of the country within the region and globally.

Annex 5A. Methodology and Data

Overall Approach

The first step is the data collection process, which was focused on a predefined network that covers direct links (a) among main cities within a country, (b) from capital cities in a specific country to capital cities of its neighboring countries, and (c) from a capital city to key air and maritime hubs. This analysis measures transport services as opposed to physical assets. Thus, the kilometers of roads, or number of airports or ports, is less relevant than observable transport service attributes such as cost, time, reliability, and frequency, among others.

Several measures have been suggested to look at transport connectivity, with most of them focusing on physical infrastructure. Aggregate statistics such as the total road or rail track length in a country, or distance to high-quality infrastructure (such as airports, ports, highways), are examples of measures of connectivity based on the physical properties of a transport network. Using the presence of transport infrastructure, or its capacity, as a measure of connectivity is a poor proxy for the quality of transport services or accessibility to a given location.[19] In the case of airports, for example, capacity-based measures of transport connectivity "tend to underestimate the importance of small airports and overestimate it for large airports. Small airports may have high accessibility levels if they have few flights to well-connected hub airports" (Burghouwt and Redondi 2013, 36).

Similarly, Briceno-Garmendia, Moroz, and Rozenberg (2015) illustrate the problem of traditional capacity-based measures in the context of road transport. They find that while the South Asia region is ranked as the best performer for road density, it is the worst performer in terms of perceived road quality (based on the World Economic Forum's road quality perception ranking). These contradictions imply that a more nuanced measure of transport connectivity should cover not only the availability and capacity of transport infrastructure, but also the quality of transport services on the transport network. Furthermore, viewing transport in terms of proxies for user experiences—and not only in terms of the stock of infrastructure capital—is a key part of any effort aimed at understanding connectivity.

For metrics purposes, connectivity, among other transport services, is measured as the cost and time for delivering a container to a destination and the cost and time for a passenger to reach a destination. The costs are the "out-of-pocket" payments made by a consumer for sending a container or by a passenger for using transportation, in other words, the "visible price" faced by end-users in the market. An exception is the cost of using private cars over the road network. Car travel out-of-pocket costs are represented by the cost of fuel, a function of the fuel consumption that is linked to the vehicle speed and cost of fuel per liter.[20]

Data Collection

Cost and time statistics were collected to capture both freight and passenger services along each country's internal core transport network (domestic connectivity), the nodes connecting it to its neighbors (neighbor connectivity), and international transportation hubs (global connectivity). The modes of transport covered include road, rail, air, maritime, and multimodal. The data come from observable open sources, which should make results replicable and scalable.

For data collection purposes, a country's core network is defined as the road and rail network connecting the main city (capital or main commercial center) to the four most populated cities in each country, the main airport, the main port, key border crossings, and key urban roads (e.g., ring roads). In general, the cities considered were the five most populated cities in each country, with some exceptions for larger countries for which more than five cities were evaluated.[21] For each country, a main city was defined, which in most cases corresponded to the capital. In some exceptions, a second or alternative city was chosen given its economic importance. That is the case, for example, of Frankfurt in Germany and Istanbul in Turkey.

Primary data were collected on the time required to connect from node A to B (the main cities) and the out-of-pocket cost to connect from node A to B.[22]

Data were collected from open sources, hence, values and eventual results can be replicated and used in other countries and continents. Sources of primary data collected include open source platforms (i.e., Google Maps), logistics service providers (i.e., UPS), travel sites (i.e., rome2rio, Skyscanner), online freight forwarders, price estimates, and bus schedules, among others.

Geographic Scope and Coverage

The countries covered in this study include those in the ECA space: 50 countries comprising the European Union, Eastern Europe and the Western Balkans, Turkey and the South Caucasus, and Russia and Central Asia.[23]

The country sample is diverse in terms of income, economic activity, trade orientation, geography, and population. To facilitate the analysis of the data and the characterization of patterns and messages, the chapter uses typologies representing geopolitical, geographic, and socioeconomic angles. Three main typologies are used: region, location, and income (map 5A.1).[24]

Extending the Set of ECA Countries to China

One extension would be the addition of China in the set of countries to reach through the transport network. It is important given the sizable trade flows between China and the EU countries and given the geographic location of Central Asian countries that are neighboring China. Focusing only on the ECA countries delivers a truncated perspective, especially for Central Asia. Adding China and access to ports south of Central Asia would reveal different opportunities for those countries. Additional work would help in positioning Central Asia differently, especially within the context of the BRI. In this study, Central Asia is shown at the "far end" of the ECA region. Other work could add a different set of countries south and east of Central Asia.

MAP 5A.1 Typologies used in the analysis

a. Regions

Region
- Advanced (Western, Northern, and Southern) Europe
- Central Europe
- Eastern Europe
- Western Balkans
- Turkey
- Russian Federation
- South Caucasus
- Central Asia

continued

MAP 5A.1 *continued*

b. Location

continued

However, it remains challenging for Central Asia to access China nowadays. Central Asia is the region with the largest costs to send containers both to the main maritime hubs and to Shanghai compared with other ECA regions (figure 5A.1). Given that freight transport does not cover bulk trade, few containers are currently shipped from Central Asian countries toward China. Therefore, expanding this analysis to China does not improve the connectivity of Central Asian countries given the lack of affordable transport services toward the Chinese hub.

The Way Forward

The modes considered for this analysis include, for passengers, roads (personal cars and buses) and rail. For freight, the approach is slightly different and the breakdown is defined in terms of the packaging, that is, whether the freight goes in containers or parcel. The movement of a container is, by nature, multimodal. The data originally included data for parcel, but the analysis was inconclusive. The mode choice in each country depends on the availability of infrastructure as well

MAP 5A.1 *continued*

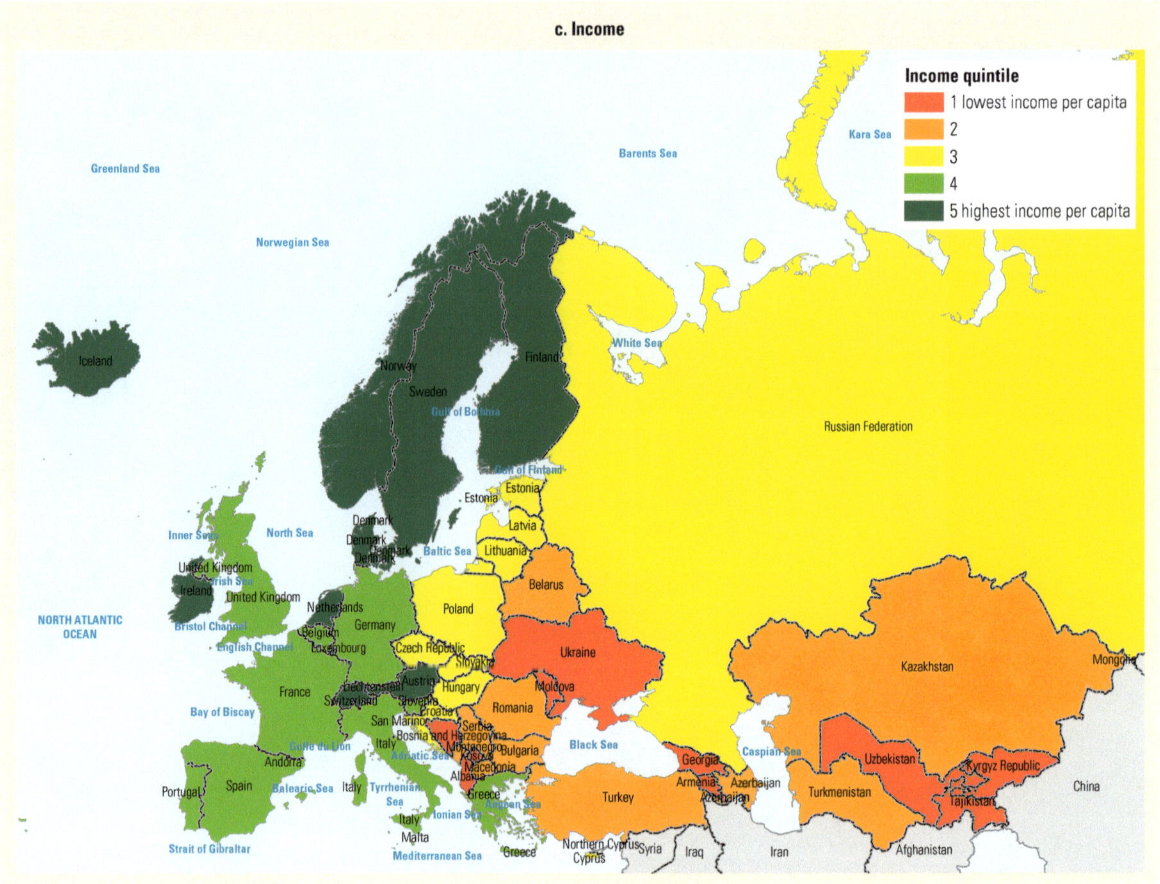

c. Income

Income quintile
- 1 lowest income per capita
- 2
- 3
- 4
- 5 highest income per capita

Note: In panel a, "Advanced Europe" refers to the group of countries that signed the 1993 Maastricht Treaty or joined the European Union before 1995. Panel c classifies countries according to their quintiles in the distribution of GDP per capita in the ECA region.

as freight rates, frequency, and reliability. For example, a multimodal transport chain in countries such as the Netherlands, Belgium, and the Western Balkans is likely to involve an inland waterway or railway leg to transport a container domestically or regionally, whereas in other countries it might only involve one mode, mostly trucking. While knowing each leg of the transport chain allows for a richer analysis, our data capture the most relevant information for shippers whose main interest is the market (equilibrium) price and shipment time rather than individual components of the mode used to move their cargo. Seen this way, the data are comprehensive enough to characterize the level of transport connectivity for containerized cargo. An alternative approach would be to collect data on freight by mode but an economic model would be required to find the optimal choice of modes along the transport chain.

The analysis of freight transport connectivity is based on the cost and shipment time of sending a container. Conspicuously missing are data for bulk, given that the share of containerized cargo movements versus bulk movements varies greatly in the ECA region. Eastern European and Central Asian economies mainly export minerals and agricultural products, which rely more heavily on

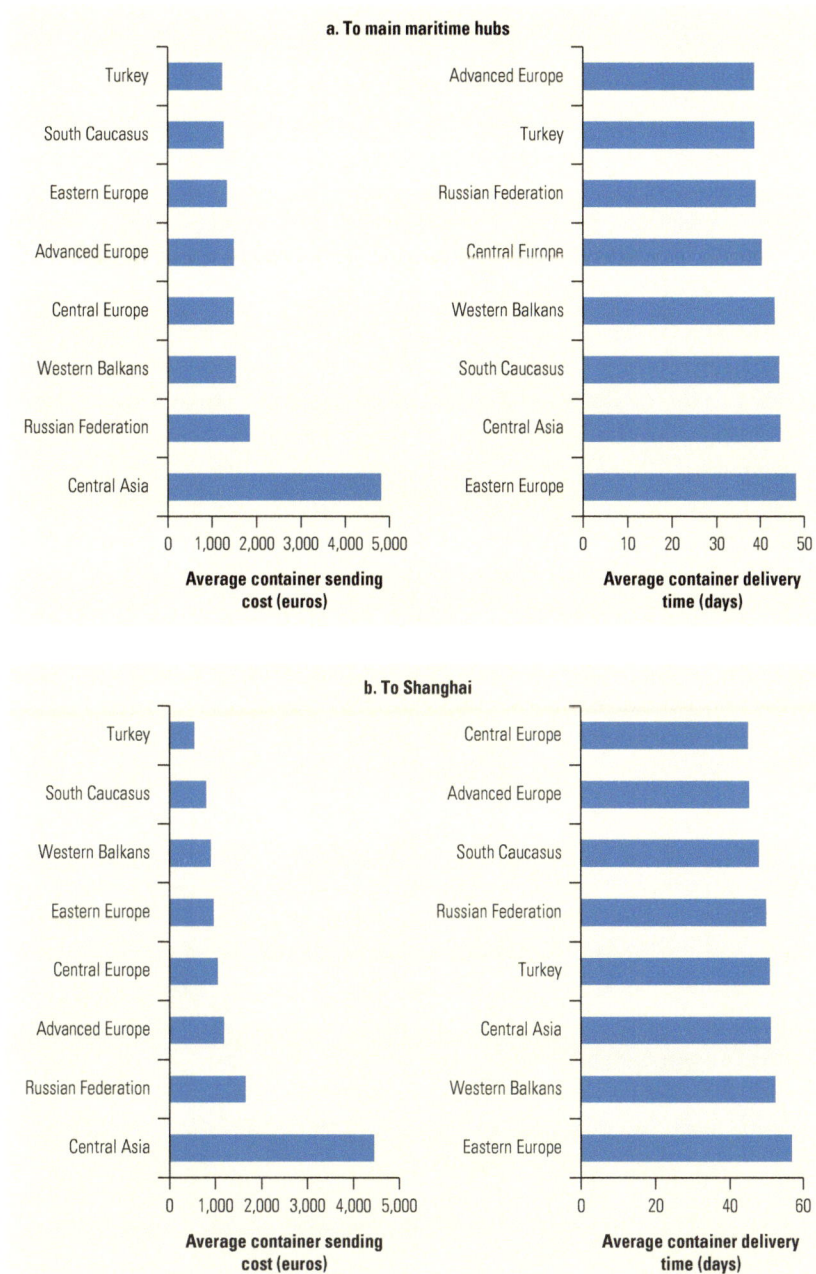

FIGURE 5A.1 Cost of and time required for freight transport services
Averages per region

a. To main maritime hubs

Average container sending cost (euros) — regions (top to bottom): Turkey, South Caucasus, Eastern Europe, Advanced Europe, Central Europe, Western Balkans, Russian Federation, Central Asia

Average container delivery time (days) — regions (top to bottom): Advanced Europe, Turkey, Russian Federation, Central Europe, Western Balkans, South Caucasus, Central Asia, Eastern Europe

b. To Shanghai

Average container sending cost (euros) — regions (top to bottom): Turkey, South Caucasus, Western Balkans, Eastern Europe, Central Europe, Advanced Europe, Russian Federation, Central Asia

Average container delivery time (days) — regions (top to bottom): Central Europe, Advanced Europe, South Caucasus, Russian Federation, Turkey, Central Asia, Western Balkans, Eastern Europe

Note: Freight connectivity to hubs for a given country is measured as the average price to send a container from its capital city to representative intercontinental global hubs: Los Angeles, Rotterdam, and Shanghai. "Advanced Europe" comprises countries in Northern, Southern, and Western Europe.

modes that transport bulk freight. Kazakhstan, Russia, and Ukraine have some of the world's most extensive freight railway systems. It is possible to get a different ranking favoring these countries had one looked at the cost and time of sending bulk commodities. It is important to note that while containerized cargo is a small share of exports from these countries, it constitutes a large share of their imports of consumer and industrial products, which rely on intermodal transport. The freight connectivity analysis is, therefore, relevant for all countries in the sample.

When defining costs as out-of-pocket and using time from origin to destination, the study focuses on the variable observables by a user or decision maker. A deeper decomposition of the costs and time structure would be necessary to identify the bottlenecks and key elements for policy recommendations. Notably, institutional costs and red tape are embedded in the costs and times observed or faced by the user. It would also be interesting to consider the impact of border crossings and market structures like the presence of cartels on transport prices and time. A natural extension is to clarify the structure of the markups created by various institutional and market issues. For example, Atkin and Donaldson (2015) use the spatial distribution of prices to obtain an estimate of the whole transport costs. These costs include the distance factor as well as the markup due to the structure of the transport sector.

The study does not explicitly consider border crossing times and costs separately. Conceivably, given the diversity of countries and presence of various economic blocs in the sample, these variables have different degrees of importance. While border-crossing delays and costs are major issues in the Western Balkans and countries such as Belarus, they are irrelevant for intra-EU movements. The shipment time and travel time data, which are gathered from open source websites should, in theory, reflect the difference in border crossing across countries. They are, however, likely to underestimate the time for inspections and customs clearance, especially for countries outside of the EU region. In addition to prolonging travel and shipment times, border-crossing problems lead to reliability issues, which have important implications for mode choice in particular and the level of realized connectivity in general. Our cost and time (speed)–based connectivity ranking could be biased upward for countries where there are well-known border-crossing problems such the Western Balkans. For others, for example, the Netherlands and Belgium, it could be biased downward where cargo moves reliably albeit at a slower speed. Open source data can be completed with survey-based data when available.

The car travel out-of-pocket cost, which is estimated as a function of vehicle speed and fuel prices in each country, does not include tolls. Accounting for tolls would make the analysis richer but would require knowledge of specific routes and segments of the road system used to net out their effect, which is a tall order within the scope of the current study. While tolls are not applied universally in the ECA region, they are becoming common for new motorways in some countries. To the extent that tolls are indicators of higher levels of service, the simple cost function should still reflect differences between countries through the speed variable.

In terms of metrics, the study uses cost and time. It is known that reliability is a third key metric entering the decision making of transport users. For example, the Netherlands is poorly rated in terms of speed for freight and passenger connectivity. However, the country would rank very well when looking at reliability. Participants in global value chains have to send parts and components to the next stage on time. An accumulation of delays caused by unreliable transport services will disturb the whole supply chain. Having reliable transport services is essential for countries and to decision makers. Further work should add reliability to time and costs as metrics for connectivity to get a more complete picture.

The current study presents the material as separate connectivity indexes for each of the aspects analyzed, that is, domestic and regional indicators, time and cost connectivity, as well as passenger and freight. The team made the decision not to create a global integrative connectivity index. Further thinking is necessary to determine whether an integrated index makes sense and if so, which methodology to use. Merging time and costs can be done using generalized cost methods, but difficulties emerge with properly defining the opportunity costs for all the cases. Among others, the principal component approach could be used to aggregate elements into a unique connectivity measure per country. Having three indicators for domestic and regional connectivity is probably the highest level of aggregation to hope for at this stage.

Finally, the resulting indexes in this report can be used to answer key analytic questions about the role of transport services in boosting social and economic outcomes. A gender perspective would help assess to what extent men and women have the same opportunities in using transport services. Obstacles for women to efficiently use transport services can lower their economic opportunities. Measuring the penetration of transport services in the whole territory can be used to gauge the extent to which less connected populations benefit less from the gains of border opening and cheaper products (Atkin and Donaldson 2015). In addition to trade opportunities, transport services also matter for people to access jobs and different services such as education and health. It could also help for cost-benefit and country-specific analyses. Thinking about strategic connectivity is particularly important for countries that are landlocked, like most countries in Central Asia. Measures of centrality and criticality help provide an understanding of the dynamics of the whole network instead of only focusing on links to neighboring countries or large hubs. In general, these indexes provide quantified tools to help develop thinking about sectoral and country strategies.

The natural extensions of this chapter include considering other groupings or adding countries outside ECA to the sample pool. As it is, the chapter mostly looks at three main economic poles or gravity centers in ECA (Russia, Turkey, and the EU) or to reach groupings defined by economic criteria. Further work could be done to analyze other key groupings defined by their historical or cultural links or prospective impact. For example, the countries of the Commonwealth of Independent States and their historic links or the involvement of China and its role in promoting projects within the BRI could be explored. China is important for most ECA countries as a major trading partner or a neighbor with large potential for trade and investment. Including other regions and considering the connectivity of ECA countries with these other regions would add more insights. The analysis would also benefit from including connections with the United States and other subsets of the ECA region. Spain and Portugal have intense connectivity with Central and South American countries. France has historical links with Maghreb countries. Central Asian countries have historical links with Middle Eastern and South Asian countries. A broader set of countries would enrich the connectivity analysis and allow for more meaningful benchmarking.

Notes

1. The BRI is an ambitious project that will reach 65 countries and 4.4 billion people, and leverage 40 percent of the world's GDP. Billions of dollars' worth of investments will be channeled toward infrastructure projects across Asia, Africa, and Europe. Six new land corridors will be rehabilitated, and the maritime connectivity, which consists of a network of planned ports and other coastal infrastructure projects, will be improved. This project will be transformative for all cities along the new corridors and will bring unprecedented opportunities for their economies.

2. The Trans-European Transport Network is an initiative of the EU consisting of hundreds of projects (studies and civil works). The project's main purpose is ensuring the cohesion, interconnection, and interoperability of the network, as well as access to it. Once completed, the Trans-European Transport Network projects will touch every EU member state and all modes of transport (European Commission 2017).

3. Data were also collected for connections to main air and maritime hubs but are not included in this analysis because of representativeness issues.

4. Data collected are that of transport prices or out-of-pocket costs, and may be influenced by subsidies and affected by the degree of competition in transport services markets (e.g., the potential for collusive practices by service providers).

5. While the results are not presented here, domestic connectivity can appear very different from the perspective of a global passenger than a domestic passenger. For global passengers, higher speeds are strongly correlated with higher unitary prices. The few exceptions include the Czech Republic, Kazakhstan, Poland, Ukraine, and Uzbekistan, where passenger transport services are subsidized, a legacy effect from the Soviet era. Based on these metrics, countries in ECA with the highest GDP per capita—such as France, Spain, Denmark, Holland, Sweden, Switzerland, and Germany—that are known for their advanced highway and railway systems (using speed as proxy) are affordable for local passengers but not necessarily for an average passenger from the rest of ECA. In sharp contrast, countries like Azerbaijan, Georgia, FYR Macedonia, Armenia, Tajikistan, and Kosovo provide very low-priced passenger transport services for global passengers but with an apparent diminished quality (using speed as proxy).

6. INRIX traffic scorecard: http://www.dutchdailynews.com/netherlands-named-second-worst-country-for-traffic-congestion/. The high share of inland waterways in these countries can also be a factor for slower movement of cargo.

7. While results are not presented here, the story of neighbor connectivity can change significantly from the perspective of a global passenger rather a domestic passenger (if nominal unit costs are used instead of the unit costs adjusted by the purchasing power parity of the country of origin of the passenger). From the perspective of a global passenger, richer countries like France, Belgium, and the United Kingdom perform well in speed ranking but badly in cost ranking, and vice versa for poorer countries such as Armenia, the Kyrgyz Republic, Georgia, and Azerbaijan. The story shifts when unit costs are adjusted by purchasing power parity, as shown in the text. This has important implications. Essentially in terms of affordability, passengers from advanced European economies such as France, Belgium, Germany, and the Scandinavian countries—among others—are the most mobile in ECA, they can afford to travel to neighboring countries. Sadly, that is not the case for passengers from Central Asia, the South Caucasus, and the Western Balkans, who are largely trapped because of affordability issues.

8. The Democratic Republic of Korea and Mongolia are not included in the data.

9. Unfortunately freight costs for bulk cargo were not collected.

10. Earlier studies have shown that coastal countries may have poor accessibility if infrastructure (ports) is not adequate (i.e., only minor ports are located nearby or connections are expensive).

11. Other important poles such as the United States and China are not considered here. More information is provided about connectivity to China in annex 5A.

12. The largest ECA economies that are considered here are France, Germany, Russia, the United Kingdom, and Italy.

13. A country's level of production sophistication is defined using the index of complexity (Hausmann and Hidalgo 2014). The Economic Complexity Index measures the knowledge intensity of an economy by considering the knowledge intensity of the products it exports. This index is used to find, for each country, the eight economies with similar levels of production sophistication. Each country is compared with a different set of economies. The index only depends on the pattern of exports, which is used as a proxy for production factors, the stock of knowledge, the institutional and regulatory environment, and the rest of production capacities. The most complex economies differ from the largest markets. According to the 2015 ranking of the *MIT Atlas of Complexity*, the five countries with the highest knowledge intensity are Switzerland, Austria, the Czech Republic, Germany, and Sweden.

14. How Central Asia connects with China, and how it can benefit from that economic gravity center, was, unfortunately, not included in this study, which limits the scope of analysis and data collection to ECA countries. This is a natural extension of this work and of the applicaiton of the proposed methodology to measure and assess connectivity.

15. Considering freight services toward China does not improve the connectivity of Central Asian countries. Prices to send containers toward Shanghai are much higher in Central Asian countries than in the rest of ECA (see "Extending the Set of ECA Countries to China" in annex 5A).

16. See chapter 1 for the analysis of the economic benefits of greater connectivity and the complementarity of different types of connections.

17. See "The Way Forward" in annex 5A.

18. "Properly managed" is an important nuance as a country cannot attract more traffic than it is able to handle domestically with its current infrastructure and services. Otherwise the infrastructure will collapse or start struggling with congestion.

19. Deichmann et al. (2004) note that summary statistics such as the total road length in a state or province or straight-line distance to ports or urban agglomerations are poor proxies for the complexity inherent in a national or regional transportation network.

20. If more time and resources were available, HDM-4 could be used to estimate more elaborate road and vehicle user costs considering aspects such as terrain, standard and class of each road link, and so on. For an exercise of this scope, the HDM-4 was not practical or affordable.

     Out-of-pocket costs or prices faced by users reflect the quality of infrastructure and services. They also internalize issues pertaining to market structure of service providers and regulatory issues. Note that all these elements have an impact on the resulting "connectivity" faced by users. A natural follow-up analysis would be to assess the drivers of the proposed connectivity index, singling out as much as possible aspects pertaining to market structure, regulation, and institutions. Also, it is possible to use metrics in addition to time and costs, such as frequency and reliability, which could be the subject of further analysis.

21. In Russia ten cities were considered. In France, Germany, Italy, Kazakhstan, Poland, Spain, Turkey, Ukraine, and the United Kingdom, seven cities were included. In Greece, only cities on the mainland were considered. In Cyprus, Luxembourg, Malta, and Montenegro, only three cities were considered. For Germany, Kazakhstan, Switzerland, and Turkey, commercial centers (Frankfurt, Almaty, Zurich, Istanbul) were included instead of the capital cities.

22. Other variables collected but not used in this specific analysis include connection frequency, and reliability (or variance) as from rush hour to non–rush hour time, or from daytime to nighttime.

   In the original data collection, nodes were also defined as hubs. Two sets of hubs were defined. Frankfurt, Istanbul, and Moscow were selected as air hubs. Los Angeles, Rotterdam, and Shanghai were selected as the "illustrative" maritime hubs. This is perhaps the most controversial element of the proposed approach because the selection of hubs is exogenous to the data collection. Which cities are considered hubs, how many international hubs to include, and their regional representativeness are all elements open to debate. For instance, Frankfurt, Istanbul, and Moscow are illustrative air hubs rather than representative ones. London, Paris, and Rome could have also been included. Given that the validaton of the pre-selected hubs was not widely discussed, the analysis of that data is excluded.

23. Albania, Armenia, Austria, Azerbaijan, Belarus, Belgium, Bosnia and Herzegovina, Bulgaria, Croatia, Cyprus, the Czech Republic, Denmark, Estonia, Finland, France, Georgia, Germany, Greece, Hungary, Iceland, Ireland, Italy, Kazakhstan, Kosovo, the Kyrgyz Republic, Latvia, Lithuania, Luxembourg, FYR Macedonia, Malta, Moldova, Montenegro, the Netherlands, Norway, Poland, Portugal, Romania, Russia, Serbia, the Slovak Republic, Slovenia, Spain, Sweden, Switzerland, Tajikistan, Turkey, Turkmenistan, Ukraine, the United Kingdom, and Uzbekistan.

24. Other categories such as EU or European Economic Association membership, the size of the country, the density, and the level of inequality were considered. The final analysis only focuses on three dimensions.

References

Arrow, Kenneth J. 1969. "Classificatory Notes on the Production and Transmission of Technological Knowledge." *American Economic Review* 59 (2): 29–35.

Atkin, David, and Dave Donaldson. 2015. "Who's Getting Globalized? The Size and Implications of Intranational Trade Costs." Working Paper 21439, National Bureau of Economic Research, Cambridge, MA. http://www.nber.org/papers/w21439.

Bahar, Dany, Ricardo Hausmann, and César Hidalgo. 2014. "Neighbors and the Evolution of the Comparative Advantage of Nations: Evidence of International Knowledge Diffusion?" *Journal of International Economics* 92 (1): 111–23.

Briceno-Garmendia, C., H. Moroz, and J. Rozenberg. 2015. *Road Networks, Accessibility, and Resilience: The Cases of Colombia, Ecuador, and Peru.* An LCR Regional Study. Washington, DC: World Bank.

Burghouwt, G., and R. Redondi. 2013. "Connectivity in Air Transport Networks: An Assessment of Models and Applications." *Journal of Transport Economics and Policy* 47 (1): 35–53.

Deichmann, U., M. Fay, J. Koo, and S. Lall. 2004. "Economic Structure, Productivity, and Infrastructure Quality in Southern Mexico." *Annals of Regional Science* 38 (3): 361–85.

European Commission. 2017. *TEN-T Projects.* https://ec.europa.eu/inea/en/ten-t/ten-t-projects.

Hausmann, Ricardo, and César Hidalgo. 2014. *The Atlas of Economic Complexity: Mapping Paths to Prosperity.* Cambridge, MA: MIT Press.

Hummels, David L., and Georg Schaur. 2013. "Time as a Trade Barrier." *American Economic Review* 103 (7): 2935–59.

6

Supply Chains in Europe and Central Asia: Connectivity through Cross-Border Production Fragmentation

Cross-border production fragmentation, or specialization across stages of the production process, has accelerated in recent decades. Many goods that were produced in single countries are now sliced in different bundles that are assigned to plants in different countries, as countries import intermediate inputs to combine them with domestic value added and reexport the whole product as a final good or as an input into the rest of the production process. This chapter is organized in three sections. The first addresses the rise in production fragmentation among European countries, creating the cluster "Factory Europe" that competes with "Factory Asia" and "Factory North America." The second section investigates the different channels and implications of cross-country knowledge sharing when production is fragmented across countries, focusing on the existence of input-output linkages across sectors from different countries. The third discusses policies to increase the gains from participating in global value chains (GVCs).

Main Messages

- The expansion of supply chains has enabled more developing country firms to participate in the production of advanced products by specializing in one or several stages of the chain, and thus gain from foreign knowledge and learning by doing. Knowledge diffusion requires more direct forms of interaction than just trade and is heightened in supply chains that involve both movement of goods and know-how transfers, as well as movement of managers across stages

of production. Thus, despite large improvements in transport and information flows between countries, geographic proximity continues to be important to the coordination of input production as well as the transfer of "tacit knowledge." Cultural proximity and migration networks have facilitated the development of successful regional supply chains in Europe.

- Productivity growth in supply chains depends on the extent to which countries are close to or well connected with the most productive countries to reap the benefits of cross-border knowledge sharing. Integration into the trade network and GVC participation are drivers of productivity growth. At the same time, the rise of trade in intermediate goods and services tends to increase the interdependence of countries and to make economies more volatile.

- Different policies may be useful for increasing participation in supply chains through importing intermediate goods versus increasing exports of intermediate goods. A large set of policies, from removing barriers to trade and foreign direct investment (FDI) to strengthening intellectual property protection and competitiveness reforms, are needed to participate and make the most of cross-border production fragmentation.

Factory Europe

Many supply chains can be described as "regional" production chains rather than global value chains, since they are composed of geographically proximate countries. The production chains associated with auto parts trade in North America and the production and assembly of electronic components in Asia are the most famous ones. Other regional production chains are located in Europe and Central Asia (ECA). Siemens has divided its activities between engineering in Western Europe and assembly in Eastern Europe. French and German car makers have raised their productivity by offshoring part of their production in Eastern countries (Gill and Raiser 2011; Marin 2010). Skoda in the Czech Republic makes high-tech components for Volkswagen, and Renault has opened assembly firms in Romania.

This section focuses on "Factory Europe" and the importance of geographic proximity in the development of supply chains. Despite dramatic declines in transportation costs, proximity remains important in channeling knowledge and facilitating the coordination of production stages across borders. In addition, geographic proximity is associated with similarities in culture and language, as well as migration networks, that matter even more for production fragmentation than for traditional trade. These diverse forms of proximity facilitate the movement of "tacit knowledge" along production stages across borders.

Factory Europe in a Multipolar Economy

The rise of production fragmentation as an important global phenomenon began in developed countries. For example, the 1965 Auto Pact between the United States and Canada increased trade and improved the efficiency of their auto-parts supply chain. Between 1985 and 1995 trade in supply chains grew between high-tech and low-wage countries, referred to as "globalization's second unbundling" (Amador and Cabral 2009; Baldwin and Lopez-Gonzalez 2015). Three regional clusters have emerged as zones of intense production fragmentation: "Factory Asia," "Factory North America," and "Factory Europe" (Baldwin and Lopez-Gonzalez 2015). These zones are composed of headquarters economies such as Germany, the United States, and China, which offshore part of their production to nearby "factory" economies with lower wages.

Participation in supply chains is measured in terms of value-added flows rather than gross export flows across countries.[1] Data on value-added flows from the Organisation for Economic Co-operation and Development (OECD) Trade in Value Added (TiVA) database[2] can be used to construct visual network representations[3] that capture the integration of countries into the global network of trade in value added (figure 6.1). The size of the country is given by a measure of its centrality in the network (figure 6.1 only shows the backbone of the network rather than all the flows across countries).

In 2011, three groupings emerged around three central economies: Germany for the ECA region, China in Asia, and the United States for North America. The emergence of China as a main node for the Asian regional cluster is relatively recent when compared to the same network in 1995 in which the Asia cluster was

FIGURE 6.1 **Three clusters of countries emerge: "Factory Europe" around Germany, "Factory North America" around the United States, and "Factory Asia" around China**
Minimal spanning tree, value-added network, 2011

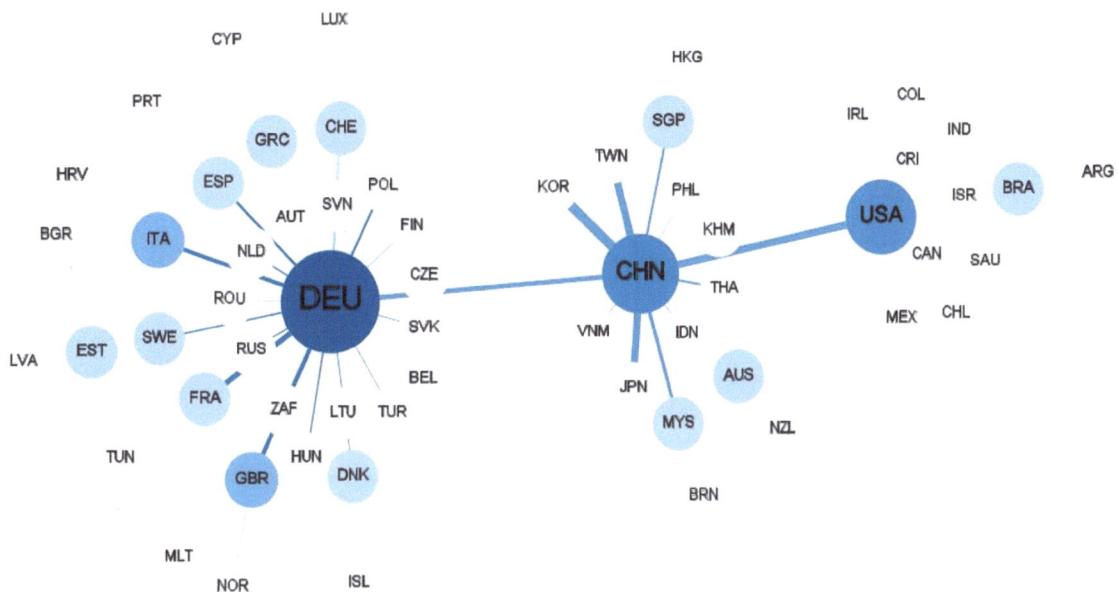

Source: Santoni and Taglioni 2015.
Note: The minimal spanning tree is a network analysis technique that keeps only a subset of the links between all countries in the network of value-added flows. All countries are connected through a path that favors links that represent major flows of value added. Node size is given by the centrality measure in the network.

FIGURE 6.2 Smaller European countries, like the Czech Republic, are dominated by trade with Germany, while Germany is the headquarters of "Factory Europe," which trades more globally

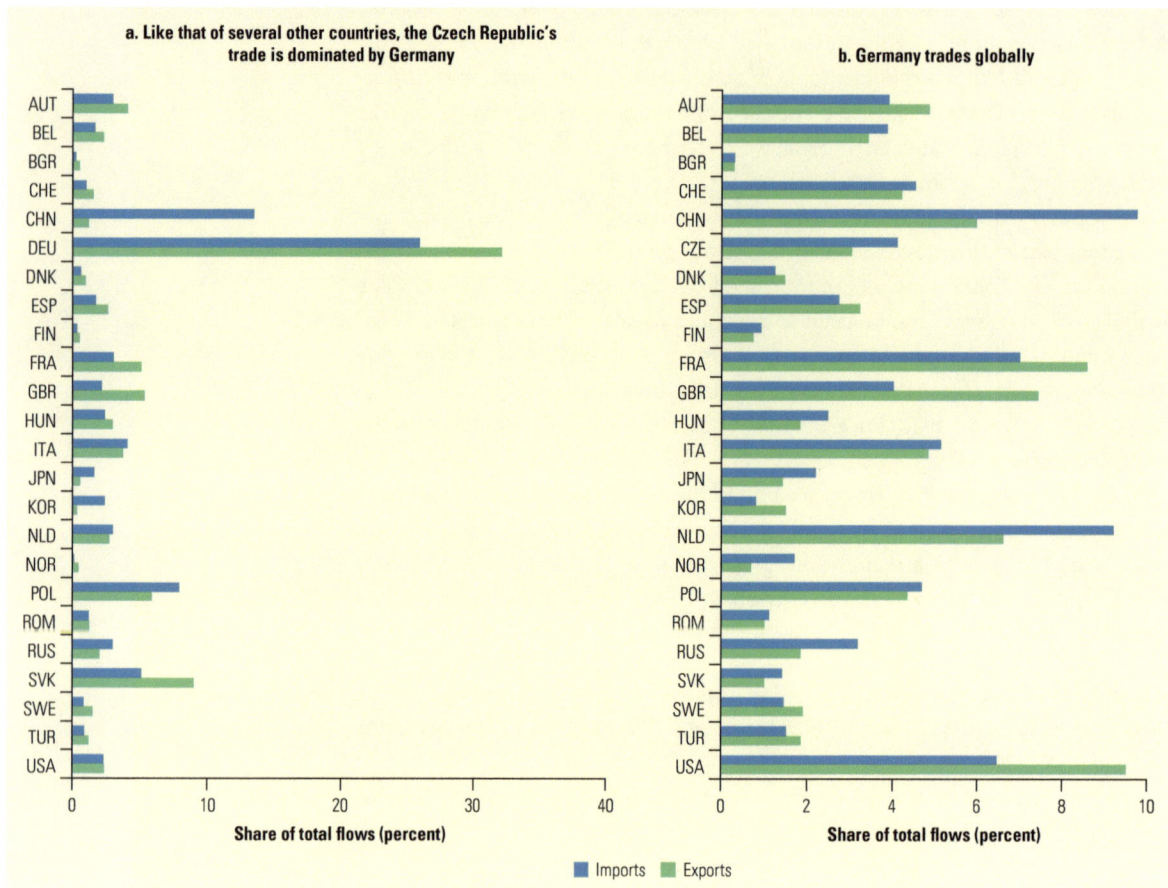

a. Like that of several other countries, the Czech Republic's trade is dominated by Germany

b. Germany trades globally

■ Imports ■ Exports

Source: UN Comtrade data on the import and export structure of the Czech Republic and Germany, 2015.

not apparent (Santoni and Taglioni 2015). Germany's role as the headquarters economy of a large European cluster can be illustrated by comparing the export and import destinations for Germany and the Czech Republic (figure 6.2). Similar to other small European countries, the bulk of imports to and exports from the Czech Republic go to Germany, whereas Germany has a balanced portfolio of trade partners in the world.

Asia and North America have similar patterns to those observed in Europe, although Europe has moved much more in terms of political and economic cooperation, particularly under the European Union (EU). Germany, like the United States, does a great deal of supply-chain trade with its lower-wage neighbors. Several countries, such as the Czech Republic and Poland, import intermediate and final goods from Germany, and export intermediate products to Germany, where they undergo final processing for sale to third countries. However, Germany also engages in supply-chain trade with many other high-wage neighboring nations (Austria, the Netherlands, and France). Unlike other regional supply chains, Factory Europe has three high-technology nations (other than the main node, Germany) with large manufacturing sectors: the United Kingdom, France and Italy.

Production Fragmentation and Exports of Value Added as an Indicator of GVCs

Production fragmentation has increased in Europe. Comparing data on trade measured by gross and value-added flows shows the fragmentation of production through trade in intermediate goods. Traditionally, exports are simply measured by their gross value, which masks the value of imported component inputs.[4] For example, a country that imports high-value-added inputs and assembles them into a final good may only provide a small domestic value-added contribution while exporting high-value goods. Trade statistics count the whole product as an export, whereas value-added trade flows only count the smaller domestic contribution. We use the ratio of gross exports to value-added exports to quantify the fragmentation of the production process due to the presence of supply chains.[5] An increase in this ratio over time means that the importance of production fragmentation and supply chains are likely increasing.

Overall, increased participation in supply chains (production fragmentation) is associated with more rapid growth in value added in exports. Production fragmentation (an increase in the ratio of gross exports to domestic value-added exports) increased between 2000 and 2011 for both Asia and Europe (but not in the North American Free Trade Agreement [NAFTA] region),[6] with the largest increase in Asia (figure 6.3, panel a). At the same time, panel b of figure 6.3 shows that those regions with larger percentage point increases in production fragmentation also experienced greater average growth in overall value added in exports. Thus, higher growth in gross exports than in domestic value added is associated with more rapid growth of domestic value added in exports than in regions where the fragmentation of production occurred more slowly. EU advanced countries (EU15) and transition economies (EU13) are the second- and third-highest beneficiaries of this process, after Asia. Value added in exports is a better measure of the importance of participation in international trade than gross value of exports, because it encompasses the potential benefits in terms of domestic employment and productivity growth.

Greater production fragmentation in the EU13 countries and in Turkey was associated with more rapid growth of total value added in exports. Over the period 2000–11, Turkey and Poland experienced among the largest percentage increases in both production fragmentation (figure 6.4, panel a) and growth rate of exports of value added (figure 6.4, panel b). The Czech Republic, Bulgaria, and the Slovak Republic also experienced greater than average rates of increase in production fragmentation and exports of value added. In Romania, the increase in production fragmentation was moderate but exports of value added grew rapidly. Finally, Slovenia, the Russian Federation, and Hungary experienced decreases in production fragmentation and modest growth of exports of value added.

FIGURE 6.3 Higher production fragmentation due to supply chains is associated with more rapid growth in value added in exports over 2000–11

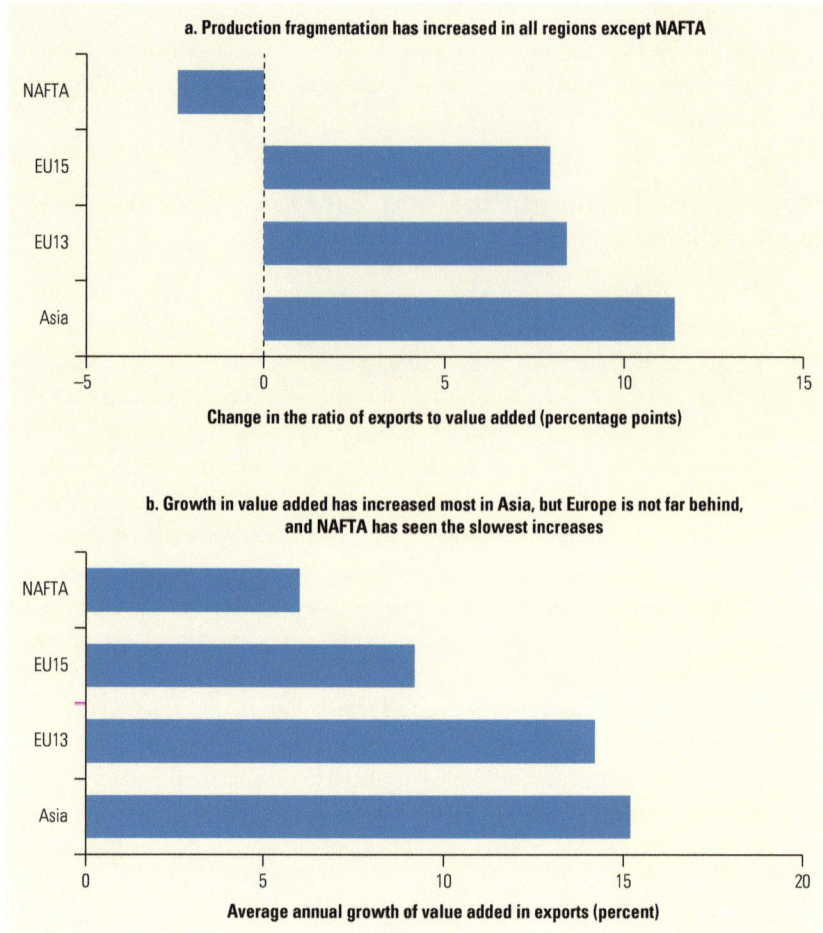

a. Production fragmentation has increased in all regions except NAFTA

Change in the ratio of exports to value added (percentage points)

b. Growth in value added has increased most in Asia, but Europe is not far behind, and NAFTA has seen the slowest increases

Average annual growth of value added in exports (percent)

Source: Organisation for Economic Co-operation and Development Trade in Value Added database.
Note: NAFTA (the North American Free Trade Agreement) includes Canada, Mexico, and the United States. Asia includes China; Hong Kong SAR, China; Japan; Korea; and Taiwan, China. EU = European Union.

Participation in Supply Chains: Backward and Forward Linkages

The form of participation in supply chains differs in terms of the value added embodied in imports and exports (Hummels, Ishii, and Yi 2001; Koopman, Wang, and Wei 2012). Countries can participate in supply chains as importers of foreign value added produced in other countries (backward links—such as importing inter-mediate inputs) and exporters of domestic value added to other countries (forward links—such as exporting intermediate inputs). Backward links are measured as the percentage of foreign value added in domestic exports. Forward links are mea-sured as the percentage of domestic value added used as inputs in third-country exports. Countries that are specialized in sophisticated tasks that add more value to goods, like research and development, tend to have strong forward linkages. Countries that focus on low-value-added tasks, like assembly, tend to depend

a. Production fragmentation, 2000–11

Change in the ratio of exports to value added (percentage points)

b. Exports of value added, 2000–11

Average growth per year (percent)

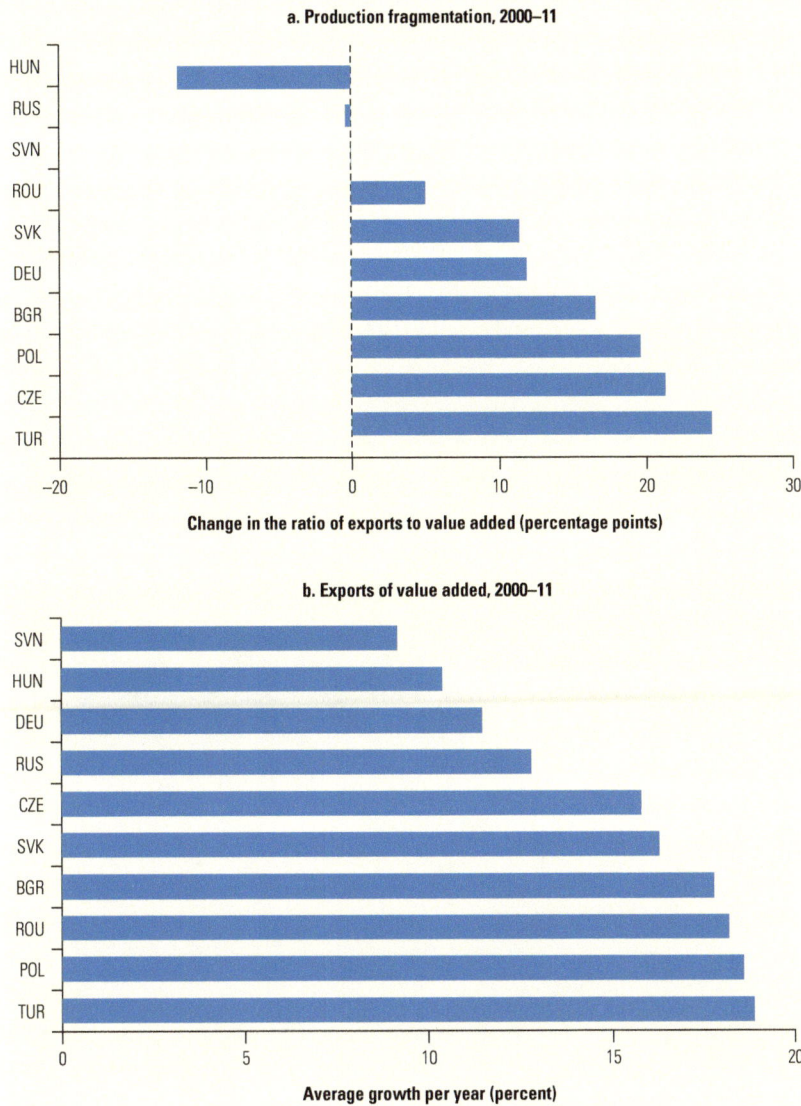

FIGURE 6.4 Among the transition EU13 countries, greater production fragmentation is associated with a more rapid increase in the flows of value added in exports

Source: Calculations based on Organisation for Economic Co-operation and Development Trade in Value Added database.
Note: Germany and Russia are included as reference countries.

more on foreign value added and have higher backward linkages. For example, 32.4 percent of the gross exports of the EU28 countries are foreign value added (backward participation) whereas 20.8 percent of third countries' exports are value added from the EU28 (forward participation) (table 6.1). The NAFTA region has the lowest share of foreign value added in gross exports (23.4 percent), or the lowest backward participation, and the lowest share of domestic value added in third countries' exports (19.7 percent), or the lowest forward participation. Such aggregate numbers can partly be explained by the size of countries in each zone. Bigger countries tend to trade less and to participate less in international supply chains

TABLE 6.1 The Importance of Imported Value Added in Exports (Backward Linkages) and Exported Value Added in Third Countries' Exports (Forward Linkages) Differs by Region

Backward and forward linkages, 2011

Region	Backward linkages Foreign value added as a percentage of gross exports	Forward linkages Domestic value added as a percentage of third countries' exports
NAFTA	23.4	19.7
EU28	32.4	20.8
Asia	34.5	20.9

Source: Organisation for Economic Co-operation and Development Trade in Value Added database.
Note: EU = European Union; NAFTA = North American Free Trade Agreement.

FIGURE 6.5 EU countries buy more foreign value added (backward linkages) than they sell to third countries (forward linkages)

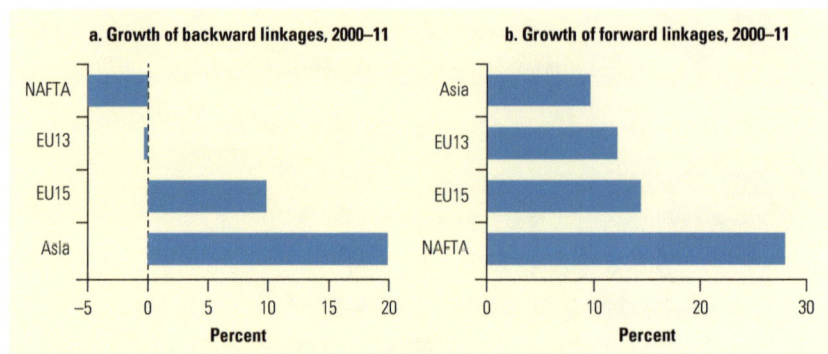

Source: Organisation for Economic Co-operation and Development Trade in Value Added database. Simple averages across countries are calculated for each region.
Note: EU = European Union; NAFTA = North American Free Trade Agreement.

(OECD 2015a). Backward and forward linkages are the lowest for NAFTA, which gathers large countries with relatively lower participation in supply chains.

These measures reflect different forms of involvement in value chains. A country that mostly assembles imported inputs (such as auto parts) into final goods and then exports them will have a high backward-participation index but a small forward-participation index. In contrast, a country that mostly produces intermediate inputs (such as auto parts) and exports them to be assembled and reexported abroad will have a low backward-participation index but a high forward-participation index (figure 6.5).

Compared with other countries, EU13 countries tend to import relatively more foreign value added for their exports than they export domestic value added to third countries' exports. On average, EU13 countries contribute less (than EU15 countries and NAFTA) to the production of the goods or services they export and rely more on foreign contributions (figure 6.5). They also contribute less to the production of exports of third countries. Between 2000 and 2011, all regions except NAFTA increased their participation in supply chains as importers of foreign value added as well as exporters of domestic value added. The largest increase in backward linkages (left panel of figure 6.5) happened in Factory Asia

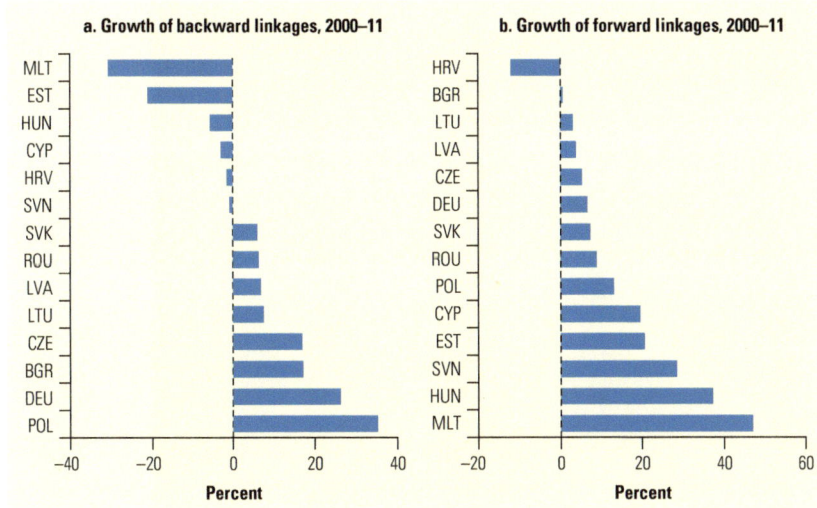

FIGURE 6.6 Participation in supply chains is heterogeneous among ECA countries

Source: Organisation for Economic Co-operation and Development Trade in Value Added database.

and the largest increase in forward linkages (right panel) happened in Factory North America (NAFTA countries).

Almost all ECA countries increased their supply-chain participation as exporters of domestic value added from 2000 to 2011, but only half have increased their participation as importers of foreign value added. Countries in Factory Europe, such as Poland, Bulgaria, and the Czech Republic, experienced the largest increase in participation as importers of foreign value added and an increase in participation as exporters of domestic value added (figure 6.6). Other countries, such as Slovenia, Hungary, Malta, Cyprus, and Romania, mostly experienced large increases in participation as exporters of domestic value added. This may suggest that the recent integration of countries into the EU has increased their participation in supply chains.

The Role of Geographic Proximity

Despite the fall in transport and information costs, geographic proximity continues to play an important role in production fragmentation across countries. Distance is a friction for both bilateral gross exports and value added in exports (Johnson and Noguera 2017). Overall, the fragmentation intensity elasticity with respect to distance has remained stable since 1995, except for a dip in the first half of the 2000s for EU13 countries (figure 6.7).[7]

The effect of distance on production fragmentation remains important. While distance depresses the flows of both gross exports and value added in exports, gross exports fall more strongly with distance than do value-added exports—that is, the absolute value of the distance coefficient on gross exports is larger than the coefficient on value-added exports in all years (table within figure 6.7). The ratio of gross exports to value-added exports, that is, the index

FIGURE 6.7 **Supply chain trade with close partners remains high**
Elasticity of the ratio of gross exports to value-added exports with respect to distance

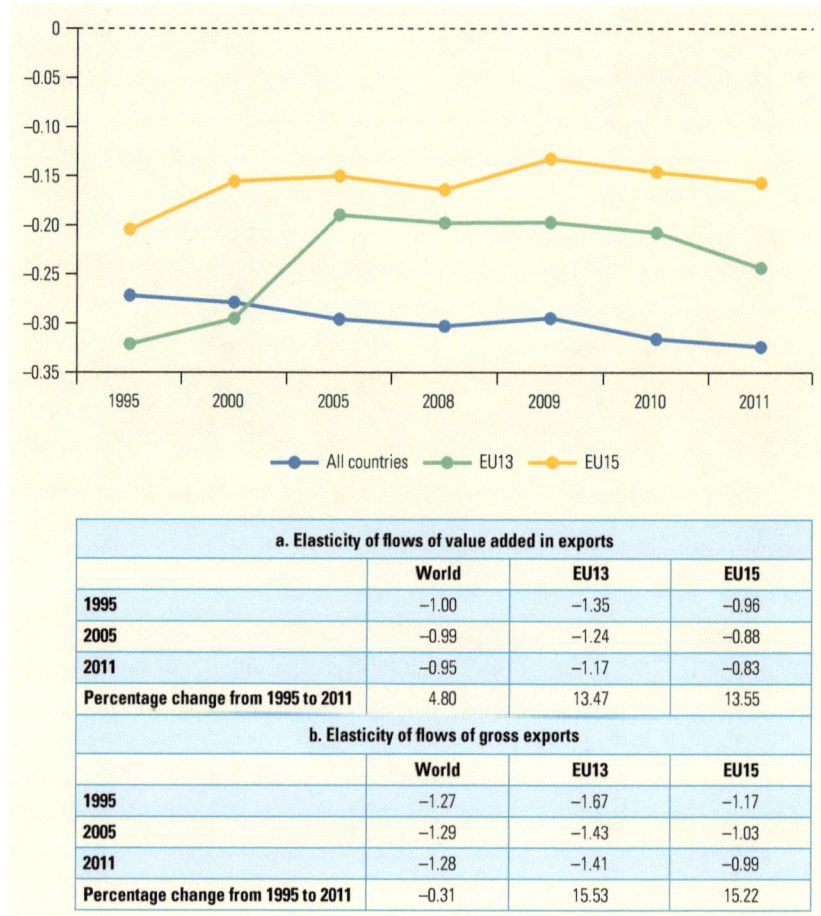

a. Elasticity of flows of value added in exports			
	World	**EU13**	**EU15**
1995	−1.00	−1.35	−0.96
2005	−0.99	−1.24	−0.88
2011	−0.95	−1.17	−0.83
Percentage change from 1995 to 2011	4.80	13.47	13.55
b. Elasticity of flows of gross exports			
	World	**EU13**	**EU15**
1995	−1.27	−1.67	−1.17
2005	−1.29	−1.43	−1.03
2011	−1.28	−1.41	−0.99
Percentage change from 1995 to 2011	−0.31	15.53	15.22

Source: Data from the Organisation for Economic Co-operation and Development Trade in Value Added database.
Note: The elasticities depicted in the figure result from a regression of each flow on the distance between origin and destination countries, with additional controls. Annex 6A provides additional details. "All countries" covers all countries included in the OECD database.

of production fragmentation, decreases with distance (figure 6.7). Overall the tendency was an increase in the deterring effect of distance on the extent of production fragmentation in trade flows, suggesting an increase in regional supply chains at the expense of global supply chains. Regarding ECA, the effect of distance is stronger for EU13 countries than for EU15 countries. Between 2000 and 2005, the patterns of participation in supply chains of EU13 and EU15 countries converged as production fragmentation became less dependent on distance for EU13 countries. One reason could be the entry of these countries into the EU and the deepening of supply chain links with richer EU countries like Germany. The role of regional trade agreements in increases in production fragmentation among adopting partners has been shown for the EU and other agreements too (Johnson and Noguera 2017).

Why Does Distance Matter for Supply Chains?

Despite the fall of transport and information and communication technology costs, geographic distance remains an important factor in shaping the information flows and connections required for supply chains. Two explanations are explored here: (a) the need for rapid transport, coordination, and agglomeration to support supply chains and (b) the association between distance and language or cultural similarities, as well as migrant diaspora proximity between the home and host countries.

Transport, Coordination, and Agglomeration in Supply Chains

Coordination costs, timeliness and agglomeration forces partly explain the continued importance of proximity. In order to understand firms' location and trade decisions, three types of costs should be distinguished: transport costs, coordination costs, and wage costs. The fall of transport costs and lower foreign wages tends to increase the role of global supply chains, whereas higher coordination costs tend to reduce the importance of global supply chains and induce firms to locate production close to large markets. One difference between trade linked to production fragmentation and traditional trade is the importance of coordination costs in shaping the geographic patterns of trade. Timeliness in the shipping and receipt of inputs is more important across production value chains than it is for traditional final goods trade. The absence of key intermediate inputs as a result of shipping delays or quality defects can have an important adverse impact on the whole supply chain (Hummels and Schaur 2013), and time costs are magnified by the number of stages in supply chains. Therefore, lead firms face trade-offs between reliability and cost effectiveness, particularly when choosing where to locate their activities (Nicita, Ognivtsev, and Shirotori 2013; Taglioni and Winkler 2016). The benefits of agglomeration also play a role and may exceed the gains from using suppliers in more distant markets because they have lower wages and other natural endowments. Agglomeration externalities are due to better allocation of production factors across firms, easier transfer of knowledge across plants, and more efficient use of infrastructure and other public goods. Similar to results found in the "New Economic Geography" literature, lowering trade costs such as transport costs when they are high can produce a concentration of economic activity.

> Timeliness . . . is more important across production value chains than it is for traditional final goods trade.

The existence of tacit or noncodified knowledge transfers partly explains the importance of proximity for supply chains. Firms' knowledge-based capital reflects their history of technology investments, their successes and failures, and the interactions between their workers and other types of capital. Part of this knowledge, such as technological knowledge or knowledge that can be codified as standards or well-defined routines, can be replicated. Management know-how and techniques for reducing the cost of production can be transferred to suppliers. However, firm-specific knowledge can be difficult to replicate when it contains complex and abstract notions or when it is embodied in specific employees or corporate systems (OECD 2013; Polanyi 1962). This "tacit knowledge" cannot be captured by blueprints or instruction manuals and requires more direct forms of human interaction than just trade to be diffused (Arrow 1969; Bahar, Hausmann, and Hidalgo 2014; Polanyi 1962). To avoid imitation by other firms, firms tend to increase the share of tacit knowledge and noncodified know-how (Thoenig and Verdier 2003). Thus, the exchange of complex tacit information accompanied by frequent face-to-face interactions is an important part of knowledge sharing across countries that participate in supply chains.

Geographic Proximity Is Associated with Other Types of Proximity

Other noneconomic and nongeographic issues, such as language, culture, social norms, or migration networks, may explain the continued importance of proximity for participation in supply chains. Countries that are near each other often have other similarities, such as a common language, culture, or social norms. Migration networks and diaspora ties, which can be important for trade and investment (Aleksynska and Peri 2014; Burchardi, Chaney, and Hassan 2016; Felbermayr and Toubal 2012; Gould 1994; Rauch and Trindade 2002), may also be stronger between countries located close to each other. Such ties may be more important within supply chains than for traditional trade, given the role of face-to-face interactions in transferring tacit knowledge across production stages. Cultural and language proximity makes it easier for managers to move and transfer knowledge across stages of production and for workers and firms to absorb it. In addition, the nature of the contracts between stages in supply chains (Antràs 2003; Helpman, Antràs, and Helpman 2008) and the often-differentiated nature of the products explain why such ties can be useful. When product specifications cannot be fully codified, so that cooperation relies on the transfer of tacit knowledge, it is difficult to write complete contracts to protect transactions. This increases the importance of reputation, social and spatial proximity, family and ethnic ties, and the like in managing transactions (Gereffi and Humphrey 2005).

> Cultural and language proximity makes it easier for managers to move and transfer knowledge across stages of production and for workers and firms to absorb it.

The Role of Regional Agreements

The rise of regional agreements in the past two decades also has contributed to the development of regional supply chains. Integration agreements have been shown to be one of the forces behind the development of production linkages across countries (Blyde, Graziano, and Volpe Martincus 2015; Hayakawa and Yamashita 2011; Johnson and Noguera 2017; Orefice and Rocha 2014). The 1965 US-Canada Auto Agreement, for example, was crucial to building supply chains involving US exports of engines and parts to Canada and Canadian assembly and exports of finished cars and trucks to the United States (Hummels, Rapoport, and Yi 1998). Deep regional agreements (those, like the EU, that cover many economic dimensions beyond trade policies—see chapter 7) have played an important role in the development of supply chains. In addition to reducing customs barriers and the likelihood of future protectionist measures, deep regional agreements can promote production fragmentation by encouraging FDI flows (see the spotlight to chapter 2). Figure 6.8 shows the rise in FDI flows to new EU entrants.

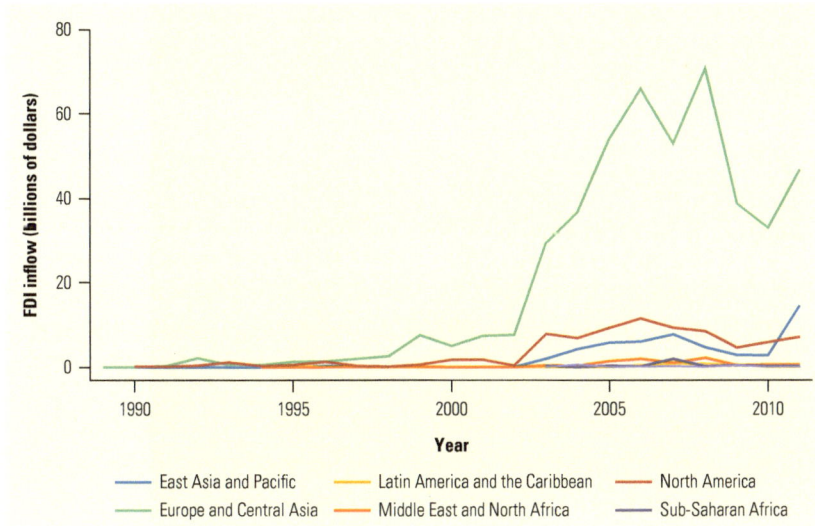

FIGURE 6.8 European FDI inflows into the EU13 countries increased dramatically after the 2003 entry of those countries into the European Union
Inflows of FDI into the EU13

Source: Calculations based on data from Peterson Institute for International Economics, Transactional FDI Dataset (created by Jacob F. Kirkegaard; see Kirkegaard 2013).
Note: FDI = foreign direct investment.

Are There Only Benefits from Increased Interdependence of Countries?

Globalization's second unbundling has not just involved more goods crossing borders; it also has heightened international mobility of managerial and manufacturing know-how. When Volkswagen makes car parts in Poland, they do not only rely on local know-how; they bring Volkswagen technology, Volkswagen management, Volkswagen logistics, and other types of know-how needed. Polish-made parts must fit with precision into the German company's production network. A country's capacity to benefit from this knowledge sharing depends on its integration in trade, FDI, capital, and migration networks and its links with countries or sectors that are large producers of ideas or innovations. The extent to which countries benefit from these knowledge transfers also depends on their capacity to receive and absorb this knowledge.

This section investigates the different channels of cross-country knowledge sharing linked to production fragmentation. It discusses whether the most central sectors or countries given their international input-output linkages are sectors or countries that are likely to produce new ideas. It also considers whether the increasing interdependence of countries through trade is conducive to more positive or negative shocks and increases the vulnerability of economies.

Productivity Growth, Value-Added Growth, and Participation in Global Production Networks

Firms exchange know-how through supply chains, which increases productivity and spurs innovation. Along the stages of production in different countries, the lead firms and the key suppliers exchange blueprints, technicians, managerial practices, and productivity-enhancing techniques. Compared to trade in final goods, supply chains can facilitate the transfer of "tacit knowledge" and learning at a more rapid pace (Taglioni and Winkler 2016). Traditional trade of goods allows countries to learn new things through the technology embodied in the goods. In a supply-chain framework, slicing the production requires frequent interaction between the staff of the suppliers at one stage and the managers of the lead firms or those of firms at other stages of the production chain.

Production fragmentation across countries can increase output, productivity, value added, and job creation through several channels. First, increasing supply chain participation can boost productivity of firms that have access to cheaper and better inputs (backward links) and boost the sales of domestic intermediates used in third countries' exports (forward links). Productivity gains may also come from a finer division of tasks (similar to factor-augmenting technical change; Grossman and Rossi-Hansberg 2008), increased competition, and a greater diversity of input varieties. The entry of foreign firms or new opportunities of importing better inputs may have a procompetitive effect on domestic firms. Second, participation in supply chains leads to knowledge transfers through the movement of goods, capital, and people and skill upgrading through increased demand for skilled labor (Baldwin and Robert-Nicoud 2014; Li and Liu 2005). FDI spillovers from foreign affiliates to local firms are discussed in chapter 3. Finally, supply chain participation may increase investments in infrastructure that benefit the whole economy (see box 6.1).

BOX 6.1 Global Value Chain Spillovers in Romania

H.Essers and Oracle are two examples of foreign companies investing in Romania that illustrate the benefits from foreign investments.

H.Essers is a leading European logistics firm focusing on chemicals, pharmaceuticals, health care, and high-quality products, with headquarters in Belgium. After its integration with a Dutch company located in Romania, the Belgian firm increased its presence in Romania, increasingly looking toward Eastern Europe and Central Asia. Knowledge and know-how coming from traditional logistics hubs like the Netherlands and Belgium benefited Romania by improving its logistics performance. Logistics is the backbone of supply chains, as it makes production fragmentation and the smooth coordination of its stages possible. Knowledge spillovers happen through clients being educated about good practices on norms, information technology, and cold chains.

Oracle is a major multinational company headquartered in the United States, specialized in developing and marketing database software and technology, cloud-engineered systems, and enterprise software products. In the mid-2000s, it created a branch in Bucharest and began to hire local software engineers for its routine software development. In addition to short-term spillovers, its entry has spurred a new generation of entrepreneurs, who got their start at Oracle in Bucharest, to create their own businesses. One of them is Softelligence, a Romanian software company designing tailored mobile applications for financial institutions. The low cost of entry for new entrepreneurs in this industry, coupled with low wages, a qualified workforce, and an excellent internet network, has boosted this sector and diversified the economy.

Participation in value chains also is associated with greater labor productivity.[8] Participation in supply chains is broader than just trade integration and contributes to labor productivity through multiple channels: FDI spillovers, exchange of managerial know-how, or increasing competition, as discussed in earlier chapters. In OECD countries, growth in participation in supply chains is positively correlated with growth in real labor productivity by country and year (figure 6.9).[9] An increase of 1 point of growth in GVC participation is associated with a significant increase of 0.27 point of growth in labor productivity.[10] This association does not prove that participation in supply chains causes increased productivity, as more productive countries may also be more likely to participate in supply chains. Addressing endogeneity is difficult, although Constantinescu, Mattoo, and Ruta (2017) find that participation in GVCs boosts productivity. Based on a panel estimation covering 13 sectors in 40 countries over 15 years, they find that participation in GVCs is a significant driver of labor productivity. Backward participation emerges as particularly important. An increase of 10 percent in the level of GVC participation increased average productivity by 1.7 percent. They also suggest that trade that is not GVC related also has a positive impact on productivity, but the relationship is less robust. Which channels are the most important remains to be determined.

Participation in value chains is also associated with higher domestic value added at the sector level (figure 6.10). Causality issues are addressed by Kummritz (2016), who confirms a positive effect of GVC participation for sectors. In addition, GVC participation measured by both forward- and backward-linkage indicators generates robust gains for participating countries with a larger effect coming from forward linkages. Such gains are also independent of country's per capita income level (Kummritz 2016). This sheds light on current debates on the transmission

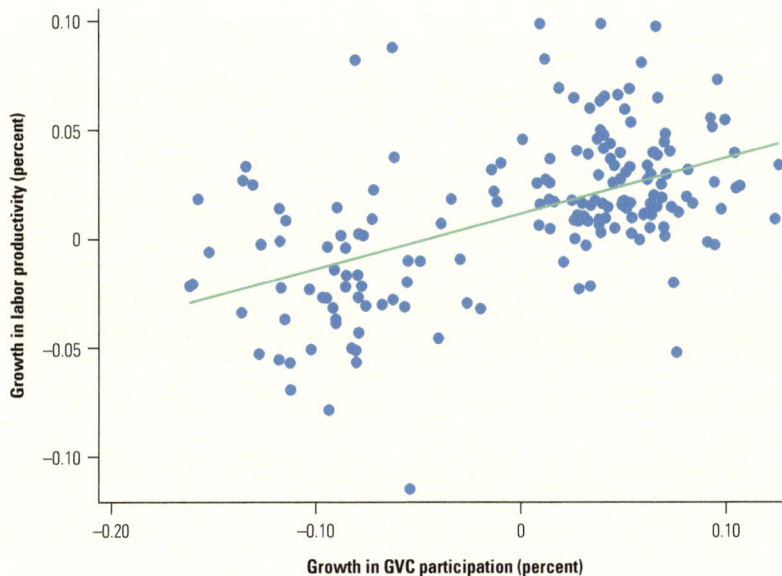

FIGURE 6.9 Participation in global value chains is correlated with higher labor productivity
Growth in labor productivity versus growth in global value chain participation, 2009–11

Source: World Bank labor productivity data and country global value chain participation index for member countries of the Organisation for Economic Co-operation and Development over the period 2009–11.
Note: Each dot in the figure represents one country for one year. GVC = global value chain.

FIGURE 6.10 Participation in global value chains is correlated with higher domestic value added at the sector level

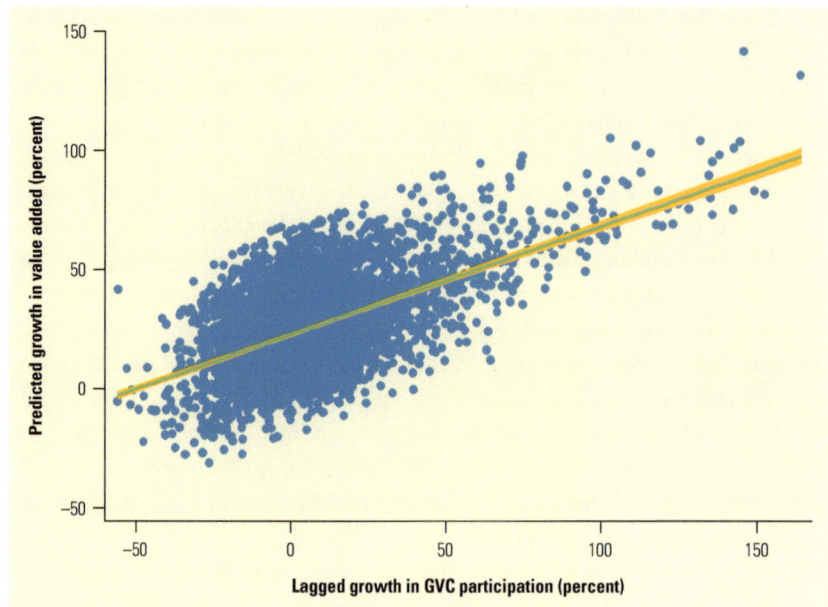

Source: Sectoral global value chain and domestic value-added data for Organisation for Economic Co-operation and Development (OECD) countries for 1995, 2000, 2005, 2008, 2009, and 2011 from the OECD's Trade in Value Added database (ISIC 3).
Note: Each dot represents a sector-country-year pair of global value chain (GVC) participation and value added. GVC participation is defined as the sum of the backward and forward linkages. The predicted growth of value added results from a simple ordinary least squares regression with industry and country fixed effects. The figure also reports the confidence interval surrounding the linear fit. Growth in GVC participation is lagged to minimize the reverse-causality problem.

channels between GVC participation and development as well as some current debates on the nature of the gains or losses from GVC participation.

Input and Output Linkages: An Increasing Interdependence of Countries

Greater participation in supply chains can increase firms' dependence on other sectors and economies. The acceleration of production fragmentation has created a global economy in which some sectors increasingly rely on other sectors through the supply of inputs for their own production and exports. Recent studies have focused on the fact that significant aggregate fluctuations may originate from sector or firm shocks (Carvalho et al. 2012). Economic transmission can happen through demand-side shocks (to input-supplying industries) or through supply-side shocks (to customer industries). The structure of economies in which sectors are becoming more interdependent might create "cascade effects" where shocks can propagate to a large part of the economy and across borders. Recently, "the Dieselgate" scandal not only directly affected the activities of Volkswagen in Germany, but also indirectly affected the multiple suppliers of its production chain in Germany and in other European countries. Large multinationals whose external suppliers and affiliates are spread all over European countries are a major channel for propagation of shocks.

This section examines the interdependence of sectors through their participation in production networks. If the production network is dominated by a few sectors, fluctuations in these sectors are likely to propagate and affect economic

FIGURE 6.11 Sectors from advanced EU15, transition EU13, and non-EU countries are interdependent, but the most central sectors are from EU15 countries

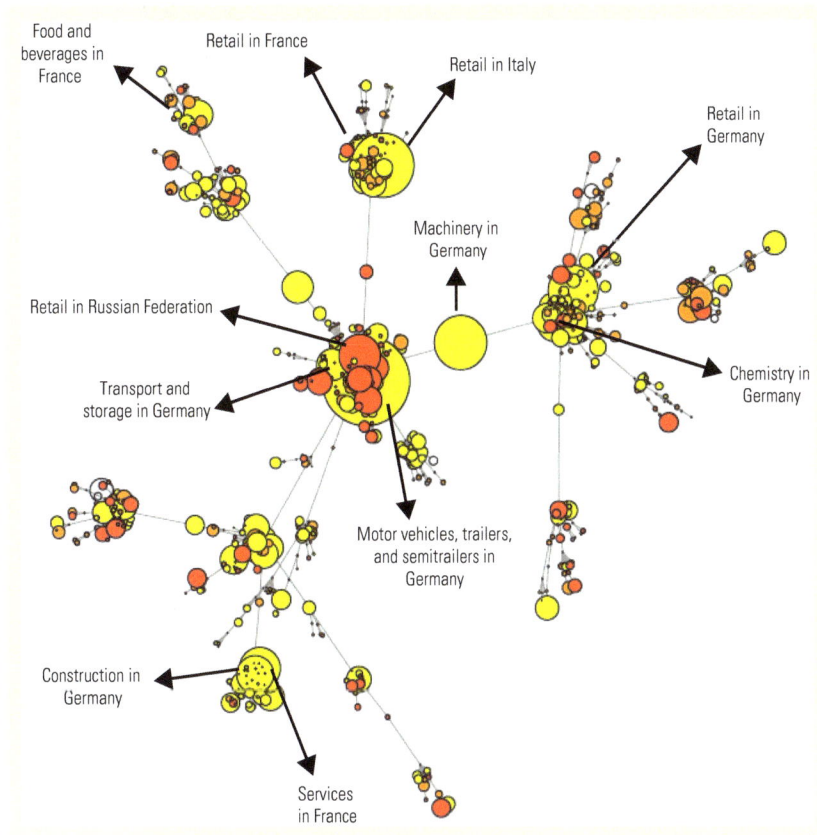

Note: The figure shows a network visualization of the 2011 input-output network for Europe and Central Asia (ECA) member countries of the Organisation for Economic Co-operation and Development using the minimum spanning tree method. EU15 countries are shown in yellow, EU13 countries in orange, and ECA non-EU countries in red. Node size is determined by the PageRank measure in the ECA production network. The most central sectors in the ECA production network are motor vehicles, trailers, and semitrailers in Germany; wholesale and retail trade in Italy; machinery and equipment in Germany; wholesale and retail trade in Germany; and wholesale and retail trade in France.

aggregates.[11] In addition to the benefits from knowledge transfers and increased trade opportunities, increased production fragmentation could increase the volatility of sectors or large economies, driven by shocks coming from different sectors or from different countries. It is therefore important for countries to adapt their economic and social structures to a potential for increasing volatility.

Finding the central sectors and the major cross-border links is important to gaining an understanding of how positive or adverse shocks spread through production networks in the ECA region. We can use the tools of network analysis to determine the extent to which sectors and countries are central and influence this network. We compute a measure of influence in the network similar to that used in chapter 1, the PageRank centrality, based on the flows of inputs going from one country-sector pair to another.[12] A country or a sector that is central might be able to spread ideas to the rest of the network, but might also more frequently receive shocks from the rest of the network.

The ECA production network is organized around several clusters that include sectors from different parts of the region (figure 6.11). Each color

> Finding the central sectors and the major cross-border links is important to gaining an understanding of how positive or adverse shocks spread through production networks.

TABLE 6.2 What Sectors or Countries Are Expected to Have the Largest Impact on the Rest of the ECA Economies When They Face Either a Positive or a Negative Shock?

Ranking	Country/sector	Country/sector outside EU15	Country (average)	Country outside EU15 (average)	Sectors (average)
1	Germany/vehicles	Russian Federation/retail	Germany	Russia	Retail
2	Italy/retail	Poland/retail	Italy	Turkey	Construction
3	Germany/machinery	Russian Federation/construction	France	Poland	Transport
4	Germany/retail	Turkey/retail	Russian Federation	Czech Republic	Food and beverages
5	France/retail	Russian Federation/transport	Turkey	Croatia	R&D
6	Russian Federation/retail	Turkey/transport	Spain	Lithuania	Machinery
7	Germany /construction	Turkey/food and beverages	Sweden	Latvia	Government
8	Germany/food	Russian Federation/government	Poland	Cyprus	Hotels/restaurants
9	France/R&D	Poland /construction	Finland	Bulgaria	Real estate
10	France/ construction	Poland/food and beverages	Belgium	Hungary	Others

Source: Organisation for Economic Co-operation and Development Structural Analysis database, 2011.
Note: EU = European Union; R&D = research and development.

represents one of the three regions of ECA (EU15, EU13, and the non-EU area). Having sectors from different regions in the same production cluster illustrates the interdependence of country-sectors across most countries of ECA through input-output linkages. Table 6.2 ranks the most important pairs of country-sectors in the ECA region and in the ECA region excluding EU15 countries. It also indicates the most central countries and sectors in the ECA production network. Interestingly, the motor vehicle sector in Germany is the most central in the ECA production network. This sector largely relies on regional value chains to organize its production. The retail sectors in Italy, Germany, France and Russia are all very central. The machinery and equipment sector in Germany is also among the most central sectors. Outside of the EU15 countries, sectors in Russia, Turkey, and Poland appear the most central in the production network. Germany, Italy, and France are the most central countries in the ECA trade production network, followed by Russia and Turkey (table 6.2, map 6.1). The least central countries are Portugal, the Baltic countries, and Eastern European countries.

Interdependence in the Global Network and Volatility

The intensification of trade links between sectors across the ECA region has increased the interdependence of sectors. Countries or sectors that are more integrated into a trade network (measured by using network analysis tools to compute an integration index for sectors in the input-output trade network) tend to have output growth rates that are more correlated (annex 6B and figure 6.12).[13] Thus, trade integration seems to increase output interdependence across sectors. Indeed, a sector that produces goods or services that are increasingly demanded will import more inputs from other sectors. A sector producing intermediate goods that experiences a positive productivity shock will export cheaper or better inputs. By contrast, a negative shock in a final-product sector or an intermediate-product sector will negatively affect the sectors that are using these products or selling products to them. Production fragmentation by dividing stages of production

MAP 6.1 Which countries are the most central in the ECA production network?
Average centrality per country, 2011

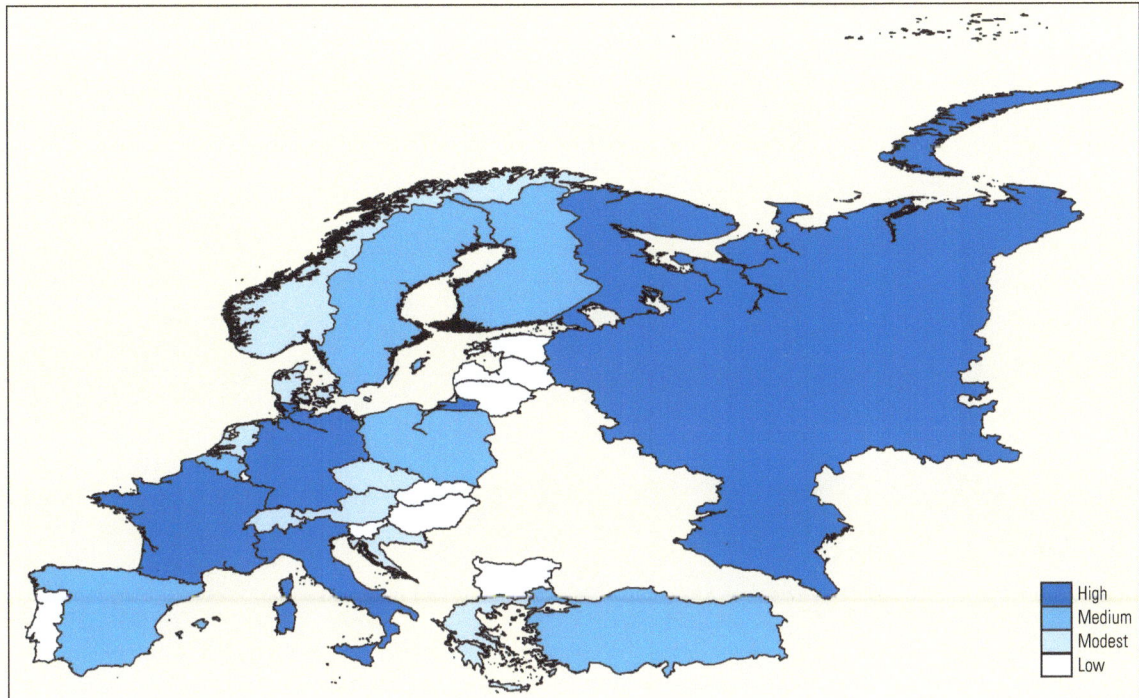

High
Medium
Modest
Low

Note: The map shows average centrality measured across sectors at the country level: the darker the color (and thus the higher the number for centrality), the higher the importance of the country in the Europe and Central Asia (ECA) network, given sector linkages. Some ECA countries are not included in the analysis for data availability reasons.

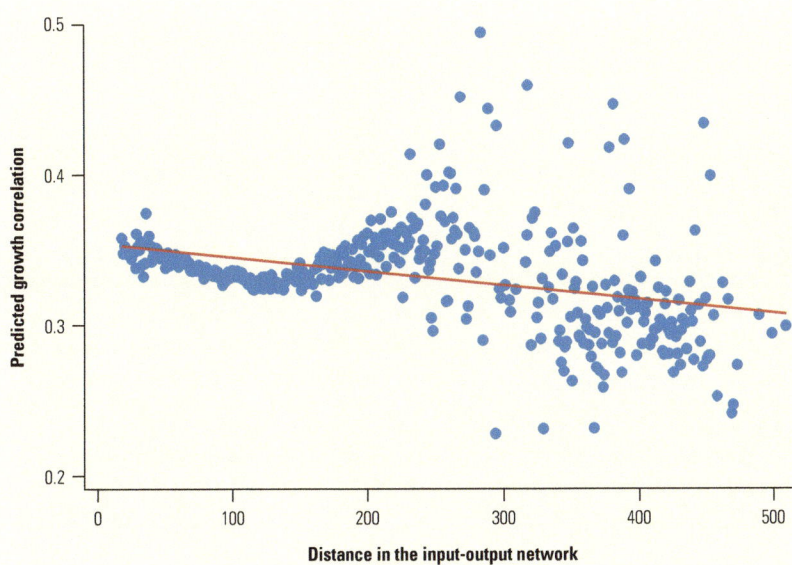

FIGURE 6.12 Sectors that are more integrated in a production trade network move more together
ECA region

Source: Calculations using data from the Organisation for Economic Co-operation and Development.
Note: The red line in the figure represents the best linear fit. A shorter distance in the input-output network means that sectors are more integrated.

FIGURE 6.13 Imports of intermediate goods are more volatile than imports of final goods

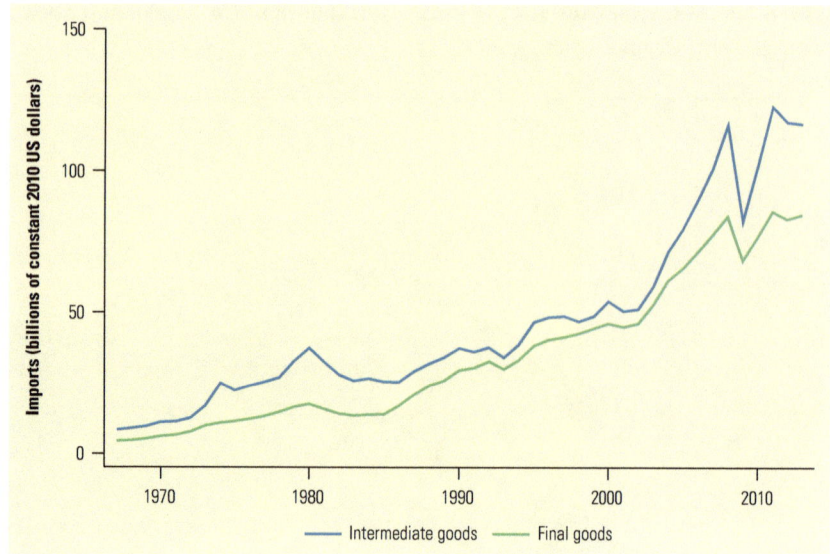

Source: United Nations Commodity Trade Statistics Database data using Broad Economic Categories classifications.

across countries tends to increase the interdependence of sectors across borders. Economies might therefore become increasingly vulnerable to external shocks.

Finally, trade in intermediate goods tends to be more volatile than trade in final (capital and consumption) goods (Sturgeon and Memedovic 2011). From 1967 to 2014, imports of intermediate goods appear to have been more volatile than trade in final goods, given the higher variation observed during major crises (the oil shock of 1979, the Asian crisis, and the global financial crisis in 2008) or sectoral bubbles (for example, the 2001 internet bubble) (figure 6.13). This supports the notion of "bullwhip" effects of recessions and business cycles. Parts and components shipments are more affected than final goods shipments, because final goods producers tend to draw down parts inventories and delay reordering during periods of uncertainty (Escaith, Lindenberg, and Miroudot 2010).

Different Policies for GVC Upgrading

Participating in value chains can be growth enhancing, especially by creating channels for knowledge transfers, but not all countries have fully benefited from the rise of cross-border production fragmentation. Different types of economic upgrading and participation in value chains call for different policies and depend on each country's stage of development. Policies that play a role in economic upgrading should reinforce physical connectivity (infrastructure, trade, and investment policies), improve the productivity of labor (education and skills policies), and improve the overall domestic economic environment (business climate, labor market flexibility, financial institutions, and so on).

Diverse policies support increasing supply chain integration by strengthening backward and forward linkages (Kummritz and Quast 2016; Kummritz, Taglioni, and Winkler 2017). A wide spectrum of policies can play a role for increasing GVC participation. Importing more foreign inputs requires increasing connectivity by improving infrastructure as well as trade and investment policies (backward participation). Exporting domestic value added that is integrated into third countries' exports (forward participation) requires countries to increase productivity to be more competitive in the global marketplace (Kummritz, Taglioni, and Winkler 2017). Higher GVC participation is associated with a higher share of manufacturing, better logistics, and lower trade barriers (see annex 6c for empirical results). Large countries tend to have lower participation in GVCs. Beyond trade or investment policies, broader policies are necessary to upgrade GVC participation, in order to increase productivity or domestic value added. Upgrading forward linkages, rather than backward linkages, contributes more to increasing the broad economic gains (Kummritz, Taglioni, and Winkler 2017). Higher forward linkages are strongly associated with better Doing Business indicators. Other nontraditional policies, such as business climate and institutions, financial development, labor market policy, education and skills, product standards and innovation, as well as labor, social, and environmental standards, have been shown to play a role in upgrading value chain participation (Kummritz, Taglioni, and Winkler 2017).

Policies for Countries in Factory Europe

Different policies are appropriate for countries at different stages of GVC upgrading. Figure 6.14 shows that most countries are more integrated as buyers of foreign value added (backward linkages) than as sellers of domestic value added (forward linkages). Some countries, such as Croatia and Romania, have low backward participation. Improving their connectivity and their trade and investment policies could lead to higher backward linkages. Some countries, like Hungary, the Slovak Republic, the Czech Republic, Bulgaria, and Slovenia, have high backward participation but lower forward participation. If they target increasing their forward

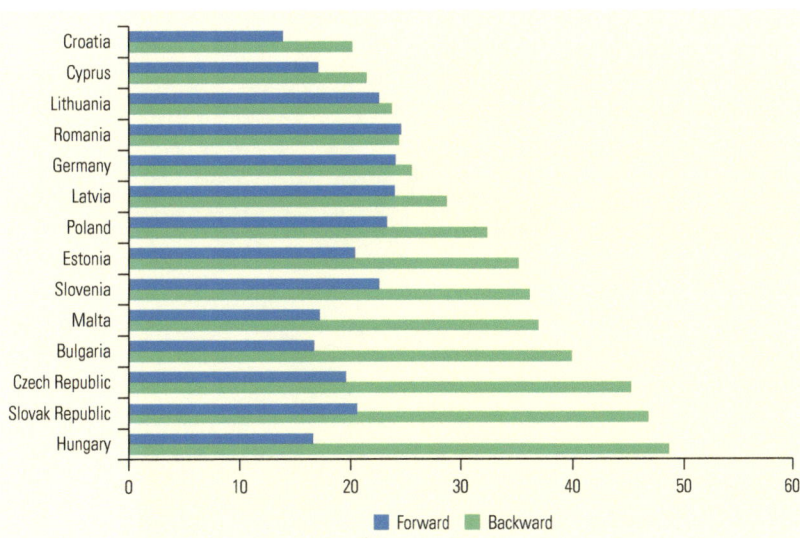

FIGURE 6.14 Many EU13 countries have high backward participation but low forward participation
Backward- and forward-participation indexes across countries, 2011

Source: Organisation for Economic Co-operation and Development Trade in Value Added database.

linkages, the focus should be on improving the productivity of their firms to increase the exported value added in third countries' exports.

For the rest of the ECA countries, participation in supply chains remains limited. While EU13 countries and Turkey have increased their imports of intermediates as well as their exports, other countries tend to import many final goods and export relatively little outside of raw materials. Figure 6.15 looks at three key GVCs that are important for the ECA region: apparel and footwear, electronics, and automotive goods. The electronics and automotive industries have been extremely important drivers of supply chain development (Sturgeon and Memedovic 2011). Different patterns of integration emerge across the different regions in ECA (excluding the high-income countries). EU13 countries and Turkey have increased their participation in the automotive and electronics production chains through a rise in both imports and exports and in both intermediate and final goods. The largest exports are for final electronics, final vehicles, and intermediate vehicles.

In contrast, ECA non-EU countries have substantially increased their imports, mostly in final electronics and final vehicles, but have only slightly increased their exports in these manufactured goods. They also import few intermediate products. This pattern differs greatly from the integration pattern observed in the EU13 countries and Turkey, which have successfully integrated into regional and global supply chain trade.

Despite large heterogeneity of firms' supply chain participation across the ECA region, both domestic and foreign firms have stronger backward linkages as buyers of value added than forward linkages as sellers of value added. At the firm level, figure 6.16 shows the intensive and extensive margins for both imports (left panels) and exports (right panels) for domestic versus foreign firms. In most regions

FIGURE 6.15 ECA Non-EU countries mainly import final goods and export little
Imports and exports for ECA non-EU countries

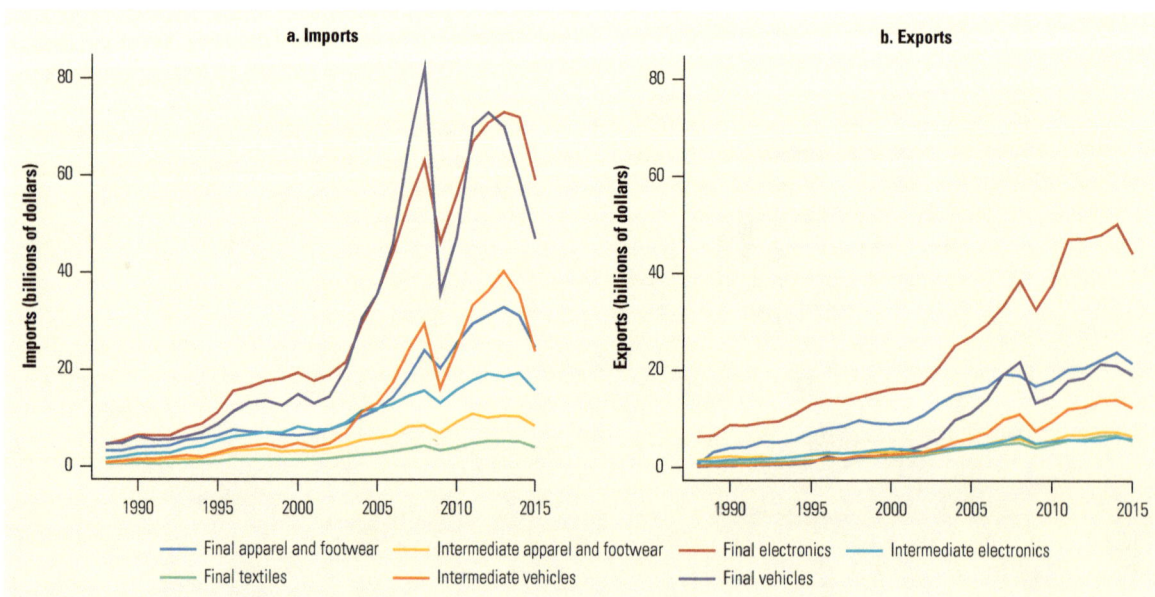

Source: World Bank, Global Value Chain database.

FIGURE 6.16 Heterogeneous participation in trade of domestic and foreign firms

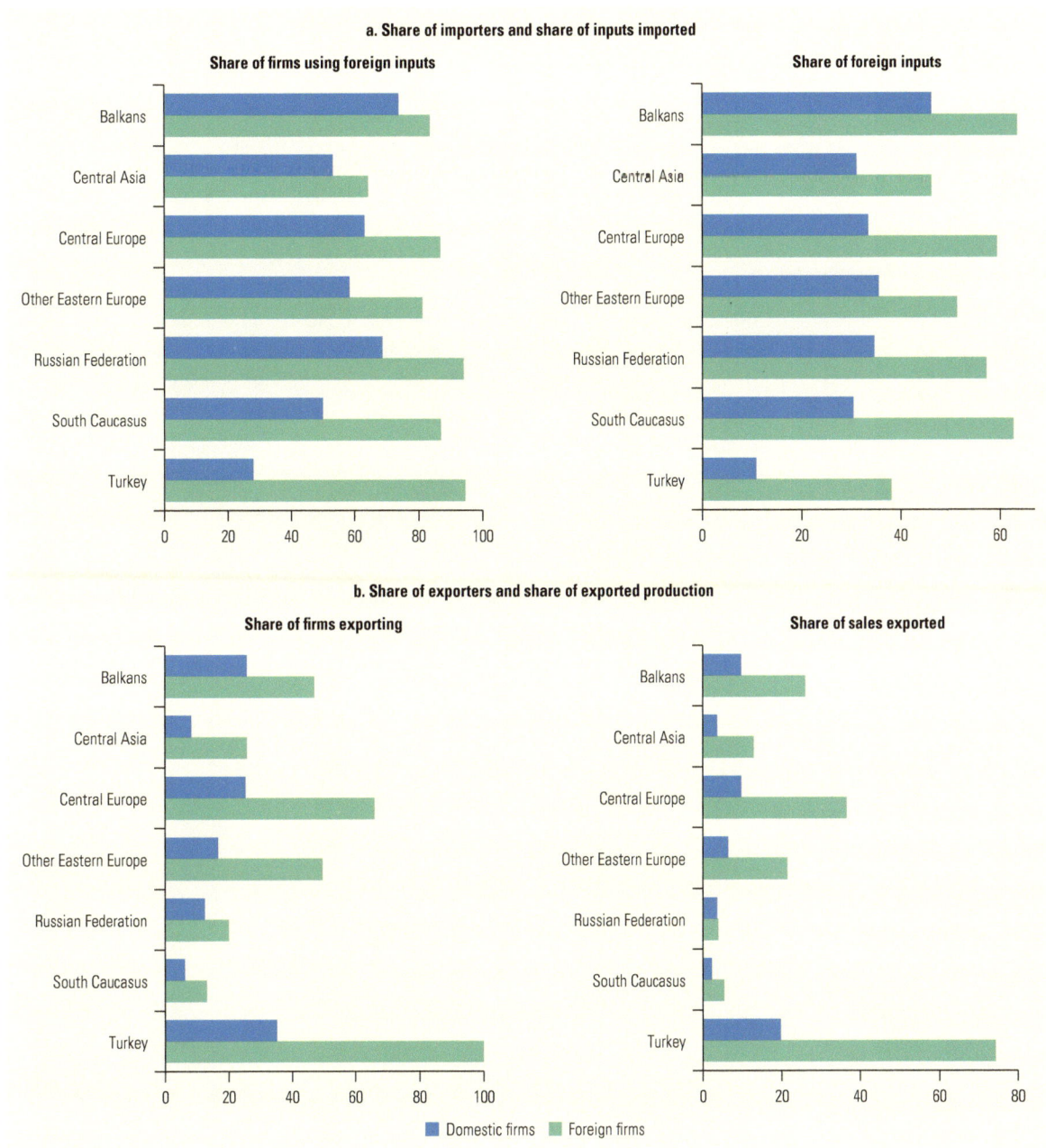

a. Share of importers and share of inputs imported

Share of firms using foreign inputs

Share of foreign inputs

b. Share of exporters and share of exported production

Share of firms exporting

Share of sales exported

■ Domestic firms   ■ Foreign firms

Source: World Bank, Enterprise Survey database.

(excluding the EU15 countries), a large share of foreign-owned firms' inputs are foreign inputs. However, few of them export, and they export a small part of their production. Overall, foreign firms tend to first target the domestic market rather than looking to reexport their production. This shows that the primary purpose of these foreign firms is not to be involved in global production chains. One exception is that most foreign firms in Turkey export, and they export a large share of their production (figure 6.16, panel b). They seem to be well integrated in supply chains, especially in the automobile and textile industries. Except for Turkey, domestic firms in ECA rely more on importing foreign inputs than on exporting their production (they have stronger backward linkages than forward linkages). This reflects a lack of competitiveness of domestic firms in many ECA countries that do not or cannot compete with other firms in foreign markets.

Most ECA countries outside the EU need to improve their connectivity, their trade and investment policies, and their business climates. Figure 6.17 shows the current levels of policies regarding trade, logistics, and the business climate. Central Asian countries (Tajikistan, Kazakhstan, and the Kyrgyz Republic) as well as Russia and Ukraine perform poorly compared with the rest of ECA. In this group, the Kyrgyz Republic performs better in terms of trade policies, while Russia and Kazakhstan have better business climates. Turkey is an outsider that should improve its business climate and its trade policies. A second cluster is formed by the Balkans and South Caucasus countries (FYR Macedonia, Serbia, Montenegro, Albania, Georgia, and Armenia). They overall have good trade policies but poor-quality logistics. The business climate varies a lot in this group, with Albania and Serbia having the poorest regulatory environment. Eastern European EU members (the Czech Republic, Hungary, the Slovak Republic, and Slovenia) could still improve their business climates, with Doing Business indicators between 70 and 80 on a 100-point scale. Compared with the others, Bulgaria performs poorly in terms of logistics performance. Such various policies are complementary to GVC participation to increase the broader economic gains for each country (Kummritz, Taglioni, and Winkler 2017).

FIGURE 6.17 Many ECA countries can still reduce trade barriers and improve logistics and the business environment to increase their supply chain participation
Trading across Borders, Logistics Performance, and Doing Business Indexes

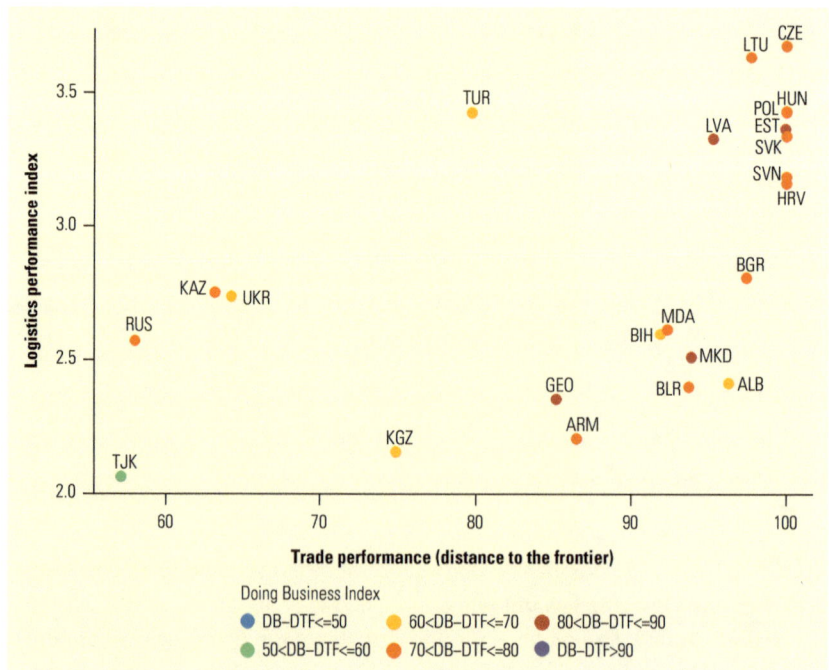

Source: World Bank, Trading across Borders, Logistics Performance, and Doing Business Indexes (most recent data available).
Note: The Doing Business (DB – DTF) and Trading across Borders Indexes are given by the distance to the frontier index for each country. A higher number for a country means that it is closer to best practices.

Conclusion

Cross-border production fragmentation has increased connectivity across countries in Europe and Central Asia. Countries can benefit from being better connected by improving their access to ideas and innovations that support economic growth. Supply chains not only increase trade in goods or services, but also enhance movement of capital, people, and ideas. In particular, they promote the transfer of "tacit knowledge" across production stages as well as more traditional forms of knowledge sharing through increasing participation in the trade and FDI global networks. Policies to increase supply chain participation should be tailored to the needs and particularities of each country. However, an increasing interdependence of countries might also tend to increase the volatility of their economies. Complementary policies should be adopted to minimize the risks from increased global interdependence to fully reap the benefits of participation in supply chains.

Annex 6A. Elasticities of Value Added in Exports, Gross Exports, and Fragmentation Intensity

Following Johnson and Noguera (2017), this annex describes how changes in bilateral value added exports versus gross exports are shaped by bilateral trade frictions. The analysis here focuses on one common proxy for bilateral frictions: distance.

FIGURE 6A.1 Elasticities of exports of value added and gross exports, and of the ratio of gross exports to value added, for the EU13, EU15, and all countries

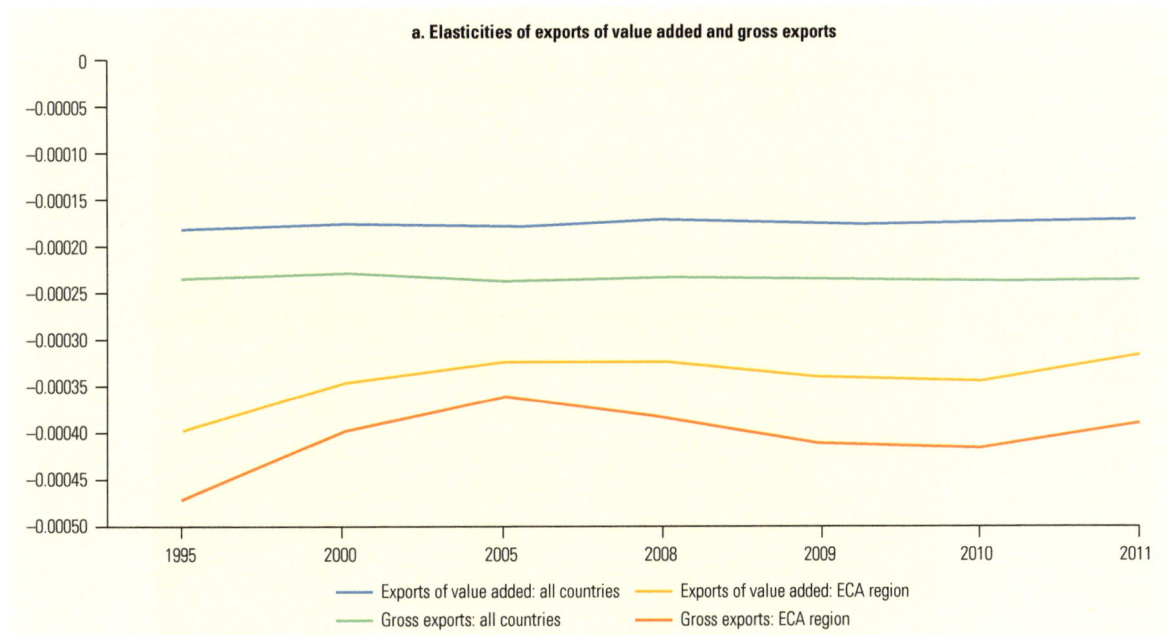

a. Elasticities of exports of value added and gross exports

Legend:
- Exports of value added: all countries
- Exports of value added: ECA region
- Gross exports: all countries
- Gross exports: ECA region

continued

FIGURE 6A.1 *continued*

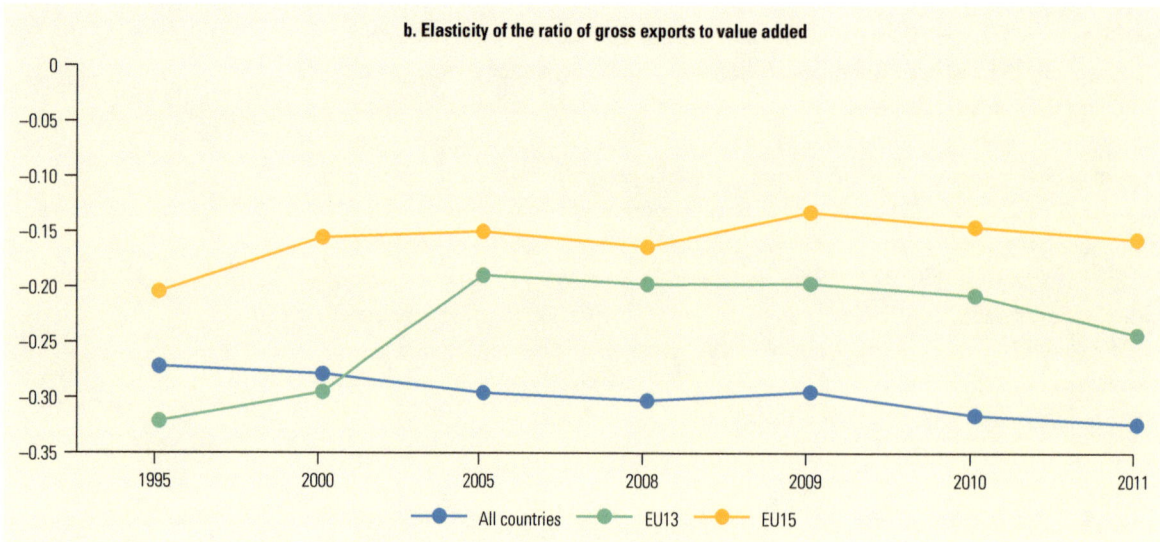

b. Elasticity of the ratio of gross exports to value added

Source: Organisation for Economic Co-operation and Development Trade in Value Added database.
Note: Elasticities of value added and exports with respect to distance (*dist*) are given by

$$\varepsilon^{VAX} = \frac{\partial(VA)/VA}{\partial\,dist/dist} = \beta^{VA},$$

$$\varepsilon^{X} = \frac{\partial(EXP)/EXP}{\partial\,dist/dist} = \beta^{X}.$$

The elasticity of the production fragmentation intensity with respect to distance (*dist*) is defined by the following formula:

$$\varepsilon^{VAX} = \frac{\partial\left(\dfrac{EXP}{VA}\right) \Big/ \dfrac{EXP}{VA}}{\partial\,dist/dist} = \beta^{VAX} = \beta^{X} - \beta^{VA}.$$

Elasticities are measured for all countries and for ECA countries only.

To measure the elasticity of production fragmentation with respect to distance, we look at how gross exports (x_{ijt}), value-added exports (va_{ijt}), and gross-exports-to-value-added-in-exports ratios from country i to country j at time t respond to bilateral distance. To answer these questions, we estimate gravity-style regressions for each of the three variables of interest:

$$\log\left(y_{ijt}\right) = \phi_{it}^{y} + \phi_{jt}^{y} + \beta_{t}^{y}\log\left(dist_{ij}\right) + \varepsilon_{ijt}.$$

The terms $y_{ijt} \in \left\{x_{ijt},\ va_{ijt}, VAX_{ijt}\right\}, \left\{\phi_{it}^{y},\phi_{jt}^{y}\right\}$ are importer-year and exporter-year fixed effects and β_{t}^{y} the time-varying coefficient on bilateral distance ($dist_{ij}$) for outcome y_{ijt}.

Annex 6B. Interdependence of Countries

Using the OECD Input-Output database, distance measures are given by the closeness network measures in the input-output network in 2005. Correlations across sectoral output growth come from the OECD Structural Analysis database and cover the years from 1995 to 2011. The regression table includes the measure of supply chain integration from the 2005 input-output network and shows its correlation over the whole period with sectoral value-added growth. Country, sector, and interaction sector dummies are added as controls.

TABLE 6B.1 Sectors That Are More Integrated in the Production Network Are More Correlated

| Variable | Sector comovement | |
	(1)	(2)
Integration index	1.58e−05*	1.63e−05*
	(9.50e−06)	(9.47e−06)
Constant	0.275***	0.379***
	(0.00881)	(0.0139)
Number of observations	76,452	76,452
R^2	0.047	0.069
Country dummies	Yes	Yes
Sector dummies	Yes	Yes
Interaction dummies	No	Yes

Note: Robust standard errors are in parentheses. Comovement is measured by the correlation of sectoral outputs over the chosen period. The integration index measures the distance in the input-output network based on observed contributions of one sector in another.
Significance level: * = 10 percent, *** = 1 percent.

Annex 6C. Regression of Backward- and Forward-Participation Indexes over a Set of Policy Variables

The variables to explain are the backward- and forward-participation indexes using the OECD Trade in Value Added database.

- Country variables: gross domestic product (GDP), the size of the manufacturing sector, the population (POP), the total tax rate as a percentage of commercial profits, the minimum distance to a headquarters economy (Germany, China, or the United States).
- Connectivity variables: the quality of logistics (the Logistics Performance Index), trade policies measured by Trading across Borders indexes, investment policies measured by FDI restrictions.
- Business Climate variables: the Doing Business index.
- Year fixed effects: 2008–09–10–11.
- Countries covered: EU countries.

TABLE 6C.1 Variables for Global Value Chain Participation and Forward Linkages

Variable	Global value chain participation	Forward linkages
Log of GDP	−3.604***	0.724
Share of manufacturing in GDP	0.415***	−0.007
Population	−2.11e−08	7.03e−09
Simple tax policies	−0.025	0.071*
Geographic distance	−0.003	−0.001
FDI restrictions	−23.623	2.497
LPI	10.53***	−4.027*
Trading across Barriers	−0.444***	−0.165
Doing Business	−0.037	0.447***
Contiguity to Germany	1.647	1.723
Constant	155.5**	−5.493
Number of observations	95	95
R^2	0.633	0.415
Time fixed effects	Yes	Yes

Note: FDI = foreign direct investment; LPI = Logistics Performance Index.
Significance level: * = 10 percent, ** = 5 percent, *** = 1 percent.

Notes

1. Final goods and services are composed of inputs from several countries. The flows of goods and services within supply chains are not reflected in conventional measures of international trade.
2. Recent initiatives to measure supply chain activity using harmonized intercountry input-output tables (OECD 2015b; Timmer et al. 2014) led to the release of the OECD TiVA database in 2013. It provides a decomposition of gross trade flows into domestic and foreign value added.
3. Santoni and Taglioni (2015) use the Katz-Bonacich metrics as a measure of integration and show a simplified version of the whole network using the minimal spanning tree method.
4. To measure the flows of value added, national input-output tables are linked together using bilateral trade data to form a global input-output table that shows both final and intermediate good shipments between countries. All domestic contributions are tracked to determine the value-added content of exports until the final good reaches the final demand.
5. The inverse ratio of value-added exports to gross exports can also be found in the literature on supply chains.
6. Production fragmentation started earlier in NAFTA than in the other regions. In addition, trade flow measures are biased by the fact that the United States is only one country and interstate trade is not considered.
7. Annex 6A shows the details of the computation.
8. We consider total factor productivity (TFP) and labor productivity separately because of the difficulties in measuring productivity (for example, indexes of TFP suffer from measurement errors). Since TFP and labor productivity are measured differently, showing that both are related to supply chain participation provides greater confidence in empirical findings.
9. Participation in supply chains is measured as the sum of the foreign value added embodied in exports (backward linkages) and the domestic value added in exports that the direct importer exports further or that returns home as imports (forward linkages).

10. This results from regressing growth in labor productivity on growth in GVC participation with country fixed effects over the given period. The coefficient of the regression is significant and equal to 0.27.

11. A recent strand of the economic literature has studied how the structure of domestic production networks can affect aggregate performance (Acemoglu and Jensen 2015; Carvalho 2014). A few recent studies have focused on the importance of interconnections between firms to understand how micro disturbances can affect macro performance (Carvalho and Grassi 2015). For example, the 2007–09 global financial crisis showed how the linkages between financial institutions contributed to the impact on economic growth and unemployment in most ECA countries. Other references on global supply chains include Antràs and Chor 2013; Chaney 2014; Costinot, Vogel, and Wang 2013; and di Giovanni and Levchenko 2012.

12. The contribution of the sector to another sector determines the strength of a link in the global network. We use the OECD input-output network in 2011 to highlight the most influential sectors, and then the most influential countries in this network.

13. Distance measures are given by the network closeness measures in 2005. Correlations across sectoral outputs come from the OECD Structural Analysis database and cover the years from 1995 to 2011. For more details, see annexes 6B and 6C.

References

Aleksynska, M., and G. Peri. 2014. "Isolating the Network Effect of Immigrants on Trade." *World Economy* 37 (3): 434–55. https://doi.org/10.1111/twec.12079.

Amador, J., and S. Cabral. 2009. "Vertical Specialization across the World: A Relative Measure." *North American Journal of Economics and Finance* 20 (3): 267–80. https://doi.org/10.1016/j.najef.2009.05.003.

Antràs, P. 2003. "Firms, Contracts, and Trade Structure." *Quarterly Journal of Economics* 118 (4): 1375–1418.

Antràs, P., and D. Chor. 2013. "Organizing the Global Value Chain." *Econometrica* 81 (6): 2127–204. https://doi.org/10.3982/ECTA10813.

Arrow, K. J. 1969. "Classificatory Notes on the Production and Transmission of Technological Knowledge." *American Economic Review* 59 (2): 29–35.

Bahar, D., R. Hausmann, and C. Hidalgo. 2014. "Neighbors and the Evolution of the Comparative Advantage of Nations: Evidence of International Knowledge Diffusion?" *Journal of International Economics* 92 (1): 111–23.

Baldwin, R., and J. Lopez-Gonzalez. 2015. "Supply-Chain Trade: A Portrait of Global Patterns and Several Testable Hypotheses." *World Economy* 38 (11): 1682–721. https://doi.org/10.1111/twec.12189.

Baldwin, R., and F. Robert-Nicoud. 2014. "Trade-in-Goods and Trade-in-Tasks: An Integrating Framework." *Journal of International Economics* 92 (1): 51–62. https://doi.org/10.1016/j.jinteco.2013.10.002.

Blyde, J., A. Graziano, and C. Volpe Martincus. 2015. "Economic Integration Agreements and Production Fragmentation: Evidence on the Extensive Margin." *Applied Economics Letters* 22 (10): 835–42. https://doi.org/10.1080/13504851.2014.980569.

Burchardi, K. B., T. Chaney, and T. A. Hassan. 2016. "Migrants, Ancestors, and Investments." Working Paper 21847, National Bureau of Economic Research, Cambridge, MA.

Carvalho, V. 2014. "From Micro to Macro via Production Networks." *Journal of Economic Perspectives* 28 (4): 23–48. https://doi.org/10.1257/jep.28.4.23.

Carvalho, V., D. Acemoglu, A. Ozdaglar, and A. Tahbaz-Salehi. 2012. "The Network Origins of Aggregate Fluctuations." *Econometrica* 80 (5): 1977–2016.

Carvalho, V., and B. Grassi. 2015. "Large Firm Dynamics and the Business Cycle." Working Papers in Economics 1556, Faculty of Economics, Cambridge University, Cambridge, UK.

Chaney, T. 2014. "The Network Structure of International Trade." *American Economic Review* 104 (11): 3600–34. https://doi.org/10.1257/aer.104.11.3600.

Constantinescu, C., A. Mattoo, and M. Ruta. 2017. "Does Vertical Specialization Increase Productivity?" Policy Research Working Paper 7978, World Bank, Washington, DC.

Costinot, A., J. Vogel, and S. Wang. 2013. "An Elementary Theory of Global Supply Chains." *Review of Economic Studies* 13 (80): 109–44. https://doi.org/10.1093/restud/rds023.

di Giovanni, J., and A. A. Levchenko. 2012. "Country Size, International Trade, and Aggregate Fluctuations in Granular Economies." *Journal of Political Economy* 120 (6): 1083–132. https://doi.org/10.1086/669161.

Escaith, H., N. Lindenberg, and S. Miroudot. 2010. "International Supply Chains and Trade Elasticity in Times of Global Crisis." MPRA Paper 20478, University Library of Munich, Munich, Germany.

Felbermayr, G. J., and F. Toubal. 2012. "Revisiting the Trade-Migration Nexus: Evidence from New OECD Data." *World Development* 40 (5): 928–37. https://doi.org/10.1016/j.worlddev.2011.11.016.

Gereffi, G., and J. Humphrey. 2005. "The Governance of Global Value Chains." *Review of International Political Economy* 12.70–104. https://doi.org/10.1000/09692290500049805.

Gill, I. S., and M. Raiser. 2011. *Golden Growth.* Washington, DC: World Bank. https://doi.org/10.1596/978-0-8213-8965-2.

Gould, D. 1994. "Immigrant Links to the Home Country: Empirical Implications for U.S. Bilateral Trade Flows." *Review of Economics and Statistics* 76 (2): 302–16.

Grossman, G. M., and E. Rossi-Hansberg. 2008. "Trading Tasks: A Simple Theory of Offshoring." *American Economic Review* 98 (5): 1978–97. https://doi.org/10.1257/aer.98.5.1978.

Hayakawa, K., and N. Yamashita. 2011. "The Role of Preferential Trade Agreements (PTAs) in Facilitating Global Production Networks." Discussion Paper 280, Institute of Developing Economies, Japan External Trade Organization (JETRO), Tokyo.

Helpman, E., P. Antràs, and E. Helpman. 2008. *The Organization of Firms in a Global Economy.* Cambridge, MA: Harvard University Press.

Hummels, D. L., J. Ishii, and K.-M. Yi. 2001. "The Nature and Growth of Vertical Specialization in World Trade." *Journal of International Economics* 54 (1): 75–96. https://doi.org/10.1016/S0022-1996(00)00093-3.

Hummels, D. L., D. Rapoport, and K.-M. Yi. 1998. "Vertical Specialization and the Changing Nature of World Trade." *Economic Policy Review* 4 (2): 79–99.

Hummels, D. L., and G. Schaur. 2013. "Time as a Trade Barrier." *American Economic Review* 103 (7): 2935–59. https://doi.org/10.1257/aer.103.7.2935.

Johnson, R., and G. Noguera. 2017. "A Portrait of Trade in Value-Added over Four Decades." *Review of Economics and Statistics* 99 (5): 896–911.

Kirkegaard, J. F. 2013. "New Avenues for Empirical Analysis of Cross-Border Investments: An Application for the ASEAN Members and Middle and Low Income Country Outward Investments." PhD dissertation, Johns Hopkins University, Baltimore, MD.

Koopman, R., Z. Wang, and S.-J. Wei 2012. "Estimating Domestic Content in Exports When Processing Trade Is Pervasive." *Journal of Development Economics* 99: 178–89.

Kummritz, V. 2016. "Do Global Value Chains Cause Industrial Development?" Working Paper 2016-01, Centre for Trade and Economic Integration, The Graduate Institute, Geneva.

Kummritz, V., and B. Quast. 2016. "Global Value Chains in Low and Middle Income Countries." Working Paper 2016-10, Centre for Trade and Economic Integration, The Graduate Institute, Geneva.

Kummritz, V., D. Taglioni, and D. Winkler. 2017. "Economic Upgrading through Global Value Chain Participation: Which Policies Increase the Value Added Gains?" Policy Research Working Paper 8007, World Bank, Washington, DC.

Li, X., and X. Liu. 2005. "Foreign Direct Investment and Economic Growth: An Increasingly Endogenous Relationship." *World Development* 33 (3): 393–407. https://doi .org/10.1016/j.worlddev.2004.11.001.

Marin, Dalia. 2010. "The Opening Up of Eastern Europe at 20—Jobs, Skills, and 'Reverse Maquiladoras' in Austria and Germany." Working Paper 421, Bruegel, Brussels.

Nicita, A., V. Ognivtsev, and M. Shirotori. 2013. "Global Supply Chains: Trade and Economic Policies for Developing Countries." Blue Papers Series 55, United Nations Conference on Trade and Development, Geneva.

OECD (Organisation for Economic Co-operation and Development). 2013. *Interconnected Economies*. Paris: OECD. https://doi.org/10.1787/9789264189560-en.

———. 2015a. "The Participation of Developing Countries in Global Value Chains: Implications for Trade and Trade Policy." Trade Policy Note, OECD, Paris.

———. 2015b. Trade in Value Added (TIVA) Indicators Database (October). OECD, Paris. https://doi.org/10.1787/tiva-data-en.

Orefice, G., and N. Rocha. 2014. "Deep Integration and Production Networks: An Empirical Analysis." *World Economy* 37 (1): 106–36. https://doi.org/10.1111/twec.12076.

Polanyi, M. 1962. "Tacit Knowing: Its Bearing on Some Problems of Philosophy." *Reviews of Modern Physics* 34 (4): 601–16. https://doi.org/10.1103/RevModPhys.34.601.

Rauch, J. E., and V. Trindade. 2002. "Ethnic Chinese Networks in International Trade." *Review of Economics and Statistics* 84 (1): 116–30. https://doi.org/10.1162/003 465302317331955.

Santoni, Gianluca, and Daria Taglioni. 2015. "Networks and Structural Integration in Global Value Chains." In *The Age of Global Value Chains*, ed. João Amador and Filippo di Mauro. London: Centre for Economic Policy Research.

Sturgeon, T. J., and O. Memedovic. 2011. "Mapping Global Value Chains: Intermediate Goods Trade and Structual Change in the World Economy." UNIDO Working Paper 5: 52.

Taglioni, D., and D. Winkler. 2016. *Making Global Value Chains Work for Development*. Washington, DC: World Bank. https://doi.org/10.1596/978-1-4648-0157-0.

Thoenig, M., and T. Verdier. 2003. "A Theory of Defensive Skill-Biased Innovation and Globalization." *American Economic Review* 93 (3): 709–28. https://doi.org/10.1257 /000282803322157052.

Timmer, M. P., A. A. Erumban, B. Los, R. Stehrer, and G. J. de Vries. 2014. "Slicing Up Global Value Chains." *Journal of Economic Perspectives* 28 (2): 99–118. https://doi .org/10.1257/jep.28.2.99.

7

ECA Policies for Improving Connectivity

Countries in Europe and Central Asia (ECA) have made important progress in furthering regional and global connectivity along the several policy dimensions discussed in this report, including trade, foreign direct investment (FDI), supply chains, migration, internet and telecommunications, and transport. ECA countries have taken critical steps to increase integration and connectivity along many of these dimensions, yet important challenges remain. This chapter considers the historical, political, and economic developments that have led to greater connectivity in many parts of ECA and how policies influenced this connectivity. We consider data on selected connectivity-related policies in the ECA region and comparator countries and regions including tariffs, FDI policies, preferential trade agreements (PTAs), bilateral investment treaties (BITs), product market regulations (PMRs), and domestic regulatory reforms in transition countries (transition indicators). In addition, comovements across the different policy areas for ECA as a whole and ECA subregions are analyzed as a means to understand whether connectivity policies pursued by ECA countries are moving in the same direction or are at odds with each other.

Main Messages

- ECA countries generally have supported greater international connectivity through reductions in most-favored-nation (MFN) tariffs, increased numbers of

PTAs and BITs, reductions in regulatory restrictions on FDI, improved domestic economic governance in general and the regulation of key network sectors in particular, and a process of policy transition toward Organisation for Economic Co-operation and Development (OECD) standards. Regional integration through PTAs has been faster in ECA than elsewhere, although less so with BITs. However, ECA is less successful than other regions in domestic product market governance.

- The trend in policies that improve connectivity in ECA slowed significantly after the early 2000s. Little change is observed in tariff liberalization (as of the beginning of the 2000s), the use of BITs (as of the end of the 2000s), and reductions of FDI regulatory restrictions and product market liberalization (as of 2010).
- Policies toward regional integration have varied greatly across ECA countries. Northern, Southern, and Western European high-income countries tend to have lower tariffs, higher global and extraregional integration through PTAs, and lower regulatory restrictions on FDI. Former centrally planned economies in Central and Eastern Europe still rank lower on the quality of domestic governance in infrastructure sectors than countries in other ECA subregions. Countries tend to be consistent in their policies aimed at improving connectivity; decreases in MFN tariffs and increases in the number of BITs go hand in hand. However, some country groups, particularly the non-high-income ECA countries in Eastern Europe and Central Asia, tend not to consistently implement connectivity-friendly policies across different dimensions.

Introduction

The set of policies that are relevant for international connectivity is multidimensional, encompassing measures that affect trade, FDI, supply chains, migration, and transport infrastructure. While policies affecting connectivity are determined on an autonomous, independent basis by governments, they have implications for foreign countries, and thus are often the focus of international agreements and cooperation. The ECA region has a rich history of progress on enhancing international connectivity. The region is unique both in the distinct character of connectivity-related initiatives that have been pursued over time and more generally the integration of countries in this region into the broader world economy.

An important dimension of this uniqueness is the role that has been played—and continues to be played—by formal regional integration arrangements between subsets of ECA countries. The most prominent feature of international economic policy cooperation in ECA is undoubtedly the gradual expansion of what is now the European Union (EU). Starting with a sectoral integration initiative among six European states—the 1951 European Coal and Steel Community—and a much more ambitious agreement to form a European Economic Community in 1957, over time the European Economic Community grew incrementally both in terms of issue coverage and the depth of policy cooperation. It is now an economic union spanning the free movement of goods, services, capital, and people with associated supra-national common institutions and a common currency that has been adopted by 19 EU member states.

Concurrently with the gradual process of deepening economic cooperation between EU member states there has been a process of widening the EU to encompass additional countries. Currently membership stands at 28, with 7 countries formally accepted as accession candidates.[1] A major feature of European integration in the past 20 years has been the process of accession—most notably by 10 Baltic and Central European countries (Estonia, Latvia, Lithuania, Poland, Hungary, the Czech Republic, the Slovak Republic, and Slovenia in 2004, followed by Bulgaria and Romania in 2007). Until the dissolution of the former Soviet Union, these countries had been part of the second major regional bloc that dominated the ECA region: the Council for Mutual Economic Assistance (CMEA or COMECON), led by the former Soviet Union. The 10 nations that acceded to the EU in 2004–07 had all been CMEA members in one form or another until it ceased to operate in 1991 following the breakup of the Soviet Union.

The demise of the Soviet Union was followed by a looser form of economic integration and cooperation between the Russian Federation and the former Soviet Republics—the Commonwealth of Independent States (CIS). Starting late in the first decade of the 2000s, Russia sought to deepen the CIS into a common market and economic union and pursued a process of deepening economic integration with a subset of its neighbors, through the creation of a Eurasian Economic Union. This currently comprises Armenia, Belarus, Kazakhstan, and Russia.

Trade agreements have been a central feature of the EU's engagement with countries in the "European neighborhood," both those that were (are) eligible for EU membership and those that are not. The EU currently has more than 50 PTAs in place, with another 80 or so in the pipeline—both agreements that have been negotiated and are waiting ratification and agreements that are in the process of negotiation.[2] The EU's approach toward reciprocal trade agreements has shifted over time from "shallow" trade agreements that centered mostly on the liberalization of merchandise trade toward deeper agreements that also liberalize trade in services, public procurement markets, and cross-border investment and include disciplines on the implementation of national regulatory regimes.

EU trade agreements vary across partners in depth and design. The EU has customs union agreements with a small number of neighboring states, such as Turkey, and deeper arrangements with European countries that have elected not to join the EU—for example, Norway and Switzerland—that provide these countries with full access to the European Single Market through the European Economic Association agreement.

The EU has developed so-called deep and comprehensive free trade agreements (DCFTAs) that include various elements of EU law (the *acquis communautaire*). These are on offer to neighboring countries and are intended to be instruments to support convergence in the partner with specific areas of EU legislation and regulation that pertain to the operation of the Single Market (Hoekman 2016). DCFTAs differ from earlier-vintage EU trade agreements with neighboring countries in having less "soft law" language and establishing specific, binding (enforceable) disciplines that aim at the (gradual) convergence of policies in covered areas with those of the EU (Langbein and Wolczuk 2012). An implication of DCFTAs anchored on adoption

> Trade agreements have been a central feature of the EU's engagement with countries in the "European neighborhood," both those that were (are) eligible for EU membership and those that are not.

of the *acquis* is that partner countries would move away from Russian regulatory standards, raising worries by Russian enterprises that they would be negatively affected by the adoption of EU norms and standards by European neighborhood countries (Hoekman, Jensen, and Tarr 2013).

A recent development has been a shift toward a less EU-norm centric, more pragmatic strategy when pursuing DCFTAs, reflected in less emphasis on making EU law the focal point for deep agreements (Hoekman 2016). There is increasing recognition among European policy makers that the approaches pursued by the EU since the collapse of the Soviet Union that were centered on the concept of a "normative power Europe" and a focus on exporting European values and regulatory norms to partner countries has not delivered the desired results (Langbein 2014; European Commission 2015). The EU itself is becoming more contested by European polities. Proposals by the European Commission to revamp long-standing approaches toward investor-state disputes under BITs are another indication of a recognition that new approaches are needed to govern international economic cooperation. The decision by the UK government in 2016 to leave the EU will require the remaining 27 member states to determine how to structure a deep economic integration arrangement with the United Kingdom. This may build on recent agreements that have been concluded with Canada and Japan or be substantially more ambitious—the eventual outcome will depend on the objectives of the UK government, which have yet to be fully articulated.

While the EU is in a state of flux, confronting major challenges and questions regarding the future of further deepening of cooperation as opposed to reducing the extent of integration both among the membership and with non-EU countries, it has played a major role in providing a focal point for efforts to enhance regional connectivity. The primary purpose of this chapter is to provide a descriptive analysis of a set of policy indicators that are salient from a connectivity perspective, focusing on both domestic policies and the extent to which countries have engaged in international agreements with partners that entail disciplines and liberalization of the relevant policy.

Trade Costs as a Focal Point for Connectivity

Extensive research has shown that from a development and growth perspective, lowering trade and transactions costs for firms is a key dimension of enhancing connectivity. High trade costs reduce competitiveness of firms and the ability of an economy as a whole to exploit its comparative advantages. Trade costs are a function of a mix of exogenous variables (e.g., location) and policy (Moïse and Le Bris 2015). Restrictive trade policies, markets that are difficult for new entrants to contest because of restrictive business practices of a dominant supplier or state-owned enterprise, PMR that impedes entry as opposed to addressing market failures, barriers to FDI, and restrictive visa regimes that make it difficult for employees and professionals to cross borders to supply services or establish contacts with potential suppliers or customers (see chapter 4) are all examples of policies that raise trade-related operating costs for firms, which in turn may increase the prices of goods and services for consumers and reduce the demand for workers and thus negatively affect household incomes.

A challenge for analysts (and policymakers) is to differentiate between trade cost–creating measures that generate social waste and those that do not. Abstracting from tariffs, which remain a burden on international exchange even though the average level of tariffs has dropped substantially in the past 30 years, most trade policy instruments used by countries comprise nontariff measures (NTMs): regulatory policies pertaining to product quality, health, and safety standards for goods and services (e.g., transport, logistics, finance, and professionals).[3] Taking action to reduce trade costs by facilitating the movement of goods, services, investment, and people by necessity implies focusing on the substance and implementation (enforcement) of NTMs.

Many NTMs have been put in place for good reasons, that is, to address market failures or to pursue specific noneconomic social objectives. Policy consistency requires that efforts to reduce trade costs not undercut the realization of the legitimate objectives that motivate the regulatory policies (NTMs) a country has put in place. International cooperation is one mechanism governments can use to balance a process aimed at reducing the trade costs generated by differences in regulatory regimes that affect connectivity. The demand for such balancing has increased as a result of the growth in international value chain–based production networks in recent decades. This has led to an increasing number of firms supporting trade facilitation initiatives broadly defined as opposed to lobbying for policies to restrict trade and factor movement (Gawande, Hoekman, and Cui 2014; Baldwin 2016).

The policy agenda has shifted toward efforts to facilitate trade and to reduce the trade costs created by regulatory heterogeneity while ensuring that regulatory objectives (such as health and safety) are met. This is a more complex agenda than one that centers on removing welfare-reducing border barriers such as tariffs. Trade policy today increasingly involves the use of NTMs that are not necessarily designed to restrict or to encourage trade but that address nontrade regulatory objectives such as product safety, environmental protection, national security, or intellectual property protection. Trade agreements, both those at the multilateral level of the World Trade Organization (WTO) and bilateral and regional PTAs, are the instrument of choice for governments to pursue reductions in NTM-related trade costs. One function of trade agreements is to establish what types of NTMs should be banned because they are simply protectionist. An example is quantitative restrictions. These are prohibited in principle by the WTO and EU PTAs outside of agriculture where tariff rate quotas continue to prevail for some products. More generally, trade agreements provide frameworks regulating the use of NTMs.

> The policy agenda has shifted toward efforts to facilitate trade and to reduce the trade costs created by regulatory heterogeneity while ensuring that regulatory objectives are met.

For example, a common form of NTMs is product standards, and, more generally, PMR. These are generally aimed at ensuring the health and safety of consumers. The WTO imposes rules on countries regarding how they may pursue such regulation, for example, by encouraging the use of international standards where they exist and requiring countries to notify the WTO regarding new product standards if they are not compliant with or based on internationally agreed standards that have been developed by specialized international bodies. The extent to which countries notify regarding noncompliant standards is one indicator of integration (connectivity) of their economies as it reveals implicitly to what extent a WTO member has chosen to adopt national norms that diverge from international standards.

Agreeing to a common set of rules on the use and implementation of NTMs without undercutting the ability to pursue legitimate regulatory objectives enhances joint welfare. International cooperation and rules on NTMs generate not just benefits in terms of economic gains associated with lower trade costs, but also in terms of connectivity, interconnection, and the reduction of coordination externalities related to public goods such as environmental and labor standards. No matter what a country's strategy is with respect to industrial policy and trade or the extent to which it makes use of NTMs, minimizing the transactions costs and uncertainty associated with their implementation is important in reducing the real resource (welfare) costs of NTMs. There is therefore a strong connection between efforts to streamline and rationalize the use of NTMs (e.g., Cadot, Malouche, and Sáez 2012) and enhancing connectivity.

Connectivity and trade cost concerns often are reflected in a focus on trade in goods and related FDI flows. The need to also consider services trade costs is often neglected. Services directly matter for connectivity, as many of the networks that define connectivity levels comprise services sectors. But they also matter more generally because all firms use services as inputs into production. Input costs that are higher than they would be in an environment in which services trade costs were lower act as a tax on domestic industries and reduce their competitiveness. The stylized fact here is that trade costs for services are much higher than trade costs for goods (Miroudot and Shepherd 2016). The result is to reduce the volume of trade in services, and thus to reduce the access firms and households have to low-cost services.

Services trade costs are high in part because of the characteristics of services: trade often requires movement of people or establishment of a commercial presence (FDI). This implies that many policies and their administration may affect trade costs. Two dimensions are important in this regard: (a) regulatory policies that apply to all firms, both national and foreign; and (b) policies that are designed to discriminate against foreign providers or consumption abroad. Regulatory policies vary across countries for any given sector and the resulting heterogeneity is an important source of international trade costs. High services trade costs also reflect in part that regulatory policies may discriminate against foreign providers. Examples include nationality requirements or banning access to markets as is the case in many countries for segments of the transport, communications, or professional services sectors. Research has shown that barriers to trade and investment in services are often much higher than for goods. Although information on services trade policy is limited, recent compilations of prevailing policies across countries by the OECD and the World Bank have shown that barriers to trade in services are often high, with significant variation across countries and sectors, translating into estimates of ad valorem tariff equivalents that are greater than trade barriers for goods (Jafari and Tarr 2017).[4]

The effect of trade and FDI policy instruments is in part determined by institutional variables (e.g., Rodriguez and Rodrik 2001; Freund and Bolaky 2008; Fiorini and Hoekman 2017a, 2017b). Beverelli, Fiorini, and Hoekman (2017) show that the economic effects of services trade policies on manufacturing industries are moderated by the quality of economic governance institutions in the importing country.

Lower services trade restrictiveness is found to increase downstream manufacturing productivity only in countries with good economic governance (as proxied by indicators of control of corruption, rule of law, and the quality of regulatory institutions). This moderating effect prevails with respect to trade policies that target services provision through foreign establishment (FDI) more than cross-border trade in services. This result reflects the intangibility and nonstorability of services, which mean that foreign providers must invest in local production facilities (establish a commercial presence) to be able to contest the relevant market. The bottom line is that regulatory regimes for products matter—they help determine the ability of firms to benefit from actions that aim to integrate markets. Thus, PMR is one policy area that should be considered a determinant of the level of effective connectivity that prevails in a market.

Indicators of Trade Cost–Related Policies

What follows focuses on six policy areas that affect the cost of interaction between pairs of countries and between countries and the rest of the world: import tariffs, engagement in trade agreements that reduce tariffs on a preferential basis, policies toward inward FDI, the use of BITs to provide protection to investors from expropriation and adverse changes in investment policies, PMRs, and European Bank for Reconstruction and Development (EBRD) transition indicators (on sectoral domestic regulation). Policies regulating international mobility of people (visa regimes) and policies toward integration of migrants are discussed in chapter 4. The time periods and country coverage for these variables are listed in table 7.1.

The choice of these specific variables reflects in part data availability but more important is that they relate closely to the trade cost discussion in the previous section and the different dimensions of connectivity that are the focus of previous chapters of this report.[5] Some of the variables measure policies that apply at the border and increase costs—for example, tariffs. Tariffs are of course less important today than a few decades ago, but differences in average tariff levels provide information on the extent to which countries have opened their markets to foreign competition. Unfortunately, comprehensive comparable time series data on NTMs do not exist. However, as noted above, NTMs are highly correlated with PMR, and the intensity with which a country has pursued PTAs is a good indicator of the degree to which countries are willing to agree to disciplines on the use of NTMs. The same is true for the extent of BITs negotiated—BITs are an instrument that affects FDI policies, and BITs are concluded to improve the investment climate confronting foreign firms. Measures of the degree to which FDI is restricted is particularly salient as a proxy for barriers to trade in services, as FDI is a major "mode of supply" for services firms. Measures of PMR are similarly a good proxy for connectivity because they capture the extent of barriers to entry and the extent to which a nation has put in place good regulatory practices. For many ECA countries there is a unique time series measure of convergence toward good regulatory practices compiled by the EBRD—the so-called transition indicators.

Tariffs are of course less important today than a few decades ago, but differences in average tariff levels provide information on the extent to which countries have opened their markets to foreign competition.

TABLE 7.1 Policy Measures and Indicators

Variable	Starting year	Ending year	Countries covered
Tariffs	1988	2015	186
FDI restrictiveness	1997	2015	59
PTAs	1988	2015	189
BITs	1988	2015	177
Horizontal PMR	1998	2013	47
Sectoral PMR	1975	2013	47
Transition EBRD	1989	2012	20

Sources: Tariff data are from World Bank, World Integrated Trade Solution. Foreign direct investment (FDI) policy measures are sourced from the Organisation for Economic Co-operation and Development (OECD) FDI Regulatory Restrictiveness Indicators (FDIRRI) database. Preferential trade agreement (PTA) data come from the World Bank database on Content of Deep Trade Agreements (http://data .worldbank.org/data-catalog/deep-trade-agreements). Data on bilateral investment treaties (BITs) are from the United Nations Conference on Trade and Development investment hub database. Horizontal product market regulation (PMR) is sourced from the OECD's PMR Economy Wide Database. Sectoral PMR indicators are from the OECD's PMR Energy, Transport, and Communications Database. Transition EBRD data are from the Transition Indicators Database of the European Bank for Reconstruction and Development (EBRD).

Note: The simple average most-favored-nation tariff is taken as the measure for "Tariffs." The "FDI restrictiveness" indicator measures statutory restrictions on inward FDI; a higher value means more restrictions. To capture integration through PTAs (BITs), the number of trade agreements (investment treaties) to which each country belongs is used. "Horizontal PMR" refers to indicators of the restrictiveness of product market regulation that applies to the economy as a whole, that is, measures that pertain to all types of economic activity, independent of sector; a higher value indicates more restrictive regulation. "Sectoral PMR" is the aggregate restrictiveness of product market regulation that is specific to sectors that matter for connectivity: energy, telecommunications, transport, and distribution, a higher value reflects more restrictive regulation. "Transition EBRD" refers to the transition indicators compiled by the EBRD, which measure the degree to which policies are equivalent to the standards prevailing in industrial market economies; higher values imply greater convergence toward best practice.

The data reveal several patterns. First, there is a clear trend toward a policy environment that is supportive of greater international connectivity. This is apparent across all policy instruments for which data are reported before 2000. Across the different time spans for which data on respective policies are reported, ECA countries have on average decreased MFN tariffs, increased the number of PTAs and BITs, unilaterally reduced regulatory restrictions to FDI, improved domestic economic governance in general and the regulation of key network sectors in particular, and undergone a process of policy transition toward OECD standards.

Comparing the evolution of ECA countries' policy stances with those in the rest of the world, on average ECA as a whole (including the EU) is a leader in cooperating with partner countries through PTAs and BITs, reflecting a relatively faster pace of intraregional integration than elsewhere. Conversely, the average ECA country is more of a follower and more restrictive than non-ECA regions when it comes to domestic economic governance.

For many policy instruments, the observed positive trend toward a more connectivity-friendly policy environment in ECA slowed significantly after the early 2000s. In some cases, the data reveal convergence toward a "steady state" with little change observed. This is the case for tariff liberalization (as of the beginning of the 2000s), the use of BITs (as of the end of the 2000s), and reductions of FDI regulatory restrictions and product market liberalization (as of 2010).

Disaggregating these trends and patterns across subsets of ECA countries, whether on the basis of geography or per capita incomes, often reveals very heterogeneous policy stances across country groups. Northern, Southern, and Western European high-income countries (HICs) converge on lower tariffs and higher global and extraregional integration through PTAs and have lower regulatory restrictions on FDI. Transition to higher quality of domestic governance in infrastructure sectors is observed for Central and Northern Europe compared with former Soviet Union countries in other ECA subregions.

Analysis of comovements across policy instruments reveals the extent to which there is balance in connectivity-related policies—that is, whether for a given country, subregion or subgroup policies tend to move in the same (complementary) direction over time. Insofar as divergent policy trajectories are observed across instruments, there is a lack of policy consistency in terms of supporting greater connectivity. On average at the global level, countries would pursue balanced connectivity if they implement reforms that are consistent with each other and this pattern increases over time. The data reveal that different policies often move in the same direction, suggesting a balanced connectivity objective—for example, countries decrease MFN tariffs and at the same time increase the number of BITs.

Some country groups, however, seem to move in the opposite direction and fail to consistently implement connectivity-friendly policies across different dimensions. This is the case especially among the non-HIC ECA countries. The data show substantial heterogeneity in the comovement of MFN tariffs and BITs between the two large ECA subregions defined by the World Bank: (a) Europe + Western Balkans; and (b) Eastern Europe + Central Asia. Only the first of these subregions demonstrates policy consistency.

MFN Tariffs

Figure 7.1 reports data on simple average MFN import tariffs, using the World Integrated Trade Solution database.[6] The data are aggregated to simple averages for seven global regions, including ECA, and for three time periods. In comparison with other regions, the aggregate pattern in ECA tariff evolution is very stable, characterized by a smooth trend toward higher integration. All other regions but North America (Canada and the United States) display higher average levels of tariff protection. Within the ECA region there are heterogeneous patterns. While convergence to lower tariffs is almost ubiquitous, significantly higher integration is reached by the EU and Western Balkans region (figure 7.2) driven by Western, Southern, and Northern Europe. As shown in figure 7.3, these three subregions converged on a policy steady state of less than 5 percent as of the beginning of the 2000s. This is the case in particular for ECA HICs (figure 7.4).

Although tariffs are just one type of trade policy, focusing on trends in average MFN tariffs is relevant because tariffs are particularly important as a barrier to value chain participation. The three world regions with the lowest tariffs (North America, ECA, and East Asia and Pacific) are the most regionally integrated and the dominant users of regional supply chains (Baldwin 2016). Low MFN tariffs are often

FIGURE 7.1 Tariffs across global regions

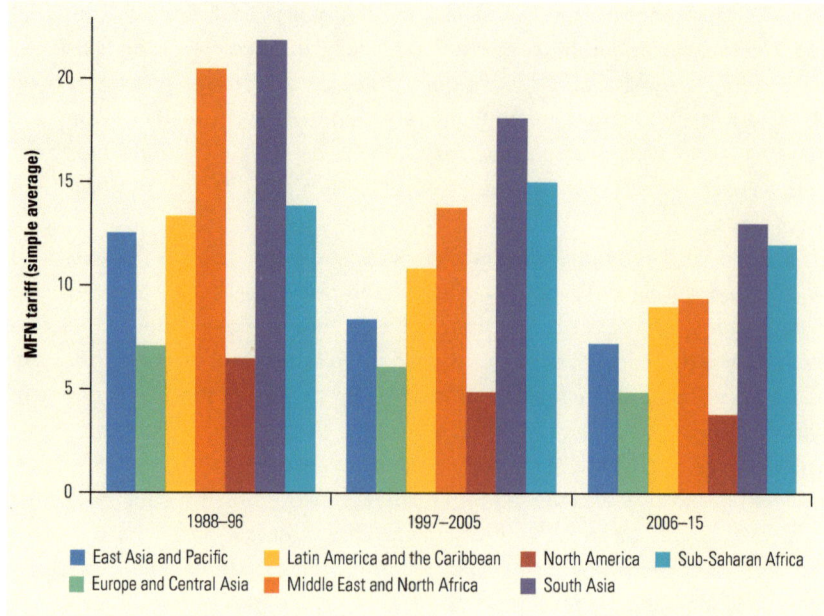

Note: MFN = most favored nation.

FIGURE 7.2 Tariffs in the main ECA subregions

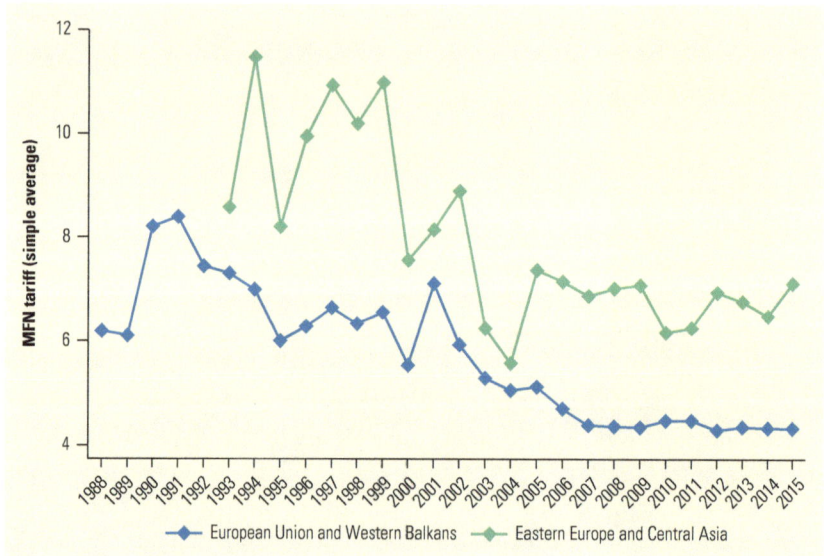

Note: MFN = most favored nation.

complemented by zero bilateral tariffs because of PTAs. They may be offset by NTMs—some countries have been shown to replace tariffs with various NTMs—but as noted above comprehensive data on NTMs are not available. The PTA, FDIRRI, PMR, and EBRD indicators are all proxies for the level of and trends in applied NTMs across countries.

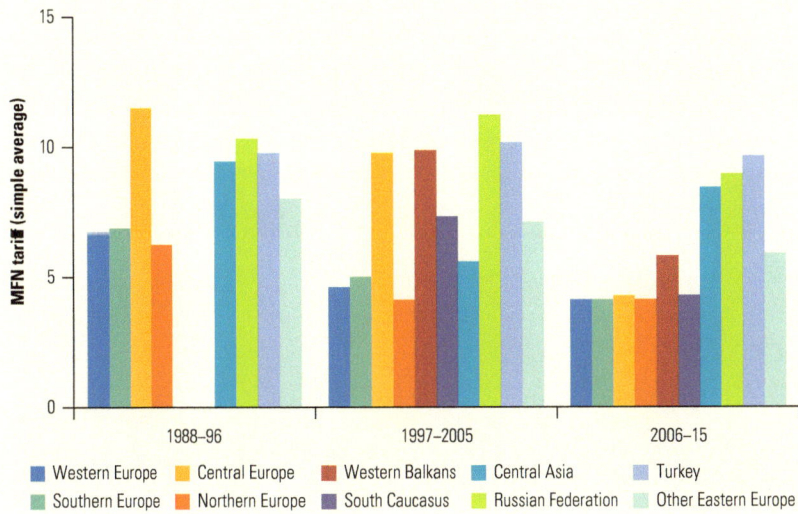

FIGURE 7.3 Tariffs in ECA regions

Note: MFN = most favored nation.

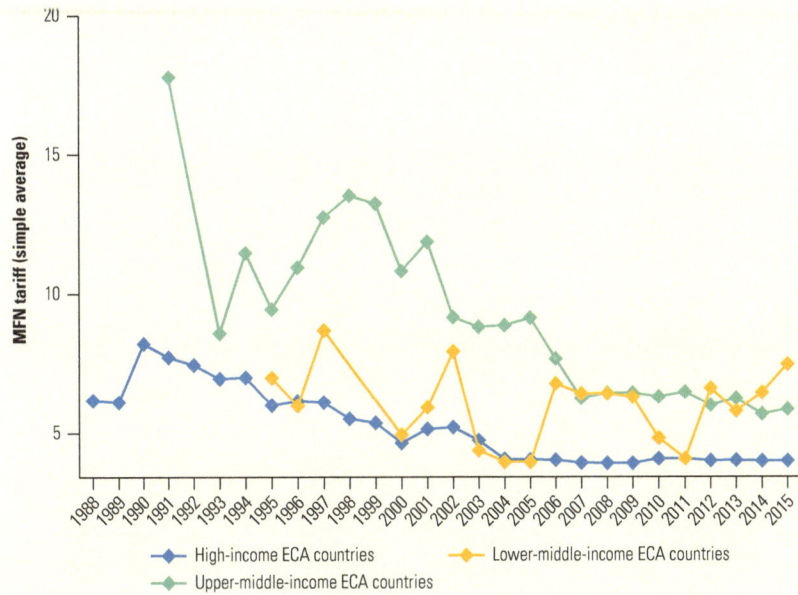

FIGURE 7.4 Tariffs in ECA countries by income group

Note: ECA = Europe and Central Asia; MFN = most favored nation.

Foreign Direct Investment Policies

The OECD has developed an aggregate indicator of a variety of regulatory policies that restrict inward foreign investment, the FDI Regulatory Restrictiveness

Index (FDIRRI). What follows uses the most aggregate version of the index, which encompasses equity restrictions, restrictions in the form of screening and approval requirements, and restrictions on the nationality of key personnel. The indicator takes values between 0 and 1, with 0 denoting no restrictions and 1 maximum restrictiveness. An important limitation for the scope of the analysis is that the country coverage of the database is not complete when it comes to the ECA region. In particular, there exists no information for countries in the Western Balkans and the South Caucasus subregions.

The average ECA country (among those covered in the database) shows a very high degree of integration, with restrictiveness scores among the lowest in the database (figure 7.5). Since the mid-2000s, ECA has maintained less restrictive policies than the United States, Canada, Brazil, India, and China.

Figures 7.6–7.8 unpack the average ECA scores across subregions and income groups. All four European regions show a pattern of openness starting in 1997, converging to stable and relatively similar scores, all below 0.05, in 2010. Turkey and Russia show a similar pattern, with the former converging to a degree of restrictiveness slightly above that of Western Europe and the latter to a relatively much more restrictive regulatory framework (score slightly below 0.2). After 2010, progress toward further integration (liberalization) seems to have stopped in both HICs and upper-middle-income countries (UMICs). The average ECA lower-middle-income country (LMIC) instead reveals some policy progress toward removing FDI regulatory barriers between 2010 and 2015.

Figures 7.9–7.12 replicate the descriptive analysis of figures 7.6–7.8 for the FDIRRI scores for two specific services sectors that are particularly relevant for connectivity: transport and telecommunications. The main patterns hold for these two services sectors with the main difference being that restrictions for FDI in transport

FIGURE 7.5 **FDIRRI in ECA and selected countries**

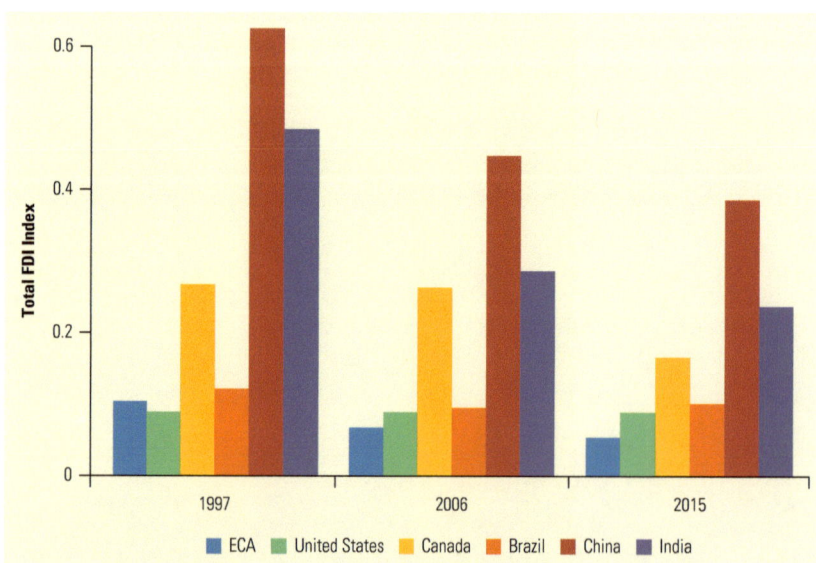

Note: ECA = Europe and Central Asia; FDIRRI = Foreign Direct Investment Regulatory Restrictiveness Index.

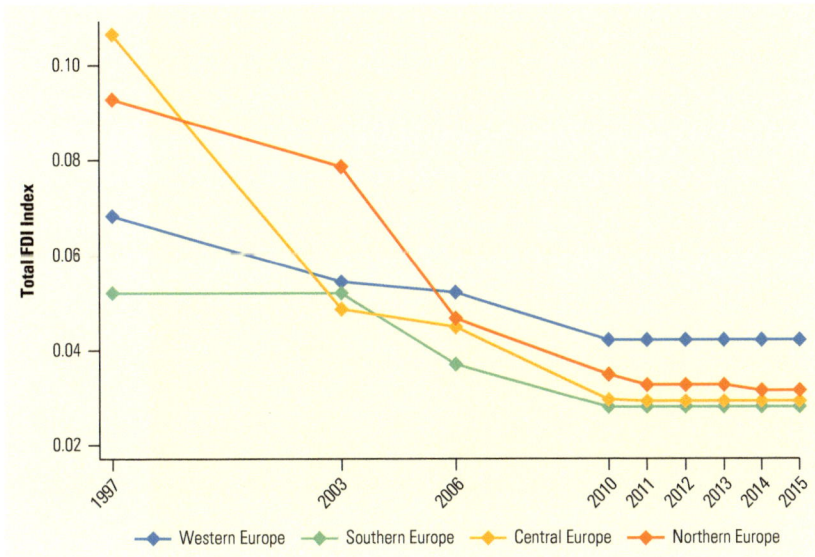

FIGURE 7.6 **FDIRRI in ECA subregion I**

Note: ECA = Europe and Central Asia; FDIRRI = Foreign Direct Investment Regulatory Restrictiveness Index.

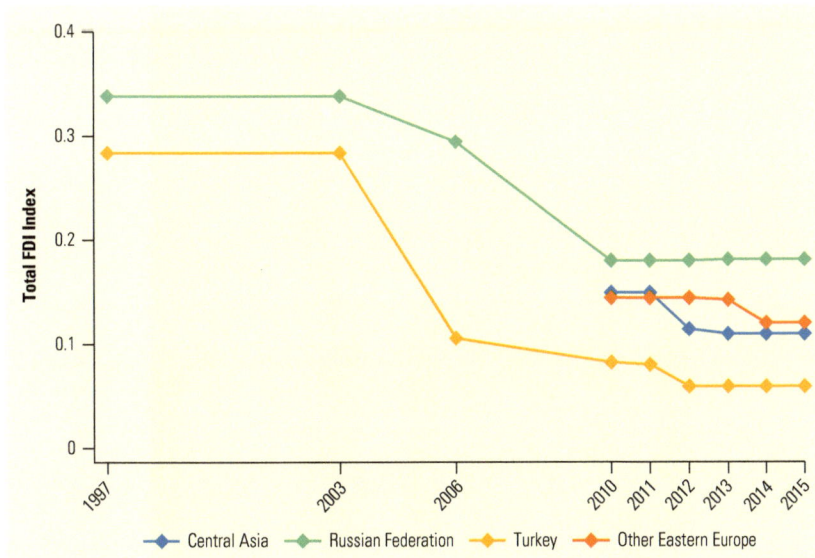

FIGURE 7.7 **FDIRRI in ECA subregion II**

Note: ECA = Europe and Central Asia; FDIRRI = Foreign Direct Investment Regulatory Restrictiveness Index.

services appear to be of a significantly greater magnitude. It is also worth noticing how the two subregions Central Asia and Other Eastern Europe tend to out-perform Russia and Turkey in terms of openness toward FDI in transport services (see 2015 data in figure 7.10).

FIGURE 7.8 FDIRRI in ECA
countries by income group

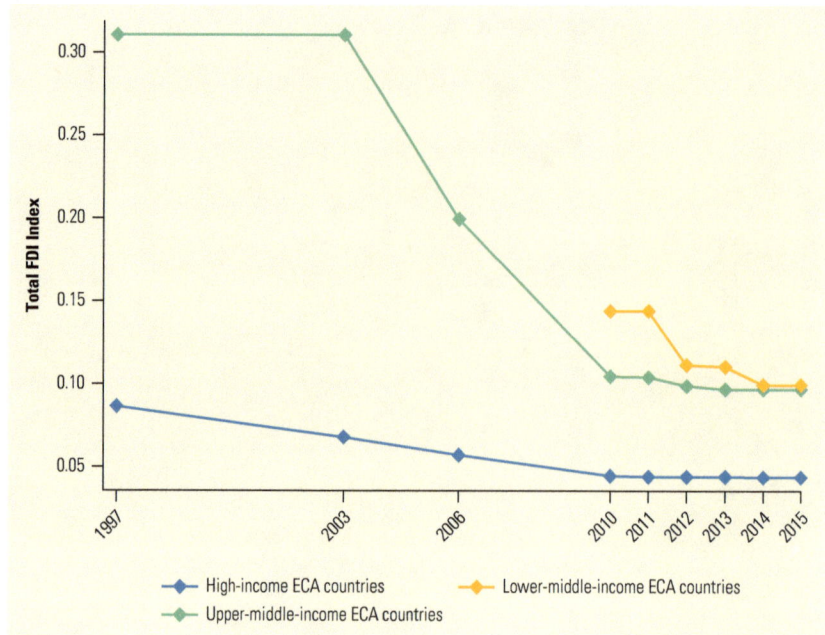

Note: ECA = Europe and Central Asia; FDIRRI = Foreign Direct Investment Regulatory Restrictiveness
Index.

FIGURE 7.9 FDIRRI for
communications and
transport in ECA and
selected countries

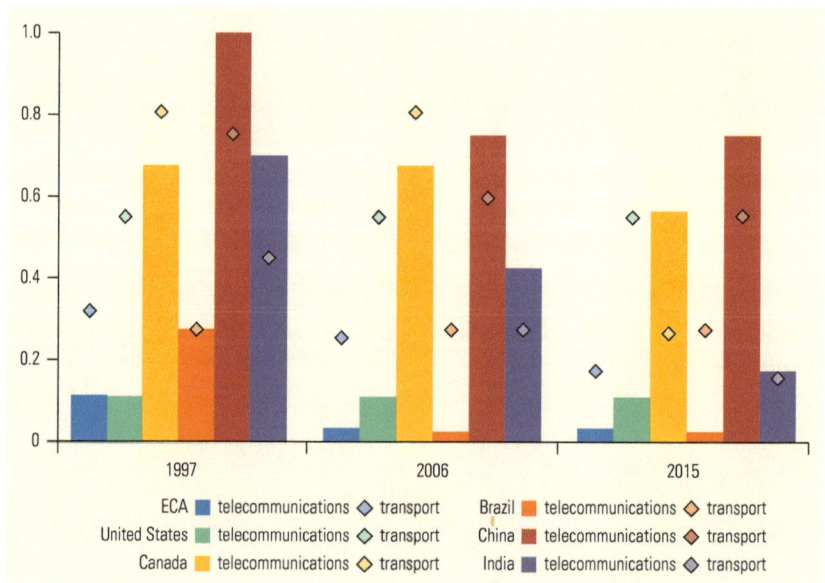

Note: ECA = Europe and Central Asia; FDIRRI = Foreign Direct Investment Regulatory Restrictiveness
Index.

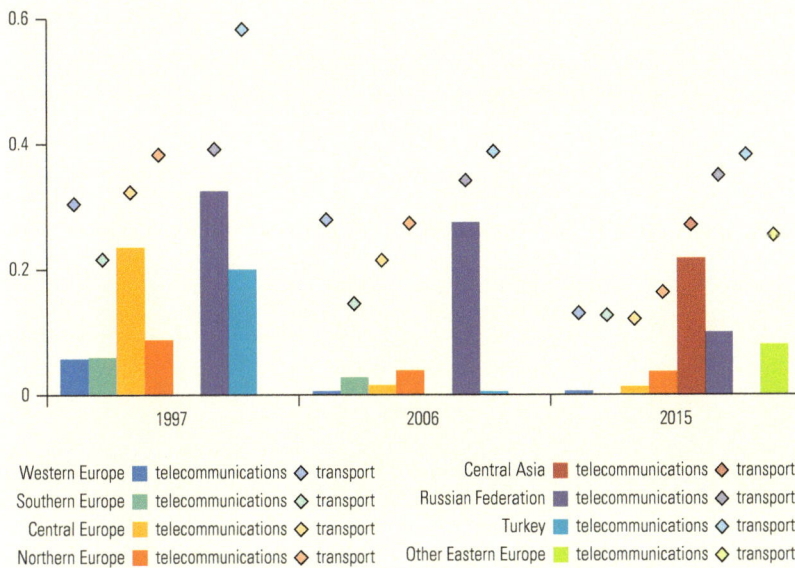

FIGURE 7.10 FDIRRI for communications and transport in ECA subregions

Note: ECA = Europe and Central Asia; FDIRRI = Foreign Direct Investment Regulatory Restrictiveness Index.

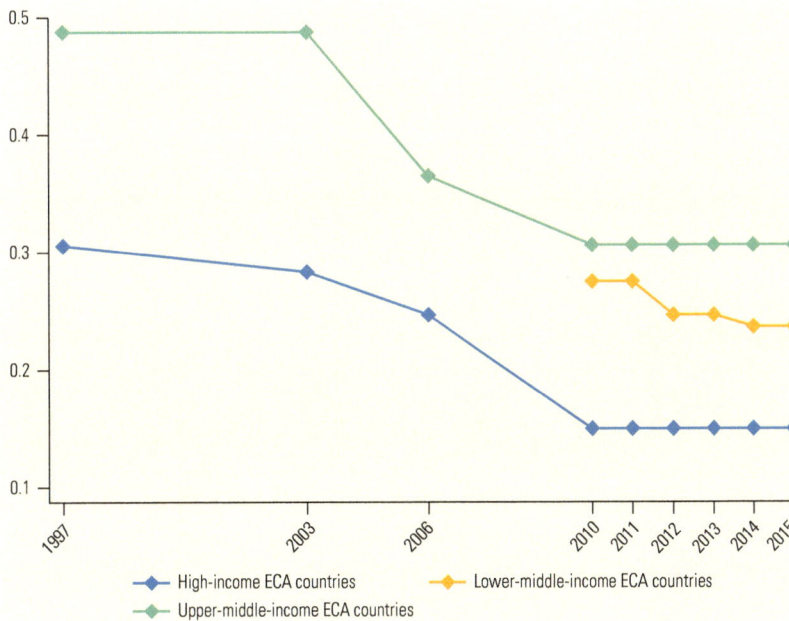

FIGURE 7.11 FDIRRI for transport in ECA countries by income group

Note: ECA = Europe and Central Asia; FDIRRI = Foreign Direct Investment Regulatory Restrictiveness Index.

FIGURE 7.12 FDIRRI for communications in ECA countries by income group

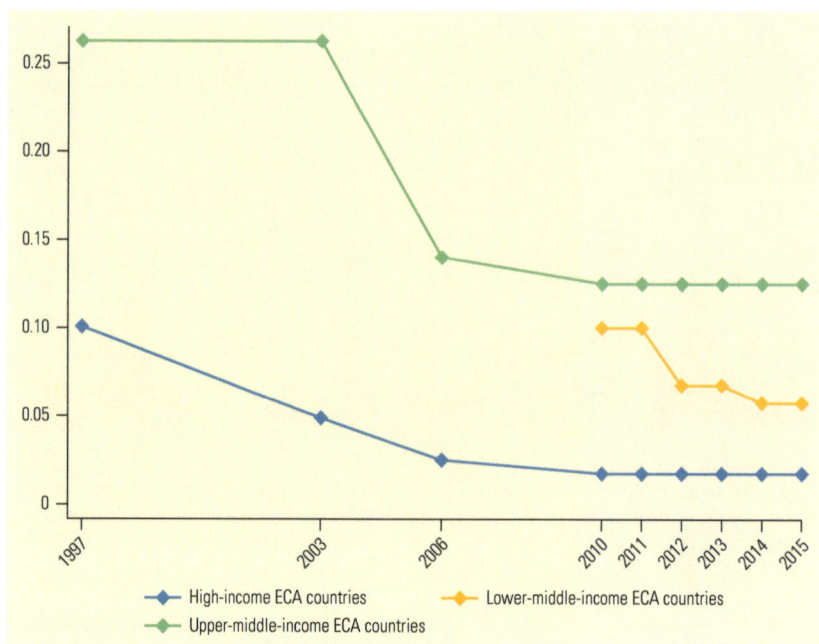

Note: ECA = Europe and Central Asia; FDIRRI = Foreign Direct Investment Regulatory Restrictiveness Index.

Preferential Trade Agreements

The number of PTAs a country has concluded is an important country-specific measure of policy toward integration and (regional) connectivity. As discussed in the introduction, PTAs are instruments to lower trade costs of a regulatory nature, as well as mechanisms to remove MFN tariffs for trade among the partners. The data that follow simply show the existence of PTAs and do not consider the coverage or depth of the PTAs. This is obviously a very important factor from a connectivity and integration perspective. Ideally, we would like to weight PTAs according to how comprehensive they are and the degree to which they are binding (enforceable). We use a simple count measure here to avoid subjective assessments of which PTAs are more "serious" than others. Analysis of the depth of PTAs is addressed in a World Bank project that comprehensively codes the content of PTAs (Hofmann, Osnago, and Ruta 2017). This permits deeper analysis of the differences across countries in this regard and their effects—a task that is not undertaken here. As a rule of thumb, PTAs between HICs tend to be more comprehensive than PTAs between developing countries. Agreements with the EU as a partner will always cover NTMs as well as tariffs, but they vary substantially in terms of coverage of services trade and investment policies and public procurement. Chapter 3 considers the impact of deep PTAs on attracting FDI.

We construct a measure of the intensity of the use of PTAs from the database on PTAs compiled by the World Bank (see Hofmann, Osnago, and Ruta 2017). ECA stands out as the region with the highest use of PTAs. In the period 2000–15, ECA countries on average were members of almost 20 PTAs that were in force

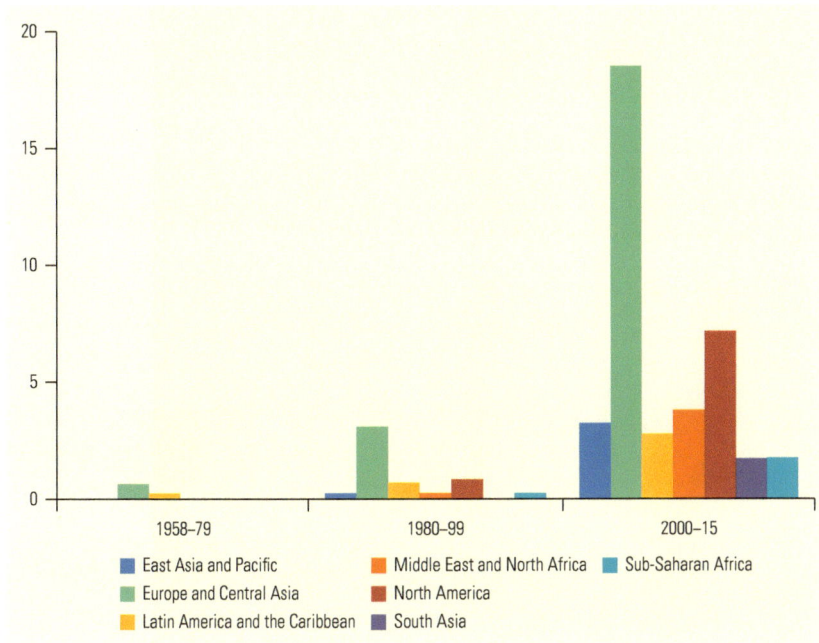

FIGURE 7.13 Preferential
trade agreements across
global regions
*Number of enforced
preferential trade
agreements*

(implemented) (see figure 7.13 plotting the number of enforced PTAs averaged across countries within each region and across years within each period). This comparative pattern with respect to other regions holds across intra- and extraregional integration as shown respectively in figure 7.14 and figure 7.15. European countries are market leaders in their pursuit of regional integration: the average score of ECA countries dwarfs those of all other regions.

The aggregate policy performance of ECA hides important heterogeneity across subregions and income groups. The rapid pace toward greater regional integration has been driven by EU member states plus—to a lesser extent—Turkey and Russia (see figure 7.16). The growth in Russian PTAs during the last period is a reflection of the demise of the former Soviet Union and the creation of the CIS and associated new PTAs. From an income group perspective PTAs are dominated by HICs (figure 7.17), but the average number of PTAs signed by upper- and lower-middle-income ECA countries is always higher than for other regions, with the exception of North America. One reason for the spike in HIC PTAs is the decision by the EU to reengage in PTA negotiations in 2006, following the adoption of the 2006 Global Europe communication, which removed a de facto moratorium on new PTAs in favor of cooperation through the WTO.

As shown in figures 7.18 and 7.19, all non-EU ECA subregions except for Turkey and—from an income perspective—LMICs, have signed PTAs only with other ECA countries. EU countries were the leading actors in extraregional PTA integration at the end of the 1970s, but their pursuit of extraregional integration accelerated substantially since the mid-1990s. The result is an equal distribution of PTAs within and beyond the ECA region in 2015.

FIGURE 7.14 Preferential trade agreements across global regions: Intraregional integration
Number of enforced preferential trade agreements within the region

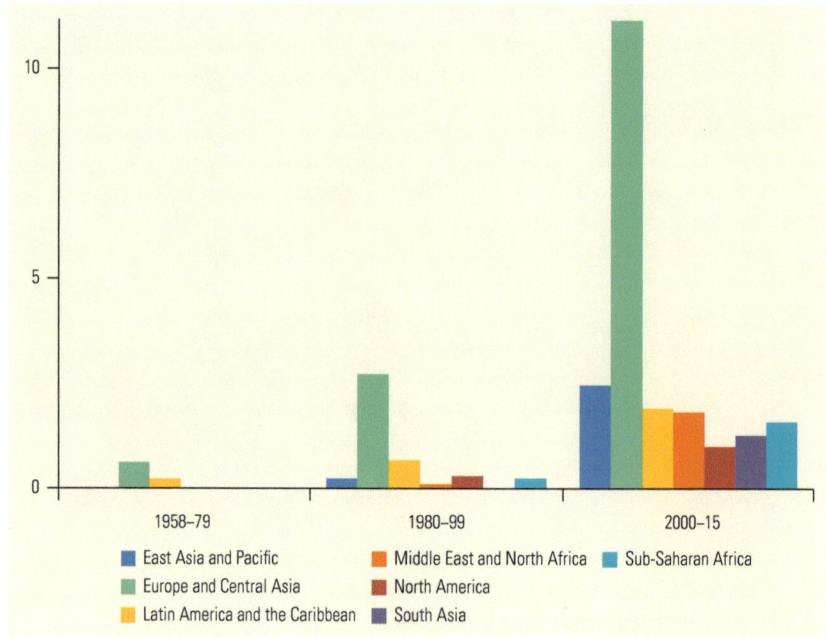

FIGURE 7.15 Preferential trade agreements across global regions: Extraregional integration
Number of enforced preferential trade agreements beyond the region

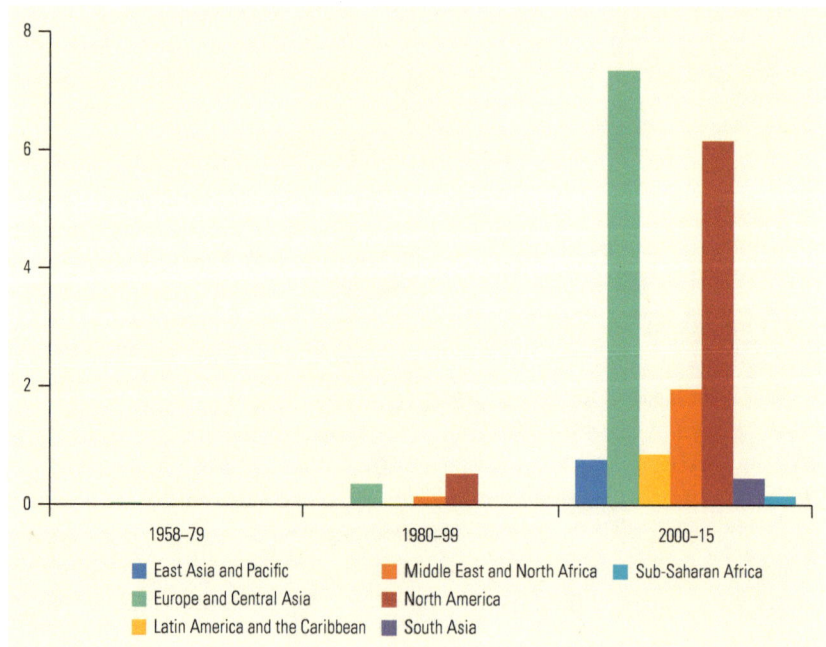

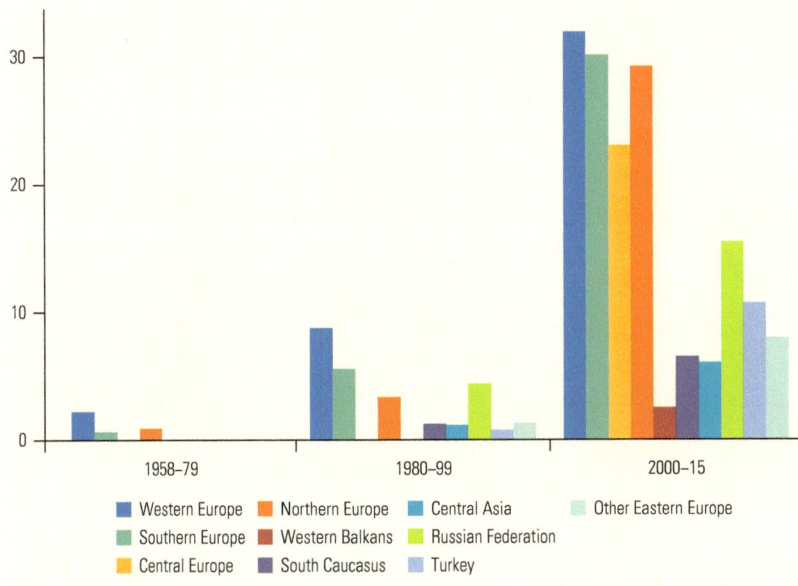

FIGURE 7.16 Preferential trade agreements in ECA subregions
Number of enforced preferential trade agreements

Legend:
- Western Europe
- Southern Europe
- Central Europe
- Northern Europe
- Western Balkans
- South Caucasus
- Central Asia
- Russian Federation
- Turkey
- Other Eastern Europe

Note: ECA = Europe and Central Asia.

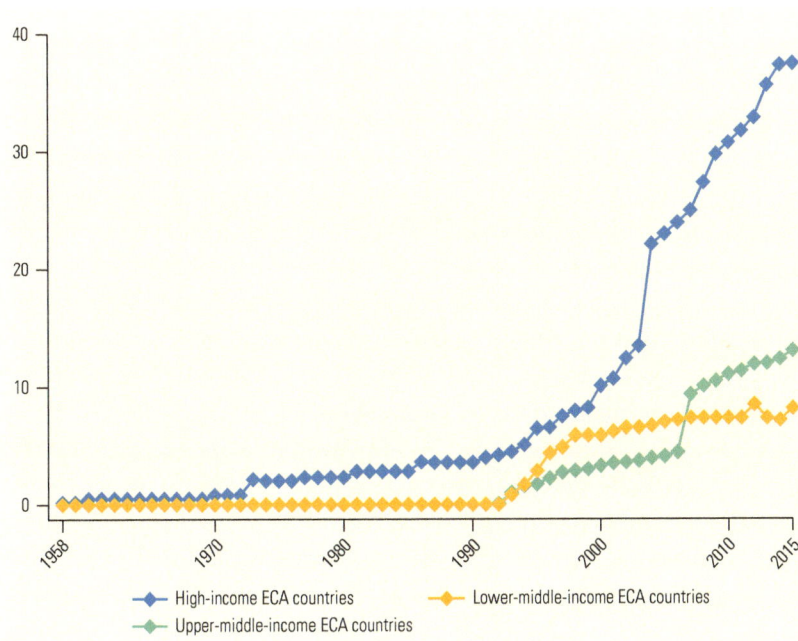

FIGURE 7.17 Preferential trade agreements in ECA countries by income group
Number of enforced preferential trade agreements

Legend:
- High-income ECA countries
- Upper-middle-income ECA countries
- Lower-middle-income ECA countries

Note: ECA = Europe and Central Asia.

FIGURE 7.18 Preferential
trade agreements in ECA
subregions: Intra- versus
extraregional integration
*Percentage of enforced
preferential trade agrements
with ECA countries*

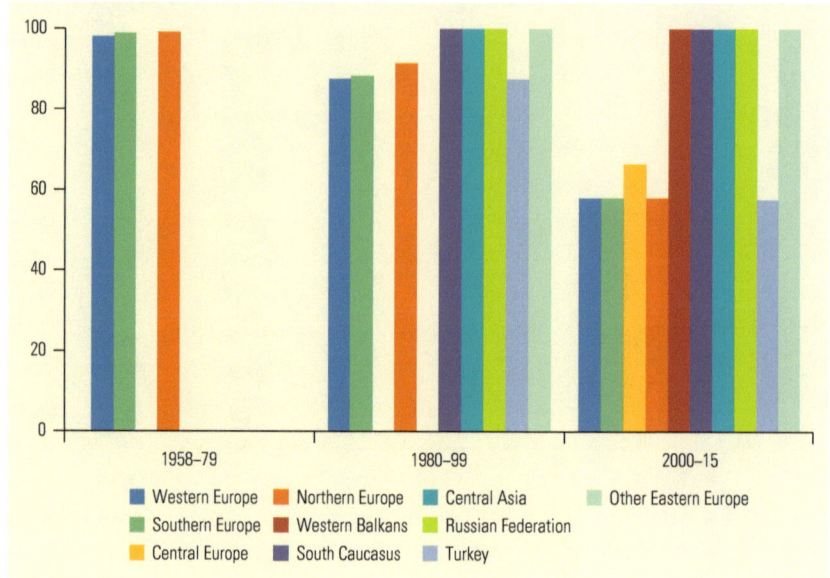

Note: ECA = Europe and Central Asia.

FIGURE 7.19 Preferential
trade agreements in ECA
countries by income group:
Intra- versus extraregional
integration
*Percentage of enforced
preferential trade
agreements with ECA
countries*

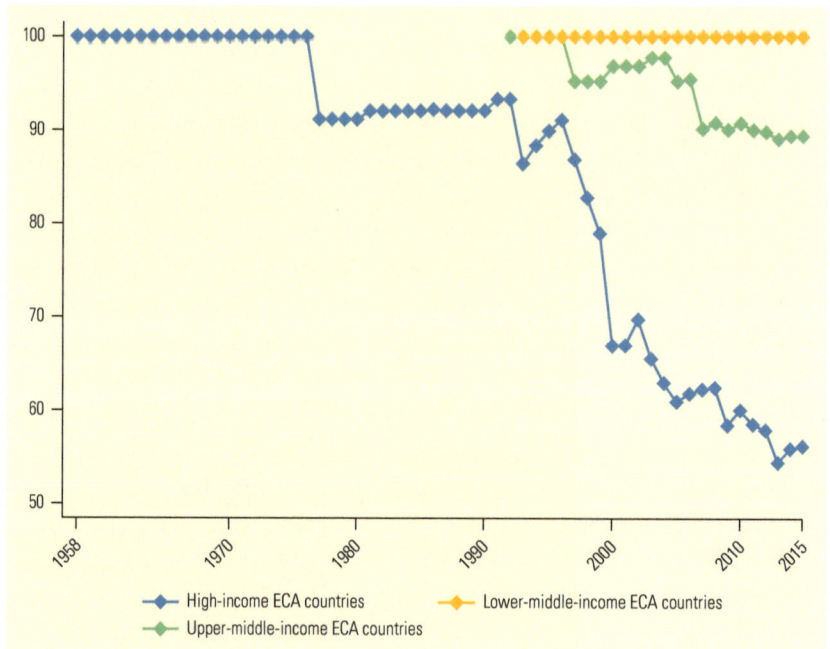

Note: ECA = Europe and Central Asia.

Bilateral Investment Agreements

Similar patterns to those observed for PTAs emerge when looking at BITs.
The descriptive analysis in this section relies on the UNCTAD investment hub database, which includes some 3,000 BITs.[7] Investment agreements are instruments to
reduce uncertainty for foreign investors regarding the policy environment they will
confront after investing and that provide investors with security that they will be

given fair and equitable treatment and not be expropriated without obtaining adequate compensation. In general, there is a great deal of commonality across most BITs in terms of substantive obligations.

This has been changing in recent years following public concern regarding the use (perceived abuse) of arbitration to address disputes between investors and host governments regarding actions by governments that are deemed by investors to violate the provisions of the BIT. The major developments in this area have been quite recent and center on the allocation of responsibility for BITs to the European Commission (as opposed to the member states) and the EU decision in 2016 to shift away from providing for arbitration to settle disputes toward the use of an investment court system.

Figure 7.20 plots regional averages for the number of enforced BITs a country in the region is part of (averaged across years in three periods). ECA emerges as the first region in terms of integration though the BIT as a policy tool. Looking at the average number of enforced BITs with other countries in the same region and in other regions, respectively, it is apparent how ECA's leading position is driven by intraregional integration (figures 7.21 and 7.22). Indeed, almost 60 percent of all BITs signed by the average ECA country involve a partner in ECA.

Figure 7.23 reveals a shift from almost zero use of BITs in the first period to a policy stance in which the average ECA country is a partner in almost 50 BITs on average between 2000 and 2016. With the exception of Western Europe clearly anticipating these patterns, the transition phase started at the beginning of the 1990s and finished at the end of the first decade of the 2000s for all ECA subregions. After that, the average number of BITs is rather constant, with the resulting policy steady states spanning a range from a minimum of 30 BITs signed on average in Central Asia to a maximum of almost 80 in Western Europe. Figure 7.24

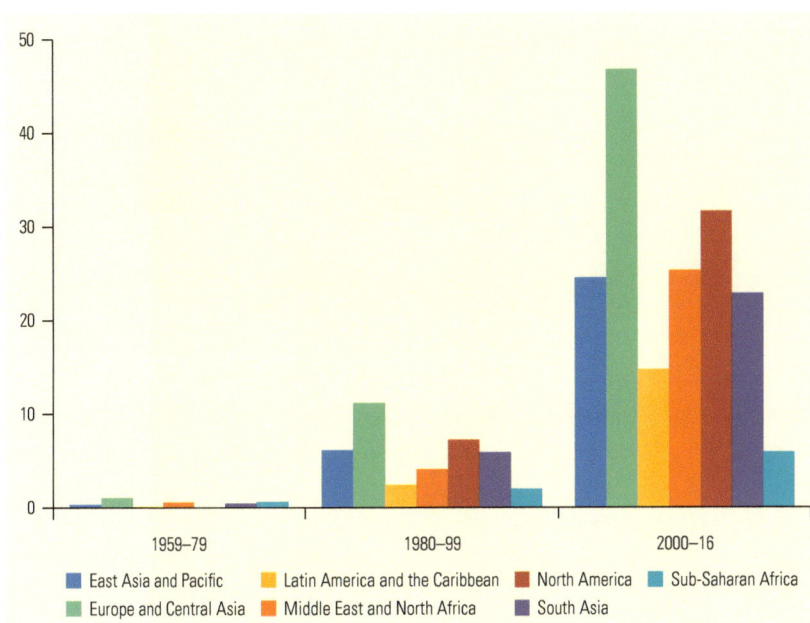

FIGURE 7.20 Bilateral investment treaties across global regions
Number of enforced bilateral investment treaties

FIGURE 7.21 Bilateral
investment treaties across
global regions:
Intraregional integration
*Number of enforced bilateral
investment treaties within the
region*

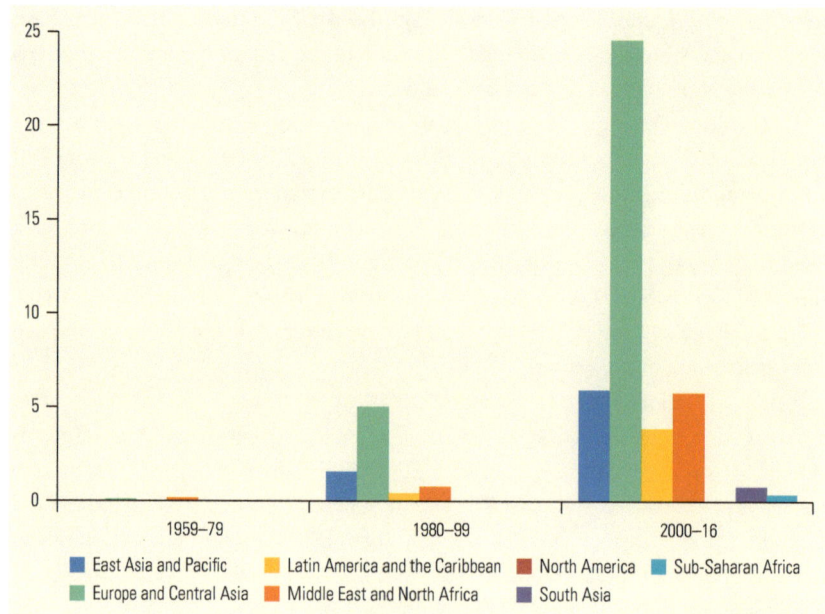

FIGURE 7.22 Bilateral
investment treaties across
global regions:
Extraregional integration
*Number of bilateral
investment treaties beyond
the region*

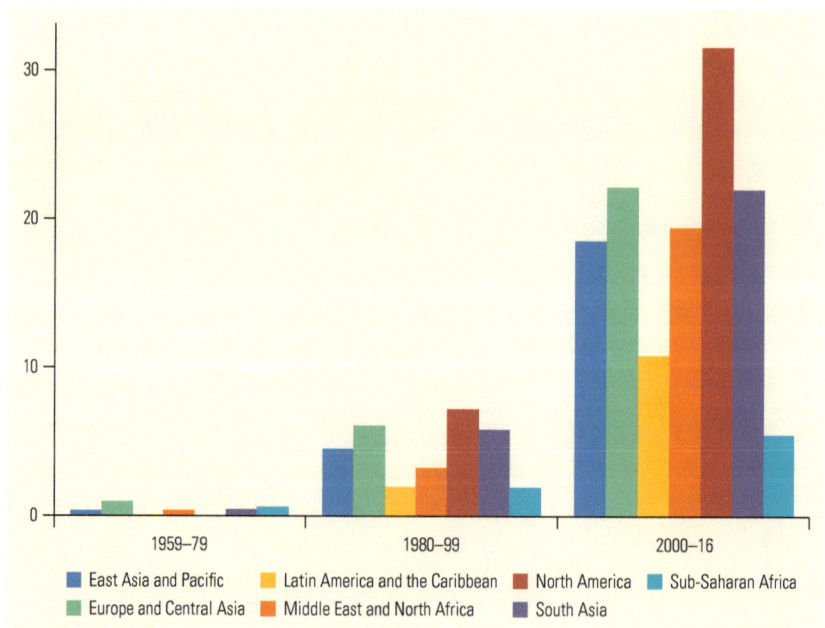

summarizes these patterns showing that an anticipated transition and a higher
steady-state level of integration characterizes the average ECA HIC with respect
to the average UMIC and LMIC.

As for intra- versus extra-ECA integration, Western and Northern Europe and
HICs show a clear pattern from disproportionate extraregional use of BIT toward a
rather balanced mix of intra- and extraregional integration (see figure 7.25 and
figure 7.26). When considering the average HIC in ECA, half of its BITs are signed

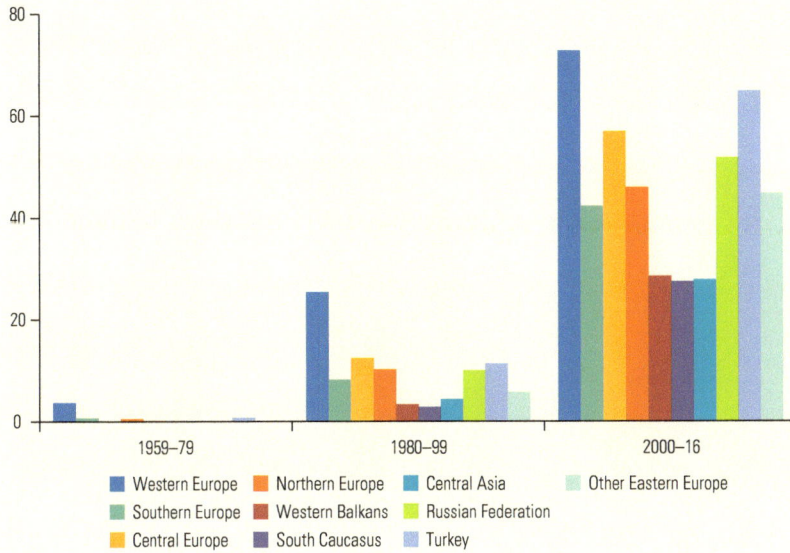

FIGURE 7.23 Bilateral investment treaties in ECA subregions
Number of enforced bilateral investment treaties

Note: ECA = Europe and Central Asia.

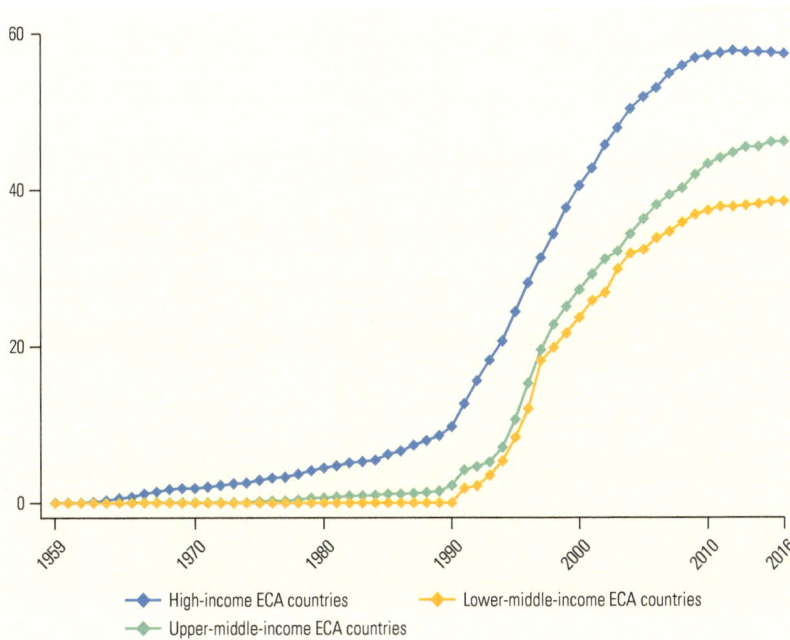

FIGURE 7.24 Bilateral investment treaties in ECA countries by income group
Number of enforced bilateral investment treaties

Note: ECA = Europe and Central Asia.

with other ECA countries and half with non-ECA ones. Similar balanced stances are reached by Southern and Central Europe as well as by Turkey and Russia with the difference that they were starting from a disproportionate intraregional use of the BIT policy tool. A rather strong average bias toward intraregional BITs is apparent for the Western Balkans, the South Caucasus, Central Asia, Other Eastern Europe, and, from the perspective of income categories, for both UMICs and LMICs.

FIGURE 7.25 Bilateral
investment treaties in ECA
subregions: Intra- versus
extraregional integration
*Percentage of enforced
bilateral investment treaties
with ECA countries*

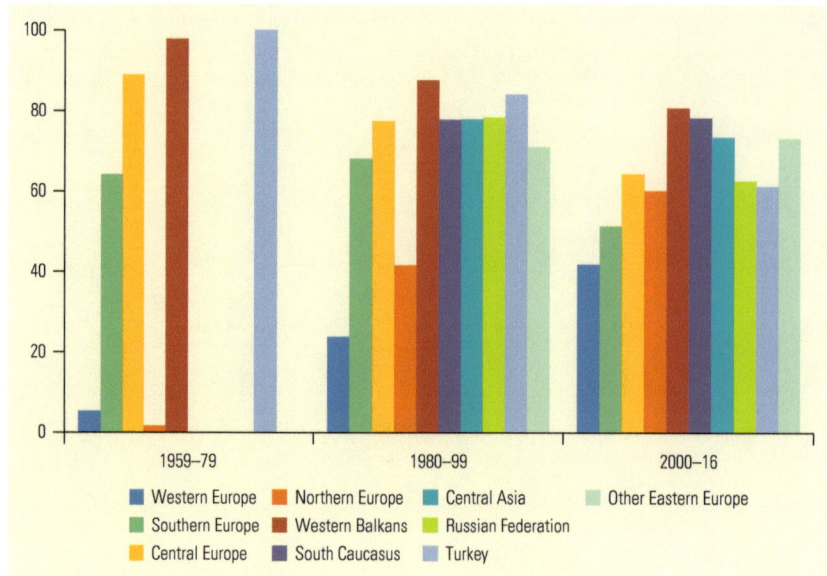

Note: ECA = Europe and Central Asia.

FIGURE 7.26 Bilateral trade
agreements in ECA countries
by income group: Intra-
versus extraregional
integration
*Percentage of enforced
bilateral investment treaties
with ECA countries*

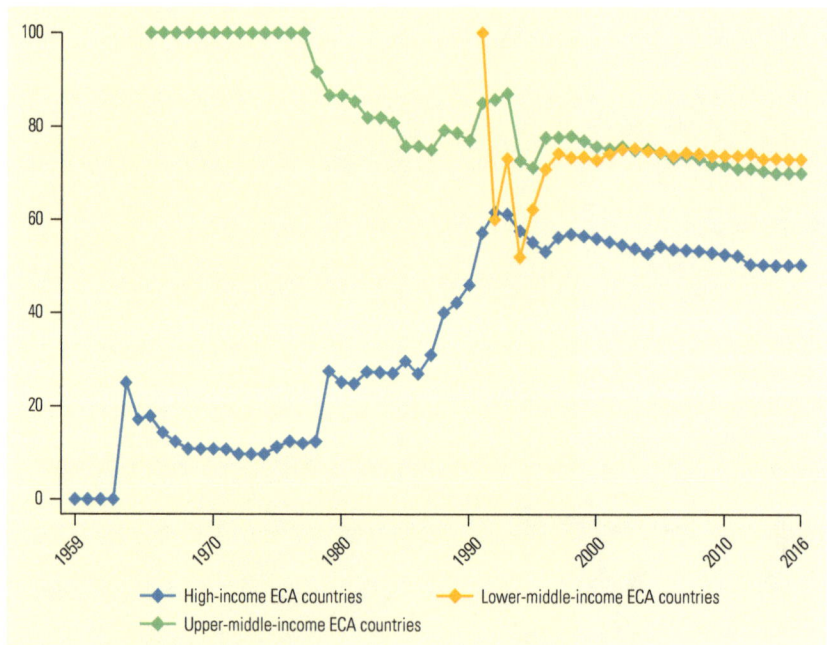

Note: ECA = Europe and Central Asia.

Product Market Regulation

This section provides some descriptive evidence on the patterns characterizing domestic PMR and regulatory reforms over time that are potentially relevant for various dimensions of connectivity. It discusses indicators of PMR developed by the OECD, focusing both on horizontal and sectoral regulation. The broader economy-wide regulation of product markets is relevant from a connectivity dimension—for example, the role of the state in the economy and the extent to which regulatory regimes impede entry into sectors by new firms. If a country has relatively closed markets internally, this will have an impact on external connectivity by affecting international competitiveness. Moreover, as discussed in the introduction, horizontal regulation and the quality of economic governance in a country have been found to determine the effect of efforts to integrate economies with the rest of the world. More directly relevant to connectivity is sectoral regulation of activities that directly affect connectivity and trade costs: regulation of entry into and the operation of energy, transport, and telecommunications network industries. We also present data on the use of product standards by ECA and comparator countries, focusing on the extent to which countries notify the WTO regarding standards that diverge from international norms. These data provide an indication of the degree to which countries adopt international standards and participate in the WTO.

Product Market Regulation: Aggregate "Horizontal" Indicators

The data used in this subsection come from the PMR Economy Wide database, which contains measures of the degree of policy restrictiveness implied by domestic regulatory regimes. More precisely, it captures horizontal barriers to entrepreneurship, barriers to trade and investment, and barriers embedded in the scope and nature of state control of the economy. All indicators range from 0 (no restrictions) to 6 (maximum restrictiveness). As with other OECD databases, the country coverage of the ECA region is not complete—there is no consistent information on the Western Balkans, the South Caucasus, Central Asia, Other Eastern Europe, and Russia. The time dimension of the data consists of four observations: 1998, 2003, 2008, and 2013.

Figure 7.27 plots the values of PMR Economy Wide overall score (horizontal PMR) for the average covered ECA country and compares it with the same score in a number of selected non-ECA countries (China and India are not observed at the beginning of the sample while the United States is not observed for 2013). While relatively less restrictive than Brazil, China, and India, the average ECA country imposes higher restrictions than either Canada or the United States. Moreover, figure 7.27 reveals a very slow pace of policy progress for the average ECA country (especially between 2008 and 2013).

A low degree of policy progress appears also across available subregions in ECA, in particular for Western and Northern Europe since 2008 (figure 7.28). This pattern is reflected in the almost negligible change between the 2008 score for HICs and the 2013 one (figure 7.29).

Product Market Regulation: Sectoral Indicators

This subsection uses a different PMR database denoted as the PMR ETCR database. PMR ETCR contains annual measures of the degree of policy restrictiveness implied by domestic regulatory regimes for specific sectors (energy, transport,

FIGURE 7.27 Horizontal product market regulation in ECA and selected countries
Index, 0 (least restrictive) to 6 (most restrictive)

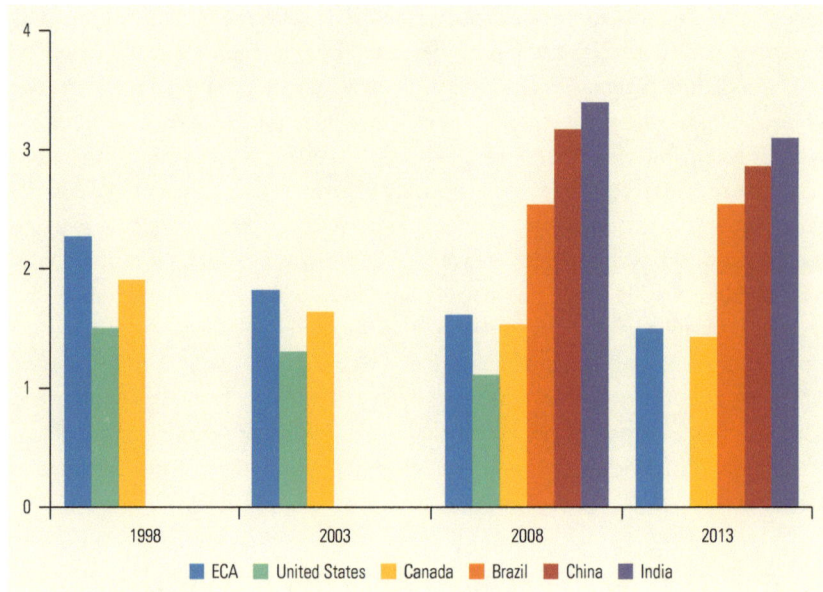

Note: ECA = Europe and Central Asia.

FIGURE 7.28 Horizontal product market regulation in ECA subregions
Index, 0 (least restrictive) to 6 (most restrictive)

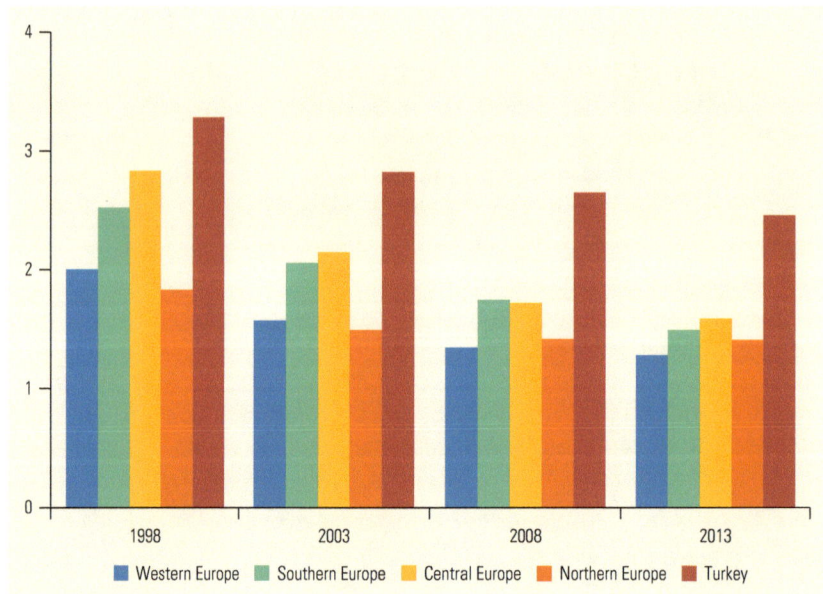

Note: ECA = Europe and Central Asia.

and communications) from 1975 to 2013. As was true for the economy-wide PMR, indicators range from 0 (no restrictions) to 6 (maximum restrictiveness). The country coverage of the ECA region is again limited.

Figure 7.30 plots the PMR ETCR overall score for the average covered ECA country as well as for a number of selected non-ECA countries (China, India, and the United States are not observed at the beginning of the sample).

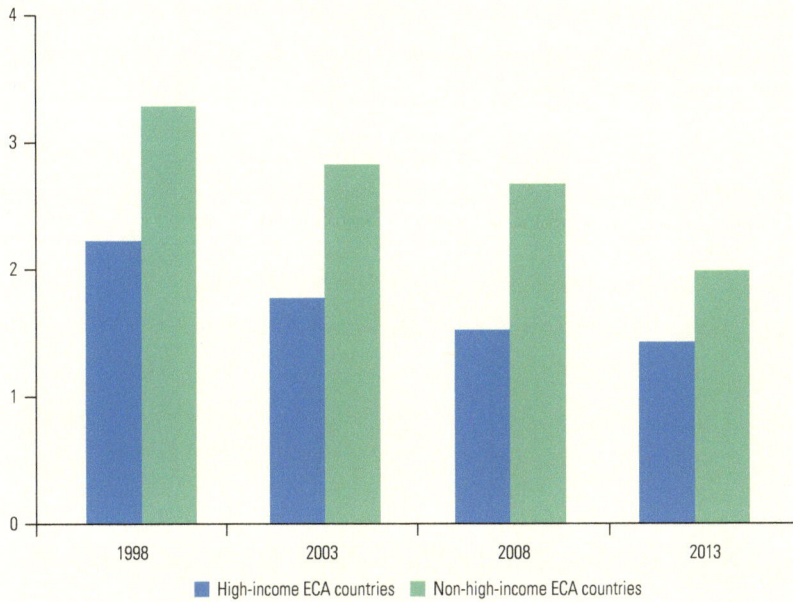

FIGURE 7.29 Horizontal product market regulation in ECA countries by income group
Index, 0 (least restrictive) to 6 (most restrictive)

Note: ECA = Europe and Central Asia.

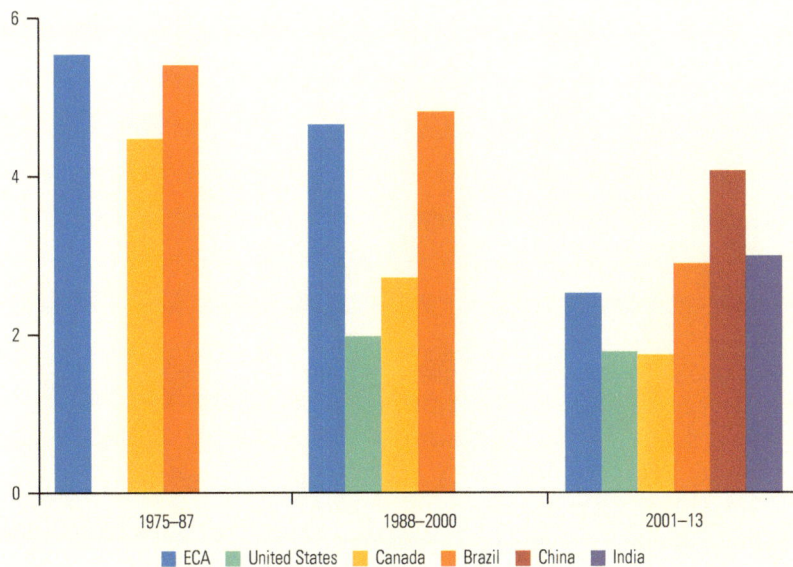

FIGURE 7.30 Product market regulation: Aggregate energy, transport, and communications regulations in ECA and selected countries
Index, 0 (least restrictive) to 6 (most restrictive)

Note: ECA = Europe and Central Asia.

Figure 7.30 reveals that in terms of PMRs the average ECA country is always more restrictive than either Canada or the United States. Moreover, a halt in policy progress is observed at the end of the sample for the average ECA country.

Figures 7.31–7.34 plot the average score for PMR ETCR aggregate (time series), airlines, rail, and telecoms (averages across periods) in a number of ECA subregions. Available data confirm a number of general policy patterns. The data reveal a phase of policy progress across all sectors and all covered country groups

FIGURE 7.31 Product
market regulation:
Aggregate energy,
transport, and
communications regulations
in ECA subregions
*Index, 0 (least restrictive) to 6
(most restrictive)*

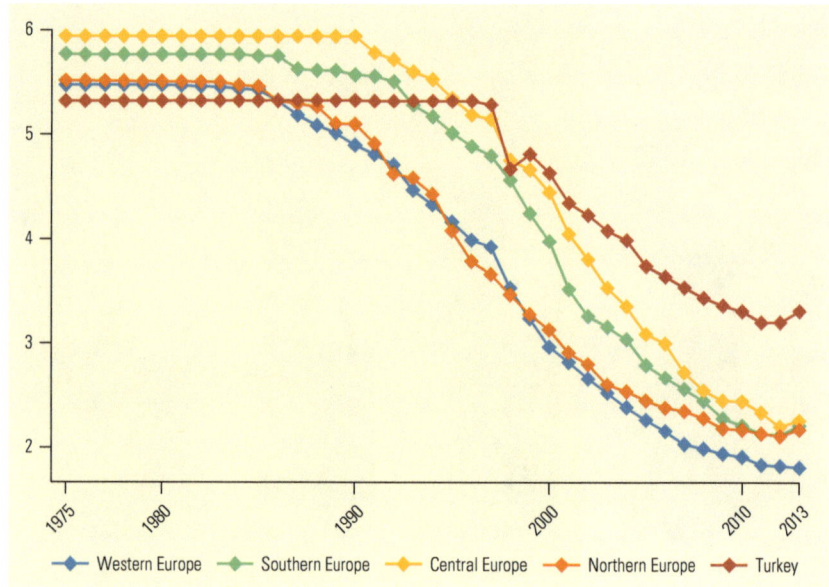

Note: ECA = Europe and Central Asia.

FIGURE 7.32 Product
market regulation:
Regulations regarding
airlines in ECA subregions
*Index, 0 (least restrictive) to 6
(most restrictive)*

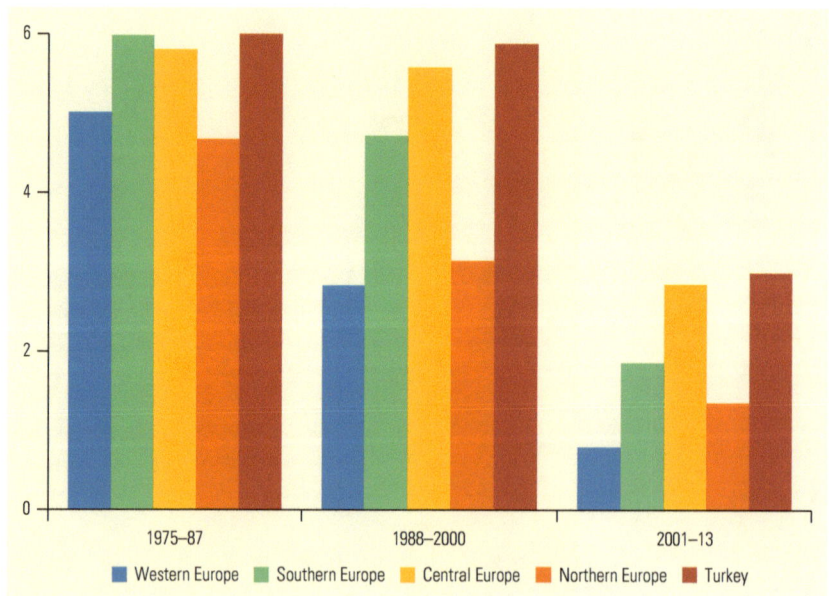

Note: ECA = Europe and Central Asia.

(with the notable exception of Turkey in the rail sector). The removal of regulatory
restrictions began in the early 1990s and in many cases stopped toward the end
of the first decade of the 2000s. Looking at the aggregate ETCR scores in figure
7.31, a small increase in restrictiveness can be observed for all subregions except
Western Europe. As shown in figure 7.35, this pattern seems to be driven by policies in HICs.

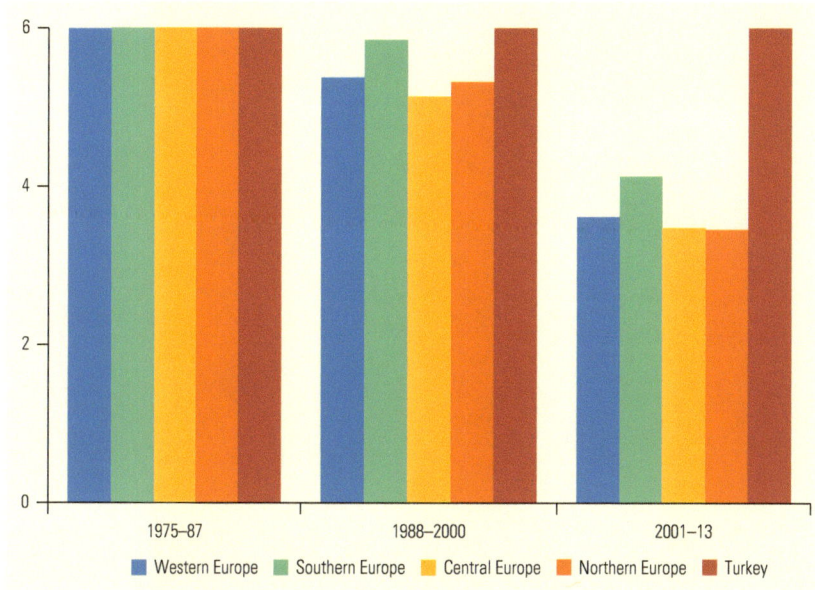

FIGURE 7.33 Product market regulation: Regulations involving railways in ECA subregions
Index, 0 (least restrictive) to 6 (most restrictive)

Note: ECA = Europe and Central Asia.

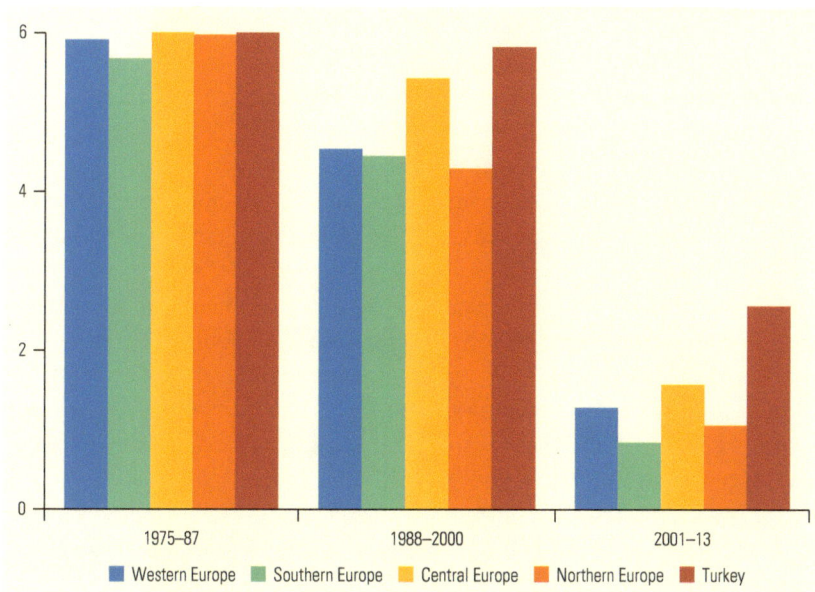

FIGURE 7.34 Product market regulation: Regulations regarding telecommunications in ECA subregions
Index, 0 (least restrictive) to 6 (most restrictive)

Note: ECA = Europe and Central Asia.

Product Market Regulation: SPS and TBT Notifications to the WTO

A final dimension of PMR that is relevant to connectivity and trade costs is convergence of national standards regimes with those prevailing internationally. There are two major types of national product standards that affect international trade and investment: health and safety norms for plants, animals, and humans—so-called sanitary and phytosanitary (SPS) measures and safety standards for

FIGURE 7.35 **Product market regulation: Aggregate energy, transport, and communications regulations in ECA countries by income group**
Index, 0 (least restrictive) to 6 (most restrictive)

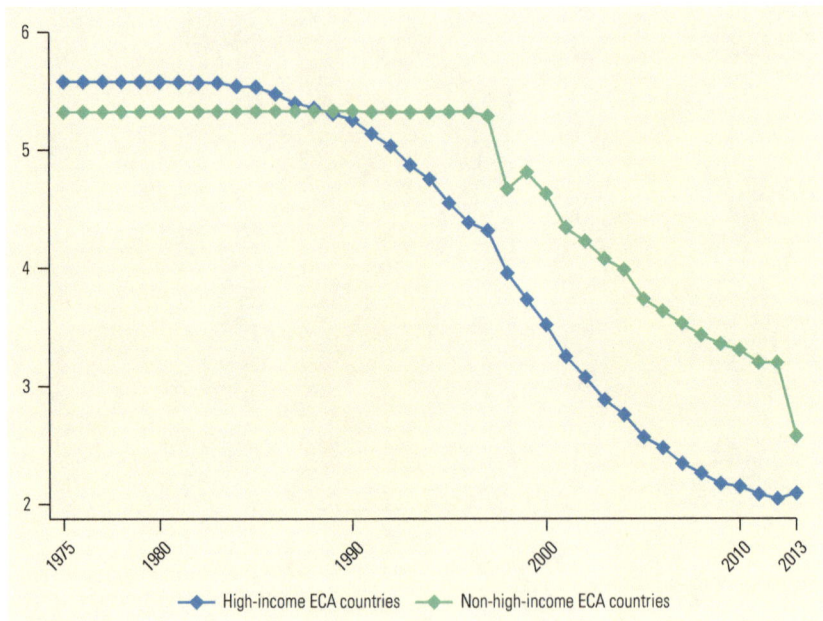

Note: ECA = Europe and Central Asia.

nonfood products—so-called technical product regulations, called technical barriers to trade (TBT) in the WTO. The WTO has specific disciplines that apply to the use of both SPS and TBT measures, including provisions that call on WTO members to adopt international standards if they exist and to notify regarding new proposed standards that may have an impact on trade and that are not based on internationally agreed-upon norms.

Figures 7.36 and 7.37 show descriptive evidence on the number of notifications of SPS and TBT measures by countries (data on notifications are taken from the WTO). More precisely, the two figures report averages across WTO member countries within groups averaged across years within three seven-year periods starting in 1995 (the year the WTO was established). Observe that for all WTO members as a whole (the "world") the number of notifications of SPS and TBT measures has been increasing steadily since 1995, especially in the most recent period (2010–17). This increase over time is an indication of the increasing prevalence of this type of NTM, although, as noted in the introduction, it does not necessarily reflect a desire to discriminate against foreign suppliers. What the data do reveal is that the EU and other WTO members make relatively more frequent use of standards that are not based on international norms—or adopt standards for which no internationally agreed-upon norms exist. The EU is the only part of ECA that notifies the WTO extensively—other ECA countries notify much less than the world (WTO-member) average. That said, Russia and Turkey have notified the WTO regarding more standards in recent years, whereas ECA countries that acceded to the EU in 2004 stopped notifying the WTO after accession, reflecting the fact that this is an EU competence (part of the common commercial policy).

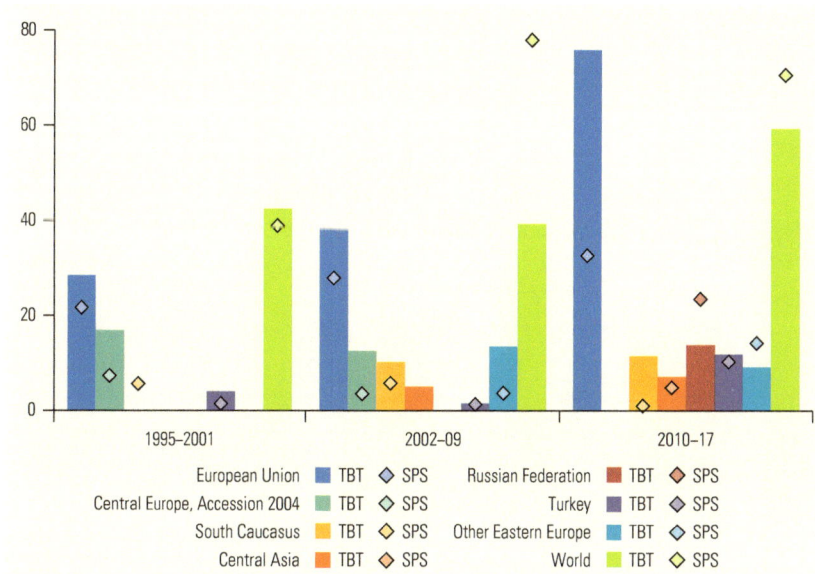

FIGURE 7.36 Technical barriers to trade and sanitary and phytosanitary notifications in ECA
Average annual number of notifications

Note: ECA = Europe and Central Asia; SPS = sanitary and phytosanitary; TBT = technical barriers to trade.

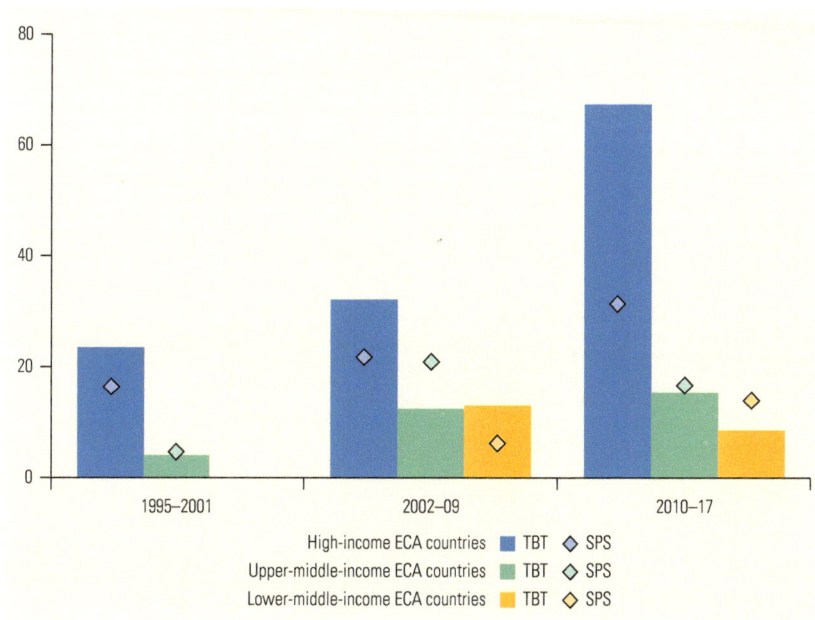

FIGURE 7.37 Technical barriers to trade and sanitary and phytosanitary notifications in ECA across income regions
Average annual number of notifications

Note: ECA = Europe and Central Asia; SPS = sanitary and phytosanitary; TBT = technical barriers to trade.

EBRD Transition Indicators

Domestic policy reforms in the former Soviet Union countries across both Europe and the Western Balkans and the Eastern ECA regions (often missing from the PMR coverage) can be analyzed empirically using the Transition Indicators Database developed and managed by the EBRD. This database contains a number of horizontal as well as sector-specific policy variables capturing the degree of transition from the policy stance in 1989. Each indicator takes the reference value of 1 in 1989. In subsequent years, indicators vary between 1 (no progress) and 4 (OECD policy standard).

Among the various indicators in the database, we report a simple average of the scores for five infrastructural sectors: electric power, railways, roads, telecommunications, and water and wastewater. Figure 7.38 plots the average scores for this aggregate indicator for different ECA subregions; figure 7.39 reports the average scores for each income group.

Former Soviet Union countries in Central and Northern Europe appear to be pioneers of transition with a steep increase in their scores from the beginning of the sample until the end of the 1990s. Since the early 2000s the pace of domestic reforms for these two groups slowed significantly, entering a slower but still positive trend of policy effort. The trend becomes flat in the second half of the 2000s for the average member of the Central Europe subregion, suggesting a stop in policy progress at levels of domestic governance still below the OECD standard.

An overall trend of policy progress emerges across all other subregions, but the usual pattern of heterogeneous policy stances holds for transition indicators as well. The distance from the OECD policy standard for the average country in Central Asia is four times the distance of the average country in Central or Northern Europe. The pattern of transition toward heterogeneous policy frameworks is confirmed when adopting an income perspective in defining subsets of countries: HICs reach higher standards in terms of domestic governance of infrastructural sectors, followed in order by UMICs and LMICs, which are relatively close to each other.

FIGURE 7.38 Aggregate EBRD Transition Indicators for infrastructure in ECA subregions

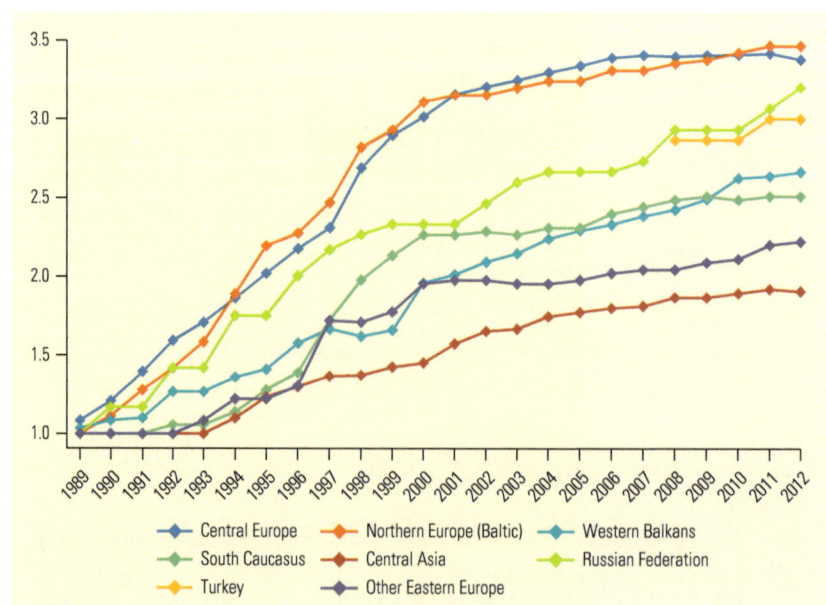

Note: EBRD = European Bank for Reconstruction and Development; ECA = Europe and Central Asia.

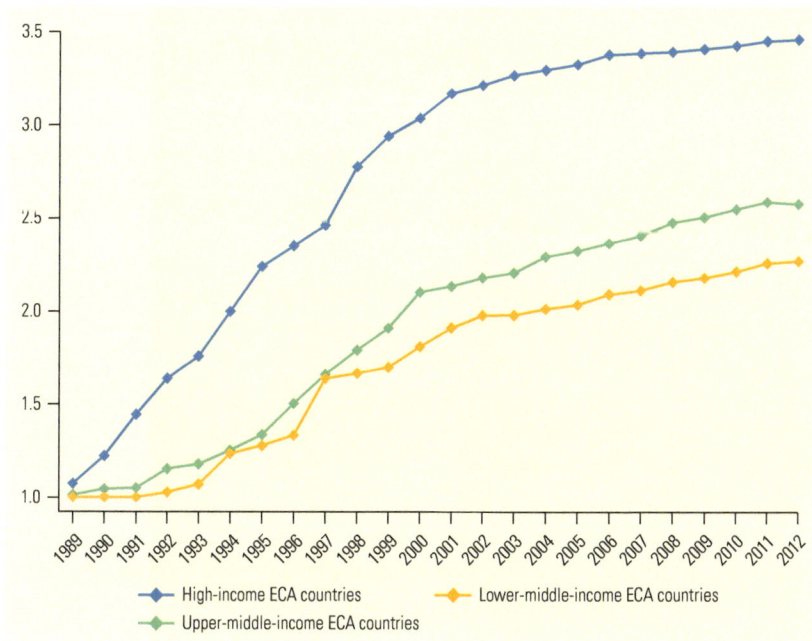

FIGURE 7.39 Aggregate EBRD Transition Indicators for infrastructure in ECA countries by income group

Note: EBRD = European Bank for Reconstruction and Development; ECA = Europe and Central Asia.

Policy Comovements—Are Policies Consistent?

This ECA flagship report establishes that balanced connectivity is an important driver of growth. Being connected along one dimension, for example, trade, is not enough to enhance growth; countries need to be connected in many dimensions to exploit complementarities between different types of connections that can enhance economic growth. This section explores whether connectivity-related policies move in the same direction within countries across time. The exercise can be interpreted as an evaluation of the extent to which countries are coherent in their policies, for example, if a country decreases tariffs over time, does it tend also to reduce barriers to mobility or lessen the restrictiveness of policies toward FDI?

We consider the connectivity-related policies discussed in the foregoing sections, plus policies on mobility restrictions and migrant integration (from chapter 4) for up to 200 countries, depending on data availability. The indicators span the simple average MFN import tariff (denoted as Tariff); the number of PTAs to which each country belongs; the average value of the horizontal and sectoral OECD PMR indicators (PMR_H and PMR_S); a measure of policies of immigrant integration—the Migrant Integration Policy Index (MIPEX); a measure of statutory restrictions on FDI; the average of several EBRD transition indicators that measure reform progress toward best practices observed in industrial market economies; the number of BITs signed by each country; and a measure of restrictiveness of visa requirements imposed by each country, the Mobility Barriers Index (MBI). Each policy variable covers a different set of countries and time period. In most cases data start in the late 1980s or early 1990s. Therefore, the sample of countries and years changes somewhat for each estimated correlation. Table 7.1 provides a description of the countries and the time coverage for each policy variable.

Table 7.2 reports overall correlations between all policies in all countries and years covered.[8] As expected, trade policies move in the same direction. Tariffs are negatively correlated with PTA and BIT, and positively correlated with FDI. Thus, lower tariffs are associated with more PTAs and BITs, and lower FDI restrictions. Moreover, FDI is negatively correlated with PTA and BIT, and positively correlated with Tariff: lower FDI restrictiveness is associated with more BITs and PTAs and lower tariffs. These correlations suggest that countries simultaneously reduce barriers to trade, both unilaterally (MFN tariffs) and through PTAs (which generally include a focus on NTMs), and increase their openness to foreign investment.

Moreover, countries more open to trade perform better in terms of reducing the restrictiveness of regulation (as measured by the PMR) and convergence toward what the EBRD defines as good market economy regulatory practice. This is reflected in the positive correlation between Tariff and PMR_H and PMR_S, respectively (more restrictive PMRs are associated with higher tariffs), and the negative correlation between Tariff and EBRD   higher tariffs are associated with lower EBRD indicators (less convergence toward good practices). The mobility of people tends to be more restricted if trade barriers are lowered, as shown by the negative correlation between openness to trade and investment and MBI/MIPEX, suggesting a political trade-off between trade and investment openness on the one hand and immigration policies on the other.

TABLE 7.2 Comovements of Connectivity Policies

	Tariff	PTA	PMR	PMR_S	MIPEX	FDIRRI	EBRD	BIT	MBI
Tariff	1.000	−0.462	0.672	0.599	−0.284	0.309	−0.503	−0.341	−0.352
PTA	−0.462	1.000	−0.447	−0.580	−0.154	−0.645	0.484	0.624	−0.581
PMR_H	0.672	−0.447	1.000	0.793	−0.458	0.283	−0.500	−0.033	−0.227
PMR_S	0.599	−0.580	0.793	1.000	−0.263	0.178	−0.876	−0.672	0.237
MIPEX	−0.284	−0.154	−0.458	−0.263	1.000	0.118	0.219	0.025	−0.176
FDIRRI	0.309	−0.645	0.283	0.178	0.118	1.000	−0.523	−0.267	0.065
EBRD	−0.503	0.484	−0.500	−0.876	0.219	−0.523	1.000	0.801	0.095
BIT	−0.341	0.624	−0.033	−0.672	0.025	−0.267	0.801	1.000	−0.156
MBI	−0.352	−0.581	−0.227	0.237	−0.176	0.065	0.095	−0.156	1.000

Note: The table reports estimates of the Spearman correlation coefficient between different connectivity policies across countries and time. Tariff is the most-favored-nation tariff. PTA is the total number of preferential trade agreements to which each country belongs. PMR_H is the average value of different Organisation for Economic Co-operation and Development (OECD) indicators of product market regulation; a higher value means more regulation. PMR_S is the average value of different OECD indicators of product market service regulation; a higher value means more regulation. MIPEX, the Migrant Integration Policy Index, measures policies regarding immigrant integration; a higher value means more favorable integration. FDIRRI is the FDI Regulatory Restrictiveness Index, which measures statutory restrictions on foreign direct investment; a higher value means more restrictions. EBRD is the average of several transition indicators that track convergence over time toward best practices; a higher value means greater convergence toward a market economy. BIT is the total number of bilateral investment treaties signed by each country. MBI, the Mobility Barriers Index, measures the strictness of visa requirements imposed by each country; a higher value means greater strictness. Each policy variable is measured for different sets of countries and for different time periods. Therefore, the sample of countries and the years used change somewhat for each correlation estimated in the table. Refer to Table 7.1 for a description of the countries and time coverage of each policy variable.

Countries with more restrictive regulatory regimes do less well in converging toward the standards of industrial market economies, reflected in a negative correlation between the PMR and the EBRD indexes. Better migration integration policies are associated with less restrictive PMR and a freer market economy, as suggested by the negative correlation between MIPEX and PMR, and a positive correlation between MIPEX and EBRD. Better migration integration policies, conversely, are associated with more restrictions on inward FDI, as indicated by the positive correlation between MIPEX and FDI restrictions. Finally, lower tariffs are associated with greater restrictions on mobility of people, given the negative correlation between Tariff and MBI.

The correlations between Tariff and PTA, BIT, and FDIRRI are a good measure of consistent international policy to the extent that it measures how countries choose to enhance connectivity through two alternative forms of market integration—trade versus investment. The correlation between Tariff and PMR, instead, is a relevant measure of consistent domestic policy to the extent that it captures how countries choose to be connected to other countries and at the same time enhance connectivity by improving internal competition.

Table 7.2 suggests that in most cases countries are relatively coherent in their policies toward connectivity. Countries that impose high tariffs tend to also sign fewer BITs. Higher tariffs are associated with lower product market liberalization, suggesting that international integration, measured by the correlation between Tariff and BIT, goes hand in hand with domestic integration, measured by the correlation between Tariff and PMR. Figure 7.40 illustrates that countries have become more policy coherent over time, with the positive correlation between Tariff and PMR increasing (lower tariffs and less restrictive PMR). Similarly, the negative correlation between Tariff and BIT has decreased over time (lower tariffs and more BITs). Figure 7.41 shows that the negative

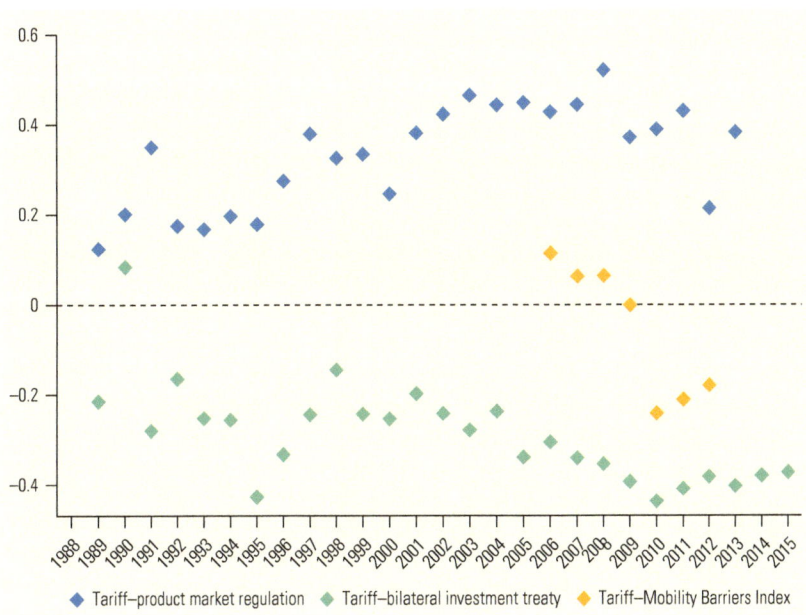

FIGURE 7.40 Global evolution of selected policy comovements
Spearman correlation coefficients

FIGURE 7.41 Evolution of selected policy comovements across income groups
Spearman correlation coefficients

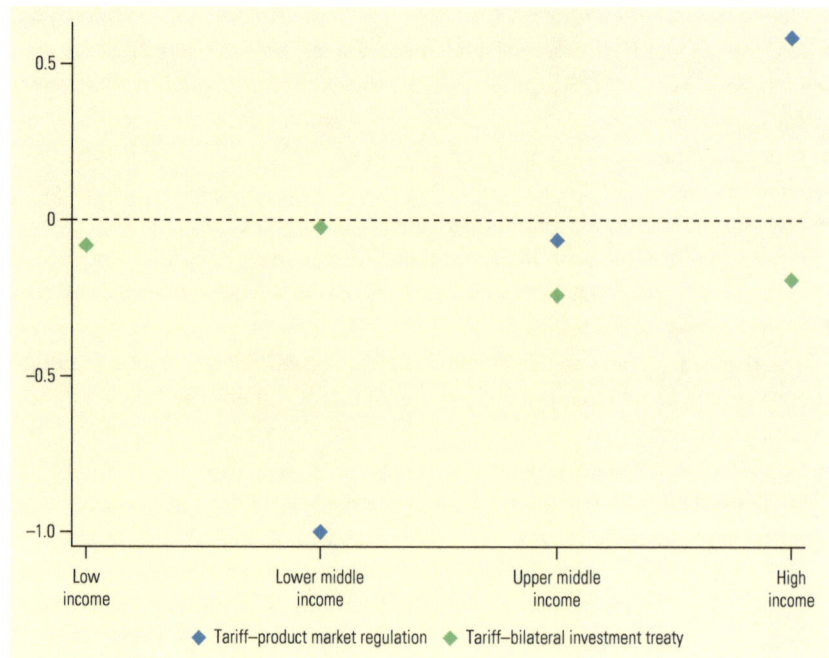

correlation between Tariff and BIT is driven by upper-middle- and high-income countries. There are substantial differences in domestic policy consistency between lower-middle-income and high-income countries. While the former show a negative correlation between Tariff and PMR, suggesting policy inconsistency, the latter show a positive correlation between the two variables, suggesting policy consistency.

Another measure of policy consistency is the correlation between the MBI and Tariff. Countries may substitute stricter movement of people for stricter movement of goods, as documented by the negative correlations between Tariff and MBI in table 7.2. Figure 7.42 shows that this applies to most HICs except Iceland, Austria, the United States, and Great Britain.

Unlike other policy variables, Tariff and BIT are measured for almost all countries and hence permit comparisons across geographic areas. Figure 7.43 shows the heterogeneity in the Tariff-BIT correlation between different geographic areas within the ECA region. All country groups within ECA are policy coherent except Central Asia, which has a strong positive correlation between Tariff and BIT (that is, higher tariffs are associated with more BITs).

Figure 7.44 compares different global regions. North America is more consistent in terms of policies, whereas ECA, Sub-Saharan Africa, and Latin America and the Caribbean show far less policy consistency. East Asia and Pacific, the Middle East and North Africa and South Asia, instead, are policy inconsistent with a positive correlation between Tariff and BIT.

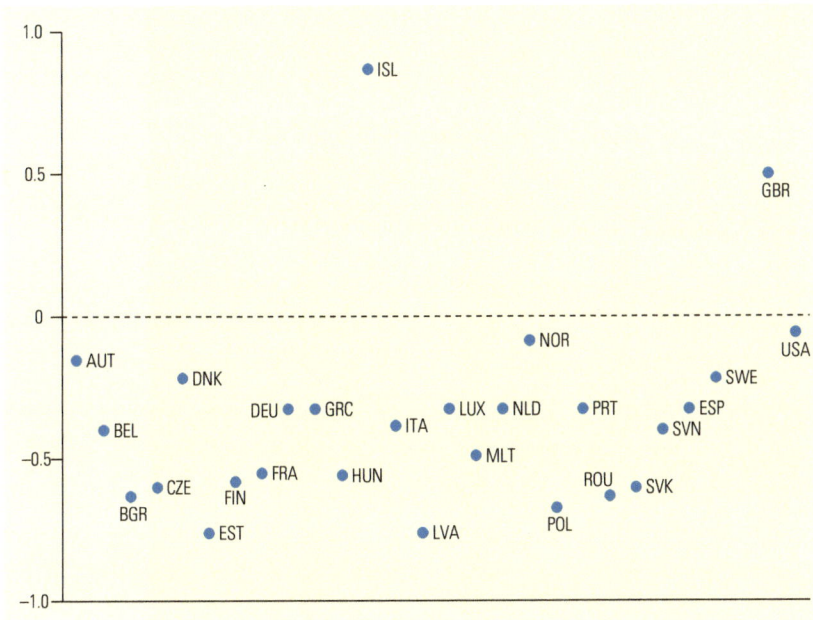

FIGURE 7.42 Tariff–Mobility Barriers Index comovements across countries imposing mobility restrictions
Spearman correlation coefficients

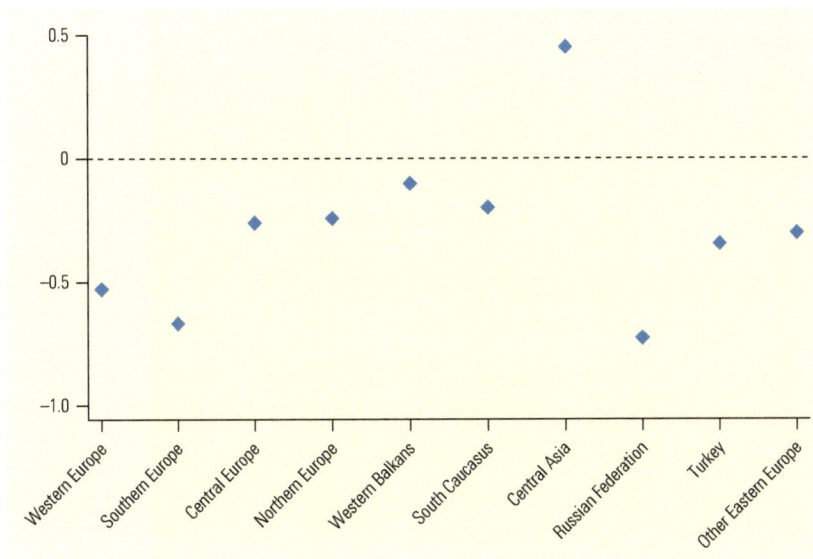

FIGURE 7.43 Tariff–bilateral investment treaty comovements across ECA subregions
Spearman correlation coefficients

Finally, figure 7.45 compares two macroregions within ECA: the EU and Western Balkans, and Eastern ECA. The correlation between Tariff and BIT is negative in the first group (policy consistency for EU and Western Balkans) and positive in the latter (policy inconsistency for Eastern ECA). This suggests substantial differences in the extent of policy consistency within the ECA region.

FIGURE 7.44 Tariff–bilateral investment treaty comovements across global regions
Spearman correlation coefficients

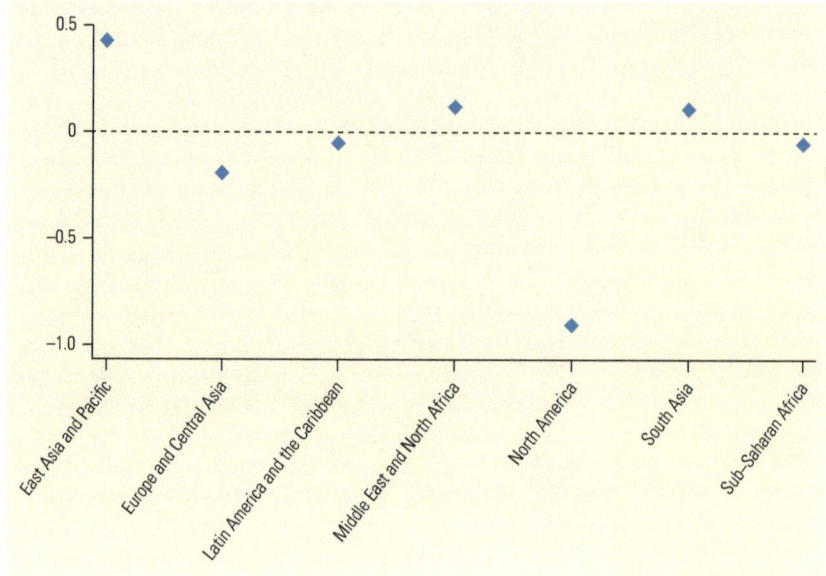

FIGURE 7.45 Tariff–bilateral investment treaty comovements across ECA macrosubregions
Spearman correlation coefficients

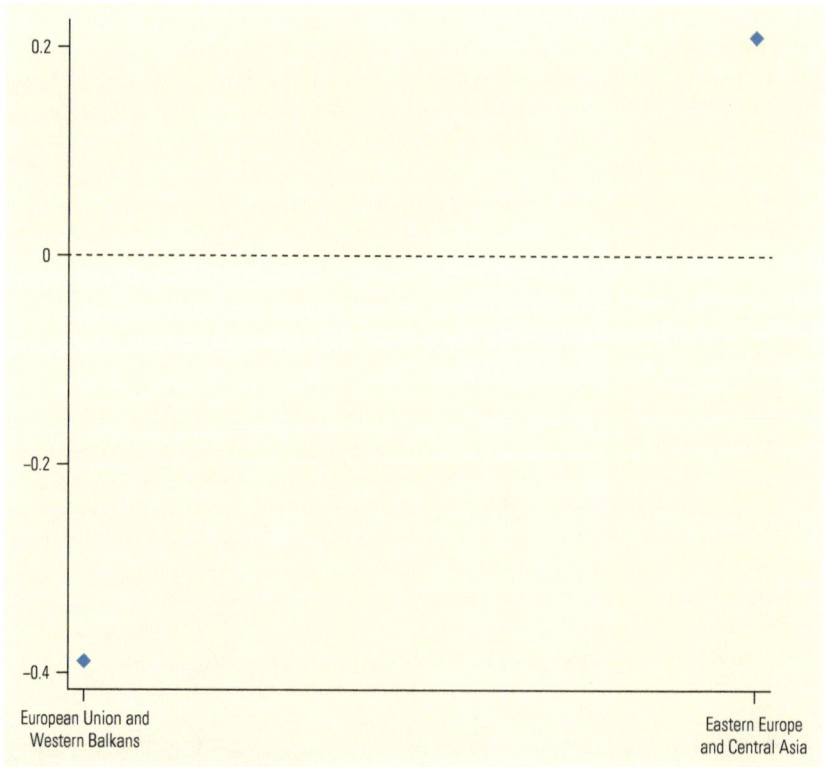

Note: ECA = Europe and Central Asia.

Conclusion

ECA countries have been global leaders in cooperation through PTAs and BITs, and among HICs in facilitating immigration. However, the average ECA country is more restrictive than non-ECA regions in domestic regulations and migrant integration policies. The trend toward more open policies slowed significantly, particularly after the first decade of this century. Little progress was made in tariff liberalization (as of the beginning of the 2000s), the use of BITs (as of the end of the 2000s), or reductions of FDI regulatory restrictions and product market liberalization (as of 2010).

It appears that ECA countries mostly pursued complementary policies across many policy dimensions of connectivity, particularly in tariff reductions, investment treaties, and lower FDI restrictions. Countries that are more open to trade also tend to have less restrictive domestic regulatory regimes. Nonetheless, lower trade barriers are not always associated with lower restrictions on immigration or product market restrictiveness, and some countries rely heavily on other ECA partners for global connectivity. Most higher-income countries have pursued complementary policies in most areas of connectivity, but LMICs less so (e.g., lower tariffs are not uniform across partner countries and are associated with higher regulatory restrictions). For the average country in Central Asia, challenges remain in improving the attractiveness of the business environment, including product market restrictions and infrastructure gaps.

Notes

1. In 2019 the number of EU member states is expected to drop to 27, following the exit of the United Kingdom.
2. See http://trade.ec.europa.eu/doclib/docs/2006/december/tradoc_118238.pdf.
3. See UNCTAD (2015) for an international classification of different forms of NTMs.
4. See Services Trade Restrictions Database (http://iresearch.worldbank.org/servicetrade /aboutData.htm) and OECD Services Trade Restrictiveness Index (http://www.oecd .org/tad/services-trade/services-trade-restrictiveness-index.htm). The negative effects of policies restricting access of foreign producers to services markets on downstream productivity performance have been estimated in country studies (e.g., Arnold et al. 2011 for the Czech Republic; Arnold et al. 2016 for India) and across countries using both firm- and industry-level data (e.g., Barone and Cingano 2011; Bourlès et al. 2013; Hoekman and Shepherd 2017).
5. The focus of this chapter is descriptive. It provides an overview of the levels and trends in applied policy that directly affect many of the dimensions of connectivity considered in this report. The aim is to provide information to help understand what has been done by ECA in different policy domains that affect connectivity of countries and to place ECA policies in a comparative context.
6. To account for measurement error, we recode as missing the values of simple average MFN import tariffs when reported as equal to 0. Within the ECA region this is the case for Estonia (1998 and 1999), the Kyrgyz Republic (1995), Turkmenistan (1998), and Switzerland (1990; 1993–2015).

7. See http://investmentpolicyhub.unctad.org/IIA.
8. It is not possible to transform all of our indicators so that they point in the same direction for ease of interpretation, that is, a higher positive (negative) number denotes
greater (lower) policy restrictiveness and connectivity. Doing so would generate incon-
sistencies in the definition and interpretation of the variables in the preceding
sections.

References

Arnold, J., B. Javorcik, M. Lipscomb, and A. Mattoo. 2016. "Services Reform and
Manufacturing Performance. Evidence from India." *Economic Journal* 126 (590): 1–39.

Arnold, J., B. Javorcik, and A. Mattoo. 2011. "Does Services Liberalization Benefit
Manufacturing Firms? Evidence from the Czech Republic." *Journal of International
Economics* 85 (1): 136–46.

Baldwin, R. 2016. *The Great Convergence: Information Technology and the New
Globalization.* Cambridge, MA: Harvard University Press.

Barone, G., and F. Cingano. 2011. "Service Regulation and Growth: Evidence from OECD
Countries." *Economic Journal* 121 (555): 931–57.

Beverelli, C., M. Fiorini, and B. Hoekman. 2017. "Services Trade Policy and Manufacturing
Productivity: The Role of Institutions." *Journal of International Economics* 104:
166 82.

Bourlès, Renaud, Gilbert Cette, Jimmy Lopez, Jacques Mairesse, and Giuseppe Nicoletti.
2013. "Do Product Market Regulations in Upstream Sectors Curb Productivity Growth?
Panel Data Evidence for OECD Countries." *Review of Economics and Statistics*
95 (5): 1750–68.

Cadot, O., M. Malouche, and S. Sáez, 2012. *Streamlining Non-tariff Measures: A Toolkit for
Policy Makers.* Washington, DC: World Bank.

European Commission. 2015. "Joint Communication to the European Parliament, the
Council, the European Economic and Social Committee and the Committee of the
Regions: Review of the European Neighbourhood Policy." JOIN(2015) 50 final,
November 11. European Commission, Brussels. http://eeas.europa.eu/archives/docs
/enp/documents/2015/151118_joint-communication_review-of-the-enp_en.pdf.

Fiorini, M., and B. Hoekman. 2017a. "Economic Governance, Regulation and Services
Trade Liberalization." Working Paper 2017/47, Robert Schuman Centre for Advanced
Studies, European University Institute, Fiesole, Italy. http://cadmus.eui.eu/bitstream
/handle/1814/48006/RSCAS_2017_47.pdf?sequence=1&isAllowed=y.

———. 2017b. "Services Trade Policy, Domestic Regulation and Economic Governance."
European Economy Discussion Paper 2017/058, Publications Office of the European
Union, Luxembourg. https://ec.europa.eu/info/sites/info/files/dp058_en.pdf.

Freund, C., and B. Bolaky. 2008. "Trade, Regulations, and Income." *Journal of Development
Economics* 87 (2): 309–21.

Gawande, K., B. Hoekman, and Y. Cui. 2015. "Global Supply Chains and Trade Policy
Responses to the 2008 Financial Crisis." *World Bank Economic Review* 29 (1): 102–28.

Hoekman, B. 2016. "Deep and Comprehensive Free Trade Agreements." Working Paper
2016/29, Robert Schuman Centre for Advanced Studies, European University Institute,
Fiesole, Italy.

Hoekman, B., J. Jensen, and D. Tarr. 2014. "A Vision for Ukraine in the World Economy:
Defining a Trade Policy Strategy that Leverages Global Opportunities." *Journal of
World Trade* 48 (4): 795–814.

Hoekman, B. and B. Shepherd. 2017. "Services Productivity, Trade Policy, and Manufacturing Exports." *World Economy* 40 (3): 499–516.

Hofmann, C., A. Osnago, and M. Ruta. 2017. "Horizontal Depth: A New Database on the Content of Preferential Trade Agreements." Policy Research Working Paper 7981, World Bank, Washington, DC.

Jafari, Y., and D. Tarr. 2017. "Estimates of Ad Valorem Equivalents of Barriers against Foreign Suppliers of Services in Eleven Services Sectors and 103 Countries." *World Economy* 40 (3): 544–73.

Langbein, J. 2014. "European Union Governance towards the Eastern Neighbourhood: Transcending or Redrawing Europe's East-West Divide?" *Journal of Common Market Studies* 52 (1): 157–74.

Langbein, J., and K. Wolczuk. 2012. "Convergence without Membership? The Impact of the European Union in the Neighbourhood: Evidence from Ukraine." *Journal of European Public Policy* 19 (6): 863–81.

Miroudot, S., and B. Shepherd. 2016. "Trade Costs and Global Value Chains in Services." In *Research Handbook on Trade in Services*, edited by M. Roy and P. Sauvé, 66–84. Cheltenham, UK: Elgar.

Moïse, E., and F. Le Bris. 2015. "Trade Costs: What Have We Learned? A Synthesis Report." OECD Trade Policy Paper 150, Paris.

Rodriguez, F., and D. Rodrik. 2001. "Trade Policy and Economic Growth: A Skeptic's Guide to the Cross-National Evidence." In *NBER Macroeconomics Annual*, edited by Ben S. Bernanke and Kenneth Rogoff, 261–325. Cambridge, MA: MIT Press.

UNCTAD (United Nations Conference on Trade and Development). 2015. "International Classification of Non-tariff Measures." UNCTAD/DITC/TAB/2012/2/Rev.1, United Nations, Geneva.